Ultimate Guide to Law Schools

Second Edition

Anne McGrath and the Staff of U.S.News & World Report

Robert Morse, Director of Data Research

Brian Kelly, Series Editor

SOURCEBOOKS, INC.
NAPERVILLE, ILLINOIS

Published by Sourcebooks, Inc.
P.O. Box 4410
Naperville, Illinois 60567-4410
(630) 961-3900 FAX: (630) 961-2168
www.sourcebooks.com

ISBN-13: 978-1-4022-0704-4
ISBN 1-4022-0704-2
Second Edition
Printed and bound in the United States of America
DR 10 9 8 7 6 5 4 3 2 1

Table of Contents

Introduction

So you want to be a lawyer.

Are you sure?

It's no idle question, given the impact choosing law will have on your life. Before walking away from three years of income (and head-on into a $100,000-plus commitment), you'd better figure out whether the reality of legal practice jibes with your vision of what your day-to-day experience will be. Many applicants, attracted by eye-popping salaries and the drama of shows such as *Law and Order*, are "woefully uninformed about what the practice of law is like," says Deborah Post, a professor at Touro College's law school in Huntington, New York, and former co-chair of the committee on admissions for the Society of American Law Teachers. Much too often, they "stumble into the law because they don't know how to find a job," says Michael Young, former dean of the George Washington University Law School in Washington, D.C., and now president of the University of Utah. "If you love it, you'll have a great life. But do you really want to spend 10 to 14 hours a day thinking about the stuff of law? If not, it might be an acceptable living, but you won't necessarily be happy."

Indeed, several studies suggest that attorneys are among the *least* happy people. A 1990 analysis of data on 104 different occupations by researchers at Johns Hopkins University, for example, found that lawyers were 3.6 times as likely as the general working population to suffer from major depression. University of Pennsylvania psychologist Martin Seligman, in his book *Authentic Happiness*, suggests three reasons: attorneys are primed to constantly anticipate "every conceivable snare and catastrophe that might occur in any transaction"; young lawyers, in particular, often hold high-pressure jobs in which they have little voice or power to make decisions; and these days lawyering often seems more about making money and crushing opponents than offering wise counsel and finding justice.

"There's been a huge change over the last 20 years," says David Stern, an attorney and head of Equal Justice Works, a Washington, D.C. advocacy group that promotes public interest law. "It's no longer a profession—it's a business. The number one priority is profits-per-partner." That's undoubtedly a major reason for the incessant lawyer jokes you'll put up with. A 2002 survey conducted for the American Bar Association found that about 70 percent of Americans think of lawyers as "greedy and manipulative," and only 19 percent have confidence in them. (Full disclosure: of the 10 professions and institutions covered in the survey, only the media inspires less confidence.)

Obviously, these conditions don't define every lawyer's job, and some attorneys thrive on the intrigue and competition. Moreover, graduates whose motivation is a strong commitment to social justice have plenty of opportunities to find work in public service, perhaps with the government, or maybe (more lucratively) through pro bono work for a law firm. The point is simply that you need to make this choice with both eyes open.

Those who *do* end up with a fancy paycheck—the median first-year salary at large firms is now $125,000 plus bonuses—are apt to work into the wee hours, researching case law and statutes, and then drafting memos for the partners (who are doing the interesting work). Partnership, the carrot dangled seven or eight years down the line that confers a share of the firm (and even more money), comes less easily than it once did, as the ranks of young associates have swelled and as firms have created alternative salaried partnership tracks. According to John Heinz and Robert Nelson, Northwestern professors who have studied the changing career paths of Chicago attorneys for the American Bar Foundation, only 16 percent of lawyers surveyed in 1995 who had started out at a large law firm had made full partner at the firm and stayed, compared with 35 percent in 1975, for example.

And the fact is that many lawyers end up in small or solo practices, making ends meet by taking on debt collections work or acting as public defenders. When the time comes, students who had planned a career in public interest law often find they can't pay off their debts and buy groceries on a $35,000-a-year salary—and so they end up at a big firm after all.

"If you love law, you'll have a great life."

How can you tell if you're among those who truly belong in law school—whether the "stuff of the law," in Young's words, really "lights you up"? He advises prospective attorneys to first expose themselves to legal ideas, if not by taking an undergraduate course in law, then by talking to lawyers and following newspaper coverage of legislation and the courts. Can't make it to the end of a *New York Times* article about a Supreme Court decision without yawning? Take that as a sign.

Tom Arthur, former dean and now professor at Emory University's law school, suggests that anybody considering law first answer these questions:

Am I truly interested in public issues?

You'd better be, because you'll be working on them; typically, the law is the vehicle by which society's knotty issues are resolved. "The environment went from a movement to statutes," says Arthur. The same thing is happening now with the issues raised by Enron and the mutual fund scandal.

Do I *really* like to read and write?

If not, be prepared to suffer. "Cases, decisions, statutes, regulations—we read all the time," says Arthur. And write: "It's always, 'When can we have a draft?'"

Do I get stage fright?

Even if you never take part in a trial, a big part of your job will entail presenting your argument cogently and credibly to partners, clients, and opposing counsel, all of whom will be judging you—and some of whom will be hostile.

How good am I with details?

Partners don't tolerate mistakes. Nor do clients. Miss a filing deadline, and you might be guilty of malpractice.

Can I separate my feelings from the facts?

Whatever your own personal value system is telling you, you'll have to step back and analyze

> *"Law is no longer a profession—it's a business. The number one priority is profits-per-partner."*

every situation rationally and objectively, and then act in your client's best interest—which may not be where your heart is.

Am I someone people can turn to for help?

There's a reason lawyers are called "counselors." If listening and empathizing and patiently advising confused people isn't part of your skill set, you might belong somewhere else.

Do I have good judgment?

Clients who assume you do will be trusting you—and paying you—to make the right decisions about what strategies they ought to follow and how much risk they ought to take to get the desired result.

● ● ●

Even if the answers to these questions point you directly to law school, consider testing your certainty by taking some time off. "I tell everybody to work for a couple years," says David Van Zandt, dean of the law school at Northwestern University in Illinois, which has adopted a policy of preferring work experience. "We feel much better about students after they've grown some, and are giving up a job and a salary," says Van Zandt. "I run into far too many 50-year-olds who were performance-oriented [in college] and got on the track seeing law school as a place where they could be rewarded. Then down the road they wake up and say 'Why did I get on the track so fast?'"

"I think anyone who applies to both Cornell and NYU hasn't got a clue what they're doing."

Once you've studied the evidence and decided law school is indeed for you, this book will help you get there. The first chapter, "Choosing the Right School," sorts through all the factors you'll need to consider: reputation, curriculum, faculty, placement services, location, and cost, among others. As those who attend the country's most elite institutions will find themselves in demand for great jobs pretty much anywhere in the country, Chapter 2 takes you inside the law schools at Yale, Harvard, Stanford, Columbia, and New York University, which regularly top the annual *U.S. News* rankings. Chapter 3 describes the attributes top schools—which have their pick of hundreds, even thousands, of qualified applicants—look for beyond grades and LSAT scores in those they accept. In Chapter 4, you'll find out how to prepare for the LSAT and put together an outstanding application; Chapter 5 advises you on how to pay

for it all. Finally, in Chapter 6, you'll read about getting that first job—and where the great opportunities are these days.

The tables that begin on page 73 allow you to compare law schools on a number of attributes key to your decision. Among them: which programs are the toughest and easiest to get into (page 75); which schools hand out the most generous financial aid (page 91); which ones leave their students with the heaviest and lightest debt loads (page 95); and which have the most success at placing graduates—and at producing new lawyers who can pass the bar exam on the first try (pages 103).

Finally, at the back of the book, you'll find detailed profiles of law schools accredited by the American Bar Association. The profiles, which are based on a comprehensive survey that *U.S. News* sends out to law schools each year, contain the most up-to-date information on everything from the academic credentials of students to programs of study and joint-degree options to the availability of financial aid and the sorts of jobs graduates land. Study it. And then go visit. Law schools are much less alike than you might think. Says Seattle-based admissions consultant Loretta DeLoggio: "I think anyone who applies to both Cornell and NYU hasn't got a clue what they're doing." This guide will clue you in.

Chapter One

Choosing the Right Law School

For many would-be attorneys, the process of picking a law school requires the coolest of calculations: apply to the most elite five or six schools within reach and enroll at the best one you can. All of those considerations that mattered so much in comparing undergraduate colleges—looking for the best campus culture, the place where you felt you fit in—get hardly a moment's thought. "I saw the choice as utilitarian—what doors will open for me for the rest of my life?—rather than as a question of how happy I'd be for the next three years," says Kimberly Parker, Harvard Law class of 1996 and now an attorney for the big corporate firm Wilmer, Cutler & Pickering in Washington, D.C. "You just cannot overestimate the importance the prestige of the degree has for your life." She speaks not only as someone for whom doors have opened, but as an attorney who has recruited young lawyers to her firm.

It's undeniable that in a profession as pedigree-conscious and tradition-bound as law, the name on your diploma will have enormous influence on the trajectory of your career. "If you have a choice between a top 15 or a second-tier school, you're *crazy* not to go to the top school—the opportunities are so much better," says David Van Zandt, law dean at Northwestern University in Illinois. Graduates of the

---

"You just cannot overestimate the importance the prestige of the degree has for your life."

---

world-class institutions that sit atop the *U.S. News* rankings year after year (see table, page 14) are wooed by the most prestigious law firms, offered plum judicial clerkships, plucked for the most visible slots in government and public service, and granted entrée to ultraselective academic jobs. Degrees from these schools hold currency in every corner of the country, and they put alumni on a national stage: these are the people working on Supreme Court cases and merging the AOLs and Time Warners, while somebody else handles the contract dispute between the local restaurant and its supplier. Says Parker: "If you want to practice on the national level, being at a top 10 or top 20 school matters *a lot*."

Anybody following that most ambitious path thus starts off with a readymade short list: Yale, Harvard, Stanford, Columbia, New York University, Chicago, and the 15 or so other truly name-brand, national institutions. What if your aspirations or LSAT scores don't point you toward the top? The quality and stature of school you choose will still be very important to your career success and your geographic flexibility—as will an exceptional performance there.

"Recruiters won't come in the same numbers," admits Patricia Adamski, former vice dean of the law school at Hofstra University in New York and now an administrator for the university. "But the top of Hofstra's class gets offers that meet those at the middle of Harvard's." Generally, she says, students who are in the top 5 or 10 people of their class at good but not name-brand law schools, or even the top 10 percent, can expect to find themselves in demand.

Below the top ranks, other factors besides a school's overall reputation may influence your chances for success. Someone who's bent on getting a public interest job, for example, should know that many cash-strapped nonprofit agencies are especially interested in graduates of law schools that offer students lots of hands-on experience working with Legal Aid clients, for example, because the agencies just don't have the budget to train beginners. Applicants contemplating a career in politics might be wise to opt for the law school at their state university. "You've got to be elected from somewhere," says Andrew Coats, dean of the University of Oklahoma College of Law. The people you meet in a law school like Oklahoma's—your class plus the two ahead of you and the two behind you—will hold many of the state's positions of power in business, law, and government when you're running for office, and they'll probably help a fellow grad regardless of their own political leanings, says Coats. He graduated from the law school himself in 1963 and has been a district attorney for Oklahoma County, a Democratic nominee from the state for the U.S. Senate, and the mayor of Oklahoma City.

For the same reason—a strong alumni network—those who are certain that they want to settle and practice in a given area of the country might want to pick a fine regional law school in that area rather than a more highly ranked law school elsewhere. Still, most say, if you can make it in the top 20, go for it.

No matter how high you're aiming, law deans, undergraduate pre-law advisors, and independent admissions consultants agree (as does *U.S. News*) that a decision about which school is the best one for you should never hang on its position in a numerical ranking alone. Though law schools may look much the same on paper—a standard first-year courseload, upper-level electives and clinics, lots of library time—comparable schools can have vastly different characters and areas of strength. There's large and impersonal, there's small and collegial, there's merely competitive, and there's "don't leave your notes around," says Stuart Rabinowitz, former dean of Hofstra's law school and now the university's president. Some schools emphasize legal theory (in an ideal system, how should the law work?); others emphasize actual practice (how the law works in reality).

So the experts suggest a more nuanced approach to thinking about quality: find the most excellent *cluster* of schools that you can get into, and within the cluster, pick the school whose character and culture and curricular strengths suit you best. "There might be 15 to 30 schools for any one candidate," says Katharine Bartlett, dean of the law school at Duke University. And within a cluster, your career opportunities are apt to be very similar. So, says George Washington University's former law dean Michael Young, you can afford to think, "Am I interested in things international? I might pick G.W. over Northwestern. Am I interested in policy formation through an economic perspective? Yale or Chicago." An applicant intrigued by the "countercultural view of the law" might pick Georgetown, says Young.

"Someone who is thinking of Yale, which is very small and 'all for one, one for all' might be very unhappy at Harvard, a big school of very competitive, very motivated, Type A people," says Mark Meyerrose, a former Harvard Law admissions officer who now advises law school applicants for AdmissionsConsultants, Inc. (www.admissions consultants.com), an independent Virginia-based counseling firm that helps clients get into college and graduate school. (The vast majority of law schools in the country—though not all—have been accredited by the American Bar Association, which means that they've met standards for legal education set by the profession. In many states, a lawyer who holds a JD from a nonapproved school is not eligible to sit for the bar exam.)

The *U.S. News* rankings—which measure schools by several yardsticks, including expert opinion of their programs, test scores and grades of students, placement record, and bar passage rate—are not intended to drive a decision between numbers three and four or five. But the rankings can help you identify your cluster. ("The difference between the [school] that ranks 4th or 7th and the one that ranks 34th or 37th? Let's not kid ourselves," says Saul Levmore, law dean at the No. 6 University of Chicago.) Then, as you narrow the

> *"If you have a choice between a top 15 or a second-tier school, you're crazy not to go to the top school."*

field in search of the right fit, a number of key questions are worth thinking about.

How big is the student body—and the typical class?

Harvard is home to some 1,700 students; Yale, to just under 600. George Washington University boasts some 1,600 full- and part-timers. Boalt Hall, the law school at the University of California–Berkeley, has a total enrollment of just under 900; Duke, about 650. Considering that all these numbers are pretty small compared to undergraduate colleges, why should you care? Because the size of the student body and the entering class affects law schools' personalities, the availability of professors outside of class, the extent to which you'll engage with your classmates, and, most likely, the breadth of the curriculum.

"You know everyone, and it didn't feel like we had to fight against each other," says Joe Lemon, a 2002 graduate of Stanford Law who went to work for a high-tech law firm in Menlo Park, California. "We formed study groups, shared notes, talked, created tests for each other." Stanford, one of the country's smaller law schools with some 550 students, has a first-year class of about 170. On the other hand, the roster of different classes offered after the first year may by necessity be much more limited at a small school. (For a peek inside Stanford, Harvard, and the other law schools at the very top of the newest *U.S. News* ranking, see Chapter 2 on page 15.)

The size of the first-year sections at the school you pick—the standard classes in civil procedure, constitutional law, torts, and criminal law—is apt to have a big impact on the quality of your experience. Many schools have focused recently on bringing section size down and on putting stu-

dents in one small seminar their first year. At Harvard, "the resources are amazing and the professors are topnotch, but it was hard to get personal attention," recalls 1996 grad Parker. Until just a few years ago, Harvard's first-year sections numbered 140 students each. Responding to criticism that the school felt too cold and impersonal, the administration has since trimmed sections to about 80, a fairly typical size among law schools. At G.W., where sections average 85 to 90 students, first-years now take at least one of their classes in a small section of 35.

At the University of Oklahoma, Dean Coats has shrunk the size of the entering class from about 225 to between 170 and 180 over the past few years, and has created four first-year sections of only 40 to 44; for instruction on legal research and writing, the class is divided into eight sections of about 20 students each. Partly as a result, the number of applicants to the school has more than doubled since 1998, and the median LSAT score and grade point average have moved steadily higher, from 152 to 157 and from 3.28 to 3.51.

You'll also want to find out how many students will be in most of the second- and third-year classes, advises David Cohen, former dean of law at Pace University in White Plains, New York. A reasonable range would be 20 to 30, he says. A related piece of data, the student–faculty ratio, offers another clue about faculty accessibility and what the chances are that your professors will actually get to know you. At most of the top schools, the ratio is somewhere around 12 to 1 or 15 to 1. At Yale, there's a professor for every 7.8 students.

What to look for in a part-time program

Is the part-time path a route for you? "How flexible is your work schedule? Do you need to be on call or take work home with you? Law school will require every other minute of your life," warns Loretta DeLoggio, an admissions consultant based in Seattle (www.deloggio.com) who specializes in helping minority students choose a school and get in. This is because you'll have no flexibility in how long you take to earn your degree; part-time means a-little-bit-less-than-full-time for four years instead of three.

Many would-be lawyers have no choice: it's their day-job salary that will pay for night school. The advantages of a full-time program—the generally much greater availability of externships, the extensive interaction with other students outside of class through study groups and extracurricular activities—don't outweigh the need for an income. Fortunately, a number of good schools offer evening programs;

you'll find detailed information about them in the directory entries at the back of this book. As you compare programs, here are the questions you should ask:

Who are the teachers? Ideally, they'll be the same people teaching the day students. At Georgetown, which was founded in 1870 as an evening program, part-timers are taught weekday evenings by members of the regular full-time faculty, and they're held to the same academic standards.

Are admissions yardsticks different for evening students? If the LSAT scores and grade point averages of students accepted into the part-time program are significantly lower than those of the day students, you might qualify for a law school that wouldn't otherwise take you. On the other hand, the level of discourse might be lower, too.

Will you get any hands-on experience? Many clinics are impossible to hold at night because the courts are closed, but there should be experiential learning going on. Look for simulation courses that involve role-playing or clinics that don't rely on courtroom experiences. Evening students at Pace often participate in securities arbitration and disability rights clinics, for example.

Will you get the same services as full-time students? Find out whether you'll have the same access as day students to career services programs, the financial aid office, the registrar, and the school's information-technology and library resources. What about student organizations? All opportunities afforded by the school should be available.

What does the school's location offer?

You'll care about location for a couple of reasons—okay, maybe three. ("It's beautiful all the time!" says Lemon of Stanford's relentlessly sunny weather.)

For starters, educational and externship opportunities may vary considerably according to where a law

---

"If you think you want to practice in Milwaukee, you might better go to Marquette than DePaul."

---

school is situated. For example, Georgetown Law Center students, whose classes meet a mere 10-minute walk from the Supreme Court, sometimes get a chance to work on Supreme Court cases. Students at the Washington, D.C., law schools also have access to externships at a whole list of federal government agencies, while those at the University of California–Los Angeles can take courses in sports and entertainment law and find externships at television and movie studios. In Grand Forks, University of North Dakota students help Native American tribal governments develop environmental programs and offer legal assistance to the Spirit Lake Tribal Court.

Secondly, bear in mind that if you're not a candidate for a national school, your future job opportunities will certainly be shaped by where you choose to enroll. The connections students make through externships or local pro bono work often lead to the permanent offers, and a school's alumni network is apt to be much stronger in its immediate region than elsewhere. "If you think you want to practice in Milwaukee, you might better go to Marquette than DePaul," says Tom Arthur, former law dean at Emory. "If you go to

Suffolk Law School, you'll be really well placed to practice in Boston and New England, but it'll take you five or 10 years of practice to establish yourself and make the leap to San Francisco," warns admissions consultant Meyerrose.

What's the culture like?

The size of the school will tell you something about its climate, but to really get a handle on the campus culture—how intense and competitive students are, for example, or how committed to social justice or to high-paying corporate law—you're going to have to visit. Even though only a tiny fraction of law schools interview applicants, most are only too happy to entertain visitors. "We want students to figure out if this is a place that will work for them," says Hannah Arterian, dean of the College of Law at Syracuse University, which regularly hosts formal programs for prospective students that start with a group meeting with her and include breakfast, a first-year class, an introduction to the career services office, a workshop on financial planning, lunch with faculty members, and tours of the law school, Syracuse's campus, and campus housing. "Not only do prospective students get an opportunity to check out our environment, we get a chance to see how they might fit in a culture that puts a high premium on maturity and interpersonal skills," says Van Zandt of Northwestern, the only major law school that tries to interview every applicant.

Sarah Russell Vollbrecht, a native of Oklahoma and a 2003 graduate of the University of Virginia's law school, applied only to institutions ranked among the *U.S. News* top 10 in the hope that her degree would take her anywhere in the country. (It worked: she graduated into a job clerking for a judge on the U.S. Court of Appeals for the 5th Circuit in Houston, after which she planned to work for a Dallas law firm.) At the outset, she expected to enroll at the most highly ranked institution that accepted her. Once she'd visited several campuses, however, she realized that distinctions in academic excellence were small, and other qualities mattered more to her than place in the pecking order.

"Duke and UVA were very similar—their facilities were impressive, the campuses were pretty, and the students were *really* friendly; they smiled and were eager to assist me," says Vollbrecht. "At Harvard it felt like everybody was rushing to do what they needed to do. Chicago might have been a better school academically than UVA, but the students seemed a lot more serious—I studied hard at Virginia, but also made time for softball." Accepted by Duke, Chicago, New York University, and UVA, Vollbrecht narrowed her picks to Duke and UVA, then made the "easy choice." She'd lived in Virginia and qualified for in-state tuition, so UVA was the cheapest by far.

"You need to talk to students—they're verbal and critical by nature," advises David Leebron, former dean of Columbia Law School and now president of Rice University. One good reason to quiz students in person (beyond seeking the inside dope about the place) is to gauge their capabilities and interests— and, by extension, the likely capabilities and interests of the people you'd be learning with next year. "I firmly believe that what makes a law school is the student body," says Robert Berring, a professor and former interim dean at Berkeley's Boalt Hall, whose students he describes as a "politically awake and less formal" bunch. "This isn't the same as the college

decision," says Leebron, who advises applicants to consider whether their classmates would challenge and excite them. "It's about making career choices. This is the most important group of people you will know for the rest of your life."

Check into how diverse the student population is, too—not just in terms of ethnic background, but also in work experience, education, age, gender,

---

"You need to talk to students—they're verbal and critical by nature."

---

and socioeconomic background. "Much of the learning happens between students, and the more perspectives you have, the richer the discussion will be," says Evan Caminker, dean and professor of law at the University of Michigan, whose methods of factoring minority status into the admissions decision won the Supreme Court's approval (for more on the Michigan decision, see page 49). "Part of being a lawyer is seeing through others' eyes. Your clients—what's motivating them? The judge— where is he coming from?" When Leebron was at Columbia, he found the school's relatively large population of Mormons and Orthodox Jews and generally rich religious mix to be a selling point: "One of my Torts students [was] a priest—what an interesting perspective!"

What are the strengths of the curriculum?

Yes, the first-year coursework will be pretty standard wherever you go, but step back and take a look at the big picture. What are the hallmarks of the schools you're considering?

Chicago is known for its academic rigor, its examination of the law through an economics filter, and its conservative viewpoint. Boalt Hall is among the most liberal schools. Yale students, who can revel in their intellectual pursuits without obsessing over grades (they either pass with honors, pass, low pass, or fail), are steeped in the theory and philosophy of the law and not in the nuts and bolts of practice. Northwestern and Duke have made a priority of transitioning students into practice by stressing teamwork and collaboration on group projects. Georgetown is noted for its large and strong program of legal clinics in which students learn by practicing with real clients. The City University of New York is devoted to public service.

As you dig more deeply into the specifics, it's important to consider the breadth and diversity of schools' second- and third-year curricula because most students who think they've settled on a practice area before they arrive change their mind. "Law school is a transforming experience—and that's true here and at the University of Baltimore night school," says Chicago's Levmore, who advises against choosing a school based solely on its areas of specialization.

On the other hand, in what is clearly an age of specialization, most law schools *do* now have areas of strength. Each year, in addition to the general ranking of law schools, *U.S. News* also ranks specialty programs based on the opinions of faculty who teach in the field; Vermont Law School regularly gets top billing for environmental law, for example, and NYU is highly ranked for international and tax law.

"It used to be that the top schools were trying to be great in everything, but now we're setting strategic priorities," says Duke's Bartlett. Her school, for example, has paid particular attention to developing four of its programs: intellectual property, telecommunications law, health and biotech law, and international and comparative law. Syracuse boasts five "centers" (in family law; indigenous law; global law; law and business enterprise; and law, technology, and management) and has launched an institute that focuses on national security. Students who complete a concentration of coursework in one of the centers receive a certificate. The University of Pittsburgh offers several certificates, including civil litigation, environmental law, and health law; the University of Missouri–Columbia offers dispute resolution, tax, European Union studies, and electronic commercial and intellectual property law.

But take note: many schools *market* an area of specialty that isn't exactly substantive. Check what the current course offerings are. It's not unheard of for courses to appear in the catalogs that haven't been offered in years.

Investigate how much emphasis is placed on the practical skills: writing, advising clients, negotiating, arguing. Employers have complained loudly that their new hires arrive ill-prepared to practice, so now many law schools are building hands-on experience into the curriculum in the form of clinics; simulation courses that have actors or students playing the roles of opposing counsel and judge, for example; and intensive first-year classes in legal research and writing. While some schools think of the practical instruction as lesser courses and assign part-timers to teach them, ideally they'll be handled by full-time faculty members who meld the teaching of practice with theory in a child advocacy clinic, for example. Look for the student-faculty ratio to be very low. The best programs limit clinics to 8 or 10 students and teach legal research and writing in small groups of 20 or 30.

"Textbooks don't tell you what clients are like or how to be in front of a judge, but that's what you need for the real world," says one recent graduate of the CUNY School of Law who spent 30 hours a week in the Family Law Clinic, where she represented a victim of domestic violence in a custody case, filing child-support orders, writing briefs, and arguing with opposing counsel before a judge. In Georgetown's clinics, participants represent a whole range of clients, from noncitizens seeking political asylum to victims of domestic violence to tenants in disputes with landlords to children accused of crimes. Some 60 percent of students take a clinic before graduation. One of the clinics at Northwestern puts students to work in the internationally recognized Center for Wrongful Convictions, where they work on cases involving claims of innocence.

As noted before, practical experience is especially valued by public interest employers, so anyone planning on a public service career will want to consider law schools whose clinical programs reflect a commitment to it. Several that get high marks include Georgetown, NYU, CUNY, Fordham, and Northeastern. Besides strong clinics, says Equal Justice Works CEO David Stern, good public interest programs tend to have full-time counselors who help students do career planning and find pro bono work; a selection of summer public interest internship opportunities; and a structured (and sometimes mandatory) pro bono program. (The truly committed schools also have generous loan-repay-

ment assistance programs. For more on how these plans work, see "How much will it cost?" on page 12.)

For more on how these plans work, see "How much will it cost?" on page 12.)

As the practice of law gets increasingly global, a growing number of students are looking for more than just a class or two in international and comparative law. Some law schools have begun to aggressively integrate discussion

> *"It used to be that the top schools were trying to be great in everything, but now we're setting strategic priorities."*

of other legal systems into courses throughout the curriculum, and a growing number make it possible for students to actually study law abroad. At Tulane, for example, students can spend anywhere from one week to a month in one of seven foreign countries, including Canada, England, France, Germany, and Greece; semester-abroad programs are also an option. Cornell students who are fluent in the language of the host country can study for a semester at one of several foreign law schools. Students at American University's law school can also take a semester abroad at several European, Canadian, or Mexican law schools or the City University of Hong Kong.

One advantage of choosing a school that is part of a university is the richness other programs can add to the law curriculum. At Penn, for example, with 12 schools on one campus, law students can study with Wharton business students in a small-business clinic and in a negotiation class; medical students and law students study together how to use the legal and medical systems to protect children's rights. The Institute for National

Profile: The politician

Chuck Larson Jr. went into politics before he went to law school, but it's his University of Iowa JD that really launched his career. Law school "has been the foundation of everything I do," says the 34-year-old Iowa native, who is a member of the state Senate, a member of the Judiciary Committee, and former head of the Iowa Republican Party.

Larson had already put aside plans for a career in business back in 1992 after a conversation with some buddies. "The economy wasn't good, and we were talking about the large part of our generation that was leaving the state because we didn't have good-paying jobs," he says. By the time the chat was over, Larson had decided not only to stay in Iowa, but to get involved in running it. He campaigned by knocking on virtually every door in his district—twice.

Shortly after winning a seat in the state House of Representatives, Larson realized that "some 40 percent of the bills that land on the governor's desk move through the Judiciary Committee," and he wanted to know how the laws would affect his constituents. So he went back to school, taking his spring semester courses in the summers so as not to miss the legislative season. "I didn't have a lot of free time," he concedes, but the hard work paid off: his understanding of the intricacies of case law and constitutionality propelled him to leadership roles on first the House and then the Senate Judiciary Committees.

Day to day, Larson tackles civil issues such as the definition of marriage ("a hot topic right now") and bankruptcy law ("it's narrow and specific and can be confusing—law school helped me put it into sharp focus"). On the criminal front, his understanding of drug laws helped when he and his colleagues drafted the nation's toughest law on methamphetamine abuse (first offense: mandatory treatment; second offense: jail).

Because of its strong alumni network in the state, the University of Iowa has been a powerful support to Larson, no small consideration when he was choosing law schools. Many of his colleagues in government are Iowa graduates—and, perhaps most importantly, so are many of his constituents. "Obviously the ties with alums across the state work politically," he says. "Iowans like their universities. Politically, it's a mark of distinction." On the other hand, he says, Iowa is "a fairly liberal school, and I'm a Republican. Some of my [professors] have contributed to my opponents." He may not have raked in political contributions on campus, but he did save some money: choosing the flagship state university allowed Larson to leave law school "relatively debt free."

As a member of the U.S. Army National Guard's Judge Advocate General corps, Larson is back from a year in Iraq, where, when he wasn't handling the legal affairs of fellow soldiers, he helped build schools and water filtration systems.

Security and Counterterrorism at Syracuse University's law school will bring together students and faculty in law, journalism, history, and public affairs to study and discuss their various perspectives on how threats to national security should be handled. And at the University of Michigan, students can take up to nine credits in graduate programs outside the law school.

At the extreme, student interest in crossdisciplinary study expresses itself in the pursuit of a joint degree, which may add an extra year or two to the educational experience but (at least theoretically) offers an edge in the ultracompetitive job market. While the most common combo degree is probably law and business, there's a whole array of possible combinations, and many schools allow students to create their own dual degrees.

At Michigan, choices include a JD/master's of science in information (for those interested in the intellectual property issues created by technology) and a JD/MS in natural resources (for anyone with a particular interest in pollution and the environment). At Duke—where fully a quarter of the law school population is enrolled in a joint-degree program—students can complete a three-year-plus-one-summer combination JD/master's degree in any of some 15 academic disciplines from English to psychology to Romance studies. They can also complete longer professional joint degrees with the divinity school, the Fuqua School of Business, and the medical school, among others.

Who's doing the teaching, and are they good?

Talking to students and sitting in on first-year classes should give you a sense of the faculty as teachers, a factor that's difficult to judge from a distance. On many campuses, there's been quite a shift since *The Paper Chase* days, toward an educational experience much friendlier to students. (The noble explanation: professors have realized that using the Socratic method to intimidate and humiliate doesn't promote learning and probably inhibits it. A more practical reason: schools are battling each other to attract the most-qualified candidates—who happen to be a more vocal and demanding bunch of consumers than previous generations.)

The result is that many deans have put a premium on good teaching and student-faculty interaction as well as a professor's legal scholarship. Vanderbilt University law profs are expected to know every student by name from the first day and to have their doors open anytime. At the University of Pennsylvania law school, which encourages informal student-professor contact, the whole faculty pretty much lunches out with students nonstop, says Dean Michael Fitts. "We all have this irrational fear that we're going to go in [to see a professor] and our question will be stupid," says Karen Tani at Penn who remembers those fears evaporating during her first term after she and a handful of other students had lunch with each of her four professors. Pace University law school in New York has introduced a merit-based pay system in which the strength of professors' syllabi, grading methods, and student evaluations counts as 35 to 40 percent of their marks for performance, along with their records of scholarship and public service. Chicago has worked at creating an "intellectual community" by holding frequent lunchtime panel discussions by faculty and seminars at professors' homes, says Levmore.

A side effect of the reform movement has been a "huge variance in the degree to which teaching is still rigorous," says Kent Syverud, dean of the law school at Washington University in St. Louis and former president of the American Law Deans' Association. He advises prospective applicants to observe the interactions in one or two first-year classes with a critical eye. As argument and analysis are such vital legal skills, "You don't want to see a replication of Psych 101, where the professor lectures, poses rhetorical questions, and walks out," he says. It should be clear that the presentation has been carefully thought through, and that the students are engaged and involved; where the Socratic method is practiced properly, students are respectfully asked to articulate and defend their arguments and are doing the talking at least a third of the time. Rather than embarrassing the unprepared by calling on students randomly, many professors now use an "on call" system that alerts those who need to be ready ahead of time.

Will your classes be led by the great legal minds who have established the school's reputation? Or are the scholars off doing their research while attorney adjuncts do the teaching? You definitely want a faculty still active out in the field and on the cutting edge of legal scholarship; the bios and vitae posted on school websites can give you some indication of professors' accomplishments and publications. Penn's Paul Robinson is a recognized scholar on criminal law who has served on the U.S. Sentencing Commission; William Banks, head of Syracuse's counterterrorism institute, is an expert in national security law who lectures around the world and has testified before the Senate Judiciary Committee on the U.S. Patriot Act.

But you also want reassurance that the scholars are the people you'll be learning from—and that they're accessible to you outside of class, too. When you quiz current students, ask them whether "when you ask to see a professor, they say 'See you in a week and a half,'" advises Andrew Popper, a professor at American University's Washington College of Law.

How much will it cost?

Take a deep breath.

Perhaps $250,000 or $300,000 or even a lot more, counting all the income you'll give up to go to school. Graduates of the top programs, where yearly tuition now runs more than $30,000, may not have to worry so much about accumulating $100,000 in debt; they can expect to be making lots of money if they choose to. But the rest of the world will need to weigh the tradeoffs of choosing an in-state public institution (tuition and fees at Ohio State's law school run under $16,000 a year for state residents; in-state tuition and fees at the University of Georgia, just a bit over $9,000); apply for financial aid; investigate the availability of merit awards based on academic credentials or commitment to public service rather than need; and check out loan repayment assistance programs. (For a complete discussion on how to pay for law school, see Chapter 5 on page 51.)

One advantage of applying to school where your LSAT scores stand out is that you might well be a candidate for a scholarship. A growing number of schools now offer merit money in an effort to attract the most talented students possible. "It's amazing," says admissions consultant Mark Meyerrose of the explosion of merit aid. "We can't *not* do it in this competitive environment," says Hofstra's Rabinowitz. The pool of aid money at Hofstra, which includes some need-based aid but is mostly awarded based on merit, tripled from $1.1 million to

$3.3 million between 1994 and 2002; merit aid accounted for the entire increase. Quinnipiac Law School in Connecticut, which has been working hard on attracting a student body with higher LSAT and GPA numbers, gave out some $3.4 million last year, up from $500,000 12 years ago. In the last four years, the 25th/75th percentile range of LSAT scores at Quinnipiac has moved from 144–151 to 155–159. Pace University law school gave out $380,000 to first-year students in 1999; a mere four years later, the pot had grown to $1.9 million.

Pace has also joined the ranks of law schools with loan repayment assistance programs. These programs, also sometimes called loan forgiveness programs, are designed to help graduates who take public interest jobs pay back their law school loans. They now exist at more than 70 schools, according to surveys by Equal Justice Works (for the list, see page 60). Under the typical plan, a graduate who takes a job at a nonprofit or government agency that pays less than a certain amount, say $40,000, is either granted or loaned money each year to cover part of his yearly debt payments. If you receive the funds as a loan, the debt is forgiven after a certain number of years as long as you stay in a public interest job and your income doesn't rise too high.

What kind of help will I get finding a job?

One stop on your campus tour should be the career services office, whose assistance (or lack thereof) may mean the difference between your graduating into a job or not. Does it appear to be a professionally run operation with counselors on staff—rather than just administrative assistants who schedule interviews? In addition to arranging for scores of employers to recruit on campus, the best place-ment services are constantly scheduling workshops on job-hunting strategies and various career paths, bringing attorneys to campus to speak about their work, sending students to recruitment fairs, and offering individual advice.

While you're there, ask how many graduates end up getting jobs after graduation, and how soon. "Most schools have extraordinarily detailed placement data that they'll share with you if asked," says Syverud of Wash U. You'll want to know the proportion of the class with a job offer at graduation and how many are working six months or nine months later; the directory entries at the back of this guide provide each school's most recent placement data. You'll want to know how many grads accepted clerkships, positions at dif-ferent sized corporate law firms, and public inter-est slots. At Yale, for example, nearly half of the 2004 graduating class accepted judicial clerkships, and 8 to 10 percent of students typically go into teaching law.

Find out where graduates end up geographi-cally, too, advises Syverud. "If your goal is to be a litigator in New York, does this school produce lit-igators in New York? If your goal is to practice employment law in San Francisco, does this school produce San Francisco lawyers?"

How much do graduates make? According to the most recent surveys by the National Association of Law Placement, the median starting pay for all JD full-time jobs has lately been $55,000; the figure for first-year associates ranged from just under $67,500 at small firms to $125,000 (plus bonus) at firms of 500 or more attorneys; for the class of 2004, median pay was only $43,000 for clerkships and $45,000 for government jobs and $38,000 for public interest positions. It may surprise aspiring lawyers to learn that, "for all full-time jobs, half of salaries were

The latest Top 20

Each year, *U.S. News & World Report* ranks the nation's accredited law schools based on such measures of excellence as the expert opinion of deans and faculty members, expenditures per student on instruction, placement success, and how well students fare on the bar exam. To see where your schools rank, check out "America's Best Graduate Schools," available on newsstands, or go to www.usnews.com. Here is this year's Top 20. Schools whose ranks are identical are tied.

1. Yale University (CT)
2. Stanford University (CA)
3. Harvard University (MA)
4. Columbia University (NY)
   New York University
6. University of Chicago
7. University of Pennsylvania
8. University of California-Berkeley
   University of Michigan–Ann Arbor
   University of Virginia
11. Duke University (NC)

12. Northwestern University (IL)
13. Cornell University (NY)
14. Georgetown University (DC)
15. University of California–Los Angeles
16. University of Texas–Austin
17. University of Southern California
    Vanderbilt University (TN)
19. University of Minnesota–Twin Cities
    George Washington University (DC)
    Washington University in St. Louis

$55,000 or less, outnumbering by a considerable margin salaries of more than $75,000."

But the actual pay packages that individuals are offered vary widely by law school and by job location. The placement office can give you the data you need, and the entries in this book provide the starting salaries reported by the class of 2004. No. 3 Harvard Law grads who went into the private sector garnered a median salary of $125,000; No. 65 University of Kentucky grads, $47,000.

Finally, check out how many graduates pass the bar exam on the first try. (For a look at how the schools stack up on this measure, see page 103.) Once you've decided to go into law—and committed all that time and money—you'll want to know your odds of clearing the final hurdle.

Chapter Two

Inside America's Top Law Schools

Last year, some 1,750 people claimed a spot in the first-year law school classes at Yale, Harvard, Stanford, Columbia, and New York University—which means that, at least in terms of their career opportunities, they pretty much have it made. Are you, too, planning on gunning for the top? Here's a peek inside the elite of the elite: The top five schools on this year's *U.S. News* law school ranking.

Number 1: Yale Law School

New Haven, Connecticut

"Anarchic" isn't a word often associated with the Ivy League. But it's how students, faculty, and even a former dean describe Yale Law. And with good reason: the traditionally grueling first term is ungraded here (and subsequent courses are graded on an honors, pass, low pass or fail basis), there are virtually no course requirements past first term, and professors are free to choose what they want to teach. The current dean, Harold Koh, an international human rights expert who served as an assistant secretary of state in the Clinton administration, recently took a class to a screening of *Runaway Jury*, during which he loudly enumerated the film's many procedural errors.

Such a freewheeling approach might be less successful if Yale weren't so small. With fewer than 600 students, the school has a student–faculty ratio of about 8 to 1, and the hallways of its rambling Gothic building near the heart of campus are abuzz with chance meetings between students and professors. Even in crowded first-year courses, where enrollment tops 100, professors call on students by name without checking seating charts. The school's size and the absence of grades or class ranking breeds a collaborative spirit and a homey informality. When Yale students express interest in a subject not accounted for in the course catalog—like maritime law or 9/11-related litigation—they simply draft a faculty advisor and create their own course, or "reading group."

The anarchic spirit extends to classroom interaction, where students challenge professors constantly and debate one another on issues such as the legitimacy of the International Criminal Court and the limits of Supreme Court power. "We take a very spacious view of the law," says Anthony T. Kronman, who served as dean for 10 years. "We don't see the law as a narrow professional enterprise, but as a vantage point from which the entire world can be viewed. It's a window into the human comedy."

Classes at Yale are thus highly theoretical; this is not the place to look for a lot of attention to the nuts and bolts of practice. "You're going to have to cram for six miserable weeks for the bar exam anyway, so why waste time preparing when you're in law school?" says Kronman. A recent contracts course included a long, spirited discussion over whether Pepsi could in theory be held liable for what amounts to a joke: its ad campaign offering a Harrier Jet to customers who collected 7,000,000 Pepsi points. At other schools, "I might spend time going over statutes, talking about black-letter law," or clear-cut legal principles, says Richard Brooks, an associate professor who teaches contracts. But this high-minded approach has its limits, students say. "Sometimes we're criticizing the doctrine before we've even learned what it is," says Matt Alsdorf, class of 2004. "I'm going to have to gain a lot of experience on the job."

Given this theoretical bent, it should come as no surprise that Yale is an incubator for academics; a 2001 Yale survey found that 10 percent of the class of 1997 had jobs in academia. The law school is home to a dozen research centers and projects, including the China Law Center, which aims to help the legal reform process in that country, and the Information Society Project, which studies the effect of the Internet on law and society. Each student is required to do original research and write a major paper of about 60 to 80 pages, which they might publish in one of Yale's student-run law journals.

Yale is known as an activist school, where students often fight legal battles in the larger world and a relatively large percentage pursue public interest law, which is emphasized by professors, career counselors, and Dean Koh. More than 70 percent of the class of 2005 took first-year summer jobs in public interest work, most of them unpaid (Yale provided funding).

Roughly half of Yale Law's graduating class traditionally take judicial clerkships—and a large chunk stay with public interest work afterward. Easing their way is Yale's generous loan repayment program for graduates making less than a certain amount, recently $44,000, which covers their loan payments for up to 10 years.

While most law schools permit students to enroll in their clinics only after the first year, Yale opens clinics to students after a single term. Fourteen distinct clinical projects cover areas such as immigration, tenant eviction proceedings, child advocacy, and legislative advocacy. The international human rights law clinic matches students with lawyers working on cases in federal and U.N. courts, and with regional human rights bodies in South America and Africa. Nearly 80 percent of Yale JD students take at least one clinical course, gaining experience in all aspects of lawyering, from writing and filing briefs to negotiating with opposing counsel to representing clients in court.

A burning commitment to law is practically a prerequisite for study at a school with virtually no requirements, no class rankings, and a hardly noticeable grading system. Which is not to suggest that Yalies aren't competitive: the median LSAT score and grade point average of the 2005 entering class were 172 and 3.88. "People here live, breathe, and eat law school—there's no competing social structure like in New York. Even if you go to a bar, you're talking law school," says Alsdorf. While the freedom is a gift for most students, it can be tough at first for the undisciplined. "Students who have always been told to climb the ladder—and who climb it really well—may be a little lost," says Kate Stith, a professor and formerly the deputy dean, "when we don't tell them which ladder to climb."

Number 2: Stanford Law School

Stanford, California

"Who could resist a world-class law school in paradise?"

That's a pretty sizable boast from former dean Kathleen Sullivan. But academically topnotch Stanford is also easily one of the nation's most beautiful law schools, situated on an 8,000-acre campus that looks more like a Spanish-colonial country club than a college. Nearly every student has a bike (and knowledge of local hiking trails). Beaches and ski slopes are just an hour or two away. Indeed, Stanford is often portrayed as a land of laid back would-be lawyers brushing up on their torts while they work on their tans. (Actually, since it's a wireless campus, this might be easily done).

But don't buy the "Dude, where's my lawn chair?" rap. "It's considered kind of cool here not to show how intense you are or how much you care," says one second-year student. "It's not that we're not really serious. We just don't flash it around." Last year, Stanford had more than 4,800 applicants for its entering class of just over 170 students. The median LSAT for accepted students was 169 and the median GPA was above a 3.87.

Those who make the cut learn quickly how much size matters at the so-called Harvard of the West. With fewer than 180 students entering each year (compared to roughly three times that at Harvard), Stanford is able to foster a level of community among students and faculty that many law schools cannot. First-year sections typically average no more than 60 students, and with an average student–teacher ratio of about 9 to 1, getting extra time with professors outside of class is easy. The entire law school is housed in one small building, and most of the faculty's office doors are routinely open. "There's a feeling that no one will be left behind," says one student who is also somewhat of an expert on graduate programs, with a master's degree in philosophy from Columbia University and a doctorate in rhetoric from the University of California–Berkeley. "The faculty have the time

---

"So many people have done really interesting non-law-related things before they come here to school."

---

and the inclination to talk to students about everything from questions that come up in class to career advice to abstract ideas. I've been to a lot of schools—a lot of good schools—and that's not always the case."

Decades younger than Harvard and Yale, the law school, like the West itself, is more cutting edge than traditional. Stanford is well known for its program in technology and law, for example; in fact, one of the few criticisms of the school is that its position at the forefront of that emerging field has come at the expense of more traditional areas of study, such as constitutional law.

Not surprisingly, Stanford's proximity to Silicon Valley has made it a magnet for scholars in Internet-age intellectual property law. The faculty includes Lawrence Lessig, a leading light in cyberlaw lured from Harvard in 2000 to head up the Center for Internet and Society, which examines the many constitutional and public policy legal issues raised by the Internet. Stanford also recently established the Center for E-Commerce to explore the field of electronic commerce law. In the school's cyberlaw clinic, students guided by full-

time faculty study legal issues such as ethics, free speech, and privacy as they prepare real cases for real clients.

All told, Stanford offers seven legal clinics, including one on civil rights, another on criminal prosecution, and one on Supreme Court litigation. At the Stanford Community Law Clinic, which serves needy people in East Palo Alto, students get a chance to put their learning into practice handling cases concerning such issues as housing, workers' rights, and immigration. They work alongside lawyers with years of experience fighting the system on behalf of low-income clients and are involved from start to finish on cases, often seeing them through to trial.

Because students at Stanford are highly encouraged to develop a broad view of the law in several contexts, the curriculum includes a large offering of interdisciplinary programs. The school's Center on Conflict and Negotiation, for instance, brings together students and faculty from all parts of the university to study mediation and conflict resolution theory and practice in domestic and international settings. The International Studies program is open to grad students in law, business, engineering, and the arts and sciences, and offers classes that explore the global nature of law, business, science, and politics, taught by faculty from several disciplines.

Another area of strength is the environmental law program, consistently mentioned among the top in the nation. The program relies heavily on situational case studies—much like those used in business schools—to bring disputes over resources and regulations to life and give students a crack at solving real problems, such as how to balance business interests and conservation. In the public interest arena, where the number of course offerings rivals those in technology and intellectual property, students are trained in such areas as racial equality, voting rights, and gender law and public policy, and have access to a full-service, public interest career counseling office. Stanford offers annual fellowships to second- and third-year students pursuing public interest careers, plus summer fellowships for those who want to do nonpaying public interest work. Graduates who take low-paying public interest jobs can have as much as 100 percent of their law school loans forgiven depending on the number of years they stay in the job. (Typically, a loan is completely forgiven after 10 years.)

With so many older students in Stanford's law school population—the average age is 24—count on an often unusual mix of experiences and some lively discussion. Former investment bankers, doctors, legislators, even dancers become law students; the mix is consistently mentioned by students and faculty as one of the most valuable aspects of a Stanford education. "So many people have done really interesting non-law-related things before they come here to school," says Gabrielle Vidal, a grad of the class of 2000, which included a former Texas legislator and a coroner. "Then when they get here, they have interesting life stories to bring to the law."

Paradise, of course, comes at a price. With annual tuition now over $35,000 coupled with the San Francisco Bay Area's high cost of living,

a Stanford Law education runs over $50,000 a year. However, stop any Stanford student and they'll tell you the investment is well worth it: they, like graduates of the other elites, are walking away with six-figure starting salaries. And don't be surprised if the student tries to interest you in a T-shirt that says "Harvard, the Stanford of the East."

> *"Who could resist a world-class law school in paradise?"*

Number 3: Harvard Law School

Cambridge, Massachusetts

With nearly 1,700 students, the "metropolis" is roughly the size of the law schools at Yale, Stanford, and the University of Chicago combined. The law library, with two million volumes, is the largest of its kind in the world. More than 80 full-time professors and about 100 part-time faculty teach 250-plus electives, providing depth in many areas—Islamic law, for example—that smaller schools simply can't achieve.

Harvard's platinum reputation rests largely on its biggest resource: a marquee faculty that includes defense attorney Alan Dershowitz, former U.S. Solicitor General Charles Fried, and constitutional scholar Laurence Tribe, to name just a few of the larger lights. The big names often teach first-year classes, bringing the material alive with war stories from the trenches. "A course with Alan Dershowitz is not criminal law—it's criminal law with Alan Dershowitz," says 2004 graduate John Doulamis. "I took constitutional law with Fried, and he'd argued the cases we were reading in front of the Supreme Court."

But one big downside of Harvard's size has long been its tendency to feel cold and impersonal to students. "The stereotype used to be that everybody wanted to come here because it was Harvard, but didn't much expect to like it," says Dean Elena Kagan. That perception started changing five years

---

"The stereotype used to be that everybody wanted to come here because it was Harvard, but didn't much expect to like it."

---

ago, when the school hired an outside management firm to direct a makeover. Responding to complaints that professors were inaccessible, administrators went on a hiring spree and halved the student–faculty ratio to about 11 to 1. First-year sections—the big groups of students who take the basic courses together—shrank from 140 to about 80. And first-year students are now divided into groups, or "law colleges," that aim to promote a sense of community by sponsoring social events. "We're never going to get an intense intimacy here, but we can make sense within this big city—we can have neighborhoods," says Kagan. "It's a much friendlier place now," says Doulamis.

Some students still see room for improvement. Small seminars for second and third years can be tough to get into, for example. "I don't have enough credits this semester because I'm on too many wait lists," is not a rare complaint. First-year sections are sometimes bundled together, forcing class size beyond 150 students. And many professors, engaged in their research, continue to be inaccessible. "One of my professors saw me as a nuisance," says one first-year

student. "He had me out of his office in 10 minutes after I'd waited two weeks to see him." Kagan hopes to extend the law college system to second and third year students and hire 15 additional faculty to drive the student–faculty ratio down even further.

While students at some smaller law schools seem uniformly bent on changing the world, many Harvard students—who coming in in 2005 had a median 3.81 undergraduate GPA and a median 173 LSAT—proudly advertise that they're here for the renowned corporate law curriculum. The program boasts nearly 20 professors, research centers in international tax, corporate governance, and international finance, plus opportunities for interdisciplinary study through the esteemed business school. Recently, though, the school has strengthened its focus on public interest law, adding a graduation requirement of pro bono work and increasing funds for students who do low- or nonpaying public interest work during the summer. While the last dean was a corporate law specialist, Kagan is a veteran of the Clinton White House.

Though some students—especially those on the corporate law track—chafe at the pro bono requirement, Kagan says "students should feel like public service is an integral part of the legal profession." Harvard's "low-income protection program" repays the loans of graduates making less than $38,000. Slightly higher-paid grads are eligible for partial loan repayments. The school also promotes public service through 20-plus courses with clinical components that have students doing such work as helping low-income area residents with immigration, housing, and

Kelly Farrell had reached the midpoint of her time at Harvard Law when it happened: she realized that she didn't want to be a lawyer. Farrell hadn't figured she'd end up at Harvard initially. Waitlisted, she'd made plans to attend the University of Virginia. "I was very excited about UVA, actually," she says. But when the phone call came, "my parents were like, 'Harvard calls,' so I went," heading off to Cambridge, Massachusetts, in the autumn of 1999 with great expectations and prepared for "a really amazing experience."

And yet, she says, her time at HLS "was only so-so. My roommate was the best thing to come out of my Harvard experience." The competitiveness on campus was part of the problem. It wasn't as if people were hoarding notes, she says, or sabotaging fellow classmates. But the classes were large and populated liberally with "gunners," always at the ready with an answer. The real pressure, she says, came from the high standards people imposed on themselves. "These expectations breed a little bit more anxiety. You're told that Harvard

is the key to unlocking all of these great doors."

Which it did: after her identity crisis, Farrell took stock and decided to use her law degree to work in politics, an interest since her days as a political science major at Duke University. First, she snagged a summer internship at Verner Liipfert, which had just been named one of the most powerful firms in Washington in a survey of Congressmen, Hill staffers, and senior White House aides. Then, upon graduation, she accepted a job with the law firm, where she spent her days on Capitol Hill lobbying members of Congress and attending hearings that related to the public policy interests of the firm's clients, which included Lockheed Martin, Visa, and British Aerospace.

In 2002, the firm merged with a larger company—and while the merger went smoothly, Farrell says, the atmosphere changed. Then a newlywed, Farrell was much more concerned about her quality of life, which was being affected by late nights and pressure to increase billable hours. "It drains you to be working 65–70

hours a week—and my hours were even more reasonable than other associates," she says.

She went next to the United States Maritime Administration, within the Department of Transportation, where as an attorney-advisor she followed legislation and new developments pertaining to initiatives such as the Maritime Security Program. For example, she worked on legislation allowing merchant marines to enter into agreements with private vessels during times of national emergency so that they can carry cargo for the government. Then she moved into space travel; as a legislative affairs specialist at NASA headquarters in Washington, she serves as a liaison with Congress on matters having to do with the space shuttle and international space station. One notable effort in which she played a part: getting Discovery off the ground again after the Columbia accident.

Farrell took a pay cut when she moved to the government, but notes that "averaged out by hours, I'm probably making about the same as I used to." The lifestyle change, of course, is just about priceless. "I was almost stunned when I didn't have to stay until 8 or 9 at night." That extra time at home has been especially precious since the birth of Jake, her first child. What's more, she loves the work. "It's kind of a nobler purpose than representing big corporations," she says. "You do your own little part for the country."

roughly 50 JD students each year in the office of the state Attorney General and in Boston's U.S. attorney's office.

Still, two-thirds of graduates end up taking private practice jobs—indeed, HLS attracts more than 700 private recruiters each year to its job bazaars. And students often snag a handful of offers in a single day.

Number 4: Columbia Law School

New York, New York

Columbia is a school that prides itself on its diversity. As a former director of admissions put it, Columbia students are "people comfortable [being] uncomfortable. They want to feel that a community is there for them, and then surround themselves with people who are different." Students typically have worked in all sorts of capacities: as Peace Corps volunteers, human rights activists, physicists, performing artists, journalists, teachers, and management consultants, among other things; only about a quarter come to campus straight from college. And though the law school is medium-sized—with some 1,200 students, it's not as big as Harvard, not as small as Yale—it's one of the most culturally diverse of the elites, with both a healthy percentage of international students and one of the largest percentages of minority students. It's religiously diverse, too, with substantial populations of Mormons, Muslims, Catholics, and Orthodox Jews. One attribute all do share: a strong academic record. The median LSAT score is 171 and the median GPA is 3.67.

By virtue of its location in the epicenter of international business, Columbia's areas of greatest strength traditionally have been corporate, comparative, and international law. Professors include such leaders in their fields as John Coffee, once named one of the country's 100 most influential lawyers by *The National Law Journal*; Harvey Goldschmid, who has served as a commissioner with the Securities and Exchange Commission; and Jose Alvarez and Lori Fisler Damrosch, both widely recognized experts in international law.

In recent years, the school has worked to build a reputation in public interest law and legal philosophy as well. The Center for Public Interest Law, offers counseling to students who want to pursue service careers and funds summer internships in human rights and public service organizations. Interested students are paid by Columbia to work in over 40 countries with groups such as the Human Rights and Equal Opportunity Commission in Australia, the International Criminal Tribunals in Yugoslavia and Rwanda, and the European Court of Human Rights in France. Others go to nonprofits and government agencies that have included the U.S. Attorney's office, the United Nations, the American Civil Liberties Union, and the NAACP Legal Defense and Education Fund.

The Center for Public Interest Law also helps students fulfill their obligation of 40 hours of pro bono work before graduation. The pro bono experience, which can range from representing death row prisoners to helping children in foster care, is rewarding enough that more than half of students put in more than the 40-hour minimum.

In the upper-class years, students can enroll in one of eight clinical programs, taught by full-time faculty members, in child advocacy, law and the arts, environmental law, human rights, lawyering in the digital age, mediation, non-profit organizations and small business, and prisoners and families. "It was definitely the best class at law school," says 2004 grad Dale Margolin, who took the child advocacy clinic and then became a clinic teaching assistant. "The highlight was when my lawyer let me handle a case that involved getting a mother out of a homeless shelter and reuniting her with all her seven children."

Though Columbia has long had a reputation for being overly competitive, students beg to differ. "Everyone's so aware of the cutthroat image that there's social pressure to act noncompetitive," says a student from Belton, Texas. Anne Ochsendorf from Elkins, West Virginia, says she found classmates friendly and actually eager to lend notes to anyone who missed a class. But that didn't surprise her as much as the closeness that often develops between students and professors. Each 1L is assigned a faculty advisor, who takes him or her out to dinner or lunch sometime during the fall. Some 130 small seminars are open to upperclassmen, all with a student-to-teacher ratio of 14 to 1. "I came from Wellesley to the big city, and I was pleased to find that professors here are very much interested in getting

"Even if you're not in the top of your class at Columbia, you still get a job."

to know and support and involve students," Ochsendorf says.

Individual attention is emphasized in career counseling, too. Essentially, students are encouraged to do what they like the first summer (typically, 32 percent of 1Ls spend the summer working for a firm), and to get serious the second summer (90 percent work for firms). More than 700 interviewers come to campus each fall. "Even if you're not in the top of your class at Columbia, you still get a job," says JaMille Jackson, class of 2005. "I did 22 interviews, got 12 callbacks, and 6 offers."

And Columbia students land their first choice job more often than not. Many grads stay on in New York, and, while Columbia, like its peers, has a loan-forgiveness program for those who take public interest jobs, the vast majority opt for private practice. It's easy to see why: first-year associates can expect to earn a median of $125,000, plus bonus—just about what you need to survive in New York City these days.

Tied for Number 4: New York University School of Law

New York, New York

Like many would-be attorneys, Liyah Brown chose her law school with an eye on finding job opportunities, not friends. Interested in using the legal system to create social change, Brown planned to

> *"I think the thing that most impressed me when I came here is just how people were uniformly very sharp."*

immerse herself in New York University law school's renowned public interest courses and clinical programs, then move on to a job as a civil rights or poverty lawyer. What's more, she was occupied with being pregnant during her first year and commuting from Brooklyn, far from the dorm scene. So she was startled when her classmates started checking in with her. "People would email me and say, 'If there's ever a day you don't feel like coming to class, if you need an assignment, just email me, and my notes are your notes,'" says Brown, class of 2004. "I feel like there's definitely more than 10 people that I'll [stay] in touch with, professors included. And that's a nice surprise."

There's no question that NYU is highly competitive: seventy-five percent of last fall's 1Ls scored 168 or higher on their LSATs and boasted undergraduate GPAs of at least 3.6. "I think the thing that most impressed me when I came here is just how people were uniformly very sharp," says Matthew Ginsberg, who previously was an organizer for a service employees' union in Baltimore and is planning a career in labor or immigration law.

But students report that success doesn't come at the next guy's expense. "People want to do well, but they want that for each other, too," says Brown. Professors, two-thirds of whom live within a five-minute walk of campus, are generally helpful and accessible, students say. Dean Richard Revesz, an Argentinian-born environmental lawyer, answers to "Ricky." Even the school's location—in a handful of brick mansions facing historic Washington Square Park in Greenwich Village, near coffeeshops and bars where both the servers and the customers often know your name—has a small-town feel.

Perhaps the collegial atmosphere should come as no surprise—one of the strengths of the NYU curriculum is that specialty dedicated to making the world a better place: public interest law. The school supplements its wide variety of courses and clinics with a weekly speakers' series, a public interest career counseling center, and financial assistance for students interested in pursuing such jobs. The school's loan repayment assistance program covers up to 100 percent of law school debt payments for as long as 10 years after graduation for students entering public interest careers and earning less than a certain amount ($58,000 for those graduating in 2005 and beyond; the salary cap is adjusted upward in year four and year seven as careers progress, to take account of inflation). And last year, the school announced it would provide several thousand dollars to every first- and second-year student who wanted to take a nonpaying summer job in a public interest organization in the United States or abroad.

Another area of distinction here is international law. In addition to its star-studded

American faculty, NYU maintains a "global faculty" from universities abroad who visit each year to teach special classes on subjects ranging from foreign tax treaties to gender issues in Islamic law. Driven by a school-wide sense that domestic lawyers increasingly will work on global issues, professors even outside the international arena often roll non-U.S. cases into their courses; a first-year student might study an Australian case asserting aboriginal rights in a course examining sovereignty, for example.

Many students are drawn to NYU by the opportunities it provides for students to practice before they graduate. All 1Ls take a one-year, ungraded course called Lawyering in which they role-play client interviews and negotiations, for example, under the guidance of tenured or tenure-track profs. Upperclassmen may apply for admission to any of about 20 clinics in which they assist real clients in such areas as immigrant rights, child welfare, and capital defense cases. Asit Panwala, class of 1999 and now a prosecutor in the Bronx, says that focusing on the facts of actual cases in his prosecution clinic while simultaneously having class discussions of the big-picture issues was the highlight of his law school experience. "Sometimes people see the forest and they don't see the trees,"

he observes. His clinic helped him see both, he says, and "that experience put me light years ahead when I started working."

Students also gain exposure to the real world through a faculty that features lawyers often quoted in the morning papers, like Noah Feldman, the Bush Administration's senior advisor for constitutional law in postwar Iraq, and Gerald

"People want to do well, but they want that for each other, too."

Lopez, author of *Rebellious Lawyering,* a seminal book on progressive law practice and Burt Neuborne, a former legal director of the ACLU.

In spite of the school's efforts to support alternative careers, most graduates pick the path of least resistance. Most accept jobs at private firms, while only a small percentage typically join public interest organizations and government agencies. Students say they have their pick of job offers. According to the career placement office, during the average school year, more than 550 employers interview on campus and the majority of graduates accept their first- or second-choice job. And, as is true at all the top schools, virtually everybody lands a job by graduation.

Chapter Three

What Law Schools Will Look For in You

The University of Chicago law school received more than 4,800 applications for 192 spots in the 2005 entering class. At the University of Pennsylvania, 6,400 people applied for about 250 slots. Georgetown fielded almost 12,000 applications last year for 450 day and 130 evening spots.

And it's not only the top 20 or 25 schools that are flooded with candidates; the competition is tougher just about everywhere. American University's Washington College of Law received about 9,000 applications last year. At Quinnipiac in Connecticut, a third-tier law school that has made improving the quality of its academic program and student body a top priority, the number of applicants rose 108 percent between 2001 and 2005.

How can you possibly stand out in such a crowd? This chapter tells you what attributes the admissions committee is looking for in a candidate and how you can best convey that you've got them. Your superior qualities are going to have to shine through in your test scores, transcript, personal statement, and letters of recommendation, because only a handful of law schools offer the

---

"The numbers matter, and anybody who says otherwise—that's ridiculous."

---

chance to impress in person. (For more detailed advice on how to tackle the application, see Chapter 4.)

Start with strong numbers

While it's not true—as many applicants fear—that your fate will hang entirely on your LSAT score, "the numbers matter, and anybody who says otherwise—that's ridiculous," says Georgetown's Cornblatt. Typically, grades and test scores serve as a kind of sorting mechanism, an efficient way for admissions staffers to mentally put applicants into one of three categories as they read through all the files: the probably admitted (unless something unexpected turns up to detract from the numbers), the probably denied (unless something unexpected turns up that makes them really appealing), and the ones who require considerable mulling over and discussion. Some schools do this analysis based on the LSAT, some do it based on the GPA, and some use both. Another option is to use an index number calculated by the Law School Admission Council (administrator of the LSAT)

that factors in LSAT score and GPA. Since schools can ask LSAC to correlate their index with the academic success of first-year law classes, the number can offer some indication of how an applicant is apt to fare during his or her first year at the school.

But contrary to popular belief about automatic acceptances and rejections, all applications generally get read—even at the very top and very bottom of the range. "In my experience, the goal of admissions is to enroll a dynamic class, and this commands a look beyond the numbers," says one person with experience both in the admissions office at an elite law school and as a private counselor. Some admissions experts believe that applications are bound to be read with even greater attention to non-numerical factors in the future. When the Supreme Court said it was legal for the University of Michigan Law School to consider race in admissions (see page 49), the justices "made clear that genuine diversity is an interest of constitutional significance—and that could include exotic languages," says Andrew Popper, a professor at American University's law school who has lots of experience reading applications himself as a member of the admissions committee. "If we're going to attempt to establish diversity, [law schools] have to really look at every file."

Indeed, some of the "probably denied" may turn out to bring unique experience to the table. One admissions dean, for example, recalls a Vietnamese applicant who spent time living under a bridge before escaping to the United States; he wouldn't have made it into law school based on numbers alone. And files of the almost-certain-to-be-admitted are typically read to be sure "they're not psycho killers," says Robert Berring, formerly interim dean at UC–Berkeley's Boalt Hall—and to check for honor code violations, for example, or whether applicants reveal themselves in their personal statement as offensively arrogant or whiny.

Some schools are much more numbers-driven than others, says Seattle-based admissions consultant Loretta DeLoggio, and one way to tell is to check the variance between the 25th percentile and the 75th percentile in LSAT and GPA scores. If the bottom of the range is just a couple of points below the top, the school may well be pushing to get its numbers higher, she says. But in general, says DeLoggio, who specializes in helping minority students choose a law school and get in, applicants "grossly misuse" the 25th–75th percentile ranges in choosing schools. It's important to remember, she says, that "the 25th percentile is not a bottom. In 200 people accepted, 50 are below it!"

On the other hand, candidates who get in with scores on the low side are sure to be exceptional in some other way. In general, "someone with a 3.0 and an average LSAT score hasn't got a chance in hell of getting admitted to a top school—I'd discourage students from wasting their money" on the application, says former University of Dayton pre-law advisor Roberta Alexander, now retired.

"We have an informal sorting mechanism based on LSAT and GPA, but every applicant gets a holistic review. We're trying to find people who will be a good fit," says Derek Meeker, associate dean for admissions and financial aid at the University of Pennsylvania law school. At the University of Chicago, applicants are admitted, denied, or held on the first reading; those who are held might be offered the opportunity to write an additional essay or explain any puzzle in their files—really high grades and a low LSAT score, for example. "We read every single application from cover to cover," says Megan Barnett, associate dean for admissions and financial aid at Yale. The best 20 percent or so are then sent to the faculty for consideration; three faculty members read each file and rate candidates on a

> *"In my experience, the goal of admissions is to enroll a dynamic class, and this commands a look beyond the numbers."*

2-to-4 scale. Of the pool of around 12,000 that Georgetown considers to admit maybe 2,000, some "2,500 are easy 'nos' and 800 are easy 'yeses,'" says admissions head Andrew Cornblatt. "Of the rest, I get to admit 1 in 9. That's where I earn my salary." Every file at Columbia is read by at least two people.

Show them you're a thinker

One characteristic of law students who succeed—the only kind admissions officers intend to accept—is that they're informed and incisive thinkers. So your application will be closely studied for evidence that you can measure up. "I try to gauge the intellectual ability of the student—who's analytically really good?" says Kate Stith, former deputy dean and professor at Yale. "I'm looking for the students who will come up with new ideas, the ones that aren't in the textbooks."

While the grades and test scores certainly indicate intellectual ability, the transcript tells a much more nuanced story. Anybody who still has maneuvering time ahead should know that grades

If your heart is set on a top school but your grades and LSAT scores won't get you there, consider enrolling elsewhere and taking another shot next year. "There are two ways to get into law school now," says Deborah Post, former co-chair of the Society of American Law Teachers' committee on admissions and a professor at Touro College's law school in Huntington, New York. "You've got the numbers, or you prove you can do the work: you go to a lower-tier school and transfer."

While they don't exactly advertise it, many highly competitive law schools rely on their transfer programs to fine-tune the composition of their student bodies and bring in appealing near-miss applicants after they've blossomed academically at another school. (Because the undergraduate grade point averages and LSAT scores of first-year students figure in the *U.S. News* law school rankings, taking less-credentialed

applicants into the second-year class is also seen by many administrators as a way to avoid putting a school's rank at risk.)

"It's a terrific, terrific program," says Robert Berring, formerly interim dean at the University of California–Berkeley's Boalt Hall, which accepts about 30 transfer students each year. "We can take people from the top of lots of little law schools, and they're often [our] best students, with fire in their eyes."

It's also a good way to "do something for your legacy and donor kids—it's a better message than 'we don't have room,'" says Andrew Cornblatt, head of admissions at Georgetown University law school, who calls transfer programs "an underreported way to get into a top place."

That fire in the eye is what admissions committees will be looking to find—a position in the top 5 or 10 percent of your law school class, and, better yet, a spot on the law review,

too. On the other hand, if you've *got* those credentials and are flourishing where you are, be sure to weigh the benefits of being at a higher-prestige institution against the likelihood that you'll give up star status.

"A transfer student might not make law review at the next school—you're giving up a very, very important credential and taking a risk," says Stuart Rabinowitz, president of Hofstra University in New York and formerly dean of its law school, which regularly loses top students to more prestigious places. Moreover, students at the very top of their classes at well-respected but not prestigious schools very often find themselves in contention for jobs on par with those offered to middling students at highly ranked schools. If you move, are you at risk of falling toward the bottom?

by themselves don't mean a whole lot: what matters is that you performed well in a curriculum of rigorous, challenging courses that required you to think, and to write. "I want to see people who

are intellectually curious and ambitious, and who have taken some courses outside their typical realm," says Penn's Meeker. "Many people have studied political science or history, and this is all fine, but it's common. A polysci major might want to take some science and math." Any patterns in your undergraduate grades will also be of great interest. "Did your grades improve over time? Is there a special explanation for a particularly weak semester?" says Evan Caminker, dean and professor of law at the University of Michigan law school.

"Some students think you have to be a polysci major—forget it!" says Cheryl Ficarra, associate dean for enrollment management at Syracuse University. "English! Or any subject that shows they've done serious analytical writing and been critiqued. These students have a serious advantage." In fact, Carol Leach, an associate professor of political science and pre-law advisor at Chicago State University, analyzed data on the undergraduate majors of the entering class at American law schools several years ago and found that the highest rates of admission were among physics majors, with history, English, economics, math, and the other sciences close behind. "I tell students to pick a major they like so they'll do well, but one that's challenging," says Leach. The bottom line, she says, is that "you have to have really good grades in hard subjects."

Put it in writing

There's no doubt about it, a bad essay speaks volumes.

The main function of the personal statement is to give the committee some insight on what kind of person you are. But your essay will also demonstrate whether you've got that all-important legal skill: the ability to marshal your arguments on paper in an articulate and persuasive fashion. So not only do you have to give information that will put you over the top, but you also must present it in a well-organized, elegant way. "Someone could have an outstanding LSAT score and GPA, and if he's not able to write compellingly or effectively, that's a *big* problem," says admissions consultant Mark Meyerrose.

> *"I'm looking for the students who will come up with new ideas, the ones that aren't in the textbooks."*

You'll get partway there by choosing your topic well; for detailed advice on coming up with a theme, see page 44. Some general tips: it's far better to talk about yourself than about legal issues, or politics, or the state of the country today. If you try to take on the world in two pages, the result is bound to sound naïve or pseudo-intellectual. But don't just describe an experience or an achievement—go a step further and explore how it's influenced you. "What have you learned? Don't just say that you've worked at a camp for disabled children, tell us how that's changed you," says Ann Perry, assistant dean for admissions at the University of Chicago's law school. Beware of overdoing it. Grandiose claims will certainly spur admissions officers to carefully search for the supporting evidence.

Then you need to structure your story effectively, express yourself clearly and artfully, perhaps use a bit of humor if you've got the touch. "Your personal statement is a writing sample in the most profound sense—there's no excuse for sloppy expression," says Berring of Boalt Hall. "Use crisp, clear sentences. Many people think legal writing is complex clauses—not true!"

"Is the use of language effective? Does it paint a picture? Does it make me and my colleagues stop and listen? If you've got a great story to tell and you don't tell it until the second page, I won't see it," says AU's Andrew Popper. It probably goes without saying—or should—that every comma and period better be in the right place, too.

> *"If you take on the world in two pages, it comes across as naïve, or pseudo-intellectual."*

Make the most of your experience

Once a candidate's academic abilities have been established, the committee wants to know if she'll arrive with a perspective that will make for informed and lively debate. "I'm looking for an interesting class," says Popper. At AU's Washington College of Law, where last year some 9,000 applicants vied for 365 full-time and about 100 part-time slots, the LSAC-calculated index number assigned to each candidate gives the admissions committee a sense of his or her capabilities. Each file is read by one of the committee members, who review about 50 applications a week apiece and meet regularly to discuss them and give a thumbs-up or thumbs-down.

Many kinds of experience may make a particular candidate interesting, depending on the mix of other people applying: ethnic or religious background, socioeconomic status, undergraduate major—even geographic location. "People from the West think differently about the role of government and individual rights than people in New York City do," says Michael Young, who served as dean of George Washington University law school before moving to the presidency of the University of Utah. "People from California and Florida understand the melting pot and the importance of legal systems that work for all cultures." An applicant whose experience as a member of a minority group has been influential may want to explore that theme in the essay because most law schools value diversity for what it brings to class discussion.

One factor that has grown increasingly important in recent years is work experience. This has happened partly because the nature of the pool is changing; due to the economic downturn, the applicant pool has been rich with experienced people returning to school. "Ten years ago, 85 percent of our students came directly from college," says Lynell Cadray, dean of admission at Emory law school. "This year, it was 50 percent."

This is also a function of a desire on the part of law deans and professors to seed their classes with wise and seasoned students attuned to the way the world operates now. "Lawyers today are part of a team, working with people whose experience is finance or human resources—it's no longer the Abe Lincoln version of law," says David Van Zandt, dean of the law school at Northwestern University, where almost everybody arrives with at least one year of work experience, and more than half typically have two or more. "What we're looking for is people who have had to work with a team or lead a team to get a project done. We've turned away people with very high LSATs who've had no work experience."

"Work experience adds to the level of what we can do with them here," says Cadray. "It's fun to have young, energetic students, but it's good to have balance. People interpret the legal sys-

Profile: The corporate lawyer

After five summers playing outfield for the Asheville Tourists, the Carolina Mudcats, and other minor league teams, David Feuerstein was ready for a change. He had graduated from Yale in 1995, grabbed his mitt, and begun the circuit of 14-hour bus trips to games up and down the East Coast. "That's a lot of baseball," he says. "As a minor leaguer, you make no money. And I was tired of it."

During the off-season, Feuerstein paid the bills by working as a paralegal for five months a year and discovered that he liked what he was doing. While he wasn't sure he wanted to be a lawyer, he figured that "a law degree [gives] you the most flexibility in the professional world. I knew I could do really whatever I wanted with it."

Because Feuerstein's girlfriend (now his wife) was living in New York City, he applied to the law schools at New York University, Columbia, and Yeshiva University. When he didn't get in to Columbia or NYU, he enrolled at Yeshiva's Benjamin N. Cardozo School of Law—though he worried that it didn't have the name recognition of the Ivies. "You take a risk not going to a top name law school, and I rolled the dice a little bit," Feuerstein says. "But I thought, 'I can do well. I can make the most of it.'"

As it turned out, he loved it. Taking a position and defending it to the bitter end appealed to the athlete in him. "My time away from higher intellectual challenges may have helped, too," he adds. In his third year, he was approached by the faculty to help organize a symposium on a subject one Cardozo professor had written extensively about: the similarities between law and baseball. The symposium drew the former commissioner and deputy commissioner of baseball, the president of the Florida Marlins, a sports writer from the *New York Times*, and, perhaps most importantly, the former dean of Cardozo Law School, Paul Verkuil. Later, when Feuerstein was searching for a job, it was Verkuil who introduced him to his future employer.

After graduation, Feuerstein joined Boies, Schiller, and Flexner in New York, where the majority of his clients were big corporations and the work involved such complex commercial litigations as antitrust cases and contract disputes. Many of Feuerstein's clients were sports organizations: the firm does work for the Yankees and NASCAR, for example.

Now, Feurerstein is an associate at Herrick, Feinstein, a general practice firm with offices in New York and New Jersey, where he hopes to continue combining his love of sports and the law.

---

tem differently depending on what they have done. And people who have worked tend to know how to work together, and want everyone to succeed."

While you might assume it's best to take a job in the legal field, perhaps as a paralegal, that's not necessarily the case. As Sandra Oakman, AU's late admissions director once put it, "It really doesn't matter what it is—you could be a bartender in Vail. Go out and work beside people and learn what it's like to be a single mother making $12 an hour. As a lawyer, you'll deal with all kinds of people, and wouldn't it be nice to know something about their culture?" Joe Lemon of the Stanford Law class of 2002 wrapped up his undergraduate studies at Brown in 1992 then

---

"Go out and work beside people and learn what it's like to be a single mother making $12 an hour."

---

managed a hotel for several years before applying to law school. In his personal statement, he wrote about how the experience taught him to handle unexpected challenges—like the time two hours before a 200-guest wedding service when the groom had a seizure. (The wedding quickly was turned into a private affair, and the party went on as planned—except that the groom took a number of breaks to lie down.)

Remember, the point is to highlight how your background will allow you to offer something to the intellectual life at the school. "There's not one formula," says Katharine Bartlett, dean of the law school at Duke University, one of whose essays simply asks applicants to discuss what they might contribute that's different. A 37-year-old mom with three kids will certainly have an unusual perspective, says consultant DeLoggio. "People who have overcome eating disorders and drug addictions often want to hide these successes because they only see the failure they were before. But tomorrow's leaders need to understand a broad swath of society—not just the one in which they grew up," she says.

Demonstrate that you're a leader

One detail law schools can often glean from your work experience is whether or not you've got what it takes to motivate other people, solve problems, and make things happen. Ideally, your essay and your letters of recommendation will work together to paint you as the type of person who takes on responsibilities and produces results, either on the job if you've had one or in your activities as a student. "We want someone who's taken ownership of a group or a project, and made a difference," says Bartlett.

"It's very common for people to write 'I went to college, I studied this because I wanted to do this. I was president of this,'" says Ann Perry of Chicago. "Better to tell us what challenges you faced. You needed funding? Tell us how you worked the system. We want to see that you're capable."

Prove you've got a passion— and compassion

It's definitely in your favor to show a passionate interest in something other than your schoolwork or your work. Otherwise, you might come across as a "not very active citizen," says admissions consultant Mark Meyerrose. "What have you done? I don't want someone who has just gone to class and gone home," says Cornblatt.

But no one will be impressed by a padded résumé of activities that shows breadth without any depth. Much better to be very involved in a couple of activities—perhaps you studied the environment as an undergraduate, have taken a lead role in your local community group's battle against rapid development, and have religiously biked to work for the past two years—than to be a dabbler in a whole list of organizations. That's because admissions people recognize that those who graduate and become leaders in their field are likely to be the ones who show true commitment. Keep in mind that your letters of recommendation can be very helpful here. "It would raise flags for me if someone talks about how active on campus they've been and the recommender doesn't mention it," says Cornblatt. "It's great stuff when the application and letter both say it."

Because public service is such a major focus of the legal profession (even if many lawyers can't afford to take the jobs) many law schools are impressed by evidence of heart. "We're definitely on the lookout for compassionate students who have worked in their communities. This is a profession of counseling, being altruistic, caring," says Lynell Cadray, Emory's admissions dean. One of the more memorable personal statements that Cadray has read came from an older applicant who had served in the military; he wrote about bravery and his own experience pulling an accident victim from a burning car. "If we'd only looked at the numbers, he'd have been put on the wait list," she says. "But this is the kind of character you want in the profession."

Chapter Four

The Application

Whether you've dreamed your whole life of becoming the next Ally McBeal or are angling to hide out in law school until the job market recovers, one thing is for sure: you're not alone. Law schools across the country are reporting record numbers of applicants, so you'll be applying during the most intensely competitive era in history.

The fact is, it's tough to get into any school, anywhere, these days.

To stand out among the overachieving, type-A masses, you'll need to submit a virtually flawless application. The four parts of the package—your academic credentials, Law School Admissions Test score, personal statement, and letters of recommendation—will demonstrate whether you're equipped (or not) with the skills you'll need to succeed in a law career: the powers of persuasion, analytical and critical thinking, and a mastery of clear, precise, and direct writing.

First, understand that you're playing a numbers game. Law school admission is largely about two stats: your undergraduate grade point average and your performance on the LSAT. Chances are it's too late to do very much about the former—although any opportunity to raise your GPA even just a point or two should be taken seriously. (Note that grades are generally considered in the context of who's granting them and in what subject. In other words, a B in physics from Yale may be more impressive than an A in physics from your local public college.) Even more important, you've got to kick butt on the LSAT. Together, "the numbers account for 80 percent of the decision," estimates Roberta Alexander, who served as director of the pre-law program at the University of Dayton before retiring and was a former president of the Midwest Association of Pre-Law Advisors.

The other 20 percent? You've got to prove that you're interesting and accomplished, as well as smart. "Making a law school class is a lot like making a guest list for a dinner party," says R. Michael Cassidy, associate professor at Boston College Law School. "We want people who will have exciting discussions." The personal statement, handled properly, will reveal something about your character that speaks to your desirability as a dinner companion, if you will—and also your abilities as an effective and fluent writer. You've also got to get your professors, bosses, ex-bosses, or anyone else who knows you well to lend credence to the impressive picture you've painted of yourself.

The advice that follows on navigating the admissions process is gleaned from interviews with dozens of people who've either been there themselves or watch it over and over, including pre-law advisors at undergraduate colleges, law school admissions officers, and students who wish they'd handled a few things differently than they did. You still can.

Get a little guidance

If you haven't already done so, stop by your college's pre-law advising office. Though pre-law advisors, unlike high school guidance counselors, don't usually write recommendations or have any say in admissions at all, they do know a lot about the priorities of the decision makers. And sometimes, they *are* in a position to help or hurt your case: "I use pre-law advisors when we're trying to make decisions to find out about curricula and an applicant's major and colleges' grading scales," says Lynell Cadray, dean of admissions at Emory University's law school in Atlanta.

Most pre-law advisors are also professors, administrators, or career counselors with all of the multiple responsibilities of two full-time jobs. As a

> *It's tough to get into any school, anywhere, these days.*

result, it can take some work to get a bit of face time, much less an hour-long appointment. But students who take the initiative early in their college career will find that a dedicated advisor can help them figure out which classes enhance a transcript, for example, or what major might make sense. Later on, an advisor might help you figure out which law schools are within your reach and which ones offer scholarships, and then review your personal statement before you send it off. Applicants who have been out of college for a while should feel free to tap the advising office at their alma mater—although they may be charged a fee for any services. (When you register for the LSAT, the Law School Admissions Council, which administers the test, will provide you with the name and contact information of the pre-law advisor on your old campus.)

Unfortunately, many students report that overtaxed pre-law advisors are no help at all. If yours hasn't been responsive, you might consider hiring a private counselor. "Applying to law school is very much about self-assessment; this introspection really can't effectively take place unless there is another person to bounce ideas off of," argues Mark Meyerrose, a former Harvard Law School admissions officer who now works for Admissions Consultants, Inc., a Virginia-based firm that offers strategy and essay editing for applicants to college and graduate schools. "Everyone needs a critical reader." The firm's soup-to-nuts packages range from $1,595 for help with three applications to $3,895 for 10 applications (www.admissionsconsultants.com).

Indeed, while seeking the feedback of a trusted friend or professor is a fine idea, applicants appear to be increasingly willing to pay for professional guidance. Test-prep behemoth Kaplan Educational Services has seen demand for its pre-law consulting services climb rapidly in recent years. The cost for its comprehensive admissions advice, usually given over the phone or by email, is anywhere from $599 for three hours of service to $1,599 for 10 hours; check out www.kaptest.com for more details. Test Masters, at www.testmasters180.com, will help you pick a topic for your personal statement and write an outline in one hour, for $200, and will continue to lend a hand as you hone your prose for an additional $150 per hour; full admissions counseling is also available at $200 for an initial hour and $150 for each hour after that The 10-hour package runs $1,250.

If you're not willing or able to cough up the fees, consider contacting current law students for their insight about what qualities matter most to a school. One current 3L at the University of Pennsylvania suggests calling or emailing student organizations you may be interested in and asking a member or two how best to market yourself. Though most schools don't offer admissions interviews, deans and other faculty members also may be willing to answer questions about their school and what they value in a candidate. "I talk to every student who wants to meet with me," says David Cohen, professor and former dean at Pace University law school.

These contacts can come in handy later, after your applications are in. Randy Reilford contacted admissions officers at all of the nine law schools he applied to in late December and January of 2001–2002, and he often got put through to the dean. "I said 'I just want to talk to you about my application, to see if I can clear up any questions you might have had,'" says Reilford, who also visited schools in Philadelphia, where he's from, and met with admissions officers, faculty members, and representatives from black student organizations. "I wanted them to have a voice to put with my application, which I think has its weight just like anything else." Reilford was accepted at six of the schools he applied to and chose the University of Wisconsin School of Law, whose admissions dean had mentioned to him that graduates of the flagship institution's law school don't have to take the bar exam to become credentialed in Wisconsin.

> *"I wanted them to have a voice to put with my application, which I think has its weight just like anything else."*

Watch your timing

The number one tip from pre-law advisors, paid and otherwise: it really helps to get your paperwork in early. Why? Better that your scintillating story about tutoring underprivileged inner-city kids be the first one a dean reads, rather than the 245th. "Earlier is always better," says Mark Meyerrose. "But there is a limit to that. I never push an applicant to get his application in by the beginning of, say, November, if that push will compromise quality. As long as the application is submitted by the December holidays, an applicant should be in good shape." See page 43 for more help with timing.

A great way to stay ahead of the game is to obtain your applications online and fill them out all at one time. The Law School Admissions Council, or LSAC—a nonprofit corporation of law schools that manages the admissions process for its members—offers two ways to apply to multiple law schools: students can fill out a common application using the "LSACD on the Web" software—on sale at www.lsac.org—that's accepted at all ABA-approved law schools; a CD-ROM version is also available. The applications can then be submitted electronically to individual schools or printed out and mailed in.

Just about every law school requires that you apply using the LSAC's Law School Data Assembly Service, or LSDAS. For a fee, the group will prepare a report (and send it to one school) that includes a summary of your undergraduate academic career, copies of all undergraduate, graduate, and law school transcripts, your LSAT score and writing sample from the test, and copies of your letters of recommendation. Reports for each additional institution cost extra. (If you specify that you want an online account when you sign up, you'll be able to view your report on the Web and proofread the personal information in it.)

LSDAS suggests that you register for the service at least six weeks before you want your applications out. You can sign up online at www.lsac.org, by getting the 2003–2004 LSAT/LSDAS Registration and Information Book from your pre-law advising office, or by phone. Law schools then contact the service directly to obtain your report.

Familiarize yourself with the LSAT

Ah, the dreaded Law School Admissions Test—the bane of every future lawyer's existence. "I hate to say it's the key factor in admissions, but it certainly predominates," says one admissions officer at a top 20 school who asked not be identified. "When other things are weak and it is really strong, [it] will often make admissions officers forgive all the weaknesses." The converse can also be true, since most top schools are choosing among thousands of students with top grades *and* scores.

Why is the test so crucial? For one thing, it offers a quick and dirty way for admissions officers to compare applicants from diverse backgrounds and different schools—it's the one thing that a pottery major from State U. and a biochemical engineer from the Ivy League have in common. In addition, the test is widely considered to be a fairly reliable predictor of success during the first year of law school (as is college performance).

Part academic exercise and part endurance test, the LSAT is a half-day exam that tests skills as opposed to knowledge. It measures critical reading, verbal reasoning, analytical thinking, and writing abilities; there's no content involved whatsoever—no math or memorizing dates, in other words. "The LSAT is all about being able to pull apart arguments and understanding how evidence works," says Justin Serrano, general manager of graduate programs at Kaplan Test Prep and Admissions, who notes that these are exactly the talents you'll need in law school and, later, on the job.

The test is organized as five, 35-minute multiple-choice sections. Logical reasoning tests your capacity to understand, analyze, and complete arguments that are presented in short paragraph form; there are two logical reasoning sections that together account for half of your score. The problems in the analytical reasoning section measure your ability to understand relationships and draw conclusions about those relationships; there are four "games" with several questions apiece, and you will likely need to sketch diagrams in your test booklet to answer them. This is by far the most feared section

of the test, say veterans; it's also the most coachable, claim test-prep experts.

Reading comprehension is similar to what you experienced on the SAT; you'll have to read four long, complex passages and answer questions about them. Finally, an experimental section tests questions for future LSATs; although it appears to be a real part of the test, it doesn't count toward

---

"The LSAT is all about being able to pull apart arguments and understanding how evidence works."

---

your score. (Unfortunately, you won't necessarily know which section is experimental when you see it on the test.) The exam wraps up with a writing sample, which doesn't count either. You'll be given two alternatives and asked to choose a position and advocate it. Though the essay is sent to law schools along with your LSDAS report, it's generally not considered an important part of the package, and might not even merit a glance. But complete it carefully, just in case, because some application readers find the essay revealing. "The only thing you can't get editing help with is the written essay on the LSAT," says Barbara Safriet, associate dean at Yale's law school. "I read it for writing skills."

There's no penalty for wrong answers on the LSAT, so you should always take a guess, educated or not. The number of questions you answer correctly is your raw score, which is then converted to a scaled mark between 120 and 180. The average score is 150, but anything over 160 is considered competitive; anything over 170 puts you at or above the 98th percentile. An interesting fact: you can often miss a question or two and still nail a perfect 180.

The LSAT is offered four times a year: on a Saturday morning in October, December, and February, and on a Monday in June. (Alternatives are available for anyone who observes the Jewish Sabbath.) You can register online at www.lsac.org, with a form from the LSAT/LSDAS Registration and Information Book or over the phone. Be sure to sign up as soon as you can; with record numbers of test takers, popular testing sites can fill up early. (You may first want to check out www.kaptest.com/test-sites, which rates various locations for the last five test dates, based on student evaluations of proctors, desk space, and the like.) Scores remain valid for five years, so anyone planning on working a year or two before applying to law school may want to tackle the exam during junior or senior year, when he or she is still in test-taking mode.

In fact, all applicants should take the test as early as possible in order to allow for further preparation and a retest, if necessary. February and June of the junior year—or one full year before you plan to matriculate—are increasingly the norm. "This is a big mindset change," says Heather Struck, pre-law advisor at Binghamton University in New York. "Students used to be able to study during the summer and take the test in October [of senior year]. But there's a lot more stress now, and it helps if you can take it in your junior year." Still, you can procrastinate until December, if necessary, and still have time to beat the final February 1 or March 1 application deadlines.

Prepare to beat the test

Though the LSAT tests for capabilities rather than knowledge, that doesn't mean you can't prepare for the exam. In fact, practicing is crucial so you'll know what types of questions and games to expect: with only 60 to 90 seconds allotted per question, there's no time for confusion. The more familiar you are with all aspects of the exam, the more confident you'll feel on test day—and the better you'll do.

Do you have enough self-discipline to set your own study schedule and stick to it? Alex Murray did. In the first week of September of his senior year at Tulane, Murray bought a test-prep book and began completing problems and taking timed practice tests on the weekends. "I started out just doing one section at a time without a time limit to get used to the questions and format," he recalls. "Then I would do one or two sections and time myself. I didn't start taking full, timed exams until about two or three weeks before the exam, because it's so time-consuming." The week before Murray sat for the exam, he took advantage of a free practice test at the local Kaplan Test Prep center, which was timed and scored for him. In the end, he raised his score from the "high 150s" on practice tests to an extremely competitive 169 on the real thing—which helped get him into the University of California–Los Angeles School of Law.

In addition to the shelves of good commercial test-prep booklets out there (those published by Kaplan and Peterson's, for example), LSAC (www.lsac.org) offers such "official" help as the $28 SuperPrep, which contains three previously administered LSATs, with explanations. The most recent exams are available there for $8 each, too. Applicants also can take free sample tests at websites such as www.ivyleagueadmission.com, a for-profit site run by former admissions counselors. (Print out the sample exams first in order to best approximate a real test-taking situation.)

There are online options for those who prefer to learn at their own pace, with 24-hour-a-day access to online instruction and practice

practice tests. In fact, due to increased demand, The Princeton Review has recently extended its web-based offerings with a course featuring live, real-time instruction for $899, a do-it-anytime online course for $599, and an express version with three hours of lessons and two practice tests for $99.

Not everyone can do this kind of prep on his own, however. If you need additional motivation in the form of a class commitment and several hours'

The application timeline

18 months prior to enrollment

- Contact your pre-law advisor to set up a meeting; attend any related seminars offered on your college campus.
- Research schools and come up with a target list.
- Take a practice, timed LSAT to see where you stand.
- Register for the June LSAT.
- Decide on the method of test prep that suits you best and start studying.

June before applying

- Take the June LSAT, and if you don't do as well as expected, re-register for October and start studying again.
- Start visiting campuses, if possible.

August–September

- Begin crafting the "story" that will become your personal statement, then write and rewrite it—and then

rewrite it again. Get feedback from an unbiased editor.
- Put together a résumé to submit with your application.
- Figure out whom you will ask for recommendations—and whether or not each will write you a positive letter.
- Send away for or download applications.

October–November

- Continue to perfect your personal statement and résumé.
- Make sure the people writing your letters of recommendation have enough source material to draw from and remind them about deadlines
- Take the October LSAT, if necessary.
- Subscribe to LSDAS and request transcripts from all undergraduate and graduate schools you've attended.
- Sign up for an LSAC online account so you can obtain a

copy of your master Law School Report from LSDAS. Proofread for any errors.
- Complete and mail your applications to schools—the earlier the better.

December

- Finish up any remaining applications.
- If you have not yet taken the LSAT or want to try it again, the December test is your last shot, assuming you want to be considered for the fall entering class.

January–February

- Request that any supplemental transcripts be sent to LSDAS.
- Check in with your schools to see if they need any additional information.
- Wait for the acceptance letters to start rolling in!

worth of homework a week, there are virtually endless opportunities. Many colleges and law schools offer their own test prep; the University of Arizona's law school, for example, gives a free four-day class to local students who demonstrate they can't afford a commercial one. Check with your pre-law advising center for similar opportunities in your area.

On the other end of the spectrum are intensive classes offered by companies such as Kaplan and The Princeton Review, the latter of which boasts an average seven-point gain for its students. They offer options for everyone from the ultraorganized student who plans to spend at least three months studying to the person holding down a full-time job who only has a couple of weeks to get ready. Those seeking more personalized attention can also purchase private, one-on-one tutoring.

The quality of tutors and programs can vary from region to region, so it's a good idea to research test prep offerings in your area before signing up for a particular company's course. Talk to different teachers and investigate their review materials to determine what approach they take, for instance, and consult friends and acquaintances who have prepped before you.

Make the most of your second time around

Didn't quite hit 175 this time? Think hard about whether you want to try again. The LSAC reports your LSAT scores (plus any decisions you make to cancel a score) over a five-year span, as well as an average score. You're also assigned a "score band" that ranges from roughly three points below to three points above your actual score—an attempt by the LSAC to recognize that there

could be statistical errors, and to discourage schools from putting too much weight on single-point differentials. When applicants take the test more than once, most schools look at the average score, not just the higher one, and so only a fairly significant jump is going to have any real impact.

Admissions officers suggest sitting for the LSAT again only if practice tests taken under realistic conditions suggest that you'll get a much higher score, or if circumstances the first time—a marching band outside the testing room, say, or a nasty case of mono—had an obvious impact on your performance. If you do take the exam twice and end up with a large discrepancy between your scores, you might want to write a note of explanation countering any suspicion of cheating (and clarifying why the higher grade makes sense).

Write a mind-blowing personal statement

Here is your chance to take the admissions committee beyond the cold, hard numbers and demonstrate why you'll be an asset to the class. Think of your personal statement as the interview you probably won't have—an opportunity to showcase your personality and drive and talk about your passions and events that have made you who you are. The idea is to demonstrate that your superlative record comes with humor, an ability to reflect, and a measure of gained wisdom.

First, you need to decide on a specific topic. "Students should really hone in on one thing—one activity they're involved in or one challenge that was significant," says Don Rebstock, associate dean for enrollment management and career strategy at Northwestern University School of Law in Illinois. Otherwise, there's an unappealing tendency to ramble. Rebstock suggests brainstorming for ideas by going to a bookstore and paging through a manual on hiring for questions intended to get at interviewees' characters. What is the defining moment of your life? What are your biggest strengths and weaknesses? Though it might be tempting to expound on the complex legal theory du jour, an academic treatise won't help your case—it doesn't really address anything about *you*. "Let us know what type of voice you'll bring," says Ann Perry, assistant dean for admissions at the University of Chicago law school. "I don't want a résumé, and I don't want to know what kind of law you want to practice."

You needn't deal directly with the law at all, in fact, to show that you've got what it takes to be a lawyer. When he applied to New York University School of Law, Paul Millen wrote about scaling a difficult stretch of rock formations while hiking in Central China. "The story illustrated a method of problem solving that analyzed information to the degree possible, but recognized that the ultimate decision required a certain amount of courage and risk-acceptance," he explains. "I highlighted my travel experiences, demonstrated my adventuresome spirit, and, in discussing the decision-making process, exhibited an ability to work [with others], since the rest of my group consisted of Chinese, Israelis, and Europeans."

Another applicant wrote about organizing hotel workers in New Orleans. Although her LSAT scores were only so-so, Washington and Lee School of Law admired her pluck, commitment, and unique experience and came through with a generous financial aid package. A Naval officer accepted by an Ivy League law school described how confounded he'd felt as judge of a local beauty pageant when he'd tried to issue orders to the crowd of 17-year-old girls with absolutely no effect. "If he'd written about the wisdom and maturity he'd gained in his naval command, he would only have put himself among everyone else with five years' work experience," says Seattle admissions consultant Loretta DeLoggio.

> *"Students should really hone in on one thing— one activity they're involved in or one challenge that was significant."*

Many admissions officers recommend staying away from potentially inflammatory subjects such as politics or religion, as you can never be sure who your reader will be. Others counter that any topic is fine, as long as you're invested in it. But there are some definite no-no's: unless the story is dramatic and compelling, you'll want to avoid predictable themes such as "Why I've dreamed of becoming a lawyer since I was 4." It's also smart to steer clear of areas that are already well-covered in your application, like your LSAT score or your grades. (Consider an addendum to the application if you really feel there's more to say on these matters, say experts.)

Writing about challenges overcome is okay, but be sure to hit the right notes. "I'm often struck by people who seem to lack perspective, and who think minor hurdles overcome were extraordinary," says Sarah Zearfoss, assistant dean and director of admissions at the University of Michigan Law School in Ann Arbor. "It's fine and good to talk about hurdles," she says, but do not make a bigger claim for yourself than the situation warrants. And the last thing you want to seem to do is whine.

Whatever the topic, your personal statement should be well-organized and compelling because effective communication is so key to the practice of law. And make sure to proofread for any goofs in grammar, spelling, or punctuation. Or worse: you don't want to say you'd be a perfect fit at Yale on your Cornell essay, for instance (a more common occurrence than you might think). Inattention to detail is unacceptable in the field of law, so why should the application process be any different? Further, think long and hard about the tone of your personal statement, as nearly every admissions officer has a horror story about a mean-spirited or arrogant essay that doomed a candidate's application. It goes without saying that the work should be wholly your own.

One dean remembers a successful essay written as a recipe, but creative writers should generally err on the side of caution; law school, after all, is a pretty conservative place. "We're open to various styles, with one caveat: it can definitely be taken too far," says Monica Ingram, assistant dean for admissions at the University of Texas–Austin. "If you're not Charles Dickens before you write your statement, this is probably not the opportunity to take a foray into creative writing."

"No one with a rhyming essay has gotten in for at least the last five years," adds Megan Barnett, Yale's dean of admissions and financial aid.

Get glowing recommendations

Now that you've presented your accomplishments, it's time to have a third party back you up. Ask people you've worked with closely to write your letters of recommendation—people who will offer enthusiastic support. You might assume that a letter from your senator or a local Pulitzer Prize–winning author will carry great weight, but if she does-n't know you from your next door neighbor, it's unlikely she can say anything about you that will have any impact. Far better to have a teaching assistant who's observed you in class comment on how smart you are and how enthusiastically you participate, or to ask a former boss to describe how you went the extra mile. Then make sure each letter writer has the necessary raw material as inspiration, including a copy of your résumé and personal statement and perhaps a particularly impressive paper you wrote for class or a project you've worked on with a colleague.

"The best advice I can give to students is that they keep papers and exams so they can furnish them to letter writers," says now-retired Dayton pre-law advisor Roberta Alexander, who kept all of her grade books from 35 years of teaching and used them to write letters of recommendation for students she taught as many as 15 years earlier. Some undergraduate institutions, such as the University of California–Berkeley, will keep letters of recommendation on file for a period of years for a fee and mail them out, as needed, for an additional cost.

Most law schools allow up to three letters of recommendation, though some request only one. Be sure to follow any directions for submitting the letters: some institutions request or require that they come through LSDAS. If so, log onto www.lasc.org to download the necessary form; anyone vouching for you will need to fill it out and return it to LSDAS along with a signed copy of the letter itself.

Interview, if you can

While most admissions officers will meet with candidates for informational meetings as time allows, only a handful of schools offer true admissions interviews. Pace University, for one, conducts up to 450 on- and off-campus interviews a year on a first-come, first-served basis; some schools make it a point to meet

Profile: The public defender

When Brian Marsicovetere enrolled in Vermont Law School, he was pretty sure he wanted to study environmental law. The school has one of the best programs in the country. But then something happened that changed his mind. "That would have been my first criminal law class," he says.

The more cases he read, the more fascinated he became with "the idea that there are limits on the government's ability to reach into people's private lives," he says. "I became really interested in the notion of privacy and of protecting people's liberty. I just really wanted to stand up for people in relation to institutions." His professor, a former prosecutor, "did a really great job of bringing out the personal elements of the cases," he says.

Vermont gave Marsicovetere the option of taking up to 18 credits of internships, so he promptly went to work in a public defender's office. By graduation, he had argued bail hearings in trial court, won his first motion to suppress an illegal search, cross-examined a police officer—and even argued an appeal before the Vermont Supreme Court. The case involved a police officer who had gone to a house to investigate a noise complaint. When the officer arrived, the homeowner refused to let him in "to the point of using force," Marsicovetere says. It was reasonably clear that it was an unlawful search, but did the homeowner have the right to resist with force?

The early immersion in the day-to-day of trial law would make Marsicovetere an attractive job candidate: before he even began scouring the want ads, he was offered an associate position doing criminal defense with the firm of Kevin W. Griffin in White River Junction, Vermont. "I had so much experience by the time I graduated," he says. "I had this well of motions already drafted, and a whole bunch of legal research for issues that would occur in case after case. I was very much ahead of the game." He also had developed people skills. Most valuable lesson? How to ask opposing counsel for what you need without triggering a hostile response or blowing the lines of communication.

Today, the firm's name has expanded to Griffin, Marsicovetere, and Wilkes. Marsicovetere spends 60 percent of his time taking on assigned public defender cases—aggravated assaults, rapes, murders, and kidnappings—and the rest devoted to a thriving private practice across the state and in New Hampshire, representing plaintiffs in civil rights lawsuits and clients in criminal cases. And he loves small-town lawyering. "You really get to see the product of your work in the community—I run into past clients all the time, walking down the street, in the diner," he says. "The fact that you see these people around town really pushes you to do a better job for them." In short, he says, he doesn't miss big-city firm life at all.

their "borderline" candidates. Such meetings are used to obtain additional information about an applicant's communication skills and more recent accomplishments.

Northwestern aims to interview as many candidates as possible, giving each a numerical rating and a page-long write-up. "We really feel that law is a very interactive profession, and no employer is going to hire anyone without interviewing them first," explains Don Rebstock. "I scratch my head [wondering] why other law schools aren't doing this." Rebstock says he won't admit recent college grads until he has a sense of their maturity and how well they'll interact with people who've been in the work force for several years.

It's a good idea to seek an interview if you can, and to prepare for it as carefully as you would a job interview. Bring a résumé, dress professionally, and be ready to answer questions about your studies, the value of any work experience you've had, and your interest in the law school—what attracted you to the program, for example. Rebstock recalls applicants who looked great on paper but who stared at the ground and had nothing to say and who did not get admitted as result. He has also interviewed wait-list candidates and been so impressed by their interpersonal skills that he has offered them admission on the spot.

Escape wait-list limbo

What if you land in that twilight zone between acceptance and rejection? Though it's become increasingly difficult to get into law school off of the wait list, it does still happen. Admissions deans counsel those in wait-list limbo to stay in touch over the summer about additional grades and honors, and to periodically let law schools know that they're still interested.

One Binghamton University student who found herself on the wait lists at Georgetown, Columbia, and NYU a few years ago started making plans to attend another New York law school, but stayed in touch with the admissions directors at the other three, sending an updated transcript and an additional recommendation letter, as well as an article about her role in a national mock trial competition. She also kept in phone and email contact with her pre-law advisor, who talked to several admissions staffers on her behalf. She eventually got the nod from NYU and decided to enroll there instead.

What minority students need to know

In June 2003, in *Grutter v. Bollinger*, the Supreme Court ruled that University of Michigan law school administrators were justified in counting an underrepresented minority applicant's race in his or her favor when making their admissions decisions. While the case concerned Michigan, every other law school sat up and took note, too.

As well they should. "I am the one admissions director in the country who can feel pretty certain that the way we do things is constitutional," says Sarah Zearfoss, assistant dean and director of admissions at Michigan, whose practices were challenged by a 49-year-old white woman—a consultant and mother of two—who'd been rejected by the school. There is no formula for admission at Michigan; deans weigh race, among other myriad factors, in a complex decision-making process. As a result, sometimes students with lower-than-average scores or grades are admitted to the school because they have other important assets such as

leadership or service experience or are from underrepresented racial backgrounds.

The larger result of *Grutter v. Bollinger* is that most schools will continue to consider minority status as one attribute among the many that influence their choices—though it cannot be an overriding factor, nor can it be assigned a specific weight through point systems or quotas. And it certainly will not compensate for generally poor performance.

How should you handle the question of race in your own application? "It's helpful to speak about race if it has meaning for you," advises Zearfoss. "It's not necessary, but it is certainly additional information that we would consider positively in reviewing a file." Tamara Gustave, a graduate of the University of Baltimore School of Law, wrote in her personal statement about why she— a multilingual Haitian woman who was the first member of her family to graduate from college in the United States—wanted to be a lawyer. "I think that all of these

qualities are positive things that added to me as a person," she explains. "I talked about the fact that my family were immigrants from Haiti, my involvement with my [undergraduate] black student union, and the fact that the law sometimes doesn't apply to everybody equally, which I saw firsthand as a black woman."

"Don't think that just marking off a box indicating your racial and ethnic identity on your application is enough," says Evangeline Mitchell, author of *The African American Pre-Law School Advice Guide: Things You Really Need to Know before Applying to Law School*. She suggests students include any race-related organizations, activities, and community service work on their résumés. If you have other topics to cover in your personal statement, she also advises submitting an additional, one- to two-page "diversity statement" that covers what race means to you, how it's shaped you, and how this may have drawn you to the law—as well as how you can contribute to the incoming class.

Chapter Five

Finding the Money

Not many pieces of paper are more expensive than a law diploma. At the priciest schools—Northwestern University Law School in Illinois and Columbia Law School in New York City, to name two—the total cost of a JD degree (including living expenses and books) now tops $150,000. How do law students cover the bills? "Loans, loans, and more loans," says one assistant director of student financial aid. Debts of $80,000 are common among law school grads—and that's not counting the load that many have taken on as undergraduates.

How can you limit the damage? Most schools award at least a little financial aid based on need, and a rapidly growing number also offer merit-based scholarships to numerically attractive candidates who would enhance the student-body profile. Uncle Sam's largesse, in the form of tax credits for the cost of higher education, can also free up some extra cash. And work-study, summer employment, or tuition reimbursement from an employer can lessen your out-of-pocket expense.

Even if you do have to borrow significant sums, you can take some comfort in the fact that education debt is still pretty cheap; through your tax deductions, Uncle Sam will chip in on the interest you do pay. And if you don't wind up with a hefty salary after graduation because you're working for a government or nonprofit agency, one of a growing number of debt-forgiveness programs can help you pay off the bills (see list, page 60). Here's what you need to know to pay for your degree.

Need-based grants might help a little—very little

As you probably recall from your undergraduate days, anyone applying for financial aid funds handed out by the federal government has to fill out the Free Application for Federal Student Aid, more commonly known as the FAFSA. That's where you'll start, but the truth is that most law schools have only a modest amount of money available for need-based grants. They assume that most students will borrow to finance their degrees and will easily be able to repay their debts once they are lawyers. Even schools with more available money generally do not meet their students' full need with grants: there simply aren't enough funds available at the graduate level to fully fund the

requirements of students no longer dependent on their parents. Apply early, generally before the end of January, if you hope to qualify for a need-based grant; some schools make their awards on a first-come, first-served basis.

You may find that your eligibility for need-based aid varies dramatically from school to school. That's because law schools, like undergraduate colleges and universities, use different formulas to calculate how big a discrepancy you've got between your resources and how much law school will cost. Under the formula used to disburse federal aid, for example, all graduate students are considered independent and supporting themselves, regardless of their age or whether they have financial help from their parents. Since most recent graduates have income levels in the $20,000s or $30,000s, schools that use the federal methodology see quite a bit of need.

But at law schools that use their own institutional formulas—such as those at Harvard, Yale, Columbia, and Syracuse University—many students are classified as dependent, which means that financial aid officers consider Mom's and Dad's resources to be available to pay the bills. Typically, a school would call you dependent if you're under age 29 or 30, say, and don't have any dependents of your own. Other schools are stricter. At Fordham, "If the parents are alive, we look at them," says Stephen Brown, director of financial aid for the law school.

Apply with an eye on the merit money

In the past decade, many law schools have boosted the amount of merit aid they award in an effort to compete for the best students; these grants are given out not on the basis of need but to reward academic performance (and to snag top candidates). The awards are usually made based on your application for admission: high LSAT scores and undergraduate grades are the predominant criteria, but schools are also looking to lure in people with interesting work and life experience, and those who would bring geographic and racial diversity to the student body. You'll have a shot at one of these scholarships if you apply to schools where your academic credentials are above average or where you stand out in some other way. At the very top law schools, where every successful applicant is a standout student, merit awards are harder to come by. (But remember: a degree from such a school is a key credential if you hope to land a job at a prestigious corporate law firm.)

More than a dozen schools now offer scholarships specifically for students who are planning careers in public interest law and have a record of community service to prove it. Boston College's Public Service Scholarships are worth two-thirds of the $33,000 tuition each year. The University of Denver offers full-tuition Chancellor's Scholarships to 12 students who have a solid record of service and aspire to practice public interest law. At some schools, law students can apply for university-wide fellowships available to graduate students. Florida State University, for instance, offers a University Fellowship that covers tuition for up to 12 credit hours a semester and pays an $18,000 stipend to cover living expenses. You may need to apply for the university-wide awards through the graduate school financial aid office rather than the law school, but your law school's financial aid counselor should know what's available.

Search for outside scholarships

Scholarships from foundations, associations, and civic organizations are not as plentiful for law students as they are for other graduate and professional students. Many outside awards are reserved for minority students, for residents of specific states, or for students concentrating in specific areas of the law. But it's well worth spending a few hours searching scholarship sites such as www.fastweb.com or www.collegenet.com to see if there's an award you might be eligible for. Also try the excellent listing of grants on Michigan State University's website at www.lib.msu.edu/harris23/grants/3subject.htm. Some examples:

- The Association of Trial Lawyers of America awards a handful of scholarships, worth $1,000 to $3,000, to students who are active ATLA student members.
- The Attorney-CPA Foundation awards 12 scholarships a year ($250 to $1,000) to law students who are also certified public accountants.
- Some state and local bar associations award scholarships. For instance, the Foundation of the State Bar of California makes awards of $2,500 to $7,500 to students at California law schools; it made 47 such awards in 2003.
- The American Bar Association Legal Opportunity Scholarship Fund offers 20 awards per year of $5,000 each to minority students.

Some law schools keep a binder of outside scholarship listings; others post listings on their websites. An undergraduate pre-law advisor may also be able to steer you to scholarship opportunities. Other possible sources of leads include state bar associations, unions, and civic groups you're

Other ways and means

Go part-time. There's nothing easy about working full-time and then going to class four nights a week. But part-time study allows some students to foot the bill, at least in part, from cash flow and perhaps to take advantage of employer-paid tuition (see below). The best part-time programs are those where the same instructors teach both full-time and part-time students. (For more on choosing a part-time program, see page 5.)

Let your employer pay for it. Many large employers offer corporate tuition benefits for employees pursuing graduate degrees. But there's a catch: most require the courses you take to be job-related. That means paralegals and legal assistants are the most likely to qualify for corporate benefits to fund a law degree. Colleges and universities also tend to be generous with their tuition benefits for employees and sometimes spouses; some prospective law students even seek out university employment for this very reason.

Live like a student. The student expense budget law schools estimate for yearly housing, food, and personal expenses is almost laughable—$12,000 to $15,000 is typical. "Food is the number one budget buster," says Stephen Brown at Fordham. "It's very easy to grab a bagel and coffee out every day and spend $900 a year."

"The living expense choices that students make will affect how much they have to borrow," says Gina Soliz, director of financial aid at Syracuse University's College of Law. Those who manage to keep their debt to a minimum are the ones who say, "I don't need digital cable right now. I can get a roommate and live like a student."

Build up some savings. If you're looking ahead to law school in the next couple of years and can set aside some savings, take advantage of the tax benefits of a state-sponsored 529 plan. While most investors use these plans to save for a child's undergraduate expenses, they generally allow you to open an account and name yourself as the beneficiary. The primary benefit is that the earnings on your savings won't be taxed, and your state may throw in a deduction for your contributions. All 529 plans include investments that are appropriate for adults who will need to tap the money soon, such as bonds and money-market accounts.

While many of the broker-sold 529 plans impose up-front sales fees that would minimize or offset any tax benefits over just a year or two, many of the direct-sold plans, such as those offered by TIAA-CREF and Vanguard, do not. Several are paying a guaranteed 3 percent or so right now. Not a bad parking place for a year or two, especially when Uncle Sam isn't claiming any of the gains.

affiliated with, as well as honor societies, fraternities, or sororities you belonged to as an undergraduate.

Be aware that if you qualify for a need-based grant from your law school, an outside scholarship probably won't just add to your kitty; it may be used to reduce the size of your grant. At such a school, say, a $2,500 award might lighten your loan burden by $1,000 and trim a need-based grant by $1,500.

Get set to borrow

Debt is a fact of life for most law students; at many pricey private law schools, the average debt at graduation now exceeds $80,000. But low interest rates definitely help ease the sting.

Federal loans. Government-guaranteed Stafford loans made directly to students are a staple for most law students; a typical full-time student takes out the annual maximum of $18,500 per year. (Overall, you can borrow up to $138,500 in Stafford loans to finance your education, including what you've borrowed as an undergraduate.) Part of that total, up to $8,500, is often a "subsidized" loan, meaning that the federal government pays the interest while you're in school and for six months after you graduate or drop below half-time status. The rest is unsubsidized, so interest accrues while you're in school. Payments on both subsidized and unsubsidized Staffords can be deferred until after graduation.

To be eligible for a subsidized loan, your FAFSA form will have to show that you can't shoulder much of the financial burden yourself—fairly easy to do with law school costs so high. If your school participates in the Federal Direct Loan Program, you'll borrow directly from the federal government. Otherwise, you can choose your own funding source using a list of preferred lenders provided by your school. While all lenders offer Stafford loans at the same interest rate, some waive the up-front origination and guarantee fees (which can run 4 percent of the loan amount), some reduce the interest rate in repayment if you sign up for automatic payments or make a certain number of payments on time, and some do both. So it can pay to shop around. Rates on these variable-rate loans change every summer, but will not exceed a cap of 8.25 percent.

Students with high financial need—that is, the FAFSA shows that they're expected to contribute very little or nothing toward their law school education—will also qualify for a Perkins loan of up to $6,000 per year at an interest rate that's fixed at 5 percent. In addition, there are no up-front origination fees. The Perkins is a subsidized loan, so no interest accrues until nine months after you graduate or drop below half-time status.

Private loans. If the federal loan limits leave you short, private lenders stand ready to lend you as much as the full cost of your education less any financial aid. (Some law schools also have their own loan programs.) Interest rates tend to be only slightly higher than the rates on Stafford loans. However, origination and other fees can be significantly higher—running as much as 8.5 percent of the loan amount—and interest begins accruing right away. Loan programs geared specifically to law students will even lend you up to $10,000 or so on top of what you need for tuition and living expenses during the school year to help cover your costs while you study for the bar exam. Some popular programs include CitiAssist from Citibank (www.studentloan.com), Law Access Loan from Access Group Inc. (www.accessgroup.org), Law Loans from Sallie Mae (www.salliemae.com/lawloans), and LawAchiever from KeyBank (www.keybank.com/educate).

To qualify for private loans, you need a clean credit history—or a cosigner. Financial aid officers recommend that prospective students pay down their debts, close unnecessary lines of credit, and check their credit histories for errors before applying for admission. Ann Weitgenant, assistant director of financial aid at Valparaiso University Law School in Indiana, says she sometimes even counsels students to work an extra year to pay down their credit cards and car loans.

Home-equity loans. For students who own a home, a home-equity line of credit is another attractive choice. Rates are low, fees are minimal, and interest on up to $100,000 in debt is tax deductible if you itemize. If you expect to graduate into a high-paying job, home-equity debt may be a better choice than other debt because you won't qualify for tax-deductible interest on government or private student loans. Interest on regular student loans will be fully tax deductible only if your income falls below $50,000 if you're a single taxpayer and below $100,000 if you file jointly. Remember, though, that a home-equity line of credit is secured by your home, so be certain you'll be able to make the payments regardless of where your career path leads after graduation.

Find help paying the money back

At current rates, the payment on $80,000 in debt is more than $900 a month over 10 years. Those payments may be easily manageable for newly minted lawyers who land high-paying jobs in the private sector. For those who don't, there are ways to ease the burden.

Flexible repayment options. While the standard term for repaying Stafford loans is 10 years, you can stretch the term in various ways to make your payments more affordable. With an extended repayment plan, for instance, you can lengthen the loan term to up to 30 years. Another option, a graduated repayment schedule that extends over 12 to 30 years, starts you off with lower payments than the standard plan and then ratchets them up annually. Income-contingent or income-sensitive repayment plans adjust your payment each year based on your income. In the end, you'll pay more interest over longer payback periods. But you can always boost your payments as your income rises to pay down the loan more quickly than you're asked to.

Loan consolidation. You may also be able to reduce the interest you pay on Stafford loans by consolidating them when interest rates are low. That locks in current interest rates instead of allowing them to fluctuate annually. You may even be able to consolidate your undergraduate and early law school loans to take advantage of low rates while you're still in school. For more details about student loan consolidation, you may wish to visit www.loanconsolidation.ed.gov at the Department of Education's website, or www.federalconsolidation.org, a website sponsored by Access Group, Inc., a private, nonprofit lender.

Student-loan interest deduction. If your income is modest, Uncle Sam will step in to help with the interest payments. You can deduct up to $2,500 a year in student-loan interest if you earn less than $50,000 as a single taxpayer or less than $100,000 if you are married and filing jointly. (You can deduct a lesser amount with income up to $65,000 filing singly or $130,000 filing jointly.)

Note to parents: you get to take this deduction if you're legally obligated to pay back the debt and you claim the student as a dependent on your tax return.

Loan repayment assistance programs. "If you get out of here with $70,000 of debt and get a job for $30,000, it's tough to pay the debt back," says Christine Falzerano, associate director of student financial services at Pace's law school. That's why more than 70 schools, 50 employers, and a number of states now offer loan repayment assistance to lawyers who practice public interest law for a non-profit agency or who work as government prosecutors or public defenders. University of Oregon law grads earning less than $45,000 a year in a public service or public interest law job can qualify for up to $25,000 in loan-repayment assistance over five years, for instance. The university lends graduates up to $5,000 per year to make payments to the government or the bank that holds their student loans, then later forgives all or part of the debt, depending on the graduate's level of income and length of time doing public interest work. Instead of forgivable loans, a few law schools make outright grants to cover student loan debt. The University of San Diego, for one, awards grants of $2,000 to $5,000 per year for up to five years to graduates in public interest jobs.

Loan repayment programs vary dramatically from school to school. Those with meager budgets may offer help to only a handful of students, may offer relatively small loans or grants, or may cap eligibility at salaries of $35,000 or less. Institutions with ample resources, such as Harvard, Yale, Columbia, and New York University, can afford to offer loan repayment help to more graduates and to graduates with higher salaries. If you're comparing LRAPs when choosing a law school, ask how much funding is available and how many eligible students receive loans or grants. Also, be aware that you may have to repay some or all of an LRAP loan if you leave your public interest job during the course of a year, and you may cease to be eligible if your income rises over a certain amount.

Find work

While the American Bar Association recommends that first-year law students do not work during the academic year, "a lot of students feel they can handle it," says Valparaiso's Ann Weitgenant. "It lets them step away from the law for awhile." In fact, students who apply for financial aid may be awarded a work-study job to meet some of their financial need; an award of $1,500 to $2,000 a year is typical, for 10 to 15 hours of work a week. Some students manage to get work-study jobs off campus providing legal services to a nonprofit organization such as Bay Area Legal Aid and the Folsom City Attorney's Office, two of the off-campus employers in UC–Berkeley's work-study program. In that case, the employer and the school, subsidized by the federal government, jointly provide the funds paid to the student.

Research assistantships are another option at some universities. At Syracuse, for instance, law students can take a graduate assistantship position anywhere in the university. "That's probably the best deal out there," says Gina Soliz, director of financial aid at Syracuse University's College of Law. "For a little bit of work, you could get part or all of your tuition paid, plus a stipend," she says. Law students would generally have to seek out such positions by knocking on faculty doors once they arrive on campus.

Summer jobs can be a way to rack up some serious earnings, especially for second- and third-year students at good schools, where corporate law firms recruit for summer positions that can pay

Profile: The child advocate

Theresa Owens knew when she decided on law school that she wanted to represent children. So she researched schools with specialized programs in juvenile law and settled on Whittier in Costa Mesa, Calif. She was swayed by Whittier's financial package and the fact that she would be eligible for summer stipends of $3,000 if she chose to do public interest work in the community. (Having grown up in New Jersey and having attended the University of Massachusetts–Amherst, Owens didn't mind the prospect of some balmy Southern California weather, either.)

Along with 20 other entering students, Owens enrolled in Whittier's children's law program, which includes courses in family law, juvenile trial advocacy, and juvenile justice in addition to the standard courses. She also took a special writing class with a focus on the research and briefs likely to be encountered in juvenile law. Monthly colloquia brought judges, doctors, and child psychologists to campus to shed light on such topics as signs of child abuse, hurdles of the adoption process, and how to interview children in court. To fulfill one of the program's requirements, she worked for one semester at the school's clinic for underprivileged families, delving into the details of domestic violence cases and restraining orders, and helping the grandparents of abandoned children file for guardianship. As the first editor-in-chief of the program's newly launched *Children and Family Law Journal* she commissioned and published articles by legal scholars on subjects that ranged from juvenile delinquency to reproductive issues such as surrogacy and custody of eggs.

As they honed their skills, Owens and her colleagues were sent into juvenile detention centers in Los Angeles to assist on civil rights cases. She recalls a talk with one child offender who was HIV positive, and was having trouble getting medication because "it wasn't the sort of thing you'd want to tell any of the staff there about." Then there were the allegations of sexual abuse of children by juvenile hall staffers. To practice questioning young witnesses, Owens and her classmates took turns playing frightened four-year-olds in mock trials.

After graduation, Owens worked frequently with the foster care system as a court-appointed lawyer helping parents get their children back. Usually, the children had been removed from their parents due to abuse or neglect, or maybe because the home was overrun with rats or roaches. In those cases, particularly if it seemed as if the parents were doing their best, she felt as if the family were in a Catch-22. "The public financial benefits don't kick in until you have your children back with you," she says. But, understandably, "the state won't return your children until you have a home with electricity, water"—and no rodents. "You look for the cases that can bring you some joy," she says, "because a lot of them are very frustrating and very hard."

$1,500 to $2,500 a week. Many students at Fordham, for instance, have summer earnings in the $32,000 range, says Stephen Brown. On the other hand, students interested in public service often pursue volunteer work, clerkships, or other public interest work that doesn't pay much at all. A job at a public interest agency may in fact pay nothing, but some law schools come up with at least some money.

Take advantage of a hand from Uncle Sam

If your income is modest, the federal government will help foot the bill for your law degree by giving you a tax credit or tax deduction for educational expenses. Most law students will want to take advantage of the Lifetime Learning tax credit, worth $2,000 a year (20 percent of the first $10,000 you spend in tuition and fees each year.) You qualify for the full credit if your income is under a certain threshold ($43,000 for single filers in 2005; $87,000 for people married and filing jointly). You qualify for a partial credit if you make somewhat more (up to $53,000 for singles in 2005 and $107,000 on joint returns. A tax credit reduces your tax bill dollar for dollar.

Full-time students aren't likely to exceed those thresholds. But if you do—perhaps as a part-time student—you may still qualify for a tax deduction for your educational expenses. In 2005, students could take a deduction for up to $4,000 in tuition and fees if their incomes don't exceed $65,000 filing singly or $130,000 filing jointly. That's worth up to $1,000 to a taxpayer in the 25 percent tax bracket. With income up to $80,000 filing singly or $160,000 filling jointly, you can deduct up to $2,000 in tuition and fees. Note: you can't take both the credit and the deduction.

While a law degree is obviously a major financial investment, chances are good you'll graduate knowing you've significantly boosted your earning power over your lifetime. Then you can move on to bigger worries—like passing the bar exam.

Law schools that help with the payments

According to the latest survey by Equal Justice Works, a Washington, D.C.–based organization that promotes public interest law, more than 70 American law schools (below) now offer or are developing loan
repayment assistance programs (LRAPs). These plans, which help graduates who take public interest jobs
repay their student loans, can differ dramatically, and some schools can only afford to fund a few students
each year. It's important to research the particulars by calling a school's admissions or financial aid office,
or by consulting "Financing the Future: Equal Justice Works 2004 Report on Loan Repayment Assistance
and Public Interest Scholarship Programs" (available at www.equaljusticeworks.org).

American Univ. Washington College of Law (DC)

Benjamin N. Cardozo Sch. of Law, Yeshiva U. (NY)

Boston College Law School

Boston University School of Law

Brooklyn Law School (NY)

Case Western Reserve Univ. School of Law (OH)

Catholic U. of America–Columbus Sch. of Law (DC)

Columbia University School of Law (NY)

Cornell University Law School (NY)

Creighton University School of Law (NE)

Duke University School of Law (NC)

Emory University School of Law (GA)

Fordham University School of Law (NY)

Franklin Pierce Law Center (NH)

George Washington University Law School (DC)

Georgetown University Law Center (DC)

Golden Gate University School of Law (CA)

Harvard Law School (MA)

Hofstra University School of Law (NY)

Lewis & Clark Coll., Northwestern Sch. of Law (OR)

Loyola Law School, Los Angeles

Loyola University, Chicago School of Law

Loyola University, New Orleans School of Law

Marquette University Law School (WI)

New York Law School

New York University School of Law

Northeastern University School of Law (MA)

Northwestern University School of Law (IL)

Ohio State Univ. Michael E. Moritz College of Law

Pace University School of Law (NY)

Penn. State Univ., The Dickinson School of Law

Pepperdine University School of Law (CA)

Regent University School of Law (VA)

Rutgers University School of Law–Camden (NJ)

Rutgers University School of Law–Newark (NJ)

Santa Clara University School of Law (CA)

Seattle University School of Law

Seton Hall University School of Law (NJ)

Southwestern University School of Law (CA)

Stanford University Law School (CA)

St. Thomas University School of Law (FL)

Suffolk University Law School (MA)

Temple Univ. James E. Beasley School of Law (PA)

Touro College: Jacob D. Fuchsberg Law Center (NY)

Tulane University School of Law (LA)

University of California–Berkeley School of Law

University of California–Davis School of Law

University of California–Hastings College of Law

Univ of Cal.–Los Angeles (UCLA) School of Law

University of Chicago Law School

University of Georgia School of Law

University of Iowa College of Law

University of Maine School of Law

University of Maryland School of Law

University of Michigan Law School

University of Notre Dame Law School (IN)

University of Oregon School of Law

Univ of the Pacific, McGeorge School of Law (CA)

University of Pennsylvania Law School

University of San Diego School of Law

University of San Francisco School of Law

University of Southern California Law School

University of Utah College of Law

University of Virginia School of Law

Valparaiso University School of Law (IN)

Vanderbilt University Law School (TN)

Vermont Law School

Wake Forest University School of Law (NC)

Washington and Lee University School of Law (VA)

Washington University School of Law

Whittier Law School (CA)

Widener University School of Law (DE)

College of William and Mary School of Law (VA)

Willamette University College of Law (OR)

Yale Law School (CT)

In addition, the following four Minnesota law schools contribute funds to LRAP Minnesota, their state program. Students who are eligible for funding apply to the state.

Hamline University School of Law

University of Minnesota Law School

University of St. Thomas School of Law

William Mitchell College of Law

Chapter Six

Getting Your First Job

The past few years were tough even at prestigious law firms, many of which have handed out pink slips by the dozen. Other firms cut back their summer associate programs, which put rising third-year law students into jobs that traditionally lead to permanent offers, and have employed fewer newly-minted JDs as well.

Alas, the good not-so-old days when law students were wooed by multiple firms with fancy dinners and promises of even fancier bonuses are over, at least for the moment.

"Two or three years ago, people had to work hard *not* to get a job," says a hiring partner at one top firm. "Now it's a different story." Today's third-year students will compete for fewer positions and will certainly not receive as many offers as they would have in previous years; some students with subpar grades might not get any.

> "Two or three years ago, people had to work hard not to get a job. Now it's a different story."

But don't tear up your law school applications just yet. Even though work has been harder to come by lately, there are still opportunities to be had. And students entering law school now may find the picture to be much rosier by the time they are out job hunting. Indeed, many schools report the same number of recruiters showing up on campus this year as they did last year, and experts in both career counseling offices and law firms say that with the economy on the rebound there is reason to be optimistic. Even firms that have cut back in recent years say that the hiring picture is decidedly brighter these days.

And new JDs, by and large, do pretty well—though how well clearly depends on the type of work you're interested in. The median starting salary for 2004 graduates was $55,000, taking into account everyone from young lawyers in public interest law, where the figure is only $38,000, to those in private practice, where median base salary—before bonuses—is now $80,000—down from about $93,000 for the class of 2002. (Starting salaries at firms in big cities such as Boston, Chicago, and Los Angeles can reach $125,000.)

To land that first job in a competitive market, you'll need impeccable credentials, and will probably have to take more initiative and be more flexible about what and where you end up practicing than young law grads of several years ago. The more prepared you are, the easier the job hunt will be. And believe it or not, the groundwork will begin almost the first day of school. That's because grades and summer work experiences play a major role in where grads end up.

Where will the jobs be?

The type of law you choose to practice clearly will have an impact on how much money you make. It may also determine how much in demand your services will be—and where. The larger the metropolis, the more specialized the law tends to be, and certain cities dominate certain practice areas. Students who specialize in corporate law may find that the best opportunities are in New York, for example, while technology centers Austin and San Francisco are still hot for intellectual property lawyers.

It's tough to predict how the employment picture might change between now, as you apply to law school, and your first round of job interviews. Consistently busy practice areas, in good times and bad, include family law and criminal law; divorce is constant, and fewer jobs and a stressed economy often equal more murders, thefts, and the like. As you look ahead for growth areas in law, here are some current winners to keep an eye on.

Litigation. It takes more than bad economic news to dampen the demand for litigators, the attorneys who argue cases in court. Litigation is the nation's favorite method for settling disputes; most clients—corporate and otherwise—sue whenever they perceive a wrong that needs to be addressed no matter what the economy happens to be doing, says Jackie Burt, former assistant dean of career services at the Benjamin N. Cardozo School of Law at Yeshiva University in New York. And each suit filed means an equal amount of work for the other side.

Young lawyers with visions of yelling, "Objection, your honor!" often gain experience in state, district, or city attorneys' offices doing legal research and preparing briefs (and may, in fact, end up settling most of their cases out of court). Starting salaries are much lower for attorneys at small- and medium-sized firms, which often represent plaintiffs on a contingency basis, than for those who work in the litigation departments of big-time firms.

Intellectual property. The prospects for IP specialists are excellent over the long term because rapid innovations in science and technology continue to drive the economy. Career opportunities can be found in patent, trademark, and copyright law, as people create new gadgets, literary works, computer programs, and logos—all of which need to be protected.

"IP continues to be a growing practice area," says Sheron Hindley-Smith, executive director of Robert Half Legal, a legal staffing firm in Menlo Park, California. "Patent prosecution is especially hot." This is particularly true in the science and technology fields, which depend so heavily on being first in research and development. As companies strive to guard their patents on new drugs, software, and the like—not to mention their

brand names—law students who fully understand the technical nature of the breakthroughs as well as the applicable law will find themselves at a premium and commanding top starting salaries. A science or engineering background is widely considered essential; patent attorneys also have to pass the patent bar exam, administered and required by the Patent and Trademark office.

> *"IP continues to be a growing practice area. Patent prosecution is especially hot."*

In IP, "you are always dealing with something complex and new," says one recent graduate of the University of Texas–Austin School of Law, who signed on with a Houston-based firm, "You are jumping from new technology to new technology." Interested graduates can work in-house for a corporation, at a firm, for a university, or for the government.

Bankruptcy. Whenever the economy sours, the demand for bankruptcy lawyers jumps. (Think Enron.) "There are some huge bankruptcies out there, and they get very complicated and very complex, and they need a lot of attorneys," says Michael Schiumo, assistant dean for career planning at Fordham University School of Law in New York City. They can also take decades to sort out. (Think Enron.) In addition, companies fail and people lose their shirts even in the brightest of boom times.

Trust and estate. This field is expanding as the first wave of baby boomers hits 60. "People want to make sure their kids get their hard-earned money," says Eric Janson, an adjunct professor at Vermont Law School in South Royalton who also has his own

Is a clerkship right for you?

Each year, roughly 12 percent of law school grads opt to spend a year or two working with a judge in one of the nation's many courts. The median wage is just $43,000, but the payoff is far greater: a judicial clerkship is a great way to see many different aspects of the law as it unfolds—as well as have an impact on it yourself. The experience also provides a lifelong résumé boost and, often, a lifelong advisor.

Jerry Noblin Jr., for one, views his clerkship with Chief Judge Robin Cauthron of the U.S. District Court for the Western District of Oklahoma as the best possible way to prepare for a career as a trial lawyer—to "learn how to run a trial, without having a real client's case on the line," and to "be involved in myriad cases with all kinds of causes of action, both civil and criminal, which is something that a firm simply could not offer."

There is a range of clerkship opportunities at every court level—federal, state, and even local—and your experience will vary with each. For example, if you work for a trial court, you'll likely be involved in every stage of a hearing, from writing jury voir dire questions and instructions to helping your judge write and edit his or her decision before it's published. The court of appeals is a more studious exercise; you'll hear oral arguments from attorneys and then help research and prepare decisions on the legal issues. Debra Strauss, author of *Behind the Bench: The Guide to Judicial Clerkships* and administrator of www.judicialclerkships.com, a site that helps students navigate the application process, suggests seeking the court that's right for you in terms of your future goals. "Federal clerkships are considered more prestigious than state, but it's great to work in the state court system if you know you want to practice law in that state, because you get to know all the attorneys and court procedures intimately," she explains. "Moreover, the highest court in a state can be just as prestigious as a federal clerkship."

Competition for all such positions is stiff. Top grades at a good school and solid writing skills are important, though some judges will pass over Ivy Leaguers in favor of in-state students who have a demonstrated interest in local legal issues. Pursuing activities such as law review and moot court can help you stand out. Strauss also suggests doing a judicial externship, like the one she oversees at the Pace University School of Law: The Federal Judicial Extern Honors Program, a yearlong course that includes a lengthy research and writing project (in which students use motion papers from federal court to write a decision, which can later serve as a writing sample for a clerkship application), places students with federal district or court of appeals judges where they act as junior clerks, of sorts.

All clerkship candidates should be proactive about the process. This includes researching what type of court you're interested in, where, as well as which judge, specifically, you'd like to work for. The recommended deadline for federal clerkship applications is now fall of the third year of law school, though that varies by court and individual judge; the cutoff date for state clerkships can be even earlier, from the spring or summer of second year on.

If you're successful, a clerkship can pay off in many ways—most ideally, in close mentorship from a judge. The post can also open doors later in your career, as firms, government agencies, and nonprofits alike actively recruit former law clerks for their varied experiences and close exposure to the court system. In addition, it's seen as an essential credential if you hope to teach. One last potential advantage: federal positions can lead to the mother of all clerkships—working for one of the nine U.S. Supreme Court justices, who typically choose clerks who have worked for peers in the U.S. Court of Appeals. Those interested should focus on working for one of the federal "feeder judges" who have sent numerous staff members to the Supreme Court in the past.

---

private practice and specializes in estate planning, wills, trusts, and probate administration. T&E lawyers, who may create living wills, plan for the eventual dispersal of billion-dollar fortunes, and arrange the transfer of long-held family businesses from one generation to the next, are needed at firms of all sizes, which handle estates of all sizes.

Employment. "Whether you are hiring or firing, a company needs lawyers," says Susan Guindi, assistant dean for career services at the University of Michigan's law school. Employment attorneys can work in-house or for a company's outside counsel, as well as for unions and government agencies. In the process, they may deal with a range of issues, including labor relations; age, race, or sex discrimination; and workplace health and safety.

Tax. Although there will almost certainly never be a sexy television show about tax attorneys, don't rule out entering this field. "Tax is always solid," says Merv Loya, assistant dean at the University of Oregon's law school in Eugene, who notes that companies and individuals need attorneys in good and bad economic cycles who enjoy digging into financial documents and interpreting the tax code; the president's tax initiative will also heat up demand. But often, Loya adds, students need a master's degree in tax law to set them apart.

• • •

Shortly after you arrive on campus, you'll want to start getting to know the people in the career counseling office; the men and women who run on-campus recruiting programs have close contacts in the field, know the experiences of all those who've come seeking employment before, and can offer the most specific, well-tailored advice on how to make your particular career goals a reality, no matter what area of law you're interested in. Stop by early and often to get help formulating your long-term plan and attend career-oriented seminars from day one on.

Make the most of the summer

It used to be that finding a substantive legal job after the first year of law school was optional, but that is no longer the case, say many career counselors. "We recommend doing anything law-related during your first summer, even if you have to do something unrelated part-time—like word processing, waiting tables, or slinging lattes at Starbucks—in order to finance some sort of volunteer gig in the legal community," says Skip Horne, former assistant dean for career services at the Santa Clara University School of Law. "The key is to get experience, and not wait until your second or third year when it will get harder and harder to overcome that initial 'I don't have any legal experience' hump."

Finding a law firm job that first summer is going to be difficult, but this is an excellent time to take advantage of opportunities in the nonprofit sector. Many law schools offer scholarships that help support students who want to do low- or non-paying public interest work for a summer. The Equal Justice America fellowship, for example, is an award for first- and second-year students who work at organizations that provide civil legal services for the poor. It's offered at more than 40 schools, including Brooklyn Law School, the University of Virginia School of Law, and Stanford. Working for a judge or doing research for a professor is another common first-year choice, as is a study-abroad program. The University of Wisconsin's law school, for one, has partnered with Thammasat University Faculty of Law in Bangkok so students can study the Thai legal system firsthand while working in international law firms.

For those interested in going into private practice—that is, the vast majority of law school students—the employment process starts in the fall of the second year of law school, with interviews for summer associate positions. These eight-week jobs allow students to get firm experience for great pay, often with the promise of future employment.

However, be forewarned: such programs are no longer the schmooze-fests recent grads may have described, where getting to know the other young associates and partners over expense-account lunches at hip restaurants and outings to baseball games or sold-out rock concerts took precedence over real work. Many firms are now working their "summers" considerably harder than in the past and evaluating them more closely. "It used to be that summer associates really had to screw up badly in order to not get an offer," says Gihan Fernando, assistant dean for career services at Georgetown University Law Center. "In past years, behaviors of all kinds were tolerated and not much work was accomplished. Now there's much more of a sense that you should put your best foot forward." Georgetown, for one, provides an intensive, one-day seminar to help prepare students for the experience, complete with panels of hiring partners and 3Ls and discussions about firm life, etiquette, and the kinds of basic research and writing assignments summer associates will be expected to handle.

No matter what you do on the job, try not to follow in the footsteps of one law student who, as a 2003 summer associate at Skadden, Arps in New York, mistakenly sent the following email, meant for a friend, to 40 people at the firm, including 20 partners: "I'm busy doing jack shit. Went to a nice 2hr sushi lunch today at Sushi Zen. Nice place. Spent the rest of the day typing emails and bullshitting with people. Unfortunately, I actually have work to do—I'm on some corp finance deal, under the global head of corp finance, which means I should really peruse these materials and not be a fuckup." The email slowly made its way around the firm, the city, and the rest of the country, and became a classic lesson in what not to do for summer associates everywhere, for all time. (Neither the student nor the firm will comment on what happened as a result.)

Finally, take heart: for those who maintain the appropriate level of decorum and impress associates and partners alike with their research, writing, and communication skills, many benefits remain—including the free food. "I worked really, really hard, but I gained like seven pounds," says one recent summer associate at a top New York firm. She also gained a full-time offer.

Get recruited

So how do you obtain such plum summer positions? Most students go through on-campus recruiting, which brings in employers to interview job candidates who are either prescreened using their résumés or selected in a lottery. The employers then call back those they're interested in hiring for a second interview at the office. This occurs in the fall, mostly, though there is some overflow in the spring. While recruiting schedules and procedures differ from school to school (meaning it's wise to check with your career center for details about how the process operates), it's true at most institutions that on-campus recruiting has become ever more competitive, as firms have limited the number of campuses they

visit and offered fewer interview slots at those they do. Still, on-campus recruiting has rebounded along with the economy.

Needless to say, the better your law school performance is, the better your chances. Often, top firms will only interview students whose GPA falls above a certain cutoff—though they do adjust that cutoff based on the name and reputation of a

"The key is to get experience, and not wait until your second or third year."

school. For example, a firm may only meet candidates with a 3.7 or higher at a second-tier institution, while those at top 20 schools simply need a 3.3; grades may not matter at all for candidates from Harvard or Yale. Hiring partners say having substantial legal experience in summer positions, as noted, also helps people stand out, as does participation in clinics, which signals that you'll bring a toolbox of practical skills to the job—not just theory learned in class.

After academics, motivation and initiative matter most of all. You can no longer rely on the on-campus interview process to find a job—be prepared to do some independent outreach, too, even if it means cold calling or sending your résumé and a cover letter out to several hundred firms across the country.

"I was extraordinarily aggressive and shameless—I sent out hundreds of letters and got rejected by so many great places," recalls Alex Wellen, a graduate of Temple University's law school in Philadelphia and the author of *Barman: Ping-Pong, Pathos, & Passing the Bar*, his account of coming out of law school into the work world. Wellen says he was "crazy about Temple," but

Profile: The prosecutor

Like many young college grads, Stephen Sincavage applied to law school for lack of a better idea. "I never had any grand plans that I wanted to go to law school or anything like that," he says. "But...I kind of realized that I wasn't sick of school, and I knew a couple of people who'd gone to law school," he says. In fact, he'd heard some horror stories of cutthroat law schools where students hoarded notes and ripped pages out of library books to thwart the competition. "There were exceptions," says Sincavage, "but generally when I talked to other people, they'd say, 'law school was hell.'" He knew that *that* wasn't the kind of experience he wanted.

And he figured he knew how to avoid it. Sincavage had so enjoyed being an undergraduate at the University of Virginia that the decision about where to go was easy: he'd stay in Charlottesville. "It's very social," he says. That sense of community was the key to his happy law school experience, Sincavage adds. The first week on campus, his class of 300 was divided into first-year sections of 30 each. If someone missed a class, other students would share notes and outlines. Regular softball games "gave everybody a focus and a reason to be together." It helped that the school's grading system centered around a B mean, notes Sincavage. "That meant that, for the most part, unless you were really brilliant on an exam—or you were really just out to lunch—you were more than likely to get a B," he adds. "I don't know how you get by in an atmosphere where everyone's out for themselves."

Sincavage began to zero in on his career path during his second summer when he clerked for a circuit judge in Loudoun County, Virginia, now the fastest-growing county in the country. His time there made him realize he liked the courtroom experience and gave him a pretty good idea of the sort of work he *didn't* want to do—domestic relations, for example. "The rancor, the hatred—that just didn't seem like something that I'd be up for," he says. The work a friend was doing in a prosecutor's office seemed a lot more appealing. So after graduating in 1993, he clerked for the Loudon County Circuit Court and, in 1997, went to work for the county prosecutor's office. It didn't hurt that he'd graduated from a "fairly local university known to be prestigious," had grown up in the county, and had spent time as a law clerk becoming known to the legal community around the old courthouse that still dominates the center of downtown Leesburg, Virginia, where the Loudoun County prosecutor's offices are located.

His office overlooking the green, campus-like lawn of the old Leesburg courthouse is as sociable a place as his alma mater; the county prosecutors share the fascinating cases and the not-so-scintillating work alike. "You're not just the traffic guy, or the white collar crime guy, or the drug guy," he says. Sincavage does tend to get a fair number of drug cases—he often carries a pager so narcotics officers can reach him 24 hours a day—but also handles everything from juvenile cases to embezzlement and identity fraud. Some days he spends in traffic court—often the most entertaining part of his week. "The excuses you always hear are: 'All of the other cars were speeding,' or 'this guy was going faster than me, why didn't he get pulled over?'" Or, his personal favorite: "I was going downhill."

When he has to juggle hearings or be in two places at once, he relies on his colleagues—and that sense of being part of a team reminds him of law school. "I think a lot of people would say we were having too much fun," he says. "I'd do those three years again in a second if I could."

that, in his experience, aiming for a top firm out of a non–Top 20 law school (Temple is currently No. 59) was "harder at every fricking step of the way—it was harder to get an interview, harder to get a callback, harder to get an offer." His determination paid off, however, and he eventually landed a job at a prestigious New York firm.

Networking is key, say many career counselors—and it should start your first year of law school. Try getting involved with a range of organizations on campus and attending local bar association and alumni events, for instance, so you can get out into the real world and interact with practicing attorneys. You never know who'll be able to lend a hand in the future, and the experience in creating and maintaining contacts will likely help you in your future practice, as well. (One of Wellen's strategies was to identify and contact all of the Temple alumni working in midsize to large New York practices.)

No matter what happens, you should bear in mind that your first job is just that—you can always move on. Indeed, even while the hiring of first-year associates was down across the board, there's been an increase in the lateral hiring of those who have at least several years of experience.

Consider public interest law

Ironically, low-paying public interest jobs can be even more difficult to land than glamorous firm positions. Just 2.9 percent of graduates find positions in the field, which encompasses nonprofit groups such as legal aid organizations and public defender offices, as well as national, state, and local government agencies. Experts attribute this not to a lack of interest, but to a dearth of entry-level openings and graduates' huge debt loads, which make a miniscule paycheck impractical. At the same time, more JDs seem to be competing for these posts than in past years, perhaps because of the difficult firm market. "If anything, the public sector has tended to stay fairly constant," says Skip Horne. "So with similar numbers of opportunities but more students interested in them, the competition is more fierce."

Demonstrated interest and experience in the public domain are essential when you're looking for nonprofit or government jobs; organizations and agencies with extremely tight budgets simply can't afford to train rank beginners. Committed students can increase their chances of finding employment by making their own opportunities. For example, volunteering at a local nonprofit organization may eventually turn into a full-time position.

There are quite a few fellowship openings, as well, offered through individual law schools and a range of private organizations, including the Skadden Fellowship Foundation, an arm of Skadden, Arps in New York (www.skadden. com/SkaddenFellowship Index.ihtml). Such pro-

> *"I was extraordinarily aggressive and shameless—I sent out hundreds of letters and got rejected by so many great places."*

grams aim to make helping others—which usually pays around $30,000 to $35,000, to start—a financial feasibility. For example, Equal Justice Works, a public interest advocacy group in Washington, D.C., offers fellowships for recent law graduates and experienced attorneys interested in giving back. Fellows receive up to $37,500, as well as generous student loan repayment assistance and work for such organizations as the National Housing Law Project in Oakland, California, Midwest Environmental Advocates in Madison, Wisconsin, Human Rights First in New York City, and the center for Children's Advocacy in Hartford, Connecticut. Get more information at www.equal justiceworks.org.

Though the post-JD job market may be tougher than in the recent past, graduates who are determined and well prepared are clearly finding jobs. Since those are attributes that every good lawyer needs, anyway, they'll serve you well even in a new age of competing offers.

How Do the Schools Stack Up?

How much competition are you facing? Here we rank schools from most to least selective based on a formula that takes into account their acceptance rates (the proportion of applicants who make the cut into the full-time program), and students' LSAT scores and grades. The 25th–75th percentile LSAT and grade-point-average ranges show you where 50 percent of enrollees fall, but remember: that means if 200 people make up the class, 50 of them fall below the bottom of the range.

Most to least selective

School	Acceptance rate	Undergraduate grade point average (25th–75th percentile)	LSAT score (25th–75th percentile)
Yale University (CT)	6%	3.79-3.95	168-175
Stanford University (CA)	8%	3.80-3.96	167-172
Harvard University (MA)	12%	3.68-3.92	170-176
University of California–Berkeley	10%	3.67-3.90	164-169
New York University	21%	3.60-3.89	168-172
Columbia University (NY)	15%	3.50-3.80	168-173
Duke University (NC)	21%	3.54-3.86	165-169
Northwestern University (IL)	17%	3.46-3.78	167-171
University of Pennsylvania	13%	3.43-3.85	166-171
Georgetown University (DC)	19%	3.42-3.80	167-170
University of Chicago	15%	3.46-3.80	168-172
University of California–Los Angeles	16%	3.51-3.82	162-169
University of Virginia	20%	3.53-3.83	167-171
Cornell University (NY)	21%	3.50-3.80	165-168
University of Michigan–Ann Arbor	19%	3.45-3.78	166-169
Baylor University (TX)	21%	3.51-3.92	161-165
Brigham Young University (Clark) (UT)	27%	3.52-3.86	161-166
George Mason University (VA)	15%	3.15-3.83	158-166
University of Southern California (Gould)	20%	3.51-3.78	164-167
Vanderbilt University (TN)	23%	3.52-3.85	163-167
Southern Methodist University (TX)	23%	3.31-3.86	155-164
University of Texas–Austin	19%	3.41-3.83	161-168
University of North Carolina–Chapel Hill	15%	3.47-3.84	158-164
Boston College	20%	3.44-3.79	161-166
College of William and Mary (Marshall-Wythe) (VA)	22%	3.31-3.80	160-165
George Washington University (DC)	19%	3.45-3.80	163-166
University of Washington	21%	3.51-3.84	159-165
Washington and Lee University (VA)	21%	3.25-3.79	163-167
Washington University in St. Louis	25%	3.20-3.70	161-167
Boston University	24%	3.48-3.77	163-166
University of Colorado–Boulder	25%	3.43-3.82	160-164
Fordham University (NY)	21%	3.37-3.76	164-167
University of Notre Dame (IN)	18%	3.28-3.78	163-167
University of Florida (Levin)	24%	3.40-3.86	157-164
University of California–Davis	23%	3.46-3.79	158-164
University of California (Hastings)	24%	3.38-3.69	160-164
University of Georgia	23%	3.28-3.80	158-164
University of Minnesota–Twin Cities	28%	3.30-3.78	162-167
University of Tennessee–Knoxville	20%	3.36-3.86	155-161

What are the hardest and easiest law schools to get into?

Most to least selective

School	Acceptance rate	Undergraduate grade point average (25th–75th percentile)	LSAT score (25th–75th percentile)
Cardozo-Yeshiva University (NY)	24%	3.19-3.72	162-166
University of Maryland	16%	3.35-3.76	158-164
University of Utah (S.J. Quinney)	31%	3.46-3.81	158-162
University of Wisconsin–Madison	24%	3.30-3.77	158-163
University of Cincinnati	37%	3.29-3.83	156-162
University of Toledo (OH)	19%	2.98-3.76	155-162
Wake Forest University (NC)	24%	3.17-3.62	162-166
Emory University (GA)	29%	3.28-3.63	161-165
University of Alabama–Tuscaloosa	26%	3.18-3.71	160-164
University of Arizona (Rogers)	24%	3.28-3.78	159-164
University of Iowa	39%	3.39-3.77	158-163
Villanova University (PA)	32%	3.30-3.66	161-163
Illinois Institute of Technology (Chicago-Kent)	26%	3.29-3.70	159-163
Rutgers State University–Camden (NJ)	14%	3.10-3.65	159-163
University of Illinois–Urbana-Champaign	15%	3.04-3.66	162-167
University of Nevada–Las Vegas (Boyd)	12%	3.55-3.67	155-160
Brooklyn Law School (NY)	25%	3.15-3.64	161-164
Ohio State University (Moritz)	28%	3.33-3.72	158-164
University of Connecticut	17%	3.23-3.63	159-163
University of Kentucky	35%	3.30-3.81	157-163
American University (Washington) (DC)	24%	3.20-3.66	160-163
Indiana University–Bloomington	38%	3.03-3.72	158-164
Pepperdine University (McConnell) (CA)	25%	3.38-3.71	157-161
University of Houston	25%	3.22-3.73	157-162
University of Kansas	26%	3.27-3.77	154-160
DePaul University (IL)	26%	3.12-3.66	158-161
Loyola University Chicago	26%	3.15-3.68	159-163
St. John's University (NY)	31%	3.18-3.72	158-163
University of San Diego	25%	3.11-3.54	160-164
Florida State University	23%	3.21-3.67	158-161
Northeastern University (MA)	27%	3.10-3.58	159-163
University of Missouri–Columbia	32%	3.31-3.74	156-160
University of Nebraska–Lincoln	41%	3.30-3.83	153-159
Arizona State University	27%	3.10-3.69	154-161
Temple University (Beasley) (PA)	29%	3.09-3.61	160-163
University of Hawaii (Richardson)	19%	3.03-3.66	156-161
University of Oklahoma	26%	3.32-3.76	154-160
Lewis and Clark College (Northwestern) (OR)	38%	3.04-3.65	158-164
Seton Hall University (NJ)	25%	3.00-3.60	158-162
St. Louis University	40%	3.35-3.77	154-160
University of Denver (Sturm)	24%	3.10-3.60	155-162
Georgia State University	21%	3.16-3.66	156-161
University of Oregon	37%	3.17-3.66	156-160
University of Pittsburgh	29%	3.12-3.63	157-161
University of Richmond (VA)	26%	3.10-3.54	160-163
Case Western Reserve University (OH)	25%	3.13-3.57	157-161
Loyola Law School (CA)	23%	3.05-3.50	160-163
Indiana University–Indianapolis	30%	3.32-3.76	152-158
Santa Clara University (CA)	37%	3.21-3.60	157-161
University of Akron (OH)	31%	3.12-3.67	156-160
University of San Francisco	32%	3.13-3.59	157-161
Wayne State University (MI)	40%	3.33-3.72	153-159

What are the hardest and easiest law schools to get into?

Most to least selective

School	Acceptance rate	Undergraduate grade point average (25th–75th percentile)	LSAT score (25th–75th percentile)
Louisiana State University–Baton Rouge	28%	3.23-3.77	154-159
University of Louisville (Brandeis) (KY)	29%	3.43-3.68	155-159
University of South Carolina	34%	3.19-3.68	154-160
University of Mississippi	27%	3.26-3.77	151-158
Rutgers State University–Newark (NJ)	24%	3.06-3.55	154-161
Seattle University	26%	3.17-3.63	152-159
University of Arkansas–Little Rock (Bowen)	16%	3.20-3.73	151-158
University of Miami (FL)	37%	3.22-3.64	156-160
University of New Mexico	21%	3.07-3.65	150-159
Catholic University of America (Columbus) (DC)	32%	3.06-3.53	156-160
Hofstra University (NY)	38%	3.03-3.64	155-160
Mercer University (GA)	30%	3.02-3.67	153-158
Stetson University (FL)	23%	3.28-3.71	152-156
Texas Tech University	35%	3.28-3.75	151-158
Cleveland State University (Cleveland-Marshall)	31%	3.14-3.59	151-157
University of Arkansas–Fayetteville	24%	3.09-3.69	152-159
University of Memphis (Humphreys)	23%	3.07-3.61	154-158
Marquette University (WI)	40%	3.14-3.62	155-159
Michigan State University	35%	3.04-3.66	155-161
Northern Illinois University	35%	3.05-3.63	154-158
Pennsylvania State University (Dickinson)	29%	3.11-3.67	154-157
University of Idaho	31%	3.10-3.58	152-159
Willamette University (Collins) (OR)	35%	3.12-3.62	153-157
Chapman University (CA)	30%	3.01-3.61	154-158
New York Law School	39%	3.12-3.61	153-157
Southwestern University School of Law (CA)	26%	3.11-3.60	154-158
Hamline University (MN)	40%	3.16-3.61	153-159
University at Buffalo–SUNY	36%	3.15-3.64	152-157
University of the Pacific (McGeorge) (CA)	31%	3.00-3.51	156-160
Campbell University (Wiggins) (NC)	20%	3.03-3.50	153-158
Creighton University (NE)	36%	3.21-3.72	150-156
Northern Kentucky University (Chase)	25%	3.01-3.57	152-158
Quinnipiac University (CT)	23%	3.08-3.53	155-159
Southern Illinois University–Carbondale	37%	3.13-3.67	152-157
University of Missouri–Kansas City	38%	3.14-3.66	152-156
Drake University (IA)	42%	3.14-3.69	153-156
Duquesne University (PA)	44%	3.23-3.61	153-156
Ohio Northern University (Pettit)	27%	3.15-3.69	150-155
University of Maine	40%	3.16-3.58	153-159
University of Montana	38%	3.17-3.70	151-157
Suffolk University (MA)	42%	3.10-3.60	154-158
William Mitchell College of Law (MN)	48%	3.24-3.66	151-158
Pace University (NY)	33%	3.09-3.50	153-156
Samford University (Cumberland) (AL)	32%	2.98-3.52	154-158
Gonzaga University (WA)	37%	3.13-3.56	152-156
Syracuse University (NY)	34%	3.12-3.54	153-157
University of Wyoming	26%	3.06-3.65	149-156
Valparaiso University (IN)	21%	2.97-3.58	150-155
West Virginia University	39%	3.19-3.79	148-155
Texas Wesleyan University	29%	2.89-3.50	153-157
Washburn University (KS)	36%	3.04-3.66	151-155
Albany Law School-Union University (NY)	40%	2.89-3.53	153-157

What are the hardest and easiest law schools to get into?

Most to least selective

School	Acceptance rate	Undergraduate grade point average (25th–75th percentile)	LSAT I Verbal (25th–75th percentile)
California Western School of Law	37%	2.98-3.56	151-156
University of Dayton (OH)	27%	2.87-3.45	152-156
University of North Dakota	45%	3.25-3.74	147-154
University of South Dakota	35%	2.95-3.74	150-156
Capital University (OH)	38%	2.96-3.50	151-156
Franklin Pierce Law Center (NH)	38%	3.00-3.60	150-156
Howard University (DC)	23%	2.93-3.57	148-155
Regent University (VA)	45%	3.08-3.72	150-156
University of Baltimore	30%	2.98-3.52	152-156
South Texas College of Law	37%	2.98-3.50	151-156
Golden Gate University (CA)	36%	3.00-3.47	150-155
Roger Williams University (Papitto) (RI)	41%	2.94-3.54	151-155
St. Mary's University (TX)	37%	2.81-3.42	151-156
John Marshall Law School (IL)	36%	2.80-3.38	152-156
New England School of Law (MA)	37%	3.12-3.56	150-153
Whittier Law School (CA)	30%	2.86-3.32	152-155
Ave Maria School of Law (MI)	67%	2.80-3.50	150-160
CUNY–Queens College	21%	3.03-3.52	149-156
Vermont Law School	51%	2.89-3.47	151-158
Florida Coastal School of Law	37%	2.88-3.49	150-154
University of Tulsa (OK)	34%	2.80-3.50	150-154
Western New England College (MA)	43%	2.70-3.32	151-156
Thomas Jefferson School of Law (CA)	24%	2.74-3.39	151-156
Widener University (DE)	36%	2.81-3.46	150-154
Mississippi College	39%	2.99-3.51	149-153
Nova Southeastern University (Broad) (FL)	28%	2.93-3.37	148-152
Touro College (Fuchsberg) (NY)	35%	2.87-3.44	150-153
University of Detroit Mercy	46%	3.00-3.50	147-153
University of the District of Columbia (Clarke)	23%	2.76-3.23	149-155
Oklahoma City University	41%	2.78-3.43	148-152
North Carolina Central University	20%	2.80-3.50	143-152
St. Thomas University (FL)	39%	2.58-3.33	147-152
Thomas M. Cooley Law School (MI)	69%	2.72-3.39	146-152
Texas Southern University (Marshall)	22%	2.58-3.23	144-149

As you compare schools, you'll want to pay attention to the total enrollment, the size of first-year sections, the availability of small classes, and the student–faculty ratio. All will have an impact on the schools' personalities, the availability of professors outside of class, the extent to which you engage with your classmates, and the breadth of the curriculum. Schools are ranked here by total enrollment.

School	Total full- and part-time enrollment	Full-time enrollment	Part-time enrollment	Size of first-year class	Typical first-year section size	Public or private	Student to faculty ratio	% classes under 25	% classes 25–100	% classes over 100	Number of course offerings after first year
Thomas M. Cooley Law School (MI)	3,252	503	2,749	1,514	N/A	Private	23.6	67%	29%	4%	195
Georgetown University (DC)	1,940	1,580	360	583	112	Private	14.7	61%	34%	5%	307
Harvard University (MA)	1,712	1,712	N/A	557	80	Private	11.0	45%	44%	11%	267
Suffolk University (MA)	1,671	1,058	613	554	91	Private	17.1	56%	38%	6%	290
George Washington University (DC)	1,636	1,366	270	535	100	Private	15.1	61%	35%	4%	189
Widener University (DE)	1,571	997	574	550	75	Private	17.5	57%	42%	1%	203
Fordham University (NY)	1,516	1,170	346	483	80	Private	15.9	63%	33%	3%	205
Brooklyn Law School (NY)	1,490	1,134	356	305	51	Private	20.5	53%	41%	6%	149
John Marshall Law School (IL)	1,485	1,133	352	541	85	Private	21.8	68%	32%	0%	201
New York Law School	1,480	1,106	374	538	120	Private	20.3	48%	45%	7%	190
New York University	1,424	1,424	N/A	448	112	Private	11.1	43%	49%	8%	253
American University (Washington) (DC)	1,404	1,128	276	464	91	Private	14.3	58%	41%	0%	292
University of Texas–Austin	1,387	1,387	N/A	442	106	Public	16.7	56%	35%	9%	138
Loyola Law School (CA)	1,319	994	325	410	89	Private	16.1	67%	28%	5%	136
South Texas College of Law	1,262	959	303	453	90	Private	19.7	50%	50%	0%	127
University of California (Hastings)	1,251	1,251	N/A	419	85	Public	20.4	62%	37%	1%	131
Columbia University (NY)	1,242	1,242	N/A	378	109	Private	11.7	48%	37%	14%	211
University of Denver (Sturm)	1,242	814	428	349	90	Private	14.1	71%	29%	0%	147
University of Michigan–Ann Arbor	1,179	1,179	N/A	366	95	Public	16.9	32%	55%	13%	130
DePaul University (IL)	1,158	804	354	330	86	Private	17.9	59%	40%	1%	161
University of Florida (Levin)	1,156	1,156	N/A	207	100	Public	15.4	48%	45%	7%	192
University of Miami (FL)	1,151	1,099	52	415	100	Private	19.6	42%	48%	10%	156
Seton Hall University (NJ)	1,142	766	376	367	80	Private	14.9	43%	57%	0%	140
University of Virginia	1,118	1,118	N/A	374	65	Public	13.0	47%	41%	12%	242
William Mitchell College of Law (MN)	1,114	732	382	271	78	Private	23.6	42%	58%	0%	125
Seattle University	1,109	874	235	365	86	Private	15.6	55%	44%	1%	145
New England School of Law (MA)	1,095	699	396	382	135	Private	25.2	43%	53%	4%	125
University of San Diego	1,066	763	303	365	85	Private	14.3	61%	38%	1%	125
Florida Coastal School of Law	1,048	834	214	449	75	Private	17.8	50%	50%	0%	140
Illinois Institute of Technology (Chicago-Kent)	1,047	800	247	335	52	Private	12.4	74%	24%	2%	126
Cardozo-Yeshiva University (NY)	1,046	931	115	364	50	Private	15.8	42%	50%	8%	144
Michigan State University	1,044	825	219	280	73	Private	20.7	58%	41%	1%	154
Temple University (Beasley) (PA)	1,044	796	248	323	64	Public	14.7	68%	31%	1%	174
University of the Pacific (McGeorge) (CA)	1,042	641	401	340	82	Private	16.1	47%	51%	2%	129
Hofstra University (NY)	1,038	835	203	386	115	Private	17.7	45%	45%	10%	123
University of Houston	1,037	838	199	318	80	Public	20.8	53%	47%	0%	204
Stetson University (FL)	987	757	230	345	68	Private	17.5	74%	26%	0%	129
University of Baltimore	986	674	312	323	64	Public	21.9	73%	26%	1%	119
University of California–Los Angeles	970	970	N/A	317	80	Public	11.8	54%	44%	2%	151

What are the largest and smallest law schools?

School	Total full- and part-time enrollment	Full-time enrollment	Part-time enrollment	Size of first-year class	Typical first-year section size	Public or private	Student to faculty ratio	% classes under 25	% classes 25–100	% classes over 100	Number of course offerings after first year
Santa Clara University (CA)	955	721	234	310	82	Private	18.5	64%	36%	0%	244
St. John's University (NY)	952	756	196	325	79	Private	17.2	65%	33%	2%	102
Catholic University of America (Columbus) (DC)	949	688	261	329	80	Private	16.3	74%	26%	0%	132
Nova Southeastern University (Broad) (FL)	943	744	199	336	59	Private	13.4	71%	29%	0%	129
Southwestern University School of Law (CA)	931	658	273	334	71	Private	15.7	53%	47%	1%	141
Indiana University–Indianapolis	913	642	271	277	100	Public	18.0	47%	52%	1%	131
St. Louis University	880	664	216	300	0	Private	17.6	44%	49%	8%	96
University of California–Berkeley	874	874	N/A	264	95	Public	14.2	73%	24%	3%	207
Whittier Law School (CA)	871	499	372	273	64	Private	16.6	67%	33%	0%	85
Boston University	860	860	N/A	294	96	Private	12.1	45%	48%	7%	119
California Western School of Law	855	745	110	347	98	Private	18.7	61%	36%	3%	110
Golden Gate University (CA)	851	669	182	321	59	Private	22.4	74%	26%	0%	181
Loyola University Chicago	843	602	241	259	62	Private	16.8	49%	51%	0%	136
University of Wisconsin–Madison	839	801	38	271	70	Public	13.1	63%	35%	2%	169
Southern Methodist University (TX)	829	618	211	290	95	Private	15.4	43%	55%	2%	123
Boston College	809	807	2	275	90	Private	13.9	68%	32%	1%	143
University of Maryland	809	666	143	258	67	Public	11.9	74%	25%	1%	136
University of Minnesota–Twin Cities	808	808	N/A	273	112	Public	12.5	58%	40%	3%	193
St. Thomas University (FL)	806	806	N/A	328	70	Private	20.2	69%	31%	1%	97
Rutgers State University–Newark (NJ)	804	564	240	249	60	Public	15.4	55%	44%	1%	115
Thomas Jefferson School of Law (CA)	803	609	194	276	70	Private	21.9	25%	70%	5%	96
Rutgers State University–Camden (NJ)	787	571	216	261	85	Public	15.7	61%	37%	2%	102
University of Pennsylvania	777	777	N/A	243	85	Private	12.8	38%	56%	6%	92
Florida State University	772	772	N/A	284	74	Public	13.8	49%	45%	6%	108
Northwestern University (IL)	772	772	N/A	243	65	Private	11.9	43%	57%	1%	198
St. Mary's University (TX)	762	762	N/A	267	67	Private	23.5	45%	55%	0%	115
Touro College (Fuchsberg) (NY)	761	521	240	298	71	Private	17.4	56%	42%	2%	70
Syracuse University (NY)	756	749	7	266	68	Private	15.7	66%	32%	2%	141
Lewis and Clark College (Northwestern) (OR)	748	549	199	232	76	Private	14.1	53%	46%	1%	119
Villanova University (PA)	748	748	N/A	245	109	Private	17.7	59%	37%	3%	109
Washington University in St. Louis	745	743	2	222	85	Private	13.2	59%	35%	6%	123
Pace University (NY)	743	495	248	260	53	Private	15.4	71%	29%	1%	137
Albany Law School-Union University (NY)	739	702	37	247	69	Private	14.8	55%	36%	9%	117
University of South Carolina	739	739	N/A	231	75	Public	17.8	44%	52%	4%	105
University at Buffalo–SUNY	731	731	N/A	247	83	Public	13.2	68%	32%	0%	200
Capital University (OH)	730	457	273	255	85	Private	16.3	53%	45%	2%	109
University of San Francisco	729	599	130	259	94	Private	16.7	46%	54%	0%	71
Cleveland State University (Cleveland-Marshall)	724	463	261	236	58	Public	12.7	56%	44%	0%	71
Ohio State University (Moritz)	723	723	N/A	217	75	Public	14.1	41%	57%	2%	80
George Mason University (VA)	717	414	303	216	94	Public	16.5	78%	21%	1%	145
Marquette University (WI)	715	569	146	215	80	Private	17.3	60%	40%	0%	132
University of North Carolina–Chapel Hill	715	715	N/A	231	77	Public	16.9	49%	46%	4%	106
Wayne State University (MI)	711	549	162	238	89	Public	19.6	40%	53%	7%	72
Hamline University (MN)	710	516	194	226	60	Private	18.5	63%	37%	0%	109
University of Detroit Mercy	708	519	189	254	72	Private	17.8	49%	51%	0%	79
Pepperdine University (McConnell) (CA)	704	704	N/A	243	80	Private	19.8	60%	38%	2%	109
Texas Tech University	701	701	N/A	270	60	Public	16.6	51%	43%	5%	95
University of Georgia	694	694	N/A	210	69	Public	15.3	55%	39%	5%	114
Case Western Reserve University (OH)	692	667	25	225	75	Private	14.7	66%	33%	1%	178
University of Pittsburgh	691	691	N/A	243	84	Public	14.4	67%	28%	5%	162
Georgia State University	685	494	191	219	70	Public	16.2	57%	43%	0%	101

What are the largest and smallest law schools?

School	Total full- and part-time enrollment	Full-time enrollment	Part-time enrollment	Size of first-year class	Typical first-year section size	Public or private	Student to faculty ratio	% classes under 25	% classes 25–100	% classes over 100	Number of course offerings after first year
Oklahoma City University	684	546	138	217	84	Private	18.6	54%	46%	0%	85
Emory University (GA)	680	680	N/A	235	71	Private	13.3	60%	38%	2%	124
University of Connecticut	671	497	174	199	64	Public	11.8	57%	43%	0%	115
Texas Wesleyan University	670	432	238	253	98	Private	17.9	59%	41%	1%	88
Indiana University–Bloomington	663	662	1	228	75	Public	14.1	61%	36%	4%	110
Texas Southern University (Marshall)	657	657	N/A	236	60	Public	16.3	55%	45%	0%	112
University of Iowa	656	656	N/A	225	75	Public	12.2	49%	51%	0%	108
Arizona State University	650	650	N/A	256	105	Public	11.1	59%	40%	1%	113
Duke University (NC)	648	617	31	199	72	Private	12.6	62%	35%	3%	135
Louisiana State University–Baton Rouge	647	630	17	218	72	Public	16.6	39%	60%	1%	98
University of Illinois–Urbana-Champaign	640	640	N/A	188	77	Public	12.6	71%	27%	2%	147
University of Southern California (Gould)	628	628	N/A	207	70	Private	13.0	53%	43%	5%	86
Vanderbilt University (TN)	627	626	1	200	100	Private	16.4	57%	40%	2%	132
Northeastern University (MA)	623	623	N/A	212	72	Private	17.0	60%	39%	1%	72
Roger Williams University (Papitto) (RI)	608	511	97	198	92	Private	19.9	52%	48%	0%	130
College of William and Mary (Marshall-Wythe) (VA)	607	607	N/A	205	70	Public	15.7	75%	24%	1%	120
University of Tulsa (OK)	591	506	85	208	76	Private	16.3	62%	38%	N/A	96
University of Chicago	589	589	N/A	192	96	Private	9.5	30%	64%	6%	155
Yale University (CT)	586	585	1	199	65	Private	7.8	30%	66%	4%	143
Cornell University (NY)	580	580	N/A	193	97	Private	10.3	35%	61%	5%	120
Pennsylvania State University (Dickinson)	580	580	N/A	205	60	Private	13.8	52%	47%	1%	131
Northern Kentucky University (Chase)	579	296	283	188	108	Public	17.4	57%	42%	1%	62
Gonzaga University (WA)	578	556	22	192	80	Private	18.0	60%	39%	1%	81
Western New England College (MA)	576	416	160	192	70	Private	16.5	48%	52%	0%	92
University of California–Davis	571	571	N/A	194	65	Public	13.5	43%	49%	9%	77
Duquesne University (PA)	565	422	143	193	86	Private	16.3	56%	44%	0%	108
Vermont Law School	564	562	2	196	68	Private	13.3	66%	34%	0%	120
University of Washington	561	561	N/A	180	62	Public	10.9	52%	48%	N/A	96
Chapman University (CA)	556	515	41	194	65	Private	17.7	67%	33%	0%	83
University of Mississippi	554	553	1	187	57	Public	16.9	35%	62%	3%	67
Quinnipiac University (CT)	548	383	165	132	44	Private	14.5	69%	31%	0%	105
University of Notre Dame (IN)	539	538	1	175	89	Private	14.3	51%	48%	1%	109
Barry University (FL)	537	351	186	204	80	Private	17.9	73%	27%	0%	61
Samford University (Cumberland) (AL)	532	527	5	175	58	Private	18.2	50%	50%	0%	94
Stanford University (CA)	527	527	N/A	173	60	Private	9.2	61%	38%	1%	137
University of Oregon	526	526	N/A	179	65	Public	19.7	34%	64%	2%	94
Valparaiso University (IN)	526	479	47	199	93	Private	15.5	58%	39%	2%	99
University of Akron (OH)	525	309	216	182	34	Public	13.9	59%	41%	0%	85
University of Missouri–Kansas City	523	499	24	178	60	Public	20.4	59%	41%	0%	94
University of Oklahoma	516	516	N/A	174	43	Public	15.3	48%	52%	0%	121
University of Toledo (OH)	510	351	159	174	57	Public	13.4	72%	28%	0%	84
University of Colorado–Boulder	499	495	4	168	83	Public	12.7	57%	43%	0%	91
University of Kansas	497	497	N/A	157	68	Public	13.4	65%	34%	1%	87
Mississippi College	490	490	N/A	199	92	Private	21.4	54%	46%	0%	63
Regent University (VA)	489	444	45	161	80	Private	18.3	69%	31%	0%	71
Wake Forest University (NC)	488	468	20	154	40	Private	10.2	49%	51%	N/A	87
University of Richmond (VA)	485	483	2	171	85	Private	14.3	68%	32%	0%	82
University of Alabama–Tuscaloosa	484	484	N/A	157	50	Public	10.3	71%	27%	2%	122
University of Nevada–Las Vegas (Boyd)	479	322	157	151	63	Public	15.0	74%	26%	0%	71
North Carolina Central University	476	372	104	201	84	Public	18.8	64%	32%	3%	58
Brigham Young University (Clark) (UT)	472	472	N/A	153	106	Private	18.9	42%	51%	7%	98

What are the largest and smallest law schools?

School	Total full- and part-time enrollment	Full-time enrollment	Part-time enrollment	Size of first-year class	Typical first-year section size	Public or private	Student to faculty ratio	% classes under 25	% classes 25-100	% classes over 100	Number of course offerings after first year
University of Arkansas–Little Rock (Bowen)	472	312	160	143	90	Public	16.9	71%	29%	0%	90
Drake University (IA)	471	462	9	145	72	Private	17.8	72%	27%	1%	140
Creighton University (NE)	469	451	18	161	80	Private	15.4	72%	28%	1%	80
University of Dayton (OH)	469	468	1	119	80	Private	15.4	66%	34%	0%	68
West Virginia University	467	463	4	152	75	Public	23.2	40%	57%	3%	73
University of Tennessee–Knoxville	457	457	N/A	158	52	Public	12.1	74%	26%	0%	94
University of Arizona (Rogers)	456	456	N/A	151	84	Public	12.7	81%	18%	1%	125
University of Kentucky	453	453	N/A	172	72	Public	16.3	37%	63%	0%	56
Howard University (DC)	451	451	N/A	159	54	Private	13.0	N/A	N/A	N/A	N/A
Washburn University (KS)	451	451	N/A	152	75	Public	14.4	51%	49%	0%	83
University of Missouri–Columbia	446	440	6	150	72	Public	13.2	70%	30%	0%	126
Willamette University (Collins) (OR)	443	438	5	145	70	Private	15.6	56%	42%	1%	96
Franklin Pierce Law Center (NH)	440	437	3	143	70	Private	18.5	64%	35%	1%	85
University of Arkansas–Fayetteville	440	440	N/A	143	81	Public	13.2	60%	37%	3%	81
CUNY–Queens College	437	436	1	166	90	Public	12.5	44%	55%	2%	55
Baylor University (TX)	435	435	N/A	80	57	Private	16.9	53%	46%	1%	76
University of St. Thomas (MN)	418	418	N/A	148	73	Private	15.1	78%	22%	0%	67
Mercer University (GA)	408	407	1	155	72	Private	13.5	73%	27%	0%	95
University of Memphis (Humphreys)	400	368	32	145	70	Public	14.2	48%	49%	2%	75
University of Utah (S.J. Quinney)	398	398	N/A	127	44	Public	11.5	54%	46%	0%	96
University of Cincinnati	397	397	N/A	133	76	Public	11.8	66%	29%	5%	113
University of Louisville (Brandeis) (KY)	396	296	100	137	50	Public	15.0	50%	50%	0%	59
University of Nebraska–Lincoln	394	389	5	136	70	Public	13.7	45%	55%	N/A	64
Florida A&M University	393	231	162	172	35	Public	15.0	67%	33%	0%	45
Washington and Lee University (VA)	387	387	N/A	136	57	Private	10.5	54%	46%	0%	72
Southern Illinois University–Carbondale	377	377	N/A	122	65	Public	12.6	64%	36%	0%	75
Ave Maria School of Law (MI)	360	360	N/A	147	75	Private	14.0	72%	28%	0%	67
University of New Mexico	357	357	N/A	119	59	Public	11.4	50%	50%	0%	81
Campbell University (Wiggins) (NC)	340	340	N/A	119	83	Private	17.0	49%	49%	3%	83
Northern Illinois University	334	320	14	132	53	Public	18.4	49%	51%	0%	53
Florida International University	332	176	156	120	64	Public	13.3	74%	26%	N/A	52
Ohio Northern University (Pettit)	324	324	N/A	116	65	Private	14.8	70%	30%	0%	60
University of Hawaii (Richardson)	305	305	N/A	96	95	Public	13.6	72%	27%	1%	61
University of Idaho	297	297	N/A	104	52	Public	16.8	52%	48%	0%	53
University of Maine	254	249	5	75	84	Public	15.5	67%	33%	0%	48
University of South Dakota	250	247	3	91	73	Public	16.1	47%	53%	N/A	41
University of Montana	237	237	N/A	85	43	Public	18.2	N/A	N/A	N/A	N/A
University of the District of Columbia (Clarke)	232	232	N/A	81	85	Public	11.5	64%	36%	0%	45
University of Wyoming	227	227	N/A	80	78	Public	17.2	67%	33%	0%	56
University of North Dakota	224	224	N/A	90	76	Public	19.0	63%	37%	N/A	47

What are the most and least diverse law schools?

If you're looking for a law school culture that features students from a wealth of backgrounds, the *U.S. News* diversity index can point you to institutions with both a significant proportion of minority students and a mix of different ethnic groups. The closer the index number is to 1.0, the more likely you are to interact with people of a different ethnicity than you.

School	Diversity index	American Indian	Asian	Black	Hispanic	White	International	Men	Women	Minority faculty	Male faculty	Female faculty
Texas Southern University (Marshall)	0.66	0.3%	7.5%	49.6%	22.5%	20.1%	0.0%	44.1%	55.9%	85.4%	61.0%	39.0%
Florida A&M University	0.65	1.3%	2.5%	41.0%	15.0%	40.2%	0.0%	41.0%	59.0%	73.9%	65.2%	34.8%
University of the District of Columbia (Clarke)	0.63	1.3%	6.5%	30.6%	9.1%	46.6%	6.0%	38.4%	61.6%	55.2%	62.1%	37.9%
Florida International University	0.61	0.6%	2.7%	10.2%	40.7%	45.8%	0.0%	53.0%	47.0%	44.2%	65.1%	34.9%
Rutgers State University–Newark (NJ)	0.59	0.4%	13.1%	14.1%	11.8%	58.2%	2.5%	56.7%	43.3%	16.7%	62.8%	37.2%
Santa Clara University (CA)	0.58	0.4%	26.7%	4.0%	10.6%	58.1%	0.2%	50.9%	49.1%	15.2%	61.9%	38.1%
University of New Mexico	0.58	10.6%	2.2%	3.6%	24.4%	59.1%	0.0%	49.6%	50.4%	26.3%	61.4%	38.6%
North Carolina Central University	0.57	1.1%	3.6%	45.6%	2.5%	47.3%	0.0%	39.3%	60.7%	42.4%	51.5%	48.5%
Loyola Law School (CA)	0.56	0.7%	24.6%	3.7%	10.5%	60.2%	0.4%	52.2%	47.8%	13.0%	67.9%	32.1%
St. Thomas University (FL)	0.56	0.4%	4.7%	7.2%	27.4%	58.3%	2.0%	57.1%	42.9%	23.8%	58.3%	41.7%
University of Southern California (Gould)	0.56	0.3%	19.4%	9.1%	8.8%	61.5%	1.0%	51.9%	48.1%	14.4%	70.5%	29.5%
Whittier Law School (CA)	0.54	0.2%	19.4%	4.6%	11.6%	63.7%	0.5%	48.6%	51.4%	15.9%	56.5%	43.5%
CUNY–Queens College	0.53	0.2%	14.2%	8.7%	10.1%	63.2%	3.7%	33.2%	66.8%	45.5%	50.0%	50.0%
Southwestern University School of Law (CA)	0.53	1.0%	19.5%	4.0%	10.6%	63.3%	1.6%	48.7%	51.3%	15.3%	72.9%	27.1%
University of California–Davis	0.53	0.7%	23.5%	1.8%	10.7%	62.5%	0.9%	39.6%	60.4%	24.0%	66.7%	33.3%
University of Hawaii (Richardson)	0.53	1.3%	55.4%	1.0%	2.0%	38.0%	2.3%	52.8%	47.2%	38.9%	58.3%	41.7%
Stanford University (CA)	0.52	1.1%	11.2%	7.8%	12.3%	64.7%	2.8%	56.0%	44.0%	N/A	N/A	N/A
University of California–Berkeley	0.52	1.0%	19.1%	4.5%	9.7%	65.7%	0.0%	40.8%	59.2%	N/A	N/A	N/A
University of Illinois–Urbana-Champaign	0.52	0.6%	18.0%	6.9%	8.0%	64.7%	1.9%	61.1%	38.9%	14.6%	67.7%	32.3%
American University (Washington) (DC)	0.51	0.7%	12.3%	8.0%	11.5%	66.9%	0.7%	43.2%	56.8%	13.9%	59.7%	40.3%
Columbia University (NY)	0.51	0.6%	14.7%	8.6%	6.1%	61.0%	8.9%	54.8%	45.2%	9.6%	70.0%	30.0%
Yale University (CT)	0.51	0.0%	13.1%	8.9%	9.6%	64.3%	4.1%	55.6%	44.4%	15.7%	74.1%	25.9%
University of California (Hastings)	0.50	0.3%	23.7%	2.6%	7.0%	65.1%	1.2%	46.0%	54.0%	11.5%	64.5%	35.5%
University of Chicago	0.50	0.3%	13.1%	7.5%	10.4%	68.3%	0.5%	55.2%	44.8%	8.3%	82.6%	17.4%
University of San Francisco	0.50	0.7%	18.5%	4.3%	8.6%	67.4%	0.5%	48.1%	51.9%	24.6%	58.5%	41.5%
Cornell University (NY)	0.49	0.7%	16.7%	7.8%	5.2%	65.0%	4.7%	51.7%	48.3%	N/A	N/A	N/A
Northwestern University (IL)	0.49	0.3%	15.5%	7.1%	7.9%	69.2%	0.0%	52.6%	47.4%	8.7%	74.8%	25.2%
University of Arizona (Rogers)	0.49	5.3%	10.5%	3.7%	10.7%	68.9%	0.9%	49.6%	50.4%	12.9%	70.1%	29.9%
University of Pennsylvania	0.49	0.6%	14.2%	7.9%	6.8%	66.8%	3.7%	54.6%	45.4%	11.5%	75.2%	24.8%
University of Texas–Austin	0.49	0.8%	6.1%	5.7%	19.3%	68.2%	0.0%	56.8%	43.2%	8.9%	69.6%	30.4%
Harvard University (MA)	0.48	0.6%	12.4%	10.3%	5.7%	67.3%	3.7%	56.0%	44.0%	9.0%	75.4%	24.6%
University of California–Los Angeles	0.48	1.8%	15.9%	4.3%	7.9%	69.1%	1.0%	50.3%	49.7%	8.8%	74.7%	25.3%
University of Maryland	0.48	0.4%	10.8%	14.5%	4.7%	68.7%	1.0%	42.6%	57.4%	12.0%	62.7%	37.3%
Northeastern University (MA)	0.47	1.3%	12.4%	7.4%	8.2%	70.6%	0.2%	38.7%	61.3%	17.9%	42.9%	57.1%
Nova Southeastern University (Broad) (FL)	0.45	0.2%	3.0%	5.8%	19.4%	70.0%	1.6%	49.2%	50.8%	16.0%	64.9%	35.1%
St. Mary's University (TX)	0.45	1.6%	4.3%	2.5%	20.6%	71.0%	0.0%	58.4%	41.6%	18.2%	65.2%	34.8%
University of Michigan–Ann Arbor	0.45	2.6%	10.9%	6.3%	6.4%	69.2%	4.6%	54.5%	45.5%	10.3%	66.4%	33.6%
University of San Diego	0.45	0.7%	14.4%	3.3%	9.2%	72.0%	0.4%	54.6%	45.4%	10.6%	77.7%	22.3%
Arizona State University	0.44	4.6%	4.2%	3.5%	14.6%	71.7%	1.4%	56.2%	43.8%	12.3%	83.1%	16.9%

What are the most and least diverse law schools?

School	Diversity index	American Indian	Asian	Black	Hispanic	White	International	Men	Women	Minority faculty	Male faculty	Female faculty
California Western School of Law	0.44	1.2%	13.1%	3.0%	9.6%	72.2%	0.9%	48.1%	51.9%	10.3%	58.8%	41.2%
Emory University (GA)	0.44	0.0%	9.4%	9.7%	6.9%	72.2%	1.8%	49.7%	50.3%	11.3%	76.3%	23.8%
George Washington University (DC)	0.44	0.6%	9.9%	8.8%	7.5%	72.5%	0.7%	55.3%	44.7%	12.8%	65.1%	34.9%
Chapman University (CA)	0.42	0.9%	18.0%	0.7%	7.0%	73.2%	0.2%	50.2%	49.8%	9.3%	68.5%	31.5%
Fordham University (NY)	0.42	0.7%	10.8%	5.5%	8.0%	75.0%	0.0%	53.2%	46.8%	14.3%	66.3%	33.7%
New York University	0.42	0.0%	10.3%	8.6%	5.6%	72.2%	3.3%	54.3%	45.7%	9.1%	71.1%	28.9%
St. John's University (NY)	0.42	0.1%	9.2%	7.1%	7.7%	72.2%	3.7%	52.7%	47.3%	11.6%	69.6%	30.4%
Touro College (Fuchsberg) (NY)	0.42	0.5%	8.9%	9.3%	6.2%	74.2%	0.8%	55.6%	44.4%	12.3%	63.2%	36.8%
University of Houston	0.42	0.8%	12.2%	3.9%	8.8%	74.2%	0.2%	54.0%	46.0%	8.1%	72.3%	27.7%
University of Wisconsin–Madison	0.42	2.0%	6.6%	8.1%	7.7%	73.4%	2.1%	52.9%	47.1%	10.3%	57.8%	42.2%
Brooklyn Law School (NY)	0.41	0.1%	14.7%	4.8%	5.0%	74.6%	0.8%	51.1%	48.9%	8.2%	60.7%	39.3%
Georgetown University (DC)	0.41	0.2%	9.6%	9.0%	4.7%	72.7%	3.9%	56.1%	43.9%	6.8%	75.6%	24.4%
Golden Gate University (CA)	0.41	0.8%	16.2%	2.5%	5.6%	74.0%	0.8%	43.4%	56.6%	23.9%	58.7%	41.3%
Seattle University	0.41	1.5%	13.4%	4.1%	5.3%	74.5%	1.1%	44.5%	55.5%	17.4%	65.2%	34.8%
Temple University (Beasley) (PA)	0.40	0.4%	11.4%	8.0%	4.2%	75.1%	1.0%	52.0%	48.0%	N/A	N/A	N/A
Thomas M. Cooley Law School (MI)	0.40	0.4%	6.3%	11.6%	4.9%	74.0%	2.9%	52.7%	47.3%	6.4%	65.7%	34.3%
University of Miami (FL)	0.40	0.4%	4.1%	7.2%	11.8%	75.1%	1.4%	56.0%	44.0%	14.8%	73.4%	26.6%
University of Nevada–Las Vegas (Boyd)	0.40	0.6%	12.3%	3.8%	7.1%	76.2%	0.0%	51.4%	48.6%	16.3%	63.3%	36.7%
Duke University (NC)	0.39	0.6%	6.8%	10.6%	3.9%	73.0%	5.1%	54.3%	45.7%	8.5%	73.6%	26.4%
Ohio State University (Moritz)	0.39	0.4%	10.2%	8.3%	3.6%	75.8%	1.7%	58.5%	41.5%	N/A	N/A	N/A
University of Florida (Levin)	0.39	0.3%	4.9%	6.6%	9.9%	72.8%	5.4%	54.5%	45.5%	8.0%	65.0%	35.0%
University of Notre Dame (IN)	0.39	1.1%	8.2%	5.6%	7.6%	76.1%	1.5%	58.3%	41.7%	8.7%	63.0%	37.0%
Northern Illinois University	0.38	0.6%	6.6%	8.4%	6.9%	77.2%	0.3%	48.2%	51.8%	30.8%	73.1%	26.9%
Pennsylvania State University (Dickinson)	0.38	0.2%	7.2%	7.4%	7.2%	77.4%	0.5%	53.6%	46.4%	9.9%	70.3%	29.7%
University of Arkansas–Fayetteville	0.38	2.3%	2.7%	15.9%	1.8%	76.8%	0.5%	56.4%	43.6%	15.8%	63.2%	36.8%
Boston College	0.37	0.1%	10.9%	4.9%	5.3%	77.0%	1.7%	50.1%	49.9%	10.2%	67.6%	32.4%
Boston University	0.37	0.2%	14.2%	3.7%	3.6%	75.0%	3.3%	49.5%	50.5%	N/A	N/A	N/A
Illinois Institute of Technology (Chicago-Kent)	0.37	0.5%	10.1%	5.5%	5.5%	77.2%	1.1%	54.8%	45.2%	6.0%	69.3%	30.7%
Rutgers State University–Camden (NJ)	0.37	0.1%	8.1%	6.4%	7.1%	77.3%	1.0%	59.7%	40.3%	8.2%	70.9%	29.1%
University of Colorado–Boulder	0.37	3.0%	8.8%	3.2%	6.6%	78.2%	0.2%	48.1%	51.9%	9.6%	71.2%	28.8%
University of North Carolina–Chapel Hill	0.37	1.7%	5.2%	10.5%	4.1%	78.6%	0.0%	51.9%	48.1%	18.0%	68.0%	32.0%
University of Oklahoma	0.37	9.7%	2.7%	5.2%	3.7%	78.5%	0.2%	55.2%	44.8%	6.9%	75.9%	24.1%
University of the Pacific (McGeorge) (CA)	0.37	1.1%	12.4%	2.3%	5.7%	76.4%	2.2%	53.3%	46.7%	13.0%	64.0%	36.0%
New York Law School	0.36	0.4%	7.7%	6.0%	6.9%	78.0%	1.0%	46.0%	54.0%	9.1%	63.0%	37.0%
Southern Methodist University (TX)	0.36	0.8%	8.1%	4.5%	7.4%	78.6%	0.6%	52.6%	47.4%	12.5%	66.7%	33.3%
South Texas College of Law	0.36	0.7%	9.4%	3.4%	7.8%	78.6%	0.2%	53.6%	46.4%	10.6%	72.1%	27.9%
University of Connecticut	0.36	0.6%	5.8%	6.0%	8.6%	78.4%	0.6%	49.6%	50.4%	8.8%	73.6%	26.4%
Vanderbilt University (TN)	0.36	0.5%	6.1%	9.9%	3.7%	76.4%	3.5%	54.2%	45.8%	9.8%	72.5%	27.5%
Wayne State University (MI)	0.36	1.1%	6.0%	10.1%	3.8%	78.9%	0.0%	50.1%	49.9%	6.3%	72.2%	27.8%
DePaul University (IL)	0.35	0.2%	7.0%	6.1%	6.8%	79.9%	0.0%	49.8%	50.2%	N/A	N/A	N/A
Hofstra University (NY)	0.35	0.4%	6.4%	7.4%	5.8%	77.9%	2.1%	52.1%	47.9%	3.6%	79.1%	20.9%
Texas Wesleyan University	0.35	1.0%	7.3%	4.0%	7.9%	79.1%	0.6%	49.3%	50.7%	8.7%	71.0%	29.0%
Cardozo-Yeshiva University (NY)	0.34	0.1%	9.6%	3.1%	6.2%	78.5%	2.6%	52.3%	47.7%	5.2%	74.1%	25.9%
Georgia State University	0.34	0.4%	6.3%	10.9%	2.3%	80.0%	0.0%	52.0%	48.0%	14.9%	63.8%	36.2%
Seton Hall University (NJ)	0.34	0.3%	8.5%	4.0%	6.2%	79.0%	2.0%	56.2%	43.8%	15.5%	70.1%	29.9%
Stetson University (FL)	0.34	0.5%	2.3%	5.8%	11.3%	79.5%	0.5%	46.5%	53.5%	10.8%	64.5%	35.5%
University of Baltimore	0.34	0.5%	4.9%	12.3%	2.3%	79.3%	0.7%	50.8%	49.2%	13.9%	72.1%	27.9%
University of Georgia	0.34	0.3%	3.5%	14.1%	2.2%	80.0%	0.0%	49.3%	50.7%	N/A	N/A	N/A
University of Washington	0.34	2.5%	13.0%	1.6%	2.3%	76.3%	4.3%	41.5%	58.5%	10.4%	68.9%	31.1%
Barry University (FL)	0.33	2.0%	3.5%	6.0%	7.4%	81.0%	0.0%	50.3%	49.7%	16.1%	71.0%	29.0%
Florida State University	0.33	1.0%	4.1%	5.3%	8.3%	79.7%	1.6%	54.4%	45.6%	7.0%	63.2%	36.8%

What are the most and least diverse law schools?

School	Diversity index	American Indian	Asian	Black	Hispanic	White	International	Men	Women	Minority faculty	Male faculty	Female faculty
Franklin Pierce Law Center (NH)	0.33	0.0%	10.5%	4.3%	3.6%	77.7%	3.9%	59.5%	40.5%	3.2%	66.7%	33.3%
Oklahoma City University	0.33	7.0%	3.8%	3.1%	4.5%	80.8%	0.7%	60.1%	39.9%	10.4%	70.8%	29.2%
Pepperdine University (McConnell) (CA)	0.33	0.3%	9.9%	4.7%	3.8%	81.3%	0.0%	47.6%	52.4%	7.9%	65.8%	34.2%
Syracuse University (NY)	0.33	1.1%	7.8%	4.9%	4.2%	78.6%	3.4%	54.1%	45.9%	13.0%	71.0%	29.0%
University of Denver (Sturm)	0.33	4.5%	5.1%	4.5%	4.6%	81.3%	0.0%	54.2%	45.8%	12.8%	69.7%	30.3%
Lewis and Clark College (Northwestern) (OR)	0.32	1.9%	9.0%	2.0%	5.3%	80.1%	1.7%	50.7%	49.3%	4.8%	69.8%	30.2%
University of Kansas	0.32	3.0%	6.2%	2.6%	6.0%	79.3%	2.8%	56.9%	43.1%	6.3%	69.8%	30.2%
University of Oregon	0.32	1.5%	7.8%	3.2%	5.1%	80.8%	1.5%	58.2%	41.8%	9.4%	62.5%	37.5%
Brigham Young University (Clark) (UT)	0.31	1.1%	8.1%	1.3%	7.0%	81.4%	1.3%	62.1%	37.9%	7.5%	76.1%	23.9%
Catholic University of America (Columbus) (DC)	0.31	0.3%	8.2%	3.9%	5.3%	81.3%	0.9%	49.6%	50.4%	12.8%	71.6%	28.4%
Texas Tech University	0.31	0.7%	4.0%	2.9%	10.1%	82.0%	0.3%	50.6%	49.4%	18.9%	73.6%	26.4%
Washington University in St. Louis	0.31	0.5%	9.0%	6.4%	1.2%	78.7%	4.2%	58.7%	41.3%	9.8%	67.8%	32.2%
George Mason University (VA)	0.30	0.8%	7.7%	3.3%	4.7%	80.8%	2.6%	61.6%	38.4%	5.7%	78.7%	21.3%
Loyola University Chicago	0.30	0.1%	8.9%	3.7%	3.8%	82.0%	1.5%	46.9%	53.1%	5.4%	53.3%	46.7%
Thomas Jefferson School of Law (CA)	0.30	0.4%	7.8%	1.6%	7.3%	82.8%	0.0%	56.7%	43.3%	5.6%	63.0%	37.0%
University of Cincinnati	0.30	1.0%	5.5%	7.6%	2.8%	83.1%	0.0%	49.9%	50.1%	11.2%	71.9%	28.1%
University of Virginia	0.30	0.5%	7.5%	7.3%	1.6%	82.7%	0.3%	59.3%	40.7%	5.2%	82.3%	17.7%
Villanova University (PA)	0.30	0.4%	7.1%	4.5%	4.8%	82.2%	0.9%	52.0%	48.0%	8.0%	67.8%	32.2%
Indiana University–Bloomington	0.29	0.2%	6.2%	6.2%	3.6%	83.7%	0.3%	60.8%	39.2%	6.6%	68.9%	31.1%
University at Buffalo–SUNY	0.29	0.5%	7.7%	4.8%	3.6%	83.4%	0.0%	49.8%	50.2%	12.2%	67.9%	32.1%
University of Iowa	0.29	1.1%	5.6%	4.7%	4.6%	83.4%	0.6%	53.5%	46.5%	7.1%	63.5%	36.5%
University of Minnesota–Twin Cities	0.29	0.6%	9.2%	2.4%	4.1%	81.3%	2.5%	56.8%	43.2%	8.3%	60.5%	39.5%
Vermont Law School	0.29	1.2%	2.5%	6.6%	5.7%	83.3%	0.7%	49.5%	50.5%	4.3%	57.1%	42.9%
Indiana University–Indianapolis	0.28	0.3%	3.9%	6.7%	4.5%	82.4%	2.2%	51.5%	48.5%	7.4%	66.2%	33.8%
John Marshall Law School (IL)	0.28	0.7%	5.7%	4.7%	4.3%	83.2%	1.3%	57.1%	42.9%	10.9%	75.2%	24.8%
Pace University (NY)	0.28	0.1%	7.9%	2.8%	4.7%	83.0%	1.3%	43.2%	56.8%	8.2%	60.3%	39.7%
Albany Law School-Union University (NY)	0.27	0.0%	6.2%	4.5%	4.3%	83.2%	1.8%	50.1%	49.9%	9.2%	64.4%	35.6%
Ave Maria School of Law (MI)	0.27	1.4%	6.1%	1.7%	5.3%	82.5%	3.1%	68.9%	31.1%	6.7%	76.7%	23.3%
University of Memphis (Humphreys)	0.27	0.0%	1.3%	13.5%	1.0%	84.3%	0.0%	55.3%	44.8%	10.5%	68.4%	31.6%
Washington and Lee University (VA)	0.27	1.3%	7.0%	5.2%	1.0%	82.9%	2.6%	58.4%	41.6%	N/A	N/A	N/A
College of William and Mary (Marshall-Wythe) (VA)	0.26	0.2%	5.1%	8.2%	1.3%	85.2%	0.0%	54.5%	45.5%	N/A	N/A	N/A
Florida Coastal School of Law	0.26	1.1%	2.2%	6.8%	4.2%	85.7%	0.0%	53.0%	47.0%	10.8%	59.8%	40.2%
Howard University (DC)	0.26	0.7%	3.8%	79.8%	2.7%	6.2%	6.9%	40.4%	59.6%	80.3%	62.1%	37.9%
University of Dayton (OH)	0.26	0.9%	5.8%	4.7%	3.0%	85.7%	0.0%	54.6%	45.4%	10.0%	72.0%	28.0%
University of St. Thomas (MN)	0.26	1.0%	6.2%	4.1%	3.3%	85.4%	0.0%	48.6%	51.4%	5.7%	58.6%	41.4%
Case Western Reserve University (OH)	0.25	0.3%	9.5%	3.2%	0.7%	83.8%	2.5%	61.6%	38.4%	4.9%	64.4%	35.6%
Mercer University (GA)	0.25	0.7%	3.2%	9.1%	1.0%	86.0%	0.0%	55.4%	44.6%	7.3%	76.4%	23.6%
University of Pittsburgh	0.25	0.1%	5.2%	6.5%	2.2%	86.0%	0.0%	54.7%	45.3%	6.7%	67.2%	32.8%
University of Tennessee–Knoxville	0.25	0.4%	0.9%	12.9%	0.4%	85.3%	0.0%	49.2%	50.8%	6.3%	60.4%	39.6%
Wake Forest University (NC)	0.25	0.0%	2.9%	6.4%	4.7%	85.0%	1.0%	54.7%	45.3%	5.5%	67.3%	32.7%
Washburn University (KS)	0.25	1.1%	4.0%	4.2%	4.4%	85.4%	0.9%	57.4%	42.6%	10.2%	74.6%	25.4%
Baylor University (TX)	0.24	1.1%	4.8%	1.1%	6.0%	86.9%	0.0%	54.9%	45.1%	1.8%	89.1%	10.9%
University of Tulsa (OK)	0.24	5.2%	1.9%	2.7%	3.0%	86.5%	0.7%	63.5%	36.5%	8.1%	62.9%	37.1%
Cleveland State University (Cleveland-Marshall)	0.23	0.4%	3.6%	6.2%	2.2%	86.7%	0.8%	50.8%	49.2%	3.3%	71.7%	28.3%
Hamline University (MN)	0.23	0.6%	4.4%	3.5%	3.9%	86.8%	0.8%	46.2%	53.8%	7.2%	65.8%	34.2%
Regent University (VA)	0.23	0.6%	3.7%	5.9%	2.0%	87.1%	0.6%	51.9%	48.1%	14.0%	74.4%	25.6%
Widener University (DE)	0.23	0.3%	5.6%	4.6%	1.8%	87.0%	0.7%	54.2%	45.8%	3.7%	62.2%	37.8%
Michigan State University	0.22	1.1%	3.8%	4.4%	2.2%	84.5%	4.0%	55.0%	45.0%	6.7%	68.9%	31.1%
Roger Williams University (Papitto) (RI)	0.22	0.7%	4.8%	3.3%	3.3%	87.5%	0.5%	50.5%	49.5%	N/A	N/A	N/A
Valparaiso University (IN)	0.22	0.4%	1.9%	5.3%	4.2%	87.1%	1.1%	54.2%	45.8%	1.4%	67.6%	32.4%
Gonzaga University (WA)	0.21	1.2%	6.7%	0.3%	3.3%	88.4%	0.0%	55.4%	44.6%	4.6%	67.8%	32.2%

What are the most and least diverse law schools?

School	Diversity index	American Indian	Asian	Black	Hispanic	White	International	Men	Women	Minority faculty	Male faculty	Female faculty
Samford University (Cumberland) (AL)	0.21	1.1%	0.9%	7.1%	2.1%	88.7%	0.0%	59.4%	40.6%	11.1%	73.3%	26.7%
Suffolk University (MA)	0.21	0.3%	5.7%	2.6%	2.4%	87.4%	1.6%	52.0%	48.0%	7.6%	73.6%	26.4%
University of Arkansas–Little Rock (Bowen)	0.21	1.3%	0.6%	7.8%	1.9%	88.1%	0.2%	49.8%	50.2%	N/A	N/A	N/A
William Mitchell College of Law (MN)	0.21	0.4%	4.8%	3.7%	2.4%	88.1%	0.5%	48.1%	51.9%	16.8%	56.4%	43.6%
Capital University (OH)	0.20	0.3%	2.2%	6.8%	1.6%	88.4%	0.7%	54.1%	45.9%	8.0%	79.3%	20.7%
Creighton University (NE)	0.20	0.9%	3.4%	2.3%	4.3%	88.9%	0.2%	54.2%	45.8%	7.7%	76.9%	23.1%
Louisiana State University–Baton Rouge	0.20	0.2%	1.4%	8.5%	1.1%	88.6%	0.3%	49.9%	50.1%	7.6%	84.8%	15.2%
Drake University (IA)	0.19	0.6%	3.0%	3.8%	2.5%	88.3%	1.7%	51.2%	48.8%	8.5%	61.7%	38.3%
Ohio Northern University (Pettit)	0.19	0.0%	2.8%	6.5%	1.2%	89.5%	0.0%	50.6%	49.4%	4.2%	66.7%	33.3%
St. Louis University	0.19	0.6%	3.1%	4.4%	2.2%	89.4%	0.3%	49.1%	50.9%	5.5%	65.8%	34.2%
University of Akron (OH)	0.19	0.0%	3.0%	5.1%	1.7%	89.7%	0.4%	59.8%	40.2%	7.7%	57.7%	42.3%
University of Alabama–Tuscaloosa	0.19	0.8%	1.0%	7.6%	1.0%	89.5%	0.0%	63.2%	36.8%	7.1%	83.3%	16.7%
University of Mississippi	0.19	0.5%	0.9%	8.8%	0.2%	89.5%	0.0%	54.3%	45.7%	11.1%	72.2%	27.8%
University of Missouri–Columbia	0.19	1.1%	2.5%	4.9%	1.6%	89.2%	0.7%	60.5%	39.5%	11.6%	62.8%	37.2%
University of Missouri–Kansas City	0.19	0.8%	4.4%	3.3%	1.9%	89.1%	0.6%	55.8%	44.2%	6.7%	75.3%	24.7%
University of Nebraska–Lincoln	0.19	1.0%	2.8%	3.6%	2.8%	88.8%	1.0%	54.1%	45.9%	3.2%	69.8%	30.2%
University of North Dakota	0.19	2.7%	3.6%	1.8%	1.8%	87.1%	3.1%	53.6%	46.4%	6.5%	58.1%	41.9%
University of South Carolina	0.19	0.1%	1.8%	6.4%	1.8%	88.2%	1.8%	57.2%	42.8%	5.4%	66.3%	33.7%
University of Utah (S.J. Quinney)	0.19	1.0%	4.3%	0.8%	4.3%	88.9%	0.8%	62.1%	37.9%	12.8%	63.8%	36.2%
New England School of Law (MA)	0.18	0.1%	3.7%	2.3%	3.4%	90.6%	0.0%	48.6%	51.4%	3.4%	60.3%	39.7%
Western New England College (MA)	0.18	0.2%	3.3%	2.3%	3.6%	86.3%	4.3%	54.3%	45.7%	4.7%	60.9%	39.1%
University of Idaho	0.17	1.0%	4.7%	1.0%	2.0%	90.9%	0.3%	59.9%	40.1%	.0%	76.7%	23.3%
Willamette University (Collins) (OR)	0.17	1.8%	3.8%	0.9%	2.7%	90.5%	0.2%	55.8%	44.2%	9.0%	76.1%	23.9%
Marquette University (WI)	0.16	0.6%	2.7%	2.7%	2.7%	89.9%	1.5%	56.6%	43.4%	4.6%	62.9%	37.1%
Mississippi College	0.16	0.2%	0.4%	7.3%	0.6%	91.4%	0.0%	60.8%	39.2%	4.7%	71.9%	28.1%
Quinnipiac University (CT)	0.16	0.4%	4.4%	1.8%	1.6%	91.2%	0.5%	48.4%	51.6%	6.3%	68.8%	31.3%
University of Richmond (VA)	0.16	0.4%	4.1%	3.9%	0.2%	90.1%	1.2%	57.5%	42.5%	5.9%	67.8%	32.2%
Northern Kentucky University (Chase)	0.15	0.9%	0.9%	4.5%	1.9%	91.9%	0.0%	54.2%	45.8%	9.4%	68.8%	31.3%
Southern Illinois University–Carbondale	0.15	0.8%	3.2%	2.4%	1.6%	92.0%	0.0%	62.1%	37.9%	5.7%	62.9%	37.1%
University of Detroit Mercy	0.15	0.0%	2.0%	3.8%	1.3%	81.8%	11.2%	52.8%	47.2%	N/A	N/A	N/A
University of Kentucky	0.15	0.0%	2.0%	4.9%	1.1%	92.1%	0.0%	58.1%	41.9%	5.4%	78.4%	21.6%
University of Louisville (Brandeis) (KY)	0.15	0.3%	2.8%	3.3%	1.8%	91.7%	0.3%	52.0%	48.0%	14.7%	73.5%	26.5%
University of Montana	0.15	5.5%	1.7%	0.4%	0.4%	92.0%	0.0%	48.9%	51.1%	N/A	N/A	N/A
West Virginia University	0.15	0.6%	1.1%	4.9%	1.3%	91.4%	0.6%	50.7%	49.3%	7.5%	70.0%	30.0%
Campbell University (Wiggins) (NC)	0.14	0.9%	2.1%	2.4%	1.8%	92.6%	0.3%	55.0%	45.0%	N/A	N/A	N/A
University of Wyoming	0.14	1.8%	1.3%	0.9%	3.5%	90.7%	1.8%	56.4%	43.6%	12.5%	56.3%	43.8%
University of Toledo (OH)	0.13	0.6%	2.2%	2.7%	1.4%	92.7%	0.4%	58.8%	41.2%	3.0%	71.6%	28.4%
University of Maine	0.11	0.0%	3.1%	2.0%	0.4%	93.3%	1.2%	46.9%	53.1%	2.2%	63.0%	37.0%
University of South Dakota	0.10	2.0%	0.8%	0.4%	2.0%	94.4%	0.4%	56.8%	43.2%	7.1%	78.6%	21.4%
Duquesne University (PA)	0.09	0.0%	0.7%	3.0%	0.7%	95.4%	0.2%	55.6%	44.4%	8.7%	76.1%	23.9%

Who's the priciest? Who's the cheapest?

The total cost of a JD degree can easily top $150,000 at the most expensive schools, once you factor in living expenses. (And that's not counting lost income, since you won't be working full-time while you're in school.) Private law schools are listed here by tuition and fees for the 2005–2006 academic year, with the most expensive on top. Public institutions follow, sorted by in-state tuition so you can easily see what you might save by sticking close to home.

Private Schools

School	Total tuition and fees	Room and board	Books	Other expenses
Columbia University (NY)	$39,172	$13,801	$950	$3,150
Yale University (CT)	$38,800	$14,200	$950	$0
New York Law School	$38,600	$14,455	$850	$3,935
Northwestern University (IL)	$38,372	$12,078	$1,382	$6,616
University of Southern California (Gould)	$37,971	$11,006	$1,584	$3,182
Cornell University (NY)	$37,750	$9,500	$800	$5,850
New York University	$37,150	$18,400	$925	$2,720
University of Pennsylvania	$37,086	$10,884	$975	$4,555
Duke University (NC)	$36,574	$9,000	$1,030	$5,509
University of Chicago	$36,138	$12,825	$1,575	$5,937
Stanford University (CA)	$35,780	$14,966	$1,546	$2,542
Fordham University (NY)	$35,141	N/A	N/A	N/A
Harvard University (MA)	$35,100	$16,469	$1,050	$4,081
Georgetown University (DC)	$35,080	$13,710	$875	$4,235
Emory University (GA)	$35,034	$13,176	$1,852	$1,094
Washington University in St. Louis	$34,981	$11,000	$2,000	$6,300
Brooklyn Law School (NY)	$34,850	$13,880	$1,300	$3,005
Cardozo-Yeshiva University (NY)	$34,850	$18,000	$1,000	$5,055
George Washington University (DC)	$34,500	$10,700	$890	$5,450
Vanderbilt University (TN)	$34,036	$11,268	$1,484	$6,064
University of San Diego	$33,826	$10,542	$895	$5,618
Pace University (NY)	$33,782	$12,442	$1,120	$2,900
Syracuse University (NY)	$33,462	$11,268	$1,140	$3,580
Boston College	$33,176	$12,425	$840	$3,450
Hofstra University (NY)	$33,160	$9,616	$900	$2,795
American University (Washington) (DC)	$33,134	$11,754	$950	$4,655
Boston University	$32,866	$10,782	$1,166	$3,900
Northeastern University (MA)	$32,811	$13,275	$1,200	$1,323
St. John's University (NY)	$32,700	$12,400	$1,000	$4,140
Seton Hall University (NJ)	$32,620	$11,700	$1,100	$4,470
University of Notre Dame (IN)	$32,220	$6,915	$1,200	$4,940
Quinnipiac University (CT)	$32,040	$8,480	$1,200	$6,938
Case Western Reserve University (OH)	$31,880	$12,700	$1,225	$1,774
Pepperdine University (McConnell) (CA)	$31,860	$14,098	$700	$4,910
Suffolk University (MA)	$31,814	$12,406	$900	$3,536
Loyola Law School (CA)	$31,454	$10,826	$1,080	$6,366
Catholic University of America (Columbus) (DC)	$31,405	$12,600	$1,000	$7,740
Southern Methodist University (TX)	$31,238	$14,000	$1,800	$2,600
University of the Pacific (McGeorge) (CA)	$31,173	$11,520	$800	$6,432

Who's the priciest? Who's the cheapest?

Private Schools

School	Total tuition and fees	Room and board	Books	Other expenses
University of Miami (FL)	$31,094	$10,130	$1,030	$5,170
University of San Francisco	$30,650	$13,500	$900	$4,904
California Western School of Law	$30,600	$10,800	$1,088	$5,016
Illinois Institute of Technology (Chicago-Kent)	$30,237	$13,860	$890	$3,015
Albany Law School-Union University (NY)	$30,053	$7,400	$900	$5,000
Southwestern University School of Law (CA)	$29,950	N/A	N/A	N/A
Loyola University Chicago	$29,900	$12,900	$950	$5,030
Chapman University (CA)	$29,854	$9,900	$1,000	$3,330
Ave Maria School of Law (MI)	$29,700	$12,015	$1,100	$6,117
University of Denver (Sturm)	$29,388	$8,622	$1,306	$4,094
Whittier Law School (CA)	$29,230	$10,084	$1,008	$5,398
Golden Gate University (CA)	$29,100	$13,500	$1,000	$6,300
DePaul University (IL)	$28,810	$18,454	$1,000	N/A
St. Louis University	$28,610	$8,250	$1,250	$2,500
Thomas Jefferson School of Law (CA)	$28,550	N/A	N/A	N/A
Widener University (DE)	$28,300	$8,300	$1,000	$3,940
Vermont Law School	$28,114	$9,530	$950	$7,052
Baylor University (TX)	$28,105	$9,186	$1,308	$5,537
Washington and Lee University (VA)	$27,981	$8,065	$1,300	$5,674
Wake Forest University (NC)	$27,900	$8,550	$800	$6,440
Villanova University (PA)	$27,830	$12,600	$1,200	$2,975
Western New England College (MA)	$27,814	$10,065	$1,200	$3,935
Mercer University (GA)	$27,600	$7,200	$1,000	$4,800
John Marshall Law School (IL)	$27,540	$12,932	$1,400	$6,562
Franklin Pierce Law Center (NH)	$27,300	$8,814	$1,000	$5,030
Touro College (Fuchsberg) (NY)	$27,120	$15,964	$1,744	$3,706
Valparaiso University (IN)	$27,063	$6,600	$1,000	$2,610
University of Richmond (VA)	$27,060	$8,415	$1,200	$3,635
Pennsylvania State University (Dickinson)	$26,680	$8,460	$1,100	$5,418
Gonzaga University (WA)	$26,388	$3,375	$1,000	$4,740
Lewis and Clark College (Northwestern) (OR)	$26,348	$9,774	$1,006	$3,872
Stetson University (FL)	$26,280	$8,329	$1,200	$4,117
Marquette University (WI)	$26,176	$9,782	$1,113	$5,011
Michigan State University	$26,097	$7,828	$1,230	$3,600
Seattle University	$26,026	$9,918	$1,258	$3,969
Barry University (FL)	$26,000	$11,000	$1,400	$3,900
William Mitchell College of Law (MN)	$25,950	$12,400	$1,100	$800
St. Thomas University (FL)	$25,800	$10,835	$1,000	$5,705
Nova Southeastern University (Broad) (FL)	$25,780	$10,431	$1,200	$4,895
Hamline University (MN)	$25,484	$12,430	$1,300	N/A
University of St. Thomas (MN)	$25,404	N/A	N/A	N/A
Willamette University (Collins) (OR)	$25,280	$12,930	$0	$0
Florida Coastal School of Law	$25,050	$8,316	$1,100	$7,605
Samford University (Cumberland) (AL)	$24,708	$11,418	$1,380	$4,494
Drake University (IA)	$24,256	$7,125	$1,125	$3,900
New England School of Law (MA)	$24,075	$9,750	$1,150	$4,430
Ohio Northern University (Pettit)	$23,980	$7,290	$1,000	$1,600
Regent University (VA)	$23,870	$6,138	$1,372	$7,483
Duquesne University (PA)	$23,759	$10,532	$1,200	$2,000
University of Tulsa (OK)	$23,459	$7,915	$3,427	$4,058
Creighton University (NE)	$23,430	$12,500	$1,350	$2,680

Who's the priciest? Who's the cheapest?

Private Schools

School	Total tuition and fees	Room and board	Books	Other expenses
Thomas M. Cooley Law School (MI)	$23,140	$6,860	$800	$3,500
Campbell University (Wiggins) (NC)	$23,000	$5,905	$1,200	$3,115
St. Mary's University (TX)	$21,410	$7,230	$1,300	$4,852
South Texas College of Law	$20,850	$7,912	$1,200	$5,642
Texas Wesleyan University	$20,520	$9,918	$1,650	$1,908
Mississippi College	$19,514	$9,000	$900	$7,373
Howard University (DC)	$17,855	$11,855	$1,351	$3,038
Brigham Young University (Clark) (UT)	$7,450	$7,280	$1,470	$5,326

Public Schools

School	In-state tuition and fees	Out-of-state tuition and fees	Room and board	Books	Other expenses
North Carolina Central University	$4,291	$16,151	$7,500	$700	$3,100
Georgia State University	$6,484	$21,644	$9,000	$1,500	$4,474
University of Wyoming	$6,519	$13,799	$7,703	$1,200	$2,759
University of the District of Columbia (Clarke)	$7,000	$14,000	N/A	N/A	N/A
Florida A&M University	$7,158	$26,580	N/A	N/A	N/A
University of North Dakota	$7,602	$16,220	$8,200	$900	$4,500
University of Mississippi	$7,720	$14,360	$9,686	$1,300	$3,196
University of Florida (Levin)	$7,786	$27,419	N/A	N/A	N/A
University of South Dakota	$7,962	$15,927	$6,116	$1,300	$5,502
University of Alabama–Tuscaloosa	$8,660	$18,028	$7,310	$1,168	$4,818
West Virginia University	$8,690	$20,406	$8,226	$1,075	$2,637
University of Nebraska–Lincoln	$8,783	$20,449	$6,660	$1,230	$2,900
University of New Mexico	$8,816	$21,394	$7,252	$960	$4,062
University of Idaho	$8,908	$17,678	$7,038	$1,336	$3,340
University of Montana	$9,113	$18,677	$9,900	$1,050	$340
University of Georgia	$9,126	$27,102	$5,000	$1,000	$4,400
University of Memphis (Humphreys)	$9,352	$26,208	$7,084	$1,400	$3,777
University of Arkansas–Little Rock (Bowen)	$9,369	$18,819	$9,289	$1,400	$0
University of Tennessee–Knoxville	$9,412	$24,106	$7,714	$1,400	$5,074
University of Kansas	$9,528	$17,859	$8,270	$800	$4,230
University of Nevada–Las Vegas (Boyd)	$9,552	$18,452	$11,680	$850	$230
Southern Illinois University–Carbondale	$9,705	$26,085	$7,370	$1,080	$2,399
Northern Kentucky University (Chase)	$10,128	$22,104	$13,604	$1,000	$0
University of Louisville (Brandeis) (KY)	$10,198	$22,320	$5,800	$1,000	$8,216
Texas Southern University (Marshall)	$10,268	$13,688	$6,526	$1,677	$3,381
CUNY–Queens College	$10,521	$16,421	$3,931	$600	$6,809
University of Utah (S.J. Quinney)	$10,782	$22,987	$8,334	$1,592	$4,186
University of Oklahoma	$10,786	$20,053	$9,415	$1,067	$4,703
Northern Illinois University	$11,228	$20,138	$7,850	$1,500	$2,862

Who's the priciest? Who's the cheapest?

Public Schools

School	In-state tuition and fees	Out-of-state tuition and fees	Room and board	Books	Other expenses
University of Kentucky	$11,540	$21,242	$9,300	$800	$2,960
University of Wisconsin–Madison	$11,658	$28,870	$7,220	$2,040	$4,330
University of North Carolina–Chapel Hill	$11,981	$24,199	$11,128	$1,000	$3,904
Louisiana State University–Baton Rouge	$12,022	$21,118	$10,084	$2,000	$2,942
University of Hawaii (Richardson)	$12,192	$20,856	$7,550	$900	$3,000
Texas Tech University	$12,662	$19,382	$7,097	$914	$4,185
Indiana University–Indianapolis	$12,758	$26,852	$8,700	$1,600	$9,168
University of Missouri–Kansas City	$12,803	$24,504	$8,340	$3,760	$3,640
Arizona State University	$12,907	$22,089	$8,354	$1,100	$4,680
George Mason University (VA)	$12,936	$24,500	$10,570	$940	$4,558
University of Arizona (Rogers)	$13,202	$22,182	$8,060	$1,000	$5,100
University of Iowa	$13,211	$27,989	$9,000	$2,300	$4,651
University at Buffalo–SUNY	$13,484	$19,584	$9,301	$1,025	$2,799
University of Colorado–Boulder	$13,546	$28,450	$7,236	$1,306	$3,528
University of Missouri–Columbia	$13,614	$25,986	$7,590	$1,372	$5,090
University of Toledo (OH)	$13,781	$24,024	$7,635	$1,750	$4,179
University of Akron (OH)	$13,878	$21,871	$12,624	$1,024	$0
Cleveland State University (Cleveland-Marshall)	$13,988	$19,209	$10,630	$1,300	$4,332
Temple University (Beasley) (PA)	$14,100	$24,158	$10,262	$1,500	$7,492
Indiana University–Bloomington	$14,349	$28,398	$8,316	$1,416	$4,284
University of Houston	$14,366	$21,296	$8,600	$3,300	$5,250
University of Washington	$14,927	$21,857	$10,000	$1,000	$3,913
University of South Carolina	$15,264	$30,400	$9,840	$785	$4,721
College of William and Mary (Marshall-Wythe) (VA)	$15,300	$25,500	$7,368	$1,250	$850
University of Connecticut	$15,648	$33,024	$10,400	$1,090	$4,400
University of Maine	$15,750	$25,050	$7,586	$900	$3,466
Ohio State University (Moritz)	$15,909	$29,511	$6,372	$2,500	$6,112
University of Baltimore	$15,978	$28,512	N/A	N/A	N/A
University of Cincinnati	$16,210	$29,284	$7,890	$1,143	$4,388
University of Texas–Austin	$16,935	$29,291	$8,000	$1,000	$2,620
Wayne State University (MI)	$17,507	$32,570	$11,978	$1,000	$7,950
University of Illinois–Urbana-Champaign	$17,512	$28,416	$9,120	$1,190	$2,861
University of Maryland	$17,701	$28,980	$14,985	$1,725	$6,632
Rutgers State University–Newark (NJ)	$17,789	$25,382	$13,081	$1,200	$3,230
University of Oregon	$17,792	$22,400	$7,758	$1,700	$2,556
Rutgers State University–Camden (NJ)	$18,016	$25,609	$9,583	$1,200	$2,302
University of Pittsburgh	$19,602	$28,210	$12,490	$1,500	$580
University of Minnesota–Twin Cities	$19,969	$30,353	N/A	N/A	N/A
University of California (Hastings)	$22,297	$33,522	$14,031	$863	$4,506
University of California–Davis	$23,524	$35,769	$9,554	$987	$2,767
University of California–Berkeley	$24,340	$36,585	$13,610	$1,300	$4,236
University of California–Los Angeles	$24,581	$35,545	$12,381	$1,800	$4,872
University of Virginia	$28,300	$33,300	$14,045	$1,000	$555
University of Michigan–Ann Arbor	$32,919	$35,919	$9,722	$930	$4,788

What schools award the most and the least financial aid?

Compared to what you're going to need, you may be surprised at how little you get: Law schools assume that their students can afford to borrow to pay the bills because they'll easily make enough after graduation to manage the loan payments. However, students whose LSAT scores and undergraduate grades put them near the top of a law school's applicant pool may find a generous merit award on the table.

Private Schools

School	Median grant	% of students receiving grants	Grants range (25th–75th percentile)	Grants of full tuition	Grants of more than full tuition
Loyola Law School (CA)	$30,254	20%	$29,550-$30,328	5%	10%
Michigan State University	$26,664	38%	$22,329-$26,664	23%	0%
Ave Maria School of Law (MI)	$21,900	65%	$12,875-$26,600	29%	6%
Emory University (GA)	$20,726	31%	$10,000-$27,816	7%	2%
Wake Forest University (NC)	$19,800	35%	$9,900-$26,400	11%	3%
Hamline University (MN)	$17,490	43%	$11,910-$23,820	13%	0%
New York University	$17,000	28%	$10,000-$30,000	6%	0%
Mercer University (GA)	$16,000	33%	$5,000-$24,500	7%	8%
Northwestern University (IL)	$16,000	36%	$12,500-$20,000	0%	0%
Yale University (CT)	$15,990	44%	$9,995-$21,722	1%	0%
Stanford University (CA)	$15,339	43%	$9,425-$21,557	2%	0%
Boston University	$15,000	48%	$10,000-$20,000	0%	2%
Samford University (Cumberland) (AL)	$15,000	31%	$1,500-$23,758	9%	4%
St. John's University (NY)	$15,000	49%	$7,500-$29,850	12%	2%
University of San Diego	$15,000	38%	$13,000-$23,000	3%	1%
University of St. Thomas (MN)	$15,000	70%	$8,000-$23,809	25%	N/A
Harvard University (MA)	$14,755	37%	$8,013-$21,474	1%	0%
University of Miami (FL)	$14,500	36%	$8,700-$18,000	1%	1%
Loyola University Chicago	$14,200	67%	$7,150-$21,150	0%	0%
University of Pennsylvania	$14,180	36%	$8,630-$18,780	3%	0%
Seton Hall University (NJ)	$14,000	52%	$7,000-$18,000	6%	0%
St. Louis University	$14,000	48%	$8,000-$17,500	5%	0%
Vanderbilt University (TN)	$14,000	63%	$9,000-$17,000	0%	1%
University of Detroit Mercy	$13,832	13%	$6,250-$15,960	1%	0%
Chapman University (CA)	$13,436	37%	$8,366-$19,520	3%	0%
Western New England College (MA)	$13,000	58%	$7,000-$16,000	3%	0%
Cornell University (NY)	$12,750	44%	$7,900-$17,900	0%	0%
Ohio Northern University (Pettit)	$12,500	50%	$10,000-$17,500	2%	0%
California Western School of Law	$12,490	37%	$6,945-$23,541	10%	0%
Stetson University (FL)	$12,380	24%	$5,000-$24,760	3%	7%
St. Thomas University (FL)	$12,350	34%	$6,175-$18,525	0%	0%
Valparaiso University (IN)	$12,335	32%	$6,000-$18,000	10%	6%
Duquesne University (PA)	$12,298	31%	$2,000-$22,205	14%	0%
Georgetown University (DC)	$12,100	28%	$6,850-$17,950	2%	0%
Albany Law School-Union University (NY)	$12,000	37%	$4,200-$20,000	0%	0%
Oklahoma City University	$12,000	19%	$2,500-$23,400	0%	3%
Santa Clara University (CA)	$12,000	30%	$8,000-$15,000	1%	0%
University of Notre Dame (IN)	$12,000	65%	$8,000-$16,000	2%	0%
University of Southern California (Gould)	$12,000	58%	$7,500-$15,000	2%	1%

What schools award the most and the least financial aid?

Private Schools

School	Median grant	% of students receiving grants	Grants range (25th–75th percentile)	Grants of full tuition	Grants of more than full tuition
Columbia University (NY)	$11,500	48%	$5,000-$20,000	3%	0%
Brooklyn Law School (NY)	$11,033	57%	$7,163-$14,144	0%	0%
Boston College	$11,000	52%	$7,500-$15,000	0%	0%
Washington and Lee University (VA)	$11,000	76%	$6,000-$17,500	3%	0%
Cardozo-Yeshiva University (NY)	$10,000	61%	$5,000-$16,000	1%	0%
Case Western Reserve University (OH)	$10,000	48%	$7,300-$13,000	1%	0%
Catholic University of America (Columbus) (DC)	$10,000	29%	$6,800-$13,500	0%	0%
George Washington University (DC)	$10,000	41%	$9,000-$14,000	0%	0%
Golden Gate University (CA)	$10,000	35%	$4,300-$15,000	2%	0%
Hofstra University (NY)	$10,000	52%	$6,000-$15,000	4%	1%
Howard University (DC)	$10,000	69%	$7,500-$12,500	0%	7%
Pace University (NY)	$10,000	56%	$7,300-$23,650	0%	0%
Quinnipiac University (CT)	$10,000	85%	$5,000-$15,000	0%	0%
Roger Williams University (Papitto) (RI)	$10,000	41%	$5,000-$12,630	8%	0%
Southern Methodist University (TX)	$10,000	75%	$7,500-$15,000	N/A	6%
University of Dayton (OH)	$10,000	60%	$7,000-$11,000	0%	0%
University of the Pacific (McGeorge) (CA)	$10,000	59%	$5,000-$12,900	2%	1%
Washington University in St. Louis	$10,000	66%	$5,000-$20,000	1%	4%
University of Chicago	$9,900	52%	$6,600-$15,000	0%	0%
University of Denver (Sturm)	$9,600	45%	$4-$12,000	2%	0%
Willamette University (Collins) (OR)	$9,300	43%	$7,000-$13,000	0%	1%
Drake University (IA)	$9,000	54%	$5,500-$12,000	6%	0%
Lewis and Clark College (Northwestern) (OR)	$9,000	45%	$5,000-$13,000	3%	0%
Syracuse University (NY)	$8,248	86%	$5,000-$11,740	3%	0%
University of San Francisco	$8,113	30%	$3,500-$14,718	1%	0%
American University (Washington) (DC)	$8,000	34%	$3,390-$12,000	2%	0%
Capital University (OH)	$8,000	62%	$5,000-$11,000	0%	0%
DePaul University (IL)	$8,000	58%	$4,000-$12,000	0%	0%
Duke University (NC)	$8,000	72%	$5,000-$14,000	1%	0%
Gonzaga University (WA)	$8,000	91%	$4,000-$10,000	0%	0%
Southwestern University School of Law (CA)	$8,000	33%	$5,000-$11,750	0%	0%
Pennsylvania State University (Dickinson)	$7,913	49%	$2,000-$23,438	12%	0%
Thomas M. Cooley Law School (MI)	$7,507	55%	$6,187-$12,375	5%	0%
New York Law School	$7,500	48%	$4,500-$10,000	0%	0%
Illinois Institute of Technology (Chicago-Kent)	$7,000	53%	$4,000-$15,000	2%	2%
Northeastern University (MA)	$7,000	73%	$4,200-$10,670	N/A	N/A
Nova Southeastern University (Broad) (FL)	$7,000	19%	$6,468-$23,289	6%	1%
Whittier Law School (CA)	$6,938	54%	$3,500-$20,000	19%	0%
University of Tulsa (OK)	$6,500	34%	$2,000-$17,000	2%	0%
Fordham University (NY)	$6,300	29%	$4,000-$10,300	1%	0%
William Mitchell College of Law (MN)	$6,125	34%	$5,000-$15,750	2%	0%
Creighton University (NE)	$6,000	39%	$2,500-$14,000	4%	0%
John Marshall Law School (IL)	$6,000	30%	$4,000-$10,000	0%	1%
Marquette University (WI)	$6,000	39%	$3,500-$12,000	5%	0%
Seattle University	$6,000	48%	$4,000-$8,000	0%	0%
Thomas Jefferson School of Law (CA)	$6,000	64%	$2,000-$15,000	12%	0%
Barry University (FL)	$5,000	75%	$2,850-$9,000	0%	0%
Campbell University (Wiggins) (NC)	$5,000	43%	$2,000-$7,500	1%	0%
Florida Coastal School of Law	$5,000	47%	$5,000-$10,000	0%	0%
University of Richmond (VA)	$5,000	56%	$2,810-$7,500	0%	0%
Vermont Law School	$5,000	59%	$3,000-$8,000	1%	0%

What schools award the most and the least financial aid?

Private Schools

School	Median grant	% of students receiving grants	Grants range (25th–75th percentile)	Grants of full tuition	Grants of more than full tuition
Villanova University (PA)	$5,000	18%	$3,000-$12,690	1%	0%
Regent University (VA)	$4,300	85%	$1,900-$12,400	6%	1%
Mississippi College	$4,000	32%	$100-$8,500	6%	2%
Suffolk University (MA)	$4,000	54%	$2,500-$7,475	0%	0%
Touro College (Fuchsberg) (NY)	$4,000	44%	$1,500-$8,500	0%	0%
Baylor University (TX)	$3,875	88%	$3,300-$13,440	9%	3%
New England School of Law (MA)	$3,600	47%	$2,500-$11,205	9%	0%
St. Mary's University (TX)	$3,288	41%	$303-$9,377	0%	0%
Franklin Pierce Law Center (NH)	$3,000	60%	$1,400-$6,500	1%	0%
Widener University (DE)	$3,000	30%	$1,000-$10,500	2%	0%
Texas Wesleyan University	$2,500	36%	$1,000-$5,000	0%	0%
Brigham Young University (Clark) (UT)	$1,500	53%	$1,000-$2,500	3%	1%
Pepperdine University (McConnell) (CA)	$1,500	83%	$1,500-$15,000	3%	2%
South Texas College of Law	$1,461	40%	$957-$2,079	0%	0%

Public Schools

School	Median grant	% of students receiving grants	Grants range (25th–75th percentile)	Grants of full tuition	Grants of more than full tuition
University of Toledo (OH)	$11,511	48%	$1,000-$12,877	18%	15%
University of Iowa	$11,371	43%	$1,000-$11,510	20%	1%
University of Wisconsin–Madison	$10,730	31%	$8,000-$23,218	2%	4%
University of Michigan–Ann Arbor	$10,100	40%	$5,950-$14,050	0%	3%
University of Pittsburgh	$10,000	52%	$6,000-$12,000	1%	0%
University of Virginia	$10,000	50%	$6,000-$15,000	0%	1%
University of Akron (OH)	$9,550	65%	$3,000-$11,079	1%	26%
Northern Kentucky University (Chase)	$9,240	37%	$2,900-$9,240	22%	0%
University of California–Los Angeles	$8,424	61%	$3,816-$11,420	0%	2%
Northern Illinois University	$8,346	21%	$4,173-$8,346	13%	2%
University of California–Davis	$8,200	75%	$7,200-$8,200	0%	2%
University of New Mexico	$7,568	20%	$1,950-$7,568	7%	3%
University of Minnesota–Twin Cities	$7,500	56%	$2,500-$10,094	4%	0%
University of Missouri–Kansas City	$7,454	31%	$2,000-$12,510	1%	2%
University of Nevada–Las Vegas (Boyd)	$7,245	46%	$1,000-$7,245	21%	0%
University of Connecticut	$7,175	80%	$4,175-$8,000	0%	4%
University of Washington	$7,000	45%	$3,500-$8,836	0%	1%
University of Houston	$6,696	68%	$3,348-$10,044	0%	1%
University of California–Berkeley	$6,652	74%	$4,033-$8,300	1%	3%
University of Mississippi	$6,646	30%	$3,250-$10,132	0%	5%
University of Nebraska–Lincoln	$6,500	47%	$3,000-$9,000	8%	16%
Temple University (Beasley) (PA)	$6,401	45%	$2,500-$7,540	2%	0%
Georgia State University	$6,022	9%	$2,000-$6,484	5%	0%
Indiana University–Indianapolis	$6,000	47%	$3,500-$16,544	0%	1%
University of Arkansas–Fayetteville	$6,000	38%	$1,250-$8,000	6%	3%
University of Baltimore	$6,000	14%	$3,000-$8,000	0%	3%

What schools award the most and the least financial aid?

Public Schools

School	Median grant	% of students receiving grants	Grants range (25th-75th percentile)	Grants of full tuition	Grants of more than full tuition
University of Cincinnati	$6,000	64%	$4,000-$9,500	5%	0%
University of Hawaii (Richardson)	$5,724	40%	$5,724-$5,724	5%	1%
Indiana University–Bloomington	$5,650	67%	$3,000-$8,522	1%	3%
University of California (Hastings)	$5,500	72%	$5,000-$7,000	0%	0%
College of William and Mary (Marshall-Wythe) (VA)	$5,000	25%	$3,000-$5,000	0%	0%
George Mason University (VA)	$5,000	14%	$3,000-$5,000	0%	1%
Texas Tech University	$5,000	44%	$2,000-$11,426	12%	2%
University of Arizona (Rogers)	$5,000	88%	$3,000-$9,000	0%	13%
University of Louisville (Brandeis) (KY)	$5,000	42%	$3,500-$6,500	1%	0%
University of Tennessee–Knoxville	$5,000	46%	$2,500-$8,396	2%	14%
Washburn University (KS)	$5,000	42%	$2,000-$11,530	5%	6%
University of Maryland	$4,800	54%	$3,100-$11,000	1%	0%
University of Kentucky	$4,440	48%	$1,500-$9,700	2%	4%
University of Idaho	$4,300	38%	$750-$7,572	5%	1%
University of Alabama–Tuscaloosa	$4,150	41%	$2,500-$8,401	10%	5%
Cleveland State University (Cleveland-Marshall)	$4,000	42%	$2,000-$8,000	7%	0%
Florida International University	$4,000	60%	$3,000-$5,790	1%	5%
Ohio State University (Moritz)	$4,000	85%	$2,000-$6,000	0%	4%
Rutgers State University–Camden (NJ)	$4,000	40%	$1,000-$5,000	0%	0%
Rutgers State University–Newark (NJ)	$4,000	45%	$2,000-$6,000	2%	2%
University of Arkansas–Little Rock (Bowen)	$4,000	29%	$2,000-$8,819	3%	3%
University of Illinois–Urbana-Champaign	$4,000	51%	$3,000-$6,000	4%	0%
University of Maine	$4,000	51%	$1,625-$4,926	3%	0%
University of the District of Columbia (Clarke)	$4,000	78%	$2,000-$6,000	2%	1%
University of Memphis (Humphreys)	$3,500	25%	$3,000-$7,550	4%	1%
University of Missouri–Columbia	$3,500	53%	$2,000-$5,000	0%	0%
University of Kansas	$3,304	71%	$1,100-$5,000	0%	4%
North Carolina Central University	$3,175	20%	$1,105-$5,235	7%	2%
Southern Illinois University–Carbondale	$3,100	58%	$1,500-$5,100	2%	0%
Texas Southern University (Marshall)	$3,000	36%	$1,500-$3,500	0%	0%
University of Oregon	$3,000	52%	$2,500-$5,000	0%	1%
University of South Carolina	$3,000	15%	$1,200-$10,589	0%	0%
Louisiana State University–Baton Rouge	$2,926	41%	$1,500-$8,164	0%	4%
University of Colorado–Boulder	$2,500	57%	$1,200-$3,600	0%	1%
University of Oklahoma	$2,500	56%	$1,000-$6,271	1%	3%
University at Buffalo–SUNY	$2,450	76%	$2,450-$9,020	10%	1%
University of North Carolina–Chapel Hill	$2,250	72%	$1,250-$3,750	0%	2%
University of Florida (Levin)	$2,100	22%	$650-$4,250	0%	1%
University of Georgia	$2,000	31%	$1,000-$3,000	4%	1%
Wayne State University (MI)	$2,000	80%	$2,000-$3,500	1%	0%
West Virginia University	$1,800	33%	$1,000-$3,500	3%	4%
Arizona State University	$1,727	40%	$650-$5,038	2%	6%
Florida A&M University	$1,575	10%	N/A	N/A	N/A
University of Utah (S.J. Quinney)	$1,575	43%	$1,000-$4,190	0%	1%
CUNY–Queens College	$1,500	30%	$750-$2,250	3%	0%
University of Montana	$1,400	42%	$900-$2,500	0%	0%
University of Texas–Austin	$1,250	86%	$900-$2,150	1%	2%
University of North Dakota	$1,025	48%	$500-$4,000	3%	8%
Florida State University	$1,000	33%	$1,000-$2,000	0%	1%
University of Wyoming	$1,000	77%	$500-$1,750	1%	1%
University of South Dakota	$625	33%	$250-$1,450	2%	1%

Whose graduates have the most debt? The least?

How much should you expect to borrow? Debts of $70,000 to $80,000 are common for law school grads—and that's not counting any college loans. This table shows the average amount of debt incurred by borrowers in the class of 2005, as well as the proportion of the class that took out loans.

School	Average amount of law school debt	% of grads with debt
University of Chicago	$114,263	67%
New York University	$111,850	86%
Northwestern University (IL)	$110,868	76%
John Marshall Law School (IL)	$109,862	66%
American University (Washington) (DC)	$102,954	84%
University of Pennsylvania	$101,757	84%
Pepperdine University (McConnell) (CA)	$101,130	52%
Stanford University (CA)	$100,687	86%
Vermont Law School	$99,810	89%
Columbia University (NY)	$98,066	80%
California Western School of Law	$97,509	91%
University of San Francisco	$95,327	85%
Emory University (GA)	$95,161	81%
Loyola Law School (CA)	$94,800	85%
Illinois Institute of Technology (Chicago-Kent)	$94,272	85%
Fordham University (NY)	$94,004	79%
Southwestern University School of Law (CA)	$93,716	78%
University of Miami (FL)	$93,314	82%
Catholic University of America (Columbus) (DC)	$92,902	84%
Vanderbilt University (TN)	$92,809	84%
Oklahoma City University	$92,750	81%
Georgetown University (DC)	$92,675	80%
Harvard University (MA)	$92,573	83%
Villanova University (PA)	$92,263	85%
Stetson University (FL)	$92,239	90%
Campbell University (Wiggins) (NC)	$90,929	94%
Duke University (NC)	$90,903	98%
Cardozo-Yeshiva University (NY)	$90,403	73%
University of Southern California (Gould)	$90,266	85%
Yale University (CT)	$89,908	91%
Golden Gate University (CA)	$89,337	77%
DePaul University (IL)	$89,065	88%
Santa Clara University (CA)	$88,792	78%
George Washington University (DC)	$88,673	91%
Hofstra University (NY)	$88,040	87%
Brooklyn Law School (NY)	$87,920	83%
University of San Diego	$87,905	89%
Whittier Law School (CA)	$87,651	96%
University of Tulsa (OK)	$87,032	85%
Boston College	$86,980	88%
University of Michigan–Ann Arbor	$86,901	89%
Franklin Pierce Law Center (NH)	$86,766	82%
Roger Williams University (Papitto) (RI)	$86,714	84%
University of the Pacific (McGeorge) (CA)	$86,435	96%
Washington University in St. Louis	$86,371	78%
Florida Coastal School of Law	$86,193	93%

Whose graduates have the most debt? The least?

School	Average amount of law school debt	% of grads with debt
Suffolk University (MA)	$85,527	87%
Nova Southeastern University (Broad) (FL)	$84,536	82%
New York Law School	$84,325	87%
Barry University (FL)	$83,800	85%
Thomas Jefferson School of Law (CA)	$83,776	89%
Seton Hall University (NJ)	$83,500	83%
St. Mary's University (TX)	$83,104	82%
University of Denver (Sturm)	$82,077	83%
St. Thomas University (FL)	$82,000	82%
Seattle University	$81,751	91%
St. Louis University	$81,612	88%
St. John's University (NY)	$81,362	85%
New England School of Law (MA)	$81,212	83%
Quinnipiac University (CT)	$81,046	81%
Gonzaga University (WA)	$80,996	92%
Boston University	$80,509	86%
Northeastern University (MA)	$80,484	91%
Syracuse University (NY)	$80,181	88%
Baylor University (TX)	$80,033	85%
Albany Law School-Union University (NY)	$80,005	87%
Lewis and Clark College (Northwestern) (OR)	$79,769	100%
University of Notre Dame (IN)	$79,599	87%
Hamline University (MN)	$79,034	83%
Western New England College (MA)	$78,190	81%
Touro College (Fuchsberg) (NY)	$78,149	83%
Ohio Northern University (Pettit)	$78,146	98%
Duquesne University (PA)	$78,000	93%
Creighton University (NE)	$76,904	89%
Marquette University (WI)	$76,686	90%
Samford University (Cumberland) (AL)	$76,624	85%
South Texas College of Law	$76,282	78%
Thomas M. Cooley Law School (MI)	$75,762	89%
Wake Forest University (NC)	$75,418	95%
Pace University (NY)	$75,000	90%
University of Dayton (OH)	$74,930	92%
University of Richmond (VA)	$74,780	84%
Mercer University (GA)	$74,208	87%
Michigan State University	$73,230	83%
Regent University (VA)	$71,645	96%
Chapman University (CA)	$70,846	90%
Capital University (OH)	$70,806	88%
Case Western Reserve University (OH)	$70,480	77%
Drake University (IA)	$70,441	95%
Widener University (DE)	$70,429	90%
University of California (Hastings)	$69,998	85%
Pennsylvania State University (Dickinson)	$69,943	88%
William Mitchell College of Law (MN)	$69,642	90%
Indiana University–Bloomington	$68,732	98%
University of St. Thomas (MN)	$68,501	85%
University of Maryland	$68,259	85%
University of Minnesota–Twin Cities	$67,496	87%
University of Pittsburgh	$67,294	73%
University of the District of Columbia (Clarke)	$67,000	100%
Temple University (Beasley) (PA)	$66,430	83%
Mississippi College	$66,115	89%
University of Detroit Mercy	$65,507	80%

Whose graduates have the most debt? The least?

School	Average amount of law school debt	% of grads with debt
University of Missouri–Kansas City	$65,387	88%
University of Oklahoma	$63,439	64%
University of Texas–Austin	$63,240	72%
University of Maine	$62,420	84%
University of Illinois–Urbana-Champaign	$62,223	90%
University of Oregon	$62,151	87%
Texas Wesleyan University	$61,293	91%
University of California–Los Angeles	$61,000	98%
Rutgers State University–Camden (NJ)	$60,959	83%
Washington and Lee University (VA)	$60,495	86%
University of Virginia	$60,000	78%
University of Connecticut	$59,732	86%
University of Iowa	$59,665	84%
University of California–Berkeley	$59,620	73%
Rutgers State University–Newark (NJ)	$58,940	86%
University of South Dakota	$58,304	100%
University of Baltimore	$57,983	98%
University of Missouri–Columbia	$57,889	87%
Willamette University (Collins) (OR)	$57,414	81%
University of Houston	$57,071	84%
University of California–Davis	$57,057	90%
Northern Kentucky University (Chase)	$56,736	71%
University of Toledo (OH)	$56,387	87%
Washburn University (KS)	$56,200	86%
George Mason University (VA)	$55,908	77%
University of Memphis (Humphreys)	$55,673	74%
University of South Carolina	$54,865	78%
University of Colorado–Boulder	$53,623	80%
Louisiana State University–Baton Rouge	$53,544	81%
Valparaiso University (IN)	$53,454	94%
Cleveland State University (Cleveland-Marshall)	$53,165	92%
Ave Maria School of Law (MI)	$53,029	76%
Georgia State University	$52,975	68%
College of William and Mary (Marshall-Wythe) (VA)	$52,738	84%
University of North Carolina–Chapel Hill	$52,566	79%
University of Akron (OH)	$51,814	81%
Indiana University–Indianapolis	$51,676	69%
University at Buffalo–SUNY	$50,873	88%
University of Idaho	$50,719	93%
Southern Illinois University–Carbondale	$50,558	100%
University of Arkansas–Fayetteville	$50,422	84%
CUNY–Queens College	$50,382	86%
University of Montana	$50,325	85%
Arizona State University	$50,234	83%
University of Utah (S.J. Quinney)	$49,981	89%
University of Wisconsin–Madison	$49,751	82%
Florida A&M University	$49,523	84%
University of North Dakota	$49,510	94%
University of Cincinnati	$49,263	70%
University of Nevada–Las Vegas (Boyd)	$48,810	87%
University of Florida (Levin)	$48,737	65%
Texas Tech University	$48,633	81%
University of Alabama–Tuscaloosa	$48,597	71%
University of Arizona (Rogers)	$48,594	85%
Ohio State University (Moritz)	$48,573	87%
University of Washington	$48,450	88%

Whose graduates have the most debt? The least?

School	Average amount of law school debt	% of grads with debt
University of Georgia	$47,120	74%
West Virginia University	$46,953	88%
University of Hawaii (Richardson)	$46,512	69%
Florida State University	$46,486	92%
Wayne State University (MI)	$46,344	82%
University of Louisville (Brandeis) (KY)	$46,213	84%
University of Tennessee–Knoxville	$45,404	80%
University of Kansas	$44,917	71%
University of Kentucky	$43,269	86%
Northern Illinois University	$41,900	81%
Brigham Young University (Clark) (UT)	$41,000	86%
University of Nebraska–Lincoln	$40,642	80%
University of Wyoming	$38,542	81%
University of Mississippi	$37,566	78%
University of New Mexico	$33,739	97%
Southern Methodist University (TX)	$27,529	N/A
Texas Southern University (Marshall)	$19,397	100%
North Carolina Central University	$17,215	70%
Florida International University	$16,308	83%
Howard University (DC)	$9,055	95%

Whose students are the most and least likely to drop out?

If the schools you're considering have a seemingly high attrition rate, you'll want to investigate why. The reasons students leave run the gamut, of course, from an inhospitable culture and dissatisfaction with the program to personal or family problems or a lack of money. The dropout rates shown here are for students who entered in fall 2004.

School	% not returning after 1st year	% not returning after 2nd year
Florida International University	34%	4%
Whittier Law School (CA)	31%	7%
Golden Gate University (CA)	29%	8%
Touro College (Fuchsberg) (NY)	25%	4%
Thomas M. Cooley Law School (MI)	24%	11%
Capital University (OH)	23%	7%
Campbell University (Wiggins) (NC)	22%	0%
Nova Southeastern University (Broad) (FL)	21%	2%
Widener University (DE)	21%	6%
Cleveland State University (Cleveland-Marshall)	19%	2%
John Marshall Law School (IL)	19%	17%
Ohio Northern University (Pettit)	19%	6%
University of Akron (OH)	19%	2%
Gonzaga University (WA)	18%	1%
New York Law School	18%	0%
Oklahoma City University	18%	2%
Roger Williams University (Papitto) (RI)	18%	2%
Southwestern University School of Law (CA)	18%	3%
Texas Wesleyan University	18%	3%
University of San Francisco	18%	3%
Florida Coastal School of Law	16%	4%
Northern Kentucky University (Chase)	16%	16%
University of Detroit Mercy	16%	2%
Valparaiso University (IN)	16%	4%
Baylor University (TX)	15%	3%
Quinnipiac University (CT)	15%	0%
Southern Illinois University–Carbondale	15%	1%
University of the District of Columbia (Clarke)	15%	3%
Louisiana State University–Baton Rouge	14%	0%
Pace University (NY)	14%	5%
St. Thomas University (FL)	14%	2%
University of Tulsa (OK)	14%	8%
North Carolina Central University	13%	2%
Pepperdine University (McConnell) (CA)	13%	0%
St. Louis University	13%	4%
Texas Southern University (Marshall)	13%	1%
Thomas Jefferson School of Law (CA)	13%	6%
University of the Pacific (McGeorge) (CA)	13%	8%
Barry University (FL)	12%	17%
Georgia State University	12%	4%
Hofstra University (NY)	12%	1%
Rutgers State University–Newark (NJ)	12%	3%
Santa Clara University (CA)	12%	1%
Seton Hall University (NJ)	12%	2%

Whose students are the most and least likely to drop out?

School	% not returning after 1st year	% not returning after 2nd year
University of Dayton (OH)	12%	1%
University of Louisville (Brandeis) (KY)	12%	1%
University of Nevada–Las Vegas (Boyd)	12%	5%
Vermont Law School	12%	0%
CUNY–Queens College	11%	7%
Loyola Law School (CA)	11%	3%
Pennsylvania State University (Dickinson)	11%	1%
South Texas College of Law	11%	4%
St. Mary's University (TX)	11%	6%
University of Missouri–Kansas City	11%	7%
California Western School of Law	10%	0%
Franklin Pierce Law Center (NH)	10%	2%
George Mason University (VA)	10%	0%
Michigan State University	10%	2%
Northern Illinois University	10%	2%
Syracuse University (NY)	10%	0%
University of Mississippi	10%	0%
Cardozo-Yeshiva University (NY)	9%	1%
Chapman University (CA)	9%	1%
Creighton University (NE)	9%	1%
DePaul University (IL)	9%	4%
Drake University (IA)	9%	3%
Lewis and Clark College (Northwestern) (OR)	9%	5%
Mercer University (GA)	9%	0%
University of Baltimore	9%	0%
University of Idaho	9%	1%
University of Kentucky	9%	N/A
University of Memphis (Humphreys)	9%	2%
University of Missouri–Columbia	9%	3%
University of North Dakota	9%	8%
Wayne State University (MI)	9%	2%
Western New England College (MA)	9%	1%
American University (Washington) (DC)	8%	1%
Ave Maria School of Law (MI)	8%	11%
Illinois Institute of Technology (Chicago-Kent)	8%	2%
Regent University (VA)	8%	13%
Suffolk University (MA)	8%	3%
University of Miami (FL)	8%	1%
University of Nebraska–Lincoln	8%	N/A
University of San Diego	8%	2%
Willamette University (Collins) (OR)	8%	3%
Duquesne University (PA)	7%	3%
St. John's University (NY)	7%	7%
University of Alabama–Tuscaloosa	7%	1%
University of Richmond (VA)	7%	0%
University of Toledo (OH)	7%	1%
Arizona State University	6%	6%
Rutgers State University–Camden (NJ)	6%	0%
Samford University (Cumberland) (AL)	6%	5%
Seattle University	6%	1%
Washburn University (KS)	6%	1%
Washington University in St. Louis	6%	1%
William Mitchell College of Law (MN)	6%	1%
Boston College	5%	0%
Brooklyn Law School (NY)	5%	1%
George Washington University (DC)	5%	1%

Whose students are the most and least likely to drop out?

School	% not returning after 1st year	% not returning after 2nd year
Hamline University (MN)	5%	5%
Northeastern University (MA)	5%	2%
Ohio State University (Moritz)	5%	1%
University of Minnesota–Twin Cities	5%	1%
University of Southern California (Gould)	5%	0%
West Virginia University	5%	N/A
Florida State University	4%	1%
Mississippi College	4%	1%
University of California–Los Angeles	4%	1%
University of Maine	4%	3%
University of South Dakota	4%	2%
Albany Law School-Union University (NY)	3%	0%
Boston University	3%	1%
Catholic University of America (Columbus) (DC)	3%	1%
Cornell University (NY)	3%	1%
Howard University (DC)	3%	1%
Indiana University–Indianapolis	3%	3%
Temple University (Beasley) (PA)	3%	4%
University of Arkansas–Little Rock (Bowen)	3%	1%
University of Maryland	3%	2%
University of Notre Dame (IN)	3%	3%
University of Oregon	3%	2%
University of St. Thomas (MN)	3%	2%
University of Texas–Austin	3%	2%
Villanova University (PA)	3%	N/A
Duke University (NC)	2%	N/A
Georgetown University (DC)	2%	0%
Texas Tech University	2%	1%
University of Arkansas–Fayetteville	2%	1%
University of Cincinnati	2%	0%
University of Colorado–Boulder	2%	2%
University of Denver (Sturm)	2%	4%
University of Houston	2%	4%
University of New Mexico	2%	5%
University of North Carolina–Chapel Hill	2%	0%
University of South Carolina	2%	3%
Vanderbilt University (TN)	2%	5%
Brigham Young University (Clark) (UT)	1%	1%
College of William and Mary (Marshall-Wythe) (VA)	1%	3%
Emory University (GA)	1%	5%
Marquette University (WI)	1%	2%
Stanford University (CA)	1%	1%
University of California–Berkeley	1%	3%
University of California–Davis	1%	4%
University of California (Hastings)	1%	0%
University of Connecticut	1%	N/A
University of Georgia	1%	0%
University of Illinois–Urbana-Champaign	1%	7%
University of Kansas	1%	2%
University of Oklahoma	1%	0%
University of Tennessee–Knoxville	1%	1%
University of Virginia	1%	2%
University of Wyoming	1%	4%
Yale University (CT)	1%	1%
Case Western Reserve University (OH)	N/A	6%
Columbia University (NY)	N/A	N/A

Whose students are the most and least likely to drop out?

School	% not returning after 1st year	% not returning after 2nd year
Fordham University (NY)	0%	0%
Harvard University (MA)	0%	1%
Indiana University–Bloomington	0%	3%
Loyola University Chicago	0%	2%
New York University	0%	1%
Northwestern University (IL)	0%	0%
Southern Methodist University (TX)	0%	N/A
Stetson University (FL)	0%	1%
University at Buffalo–SUNY	0%	9%
University of Arizona (Rogers)	0%	4%
University of Chicago	0%	0%
University of Florida (Levin)	0%	1%
University of Hawaii (Richardson)	0%	0%
University of Iowa	0%	0%
University of Michigan–Ann Arbor	N/A	2%
University of Montana	0%	0%
University of Pennsylvania	0%	3%
University of Pittsburgh	0%	0%
University of Utah (S.J. Quinney)	0%	0%
University of Washington	N/A	3%
University of Wisconsin–Madison	0%	4%
Wake Forest University (NC)	0%	2%
Washington and Lee University (VA)	0%	10%

What schools have the best first-time bar passage rate?

How well do the schools you're considering prepare students for the bar exam? To judge, you'll need to know not only how many grads pass on their first try, but also how that compares with the overall pass rate of everybody taking the test in the same state. Schools appear under the state in which most 2004 grads sat for the bar and are then organized by their individual passage rates.

State	State's overall bar passage rate	School	School's pass rate
Alabama	81%	University of Alabama–Tuscaloosa	97%
Alabama	81%	Samford University (Cumberland)	85%
Arizona	74%	University of Arizona (Rogers)	84%
Arizona	74%	Arizona State University	75%
Arkansas	82%	University of Arkansas–Fayetteville	85%
Arkansas	82%	University of Arkansas–Little Rock (Bowen)	77%
California	61%	Stanford University	92%
California	61%	University of California–Los Angeles	86%
California	61%	University of California–Berkeley	84%
California	61%	University of California (Hastings)	81%
California	61%	University of Southern California (Gould)	81%
California	61%	University of California–Davis	76%
California	61%	Pepperdine University (McConnell)	74%
California	61%	University of San Diego	71%
California	61%	University of the Pacific (McGeorge)	69%
California	61%	Santa Clara University	68%
California	61%	Chapman University	67%
California	61%	Loyola Law School	66%
California	61%	University of San Francisco	66%
California	61%	California Western School of Law	58%
California	61%	Southwestern University School of Law	58%
California	61%	Whittier Law School	40%
California	61%	Thomas Jefferson School of Law	36%
California	61%	Golden Gate University	35%
Colorado	74%	University of Colorado–Boulder	87%
Colorado	74%	University of Denver (Sturm)	64%
Connecticut	82%	University of Connecticut	94%
Connecticut	82%	Quinnipiac University	74%
Connecticut	82%	Western New England College	68%
Florida	73%	University of Miami	82%
Florida	73%	University of Florida (Levin)	80%
Florida	73%	Florida State University	77%
Florida	73%	Stetson University	74%
Florida	73%	Florida Coastal School of Law	71%
Florida	73%	Nova Southeastern University (Broad)	62%
Florida	73%	St. Thomas University	62%
Florida	73%	Barry University	51%
Georgia	85%	Mercer University	93%
Georgia	85%	University of Georgia	93%
Georgia	85%	Georgia State University	92%
Georgia	85%	Emory University	90%
Hawaii	77%	University of Hawaii (Richardson)	76%
Idaho	76%	University of Idaho	76%
Illinois	85%	University of Chicago	99%
Illinois	85%	Northwestern University	98%

What schools have the best first-time bar passage rate?

State	State's overall bar passage rate	School	School's pass rate
Illinois	85%	University of Notre Dame	96%
Illinois	85%	Loyola University Chicago	92%
Illinois	85%	University of Illinois–Urbana-Champaign	90%
Illinois	85%	Illinois Institute of Technology (Chicago-Kent)	87%
Illinois	85%	Northern Illinois University	86%
Illinois	85%	DePaul University	84%
Illinois	85%	Southern Illinois University–Carbondale	83%
Illinois	85%	John Marshall Law School	74%
Indiana	84%	Indiana University–Bloomington	92%
Indiana	84%	Valparaiso University	83%
Indiana	84%	Indiana University–Indianapolis	80%
Iowa	86%	University of Iowa	89%
Iowa	86%	Drake University	86%
Kansas	81%	University of Kansas	82%
Kansas	81%	Washburn University	71%
Kentucky	78%	University of Kentucky	83%
Kentucky	78%	Northern Kentucky University (Chase)	79%
Kentucky	78%	University of Louisville (Brandeis)	79%
Louisiana	67%	Louisiana State University–Baton Rouge	78%
Maine	75%	University of Maine	69%
Maryland	72%	American University (Washington)	85%
Maryland	72%	University of Maryland	78%
Maryland	72%	Catholic University of America (Columbus)	72%
Maryland	72%	University of Baltimore	57%
Maryland	72%	Howard University	52%
Maryland	72%	University of the District of Columbia (Clarke)	36%
Massachusetts	84%	Boston University	95%
Massachusetts	84%	Boston College	93%
Massachusetts	84%	Northeastern University	82%
Massachusetts	84%	Suffolk University	80%
Massachusetts	84%	New England School of Law	74%
Michigan	74%	Ave Maria School of Law	100%
Michigan	74%	Wayne State University	84%
Michigan	74%	University of Detroit Mercy	69%
Michigan	74%	Michigan State University	68%
Michigan	74%	Thomas M. Cooley Law School	55%
Minnesota	91%	University of Minnesota–Twin Cities	99%
Minnesota	91%	William Mitchell College of Law	89%
Minnesota	91%	Hamline University	86%
Mississippi	90%	University of Mississippi	90%
Mississippi	90%	Mississippi College	84%
Missouri	88%	Washington University in St. Louis	96%
Missouri	88%	University of Missouri–Columbia	89%
Missouri	88%	St. Louis University	86%
Missouri	88%	University of Missouri–Kansas City	85%
Montana	83%	University of Montana	86%
Nebraska	88%	University of Nebraska–Lincoln	90%
Nebraska	88%	Creighton University	84%
Nevada	73%	University of Nevada–Las Vegas (Boyd)	65%
New Hampshire	64%	Franklin Pierce Law Center	62%
New Jersey	80%	Seton Hall University	82%
New Jersey	80%	Rutgers State University–Camden	81%
New Jersey	80%	Rutgers State University–Newark	73%
New Mexico	82%	University of New Mexico	81%
New York	75%	New York University	97%
New York	75%	Harvard University	96%

What schools have the best first-time bar passage rate?

State	State's overall bar passage rate	School	School's pass rate
New York	75%	University of Michigan–Ann Arbor	96%
New York	75%	Duke University	95%
New York	75%	Columbia University	94%
New York	75%	Yale University	94%
New York	75%	Georgetown University	93%
New York	75%	University of Pennsylvania	93%
New York	75%	Cornell University	92%
New York	75%	Fordham University	87%
New York	75%	George Washington University	87%
New York	75%	St. John's University	86%
New York	75%	Brooklyn Law School	84%
New York	75%	Cardozo-Yeshiva University	80%
New York	75%	University at Buffalo–SUNY	79%
New York	75%	Albany Law School-Union University	78%
New York	75%	Syracuse University	76%
New York	75%	Pace University	73%
New York	75%	Hofstra University	69%
New York	75%	Touro College (Fuchsberg)	65%
New York	75%	CUNY–Queens College	64%
New York	75%	New York Law School	64%
North Carolina	75%	Wake Forest University	88%
North Carolina	75%	University of North Carolina–Chapel Hill	85%
North Carolina	75%	Campbell University (Wiggins)	78%
North Carolina	75%	North Carolina Central University	72%
North Dakota	82%	University of North Dakota	84%
Ohio	81%	Ohio State University (Moritz)	91%
Ohio	81%	University of Toledo	90%
Ohio	81%	University of Cincinnati	89%
Ohio	81%	Case Western Reserve University	88%
Ohio	81%	University of Akron	79%
Ohio	81%	Capital University	75%
Ohio	81%	University of Dayton	75%
Ohio	81%	Cleveland State University (Cleveland-Marshall)	73%
Ohio	81%	Ohio Northern University (Pettit)	72%
Oklahoma	83%	University of Oklahoma	96%
Oklahoma	83%	University of Tulsa	75%
Oklahoma	83%	Oklahoma City University	72%
Oregon	72%	Willamette University (Collins)	83%
Oregon	72%	University of Oregon	75%
Oregon	72%	Lewis and Clark College (Northwestern)	68%
Pennsylvania	81%	Temple University (Beasley)	88%
Pennsylvania	81%	University of Pittsburgh	82%
Pennsylvania	81%	Duquesne University	80%
Pennsylvania	81%	Villanova University	79%
Pennsylvania	81%	Pennsylvania State University (Dickinson)	78%
Pennsylvania	81%	Widener University	72%
Rhode Island	77%	Roger Williams University (Papitto)	71%
South Carolina	84%	University of South Carolina	87%
South Dakota	74%	University of South Dakota	69%
Tennessee	82%	Vanderbilt University	91%
Tennessee	82%	University of Tennessee–Knoxville	87%
Tennessee	82%	University of Memphis (Humphreys)	86%
Texas	79%	University of Texas–Austin	92%
Texas	79%	Baylor University	91%
Texas	79%	Southern Methodist University	88%
Texas	79%	Texas Tech University	85%

What schools have the best first-time bar passage rate?

State	State's overall bar passage rate	School	School's pass rate
Texas	79%	University of Houston	85%
Texas	79%	St. Mary's University	79%
Texas	79%	South Texas College of Law	70%
Texas	79%	Texas Wesleyan University	66%
Texas	79%	Texas Southern University (Marshall)	55%
Utah	90%	Brigham Young University (Clark)	91%
Utah	90%	University of Utah (S.J. Quinney)	89%
Vermont	85%	Vermont Law School	74%
Virginia	74%	University of Virginia	91%
Virginia	74%	Washington and Lee University	86%
Virginia	74%	College of William and Mary (Marshall-Wythe)	85%
Virginia	74%	George Mason University	80%
Virginia	74%	University of Richmond	75%
Virginia	74%	Regent University	61%
Washington	79%	University of Washington	89%
Washington	79%	Seattle University	80%
Washington	79%	Gonzaga University	76%
West Virginia	78%	West Virginia University	80%
Wisconsin	84%	Marquette University	100%
Wisconsin	84%	University of Wisconsin–Madison	100%
Wyoming	68%	University of Wyoming	70%

Whose graduates are the most and least likely to land a job?

Even with the economy still limping along, many law schools in 2004 could boast that virtually the entire class had accepted a job offer by the time they'd been given their diplomas. (The schools that didn't provide information about how many graduates were immediately working appear at the end of the list, so that prospective students can see the proportion of students who were employed nine months out.)

School	% employed at graduation	% employed at 9 months
Columbia University (NY)	99%	99%
Stanford University (CA)	99%	99%
University of Chicago	99%	100%
University of Pennsylvania	99%	99%
George Mason University (VA)	98%	100%
University of Virginia	98%	99%
Cornell University (NY)	97%	98%
Harvard University (MA)	97%	100%
Northwestern University (IL)	97%	99%
University of California–Berkeley	97%	100%
University of Minnesota–Twin Cities	97%	99%
Yale University (CT)	97%	99%
New York University	96%	99%
Duke University (NC)	95%	100%
University of Michigan–Ann Arbor	95%	99%
University of Texas–Austin	95%	98%
George Washington University (DC)	94%	98%
University of California–Los Angeles	93%	100%
Seton Hall University (NJ)	92%	97%
Vanderbilt University (TN)	92%	97%
Georgetown University (DC)	90%	98%
University of Washington	89%	99%
University of Iowa	88%	99%
University of Southern California (Gould)	88%	99%
Washington University in St. Louis	88%	99%
Boston University	87%	99%
Indiana University–Bloomington	87%	96%
Rutgers State University–Camden (NJ)	87%	93%
University of Denver (Sturm)	87%	97%
University of Notre Dame (IN)	87%	98%
University of Toledo (OH)	87%	92%
Fordham University (NY)	86%	98%
College of William and Mary (Marshall-Wythe) (VA)	85%	96%
Florida State University	85%	99%
University at Buffalo–SUNY	85%	95%
American University (Washington) (DC)	83%	97%
Brigham Young University (Clark) (UT)	83%	99%
Indiana University–Indianapolis	83%	94%
Campbell University (Wiggins) (NC)	82%	84%
DePaul University (IL)	81%	94%
Emory University (GA)	81%	99%
University of California–Davis	81%	92%
Howard University (DC)	80%	86%
Southwestern University School of Law (CA)	80%	91%

School	% employed at graduation	% employed at 9 months
Duquesne University (PA)	79%	86%
Louisiana State University–Baton Rouge	78%	91%
Loyola University Chicago	78%	98%
Texas Tech University	78%	96%
University of Maryland	78%	97%
Wake Forest University (NC)	77%	92%
Washington and Lee University (VA)	77%	91%
University of Georgia	76%	99%
University of Pittsburgh	76%	97%
University of Nebraska–Lincoln	75%	92%
Cardozo-Yeshiva University (NY)	74%	97%
Loyola Law School (CA)	74%	97%
Ohio State University (Moritz)	74%	97%
Santa Clara University (CA)	74%	95%
Texas Southern University (Marshall)	74%	75%
Case Western Reserve University (OH)	73%	98%
University of Miami (FL)	73%	93%
University of Mississippi	73%	95%
University of New Mexico	73%	94%
University of Wisconsin–Madison	73%	97%
Brooklyn Law School (NY)	72%	98%
Creighton University (NE)	72%	98%
Illinois Institute of Technology (Chicago-Kent)	72%	92%
University of Colorado–Boulder	72%	90%
University of Illinois–Urbana-Champaign	72%	100%
University of North Carolina–Chapel Hill	72%	90%
Boston College	71%	97%
St. Louis University	71%	93%
University of Arizona (Rogers)	71%	93%
University of Cincinnati	71%	96%
Pennsylvania State University (Dickinson)	69%	93%
St. John's University (NY)	69%	93%
Temple University (Beasley) (PA)	69%	96%
University of Oklahoma	69%	88%
University of Utah (S.J. Quinney)	69%	91%
Syracuse University (NY)	68%	93%
University of Hawaii (Richardson)	68%	93%
Baylor University (TX)	67%	98%
Rutgers State University–Newark (NJ)	67%	95%
Villanova University (PA)	67%	98%
University of Florida (Levin)	66%	96%
University of Houston	66%	96%
University of San Diego	66%	89%
Northern Kentucky University (Chase)	65%	92%

Whose graduates are the most and least likely to land a job?

School	% employed at graduation	% employed at 9 months
University of Akron (OH)	65%	89%
Catholic University of America (Columbus) (DC)	64%	90%
Cleveland State University (Cleveland-Marshall)	64%	91%
University of Alabama–Tuscaloosa	64%	98%
University of Kentucky	64%	98%
Marquette University (WI)	62%	94%
University of Connecticut	62%	96%
University of Louisville (Brandeis) (KY)	62%	91%
University of Oregon	62%	92%
Mississippi College	60%	96%
Samford University (Cumberland) (AL)	60%	97%
Seattle University	60%	100%
University of Nevada–Las Vegas (Boyd)	60%	83%
University of Tennessee–Knoxville	60%	85%
Mercer University (GA)	59%	98%
University of Missouri–Columbia	59%	93%
University of South Carolina	59%	95%
Pepperdine University (McConnell) (CA)	58%	91%
Suffolk University (MA)	58%	87%
University of California (Hastings)	57%	92%
University of Richmond (VA)	57%	93%

School	% employed at graduation	% employed at 9 months
John Marshall Law School (IL)	56%	89%
University of Kansas	55%	89%
Western New England College (MA)	55%	80%
Whittier Law School (CA)	54%	91%
Widener University (DE)	54%	87%
William Mitchell College of Law (MN)	54%	84%
Albany Law School-Union University (NY)	53%	96%
Chapman University (CA)	53%	91%
University of Memphis (Humphreys)	53%	97%
University of Tulsa (OK)	53%	87%
Northern Illinois University	52%	90%
Stetson University (FL)	49%	91%
University of South Dakota	49%	75%
Hamline University (MN)	47%	81%
Regent University (VA)	46%	89%
University of Idaho	46%	88%
Texas Wesleyan University	43%	83%
Ave Maria School of Law (MI)	38%	85%
Valparaiso University (IN)	33%	81%
CUNY–Queens College	30%	74%
New England School of Law (MA)	28%	81%

School	% employed at 9 months
Southern Methodist University (TX)	96%
University of Arkansas–Little Rock (Bowen)	96%
University of the Pacific (McGeorge) (CA)	96%
Drake University (IA)	95%
Northeastern University (MA)	95%
University of San Francisco	95%
Arizona State University	94%
Lewis and Clark College (Northwestern) (OR)	94%
Vermont Law School	94%
Gonzaga University (WA)	93%
Florida Coastal School of Law	92%
Georgia State University	92%
Hofstra University (NY)	92%
Quinnipiac University (CT)	92%
University of Arkansas–Fayetteville	92%
Washburn University (KS)	92%
New York Law School	90%
Pace University (NY)	90%
University of Detroit Mercy	90%
University of Maine	90%
University of Montana	89%
Capital University (OH)	88%
University of Missouri–Kansas City	88%
University of North Dakota	88%

School	% employed at 9 months
Franklin Pierce Law Center (NH)	86%
Ohio Northern University (Pettit)	86%
St. Mary's University (TX)	86%
University of Dayton (OH)	86%
University of Baltimore	85%
Willamette University (Collins) (OR)	85%
California Western School of Law	84%
Wayne State University (MI)	84%
North Carolina Central University	83%
Thomas Jefferson School of Law (CA)	83%
University of Wyoming	83%
Southern Illinois University–Carbondale	82%
South Texas College of Law	80%
Michigan State University	79%
West Virginia University	79%
University of the District of Columbia (Clarke)	78%
Nova Southeastern University (Broad) (FL)	77%
Oklahoma City University	77%
Thomas M. Cooley Law School (MI)	71%
Roger Williams University (Papitto) (RI)	69%
Golden Gate University (CA)	68%
Touro College (Fuchsberg) (NY)	66%
St. Thomas University (FL)	58%

Whose graduates earn the most? The least?

According to the most recent surveys by the National Association for Law Placement, the median salary for first-year associates at law firms ranges from $67,500 in small firms to $125,000 at firms with 500 lawyers or more. But, as this table of median starting salaries for the class of 2004 shows, many make considerably more—or, if they go into the public sector, considerably less.

School	Private sector starting salary (median)	Private sector starting salary (25th–75th percentile)	Public sector starting salary (median)
Boston College	$125,000	$93,000-$125,000	$43,100
Boston University	$125,000	$110,000-$125,000	$43,222
Columbia University (NY)	$125,000	$125,000-$125,000	$52,650
Cornell University (NY)	$125,000	$125,000-$125,000	$51,348
Fordham University (NY)	$125,000	$96,250-$125,000	$47,500
Georgetown University (DC)	$125,000	$125,000-$125,000	$48,947
George Washington University (DC)	$125,000	$90,000-$125,000	$49,000
Harvard University (MA)	$125,000	$125,000-$125,000	$50,000
New York University	$125,000	$125,000-$125,000	$48,000
Northwestern University (IL)	$125,000	$125,000-$125,000	$50,000
Santa Clara University (CA)	$125,000	$75,000-$125,000	$51,000
Stanford University (CA)	$125,000	$125,000-$125,000	$50,000
University of California–Berkeley	$125,000	$125,000-$125,000	$54,282
University of California–Los Angeles	$125,000	$75,000-$125,000	$52,261
University of Chicago	$125,000	$125,000-$125,000	$50,593
University of Michigan–Ann Arbor	$125,000	$120,000-$125,000	$50,598
University of Pennsylvania	$125,000	$125,000-$125,000	$50,250
University of Southern California (Gould)	$125,000	$120,000-$125,000	$53,000
Yale University (CT)	$125,000	$125,000-$125,000	$51,635
University of Virginia	$118,000	$100,000-$128,000	$52,000
Brooklyn Law School (NY)	$115,000	$70,000-$125,000	$45,710
Duke University (NC)	$110,000	$100,000-$125,000	$45,000
University of Texas–Austin	$110,000	$100,000-$120,000	$47,000
Howard University (DC)	$105,500	$80,000-$125,000	$42,000
New York Law School	$100,000	$52,500-$125,000	$43,340
University of Georgia	$100,000	$61,000-$100,000	$48,000
University of North Carolina–Chapel Hill	$100,000	$70,000-$115,000	$44,500
University of Notre Dame (IN)	$100,000	$90,000-$125,000	$45,500
Vanderbilt University (TN)	$100,000	$83,000-$115,000	$47,500
Cardozo-Yeshiva University (NY)	$95,000	$68,000-$125,000	$49,000
College of William and Mary (Marshall-Wythe) (VA)	$95,000	$75,000-$125,000	$48,947
University of California (Hastings)	$94,500	$68,000-$125,000	$46,500
University of Houston	$90,000	$58,000-$110,000	$45,000
University of Illinois–Urbana-Champaign	$90,000	$60,000-$125,000	$45,000
Washington University in St. Louis	$90,000	$82,000-$125,000	$49,105
Emory University (GA)	$89,500	$60,000-$102,500	$45,000
George Mason University (VA)	$84,750	$60,000-$120,000	$48,947
Brigham Young University (Clark) (UT)	$83,500	$64,000-$105,000	$38,500
Washington and Lee University (VA)	$83,500	$60,000-$110,000	$48,974

Whose graduates earn the most? The least?

School	Private sector starting salary (median)	Private sector starting salary (25th–75th percentile)	Public sector starting salary (median)
Loyola University Chicago	$83,000	$57,500-$125,000	$43,222
Temple University (Beasley) (PA)	$83,000	$60,000-$107,000	$42,000
Southwestern University School of Law (CA)	$82,500	$60,000-$91,000	$45,500
University of Miami (FL)	$82,500	$63,800-$107,200	$39,100
Ohio State University (Moritz)	$82,000	$50,000-$90,000	$42,000
Pepperdine University (McConnell) (CA)	$80,000	$61,000-$105,000	$56,000
Seattle University	$80,000	$67,500-$90,000	$40,000
South Texas College of Law	$80,000	$68,000-$105,000	$48,000
University of Arizona (Rogers)	$80,000	$65,000-$95,000	$43,000
University of California–Davis	$80,000	$68,000-$125,000	$43,500
University of Washington	$80,000	$57,600-$95,000	$40,000
Villanova University (PA)	$80,000	$60,000-$107,000	$42,000
Indiana University–Bloomington	$79,000	$58,000-$115,000	$46,450
Case Western Reserve University (OH)	$78,000	$50,000-$100,000	$45,000
Hofstra University (NY)	$77,000	N/A	$48,538
Southern Methodist University (TX)	$77,000	$52,000-$123,500	$43,000
University of Nebraska–Lincoln	$77,000	$52,000-$123,500	$43,000
University of San Francisco	$75,300	$61,000-$112,800	$50,625
Franklin Pierce Law Center (NH)	$75,000	$48,000-$120,000	$41,000
University of Connecticut	$75,000	$50,000-$87,000	$46,680
University of Pittsburgh	$75,000	$46,000-$100,000	$40,000
American University (Washington) (DC)	$72,108	$50,000-$115,000	$45,000
Rutgers State University–Camden (NJ)	$72,000	$52,000-$100,000	$37,000
University of Alabama–Tuscaloosa	$71,250	$50,000-$80,000	$42,000
Arizona State University	$70,000	$60,000-$95,000	$51,000
Baylor University (TX)	$70,000	$55,000-$105,000	$42,500
Cleveland State University (Cleveland-Marshall)	$70,000	$50,000-$90,000	$44,500
Loyola Law School (CA)	$70,000	$60,000-$110,000	$54,000
Northeastern University (MA)	$70,000	$45,000-$110,000	$42,000
St. John's University (NY)	$70,000	$52,000-$125,000	$47,000
University of Baltimore	$70,000	$50,000-$80,000	$34,552
University of Cincinnati	$70,000	$52,000-$90,000	$45,000
University of Hawaii (Richardson)	$70,000	$65,000-$75,000	$45,000
University of Minnesota–Twin Cities	$70,000	$55,000-$90,000	$47,300
University of Wisconsin–Madison	$70,000	$50,000-$95,000	$40,000
Wake Forest University (NC)	$70,000	$50,000-$100,000	$40,000
Illinois Institute of Technology (Chicago-Kent)	$69,000	$55,000-$96,000	$43,222
Texas Tech University	$68,800	$39,000-$118,000	$38,000
University of San Diego	$68,000	$56,000-$100,000	$50,000
University of Iowa	$65,500	$48,000-$90,000	$45,000
Indiana University–Indianapolis	$65,280	$55,200-$80,200	$46,736
Chapman University (CA)	$65,000	$50,000-$75,000	$56,500
Georgia State University	$65,000	$52,000-$100,000	$45,500
John Marshall Law School (IL)	$65,000	$52,250-$90,000	$43,700
University of Denver (Sturm)	$65,000	$50,000-$90,000	$41,000
University of Detroit Mercy	$65,000	$49,000-$80,000	$43,500
University of Florida (Levin)	$65,000	$55,000-$80,000	$38,000
University of Nevada–Las Vegas (Boyd)	$65,000	$50,000-$78,000	$48,000
University of Utah (S.J. Quinney)	$65,000	$52,000-$90,000	$40,000
Whittier Law School (CA)	$65,000	$58,000-$75,000	$56,600
William Mitchell College of Law (MN)	$63,883	$45,000-$80,000	$40,000
Wayne State University (MI)	$63,700	$50,000-$90,000	$50,000

Whose graduates earn the most? The least?

School	Private sector starting salary (median)	Private sector starting salary (25th–75th percentile)	Public sector starting salary (median)
University of Tennessee–Knoxville	$63,000	$50,000-$83,000	$42,000
Catholic University of America (Columbus) (DC)	$62,400	$50,000-$90,000	$50,000
University of the Pacific (McGeorge) (CA)	$62,200	$55,000-$70,000	$53,000
University of South Carolina	$61,200	$50,000-$68,000	$35,143
University of Akron (OH)	$61,154	$42,769-$79,077	$40,839
California Western School of Law	$60,000	$41,600-$66,000	$52,000
Florida State University	$60,000	$48,000-$75,000	$37,500
Golden Gate University (CA)	$60,000	$47,000-$65,000	$48,102
Northern Kentucky University (Chase)	$60,000	$50,000-$81,000	$41,557
Quinnipiac University (CT)	$60,000	$41,500-$78,077	$48,000
Seton Hall University (NJ)	$60,000	$45,000-$90,000	$35,000
Suffolk University (MA)	$60,000	$42,000-$100,000	$43,000
University of Colorado–Boulder	$60,000	$45,000-$90,000	$42,000
University of Maryland	$60,000	$45,000-$95,000	$40,000
University of Memphis (Humphreys)	$60,000	$50,000-$72,000	$44,000
University of Mississippi	$60,000	$49,000-$75,000	$37,733
University of Richmond (VA)	$60,000	$52,405-$67,114	$47,658
Stetson University (FL)	$58,000	$50,000-$65,000	$38,000
Mississippi College	$57,500	$45,000-$75,000	$38,000
DePaul University (IL)	$57,000	$45,000-$70,000	$43,423
Drake University (IA)	$56,750	$40,000-$65,000	$61,250
Creighton University (NE)	$56,250	$41,250-$72,000	$40,000
Touro College (Fuchsberg) (NY)	$56,250	$47,000-$65,000	$45,000
CUNY–Queens College	$56,212	$40,000-$80,000	$45,000
St. Louis University	$56,000	$49,000-$67,500	$33,972
Pace University (NY)	$55,412	$47,941-$66,471	$48,000
Capital University (OH)	$55,000	$48,000-$90,000	$40,000
Samford University (Cumberland) (AL)	$55,000	$45,000-$70,000	$44,200
Texas Wesleyan University	$55,000	$40,000-$65,000	$44,000
University of Toledo (OH)	$55,000	$36,000-$70,000	$38,000
Widener University (DE)	$55,000	$45,000-$80,000	$40,000
Mercer University (GA)	$53,500	$47,500-$70,000	$39,250
University of Kansas	$53,000	$48,000-$80,000	$43,000
University of Missouri–Columbia	$52,500	$39,000-$78,000	$37,000
University of Oregon	$52,500	$45,500-$65,400	$40,100
Marquette University (WI)	$52,000	$42,000-$83,200	$41,148
Michigan State University	$52,000	$42,500-$67,000	$46,249
University of Maine	$52,000	$45,000-$60,000	$39,000
Nova Southeastern University (Broad) (FL)	$51,000	$45,000-$65,000	$38,000
University of Oklahoma	$51,000	$37,500-$75,000	$40,000
Hamline University (MN)	$50,000	$45,000-$62,500	$39,715
Louisiana State University–Baton Rouge	$50,000	$40,000-$66,000	N/A
Pennsylvania State University (Dickinson)	$50,000	$40,000-$70,000	$40,000
St. Thomas University (FL)	$50,000	$45,000-$60,000	$40,000
Syracuse University (NY)	$50,000	$40,000-$73,000	$41,250
Thomas Jefferson School of Law (CA)	$50,000	$45,000-$70,000	$47,633
University of New Mexico	$50,000	$40,000-$70,000	$37,877
University of Tulsa (OK)	$50,000	$42,000-$65,000	$40,000
Washburn University (KS)	$50,000	$40,000-$58,000	$40,000
Willamette University (Collins) (OR)	$50,000	$40,800-$72,500	$42,500
University of Louisville (Brandeis) (KY)	$49,750	$40,000-$72,000	$35,250
West Virginia University	$49,250	$45,000-$57,500	$37,515

Whose graduates earn the most? The least?

School	Private sector starting salary (median)	Private sector starting salary (25th–75th percentile)	Public sector starting salary (median)
St. Mary's University (TX)	$48,540	$37,500-$61,080	$40,877
Oklahoma City University	$48,526	$38,000-$65,000	$39,125
Ohio Northern University (Pettit)	$48,500	$46,000-$51,000	$40,000
Albany Law School-Union University (NY)	$48,000	$40,000-$60,000	$48,000
Lewis and Clark College (Northwestern) (OR)	$48,000	$42,000-$60,000	$41,000
University of Dayton (OH)	$48,000	$40,375-$60,000	$40,500
Western New England College (MA)	$48,000	$35,000-$75,000	$43,000
University at Buffalo–SUNY	$47,750	$40,000-$65,000	$45,000
Valparaiso University (IN)	$47,500	$40,500-$56,300	$41,000
University of Kentucky	$47,000	$40,000-$77,000	$36,500
Ave Maria School of Law (MI)	$46,240	$36,000-$90,000	$49,390
Gonzaga University (WA)	$46,000	$40,000-$60,000	$45,000
University of Wyoming	$45,714	$33,000-$88,000	$43,452
New England School of Law (MA)	$45,500	$40,000-$60,000	$43,000
Campbell University (Wiggins) (NC)	$45,000	$40,000-$55,000	$42,000
Florida Coastal School of Law	$45,000	$38,000-$60,000	$38,000
University of Arkansas–Little Rock (Bowen)	$45,000	$40,000-$50,000	$40,000
Northern Illinois University	$44,000	$40,000-$50,000	$42,000
Regent University (VA)	$42,500	$35,000-$53,000	$38,000
Roger Williams University (Papitto) (RI)	$42,500	$36,500-$70,000	$41,000
Barry University (FL)	$42,000	$40,000-$53,000	$41,608
University of Idaho	$42,000	$27,600-$65,000	$40,850
Southern Illinois University–Carbondale	$41,500	$40,000-$50,000	$39,600
University of Missouri–Kansas City	$40,000	$35,000-$60,000	$39,000
University of Montana	$40,000	$36,500-$45,000	$39,000
Vermont Law School	$40,000	$35,000-$50,000	$35,958
University of North Dakota	$39,500	$35,000-$45,000	$40,000
University of South Dakota	$38,000	$33,000-$47,000	$40,000

Where do graduates work?

You can tell a great deal about a law school by looking at where its newly minted JDs go to work. Harvard, whose corporate law program is one of its great strengths, launched 60 percent of its 2004 graduating class into law firms, for example. Yale sent 43 percent to judicial clerkships and 8 percent into government and public service. Schools are sorted by the percentage of graduates who took jobs at law firms.

School	% employed by law firms	% employed in business and industry (in legal jobs)	% employed in business and industry (in nonlegal jobs)	% employed in government	% employed in public interest jobs	% employed in judicial clerkships	% employed in academia	% employed in law school's state	% employed in foreign countries
Campbell University (Wiggins) (NC)	83%	0%	5%	8%	2%	2%	0%	87%	1%
Northwestern University (IL)	79%	4%	N/A	5%	1%	11%	0%	46%	1%
University of Memphis (Humphreys)	78%	6%	N/A	3%	4%	10%	N/A	90%	N/A
Columbia University (NY)	77%	2%	0%	4%	3%	14%	1%	65%	3%
Texas Tech University	77%	3%	0%	13%	1%	6%	1%	96%	0%
Baylor University (TX)	76%	7%	N/A	8%	1%	7%	1%	91%	0%
Cornell University (NY)	76%	1%	0%	2%	2%	13%	3%	54%	1%
University of Pennsylvania	76%	0%	2%	1%	2%	17%	1%	18%	3%
University of Virginia	75%	0%	0%	6%	3%	15%	0%	12%	2%
Samford University (Cumberland) (AL)	74%	1%	5%	11%	1%	6%	1%	65%	0%
University of North Carolina–Chapel Hill	74%	4%	0%	9%	3%	8%	2%	54%	0%
University of Michigan–Ann Arbor	73%	0%	3%	4%	5%	15%	0%	15%	1%
Vanderbilt University (TN)	73%	1%	4%	7%	3%	11%	1%	22%	0%
Duke University (NC)	72%	0%	3%	4%	3%	16%	0%	10%	3%
Fordham University (NY)	72%	1%	6%	10%	3%	4%	2%	75%	1%
Mississippi College	72%	5%	N/A	9%	1%	11%	2%	76%	0%
University of California–Los Angeles	72%	2%	2%	6%	7%	9%	2%	85%	1%
South Texas College of Law	71%	9%	0%	11%	1%	5%	2%	98%	0%
University of Houston	70%	4%	7%	7%	2%	6%	4%	91%	0%
New York University	69%	0%	3%	4%	10%	14%	0%	66%	0%
Emory University (GA)	68%	4%	5%	11%	4%	7%	2%	47%	1%
University of Chicago	68%	1%	1%	4%	4%	21%	1%	36%	3%
Boston University	67%	4%	1%	8%	4%	12%	4%	40%	2%
California Western School of Law	67%	5%	9%	9%	6%	2%	2%	69%	1%
Southern Methodist University (TX)	67%	12%	0%	9%	5%	5%	2%	86%	0%
University of Mississippi	67%	3%	3%	6%	3%	13%	3%	76%	0%
University of Tennessee–Knoxville	67%	0%	6%	15%	3%	7%	2%	65%	0%
Wayne State University (MI)	67%	18%	N/A	8%	1%	3%	1%	93%	0%
Pepperdine University (McConnell) (CA)	66%	6%	10%	10%	1%	4%	1%	75%	1%
University of Miami (FL)	66%	4%	4%	18%	3%	3%	2%	82%	0%
University of Arkansas–Fayetteville	65%	8%	N/A	14%	3%	10%	0%	63%	0%
University of Oklahoma	65%	2%	5%	21%	4%	1%	1%	74%	1%
University of Southern California (Gould)	65%	2%	10%	5%	3%	7%	2%	83%	1%
West Virginia University	65%	N/A	5%	8%	1%	18%	0%	80%	0%
Hofstra University (NY)	64%	14%	N/A	13%	1%	4%	2%	85%	0%
Mercer University (GA)	64%	0%	5%	13%	7%	10%	1%	78%	1%
St. John's University (NY)	64%	5%	6%	13%	2%	6%	4%	90%	0%
St. Thomas University (FL)	64%	6%	0%	9%	9%	7%	5%	90%	0%
University of California–Berkeley	64%	1%	2%	7%	7%	16%	2%	66%	2%

Where do graduates work?

School	% employed by law firms	% employed in business and industry (in legal jobs)	% employed in business and industry (in nonlegal jobs)	% employed in government	% employed in public interest jobs	% employed in judicial clerkships	% employed in academia	% employed in law school's state	% employed in foreign countries
DePaul University (IL)	63%	7%	10%	10%	4%	3%	2%	87%	0%
Drake University (IA)	63%	7%	5%	11%	3%	7%	2%	71%	1%
St. Mary's University (TX)	63%	1%	7%	14%	5%	5%	4%	96%	0%
University of Alabama–Tuscaloosa	63%	8%	N/A	11%	5%	10%	1%	76%	N/A
University of Arkansas–Little Rock (Bowen)	63%	11%	N/A	14%	1%	5%	6%	85%	0%
University of San Diego	63%	13%	3%	12%	3%	3%	2%	86%	0%
Valparaiso University (IN)	63%	2%	14%	12%	2%	4%	1%	47%	1%
Wake Forest University (NC)	63%	1%	4%	16%	2%	12%	1%	53%	1%
Washington University in St. Louis	63%	6%	N/A	16%	5%	9%	0%	34%	2%
Chapman University (CA)	62%	5%	10%	11%	4%	3%	4%	91%	0%
Georgia State University	62%	2%	9%	13%	6%	7%	0%	95%	0%
Marquette University (WI)	62%	10%	11%	7%	5%	5%	1%	78%	1%
North Carolina Central University	62%	9%	N/A	12%	12%	4%	1%	86%	0%
University of Georgia	62%	6%	1%	8%	4%	17%	2%	76%	0%
University of Nevada–Las Vegas (Boyd)	62%	2%	9%	6%	1%	16%	2%	90%	0%
Villanova University (PA)	62%	4%	4%	8%	1%	21%	0%	60%	1%
Georgetown University (DC)	61%	1%	4%	7%	5%	9%	2%	41%	2%
Loyola Law School (CA)	61%	3%	18%	4%	10%	3%	1%	95%	1%
St. Louis University	61%	18%	N/A	10%	5%	5%	1%	67%	N/A
University of Texas–Austin	61%	4%	3%	11%	5%	13%	1%	74%	0%
Cardozo-Yeshiva University (NY)	60%	12%	2%	12%	3%	8%	2%	83%	1%
Harvard University (MA)	60%	N/A	3%	3%	4%	29%	1%	11%	2%
University at Buffalo–SUNY	60%	11%	7%	10%	5%	3%	3%	85%	2%
University of California (Hastings)	60%	8%	0%	12%	9%	6%	1%	82%	1%
University of Detroit Mercy	60%	6%	17%	7%	4%	2%	5%	76%	20%
University of Louisville (Brandeis) (KY)	60%	3%	10%	10%	6%	8%	1%	86%	0%
Boston College	59%	3%	5%	10%	5%	17%	0%	43%	2%
Illinois Institute of Technology (Chicago-Kent)	59%	9%	8%	14%	5%	4%	2%	84%	2%
Louisiana State University–Baton Rouge	59%	3%	0%	9%	1%	21%	2%	89%	0%
Texas Southern University (Marshall)	59%	6%	13%	10%	1%	6%	4%	72%	0%
University of California–Davis	59%	8%	0%	7%	14%	10%	1%	81%	1%
University of Iowa	59%	10%	5%	7%	3%	8%	1%	38%	1%
University of Nebraska–Lincoln	59%	16%	N/A	16%	3%	6%	2%	64%	0%
University of Notre Dame (IN)	59%	1%	3%	11%	6%	20%	0%	9%	1%
Cleveland State University (Cleveland-Marshall)	58%	3%	15%	13%	3%	5%	3%	87%	0%
College of William and Mary (Marshall-Wythe) (VA)	58%	3%	1%	20%	5%	12%	1%	37%	0%
Franklin Pierce Law Center (NH)	58%	10%	10%	9%	6%	5%	2%	28%	8%
Stanford University (CA)	58%	0%	5%	2%	4%	30%	1%	46%	1%
University of Dayton (OH)	58%	13%	3%	15%	2%	4%	1%	54%	0%
University of Florida (Levin)	58%	0%	7%	19%	9%	4%	1%	82%	1%
University of Illinois–Urbana-Champaign	58%	7%	5%	10%	3%	13%	4%	66%	2%
University of Tulsa (OK)	58%	5%	8%	17%	3%	4%	5%	63%	0%
Washington and Lee University (VA)	58%	7%	N/A	5%	3%	25%	2%	33%	1%
Albany Law School-Union University (NY)	57%	5%	11%	16%	2%	6%	2%	86%	1%
Brigham Young University (Clark) (UT)	57%	3%	11%	11%	1%	15%	3%	44%	1%
John Marshall Law School (IL)	57%	14%	7%	17%	2%	2%	2%	90%	0%
Thomas Jefferson School of Law (CA)	57%	24%	0%	9%	3%	3%	3%	70%	1%
Willamette University (Collins) (OR)	57%	14%	0%	18%	2%	6%	1%	57%	0%
Brooklyn Law School (NY)	56%	11%	4%	16%	3%	7%	1%	83%	1%
Nova Southeastern University (Broad) (FL)	56%	12%	N/A	17%	6%	3%	2%	88%	0%
Southern Illinois University–Carbondale	56%	2%	4%	27%	10%	0%	1%	77%	0%

Where do graduates work?

School	% employed by law firms	% employed in business and industry (in legal jobs)	% employed in business and industry (in nonlegal jobs)	% employed in government	% employed in public interest jobs	% employed in judicial clerkships	% employed in academia	% employed in law school's state	% employed in foreign countries
Stetson University (FL)	56%	8%	0%	18%	11%	4%	3%	85%	0%
University of Pittsburgh	56%	12%	8%	11%	3%	6%	3%	72%	2%
University of the District of Columbia (Clarke)	56%	15%	N/A	3%	17%	3%	6%	39%	N/A
Duquesne University (PA)	55%	14%	1%	12%	0%	12%	1%	79%	0%
Indiana University–Bloomington	55%	14%	0%	14%	3%	9%	4%	39%	1%
Loyola University Chicago	55%	1%	16%	13%	6%	8%	2%	88%	0%
Northern Illinois University	55%	10%	N/A	24%	4%	4%	3%	81%	0%
Ohio Northern University (Pettit)	55%	0%	11%	17%	2%	6%	4%	40%	0%
Santa Clara University (CA)	55%	11%	7%	9%	2%	2%	0%	79%	0%
Touro College (Fuchsberg) (NY)	55%	9%	11%	19%	1%	5%	0%	89%	1%
University of Missouri–Kansas City	55%	7%	3%	10%	7%	12%	1%	77%	1%
University of Utah (S.J. Quinney)	55%	10%	9%	10%	3%	11%	2%	75%	0%
University of Wisconsin–Madison	55%	3%	13%	11%	7%	7%	4%	58%	2%
University of South Carolina	54%	4%	2%	9%	4%	27%	1%	86%	1%
University of Kentucky	53%	5%	1%	16%	2%	22%	1%	75%	0%
University of Minnesota–Twin Cities	53%	11%	0%	7%	4%	23%	0%	59%	2%
University of Missouri–Columbia	53%	15%	N/A	17%	3%	11%	1%	85%	0%
Whittier Law School (CA)	53%	9%	18%	10%	5%	0%	5%	89%	2%
Case Western Reserve University (OH)	52%	7%	9%	12%	6%	4%	6%	56%	1%
Ohio State University (Moritz)	52%	8%	6%	15%	3%	12%	4%	71%	1%
Pace University (NY)	52%	26%	0%	13%	2%	5%	2%	78%	2%
Roger Williams University (Papitto) (RI)	52%	11%	N/A	11%	9%	14%	3%	46%	3%
Texas Wesleyan University	52%	17%	0%	14%	4%	2%	5%	N/A	N/A
University of Colorado–Boulder	52%	10%	0%	12%	7%	16%	4%	79%	0%
University of the Pacific (McGeorge) (CA)	52%	1%	11%	14%	12%	6%	3%	89%	0%
Creighton University (NE)	51%	15%	5%	16%	6%	6%	1%	61%	0%
George Washington University (DC)	51%	5%	N/A	17%	4%	11%	1%	42%	2%
Gonzaga University (WA)	51%	2%	12%	16%	4%	11%	4%	62%	0%
Southwestern University School of Law (CA)	51%	21%	N/A	6%	4%	2%	2%	84%	0%
Suffolk University (MA)	51%	9%	12%	11%	2%	10%	1%	71%	0%
University of Kansas	51%	8%	4%	20%	4%	9%	3%	53%	1%
University of Richmond (VA)	51%	14%	1%	8%	3%	21%	1%	71%	1%
Indiana University–Indianapolis	50%	3%	13%	11%	3%	4%	4%	88%	0%
Oklahoma City University	50%	17%	N/A	22%	0%	1%	1%	56%	0%
Seattle University	50%	26%	0%	11%	6%	4%	3%	90%	1%
University of Connecticut	50%	3%	11%	11%	4%	18%	3%	62%	1%
University of Denver (Sturm)	50%	4%	9%	17%	2%	11%	1%	76%	1%
University of Washington	50%	7%	N/A	18%	4%	16%	4%	74%	1%
Arizona State University	49%	3%	3%	24%	6%	10%	5%	81%	0%
Florida Coastal School of Law	49%	14%	0%	19%	11%	1%	2%	81%	1%
Michigan State University	49%	17%	0%	12%	4%	10%	6%	55%	3%
Syracuse University (NY)	49%	6%	6%	14%	4%	18%	2%	45%	3%
University of San Francisco	49%	5%	19%	12%	5%	4%	1%	79%	0%
Capital University (OH)	48%	10%	7%	24%	8%	2%	1%	94%	0%
Golden Gate University (CA)	48%	18%	0%	7%	8%	3%	5%	63%	1%
Hamline University (MN)	48%	4%	15%	8%	5%	18%	1%	82%	1%
Temple University (Beasley) (PA)	48%	6%	11%	14%	7%	9%	2%	77%	1%
University of Montana	48%	5%	5%	12%	2%	28%	0%	75%	1%
University of North Dakota	48%	12%	N/A	8%	8%	24%	N/A	65%	N/A
Washburn University (KS)	48%	6%	14%	19%	6%	6%	N/A	65%	1%
Barry University (FL)	47%	18%	N/A	22%	6%	0%	4%	96%	0%

Where do graduates work?

School	% employed by law firms	% employed in business and industry (in legal jobs)	% employed in business and industry (in nonlegal jobs)	% employed in government	% employed in public interest jobs	% employed in judicial clerkships	% employed in academia	% employed in law school's state	% employed in foreign countries
University of Wyoming	47%	5%	0%	22%	5%	22%	0%	63%	0%
Howard University (DC)	46%	5%	5%	12%	9%	16%	4%	42%	3%
Lewis and Clark College (Northwestern) (OR)	46%	11%	N/A	17%	11%	14%	1%	61%	1%
University of Cincinnati	46%	13%	0%	12%	6%	15%	6%	64%	2%
University of South Dakota	46%	6%	N/A	19%	2%	27%	N/A	63%	0%
Northern Kentucky University (Chase)	45%	24%	0%	13%	9%	6%	3%	41%	0%
Thomas M. Cooley Law School (MI)	45%	16%	N/A	18%	10%	8%	3%	N/A	N/A
University of Maine	45%	3%	15%	15%	6%	15%	1%	77%	0%
Yale University (CT)	45%	0%	2%	3%	5%	43%	2%	7%	2%
Florida State University	44%	1%	5%	32%	5%	8%	2%	81%	0%
George Mason University (VA)	44%	10%	4%	19%	6%	13%	4%	47%	1%
Rutgers State University–Newark (NJ)	44%	3%	10%	4%	4%	33%	2%	70%	1%
University of Akron (OH)	44%	2%	18%	17%	4%	6%	8%	83%	0%
University of Arizona (Rogers)	44%	4%	3%	28%	3%	20%	1%	68%	0%
University of Baltimore	43%	15%	N/A	16%	1%	23%	2%	N/A	N/A
University of Toledo (OH)	43%	14%	0%	15%	7%	11%	6%	68%	0%
University of Oregon	42%	5%	6%	17%	7%	18%	5%	51%	1%
University of St. Thomas (MN)	42%	12%	N/A	8%	15%	18%	2%	80%	2%
William Mitchell College of Law (MN)	42%	5%	22%	13%	7%	8%	1%	90%	0%
Quinnipiac University (CT)	41%	13%	8%	19%	1%	7%	3%	78%	0%
Regent University (VA)	41%	0%	20%	17%	9%	7%	6%	61%	0%
New England School of Law (MA)	40%	10%	12%	11%	1%	6%	0%	60%	1%
Seton Hall University (NJ)	40%	13%	1%	5%	1%	40%	0%	80%	0%
Vermont Law School	40%	18%	0%	12%	13%	14%	3%	25%	0%
American University (Washington) (DC)	39%	16%	5%	13%	11%	15%	1%	48%	1%
New York Law School	39%	13%	4%	13%	4%	7%	1%	71%	1%
Pennsylvania State University (Dickinson)	39%	12%	0%	17%	5%	23%	0%	51%	0%
Western New England College (MA)	39%	5%	24%	17%	3%	11%	1%	45%	0%
Widener University (DE)	39%	3%	19%	14%	2%	19%	1%	18%	0%
Northeastern University (MA)	37%	8%	0%	17%	18%	18%	2%	66%	1%
University of Idaho	37%	0%	5%	20%	8%	28%	2%	53%	1%
University of New Mexico	37%	6%	0%	24%	20%	12%	0%	84%	0%
CUNY–Queens College	34%	5%	4%	12%	26%	12%	5%	70%	2%
Rutgers State University–Camden (NJ)	33%	7%	6%	6%	2%	40%	1%	56%	0%
Catholic University of America (Columbus) (DC)	32%	13%	8%	26%	3%	11%	0%	49%	0%
University of Maryland	32%	9%	6%	22%	6%	19%	7%	70%	1%
Ave Maria School of Law (MI)	29%	27%	N/A	27%	2%	13%	2%	24%	2%
University of Hawaii (Richardson)	23%	8%	N/A	14%	9%	41%	5%	87%	2%

The U.S.News & World Report

Ultimate Law School Directory

How to use the directory

In the following pages, you'll find exhaustive profiles of the country's American Bar Association–accredited law schools, based on a survey that *U.S. News* conducts each year. The directory is organized by state, and schools are presented alphabetically within each state. The online version of the directory at www.usnews.com allows you to do a customized search of our database. Want to know which law schools specialize in tax law and are located within 100 miles of your home? Enter those criteria and pull up a list.

The vital statistics shown in each directory entry are explained below. The data were collected from the schools during late 2003 and early 2004. If a law school did not supply the data requested, you'll see a N/A, for "not available." If a school did not return the full *U.S. News* questionnaire, it appears at the end of the directory on page 482 with limited information, gathered by calling the schools and consulting their websites.

Addresses and Essential Stats

In addition to the law school's address and the year the school was founded, you'll find key facts and figures here.

Website: Use the website to research the law school's programs.

Tuition: Figures cited for tuition are for the 2005–2006 academic year.

Enrollment: The number represents full-time students during the 2005–2006 academic year.

U.S. News ranking: A school's overall rank, shown in the lower-right-hand corner of the gray

box, indicates where it sits among its peers in the 2007 ranking of law schools published by *U.S. News* at www.usnews.com and in its annual guide "America's Best Graduate Schools." Law schools among the top 100 are ranked numerically. Other schools are grouped in tiers. The school's ranking in various specialty areas (clinical training, dispute resolution, environmental law, healthcare law, intellectual property law, international law, tax law, and trial advocacy) is presented as well.

GPA and LSAT: The Law School Admission Test scores and grade point averages shown are for the Fall 2005 entering class and represent the range within which half of the students scored. In other words, 25 percent of students scored at or below the lower end of the range, and 25 percent scored at or above the upper end of the range.

Acceptance rate: The percentage of applicants accepted is provided for the full-time class entering in Fall 2005.

Admissions

Use the admissions phone number or the admissions email address to request information or an application. Many law schools also allow you to complete and submit an application online.

Application deadline: The application deadline for Fall 2007 admission is reported. Some schools allow students to enter at times other than the fall term; those entry points are also listed.

Applicants and acceptees: The admissions statistics provided—numbers of applicants and people accepted, and their credentials—are for the fall

2003 entering class. If the law school has a part-time option, the admissions data is presented for both full-time and part-time programs.

Financial Aid

Call the financial aid office with questions or requests for applications. Note that the deadlines for a school's financial aid form may not be the same as deadlines to apply for federal and state aid.

Tuition and other expenses: The tuition figures are for the 2005–2006 academic year. For public schools, we list both in-state and out-of-state tuition and the estimated cost of books and other miscellaneous living expenses. Whether or not the university offers student housing for law students is also noted.

Financial aid profile: The data on financial aid packages are for the 2004–2005 academic year. Grants are awarded by the university to full- or part-time students who either show need or have excellent academic records. We also list here the average amount of law-school debt borrowers in the Class of 2005 graduated with, and the proportion of students who took out at least one loan.

Academic Programs

Calendar: We tell you whether the school operates on a traditional semester schedule or a quarter system.

Joint degrees awarded: Many law students pursue a second degree in another university department to marry their interests or gain an edge in the job market. One common joint degree, the JD/MBA, combines law and business. Some people get a JD and master's or PhD degree in any of a number of arts or humanities or science disciplines. Other degree combos include the JD/MD (medicine) and the JD/MPH (public health).

Curricular offerings: What are the classes like? This section provides information on the size of both first-year and upper-level classes as well as the breadth of the curriculum during the 2004–2005 academic year. (If the school has a part-time program, its data is broken out.) If first-year students have the opportunity to take a class other than Legal Writing in a small section, that fact is noted. While the first-year curriculum is standard at most schools, the offerings in the second and third year vary widely. The number of course titles refers only to classroom courses offered, not to clinical or field placement offerings. Class-size figures include full- and part-time programs and exclude seminars.

Areas of specialization: A school listed any of the following: appellate advocacy, clinical training, dispute resolution, environmental law, healthcare law, intellectual property law, international law, tax law, and trial advocacy.

Faculty profile: Here, you'll find the total number of full-time tenured or tenure-track faculty (not including professors on leave or on sabbatical) plus part-time faculty during 2005–2006, as well as a breakdown. Part-timers include adjuncts, permanent part-time, and emeritus part-time. The student/faculty ratio (for Fall 2005) gives some indication of how accessible professors are likely to be.

Special programs: The text describing special programs was written by the schools. *U.S. News* edited this text for style but did not verify the information.

Student Body

What will your classmates be like? This section supplies the breakdown of full-time and part-time students, the male and female enrollments, and the ethnic makeup of the student body. All figures are for the 2005–2006 academic year. Note that students who did not identify themselves as members of any demographic group are classified by schools as "White" and that numbers may not add up to 100 percent because of rounding.

Attrition rates: The attrition rates indicate the percentage of students who chose not to come back to the law school during the 2004–2005 academic year. Students who transferred or left for health or financial reasons are included in the count. The percentage of full- and part-time students who left the law school during the 2004–2005 academic year is broken down by gender and by their year in school.

Library resources: In this section, you'll find key stats about the size of the library's collection at the end of the 2004–2005 academic year. Titles are those items that have their own bibliographic record. Subscriptions refers to active subscriptions, regardless of format, for which the library maintains an active record. Total volumes includes any printed, typewritten, mimeographed, or processed work including microforms that are contained in a single binding. The total number of seats includes carrel and non-carrel seats.

Information technology: How many wired network connections are available to students? Is there a wireless network? How many users can access the wireless network at the same time? Are students required to lease or own a computer? These questions are answered in this section.

Employment and Salaries

This section provides data on the employment status of the 2004 graduating class both at the time of their graduation and nine months later. (Some schools did not know the status or location of all graduates, so the data may not be a complete reflection of the graduating class.) Salary information is provided for graduates working in the private sector, which includes law firms and any for-profit company. We also list the median salary and the 25th–75th percentile salary range. Salary figures are also listed for the public service sector, which includes government, judicial clerkships, academic posts, and non-profit jobs.

Occupational breakdown by type: The employment data listed here includes both part-time and full-time jobs. Graduates working in the government are employed by federal, state, or local entities. Public interest work includes Legal Aid groups and other non-profits. The unknown category includes graduates who reported to the school that they were employed but did not note the type of employment.

Employment location: We show the percentage of 2004 employed graduates who are employed in the same state as the law school, the percentage whose jobs are located outside of the United States, and the number of states in which the remaining graduates work. We also show the percentage employed in each of the following geographic areas: New England (Connecticut, Maine, Massachusetts, New Hampshire, Rhode Island, Vermont); Middle Atlantic (New York, New Jersey, and Pennsylvania); East North Central (Illinois, Indiana, Michigan, Ohio, and Wisconsin); South Atlantic (Delaware, District of Columbia, Florida, Georgia, Maryland, North Carolina, South Carolina, Virginia, and West Virginia); East South Central (Alabama, Kentucky, Mississippi, and Tennessee); West South Central (Arkansas,

Louisiana, Oklahoma, and Texas); Mountain (Arizona, Colorado, Idaho, Montana, Nevada, New Mexico, Utah, and Wyoming); and Pacific (Alaska, California, Hawaii, Oregon, and Washington).

Bar Passage Rates

Bar passage statistics are based on 2004 graduates taking either the Summer 2004 or Winter 2005 bar exams. Schools reported the bar passage rates and state in which the largest number of their 2004 graduates took the bar exam. So that you can see how a school's graduates fared compared to all first-time test-takers in the state, we also show the state's overall pass rates.

Albany Law School—Union University

- 80 New Scotland Avenue, Albany, NY, 12208-3494
- http://www.als.edu
- Private
- **Year founded:** 1851
- **2005-2006 tuition:** full-time: $30,053; part-time: $22,562
- **Enrollment 2005-06 academic year:** full-time: 702; part-time: 37
- **U.S. News 2007 law specialty ranking:** N/A

2.89-3.53 GPA, 25TH-75TH PERCENTILE

153-157 LSAT, 25TH-75TH PERCENTILE

40% ACCEPTANCE RATE

Tier 3 2007 U.S. NEWS LAW SCHOOL RANKING

ADMISSIONS

Admissions phone number: **(518) 445-2326**
Admissions email address: **admissions@mail.als.edu**
Application website: **N/A**
Application deadline for Fall 2007 admission: **3/15**

Admissions statistics:

Number of applicants for Fall 2005: **2,175**
Number of acceptances: **876**
Number enrolled: **247**
Acceptance rate: **40%**
GPA, 25th-75th percentile, entering class Fall 2005: **2.89-3.53**
LSAT, 25th-75th percentile, entering class Fall 2005: **153-157**

FINANCIAL AID

Financial aid phone number: **(518) 445-2357**
Financial aid application deadline: **N/A**
Tuition 2005-2006 academic year: full-time: **$30,053**; part-time: **$22,562**
Room and board: **$7,400**; books: **$900**; miscellaneous expenses: **$5,000**
Total of room/board/books/miscellaneous expenses: **$13,300**
University does not offer graduate student housing for which law students are eligible.

Financial aid profile

Percent of students that received grants for the 2004-2005 academic year: full-time: **37%**; part-time **59%**
Median grant amount: full-time: **$12,000**; part-time: **$4,700**
The average law-school debt of those in the Class of 2005 who borrowed: **$80,005**. Proportion who borrowed: **87%**

ACADEMIC PROGRAMS

Calendar: **semester**
Joint degrees awarded: **J.D./M.B.A.; J.D./M.P.A.; J.D./M.R.P.**
Typical first-year section size: Full-time: **69**

Is there typically a "small section" of the first year class, other than Legal Writing, taught by full-time faculty?: Full-time: **yes**
Number of course titles, beyond the first year curriculum, offered last year: **117**
Percentages of upper division course sections, excluding seminars, with an enrollment of:
Under 25: **55%**   25 to 49: **23%**
50 to 74: **10%**   75 to 99: **4%**
100+: **9%**
Areas of specialization: appellate advocacy, clinical training, dispute resolution, environmental law, healthcare law, intellectual property law, international law, tax law, trial advocacy

Fall 2005 faculty profile

Total teaching faculty: **87**. Full-time: **47%**; **51%** men, **49%** women, **12%** minorities. Part-time: **53%**; **76%** men, **24%** women, **7%** minorities
Student-to-faculty ratio: **14.8**

SPECIAL PROGRAMS (as provided by law school):

The Clinical Legal Studies Program provides free legal services to eligible clients in New York's capital region. Law students work closely with clinical faculty and practicing attorneys in projects addressing legal concerns related to AIDS and other chronic health conditions; civil rights and disabilities; domestic violence; disputes with the Internal Revenue Service; unemployment insurance issues; and securities arbitration matters. The Field Placement Program provides placement for credit to students with state and federal courts; government agencies; and not-for-profit organizations. Over three-quarters of our students elect to participate in clinical programs during their second or third year of study.

The Government Law Center promotes interdisciplinary study and research in the problems facing government; introduces law students to methods of policy analysis and to public service; and serves as a resource to government at all levels. The law school's Summer in Government program is a unique opportunity for law students from across the country to explore New York State government via customized internships.

Semester in Government and Semester in Practice programs place students in semester-long, full-time legal internships in state and federal government agencies and public-interest organizations in Albany and Washington, D.C.

Students also have the opportunity to provide legal services to start-up ventures and early-stage technology companies throughout New York by working with attorneys at the law school's Science and Technology Law Center.

The International Law Society organizes conferences and a speaker series, and multiple study abroad options foster the study of international law.

The International Human Rights Internship Program awards stipends to students who secure summer internships in human-rights law outside the United States. Summer study is also available in Nairobi, Kenya. The University of Paris Exchange Program offers a semester focusing on international and comparative law.

Albany Law School's curriculum includes an innovative professional skills program that arms students with tools to serve clients. The cornerstone of the program is Introduction to Lawyering, a course in which first-year students are assigned a hypothetical case with transactional and litigation elements. Second- and third-year students continue to hone their pretrial lawyering skills in advanced simulation courses.

The Academic Success Program (ASP) is an integral part of Albany Law School's commitment to provide the opportunity for all students to succeed in law school. The ASP is a collaborative effort involving law school administration, faculty and students with the goal of assisting students in developing and enhancing the critical skills necessary for academic success in school, success on the bar exam and as an attorney. Our academic support services are coordinated by the Associate Professor of Academic Success.

STUDENT BODY

Fall 2005 full-time enrollment: 702

Men: 50%	Women: 50%
African-American: 4.4%	American Indian: 0.0%
Asian-American: 6.4%	Mexican-American: 0.6%
Puerto Rican: 1.4%	Other Hisp-Amer: 2.4%
White: 81.5%	International: 1.9%
Unknown: 1.4%	

Fall 2005 part-time enrollment: 37

Men: 46%	Women: 54%
African-American: 5.4%	American Indian: 0.0%
Asian-American: 2.7%	Mexican-American: 0.0%
Puerto Rican: 0.0%	Other Hisp-Amer: 2.7%
White: 86.5%	International: 0.0%
Unknown: 2.7%	

Attrition rates for 2004-2005 full-time students

Percent of students discontinuing law school:

Men: 1%	Women: 2%
First-year students: 3%	Second-year students: 0%
Third-year students: N/A	

LIBRARY RESOURCES

The library holds 101,502 and receives 3,061 current subscriptions.

Total volumes: 660,074

Percentage of the titles in the online catalog: 100%

Total seats available for library users: 472

INFORMATION TECHNOLOGY

Number of wired network connections available to students: 866 total (in the law library, excluding computer labs: 129; in classrooms: 700; in computer labs: 2; elsewhere in the law school: 35)

Law school has a wireless network.

Approximate number of simultaneous users that can be accommodated on wireless network: 425

Students are not required to own a computer.

EMPLOYMENT AND SALARIES

Proportion of 2004 graduates employed at graduation: 53%

Employed 9 months later, as of February 15, 2005: 96%

Salaries in the private sector (law firms, business, industry): $40,000–$60,000 (25th-75th percentile)

Median salary in the private sector: $48,000

Percentage in the private sector who reported salary information: 85%

Median salary in public service (government, judicial clerkships, academic posts, non-profits): $48,000

Percentage of 2004 graduates in:

Law firms: 57%	Bus./industry (legal): 5%
Bus./industry (nonlegal): 11%	Government: 16%
Public interest: 2%	Judicial clerkship: 6%
Academia : 2%	Unknown: 0%

2004 graduates employed in-state: 86%

2004 graduates employed in foreign countries: 1%

Number of states where graduates are employed: 15

Percentage of 2004 graduates working in: New England: 2%, Middle Atlantic: 91%, East North Central: 1%, West North Central: 0%, South Atlantic: 2%, East South Central: 1%, West South Central: 1%, Mountain: 1%, Pacific: 1%, Unknown: 0%

BAR PASSAGE RATES

Based on 2004 graduates taking Summer 2004 or Winter 2005 exams. Most of the school's first-time test takers took the bar in New York.

78%

School's bar passage rate for first-time test takers

75%

Statewide bar passage rate for first-time test takers

American University (Washington)

- 4801 Massachusetts Avenue NW, Washington, DC, 20016-8192
- http://www.wcl.american.edu
- Private
- Year founded: 1896
- 2005-2006 tuition: full-time: $33,134; part-time: $1,202/credit hour
- Enrollment 2005-06 academic year: full-time: 1,128; part-time: 276
- U.S. News 2007 law specialty ranking: clinical training: 2, international law: 7, trial advocacy: 11

3.20-3.66 GPA, 25ᵀᴴ-75ᵀᴴ PERCENTILE

160-163 LSAT, 25ᵀᴴ-75ᵀᴴ PERCENTILE

24% ACCEPTANCE RATE

43 2007 U.S. NEWS LAW SCHOOL RANKING

ADMISSIONS

Admissions phone number: **(202) 274-4101**
Admissions email address: **wcladmit@wcl.american.edu**
Application website: **http://www.wcl.american.edu/admiss/**
Application deadline for Fall 2007 admission: **3/01**

Admissions statistics:

Number of applicants for Fall 2005: **7,710**
Number of acceptances: **1,849**
Number enrolled: **365**
Acceptance rate: **24%**
GPA, 25th-75th percentile, entering class Fall 2005: **3.20-3.66**
LSAT, 25th-75th percentile, entering class Fall 2005: **160-163**

Part-time program:

Number of applicants for Fall 2005: **1,154**
Number of acceptances: **217**
Number enrolled: **99**
Acceptance rate: **19%**
GPA, 25th-75th percentile, entering class Fall 2005: **3.08-3.57**
LSAT, 25th-75th percentile, entering class Fall 2005: **154-160**

FINANCIAL AID

Financial aid phone number: **(202) 274-4040**
Financial aid application deadline: **3/01**
Tuition 2005-2006 academic year: full-time: **$33,134**; part-time: **$1,202/credit hour**
Room and board: **$11,754**; books: **$950**; miscellaneous expenses: **$4,655**
Total of room/board/books/miscellaneous expenses: **$17,359**
University offers graduate student housing for which law students are eligible.

Financial aid profile

Percent of students that received grants for the 2004-2005 academic year: full-time: **34%**; part-time **7%**
Median grant amount: full-time: **$8,000**; part-time: **$2,800**

The average law-school debt of those in the Class of 2005 who borrowed: **$102,954**. Proportion who borrowed: **84%**

ACADEMIC PROGRAMS

Calendar: **semester**
Joint degrees awarded: **J.D./M.A.; J.D./M.B.A.; J.D./M.S.**
Typical first-year section size: Full-time: **91**; Part-time: **94**
Is there typically a "small section" of the first year class, other than Legal Writing, taught by full-time faculty?: Full-time: **yes**; Part-time: **yes**
Number of course titles, beyond the first year curriculum, offered last year: **292**
Percentages of upper division course sections, excluding seminars, with an enrollment of:

Under 25: **58%**	25 to 49: **23%**
50 to 74: **9%**	75 to 99: **9%**
100+: **0%**	

Areas of specialization: appellate advocacy, clinical training, dispute resolution, environmental law, healthcare law, intellectual property law, international law, tax law, trial advocacy

Fall 2005 faculty profile

Total teaching faculty: **273**. Full-time: **32%**; **48%** men, **52%** women, **17%** minorities. Part-time: **68%**; **65%** men, **35%** women, **12%** minorities
Student-to-faculty ratio: **14.3**

SPECIAL PROGRAMS (as provided by law school):

Available clinical experiences include: landlord-tenant and small-claims court; civil practice; women and the law; domestic violence; tax; international human rights; intellectual property; criminal justice; and community and economic development.

The law school has centers and programs in human rights and humanitarian law, international environmental law, women and the law, Innocence Project, international arbitration and Graduate Programs for foreign lawyers in International Legal Studies and Law and Government; Summer study opportunities are available on campus and abroad. In addition to the general summer curriculum, the Human Rights Academy offers a 10-week summer session in English and Spanish. Other summer sessions are offered in Environmental Law and International Arbitration.

Study abroad programs include summers in Chile, Argentina, London, Paris, Geneva, and Istanbul; students can spend one semester abroad in more than 18 countries. The law school has JD dual degree programs with schools in Spain, Canada and France. Other opportunities include impact litigation before the Inter-American system, work in Geneva with the UNCAT Committee, War Crimes Research Office, international and local externships, Moot Court competitions in the U.S. and in France, among others.

STUDENT BODY

Fall 2005 full-time enrollment: 1,128

Men: 42%	Women: 58%
African-American: 7.1%	American Indian: 0.8%
Asian-American: 12.6%	Mexican-American: 2.7%
Puerto Rican: 0.6%	Other Hisp-Amer: 9.5%
White: 65.2%	International: 0.8%
Unknown: 0.8%	

Fall 2005 part-time enrollment: 276

Men: 48%	Women: 52%
African-American: 11.6%	American Indian: 0.4%
Asian-American: 10.9%	Mexican-American: 0.7%
Puerto Rican: 0.7%	Other Hisp-Amer: 4.7%
White: 67.8%	International: 0.4%
Unknown: 2.9%	

Attrition rates for 2004-2005 full-time students

Percent of students discontinuing law school:

Men: 3%	Women: 2%
First-year students: 8%	Second-year students: 1%
Third-year students: 0%	

LIBRARY RESOURCES

The library holds 234,826 and receives 6,729 current subscriptions.
Total volumes: 568,391
Percentage of the titles in the online catalog: 100%
Total seats available for library users: 672

INFORMATION TECHNOLOGY

Number of wired network connections available to students: 1,664 total (in the law library, excluding computer labs: 390; in classrooms: 1,076; in computer labs: 78; elsewhere in the law school: 120)
Law school has a wireless network.
Approximate number of simultaneous users that can be accommodated on wireless network: 1,440
Students are not required to own a computer.

EMPLOYMENT AND SALARIES

Proportion of 2004 graduates employed at graduation: 83%
Employed 9 months later, as of February 15, 2005: 97%
Salaries in the private sector (law firms, business, industry): $50,000–$115,000 (25th-75th percentile)
Median salary in the private sector: $72,108
Percentage in the private sector who reported salary information: 79%
Median salary in public service (government, judicial clerkships, academic posts, non-profits): $45,000

Percentage of 2004 graduates in:

Law firms: 39%	Bus./industry (legal): 16%
Bus./industry (nonlegal): 5%	Government: 13%
Public interest: 11%	Judicial clerkship: 15%
Academia : 1%	Unknown: 0%

2004 graduates employed in-state: 48%
2004 graduates employed in foreign countries: 1%
Number of states where graduates are employed: 24
Percentage of 2004 graduates working in: New England: 4%, Middle Atlantic: 11%, East North Central: 2%, West North Central: 0%, South Atlantic: 75%, East South Central: 0%, West South Central: 1%, Mountain: 2%, Pacific: 4%, Unknown: 0%

BAR PASSAGE RATES

Based on 2004 graduates taking Summer 2004 or Winter 2005 exams. Most of the school's first-time test takers took the bar in Maryland.

85%
School's bar passage rate for first-time test takers

72%
Statewide bar passage rate for first-time test takers

Arizona State University

- Box 877906, Tempe, AZ, 85287-7906
- http://www.law.asu.edu
- Public
- Year founded: 1969
- 2005-2006 tuition: In-state: full-time: $12,907, part-time: N/A; Out-of-state: full-time: $22,089
- Enrollment 2005-06 academic year: full-time: 650
- U.S. News 2007 law specialty ranking: N/A

3.10-3.69 GPA, 25TH-75TH PERCENTILE

154-161 LSAT, 25TH-75TH PERCENTILE

27% ACCEPTANCE RATE

53 2007 U.S. NEWS LAW SCHOOL RANKING

ADMISSIONS

Admissions phone number: **(480) 965-1474**
Admissions email address: **law.admissions@asu.edu**
Application website: **http://www.asu.edu/gradapp**
Application deadline for Fall 2007 admission: **2/15**

Admissions statistics:

Number of applicants for Fall 2005: **3,039**
Number of acceptances: **831**
Number enrolled: **256**
Acceptance rate: **27%**
GPA, 25th-75th percentile, entering class Fall 2005: **3.10-3.69**
LSAT, 25th-75th percentile, entering class Fall 2005: **154-161**

FINANCIAL AID

Financial aid phone number: **(480) 965-1474**
Financial aid application deadline: **3/01**
Tuition 2005-2006 academic year: In-state: full-time: **$12,907**, part-time: N/A; Out-of-state: full-time: **$22,089**
Room and board: **$8,354**; books: **$1,100**; miscellaneous expenses: **$4,680**
Total of room/board/books/miscellaneous expenses: **$14,134**
University offers graduate student housing for which law students are eligible.

Financial aid profile

Percent of students that received grants for the 2004-2005 academic year: full-time: **40%**
Median grant amount: full-time: **$1,727**
The average law-school debt of those in the Class of 2005 who borrowed: **$50,234**. Proportion who borrowed: **83%**

ACADEMIC PROGRAMS

Calendar: **semester**
Joint degrees awarded: **J.D./M.B.A.; J.D./Ph.D in Justice Studies; J.D./MD; J.D./MHSM; J.D./MS in Economics; J.D./Ph.D Law and Psychology**
Typical first-year section size: Full-time: **105**

Is there typically a "small section" of the first year class, other than Legal Writing, taught by full-time faculty?: Full-time: **yes**
Number of course titles, beyond the first year curriculum, offered last year: **113**
Percentages of upper division course sections, excluding seminars, with an enrollment of:
Under 25: **59%**   25 to 49: **30%**
50 to 74: **5%**   75 to 99: **5%**
100+: **1%**
Areas of specialization: appellate advocacy, clinical training, dispute resolution, environmental law, healthcare law, intellectual property law, international law, tax law, trial advocacy

Fall 2005 faculty profile

Total teaching faculty: **65**. Full-time: **49%**; **81%** men, **19%** women, **25%** minorities. Part-time: **51%**; **85%** men, **15%** women, **0%** minorities
Student-to-faculty ratio: **11.1**

SPECIAL PROGRAMS (as provided by law school):

The Center for the Study of Law, Science, and Technology is the oldest, largest and most comprehensive center focusing on the intersection of law and science in the country. Students may pursue specialized certificates in environmental law, genomics and biotechnology, health care law, and intellectual property. Center Faculty Fellows are distinguished, science-trained law faculty who co-publish with the American Bar Association, the prestigious, peer-refereed Jurimetrics: The Journal of Law, Science, and Technology, the oldest and most-widely circulated journal in the field of law and science.

The highly respected Indian Legal Program offers more than a dozen Indian law courses that provide the necessary foundation for practice in Indian law. An extraordinary faculty and long-term partnerships with tribal governments buttress the College's reputation in this area. More than 30 of the College's students are Native American, representing 20 tribes.

The College has developed a significant strength in International Law with 11 highly respected faculty members. Students can focus on the international aspects of Commercial

Law, Homeland Security, Human Rights, Immigration, Intellectual Property and Biotechnology, Public International Law, Tax, Trade, and Treaty Negotiation.

Recent additions to the innovative Joint Degree programs include: The J.D./M.D. with Mayo Medical School in Rochester, Minnesota and the J.D./Ph.D. in psychology.

ASU College of Law offers three cutting edge Graduate Programs programs: LL.M. in biotechnology and genomics, the first of its kind in the world; LL.M. in tribal policy, law, and government, and MLS (master of legal studies) program for non-lawyers.

The Clinical Program is one of the nation's most comprehensive with seven live-client clinics: Civil Justice Clinic, Criminal Practice Clinic, Immigration Law & Policy Clinic, Indian Legal Clinic, Mediation Clinic, Public Defender Clinic and Technology Ventures Clinic.

The Legal Research and Writing Program faculty provides intensive instruction to first year law students. Upper-level students can take advantage of advanced research and writing courses.

The College is home to the Committee on Law and Philosophy which creates and maintains an active intellectual community in such areas as criminal law theory, punishment, forgiveness, constitutional interpretation, human rights theory, law and literature, law and religion, and political obligation.

STUDENT BODY

Fall 2005 full-time enrollment: 650

Men: 56%	Women: 44%
African-American: 3.5%	American Indian: 4.6%
Asian-American: 4.2%	Mexican-American: 1.4%
Puerto Rican: 0.0%	Other Hisp-Amer: 13.2%
White: 64.0%	International: 1.4%
Unknown: 7.7%	

Attrition rates for 2004-2005 full-time students
Percent of students discontinuing law school:

Men: 3%	Women: 5%
First-year students: 6%	Second-year students: 6%
Third-year students: N/A	

LIBRARY RESOURCES

The library holds 118,905 and receives 4,031 current subscriptions.
Total volumes: 413,877
Percentage of the titles in the online catalog: 100%
Total seats available for library users: 530

INFORMATION TECHNOLOGY

Number of wired network connections available to students: 44 total (in the law library, excluding computer labs: 20; in classrooms: 10; in computer labs: 12; elsewhere in the law school: 2)
Law school has a wireless network.
Approximate number of simultaneous users that can be accommodated on wireless network: 1,000
Students are not required to own a computer.

EMPLOYMENT AND SALARIES

Proportion of 2004 graduates employed at graduation: N/A
Employed 9 months later, as of February 15, 2005: 94%
Salaries in the private sector (law firms, business, industry): $60,000–$95,000 (25th-75th percentile)
Median salary in the private sector: $70,000
Percentage in the private sector who reported salary information: 64%
Median salary in public service (government, judicial clerkships, academic posts, non-profits): $51,000

Percentage of 2004 graduates in:

Law firms: 49%	Bus./industry (legal): 3%
Bus./industry (nonlegal): 3%	Government: 24%
Public interest: 6%	Judicial clerkship: 10%
Academia : 5%	Unknown: 0%

2004 graduates employed in-state: 81%
2004 graduates employed in foreign countries: 0%
Number of states where graduates are employed: 18
Percentage of 2004 graduates working in: New England: 0%, Middle Atlantic: 0%, East North Central: 4%, West North Central: 1%, South Atlantic: 2%, East South Central: 0%, West South Central: 2%, Mountain: 86%, Pacific: 4%, Unknown: 0%

BAR PASSAGE RATES

Based on 2004 graduates taking Summer 2004 or Winter 2005 exams. Most of the school's first-time test takers took the bar in Arizona.

75%
School's bar passage rate for first-time test takers

74%
Statewide bar passage rate for first-time test takers

Ave Maria School of Law

- 3475 Plymouth Road, Ann Arbor, MI, 48105-2550
- http://www.avemarialaw.edu
- Private
- Year founded: 2000
- 2005-2006 tuition: full-time: $29,700; part-time: N/A
- Enrollment 2005-06 academic year: full-time: 360
- U.S. News 2007 law specialty ranking: N/A

2.80-3.50 GPA, 25TH-75TH PERCENTILE

150-160 LSAT, 25TH-75TH PERCENTILE

67% ACCEPTANCE RATE

Tier 4 2007 U.S. NEWS LAW SCHOOL RANKING

ADMISSIONS

Admissions phone number: **(734) 827-8063**
Admissions email address: **info@avemarialaw.edu**
Application website:
 http://www.avemarialaw.edu/appl/appStart.cfm
Application deadline for Fall 2007 admission: **4/01**

Admissions statistics:

Number of applicants for Fall 2005: **906**
Number of acceptances: **610**
Number enrolled: **147**
Acceptance rate: **67%**
GPA, 25th-75th percentile, entering class Fall 2005: **2.80-3.50**
LSAT, 25th-75th percentile, entering class Fall 2005: **150-160**

FINANCIAL AID

Financial aid phone number: **(734) 827-8051**
Financial aid application deadline: **6/01**
Tuition 2005-2006 academic year: full-time: **$29,700**; part-time: **N/A**
Room and board: **$12,015**; books: **$1,100**; miscellaneous expenses: **$6,117**
Total of room/board/books/miscellaneous expenses: **$19,232**
University does not offer graduate student housing for which law students are eligible.

Financial aid profile

Percent of students that received grants for the 2004-2005 academic year: full-time: **65%**
Median grant amount: full-time: **$21,900**
The average law-school debt of those in the Class of 2005 who borrowed: **$53,029**. Proportion who borrowed: **76%**

ACADEMIC PROGRAMS

Calendar: **semester**
Joint degrees awarded: **N/A**
Typical first-year section size: Full-time: **75**
Is there typically a "small section" of the first year class, other than Legal Writing, taught by full-time faculty?: Full-time: **no**

Number of course titles, beyond the first year curriculum, offered last year: **67**
Percentages of upper division course sections, excluding seminars, with an enrollment of:

Under 25: **72%**   25 to 49: **27%**
50 to 74: **0%**   75 to 99: **1%**
100+: **0%**

Areas of specialization: appellate advocacy, clinical training, dispute resolution, environmental law, healthcare law, intellectual property law, international law, tax law, trial advocacy

Fall 2005 faculty profile

Total teaching faculty: **30**. Full-time: **53%**; **69%** men, **31%** women, **13%** minorities. Part-time: **47%**; **86%** men, **14%** women, **0%** minorities
Student-to-faculty ratio: **14.0**

SPECIAL PROGRAMS *(as provided by law school):*

Ave Maria School of Law offers students a live-client opportunity through its clinical programs. In the Asylum Clinic, students review the basics of asylum law and procedure and develop various professional skills by representing asylum seekers, by rendering legal assistance to families in immigration matters, and by preparing and submitting appellate briefs for the Board of Immigration Appeals. In the Women's Immigrant Rights Law Clinic, students review the basics of relevant immigration law and procedure focusing on protection of women. Students also develop various professional skills (e.g., interviewing and counseling). In this course, students represent immigrants who have been the victims of domestic violence, sex trafficking, forced sterilization, female genital mutilation and other types of persecution that uniquely impact women. Advanced students in these clinics are eligible to enroll in Advanced Clinical Law.

The Externship Program at Ave Maria allows students to gain valuable hands-on experience while earning academic credit. It is administered by a full-time Externship Coordinator. Rigorous standards ensure that students have rewarding educational experiences. The Program seeks to place students in organizations where practical learning opportunities enhance their professional development. Externs have the choice of pursuing either one or two pass/fail credits for summer or school-year externships, depending on the number of hours spent with the organization. The Program offers a broad array of placements, both within and outside the State of Michigan, including state and federal courts, U. S. Attorneys' offices, state prosecutors' and public defenders' offices, corporations, government agencies, and public interest organizations.

STUDENT BODY

Fall 2005 full-time enrollment: 360

Men: 69%	Women: 31%
African-American: 1.7%	American Indian: 1.4%
Asian-American: 6.1%	Mexican-American: 1.7%
Puerto Rican: 0.3%	Other Hisp-Amer: 3.3%
White: 82.5%	International: 3.1%
Unknown: 0.0%	

Attrition rates for 2004-2005 full-time students
Percent of students discontinuing law school:

Men: 6%	Women: 10%
First-year students: 8%	Second-year students: 11%
Third-year students: N/A	

LIBRARY RESOURCES

The library holds 177,204 and receives 4,501 current subscriptions.
Total volumes: 458,012
Percentage of the titles in the online catalog: 100%
Total seats available for library users: 285

INFORMATION TECHNOLOGY

Number of wired network connections available to students: 569 total (in the law library, excluding computer labs: 215; in classrooms: 294; in computer labs: 22; elsewhere in the law school: 38)
Law school doesn't have a wireless network.
Approximate number of simultaneous users that can be accommodated on wireless network: N/A
Students are not required to own a computer.

EMPLOYMENT AND SALARIES

Proportion of 2004 graduates employed at graduation: 38%
Employed 9 months later, as of February 15, 2005: 85%
Salaries in the private sector (law firms, business, industry): $36,000–$90,000 (25th-75th percentile)
Median salary in the private sector: $46,240
Percentage in the private sector who reported salary information: 51%
Median salary in public service (government, judicial clerkships, academic posts, non-profits): $49,390

Percentage of 2004 graduates in:

Law firms: 29%	Bus./industry (legal): 27%
Bus./industry (nonlegal): N/A	Government: 27%
Public interest: 2%	Judicial clerkship: 13%
Academia : 2%	Unknown: 0%

2004 graduates employed in-state: 24%
2004 graduates employed in foreign countries: 2%
Number of states where graduates are employed: 15
Percentage of 2004 graduates working in: New England: 0%, Middle Atlantic: 5%, East North Central: 34%, West North Central: 2%, South Atlantic: 27%, East South Central: 5%, West South Central: 9%, Mountain: 2%, Pacific: 14%, Unknown: 0%

BAR PASSAGE RATES

Based on 2004 graduates taking Summer 2004 or Winter 2005 exams. Most of the school's first-time test takers took the bar in Michigan.

100%
School's bar passage rate for first-time test takers

74%
Statewide bar passage rate for first-time test takers

Barry University

■ 6441 E. Colonial Drive, Orlando, FL, 32807
■ http://www.barry.edu/law/
■ Private
■ Year founded: 1995
■ 2005-2006 tuition: full-time: $26,000; part-time: $19,600
■ Enrollment 2005-06 academic year: full-time: 351; part-time: 186
■ U.S. News 2007 law specialty ranking: N/A

2.73-3.28 GPA, 25TH-75TH PERCENTILE

149-152 LSAT, 25TH-75TH PERCENTILE

35% ACCEPTANCE RATE

Unranked 2007 U.S. NEWS LAW SCHOOL RANKING

ADMISSIONS

Admissions phone number: **(866) 532-2779**
Admissions email address: **lawinfo@mail.barry.edu**
Application website: **http://www.barry.edu/law/pdf/application.pdf**
Application deadline for Fall 2007 admission: **4/01**

Admissions statistics:

Number of applicants for Fall 2005: **1,960**
Number of acceptances: **681**
Number enrolled: **167**
Acceptance rate: **35%**
GPA, 25th-75th percentile, entering class Fall 2005: **2.73-3.28**
LSAT, 25th-75th percentile, entering class Fall 2005: **149-152**

Part-time program:

Number of applicants for Fall 2005: **138**
Number of acceptances: **78**
Number enrolled: **37**
Acceptance rate: **57%**
GPA, 25th-75th percentile, entering class Fall 2005: **2.71-3.36**
LSAT, 25th-75th percentile, entering class Fall 2005: **149-154**

FINANCIAL AID

Financial aid phone number: **(321) 206-5621**
Financial aid application deadline: **4/01**
Tuition 2005-2006 academic year: full-time: **$26,000**; part-time: **$19,600**
Room and board: **$11,000**; books: **$1,400**; miscellaneous expenses: **$3,900**
Total of room/board/books/miscellaneous expenses: **$16,300**
University does not offer graduate student housing for which law students are eligible.

Financial aid profile

Percent of students that received grants for the 2004-2005 academic year: full-time: **75%**; part-time **52%**
Median grant amount: full-time: **$5,000**; part-time: **$3,300**

The average law-school debt of those in the Class of 2005 who borrowed: **$83,800**. Proportion who borrowed: **85%**

ACADEMIC PROGRAMS

Calendar: **semester**
Joint degrees awarded: **J.D./M.A. Human Resource Development**
Typical first-year section size: Full-time: **80**; Part-time: **40**
Is there typically a "small section" of the first year class, other than Legal Writing, taught by full-time faculty?: Full-time: **no**; Part-time: **no**
Number of course titles, beyond the first year curriculum, offered last year: **61**
Percentages of upper division course sections, excluding seminars, with an enrollment of:
Under 25: **73%**   25 to 49: **21%**
50 to 74: **7%**   75 to 99: **0%**
100+: **0%**
Areas of specialization: appellate advocacy, clinical training, dispute resolution, environmental law, healthcare law, intellectual property law, international law, tax law, trial advocacy

Fall 2005 faculty profile

Total teaching faculty: **31**. Full-time: **71%**; **68%** men, **32%** women, **14%** minorities. Part-time: **29%**; **78%** men, **22%** women, **22%** minorities
Student-to-faculty ratio: **17.9**

SPECIAL PROGRAMS (as provided by law school):

Barry University Dwayne O. Andreas School of Law offers clinical programs focusing on children and families. Students may also obtain a concentration in the area of children and family law by taking a number of courses in the area. We also offer classes in intellectual property, such as trademarks, patents, copyrights, sports law, Internet law, and entertainment law.

STUDENT BODY

Fall 2005 full-time enrollment: 351

Men: **49%**   Women: **51%**
African-American: **3.4%**   American Indian: **2.6%**

Asian-American: 3.1% Mexican-American: 0.0%
Puerto Rican: 0.0% Other Hisp-Amer: 5.7%
White: 71.2% International: 0.0%
Unknown: 14.0%

***Fall 2005 part-time enrollment:* 186**
Men: 52% Women: 48%
African-American: 10.8% American Indian: 1.1%
Asian-American: 4.3% Mexican-American: 0.0%
Puerto Rican: 0.0% Other Hisp-Amer: 10.8%
White: 57.5% International: 0.0%
Unknown: 15.6%

Attrition rates for 2004-2005 full-time students
Percent of students discontinuing law school:
Men: 12% Women: 9%
First-year students: 12% Second-year students: 17%
Third-year students: 1%

LIBRARY RESOURCES
The library holds 110,083 and receives 1,723 current
subscriptions.
Total volumes: 259,018
Percentage of the titles in the online catalog: 100%
Total seats available for library users: 339

INFORMATION TECHNOLOGY
Number of wired network connections available to students: 0 total (in the law library, excluding computer
labs: 0; in classrooms: 0; in computer labs: 0; elsewhere
in the law school: 0)
Law school has a wireless network.
Approximate number of simultaneous users that can be
accommodated on wireless network: 512
Students are not required to own a computer.

EMPLOYMENT AND SALARIES
Proportion of 2004 graduates employed at graduation: N/A
Employed 9 months later, as of February 15, 2005: N/A

Salaries in the private sector (law firms, business, industry): **$40,000–$53,000** (25th-75th percentile)
Median salary in the private sector: **$42,000**
Percentage in the private sector who reported salary
information: 47%
Median salary in public service (government, judicial clerkships, academic posts, non-profits): **$41,608**

Percentage of 2004 graduates in:
Law firms: 47% Bus./industry (legal): 18%
Bus./industry (nonlegal): N/A Government: 22%
Public interest: 6% Judicial clerkship: 0%
Academia : 4% Unknown: 4%

2004 graduates employed in-state: 96%
2004 graduates employed in foreign countries: 0%
Number of states where graduates are employed: 0
Percentage of 2004 graduates working in: New England:
N/A, Middle Atlantic: 2%, East North Central: N/A, West
North Central: N/A, South Atlantic: 98%, East South
Central: N/A, West South Central: N/A, Mountain: N/A,
Pacific: N/A, Unknown: 0%

BAR PASSAGE RATES
Based on 2004 graduates taking Summer 2004 or
Winter 2005 exams. Most of the school's first-time test
takers took the bar in Florida.

51%
School's bar passage rate for first-time test takers

73%
Statewide bar passage rate for first-time test takers

Baylor University

- One Bear Place, Number 97288, Waco, TX, 76798-7288
- http://law.baylor.edu
- Private
- Year founded: 1857
- 2005-2006 tuition: full-time: $28,105; part-time: N/A
- Enrollment 2005-06 academic year: full-time: 435
- U.S. News 2007 law specialty ranking: trial advocacy: 6

3.51-3.92 GPA, 25TH-75TH PERCENTILE

161-165 LSAT, 25TH-75TH PERCENTILE

21% ACCEPTANCE RATE

51 2007 U.S. NEWS LAW SCHOOL RANKING

ADMISSIONS

Admissions phone number: **(254) 710-7617**
Admissions email address: **Becky_Beck@baylor.edu**
Application website:
http://law.baylor.edu/admissions/application_instructions.htm
Application deadline for Fall 2007 admission: **3/01**

Admissions statistics:

Number of applicants for Fall 2005: **2,437**
Number of acceptances: **520**
Number enrolled: **80**
Acceptance rate: **21%**
GPA, 25th-75th percentile, entering class Fall 2005: **3.51-3.92**
LSAT, 25th-75th percentile, entering class Fall 2005: **161-165**

FINANCIAL AID

Financial aid phone number: **(254) 710-2611**
Financial aid application deadline: **N/A**
Tuition 2005-2006 academic year: full-time: **$28,105**; part-time: **N/A**
Room and board: **$9,186**; books: **$1,308**; miscellaneous expenses: **$5,537**
Total of room/board/books/miscellaneous expenses: **$16,031**
University offers graduate student housing for which law students are eligible.

Financial aid profile

Percent of students that received grants for the 2004-2005 academic year: full-time: **88%**
Median grant amount: full-time: **$3,875**
The average law-school debt of those in the Class of 2005 who borrowed: **$80,033**. Proportion who borrowed: **85%**

ACADEMIC PROGRAMS

Calendar: **quarter**
Joint degrees awarded: **J.D./MPPA; J.D./M.B.A.; J.D./MTAX**
Typical first-year section size: Full-time: **57**

Is there typically a "small section" of the first year class, other than Legal Writing, taught by full-time faculty?:
Full-time: **yes**
Number of course titles, beyond the first year curriculum, offered last year: **76**
Percentages of upper division course sections, excluding seminars, with an enrollment of:
Under 25: **53%**   25 to 49: **26%**
50 to 74: **11%**   75 to 99: **9%**
100+: **1%**
Areas of specialization: appellate advocacy, clinical training, dispute resolution, environmental law, healthcare law, intellectual property law, international law, tax law, trial advocacy

Fall 2005 faculty profile

Total teaching faculty: **55**. Full-time: **40%**; **86%** men, **14%** women, **5%** minorities. Part-time: **60%**; **91%** men, **9%** women, **N/A** minorities
Student-to-faculty ratio: **16.9**

SPECIAL PROGRAMS (as provided by law school):

The curriculum at Baylor is rigorous, but the demands placed on the student are necessary to produce outstanding practicing lawyers. Students complete a broad course of study in the fundamentals of legal theory and doctrine, as well as skills training in legal writing and research, and trial and appellate advocacy. We also provide hands-on training in planning, drafting, negotiating, and client counseling skills. Students learn legal theory as it exists on a nationwide basis with specific emphasis, where appropriate, on Texas jurisprudence. The curriculum is heavily required, covering fundamental areas of law, and is structured to provide a logical progression of legal study.

The bedrock of Baylor's renowned advocacy training is the required third-year practice court course. Students study procedural law in great depth, developing the precision essential to a skilled lawyer. They also learn fundamental techniques for the trial of a jury case. Students try simulation lawsuits from beginning to end under the supervision of full-time faculty members. Their professors challenge them to become personally resilient individuals and seek to develop in them a new appreciation for precision in analysis, thought, expression, and communication—attributes that will prove invaluable to them regardless of what field of legal practice they choose to pursue.

Baylor offers six areas of concentration: general civil litigation, business litigation, criminal practice, business transactions, estate planning, and administrative practice. In each concentration, students build upon the foundational theory and doctrine of the first two years and culminate in the performance, through externships or skills exercises, of specialized lawyering tasks under the direct supervision of accomplished lawyers. No other law school in the nation offers its students a similar broad exposure to legal fundamentals and the opportunity to graduate with such a focused concentration on particular practice areas.

Baylor also offers three joint degree programs: J.D./master of business administration, J.D./master of taxation, and J.D./master of public policy and administration.

Baylor offers a two-week study abroad program at the Universidad Autonoma de Guadalajara in Mexico. Baylor's externship programs give students the advantage of practical experience in handling actual cases and dealing with clients. Criminal clinical experience may be gained in various externships, and judicial externships are available in federal and state courts.

STUDENT BODY

Fall 2005 full-time enrollment: 435

Men: 55%	Women: 45%
African-American: 1.1%	American Indian: 1.1%
Asian-American: 4.8%	Mexican-American: 3.9%
Puerto Rican: 0.7%	Other Hisp-Amer: 1.4%
White: 86.9%	International: 0.0%
Unknown: 0.0%	

Attrition rates for 2004-2005 full-time students

Percent of students discontinuing law school:

Men: 7%	Women: 6%
First-year students: 15%	Second-year students: 3%
Third-year students: N/A	

LIBRARY RESOURCES

The library holds **26,797** and receives **2,202** current subscriptions.
Total volumes: **224,929**
Percentage of the titles in the online catalog: **100%**
Total seats available for library users: **279**

INFORMATION TECHNOLOGY

Number of wired network connections available to students: **733** total (in the law library, excluding computer labs: **125**; in classrooms: **564**; in computer labs: **12**; elsewhere in the law school: **32**)
Law school has a wireless network.
Approximate number of simultaneous users that can be accommodated on wireless network: **1,360**
Students are not required to own a computer.

EMPLOYMENT AND SALARIES

Proportion of 2004 graduates employed at graduation: **67%**
Employed 9 months later, as of February 15, 2005: **98%**
Salaries in the private sector (law firms, business, industry): **$55,000–$105,000** (25th-75th percentile)
Median salary in the private sector: **$70,000**
Percentage in the private sector who reported salary information: **84%**
Median salary in public service (government, judicial clerkships, academic posts, non-profits): **$42,500**

Percentage of 2004 graduates in:

Law firms: **76%**	Bus./industry (legal): **7%**
Bus./industry (nonlegal): **N/A**	Government: **8%**
Public interest: **1%**	Judicial clerkship: **7%**
Academia : **1%**	Unknown: **0%**

2004 graduates employed in-state: **91%**
2004 graduates employed in foreign countries: **0%**
Number of states where graduates are employed: **11**
Percentage of 2004 graduates working in: New England: **0%**, Middle Atlantic: **0%**, East North Central: **2%**, West North Central: **1%**, South Atlantic: **3%**, East South Central: **1%**, West South Central: **91%**, Mountain: **2%**, Pacific: **1%**, Unknown: **0%**

BAR PASSAGE RATES

Based on 2004 graduates taking Summer 2004 or Winter 2005 exams. Most of the school's first-time test takers took the bar in Texas.

91%
School's bar passage rate for first-time test takers

79%
Statewide bar passage rate for first-time test takers

Boston College

- 885 Centre Street, Newton, MA, 02459-1154
- http://www.bc.edu/lawschool
- Private
- **Year founded:** 1929
- **2005-2006 tuition:** full-time: $33,176; part-time: N/A
- **Enrollment 2005-06 academic year:** full-time: 807; part-time: 2
- **U.S. News 2007 law specialty ranking:** clinical training: 18, environmental law: 21, intellectual property law: 21, tax law: 25

3.44-3.79	GPA, 25TH-75TH PERCENTILE
161-166	LSAT, 25TH-75TH PERCENTILE
20%	ACCEPTANCE RATE
27	2007 U.S. NEWS LAW SCHOOL RANKING

ADMISSIONS

Admissions phone number: **(617) 552-4351**
Admissions email address: **bclawadm@bc.edu**
Application website:
http://www.bc.edu/schools/law/admission
Application deadline for Fall 2007 admission: **3/01**

Admissions statistics:

Number of applicants for Fall 2005: **6,769**
Number of acceptances: **1,372**
Number enrolled: **275**
Acceptance rate: **20%**
GPA, 25th-75th percentile, entering class Fall 2005: **3.44-3.79**
LSAT, 25th-75th percentile, entering class Fall 2005: **161-166**

FINANCIAL AID

Financial aid phone number: **(617) 552-4243**
Financial aid application deadline: **3/15**
Tuition 2005-2006 academic year: full-time: **$33,176**; part-time: **N/A**
Room and board: **$12,425**; books: **$840**; miscellaneous expenses: **$3,450**
Total of room/board/books/miscellaneous expenses: **$16,715**
University offers graduate student housing for which law students are eligible.

Financial aid profile

Percent of students that received grants for the 2004-2005 academic year: full-time: **52%**
Median grant amount: full-time: **$11,000**
The average law-school debt of those in the Class of 2005 who borrowed: **$86,980**. Proportion who borrowed: **88%**

ACADEMIC PROGRAMS

Calendar: **semester**
Joint degrees awarded: **J.D./M.B.A.; J.D./M.A. Education; J.D./M.S.W.**
Typical first-year section size: Full-time: **90**

Is there typically a "small section" of the first year class, other than Legal Writing, taught by full-time faculty?: Full-time: **yes**
Number of course titles, beyond the first year curriculum, offered last year: **143**
Percentages of upper division course sections, excluding seminars, with an enrollment of:

Under 25: **68%**	25 to 49: **21%**
50 to 74: **5%**	75 to 99: **5%**
100+: **1%**	

Areas of specialization: appellate advocacy, clinical training, dispute resolution, environmental law, healthcare law, intellectual property law, international law, tax law, trial advocacy

Fall 2005 faculty profile

Total teaching faculty: **108**. Full-time: **44%**; **60%** men, **40%** women, **19%** minorities. Part-time: **56%**; **73%** men, **27%** women, **3%** minorities
Student-to-faculty ratio: **13.9**

SPECIAL PROGRAMS *(as provided by law school):*

Clinical programs: Immigration Law Practicum; Advanced Immigration Law: Seminar and Practicum; Civil Litigation Clinic (represent clients at Boston College Legal Assistance Bureau, a fully functioning law office); Criminal Justice Clinic (BC defenders represent indigent clients in District Court, while student prosecutors handle cases under a district attorney's office); Homelessness Litigation Clinic (fieldwork at Legal Assistance Bureau); Juvenile Rights Advocacy Project (represent girls in the Massachusetts justice system); Women and the Law Clinic (students are assigned two domestic cases); Attorney General Program (full-year clinical experience in the Office of the Massachusetts Attorney General). ICTY—Theory and Practice: work on-site at the International Criminal Tribunal for the Former Yugoslavia, investigating pending cases and drafting indictments. London program: take courses at King's College in London. Along with coursework, students spend up to 25 hours per week at their placements. Semester in Practice: The program is designed to help students improve their lawyering skills while observing experienced local lawyers and judges. Judge and Community Courts: examines the functioning of the judicial process in our lower-level trial courts. Judicial Process: The program allows a student to sit as an intern one day per week with a series of Superior Court judges. Dual-degree programs: J.D./M.B.A; J.D./M.S.W.; J.D./M.Ed. or M.A. in education; other dual-degree options by permission. Cross-registration: For courses not offered at BC Law, special cross-registration may be arranged with Boston-area law schools. Study abroad: In addition to the London and ICTY Programs, students may apply to study abroad at BC partner universities with law programs. Summer opportunities and internships: Oxford Comparative Corporate Governance Program (intensive two-week colloquium at Oxford University in England); summer positions for first-year students at London branches of Boston-area law firms; summer internships at ICTY; Holocaust/Human Rights Project internships (overseas); and summer stipends for selected public-interest work. Advocacy programs: ten moot court opportunities. Law Reviews: four, plus UCC Reporter-Digest. Student organizations: approx. 30. Career Services: extensive counseling.

STUDENT BODY

Fall 2005 full-time enrollment: 807

Men: 50%	Women: 50%
African-American: 5.0%	American Indian: 0.1%
Asian-American: 10.9%	Mexican-American: 0.7%
Puerto Rican: 0.2%	Other Hisp-Amer: 4.3%
White: 64.2%	International: 1.7%
Unknown: 12.8%	

Fall 2005 part-time enrollment: 2

Men: 50%	Women: 50%
African-American: 0.0%	American Indian: 0.0%
Asian-American: 0.0%	Mexican-American: 0.0%
Puerto Rican: 0.0%	Other Hisp-Amer: 0.0%
White: 100.0%	International: 0.0%
Unknown: 0.0%	

Attrition rates for 2004-2005 full-time students
Percent of students discontinuing law school:

Men: 1%	Women: 2%
First-year students: 5%	Second-year students: 0%
Third-year students: N/A	

LIBRARY RESOURCES

The library holds 74,215 and receives 3,386 current subscriptions.
Total volumes: 450,833
Percentage of the titles in the online catalog: 94%

Total seats available for library users: 653

INFORMATION TECHNOLOGY

Number of wired network connections available to students: 1,226 total (in the law library, excluding computer labs: 439; in classrooms: 608; in computer labs: 0; elsewhere in the law school: 179)
Law school has a wireless network.
Approximate number of simultaneous users that can be accommodated on wireless network: 1,950
Students are not required to own a computer.

EMPLOYMENT AND SALARIES

Proportion of 2004 graduates employed at graduation: 71%
Employed 9 months later, as of February 15, 2005: 97%
Salaries in the private sector (law firms, business, industry): $93,000–$125,000 (25th-75th percentile)
Median salary in the private sector: $125,000
Percentage in the private sector who reported salary information: 69%
Median salary in public service (government, judicial clerkships, academic posts, non-profits): $43,100

Percentage of 2004 graduates in:

Law firms: 59%	Bus./industry (legal): 3%
Bus./industry (nonlegal): 5%	Government: 10%
Public interest: 5%	Judicial clerkship: 17%
Academia : 0%	Unknown: 0%

2004 graduates employed in-state: 43%
2004 graduates employed in foreign countries: 2%
Number of states where graduates are employed: 24
Percentage of 2004 graduates working in: New England: 48%, Middle Atlantic: 25%, East North Central: 5%, West North Central: 0%, South Atlantic: 13%, East South Central: 0%, West South Central: 2%, Mountain: 1%, Pacific: 4%, Unknown: 0%

BAR PASSAGE RATES

Based on 2004 graduates taking Summer 2004 or Winter 2005 exams. Most of the school's first-time test takers took the bar in Massachusetts.

	93%

School's bar passage rate for first-time test takers

	84%

Statewide bar passage rate for first-time test takers

Boston University

- 765 Commonwealth Avenue, Boston, MA, 02215
- http://www.bu.edu/law/
- Private
- **Year founded:** 1872
- **2005-2006 tuition:** full-time: $32,866; part-time: N/A
- **Enrollment 2005-06 academic year:** full-time: 860
- **U.S. News 2007 law specialty ranking:** healthcare law: 5, intellecutal property law: 12, tax law: 7

3.48-3.77 GPA, 25TH-75TH PERCENTILE

163-166 LSAT, 25TH-75TH PERCENTILE

24% ACCEPTANCE RATE

22 2007 U.S. NEWS LAW SCHOOL RANKING

ADMISSIONS
Admissions phone number: **(617) 353-3100**
Admissions email address: **bulawadm@bu.edu**
Application website:
   http://www.bu.edu/law/admissions/apply
Application deadline for Fall 2007 admission: **3/01**

Admissions statistics:
Number of applicants for Fall 2005: **6,219**
Number of acceptances: **1,521**
Number enrolled: **294**
Acceptance rate: **24%**
GPA, 25th-75th percentile, entering class Fall 2005: **3.48-3.77**
LSAT, 25th-75th percentile, entering class Fall 2005: **163-166**

FINANCIAL AID
Financial aid phone number: **(617) 353-3160**
Financial aid application deadline: **3/01**
Tuition 2005-2006 academic year: full-time: **$32,866**; part-time: **N/A**
Room and board: **$10,782**; books: **$1,166**; miscellaneous expenses: **$3,900**
Total of room/board/books/miscellaneous expenses: **$15,848**
University offers graduate student housing for which law students are eligible.

Financial aid profile
Percent of students that received grants for the 2004-2005 academic year: full-time: **48%**
Median grant amount: full-time: **$15,000**
The average law-school debt of those in the Class of 2005 who borrowed: **$80,509**. Proportion who borrowed: **86%**

ACADEMIC PROGRAMS
Calendar: **semester**
Joint degrees awarded: **J.D./MSW; J.D./M.B.A.; J.D./MPH; J.D./MS; J.D./MA ; J.D./LLM**
Typical first-year section size: Full-time: **96**

Is there typically a "small section" of the first year class, other than Legal Writing, taught by full-time faculty?: Full-time: **yes**
Number of course titles, beyond the first year curriculum, offered last year: **119**
Percentages of upper division course sections, excluding seminars, with an enrollment of:
Under 25: **45%**   25 to 49: **30%**
50 to 74: **12%**   75 to 99: **6%**
100+: **7%**
Areas of specialization: appellate advocacy, clinical training, dispute resolution, environmental law, healthcare law, intellectual property law, international law, tax law, trial advocacy

Fall 2005 faculty profile
Total teaching faculty: **N/A**. Full-time: **N/A**; **N/A** men, **N/A** women, **N/A** minorities. Part-time: **N/A**; **N/A** men, **N/A** women, **N/A** minorities
Student-to-faculty ratio: **12.1**

SPECIAL PROGRAMS (as provided by law school):
We offer three clinical programs (civil, criminal, legislative) and three internship/externship programs. We have 10 academic-year programs that allow students to study at leading universities in Oxford, Paris, Florence, Madrid, Hong Kong, Buenos Aires, Tel Aviv, Leiden, Lyon and Hamburg.

STUDENT BODY
Fall 2005 full-time enrollment: 860
Men: **50%**   Women: **50%**
African-American: **3.7%**   American Indian: **0.2%**
Asian-American: **14.2%**   Mexican-American: **0.5%**
Puerto Rican: **0.5%**   Other Hisp-Amer: **2.7%**
White: **75.0%**   International: **3.3%**
Unknown: **0.0%**

Attrition rates for 2004-2005 full-time students
Percent of students discontinuing law school:
Men: **2%**   Women: **2%**
First-year students: **3%**   Second-year students: **1%**
Third-year students: **1%**

LIBRARY RESOURCES

The library holds 168,246 and receives 4,630 current subscriptions.

Total volumes: 661,828

Percentage of the titles in the online catalog: 98%

Total seats available for library users: 685

INFORMATION TECHNOLOGY

Number of wired network connections available to students: 0 total (in the law library, excluding computer labs: 0; in classrooms: 0; in computer labs: 0; elsewhere in the law school: 0)

Law school has a wireless network.

Approximate number of simultaneous users that can be accommodated on wireless network: 500

Students are not required to own a computer.

EMPLOYMENT AND SALARIES

Proportion of 2004 graduates employed at graduation: 87%

Employed 9 months later, as of February 15, 2005: 99%

Salaries in the private sector (law firms, business, industry): $110,000–$125,000 (25th-75th percentile)

Median salary in the private sector: $125,000

Percentage in the private sector who reported salary information: 75%

Median salary in public service (government, judicial clerkships, academic posts, non-profits): $43,222

Percentage of 2004 graduates in:

Law firms: 67%
Bus./industry (nonlegal): 1%
Public interest: 4%
Academia : 4%

Bus./industry (legal): 4%
Government: 8%
Judicial clerkship: 12%
Unknown: 0%

2004 graduates employed in-state: 40%

2004 graduates employed in foreign countries: 2%

Number of states where graduates are employed: 22

Percentage of 2004 graduates working in: New England: 45%, Middle Atlantic: 27%, East North Central: 6%, West North Central: 1%, South Atlantic: 9%, East South Central: 0%, West South Central: 1%, Mountain: 1%, Pacific: 8%, Unknown: 0%

BAR PASSAGE RATES

Based on 2004 graduates taking Summer 2004 or Winter 2005 exams. Most of the school's first-time test takers took the bar in Massachusetts.

95%

School's bar passage rate for first-time test takers

84%

Statewide bar passage rate for first-time test takers

Brigham Young University (Clark)

- 340 JRCB, Provo, UT, 84602-8000
- http://www.law.byu.edu
- Private
- Year founded: 1972
- 2005-2006 tuition: full-time: $7,450; part-time: N/A
- Enrollment 2005-06 academic year: full-time: 472
- U.S. News 2007 law specialty ranking: N/A

3.52-3.86 GPA, 25TH-75TH PERCENTILE

161-166 LSAT, 25TH-75TH PERCENTILE

27% ACCEPTANCE RATE

34 2007 U.S. NEWS LAW SCHOOL RANKING

ADMISSIONS

Admissions phone number: **(801) 422-4277**
Admissions email address: **kucharg@lawgate.byu.edu**
Application website:
http://www.law2.byu.edu/Admissions/application_form.htm
Application deadline for Fall 2007 admission: **2/01**

Admissions statistics:

Number of applicants for Fall 2005: **940**
Number of acceptances: **254**
Number enrolled: **153**
Acceptance rate: **27%**
GPA, 25th-75th percentile, entering class Fall 2005: **3.52-3.86**
LSAT, 25th-75th percentile, entering class Fall 2005: **161-166**

FINANCIAL AID

Financial aid phone number: **(801) 422-6386**
Financial aid application deadline: **N/A**
Tuition 2005-2006 academic year: full-time: **$7,450**; part-time: **N/A**
Room and board: **$7,280**; books: **$1,470**; miscellaneous expenses: **$5,326**
Total of room/board/books/miscellaneous expenses: **$14,076**
University offers graduate student housing for which law students are eligible.

Financial aid profile

Percent of students that received grants for the 2004-2005 academic year: full-time: **53%**
Median grant amount: full-time: **$1,500**
The average law-school debt of those in the Class of 2005 who borrowed: **$41,000**. Proportion who borrowed: **86%**

ACADEMIC PROGRAMS

Calendar: **semester**
Joint degrees awarded: **J.D./M.B.A.; J.D./MACC; J.D./MA Education; J.D./EdD ; J.D./MPA; J.D./MA**
Typical first-year section size: Full-time: **106**

Is there typically a "small section" of the first year class, other than Legal Writing, taught by full-time faculty?: Full-time: **yes**
Number of course titles, beyond the first year curriculum, offered last year: **98**
Percentages of upper division course sections, excluding seminars, with an enrollment of:
Under 25: **42%**   25 to 49: **32%**
50 to 74: **14%**   75 to 99: **4%**
100+: **7%**
Areas of specialization: appellate advocacy, clinical training, dispute resolution, environmental law, healthcare law, intellectual property law, international law, tax law, trial advocacy

Fall 2005 faculty profile

Total teaching faculty: **67**. Full-time: **37%**; **84%** men, **16%** women, **12%** minorities. Part-time: **63%**; **71%** men, **29%** women, **5%** minorities
Student-to-faculty ratio: **18.9**

SPECIAL PROGRAMS (as provided by law school):

Students at BYU Law School can become involved in the work of four centers:

The International Center for Law and Religion Studies works with scholars, government leaders, nongovernmental groups, and religious organizations from a variety of countries and faith traditions in promoting religious liberty and studying the relations between governments and religious organizations. Students are exposed firsthand to international law as the center provides technical analyses of emerging legislation to help the drafters avoid unnecessary encroachments on religious freedom. As hosts at conferences held by the center, students use their foreign-language skills as well as their legal skills. Participating students fill seven international clerkships, in Moscow; Frankfurt; Sao Paulo, Brazil; Mexico City; Manila, Philippines; Hong Kong; and Johannesburg, South Africa.

The World Family Policy Center promotes the natural family as the fundamental unit of society in national and international family policy. Students who work and volunteer with the center meet and interact with international policymakers and government leaders during the annual conference. They may earn externship credit by working with members of the European Union Parliament in Brussels.

The Schooley Mediation Center offers a basic mediation course that allows students to become state-certified mediators. Students mediate at the five small-claims courts in Utah County, as well as mediating disputes for the Campus Center on Conflict Resolution and parent-teen disputes for the local school district.

The Marriage and Family Law Research Grant sponsors legal research, writing, and dialogue related to family issues, with emphasis on public-policy considerations.

BYU Law School also sponsors an externship program designed to provide law students with a practical legal experience in the summer between their first year and second year of law school. Students earn one unit of credit for each 50 hours of legal work. Externships are supervised by attorneys and judges in government and judicial settings, public-interest agencies, or private law firms. During the summer of 2000, 223 externships were performed by 187 law students, including 28 internationally.

STUDENT BODY

Fall 2005 full-time enrollment: 472

Men: 62%	Women: 38%
African-American: 1.3%	American Indian: 1.1%
Asian-American: 8.1%	Mexican-American: 2.3%
Puerto Rican: 0.0%	Other Hisp-Amer: 4.7%
White: 81.4%	International: 1.3%
Unknown: 0.0%	

Attrition rates for 2004-2005 full-time students

Percent of students discontinuing law school:

Men: 1%	Women: 1%
First-year students: 1%	Second-year students: 1%
Third-year students: 1%	

LIBRARY RESOURCES

The library holds 168,256 and receives 4,447 current subscriptions.
Total volumes: 477,601
Percentage of the titles in the online catalog: 99%
Total seats available for library users: 879

INFORMATION TECHNOLOGY

Number of wired network connections available to students: 605 total (in the law library, excluding computer labs: 500; in classrooms: 78; in computer labs: 27; elsewhere in the law school: 0)
Law school has a wireless network.
Approximate number of simultaneous users that can be accommodated on wireless network: 1,000
Students are required to own a computer.

EMPLOYMENT AND SALARIES

Proportion of 2004 graduates employed at graduation: 83%
Employed 9 months later, as of February 15, 2005: 99%
Salaries in the private sector (law firms, business, industry): $64,000–$105,000 (25th-75th percentile)
Median salary in the private sector: $83,500
Percentage in the private sector who reported salary information: 51%
Median salary in public service (government, judicial clerkships, academic posts, non-profits): $38,500

Percentage of 2004 graduates in:

Law firms: 57%	Bus./industry (legal): 3%
Bus./industry (nonlegal): 11%	Government: 11%
Public interest: 1%	Judicial clerkship: 15%
Academia : 3%	Unknown: 0%

2004 graduates employed in-state: 44%
2004 graduates employed in foreign countries: 1%
Number of states where graduates are employed: 21
Percentage of 2004 graduates working in: New England: 0%, Middle Atlantic: 3%, East North Central: 3%, West North Central: 1%, South Atlantic: 8%, East South Central: 1%, West South Central: 6%, Mountain: 65%, Pacific: 12%, Unknown: 0%

BAR PASSAGE RATES

Based on 2004 graduates taking Summer 2004 or Winter 2005 exams. Most of the school's first-time test takers took the bar in Utah.

91%
School's bar passage rate for first-time test takers

90%
Statewide bar passage rate for first-time test takers

Brooklyn Law School

- 250 Joralemon Street, Brooklyn, NY, 11201
- http://www.brooklaw.edu
- Private
- **Year founded:** 1901
- **2005-2006 tuition:** full-time: $34,850; part-time: $26,187
- **Enrollment 2005-06 academic year:** full-time: 1,134; part-time: 356
- **U.S. News 2007 law specialty ranking:** clinical training: 19

3.15-3.64	GPA, 25TH-75TH PERCENTILE
161-164	LSAT, 25TH-75TH PERCENTILE
25%	ACCEPTANCE RATE
58	2007 U.S. NEWS LAW SCHOOL RANKING

ADMISSIONS

Admissions phone number: **(718) 780-7906**
Admissions email address: **admitq@brooklaw.edu**
Application website: **http://www.brooklaw.edu/admissions/howto/materials.php**
Application deadline for Fall 2007 admission: **rolling**

Admissions statistics:

Number of applicants for Fall 2005: **4,100**
Number of acceptances: **1,041**
Number enrolled: **305**
Acceptance rate: **25%**
GPA, 25th-75th percentile, entering class Fall 2005: **3.15-3.64**
LSAT, 25th-75th percentile, entering class Fall 2005: **161-164**

FINANCIAL AID

Financial aid phone number: **(718) 780-7915**
Financial aid application deadline: **4/28**
Tuition 2005-2006 academic year: full-time: **$34,850**; part-time: **$26,187**
Room and board: **$13,880**; books: **$1,300**; miscellaneous expenses: **$3,005**
Total of room/board/books/miscellaneous expenses: **$18,185**
University offers graduate student housing for which law students are eligible.

Financial aid profile

Percent of students that received grants for the 2004-2005 academic year: full-time: **57%**; part-time **16%**
Median grant amount: full-time: **$11,033**; part-time: **$6,453**
The average law-school debt of those in the Class of 2005 who borrowed: **$87,920**. Proportion who borrowed: **83%**

ACADEMIC PROGRAMS

Calendar: **semester**
Joint degrees awarded: **M.A. (Political Science); M.B.A. (Business Administration); M.P.A. (Public Administration; M.S. (Library and Information Science);**
M.S. (City and Regional Planning); M.U.P. (Urban Planning**
Typical first-year section size: Full-time: **51**; Part-time: **44**
Is there typically a "small section" of the first year class, other than Legal Writing, taught by full-time faculty?: Full-time: **yes**; Part-time: **no**
Number of course titles, beyond the first year curriculum, offered last year: **149**
Percentages of upper division course sections, excluding seminars, with an enrollment of:

Under 25: **53%**	25 to 49: **22%**
50 to 74: **12%**	75 to 99: **7%**
100+: **6%**	

Areas of specialization: appellate advocacy, clinical training, dispute resolution, environmental law, healthcare law, intellectual property law, international law, tax law, trial advocacy

Fall 2005 faculty profile

Total teaching faculty: **196**. Full-time: **38%**; **49%** men, **51%** women, **8%** minorities. Part-time: **62%**; **68%** men, **32%** women, **8%** minorities
Student-to-faculty ratio: **20.5**

SPECIAL PROGRAMS *(as provided by law school):*

Clinical Programs, recently ranked sixteenth nationally, offer opportunities in Criminal Justice, Individual Client Representation, Group and Business Representation, and Dispute Resolution. Supervised by expert faculty and practitioners, students interview clients and witnesses, conduct depositions and other pre-trial discovery activities, draft and argue motions, negotiate and mediate settlements, prepare and argue appeals, and try cases. Externship programs—Civil Practice, Criminal Practice, and Judicial Clerkship Internships—placed over 400 students last year in law offices, government agencies and judicial chambers.
International Business Law Fellows focus on U.S. and international business law, work closely with faculty, and prepare scholarly papers. During the summer, they may work for firms or institutions involved with business law issues. They participate in programs sponsored by our

Center for the Study of International Business Law which draws on the strength of our distinguished faculty and our location, to actively study and shape international business law and policy.

The Edward V. Sparer Public Interest Law Fellowship Program provides students with experience in public interest practice during the formative years of school, encourages later involvement in public interest/public service, and provides much needed legal services to those unable to afford them. Through summer internships that cultivate a host of valuable skills, over 350 Fellows have distinguished themselves throughout the world.

In two consecutive surveys *National Jurist* magazine cited us as one of the nation's top 20 law schools supporting public interest law.

The Center for Health, Science, and Public Policy, builds on our strong presence in health law. Our Health Law Practice and Policy Internship engages students in the legal issues/policy concerns confronting health care organizations.

Our Center for Law, Language and Cognition explores developments in the cognitive sciences—psychology, neuroscience and linguistics—and their dramatic implications for the theory and practice of law.

The Barry L. Zaretsky Bankruptcy and Commercial Law Roundtable features lively discussions about current bankruptcy/commercial law issues with renowned judges, lawyers, and scholars. Fellowships are awarded to students based on demonstrated academic achievement and commitment to bankruptcy/commercial law.

We offer study abroad programs in China, Germany, and Italy.

STUDENT BODY

Fall 2005 full-time enrollment: 1,134
Men: 51%	Women: 49%
African-American: 2.9%	American Indian: 0.0%
Asian-American: 15.3%	Mexican-American: 0.8%
Puerto Rican: 1.2%	Other Hisp-Amer: 3.1%
White: 75.7%	International: 0.9%
Unknown: 0.0%	

Fall 2005 part-time enrollment: 356
Men: 50%	Women: 50%
African-American: 11.0%	American Indian: 0.3%
Asian-American: 12.6%	Mexican-American: 0.3%
Puerto Rican: 1.1%	Other Hisp-Amer: 3.4%
White: 70.8%	International: 0.6%
Unknown: 0.0%	

Attrition rates for 2004-2005 full-time students
Percent of students discontinuing law school:
Men: 2%	Women: 1%
First-year students: 5%	Second-year students: 1%
Third-year students: N/A	

LIBRARY RESOURCES
The library holds 165,741 and receives 2,237 current subscriptions.
Total volumes: 544,380
Percentage of the titles in the online catalog: 100%
Total seats available for library users: 665

INFORMATION TECHNOLOGY
Number of wired network connections available to students: 1,970 total (in the law library, excluding computer labs: 216; in classrooms: 1,584; in computer labs: 110; elsewhere in the law school: 60)
Law school has a wireless network.
Approximate number of simultaneous users that can be accommodated on wireless network: 1,000
Students are not required to own a computer.

EMPLOYMENT AND SALARIES
Proportion of 2004 graduates employed at graduation: 72%
Employed 9 months later, as of February 15, 2005: 98%
Salaries in the private sector (law firms, business, industry): $70,000–$125,000 (25th-75th percentile)
Median salary in the private sector: $115,000
Percentage in the private sector who reported salary information: 45%
Median salary in public service (government, judicial clerkships, academic posts, non-profits): $45,710

Percentage of 2004 graduates in:
Law firms: 56%	Bus./industry (legal): 11%
Bus./industry (nonlegal): 4%	Government: 16%
Public interest: 3%	Judicial clerkship: 7%
Academia : 1%	Unknown: 3%

2004 graduates employed in-state: 83%
2004 graduates employed in foreign countries: 1%
Number of states where graduates are employed: 20
Percentage of 2004 graduates working in: New England: 2%, Middle Atlantic: 90%, East North Central: 1%, West North Central: 1%, South Atlantic: 4%, East South Central: 0%, West South Central: 0%, Mountain: 1%, Pacific: 2%, Unknown: 0%

BAR PASSAGE RATES
Based on 2004 graduates taking Summer 2004 or Winter 2005 exams. Most of the school's first-time test takers took the bar in New York.

84%
School's bar passage rate for first-time test takers

75%
Statewide bar passage rate for first-time test takers

California Western School of Law

■ 225 Cedar Street, San Diego, CA, 92101-3090
■ http://www.cwsl.edu
■ Private
■ Year founded: 1924
■ 2005-2006 tuition: full-time: $30,600; part-time: $21,630
■ Enrollment 2005-06 academic year: full-time: 745; part-time: 110
■ U.S. News 2007 law specialty ranking: N/A

2.98-3.56 GPA, 25TH-75TH PERCENTILE

151-156 LSAT, 25TH-75TH PERCENTILE

37% ACCEPTANCE RATE

Tier 4 2007 U.S. NEWS LAW SCHOOL RANKING

ADMISSIONS

Admissions phone number: **(619) 525-1401**
Admissions email address: **admissions@cwsl.edu**
Application website:
  http://www.cwsl.edu/main/default.asp?nav=admis-sions.asp&body=admissions/application.asp
Application deadline for Fall 2007 admission: **4/01**

Admissions statistics:
Number of applicants for Fall 2005: **3,652**
Number of acceptances: **1,353**
Number enrolled: **325**
Acceptance rate: **37%**
GPA, 25th-75th percentile, entering class Fall 2005: **2.98-3.56**
LSAT, 25th-75th percentile, entering class Fall 2005: **151-156**

Part-time program:
Number of applicants for Fall 2005: **225**
Number of acceptances: **63**
Number enrolled: **22**
Acceptance rate: **28%**
GPA, 25th-75th percentile, entering class Fall 2005: **3.18-3.51**
LSAT, 25th-75th percentile, entering class Fall 2005: **149-153**

FINANCIAL AID

Financial aid phone number: **(619) 525-7060**
Financial aid application deadline: **3/31**
Tuition 2005-2006 academic year: full-time: **$30,600**; part-time: **$21,630**
Room and board: **$10,800**; books: **$1,088**; miscellaneous expenses: **$5,016**
Total of room/board/books/miscellaneous expenses: **$16,904**
University does not offer graduate student housing for which law students are eligible.

Financial aid profile
Percent of students that received grants for the 2004-2005 academic year: full-time: **37%**; part-time **34%**
Median grant amount: full-time: **$12,490**; part-time: **$9,805**
The average law-school debt of those in the Class of 2005 who borrowed: **$97,509**. Proportion who borrowed: **91%**

ACADEMIC PROGRAMS
Calendar: **semester**
Joint degrees awarded: **J.D./M.S.W.; J.D/Ph.D. History; J.D./M.B.A.; J.D./Ph.D. Political Science**
Typical first-year section size: Full-time: **98**
Is there typically a "small section" of the first year class, other than Legal Writing, taught by full-time faculty?: Full-time: **no**; Part-time: **no**
Number of course titles, beyond the first year curriculum, offered last year: **110**
Percentages of upper division course sections, excluding seminars, with an enrollment of:
  Under 25: **61%**   25 to 49: **19%**
  50 to 74: **9%**   75 to 99: **7%**
  100+: **3%**
Areas of specialization: appellate advocacy, clinical training, dispute resolution, environmental law, healthcare law, intellectual property law, international law, tax law, trial advocacy

Fall 2005 faculty profile
Total teaching faculty: **68**. Full-time: **54%**; **57%** men, **43%** women, **19%** minorities. Part-time: **46%**; **61%** men, **39%** women, **0%** minorities
Student-to-faculty ratio: **18.7**

SPECIAL PROGRAMS (as provided by law school):
California Western School of Law students participate in a broad range of clinical and academic special programs, as well as in programs offered by centers and institutes on campus.
  Clinical internships combine practical experience with weekly seminars. More than 75 percent of third-year students

are placed in judicial, government, private practice, and in-house corporate offices.

The California Innocence Project is a two-trimester clinic dedicated to the release of people who have been wrongfully convicted. Students investigate claims, interview witnesses, draft motions, and assist faculty and criminal defense lawyers.

The Advanced Mediation Program is a one-trimester clinic that provides students with hands-on mediation experience at Juvenile Hall or Small Claims Court.

The Bail Project is a joint venture with the San Diego County public defender and offers the opportunity to represent actual clients in court. After training, students may be certified as pre-arraignment representatives of the public defender's office and represent indigent clients in bail proceedings.

Special academic programs include areas of concentration and dual-degree programs in conjunction with the University of California-San Diego (UCSD) and San Diego State University (SDSU).

Areas of concentration provide a thorough, rigorous academic and practical experience with opportunity for professional networking. The school offers areas of concentration in child, family, and elder law; creative problem solving; criminal justice; intellectual property, telecommunications, and technology regulation; international law; and labor and employment law.

The school offers a joint J.D./Ph.D. in either history or political science in conjunction with the La Jolla campus of UCSD. California Western and UCSD signed a collaborative agreement to provide additional broad, interdisciplinary opportunities. CWSL maintains dual J.D./M.B.A. and J.D./M.S.W. programs with SDSU.

CWSL offers an American Bar Association-approved study abroad program at foreign law schools. Students may also take part in a semester abroad program.

An innovative, six-week summer enrichment program is available to entering first-year students. It provides in-depth preparation for law school.

California Western is home to a number of centers and institutes, including the Center for Creative Problem Solving; the Institute for Criminal Defense Advocacy; the Trial Skills Academy; the National Center for Preventive Law; the Telecommunications and Intellectual Property Law Center; and Proyecto Acceso, a training program for Latin American lawyers and judges.

STUDENT BODY

Fall 2005 full-time enrollment: 745

Men: 50%	Women: 50%
African-American: 2.0%	American Indian: 1.2%
Asian-American: 14.0%	Mexican-American: 6.3%
Puerto Rican: 0.0%	Other Hisp-Amer: 2.4%
White: 59.1%	International: 1.1%
Unknown: 14.0%	

Fall 2005 part-time enrollment: 110

Men: 33%	Women: 67%
African-American: 10.0%	American Indian: 0.9%
Asian-American: 7.3%	Mexican-American: 10.9%
Puerto Rican: 0.9%	Other Hisp-Amer: 3.6%
White: 56.4%	International: 0.0%
Unknown: 10.0%	

Attrition rates for 2004-2005 full-time students
Percent of students discontinuing law school:

Men: 4%	Women: 2%
First-year students: 10%	Second-year students: N/A
Third-year students: N/A	

LIBRARY RESOURCES

The library holds 140,517 and receives 3,905 current subscriptions.
Total volumes: 319,819
Percentage of the titles in the online catalog: 100%
Total seats available for library users: 626

INFORMATION TECHNOLOGY

Number of wired network connections available to students: 515 total (in the law library, excluding computer labs: 303; in classrooms: 122; in computer labs: 10; elsewhere in the law school: 80)
Law school has a wireless network.
Approximate number of simultaneous users that can be accommodated on wireless network: 400
Students are not required to own a computer.

EMPLOYMENT AND SALARIES

Proportion of 2004 graduates employed at graduation: N/A
Employed 9 months later, as of February 15, 2005: 84%
Salaries in the private sector (law firms, business, industry): $41,600–$66,000 (25th-75th percentile)
Median salary in the private sector: $60,000
Percentage in the private sector who reported salary information: 58%
Median salary in public service (government, judicial clerkships, academic posts, non-profits): $52,000

Percentage of 2004 graduates in:

Law firms: 67%	Bus./industry (legal): 5%
Bus./industry (nonlegal): 9%	Government: 9%
Public interest: 6%	Judicial clerkship: 2%
Academia : 2%	Unknown: 0%

2004 graduates employed in-state: 69%
2004 graduates employed in foreign countries: 1%
Number of states where graduates are employed: 24
Percentage of 2004 graduates working in: New England: 1%, Middle Atlantic: 3%, East North Central: 1%, West North Central: 1%, South Atlantic: 7%, East South Central: 1%, West South Central: 1%, Mountain: 14%, Pacific: 70%, Unknown: 0%

BAR PASSAGE RATES

Based on 2004 graduates taking Summer 2004 or Winter 2005 exams. Most of the school's first-time test takers took the bar in California.

58%
School's bar passage rate for first-time test takers

61%
Statewide bar passage rate for first-time test takers

Campbell University (Wiggins)

- Box 158, Buies Creek, NC, 27506
- http://www.law.campbell.edu
- Private
- Year founded: 1976
- 2005-2006 tuition: full-time: $23,000; part-time: N/A
- Enrollment 2005-06 academic year: full-time: 340
- U.S. News 2007 law specialty ranking: N/A

3.03-3.50 GPA, 25ᵀᴴ-75ᵀᴴ PERCENTILE

153-158 LSAT, 25ᵀᴴ-75ᵀᴴ PERCENTILE

20% ACCEPTANCE RATE

Tier 4 2007 U.S. NEWS LAW SCHOOL RANKING

ADMISSIONS

Admissions phone number: **(910) 893-1754**
Admissions email address: **admissions@law.campbell.edu**
Application website: **http://www.applyweb.com/apply/camplaw/index.html**
Application deadline for Fall 2007 admission: **3/31**

Admissions statistics:

Number of applicants for Fall 2005: **1,118**
Number of acceptances: **229**
Number enrolled: **119**
Acceptance rate: **20%**
GPA, 25th-75th percentile, entering class Fall 2005: **3.03-3.50**
LSAT, 25th-75th percentile, entering class Fall 2005: **153-158**

FINANCIAL AID

Financial aid phone number: **(910) 893-1310**
Financial aid application deadline: **1/01**
Tuition 2005-2006 academic year: full-time: **$23,000**; part-time: **N/A**
Room and board: **$5,905**; books: **$1,200**; miscellaneous expenses: **$3,115**
Total of room/board/books/miscellaneous expenses: **$10,220**
University offers graduate student housing for which law students are eligible.

Financial aid profile

Percent of students that received grants for the 2004-2005 academic year: full-time: **43%**
Median grant amount: full-time: **$5,000**
The average law-school debt of those in the Class of 2005 who borrowed: **$90,929**. Proportion who borrowed: **94%**

ACADEMIC PROGRAMS

Calendar: **semester**
Joint degrees awarded: **J.D./M.B.A.**
Typical first-year section size: Full-time: **83**

Is there typically a "small section" of the first year class, other than Legal Writing, taught by full-time faculty?: Full-time: **yes**
Number of course titles, beyond the first year curriculum, offered last year: **83**
Percentages of upper division course sections, excluding seminars, with an enrollment of:

Under 25: **49%**   25 to 49: **32%**
50 to 74: **14%**   75 to 99: **3%**
100+: **3%**

Areas of specialization: appellate advocacy, clinical training, dispute resolution, environmental law, healthcare law, intellectual property law, international law, tax law, trial advocacy

Fall 2005 faculty profile

Total teaching faculty: **N/A**. Full-time: **N/A**; **N/A** men, **N/A** women, **N/A** minorities. Part-time: **N/A**; **N/A** men, **N/A** women, **N/A** minorities
Student-to-faculty ratio: **17.0**

SPECIAL PROGRAMS (as provided by law school):

Summer Study:

Beginning in the summer of 2004, Campbell Law School implemented its Cooperative Program for Foreign Study with Handong International Law School in South Korea. This six-week program offers courses on Globalization of Law Reform and Privatization and Comparative Asian Law and Culture. Students are required to visit a number of legal and government institutions in Korea, such as the Supreme Court, Constitutional Court, Office of the Attorney General, Judicial Trainee Institute, general counsel's office and corporate headquarters for major international corporations located in South Korea. Comparable visits are also planned in a field trip to Kyrgyzstan.

Externships:

The Externship Program allows student volunteers to work in public service positions under the direct supervision of an attorney in the participating office. Students also meet with, and prepare memoranda for, their supervising faculty member on a regular basis. Students must be in good academic standing to participate and may not receive compensation or reimbursements. To earn the one-time-only, two-hour credit, a minimum of 112 hours must be spent performing this public service work. Externships are available during the fall and spring semesters and in the summer.

Professionalism Development Program:

The School of Law conducts a year-long Professionalism Development Program for first-year students for which it received the 2003 ABA Gambrell Award for outstanding contributions to professionalism. This program encourages an action-observation-reflection model for professional development and utilizes the model in student interactions with visiting lawyers.

Juvenile Justice Project:

The Juvenile Justice Project exposes students to theoretical and practical aspects of Restorative Justice, within the context of juvenile mediation. Students consider theory relating to Restorative Justice, mediation and other dispute resolution processes. They observe, and under supervision, assist in live mediations in the local judicial district. The classroom portion is offered in the fall to second and third year students (two credit hours). Students who complete the classroom portion may continue with the clinical portion offered in both semesters. Students work with trained faculty and staff as co-mediators and assist in live cases. One hour of credit is offered in each semester for successful completion of the clinical portion.

STUDENT BODY

Fall 2005 full-time enrollment: 340

Men: 55%	Women: 45%
African-American: 2.4%	American Indian: 0.9%
Asian-American: 2.1%	Mexican-American: 0.0%
Puerto Rican: 0.0%	Other Hisp-Amer: 1.8%
White: 90.6%	International: 0.3%
Unknown: 2.1%	

Attrition rates for 2004-2005 full-time students

Percent of students discontinuing law school:

Men: 9%	Women: 9%
First-year students: 22%	Second-year students: N/A
Third-year students: N/A	

LIBRARY RESOURCES

The library holds 23,734 and receives 2,668 current subscriptions.

Total volumes: 194,501

Percentage of the titles in the online catalog: 76%

Total seats available for library users: 431

INFORMATION TECHNOLOGY

Number of wired network connections available to students: 165 total (in the law library, excluding computer labs: 165; in classrooms: 0; in computer labs: 0; elsewhere in the law school: 0)

Law school has a wireless network.

Approximate number of simultaneous users that can be accommodated on wireless network: 350

Students are not required to own a computer.

EMPLOYMENT AND SALARIES

Proportion of 2004 graduates employed at graduation: 82%

Employed 9 months later, as of February 15, 2005: 84%

Salaries in the private sector (law firms, business, industry): $40,000–$55,000 (25th-75th percentile)

Median salary in the private sector: $45,000

Percentage in the private sector who reported salary information: 87%

Median salary in public service (government, judicial clerkships, academic posts, non-profits): $42,000

Percentage of 2004 graduates in:

Law firms: 83%	Bus./industry (legal): 0%
Bus./industry (nonlegal): 5%	Government: 8%
Public interest: 2%	Judicial clerkship: 2%
Academia : 0%	Unknown: 0%

2004 graduates employed in-state: 87%

2004 graduates employed in foreign countries: 1%

Number of states where graduates are employed: 4

Percentage of 2004 graduates working in: New England: N/A, Middle Atlantic: N/A, East North Central: N/A, West North Central: N/A, South Atlantic: 98%, East South Central: N/A, West South Central: N/A, Mountain: 1%, Pacific: N/A, Unknown: N/A

BAR PASSAGE RATES

Based on 2004 graduates taking Summer 2004 or Winter 2005 exams. Most of the school's first-time test takers took the bar in North Carolina.

78%

School's bar passage rate for first-time test takers

75%

Statewide bar passage rate for first-time test takers

Capital University

■ 303 E. Broad Street, Columbus, OH, 43215-3200
■ http://www.law.capital.edu
■ Private
■ Year founded: 1903
■ 2005-2006 tuition: full-time: $855/credit hour; part-time: $855/credit hour
■ Enrollment 2005-06 academic year: full-time: 457; part-time: 273
■ U.S. News 2007 law specialty ranking: N/A

2.96-3.50 GPA, 25TH-75TH PERCENTILE

151-156 LSAT, 25TH-75TH PERCENTILE

38% ACCEPTANCE RATE

Tier 4 2007 U.S. NEWS LAW SCHOOL RANKING

ADMISSIONS

Admissions phone number: **(614) 236-6310**
Admissions email address: **admissions@law.capital.edu**
Application website: **https://secure.law.capital.edu/application/**
Application deadline for Fall 2007 admission: **5/01**

Admissions statistics:

Number of applicants for Fall 2005: **1,274**
Number of acceptances: **486**
Number enrolled: **168**
Acceptance rate: **38%**
GPA, 25th-75th percentile, entering class Fall 2005: **2.96-3.50**
LSAT, 25th-75th percentile, entering class Fall 2005: **151-156**

Part-time program:

Number of applicants for Fall 2005: **301**
Number of acceptances: **138**
Number enrolled: **87**
Acceptance rate: **46%**
GPA, 25th-75th percentile, entering class Fall 2005: **2.90-3.47**
LSAT, 25th-75th percentile, entering class Fall 2005: **150-157**

FINANCIAL AID

Financial aid phone number: **(614) 236-6350**
Financial aid application deadline: **4/01**
Tuition 2005-2006 academic year: full-time: **$855/credit hour**; part-time: **$855/credit hour**
Room and board: **$7,517**; books: **$898**; miscellaneous expenses: **$2,165**
Total of room/board/books/miscellaneous expenses: **$10,580**
University does not offer graduate student housing for which law students are eligible.

Financial aid profile

Percent of students that received grants for the 2004-2005 academic year: full-time: **62%**; part-time **34%**

Median grant amount: full-time: **$8,000**; part-time: **$3,000**
The average law-school debt of those in the Class of 2005 who borrowed: **$70,806**. Proportion who borrowed: **88%**

ACADEMIC PROGRAMS

Calendar: **semester**
Joint degrees awarded: **J.D./M.B.A.; J.D./M.S.A.; J.D./LL.M - Tax; J.D./LL.M. - Tax & Business; J.D./M.S.N.; J.D./M.T.S.; J.D./LL.M. - Business**
Typical first-year section size: Full-time: **85**; Part-time: **88**
Is there typically a "small section" of the first year class, other than Legal Writing, taught by full-time faculty?: Full-time: **yes**; Part-time: **yes**
Number of course titles, beyond the first year curriculum, offered last year: **109**
Percentages of upper division course sections, excluding seminars, with an enrollment of:

Under 25: **53%**	25 to 49: **24%**
50 to 74: **12%**	75 to 99: **9%**
100+: **2%**	

Areas of specialization: appellate advocacy, clinical training, dispute resolution, environmental law, healthcare law, intellectual property law, international law, tax law, trial advocacy

Fall 2005 faculty profile

Total teaching faculty: **87**. Full-time: **38%**; **58%** men, **42%** women, **9%** minorities. Part-time: **62%**; **93%** men, **7%** women, **7%** minorities
Student-to-faculty ratio: **16.3**

SPECIAL PROGRAMS (as provided by law school):

Capital's extensive curriculum and programs provide numerous options. Our concentrations and joint degree programs allow you to focus in an area of the law and expand your knowledge for the legal and business world. The governmental affairs concentration allows students to participate in externships with local, state, and federal courts and governmental agencies and to conduct extensive research in the area. The labor and employment law concentration is designed for law students who have an interest in studying laws and regulations governing the workplace. The small-business entities and publicly held companies concentrations give interested students an opportunity to focus part of their legal education on issues affecting businesses. The dispute resolution concentration prepares students to understand the full spectrum of settlement processes. Capital's concentration in environmental law prepares students for employment in the field. The children and family law concentration provides students an in-depth understanding of the legal rights and obligations of parents, children and family units. These innovative programs give students opportunities to explore various specialties within the legal profession, improve their skills, and provide a valuable service to the community. Complementing your classroom experience are opportunities for involvement in our National Center for Adoption Law & Policy, the only entity of its kind in the nation, and the Tobacco Public Policy Center. Opportunities abound in our legal and family advocacy clinics, externship programs, law review and moot court teams, meaning you will gain actual legal experience before leaving the academic world. The Center for Dispute Resolution is a resource for teaching, development and implementation of alternative dispute resolution methods. Expand your legal education by studying abroad in Capital's summer law programs in Germany or Greece. Capital has sister-institutional agreements with the Center for International and European Economic Law in Greece, Demokritus University of Thrace (Greece), the University of Saskatchewan (Canada), the University of Glasgow (Scotland) and the University of Passau (Germany). Capital's joint degree programs include: J.D./master of sports administration, J.D./master of business administration, J.D./master of science in nursing, J.D./LL.M. in taxation, J.D./LL.M. in business, J.D./LL.M. in business and taxation and J.D./master in theological studies.

STUDENT BODY

Fall 2005 full-time enrollment: 457

Men: 53%	Women: 47%
African-American: 5.5%	American Indian: 0.4%
Asian-American: 2.0%	Mexican-American: 0.0%
Puerto Rican: 0.0%	Other Hisp-Amer: 1.8%
White: 80.3%	International: 0.9%
Unknown: 9.2%	

Fall 2005 part-time enrollment: 273

Men: 56%	Women: 44%
African-American: 9.2%	American Indian: 0.0%
Asian-American: 2.6%	Mexican-American: 0.0%
Puerto Rican: 0.0%	Other Hisp-Amer: 1.5%
White: 78.8%	International: 0.4%
Unknown: 7.7%	

Attrition rates for 2004-2005 full-time students
Percent of students discontinuing law school:

Men: 9%	Women: 12%
First-year students: 23%	Second-year students: 7%
Third-year students: 1%	

LIBRARY RESOURCES

The library holds 48,477 and receives 2,585 current subscriptions.
Total volumes: 267,746
Percentage of the titles in the online catalog: 95%
Total seats available for library users: 460

INFORMATION TECHNOLOGY

Number of wired network connections available to students: 675 total (in the law library, excluding computer labs: 467; in classrooms: 183; in computer labs: 5; elsewhere in the law school: 20)
Law school has a wireless network.
Approximate number of simultaneous users that can be accommodated on wireless network: 720
Students are not required to own a computer.

EMPLOYMENT AND SALARIES

Proportion of 2004 graduates employed at graduation: N/A
Employed 9 months later, as of February 15, 2005: 88%
Salaries in the private sector (law firms, business, industry): $48,000–$90,000 (25th-75th percentile)
Median salary in the private sector: $55,000
Percentage in the private sector who reported salary information: 50%
Median salary in public service (government, judicial clerkships, academic posts, non-profits): $40,000

Percentage of 2004 graduates in:

Law firms: 48%	Bus./industry (legal): 10%
Bus./industry (nonlegal): 7%	Government: 24%
Public interest: 8%	Judicial clerkship: 2%
Academia : 1%	Unknown: 0%

2004 graduates employed in-state: 94%
2004 graduates employed in foreign countries: 0%
Number of states where graduates are employed: 6
Percentage of 2004 graduates working in: New England: 0%, Middle Atlantic: 1%, East North Central: 96%, West North Central: 0%, South Atlantic: 3%, East South Central: 0%, West South Central: 0%, Mountain: 0%, Pacific: 0%, Unknown: 0%

BAR PASSAGE RATES

Based on 2004 graduates taking Summer 2004 or Winter 2005 exams. Most of the school's first-time test takers took the bar in Ohio.

75%
School's bar passage rate for first-time test takers

81%
Statewide bar passage rate for first-time test takers

Cardozo-Yeshiva University

■ 55 Fifth Avenue, 10th Floor, New York, NY, 10003
■ http://www.cardozo.yu.edu
■ Private
■ Year founded: 1976
■ 2005-2006 tuition: full-time: $34,850; part-time: $34,850
■ Enrollment 2005-06 academic year: full-time: 931; part-time: 115
■ U.S. News 2007 law specialty ranking: clinical training: 30, dispute resolution: 6, intellecutal property law: 6

3.19-3.72 GPA, 25TH-75TH PERCENTILE

162-166 LSAT, 25TH-75TH PERCENTILE

24% ACCEPTANCE RATE

53 2007 U.S. NEWS LAW SCHOOL RANKING

ADMISSIONS

Admissions phone number: **(212) 790-0274**
Admissions email address: **lawinfo@yu.edu**
Application website: **http://www.cardozo.yu.edu/admissions/how_to.asp**
Application deadline for Fall 2007 admission: **4/01**

Admissions statistics:
Number of applicants for Fall 2005: **4,776**
Number of acceptances: **1,124**
Number enrolled: **247**
Acceptance rate: **24%**
GPA, 25th-75th percentile, entering class Fall 2005: **3.19-3.72**
LSAT, 25th-75th percentile, entering class Fall 2005: **162-166**

Part-time program:
Number of applicants for Fall 2005: **436**
Number of acceptances: **184**
Number enrolled: **117**
Acceptance rate: **42%**
GPA, 25th-75th percentile, entering class Fall 2005: **3.27-3.68**
LSAT, 25th-75th percentile, entering class Fall 2005: **156-160**

FINANCIAL AID

Financial aid phone number: **(212) 790-0392**
Financial aid application deadline: **4/15**
Tuition 2005-2006 academic year: full-time: **$34,850**; part-time: **$34,850**
Room and board: **$18,000**; books: **$1,000**; miscellaneous expenses: **$5,055**
Total of room/board/books/miscellaneous expenses: **$24,055**
University does not offer graduate student housing for which law students are eligible.

Financial aid profile
Percent of students that received grants for the 2004-2005 academic year: full-time: **61%**; part-time **3%**
Median grant amount: full-time: **$10,000**
The average law-school debt of those in the Class of 2005 who borrowed: **$90,403**. Proportion who borrowed: **73%**

ACADEMIC PROGRAMS

Calendar: **semester**
Joint degrees awarded: **J.D./M.S.W.**
Typical first-year section size: Full-time: **50**
Is there typically a "small section" of the first year class, other than Legal Writing, taught by full-time faculty?: Full-time: **no**
Number of course titles, beyond the first year curriculum, offered last year: **144**
Percentages of upper division course sections, excluding seminars, with an enrollment of:
Under 25: **42%**   25 to 49: **28%**
50 to 74: **13%**   75 to 99: **9%**
100+: **8%**
Areas of specialization: appellate advocacy, clinical training, dispute resolution, environmental law, healthcare law, intellectual property law, international law, tax law, trial advocacy

Fall 2005 faculty profile
Total teaching faculty: **116**. Full-time: **45%**; **71%** men, **29%** women, **8%** minorities. Part-time: **55%**; **77%** men, **23%** women, **3%** minorities
Student-to-faculty ratio: **15.8**

SPECIAL PROGRAMS (as provided by law school):
Cardozo boasts comprehensive endowed programs in intellectual property law, alternative dispute resolution, Jewish Law, family law, public service, and named centers in corporate governance, entertainment and communications law, constitutional democracy, Holocaust studies and human rights, and ethics. Extensive classroom offerings are combined with panels and speakers, research and internships, scholarship, and student-and faculty-edited journals.

Cardozo offers varied opportunities for experiential learning. Its famed client-based clinical program is home to the Innocence Project, founded by Professors Barry Scheck and Peter Neufeld, which has freed through DNA evidence more than 160 people convicted of crimes they did not commit. Also offered are criminal law clinics in prosecution, defense, and appeals; a Holocaust Claims Restitution practicum; Mediation, Tax, Immigration, and Family Court clinics; a Securities Arbitration clinic; a Human Rights and Genocide Prevention clinic; and a clinic serving elderly and/or disabled clients. A two-week Intensive Trial Advocacy Program is offered to second- and third-year students interested in acquiring litigation and trial skills.

A central New York City location fosters numerous field placements at major law firms and corporations; at city, state, and federal agencies; in judicial chambers; with district attorneys; in the U.S. Attorney's offices; in legal aid offices; and special externships in intellectual property, telecommunications, and labor and employment law. Summer programs include the Summer Institute, which combines academic study and internship, an international ADR program in Budapest and Paris, and programs in media law and corporate governance at Oxford University.

Students may pursue concentrations in Constitutional, Corporate, Commercial, Criminal, Family and Matrimonial, Intellectual Property and Communications, International and Comparative Law, Property and Real Estate, Tax Law, and General Litigation. Students may earn a Dispute Resolution certificate and may take one pre-approved law-related graduate course per semester at New School University. Joint degree programs include J.D./LL.M. and M.S.W./J.D.

Students may enter in September, January, or May. Students entering in January or May can graduate in 2 1/2 calendar years. Junior-year undergraduates can enter in May and, by studying at Cardozo during the summers before and after senior year, receive their B.A. and J.D. degrees in six years.

STUDENT BODY

Fall 2005 full-time enrollment: 931

Men: 53%	Women: 47%
African-American: 3.0%	American Indian: 0.1%
Asian-American: 8.9%	Mexican-American: 0.8%
Puerto Rican: 0.9%	Other Hisp-Amer: 4.5%
White: 79.2%	International: 2.7%
Unknown: 0.0%	

Fall 2005 part-time enrollment: 115

Men: 47%	Women: 53%
African-American: 3.5%	American Indian: 0.0%
Asian-American: 14.8%	Mexican-American: 1.7%
Puerto Rican: 1.7%	Other Hisp-Amer: 3.5%
White: 73.0%	International: 1.7%
Unknown: 0.0%	

Attrition rates for 2004-2005 full-time students

Percent of students discontinuing law school:

Men: 4%	Women: 3%
First-year students: 9%	Second-year students: 1%
Third-year students: 1%	

LIBRARY RESOURCES

The library holds 95,940 and receives 6,389 current subscriptions.
Total volumes: 515,715
Percentage of the titles in the online catalog: 100%
Total seats available for library users: 483

INFORMATION TECHNOLOGY

Number of wired network connections available to students: 104 total (in the law library, excluding computer labs: 104; in classrooms: 0; in computer labs: 0; elsewhere in the law school: 0)
Law school has a wireless network.
Approximate number of simultaneous users that can be accommodated on wireless network: 683
Students are not required to own a computer.

EMPLOYMENT AND SALARIES

Proportion of 2004 graduates employed at graduation: 74%
Employed 9 months later, as of February 15, 2005: 97%
Salaries in the private sector (law firms, business, industry): $68,000–$125,000 (25th-75th percentile)
Median salary in the private sector: $95,000
Percentage in the private sector who reported salary information: 65%
Median salary in public service (government, judicial clerkships, academic posts, non-profits): $49,000

Percentage of 2004 graduates in:

Law firms: 60%	Bus./industry (legal): 12%
Bus./industry (nonlegal): 2%	Government: 12%
Public interest: 3%	Judicial clerkship: 8%
Academia : 2%	Unknown: 1%

2004 graduates employed in-state: 83%
2004 graduates employed in foreign countries: 1%
Number of states where graduates are employed: 16
Percentage of 2004 graduates working in: New England: 2%, Middle Atlantic: 90%, East North Central: 1%, West North Central: 0%, South Atlantic: 2%, East South Central: 0%, West South Central: 0%, Mountain: 1%, Pacific: 2%, Unknown: 1%

BAR PASSAGE RATES

Based on 2004 graduates taking Summer 2004 or Winter 2005 exams. Most of the school's first-time test takers took the bar in New York.

80%
School's bar passage rate for first-time test takers

75%
Statewide bar passage rate for first-time test takers

Case Western Reserve University

- 11075 E. Boulevard, Cleveland, OH, 44106-7148
- http://www.law.case.edu
- Private
- Year founded: 1892
- 2005-2006 tuition: full-time: $31,880; part-time: $1,230/credit hour
- Enrollment 2005-06 academic year: full-time: 667; part-time: 25
- U.S. News 2007 law specialty ranking: healthcare law: 5, intellecutal property law: 19

3.13-3.57 GPA, 25TH-75TH PERCENTILE

157-161 LSAT, 25TH-75TH PERCENTILE

25% ACCEPTANCE RATE

51 2007 U.S. NEWS LAW SCHOOL RANKING

ADMISSIONS
Admissions phone number: (800) 756-0036
Admissions email address: lawadmissions@case.edu
Application website: http://www.law.case.edu/admissions/
Application deadline for Fall 2007 admission: 4/02

Admissions statistics:
Number of applicants for Fall 2005: 2,768
Number of acceptances: 699
Number enrolled: 200
Acceptance rate: 25%
GPA, 25th-75th percentile, entering class Fall 2005:
3.13-3.57
LSAT, 25th-75th percentile, entering class Fall 2005: 157-161

Part-time program:
Number of applicants for Fall 2005: 25
Number of acceptances: 25
Number enrolled: 25
Acceptance rate: 100%
GPA, 25th-75th percentile, entering class Fall 2005:
3.06-3.60
LSAT, 25th-75th percentile, entering class Fall 2005: 155-157

FINANCIAL AID
Financial aid phone number: (877) 889-4279
Financial aid application deadline: 5/01
Tuition 2005-2006 academic year: full-time: $31,880; part-time: $1,230/credit hour
Room and board: $12,700; books: $1,225; miscellaneous expenses: $1,774
Total of room/board/books/miscellaneous expenses: $15,699
University does not offer graduate student housing for which law students are eligible.

Financial aid profile
Percent of students that received grants for the 2004-2005 academic year: full-time: 48%
Median grant amount: full-time: $10,000

The average law-school debt of those in the Class of 2005 who borrowed: $70,480. Proportion who borrowed: 77%

ACADEMIC PROGRAMS
Calendar: semester
Joint degrees awarded: **J.D./M.B.A; J.D./MSSA (Social Work); J.D./MPH (Public Health); J.D./MNO (Nonprofit Management); J.D./MA (Bioethics); J.D./MD (Medicine); J.D./MS (Biochemistry); J.D./MA (Legal History)**
Typical first-year section size: Full-time: 75
Is there typically a "small section" of the first year class, other than Legal Writing, taught by full-time faculty?: Full-time: no
Number of course titles, beyond the first year curriculum, offered last year: 178
Percentages of upper division course sections, excluding seminars, with an enrollment of:
Under 25: **66%**   25 to 49: **24%**
50 to 74: **5%**   75 to 99: **4%**
100+: **1%**
Areas of specialization: appellate advocacy, clinical training, dispute resolution, environmental law, healthcare law, intellectual property law, international law, tax law, trial advocacy

Fall 2005 faculty profile
Total teaching faculty: 205. Full-time: 28%; 67% men, 33% women, 9% minorities. Part-time: 72%; 64% men, 36% women, 3% minorities
Student-to-faculty ratio: 14.7

SPECIAL PROGRAMS *(as provided by law school):*
Over the past eight years, Case School of Law has transformed the curriculum; the result is an innovative approach that ensures that our students are prepared to meet tomorrow's challenges. CaseArc—the most ambitious integrated, three-year, experiential learning program in the world—teaches skills missing from traditional courses: negotiation, business transactions, problem solving, and strategic thinking.
    With more than 300 courses (over 90% of upper-level courses have fewer than 50 students), our curriculum offers

unparalleled depth and breadth of study. Our six labs, seven clinics, and three externship programs offer students the opportunity not only to study the law in practice, but also to contribute to its development. A few examples:

• War Crimes Research Lab: Research issues for international prosecutors from the International Criminal Tribunal for the Former Yugoslavia, the International Criminal Tribunal for Rwanda, the Special Court for Sierra Leone, Iraqi Special Tribunal, or the International Criminal Court;

• Intellectual Property Entrepreneurship Clinic: Serve as legal counsel to burgeoning art entrepreneurs, drafting intellectual property strategies and confidential non-disclosure, work-for-hire, and licensing agreements;

• Global Corporate Governance Lab: Conduct research for the International Monetary Fund and the World Bank;

• Health Law Clinic: Conduct an examination of a medical expert in a social security disability claim.

Work-abroad opportunities are extensive. A sampling: the International Trade Centre (Geneva), the Foundation for Human Rights Initiative (Uganda), the Organization of American States, International Bridges to Justice (Beijing), the International Criminal Tribunal for the Former Yugoslavia, and the International Criminal Tribunal for Rwanda. Our Judicial Externship Program places students in the chambers of federal judges. And students play an integral part in our many lectures and symposia, which give them the opportunity to meet personally with the world's leading authorities on a wide range of cutting-edge legal issues.

We offer concentrations in:
-Law and Technology
-Law and the Arts
-Criminal Law
-Individual Rights and Social Reform
-Public and Regulatory Institutions
-International Law
-Business Organizations
-Litigation
-Health Law

Our dual degree programs offer opportunity for interdisciplinary study with a J.D. and: M.B.A. (management), M.A. (biochemistry), M.D. (medicine), M.N.O. (nonprofit management), M.A. (bioethics), M.A. (legal history), M.P.H. (public health).

STUDENT BODY

Fall 2005 full-time enrollment: 667

Men: 62%	Women: 38%
African-American: 3.3%	American Indian: 0.3%
Asian-American: 9.1%	Mexican-American: 0.1%
Puerto Rican: 0.0%	Other Hisp-Amer: 0.6%
White: 82.6%	International: 2.5%
Unknown: 1.3%	

Fall 2005 part-time enrollment: 25

Men: 60%	Women: 40%
African-American: 0.0%	American Indian: 0.0%
Asian-American: 20.0%	Mexican-American: 0.0%
Puerto Rican: 0.0%	Other Hisp-Amer: 0.0%
White: 80.0%	International: 0.0%
Unknown: 0.0%	

Attrition rates for 2004-2005 full-time students
Percent of students discontinuing law school:

Men: 3%	Women: 1%
First-year students: N/A	Second-year students: 6%
Third-year students: N/A	

LIBRARY RESOURCES

The library holds 107,063 and receives 5,241 current subscriptions.
Total volumes: 402,678
Percentage of the titles in the online catalog: 100%
Total seats available for library users: 346

INFORMATION TECHNOLOGY

Number of wired network connections available to students: 100 total (in the law library, excluding computer labs: 68; in classrooms: 32; in computer labs: 0; elsewhere in the law school: 0)
Law school has a wireless network.
Approximate number of simultaneous users that can be accommodated on wireless network: 700
Students are not required to own a computer.

EMPLOYMENT AND SALARIES

Proportion of 2004 graduates employed at graduation: 73%
Employed 9 months later, as of February 15, 2005: 98%
Salaries in the private sector (law firms, business, industry): $50,000–$100,000 (25th-75th percentile)
Median salary in the private sector: $78,000
Percentage in the private sector who reported salary information: 52%
Median salary in public service (government, judicial clerkships, academic posts, non-profits): $45,000

Percentage of 2004 graduates in:

Law firms: 52%	Bus./industry (legal): 7%
Bus./industry (nonlegal): 9%	Government: 12%
Public interest: 6%	Judicial clerkship: 4%
Academia : 6%	Unknown: 3%

2004 graduates employed in-state: 56%
2004 graduates employed in foreign countries: 1%
Number of states where graduates are employed: 33
Percentage of 2004 graduates working in: New England: 3%, Middle Atlantic: 12%, East North Central: 64%, West North Central: 2%, South Atlantic: 8%, East South Central: 1%, West South Central: 3%, Mountain: 3%, Pacific: 4%, Unknown: N/A

BAR PASSAGE RATES

Based on 2004 graduates taking Summer 2004 or Winter 2005 exams. Most of the school's first-time test takers took the bar in Ohio.

88%
School's bar passage rate for first-time test takers

81%
Statewide bar passage rate for first-time test takers

Catholic University of America

- Washington, DC, 20064
- http://www.law.edu
- Private
- **Year founded:** 1925
- **2005-2006 tuition:** full-time: $31,405; part-time: $22,750
- **Enrollment 2005-06 academic year:** full-time: 688; part-time: 261
- **U.S. News 2007 law specialty ranking:** clinical training: 11

3.06-3.53	GPA, 25TH-75TH PERCENTILE
156-160	LSAT, 25TH-75TH PERCENTILE
32%	ACCEPTANCE RATE
Tier 3	2007 U.S. NEWS LAW SCHOOL RANKING

ADMISSIONS

Admissions phone number: **(202) 319-5151**
Admissions email address: **admissions@law.edu**
Application website: **N/A**
Application deadline for Fall 2007 admission: **3/01**

Admissions statistics:

Number of applicants for Fall 2005: **2,716**
Number of acceptances: **860**
Number enrolled: **242**
Acceptance rate: **32%**
GPA, 25th-75th percentile, entering class Fall 2005:
3.06-3.53
LSAT, 25th-75th percentile, entering class Fall 2005:
156-160

Part-time program:

Number of applicants for Fall 2005: **786**
Number of acceptances: **200**
Number enrolled: **87**
Acceptance rate: **25%**
GPA, 25th-75th percentile, entering class Fall 2005:
2.99-3.42
LSAT, 25th-75th percentile, entering class Fall 2005:
154-158

FINANCIAL AID

Financial aid phone number: **(202) 319-5143**
Financial aid application deadline: **7/15**
Tuition 2005-2006 academic year: full-time: **$31,405**; part-time: **$22,750**
Room and board: **$12,600**; books: **$1,000**; miscellaneous expenses: **$7,740**
Total of room/board/books/miscellaneous expenses: **$21,340**
University does not offer graduate student housing for which law students are eligible.

Financial aid profile

Percent of students that received grants for the 2004-2005 academic year: full-time: **29%**; part-time **20%**

Median grant amount: full-time: **$10,000**; part-time: **$5,000**
The average law-school debt of those in the Class of 2005 who borrowed: **$92,902**. Proportion who borrowed: **84%**

ACADEMIC PROGRAMS

Calendar: **semester**
Joint degrees awarded: **J.D./MSW; J.D./MA Pol.; J.D./Phil**
Typical first-year section size: Full-time: **80**; Part-time: **80**
Is there typically a "small section" of the first year class, other than Legal Writing, taught by full-time faculty?:
Full-time: **yes**; Part-time: **yes**
Number of course titles, beyond the first year curriculum, offered last year: **132**
Percentages of upper division course sections, excluding seminars, with an enrollment of:

Under 25: **74%**	25 to 49: **13%**
50 to 74: **10%**	75 to 99: **2%**
100+: **0%**	

Areas of specialization: appellate advocacy, clinical training, dispute resolution, environmental law, healthcare law, intellectual property law, international law, tax law, trial advocacy

Fall 2005 faculty profile

Total teaching faculty: **109**. Full-time: **40%**; **61%** men, **39%** women, **16%** minorities. Part-time: **60%**; **78%** men, **22%** women, **11%** minorities
Student-to-faculty ratio: **16.3**

SPECIAL PROGRAMS (as provided by law school):

The Columbus School of Law of The Catholic University of America offers the following clinical courses: The General Practice Clinic, Families and the Law Clinic and Advocacy for the Elderly, offered by the Columbus Community Legal Services (CCLS) programs; the Criminal Prosecution Clinic; D.C. Law Students in Court; Legal Externships: Public Policy Fieldwork; the Securities and Exchange Commission Student Observer program, and a variety of simulated lawyering courses.

The Columbus School of Law of The Catholic University of America offers certificates of specialization in four practice areas of law: Communications, International, Public Policy and Securities, through its Institutes and Special Programs. Students accepted in one or more of the Institutes and Special Programs must fulfill curricular and experiential components of the program(s), and complete a research and writing requirement. The Institute for Communications Law Studies celebrates over 20 years of training students in communications regulation and policy. In its twentieth year, the Comparative and International Law Institute allows students to pursue a concentration in private and public areas of international law. The Law and Public Policy Program, established in 1984, is an academic enrichment program for students interested in careers in government, public interest law, politics, or public policy development. The Securities and Corporate Law Program offers students the opportunity to gain expertise in securities regulation and enforcement policy. Two non-certificate programs, the Interdisciplinary Program in Law and Religion provides students, faculty and alumni with a framework for scholarly exchange and public discussion on current issues at the nexus of law and religion; and, The Center for Law, Philosophy and Culture is a forum for inquiry into the meaning of law and legal institutions in relation to culture and human good. A highlight of the law school program includes, in its fifteenth year, the International Business and Trade Summer Law Program in Cracow, Poland, which has been noted as a model summer program, bringing together American, Canadian, and Polish students to study comparative international law.

STUDENT BODY

Fall 2005 full-time enrollment: 688

Men: 47%	Women: 53%
African-American: 3.3%	American Indian: 0.3%
Asian-American: 8.1%	Mexican-American: 0.4%
Puerto Rican: 0.6%	Other Hisp-Amer: 4.4%
White: 61.9%	International: 0.9%
Unknown: 20.1%	

Fall 2005 part-time enrollment: 261

Men: 56%	Women: 44%
African-American: 5.4%	American Indian: 0.4%
Asian-American: 8.4%	Mexican-American: 0.4%
Puerto Rican: 1.1%	Other Hisp-Amer: 3.4%
White: 60.2%	International: 1.1%
Unknown: 19.5%	

Attrition rates for 2004-2005 full-time students
Percent of students discontinuing law school:

Men: 1%	Women: 2%
First-year students: 3%	Second-year students: 1%
Third-year students: N/A	

LIBRARY RESOURCES

The library holds 124,404 and receives 5,276 current subscriptions.

Total volumes: 402,845
Percentage of the titles in the online catalog: 100%
Total seats available for library users: 502

INFORMATION TECHNOLOGY

Number of wired network connections available to students: 432 total (in the law library, excluding computer labs: 212; in classrooms: 170; in computer labs: 0; elsewhere in the law school: 50)
Law school has a wireless network.
Approximate number of simultaneous users that can be accommodated on wireless network: 500
Students are not required to own a computer.

EMPLOYMENT AND SALARIES

Proportion of 2004 graduates employed at graduation: 64%
Employed 9 months later, as of February 15, 2005: 90%
Salaries in the private sector (law firms, business, industry): $50,000–$90,000 (25th-75th percentile)
Median salary in the private sector: $62,400
Percentage in the private sector who reported salary information: 98%
Median salary in public service (government, judicial clerkships, academic posts, non-profits): $50,000

Percentage of 2004 graduates in:

Law firms: 32%	Bus./industry (legal): 13%
Bus./industry (nonlegal): 8%	Government: 26%
Public interest: 3%	Judicial clerkship: 11%
Academia : 0%	Unknown: 6%

2004 graduates employed in-state: 49%
2004 graduates employed in foreign countries: 0%
Number of states where graduates are employed: 22
Percentage of 2004 graduates working in: New England: 3%, Middle Atlantic: 9%, East North Central: 0%, West North Central: 0%, South Atlantic: 83%, East South Central: 1%, West South Central: 0%, Mountain: 2%, Pacific: 1%, Unknown: 0%

BAR PASSAGE RATES

Based on 2004 graduates taking Summer 2004 or Winter 2005 exams. Most of the school's first-time test takers took the bar in Maryland.

72%
School's bar passage rate for first-time test takers

72%
Statewide bar passage rate for first-time test takers

Chapman University

- 1 University Drive, Orange, CA, 92866
- http://www.chapman.edu/law
- Private
- Year founded: 1995
- 2005-2006 tuition: full-time: $29,854; part-time: $20,500
- Enrollment 2005-06 academic year: full-time: 515; part-time: 41
- U.S. News 2007 law specialty ranking: N/A

3.01-3.61	GPA, 25TH-75TH PERCENTILE
154-158	LSAT, 25TH-75TH PERCENTILE
30%	ACCEPTANCE RATE
Tier 4	2007 U.S. NEWS LAW SCHOOL RANKING

ADMISSIONS

Admissions phone number: **(714) 628-2500**
Admissions email address: **lawadm@chapman.edu**
Application website:
   http://web.chapman.edu/law_asp/RegForm.html
Application deadline for Fall 2007 admission: **6/01**

Admissions statistics:

Number of applicants for Fall 2005: **2,210**
Number of acceptances: **668**
Number enrolled: **187**
Acceptance rate: **30%**
GPA, 25th-75th percentile, entering class Fall 2005:
   3.01-3.61
LSAT, 25th-75th percentile, entering class Fall 2005:
   154-158

Part-time program:

Number of applicants for Fall 2005: **9**
Number of acceptances: **9**
Number enrolled: **7**
Acceptance rate: **100%**
GPA, 25th-75th percentile, entering class Fall 2005:
   2.98-3.15
LSAT, 25th-75th percentile, entering class Fall 2005: **151-154**

FINANCIAL AID

Financial aid phone number: **(714) 628-2510**
Financial aid application deadline: **6/01**
Tuition 2005-2006 academic year: full-time: **$29,854**; part-
   time: **$20,500**
Room and board: **$9,900**; books: **$1,000**; miscellaneous
   expenses: **$3,330**
Total of room/board/books/miscellaneous expenses:
   $14,230
University offers graduate student housing for which law
   students are eligible.

Financial aid profile

Percent of students that received grants for the 2004-2005
   academic year: full-time: **37%**; part-time **27%**

Median grant amount: full-time: **$13,436**; part-time: **$7,386**
The average law-school debt of those in the Class of 2005
   who borrowed: **$70,846**. Proportion who borrowed: **90%**

ACADEMIC PROGRAMS

Calendar: **semester**
Joint degrees awarded: **J.D./M.B.A.**
Typical first-year section size: Full-time: **65**
Is there typically a "small section" of the first year class,
   other than Legal Writing, taught by full-time faculty?:
   Full-time: **no**
Number of course titles, beyond the first year curriculum,
   offered last year: **83**
Percentages of upper division course sections, excluding
   seminars, with an enrollment of:

Under 25: **67%**	25 to 49: **16%**
50 to 74: **13%**	75 to 99: **4%**
100+: **0%**	

Areas of specialization: clinical training, dispute resolution,
   environmental law, intellectual property law, international law, tax law, trial advocacy

Fall 2005 faculty profile

Total teaching faculty: **54**. Full-time: **54%**; **59%** men, **41%**
   women, **10%** minorities. Part-time: **46%**; **80%** men,
   20% women, **8%** minorities
Student-to-faculty ratio: **17.7**

SPECIAL PROGRAMS *(as provided by law school):*

Chapman Law School has certificate programs for J.D. students
in three areas: a)Taxation; b) Environmental, Land Use & Real
Estate; and c) Advocacy & Dispute Resolution. We also have a
joint J.D./M.B.A. program. We also offer clinical programs in
elder law, taxation law and constitutional litigation. In addition,
we have a Ninth Circuit Appellate Law Clinic in which selected
students have the opportunity to brief and argue a case before
the U.S. Court of Appeals for the Ninth Circuit. Chapman Law
School is also part of a consortium of law schools that will sponsor a summer law program in England in 2005.

STUDENT BODY

Fall 2005 full-time enrollment: 515

Men: 50%	Women: 50%
African-American: 0.6%	American Indian: 1.0%
Asian-American: 17.7%	Mexican-American: 4.3%
Puerto Rican: 0.0%	Other Hisp-Amer: 2.1%
White: 54.6%	International: 0.2%
Unknown: 19.6%	

Fall 2005 part-time enrollment: 41

Men: 51%	Women: 49%
African-American: 2.4%	American Indian: 0.0%
Asian-American: 22.0%	Mexican-American: 9.8%
Puerto Rican: 0.0%	Other Hisp-Amer: 4.9%
White: 41.5%	International: 0.0%
Unknown: 19.5%	

Attrition rates for 2004-2005 full-time students
Percent of students discontinuing law school:

Men: 5%	Women: 2%
First-year students: 9%	Second-year students: 1%
Third-year students: 1%	

LIBRARY RESOURCES

The library holds 160,456 and receives 3,050 current subscriptions.
Total volumes: 279,673
Percentage of the titles in the online catalog: 100%
Total seats available for library users: 322

INFORMATION TECHNOLOGY

Number of wired network connections available to students: 577 total (in the law library, excluding computer labs: 180; in classrooms: 332; in computer labs: 40; elsewhere in the law school: 25)
Law school has a wireless network.
Approximate number of simultaneous users that can be accommodated on wireless network: 500
Students are not required to own a computer.

EMPLOYMENT AND SALARIES

Proportion of 2004 graduates employed at graduation: 53%
Employed 9 months later, as of February 15, 2005: 91%
Salaries in the private sector (law firms, business, industry): $50,000–$75,000 (25th-75th percentile)
Median salary in the private sector: $65,000
Percentage in the private sector who reported salary information: 54%
Median salary in public service (government, judicial clerkships, academic posts, non-profits): $56,500

Percentage of 2004 graduates in:

Law firms: 62%	Bus./industry (legal): 5%
Bus./industry (nonlegal): 10%	Government: 11%
Public interest: 4%	Judicial clerkship: 3%
Academia : 4%	Unknown: 1%

2004 graduates employed in-state: 91%
2004 graduates employed in foreign countries: 0%
Number of states where graduates are employed: 7
Percentage of 2004 graduates working in: New England: 0%, Middle Atlantic: 0%, East North Central: 0%, West North Central: 0%, South Atlantic: 4%, East South Central: 1%, West South Central: 1%, Mountain: 3%, Pacific: 91%, Unknown: 0%

BAR PASSAGE RATES

Based on 2004 graduates taking Summer 2004 or Winter 2005 exams. Most of the school's first-time test takers took the bar in California.

67%
School's bar passage rate for first-time test takers

61%
Statewide bar passage rate for first-time test takers

Cleveland State University (Marshall)

- 2121 Euclid Avenue, LB 138, Cleveland, OH, 44115-2214
- http://www.law.csuohio.edu
- Public
- Year founded: 1897
- 2005-2006 tuition: In-state: full-time: $13,988, part-time: $10,760; Out-of-state: full-time: $19,209
- Enrollment 2005-06 academic year: full-time: 463; part-time: 261
- U.S. News 2007 law specialty ranking: N/A

3.14-3.59 GPA, 25TH-75TH PERCENTILE

151-157 LSAT, 25TH-75TH PERCENTILE

31% ACCEPTANCE RATE

Tier 3 2007 U.S. NEWS LAW SCHOOL RANKING

ADMISSIONS

Admissions phone number: (216) 687-2304
Admissions email address: admissions@law.csuohio.edu
Application website: http://www.law.csuohio.edu/admissions/apply.html
Application deadline for Fall 2007 admission: 5/01

Admissions statistics:

Number of applicants for Fall 2005: 1,403
Number of acceptances: 431
Number enrolled: 170
Acceptance rate: 31%
GPA, 25th-75th percentile, entering class Fall 2005: 3.14-3.59
LSAT, 25th-75th percentile, entering class Fall 2005: 151-157

Part-time program:

Number of applicants for Fall 2005: 351
Number of acceptances: 110
Number enrolled: 66
Acceptance rate: 31%
GPA, 25th-75th percentile, entering class Fall 2005: 2.87-3.59
LSAT, 25th-75th percentile, entering class Fall 2005: 151-156

FINANCIAL AID

Financial aid phone number: (216) 687-2317
Financial aid application deadline: 5/01
Tuition 2005-2006 academic year: In-state: full-time: $13,988, part-time: $10,760; Out-of-state: full-time: $19,209
Room and board: $10,630; books: $1,300; miscellaneous expenses: $4,332
Total of room/board/books/miscellaneous expenses: $16,262
University offers graduate student housing for which law students are eligible.

Financial aid profile

Percent of students that received grants for the 2004-2005 academic year: full-time: 42%; part-time 20%
Median grant amount: full-time: $4,000; part-time: $3,640

The average law-school debt of those in the Class of 2005 who borrowed: $53,165. Proportion who borrowed: 92%

ACADEMIC PROGRAMS

Calendar: semester
Joint degrees awarded: J.D./M.B.A.; J.D./M.P.A.; J.D./MUPDD; J.D./MAES; J.D./MSES
Typical first-year section size: Full-time: 58; Part-time: 57
Is there typically a "small section" of the first year class, other than Legal Writing, taught by full-time faculty?: Full-time: no; Part-time: no
Number of course titles, beyond the first year curriculum, offered last year: 71
Percentages of upper division course sections, excluding seminars, with an enrollment of:

Under 25: 56%	25 to 49: 28%
50 to 74: 15%	75 to 99: 1%
100+: 0%	

Areas of specialization: appellate advocacy, clinical training, dispute resolution, environmental law, healthcare law, intellectual property law, international law, tax law, trial advocacy

Fall 2005 faculty profile

Total teaching faculty: 92. Full-time: 50%; 59% men, 41% women, 7% minorities. Part-time: 50%; 85% men, 15% women, 0% minorities
Student-to-faculty ratio: 12.7

SPECIAL PROGRAMS (as provided by law school):

Clinical programs include community advocacy, employment law, environmental law, fair housing law, and law and public policy.

Externships include judicial, independent (student designed), public interest, and U.S. attorney.

Concentrations are available in business law, civil litigation and dispute resolution, criminal law, employment and labor law, and tax.

Students may enroll in a summer program in St. Petersburg, Russia.

Joint degree programs include J.D./M.B.A. (business), J.D./M.P.A. (public administration), J.D./M.U.P.D.D. (planning, design, and development), J.D./M.A.E.S. (environmental studies), and J.D./M.S.E.S. (environmental science).

STUDENT BODY

Fall 2005 full-time enrollment: 463

Men: 52%	Women: 48%
African-American: 4.8%	American Indian: 0.6%
Asian-American: 3.7%	Mexican-American: 0.0%
Puerto Rican: 0.0%	Other Hisp-Amer: 1.7%
White: 84.2%	International: 1.1%
Unknown: 3.9%	

Fall 2005 part-time enrollment: 261

Men: 49%	Women: 51%
African-American: 8.8%	American Indian: 0.0%
Asian-American: 3.4%	Mexican-American: 0.0%
Puerto Rican: 0.0%	Other Hisp-Amer: 3.1%
White: 82.8%	International: 0.4%
Unknown: 1.5%	

Attrition rates for 2004-2005 full-time students
Percent of students discontinuing law school:

Men: 7%	Women: 6%
First-year students: 19%	Second-year students: 2%
Third-year students: N/A	

LIBRARY RESOURCES

The library holds 150,586 and receives 3,243 current subscriptions.
Total volumes: 519,176
Percentage of the titles in the online catalog: 100%
Total seats available for library users: 487

INFORMATION TECHNOLOGY

Number of wired network connections available to students: 148 total (in the law library, excluding computer labs: 148; in classrooms: 0; in computer labs: 0; elsewhere in the law school: 0)
Law school has a wireless network.

Approximate number of simultaneous users that can be accommodated on wireless network: 1,000
Students are not required to own a computer.

EMPLOYMENT AND SALARIES

Proportion of 2004 graduates employed at graduation: 64%
Employed 9 months later, as of February 15, 2005: 91%
Salaries in the private sector (law firms, business, industry): $50,000–$90,000 (25th-75th percentile)
Median salary in the private sector: $70,000
Percentage in the private sector who reported salary information: 37%
Median salary in public service (government, judicial clerkships, academic posts, non-profits): $44,500

Percentage of 2004 graduates in:

Law firms: 58%	Bus./industry (legal): 3%
Bus./industry (nonlegal): 15%	Government: 13%
Public interest: 3%	Judicial clerkship: 5%
Academia : 3%	Unknown: 0%

2004 graduates employed in-state: 87%
2004 graduates employed in foreign countries: 0%
Number of states where graduates are employed: 15
Percentage of 2004 graduates working in: New England: 1%, Middle Atlantic: 2%, East North Central: 87%, West North Central: 0%, South Atlantic: 7%, East South Central: 0%, West South Central: 1%, Mountain: 1%, Pacific: 1%, Unknown: 0%

BAR PASSAGE RATES

Based on 2004 graduates taking Summer 2004 or Winter 2005 exams. Most of the school's first-time test takers took the bar in Ohio.

73%
School's bar passage rate for first-time test takers

81%
Statewide bar passage rate for first-time test takers

College of William and Mary

- PO Box 8795, Williamsburg, VA, 23187-8795
- http://www.wm.edu/law
- Public
- Year founded: 1779
- 2005-2006 tuition: In-state: full-time: $15,300, part-time: N/A; Out-of-state: full-time: $25,500
- Enrollment 2005-06 academic year: full-time: 607
- U.S. News 2007 law specialty ranking: N/A

3.31-3.80 GPA, 25TH-75TH PERCENTILE

160-165 LSAT, 25TH-75TH PERCENTILE

22% ACCEPTANCE RATE

27 2007 U.S. NEWS LAW SCHOOL RANKING

ADMISSIONS

Admissions phone number: **(757) 221-3785**
Admissions email address: **lawadm@wm.edu**
Application website:
   http://www.wm.edu/law/prospective/admissions/jdprogram_procedure.shtml
Application deadline for Fall 2007 admission: **8/27**

Admissions statistics:

Number of applicants for Fall 2005: **4,116**
Number of acceptances: **924**
Number enrolled: **205**
Acceptance rate: **22%**
GPA, 25th-75th percentile, entering class Fall 2005:
   3.31-3.80
LSAT, 25th-75th percentile, entering class Fall 2005:
   160-165

FINANCIAL AID

Financial aid phone number: **(757) 221-2420**
Financial aid application deadline: **2/15**
Tuition 2005-2006 academic year: In-state: full-time:
   $15,300, part-time: **N/A**; Out-of-state: full-time: **$25,500**
Room and board: **$7,368**; books: **$1,250**; miscellaneous
   expenses: **$850**
Total of room/board/books/miscellaneous expenses:
   $9,468
University offers graduate student housing for which law
   students are eligible.

Financial aid profile

Percent of students that received grants for the 2004-2005
   academic year: full-time: **25%**
Median grant amount: full-time: **$5,000**
The average law-school debt of those in the Class of 2005
   who borrowed: **$52,738**. Proportion who borrowed: **84%**

ACADEMIC PROGRAMS

Calendar: **semester**
Joint degrees awarded: **J.D./M.B.A; J.D./M.P.P; J.D./M.A.**
Typical first-year section size: Full-time: **70**

Is there typically a "small section" of the first year class,
   other than Legal Writing, taught by full-time faculty?:
   Full-time: **yes**
Number of course titles, beyond the first year curriculum,
   offered last year: **120**
Percentages of upper division course sections, excluding
   seminars, with an enrollment of:
   Under 25: **75%**   25 to 49: **17%**
   50 to 74: **5%**   75 to 99: **2%**
   100+: **1%**
Areas of specialization: appellate advocacy, clinical training,
   dispute resolution, environmental law, healthcare law,
   intellectual property law, international law, tax law, trial
   advocacy

Fall 2005 faculty profile

Total teaching faculty: **N/A**. Full-time: **N/A; N/A** men, **N/A**
   women, **N/A** minorities. Part-time: **N/A; N/A** men, **N/A**
   women, **N/A** minorities
Student-to-faculty ratio: **15.7**

SPECIAL PROGRAMS *(as provided by law school):*

William and Mary Law School provides numerous externship
and clinical opportunities. They include externships with the
Virginia Attorney General, Court of Appeals, Supreme Court,
and Department of Employee Dispute Resolution, as well as in
nonprofit law, judicial clerkship, therapeutic justice, and general
practice. Clinics are offered in domestic violence, legal aid, and
federal tax practice. Students are active participants with programs
sponsored by the Institute of Bill of Rights Law and the
Courtroom 21 Project.

We offer summer study both on campus in Williamsburg
and abroad in Madrid, Spain.

The Law School offers three joint degree programs. The
J.D./master in business administration and the J.D./master of
public policy both can be completed in four years of study
(rather than the five it would require if taken separately). The
J.D./master of arts in American culture may be completed in
three years.

STUDENT BODY

Fall 2005 full-time enrollment: 607

Men: 55%	Women: 45%
African-American: 8.2%	American Indian: 0.2%
Asian-American: 5.1%	Mexican-American: 0.0%
Puerto Rican: 0.0%	Other Hisp-Amer: 1.3%
White: 74.1%	International: 0.0%
Unknown: 11.0%	

Attrition rates for 2004-2005 full-time students
Percent of students discontinuing law school:

Men: 2%	Women: 2%
First-year students: 1%	Second-year students: 3%
Third-year students: 1%	

LIBRARY RESOURCES

The library holds 167,018 and receives 4,387 current subscriptions.
Total volumes: 386,618
Percentage of the titles in the online catalog: 99%
Total seats available for library users: 427

INFORMATION TECHNOLOGY

Number of wired network connections available to students: 48 total (in the law library, excluding computer labs: 45; in classrooms: 0; in computer labs: 2; elsewhere in the law school: 1)
Law school has a wireless network.
Approximate number of simultaneous users that can be accommodated on wireless network: 2,000
Students are not required to own a computer.

EMPLOYMENT AND SALARIES

Proportion of 2004 graduates employed at graduation: 85%

Employed 9 months later, as of February 15, 2005: 96%
Salaries in the private sector (law firms, business, industry): $75,000–$125,000 (25th-75th percentile)
Median salary in the private sector: $95,000
Percentage in the private sector who reported salary information: 82%
Median salary in public service (government, judicial clerkships, academic posts, non-profits): $48,947

Percentage of 2004 graduates in:

Law firms: 58%	Bus./industry (legal): 3%
Bus./industry (nonlegal): 1%	Government: 20%
Public interest: 5%	Judicial clerkship: 12%
Academia : 1%	Unknown: 0%

2004 graduates employed in-state: 37%
2004 graduates employed in foreign countries: 0%
Number of states where graduates are employed: 26
Percentage of 2004 graduates working in: New England: 2%, Middle Atlantic: 12%, East North Central: 6%, West North Central: 2%, South Atlantic: 70%, East South Central: 2%, West South Central: 2%, Mountain: 1%, Pacific: 2%, Unknown: 1%

BAR PASSAGE RATES

Based on 2004 graduates taking Summer 2004 or Winter 2005 exams. Most of the school's first-time test takers took the bar in Virginia.

85%
School's bar passage rate for first-time test takers

74%
Statewide bar passage rate for first-time test takers

Columbia University

- 435 W. 116th Street, New York, NY, 10027
- http://www.law.columbia.edu
- Private
- **Year founded:** 1858
- **2005-2006 tuition:** full-time: $39,172; part-time: N/A
- **Enrollment 2005-06 academic year:** full-time: 1,242
- **U.S. News 2007 law specialty ranking:** clinical training: 13, intellecutal property law: 10, international law: 2, tax law: 24

3.50-3.80 GPA, 25TH-75TH PERCENTILE

168-173 LSAT, 25TH-75TH PERCENTILE

15% ACCEPTANCE RATE

4 2007 U.S. NEWS LAW SCHOOL RANKING

ADMISSIONS

Admissions phone number: **(212) 854-2670**
Admissions email address: **admissions@law.columbia.edu**
Application website: **https://www-app.law.columbia.edu/admissions/index.jsp**
Application deadline for Fall 2007 admission: **2/15**

Admissions statistics:
Number of applicants for Fall 2005: **8,020**
Number of acceptances: **1,169**
Number enrolled: **378**
Acceptance rate: **15%**
GPA, 25th-75th percentile, entering class Fall 2005: **3.50-3.80**
LSAT, 25th-75th percentile, entering class Fall 2005: **168-173**

FINANCIAL AID

Financial aid phone number: **(212) 854-7730**
Financial aid application deadline: **3/01**
Tuition 2005-2006 academic year: full-time: **$39,172**; part-time: **N/A**
Room and board: **$13,801**; books: **$950**; miscellaneous expenses: **$3,150**
Total of room/board/books/miscellaneous expenses: **$17,901**
University offers graduate student housing for which law students are eligible.

Financial aid profile
Percent of students that received grants for the 2004-2005 academic year: full-time: **48%**
Median grant amount: full-time: **$11,500**
The average law-school debt of those in the Class of 2005 who borrowed: **$98,066**. Proportion who borrowed: **80%**

ACADEMIC PROGRAMS

Calendar: **semester**
Joint degrees awarded: **M.A. ECON; M.A. HIST; M.A. PHIL; M.A. POL; M.A. PSY; M.A. SOC; M.B.A.; M.F.A.; M.I.A.; M.P.A.; M.P.H.; M.S. JOUR; M.S. URB PLAN;**
M.S.W.; PH.D. ANTH; PH.D. HIST; PH.D. PHIL; PH.D. POL; PH.D. SOC; PH.D. ECON; M.P.H.I.L.; PH.D. ENG; PH.D. RELIG; M.A. ANTH
Typical first-year section size: Full-time: **109**
Is there typically a "small section" of the first year class, other than Legal Writing, taught by full-time faculty?: Full-time: **yes**
Number of course titles, beyond the first year curriculum, offered last year: **211**
Percentages of upper division course sections, excluding seminars, with an enrollment of:
Under 25: **48%**   25 to 49: **22%**
50 to 74: **8%**   75 to 99: **8%**
100+: **14%**
Areas of specialization: appellate advocacy, clinical training, dispute resolution, environmental law, healthcare law, intellectual property law, international law, tax law, trial advocacy

Fall 2005 faculty profile
Total teaching faculty: **240**. Full-time: **45%**; **66%** men, **34%** women, **12%** minorities. Part-time: **55%**; **73%** men, **27%** women, **8%** minorities
Student-to-faculty ratio: **11.7**

SPECIAL PROGRAMS *(as provided by law school)*:

Clinics are Child Advocacy, Environmental Law, Human Rights, Prisoners and Families, Law and the Arts, Lawyering in the Digital Age, Mediation and Non-Profit Organizations/Small Business. Externship and other offerings are Environmental Collaborative Decision-Making Project, Reconsidering the Guilt of Executed Defendants Project; Federal District Court Clerkship, Federal Appellate Court Clerkship, Battered Women's Legal Services Externship, Fair Housing Externship, Legal Education in the Community, NY Attorney General Externship and United Nations Externship. The Law School has developed an exceptional Public Interest program through public interest courses and projects, innovative clinics, and cutting edge externships and pro bono projects. Columbia's Repayment Assistance Program (LRAP) has been recognized as among the five best in the nation. Public Service Fellowships provide enhanced benefits to graduates who show exceptional dedication and potential for contribution to the public good. Columbia funds summer jobs at human rights and public interest law organizations through the Human Rights Internship Program (HRIP) and Other Summer Fellowships. Now in its twentieth year, Columbia's HRIP is one of the foremost summer internship programs for American law students. Faculty directed centers serve to coordinate outward-looking endeavors, such as the organization of public lectures and scholarly and practice conferences, hosting visiting faculty and scholars, selection of student fellows, engagement with the business or legal practice domestic and international communities, and the coordination of interdisciplinary efforts. Columbia students may pursue a joint degree program with the following graduate or professional schools at the University: College of Physicians & Surgeons; Schools of Arts & Sciences; Business Administration; International & Public Affairs; Journalism; Social Work; Architecture, Planning & Preservation. Students may earn the J.D. degree from Columbia Law along with the Masters in Public Affairs degree from Princeton University's Woodrow Wilson School of Public and International Affairs. Six years ago, Columbia was the first U.S. Law School to establish a double degree program providing its participants with both a U.S. Juris Doctor and a foreign law degree: the French Maitrise en Droit. The program now includes: J.D./Maitrise Program with the Universite de Paris I-Pantheon Sorbonne; J.D./D.E.S.S. Program with the Universite de Paris I Pantheon-Sorbonne and the Institut d'etudes politiques, ëSciences-Po'; J.D./LL.M. Program with the University of London; and J.D./LL.B. Program with the University of London. Columbia currently has 12 semester study abroad programs in 10 countries available to its J.D. students.

STUDENT BODY

Fall 2005 full-time enrollment: 1,242

Men: **55%**	Women: **45%**
African-American: **8.6%**	American Indian: **0.6%**
Asian-American: **14.7%**	Mexican-American: **3.1%**
Puerto Rican: **1.4%**	Other Hisp-Amer: **1.6%**
White: **60.4%**	International: **8.9%**
Unknown: **0.6%**	

Attrition rates for 2004-2005 full-time students
Percent of students discontinuing law school:

Men: **N/A**	Women: **N/A**
First-year students: **N/A**	Second-year students: **N/A**
Third-year students: **N/A**	

LIBRARY RESOURCES

The library holds **376,758** and receives **6,472** current subscriptions.
Total volumes: **1,092,534**

Percentage of the titles in the online catalog: **100%**
Total seats available for library users: **330**

INFORMATION TECHNOLOGY

Number of wired network connections available to students: **3,132** total (in the law library, excluding computer labs: **40**; in classrooms: **2,478**; in computer labs: **188**; elsewhere in the law school: **426**)
Law school has a wireless network.
Approximate number of simultaneous users that can be accommodated on wireless network: **2,944**
Students are not required to own a computer.

EMPLOYMENT AND SALARIES

Proportion of 2004 graduates employed at graduation: **99%**
Employed 9 months later, as of February 15, 2005: **99%**
Salaries in the private sector (law firms, business, industry): **$125,000–$125,000** (25th-75th percentile)
Median salary in the private sector: **$125,000**
Percentage in the private sector who reported salary information: **100%**
Median salary in public service (government, judicial clerkships, academic posts, non-profits): **$52,650**

Percentage of 2004 graduates in:

Law firms: **77%**	Bus./industry (legal): **2%**
Bus./industry (nonlegal): **0%**	Government: **4%**
Public interest: **3%**	Judicial clerkship: **14%**
Academia : **1%**	Unknown: **0%**

2004 graduates employed in-state: **65%**
2004 graduates employed in foreign countries: **3%**
Number of states where graduates are employed: **22**
Percentage of 2004 graduates working in: New England: **3%**, Middle Atlantic: **70%**, East North Central: **3%**, West North Central: **0%**, South Atlantic: **9%**, East South Central: **0%**, West South Central: **3%**, Mountain: **0%**, Pacific: **8%**, Unknown: **0%**

BAR PASSAGE RATES

Based on 2004 graduates taking Summer 2004 or Winter 2005 exams. Most of the school's first-time test takers took the bar in New York.

94%
School's bar passage rate for first-time test takers

75%
Statewide bar passage rate for first-time test takers

Cornell University

■ Myron Taylor Hall, Ithaca, NY, 14853-4901
■ http://www.lawschool.cornell.edu
■ Private
■ Year founded: 1887
■ 2005-2006 tuition: full-time: $37,750; part-time: N/A
■ Enrollment 2005-06 academic year: full-time: 580
■ U.S. News 2007 law specialty ranking: international law: 13

3.50-3.80 GPA, 25TH-75TH PERCENTILE

165-168 LSAT, 25TH-75TH PERCENTILE

21% ACCEPTANCE RATE

13 2007 U.S. NEWS LAW SCHOOL RANKING

ADMISSIONS
Admissions phone number: **(607) 255-5141**
Admissions email address: **lawadmit@postoffice.law.cornell.edu**
Application website:
http://www.lawschool.cornell.edu/admissions
Application deadline for Fall 2007 admission: **2/01**

Admissions statistics:
Number of applicants for Fall 2005: **4,177**
Number of acceptances: **862**
Number enrolled: **193**
Acceptance rate: **21%**
GPA, 25th-75th percentile, entering class Fall 2005:
3.50-3.80
LSAT, 25th-75th percentile, entering class Fall 2005:
165-168

FINANCIAL AID
Financial aid phone number: **(607) 255-5141**
Financial aid application deadline: **3/15**
Tuition 2005-2006 academic year: full-time: **$37,750**; part-time: **N/A**
Room and board: **$9,500**; books: **$800**; miscellaneous expenses: **$5,850**
Total of room/board/books/miscellaneous expenses: **$16,150**
University offers graduate student housing for which law students are eligible.

Financial aid profile
Percent of students that received grants for the 2004-2005 academic year: full-time: **44%**
Median grant amount: full-time: **$12,750**
The average law-school debt of those in the Class of 2005 who borrowed: **N/A**. Proportion who borrowed: **100%**

ACADEMIC PROGRAMS
Calendar: **semester**
Joint degrees awarded: **J.D./LL.M. (International Legal Studies); JD/Maitrise en Droit (French Law Degree);**
J.D./D.E.S.S. (French Business Law Degree);
J.D./M.LL.P. (German Law Degree); J.D./M.B.A.;
J.D./Ph.D.; J.D./M.P.A.
Typical first-year section size: Full-time: **97**
Is there typically a "small section" of the first year class, other than Legal Writing, taught by full-time faculty?:
Full-time: **yes**
Number of course titles, beyond the first year curriculum, offered last year: **120**
Percentages of upper division course sections, excluding seminars, with an enrollment of:
Under 25: **35%**   25 to 49: **33%**
50 to 74: **23%**   75 to 99: **5%**
100+: **5%**
Areas of specialization: appellate advocacy, clinical training, dispute resolution, environmental law, healthcare law, intellectual property law, international law, tax law, trial advocacy

Fall 2005 faculty profile
Total teaching faculty: **N/A**. Full-time: **N/A**; **N/A** men, **N/A** women, **N/A** minorities. Part-time: **N/A**; **N/A** men, **N/A** women, **N/A** minorities
Student-to-faculty ratio: **10.3**

SPECIAL PROGRAMS *(as provided by law school):*
J.D. students at Cornell benefit not only from the law school's well-known collegial atmosphere and curricular breadth but also from an array of clinics, programs, institutes, and centers.

Programs of particular note are the Berger International Legal Studies Program; the Clark Center for International and Comparative Legal Studies; the Paris Summer Institute of International and Comparative Law; the Feminism and Legal Theory Project; the Gender, Sexuality, and Family Project; the Legal Information Institute; the John M. Olin Program in Law and Economics; and the Cornell Death Penalty Project.

Over 50 percent of graduates participate in live-client clinics that include a legal aid clinic and specialized clinics in labor law, prosecution, criminal defense, asylum and convention against torture, capital trial, post conviction capital litigation, government benefits, and women and the law.

In addition, students can take advantage of a range of externships and joint degree possibilities, as well as an ever expanding number of formal international exchange programs that now include Bucerius University in Hamburg, Germany; the Central European University in Budapest, Hungary; ESADE in Barcelona; Heidelberg University in Germany; University of Paris I in France; Waseda University Graduate School of Law in Tokyo; and the University of Sydney in Australia.

STUDENT BODY

Fall 2005 full-time enrollment: 580

Men: 52%	Women: 48%
African-American: 7.8%	American Indian: 0.7%
Asian-American: 16.7%	Mexican-American: 2.1%
Puerto Rican: 1.2%	Other Hisp-Amer: 1.9%
White: 65.0%	International: 4.7%
Unknown: 0.0%	

Attrition rates for 2004-2005 full-time students
Percent of students discontinuing law school:

Men: 1%	Women: 1%
First-year students: 3%	Second-year students: 1%
Third-year students: 0%	

LIBRARY RESOURCES

The library holds 214,108 and receives 6,632 current subscriptions.
Total volumes: 708,894
Percentage of the titles in the online catalog: 100%
Total seats available for library users: 430

INFORMATION TECHNOLOGY

Number of wired network connections available to students: 105 total (in the law library, excluding computer labs: 0; in classrooms: 34; in computer labs: 45; elsewhere in the law school: 26)
Law school has a wireless network.
Approximate number of simultaneous users that can be accommodated on wireless network: 320
Students are not required to own a computer.

EMPLOYMENT AND SALARIES

Proportion of 2004 graduates employed at graduation: 97%
Employed 9 months later, as of February 15, 2005: 98%
Salaries in the private sector (law firms, business, industry): $125,000–$125,000 (25th-75th percentile)
Median salary in the private sector: $125,000
Percentage in the private sector who reported salary information: 74%
Median salary in public service (government, judicial clerkships, academic posts, non-profits): $51,348

Percentage of 2004 graduates in:

Law firms: 76%	Bus./industry (legal): 1%
Bus./industry (nonlegal): 0%	Government: 2%
Public interest: 2%	Judicial clerkship: 13%
Academia : 3%	Unknown: 4%

2004 graduates employed in-state: 54%
2004 graduates employed in foreign countries: 1%
Number of states where graduates are employed: 27
Percentage of 2004 graduates working in: New England: 4%, Middle Atlantic: 58%, East North Central: 4%, West North Central: 1%, South Atlantic: 14%, East South Central: 1%, West South Central: 1%, Mountain: 2%, Pacific: 14%, Unknown: 0%

BAR PASSAGE RATES

Based on 2004 graduates taking Summer 2004 or Winter 2005 exams. Most of the school's first-time test takers took the bar in New York.

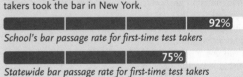

92%
School's bar passage rate for first-time test takers

75%
Statewide bar passage rate for first-time test takers

Creighton University

- 2500 California Plaza, Omaha, NE, 68178
- http://culaw2.creighton.edu/
- Private
- Year founded: 1904
- 2005-2006 tuition: full-time: $23,430; part-time: $15,154
- Enrollment 2005-06 academic year: full-time: 451; part-time: 18
- U.S. News 2007 law specialty ranking: N/A

3.21-3.72 GPA, 25TH-75TH PERCENTILE

150-156 LSAT, 25TH-75TH PERCENTILE

36% ACCEPTANCE RATE

Tier 3 2007 U.S. NEWS LAW SCHOOL RANKING

ADMISSIONS

Admissions phone number: (800) 282-5835
Admissions email address: **lawadmit@creighton.edu**
Application website: **N/A**
Application deadline for Fall 2007 admission: **5/01**

Admissions statistics:

Number of applicants for Fall 2005: **1,402**
Number of acceptances: **505**
Number enrolled: **155**
Acceptance rate: **36%**
GPA, 25th-75th percentile, entering class Fall 2005:
   3.21-3.72
LSAT, 25th-75th percentile, entering class Fall 2005:
   150-156

Part-time program:

Number of applicants for Fall 2005: **68**
Number of acceptances: **15**
Number enrolled: **6**
Acceptance rate: **22%**
GPA, 25th-75th percentile, entering class Fall 2005:
   2.91-3.75
LSAT, 25th-75th percentile, entering class Fall 2005:
   142-158

FINANCIAL AID

Financial aid phone number: **(402) 280-2352**
Financial aid application deadline: **7/01**
Tuition 2005-2006 academic year: full-time: **$23,430**; part-time: **$15,154**
Room and board: **$12,500**; books: **$1,350**; miscellaneous expenses: **$2,680**
Total of room/board/books/miscellaneous expenses: **$16,530**
University offers graduate student housing for which law students are eligible.

Financial aid profile

Percent of students that received grants for the 2004-2005 academic year: full-time: **39%**; part-time **11%**

Median grant amount: full-time: **$6,000**; part-time: **$3,000**
The average law-school debt of those in the Class of 2005 who borrowed: **$76,904**. Proportion who borrowed: **89%**

ACADEMIC PROGRAMS

Calendar: **semester**
Joint degrees awarded: **J.D./M.B.A.**
Typical first-year section size: Full-time: **80**
Is there typically a "small section" of the first year class, other than Legal Writing, taught by full-time faculty?: Full-time: **no**
Number of course titles, beyond the first year curriculum, offered last year: **80**
Percentages of upper division course sections, excluding seminars, with an enrollment of:

Under 25: **72%**	25 to 49: **16%**
50 to 74: **8%**	75 to 99: **4%**
100+: **1%**	

Areas of specialization: appellate advocacy, clinical training, dispute resolution, environmental law, healthcare law, intellectual property law, international law, tax law, trial advocacy

Fall 2005 faculty profile

Total teaching faculty: **39**. Full-time: **46%**; **72%** men, **28%** women, **11%** minorities. Part-time: **54%**; **81%** men, **19%** women, **5%** minorities
Student-to-faculty ratio: **15.4**

SPECIAL PROGRAMS *(as provided by law school):*

Milton R. Abrahams Legal Clinic: The clinic provides third-year students the opportunity to learn the lawyering process though participating in a variety of non-fee-generating civil matters, including divorce, child custody, and landlord-tenant disputes, for low-income clients.

   Internships: Upper class students are eligible to earn academic credit by participating in internships with governmental, nonprofit, and public-interest organizations in the metropolitan area.

   Combined-degree and certificate programs: In conjunction with the graduate and business schools, Creighton offers J.D.

students the opportunity to earn other graduate degrees, with some credits applying simultaneously toward both degrees. Degree programs include master of business administration, M.S. in e-commerce or information technology, and M.S. in international relations. Graduate certificates may also be earned in health services administration and international relations.

The Werner Institute for Negotiations and Dispute Resolution offers state-of-the-art training in alternative dispute resolution as well as a master's of science in dispute resolution.

STUDENT BODY

Fall 2005 full-time enrollment: 451

Men: 54%	Women: 46%
African-American: 2.4%	American Indian: 0.9%
Asian-American: 3.5%	Mexican-American: 3.1%
Puerto Rican: 0.2%	Other Hisp-Amer: 1.1%
White: 88.2%	International: 0.2%
Unknown: 0.2%	

Fall 2005 part-time enrollment: 18

Men: 50%	Women: 50%
African-American: 0.0%	American Indian: 0.0%
Asian-American: 0.0%	Mexican-American: 0.0%
Puerto Rican: 0.0%	Other Hisp-Amer: 0.0%
White: 100.0%	International: 0.0%
Unknown: 0.0%	

Attrition rates for 2004-2005 full-time students
Percent of students discontinuing law school:

Men: 2%	Women: 5%
First-year students: 9%	Second-year students: 1%
Third-year students: N/A	

LIBRARY RESOURCES

The library holds **83,362** and receives **4,627** current subscriptions.
Total volumes: **345,458**
Percentage of the titles in the online catalog: **100%**
Total seats available for library users: **363**

INFORMATION TECHNOLOGY

Number of wired network connections available to students: **70** total (in the law library, excluding computer labs: **38**; in classrooms: **24**; in computer labs: **0**; elsewhere in the law school: **8**)
Law school has a wireless network.

Approximate number of simultaneous users that can be accommodated on wireless network: **360**
Students are not required to own a computer.

EMPLOYMENT AND SALARIES

Proportion of 2004 graduates employed at graduation: 72%
Employed 9 months later, as of February 15, 2005: 98%
Salaries in the private sector (law firms, business, industry): $41,250–$72,000 (25th-75th percentile)
Median salary in the private sector: $56,250
Percentage in the private sector who reported salary information: 72%
Median salary in public service (government, judicial clerkships, academic posts, non-profits): $40,000

Percentage of 2004 graduates in:

Law firms: 51%	Bus./industry (legal): 15%
Bus./industry (nonlegal): 5%	Government: 16%
Public interest: 6%	Judicial clerkship: 6%
Academia : 1%	Unknown: 0%

2004 graduates employed in-state: 61%
2004 graduates employed in foreign countries: 0%
Number of states where graduates are employed: 24
Percentage of 2004 graduates working in: New England: 1%, Middle Atlantic: 1%, East North Central: 3%, West North Central: 76%, South Atlantic: 5%, East South Central: 2%, West South Central: 1%, Mountain: 8%, Pacific: 3%, Unknown: 0%

BAR PASSAGE RATES

Based on 2004 graduates taking Summer 2004 or Winter 2005 exams. Most of the school's first-time test takers took the bar in Nebraska.

84%
School's bar passage rate for first-time test takers

88%
Statewide bar passage rate for first-time test takers

CUNY–Queens College

- 65-21 Main Street, Flushing, NY, 11367
- http://www.law.cuny.edu/
- Public
- Year founded: 1983
- 2005-2006 tuition: In-state: full-time: $10,521, part-time: N/A; Out-of-state: full-time: $16,421
- Enrollment 2005-06 academic year: full-time: 436; part-time: 1
- U.S. News 2007 law specialty ranking: clinical training: 5

3.03-3.52 GPA, 25TH-75TH PERCENTILE

149-156 LSAT, 25TH-75TH PERCENTILE

21% ACCEPTANCE RATE

Tier 4 2007 U.S. NEWS LAW SCHOOL RANKING

ADMISSIONS

Admissions phone number: **(718) 340-4210**
Admissions email address: **admissions@mail.law.cuny.edu**
Application website: **N/A**
Application deadline for Fall 2007 admission: **3/15**

Admissions statistics:
Number of applicants for Fall 2005: **2,415**
Number of acceptances: **497**
Number enrolled: **166**
Acceptance rate: **21%**
GPA, 25th-75th percentile, entering class Fall 2005: **3.03-3.52**
LSAT, 25th-75th percentile, entering class Fall 2005: **149-156**

FINANCIAL AID

Financial aid phone number: **(718) 340-4284**
Financial aid application deadline: **5/01**
Tuition 2005-2006 academic year: In-state: full-time: **$10,521**, part-time: **N/A**; Out-of-state: full-time: **$16,421**
Room and board: **$3,931**; books: **$600**; miscellaneous expenses: **$6,809**
Total of room/board/books/miscellaneous expenses: **$11,340**
University does not offer graduate student housing for which law students are eligible.

Financial aid profile
Percent of students that received grants for the 2004-2005 academic year: full-time: **30%**
Median grant amount: full-time: **$1,500**
The average law-school debt of those in the Class of 2005 who borrowed: **$50,382**. Proportion who borrowed: **86%**

ACADEMIC PROGRAMS

Calendar: **semester**
Joint degrees awarded: **N/A**
Typical first-year section size: Full-time: **90**

Is there typically a "small section" of the first year class, other than Legal Writing, taught by full-time faculty?: Full-time: **yes**
Number of course titles, beyond the first year curriculum, offered last year: **55**
Percentages of upper division course sections, excluding seminars, with an enrollment of:
Under 25: **44%** 25 to 49: **45%**
50 to 74: **7%** 75 to 99: **2%**
100+: **2%**
Areas of specialization: appellate advocacy, clinical training, dispute resolution, environmental law, healthcare law, intellectual property law, international law, trial advocacy

Fall 2005 faculty profile
Total teaching faculty: **44**. Full-time: **66%**; **48%** men, **52%** women, **38%** minorities. Part-time: **34%**; **53%** men, **47%** women, **60%** minorities
Student-to-faculty ratio: **12.5**

SPECIAL PROGRAMS *(as provided by law school):*

CUNY'S nationally ranked clinical program offers 12-16 credits of supervised live client representation to every third-year student. In-house clinics and external placements (concentrations) include Battered Women's Rights, Criminal Defense, Immigrant and Refugees' Rights, International Women's Human Rights, Elder Law, Mediation, Equality, and Health Law. Students interested in labor law and worker representation participate in the Worker, Employment, Labor Program (WELP). Extensive academic support and a well staffed Writing Center allow students to achieve their full potential as excellent public interest lawyers. The Contemplative Lawyering program offers meditation and yoga to help students with stress and explore humanistic approaches to law. An excellent summer program is open to CUNY students and to students from other law schools.

STUDENT BODY

Fall 2005 full-time enrollment: **436**
Men: **33%** Women: **67%**
African-American: **8.7%** American Indian: **0.2%**
Asian-American: **14.2%** Mexican-American: **0.0%**

Puerto Rican: **1.8%** Other Hisp-Amer: **8.3%**
White: **54.8%** International: **3.7%**
Unknown: **8.3%**

Fall 2005 part-time enrollment: 1
Men: **100%** Women: **N/A**
African-American: **0.0%** American Indian: **0.0%**
Asian-American: **0.0%** Mexican-American: **0.0%**
Puerto Rican: **0.0%** Other Hisp-Amer: **0.0%**
White: **100.0%** International: **0.0%**
Unknown: **0.0%**

Attrition rates for 2004-2005 full-time students
Percent of students discontinuing law school:
Men: **8%** Women: **5%**
First-year students: **11%** Second-year students: **7%**
Third-year students: **N/A**

LIBRARY RESOURCES

The library holds **35,500** and receives **3,094** current
subscriptions.
Total volumes: **278,498**
Percentage of the titles in the online catalog: **100%**
Total seats available for library users: **267**

INFORMATION TECHNOLOGY

Number of wired network connections available to students: **62** total (in the law library, excluding computer
labs: **0**; in classrooms: **20**; in computer labs: **6**; elsewhere in the law school: **36**)
Law school has a wireless network.
Approximate number of simultaneous users that can be
accommodated on wireless network: **300**
Students are not required to own a computer.

EMPLOYMENT AND SALARIES

Proportion of 2004 graduates employed at graduation:
30%

Employed 9 months later, as of February 15, 2005: **74%**
Salaries in the private sector (law firms, business, indus-
try): **$40,000–$80,000** (25th-75th percentile)
Median salary in the private sector: **$56,212**
Percentage in the private sector who reported salary
information: **44%**
Median salary in public service (government, judicial clerk-
ships, academic posts, non-profits): **$45,000**

Percentage of 2004 graduates in:
Law firms: **34%** Bus./industry (legal): **5%**
Bus./industry (nonlegal): **4%** Government: **12%**
Public interest: **26%** Judicial clerkship: **12%**
Academia : **5%** Unknown: **2%**

2004 graduates employed in-state: **70%**
2004 graduates employed in foreign countries: **2%**
Number of states where graduates are employed: **2**
Percentage of 2004 graduates working in: New England:
4%, Middle Atlantic: **76%**, East North Central: **0%**, West
North Central: **0%**, South Atlantic: **4%**, East South
Central: **0%**, West South Central: **1%**, Mountain: **0%**,
Pacific: **6%**, Unknown: **8%**

DePaul University

■ 25 E. Jackson Boulevard, Chicago, IL, 60604
■ http://www.law.depaul.edu
■ Private
■ Year founded: 1912
■ 2005-2006 tuition: full-time: $28,810; part-time: $18,750
■ Enrollment 2005-06 academic year: full-time: 804; part-time: 354
■ U.S. News 2007 law specialty ranking: healthcare law: 10, intellecutal property law: 11

3.12-3.66	GPA, 25TH-75TH PERCENTILE
158-161	LSAT, 25TH-75TH PERCENTILE
26%	ACCEPTANCE RATE
80	2007 U.S. NEWS LAW SCHOOL RANKING

ADMISSIONS

Admissions phone number: (312) 362-6831
Admissions email address: **lawinfo@depaul.edu**
Application website: **http://www.law.depaul.edu/apply**
Application deadline for Fall 2007 admission: **3/01**

Admissions statistics:

Number of applicants for Fall 2005: **4,198**
Number of acceptances: **1,081**
Number enrolled: **234**
Acceptance rate: **26%**
GPA, 25th-75th percentile, entering class Fall 2005: **3.12-3.66**
LSAT, 25th-75th percentile, entering class Fall 2005: **158-161**

Part-time program:

Number of applicants for Fall 2005: **830**
Number of acceptances: **330**
Number enrolled: **96**
Acceptance rate: **40%**
GPA, 25th-75th percentile, entering class Fall 2005: **3.02-3.53**
LSAT, 25th-75th percentile, entering class Fall 2005: **154-158**

FINANCIAL AID

Financial aid phone number: (312) 362-8091
Financial aid application deadline: 3/01
Tuition 2005-2006 academic year: full-time: **$28,810**; part-time: **$18,750**
Room and board: **$18,454**; books: **$1,000**; miscellaneous expenses: **N/A**
Total of room/board/books/miscellaneous expenses: **$19,454**
University offers graduate student housing for which law students are eligible.

Financial aid profile

Percent of students that received grants for the 2004-2005 academic year: full-time: **58%**; part-time **18%**

Median grant amount: full-time: **$8,000**; part-time: **$3,000**
The average law-school debt of those in the Class of 2005 who borrowed: **$89,065**. Proportion who borrowed: **88%**

ACADEMIC PROGRAMS

Calendar: **semester**
Joint degrees awarded: **J.D./M.B.A.; J.D./M.S. Public Service Management; J.D./M.A .International Studies; J.D./M.A. Computer Science; J.D./M.S. Computer Science**
Typical first-year section size: Full-time: **86**; Part-time: **90**
Is there typically a "small section" of the first year class, other than Legal Writing, taught by full-time faculty?: Full-time: **no**; Part-time: **no**
Number of course titles, beyond the first year curriculum, offered last year: **161**
Percentages of upper division course sections, excluding seminars, with an enrollment of:

Under 25: **59%**	25 to 49: **20%**
50 to 74: **11%**	75 to 99: **10%**
100+: **1%**	

Areas of specialization: appellate advocacy, clinical training, dispute resolution, environmental law, healthcare law, intellectual property law, international law, tax law, trial advocacy

Fall 2005 faculty profile

Total teaching faculty: **N/A**. Full-time: **N/A**; **N/A** men, **N/A** women, **N/A** minorities. Part-time: **N/A**; **N/A** men, **N/A** women, **N/A** minorities
Student-to-faculty ratio: **17.9**

SPECIAL PROGRAMS *(as provided by law school):*

Center for Intellectual Property Law/Information Technology Program promotes the study and practice of intellectual property and information technology law. It supports an extensive IP curriculum and provides students with practical experience. Schiller DuCanto & Fleck Family Law Center focuses on teaching, research, law reform, and community service in all areas of family law. It supports the most extensive family law curriculum in the nation. Center for Law & Science—devoted to the gathering and distribution of information concerned with the interaction of modern science and the international legal community. Center for Justice in Capital Cases—In conjunction with the Office of the State Appellate Defender, the Center trains attorneys appointed to defend individuals charged with a capital crime. Accompanying the Center is a Death Penalty Clinic. Center for the Study of Race & Bioethics collects and makes available empirical data, and considers a broad range of topics as they relate to the physical and emotional health of minority populations. International Human Rights Law Institute—established in 1990, the Institute is dedicated to developing and promoting international human rights law and international criminal justice through fieldwork, research and documentation, publications, and advocacy. Health Law Institute—the Institute involves the study of problems facing the health care industry through an extensive curriculum offering specialty courses taught by full-time and adjunct faculty. International Aviation Law Institute—the first institute of its kind in the United States. Established in 2004, the Institute will offer courses in national and global aviation law, as well as specialized courses in aviation antitrust and tort law. It also has academic links with aviation programs at the University of Leyden, the Netherlands, and at the University of Rio de Janeiro, Brazil. Center for Rural & Urban Community Development—the Center works with communities to develop and provide the legal resources needed to stimulate increased social and economic development. Center for Church-State Studies—Co-sponsored by DePaul University Office of Mission and Values, this non-denominational Center is dedicated to expanding the dialogue about matters of religion and government. Five Legal Clinics in Asylum/Immigration, Community Development, Criminal Appeals, Death Penalty and Technology/Intellectual Property. Ten Certificate Programs in Criminal Law, Family Law, Health Law, Public Interest Law, IP: Information Technology Law, IP: Arts & Museum Law, IP: General, IPA: Patents, International & Comparative Law and Taxation. Three study abroad programs in China, Costa Rica and Ireland.

STUDENT BODY

Fall 2005 full-time enrollment: 804

Men: 49%	Women: 51%
African-American: 6.2%	American Indian: 0.2%
Asian-American: 7.2%	Mexican-American: 0.0%
Puerto Rican: 0.0%	Other Hisp-Amer: 7.1%
White: 75.9%	International: 0.0%
Unknown: 3.4%	

Fall 2005 part-time enrollment: 354

Men: 53%	Women: 47%
African-American: 5.9%	American Indian: 0.0%
Asian-American: 6.5%	Mexican-American: 0.0%
Puerto Rican: 0.0%	Other Hisp-Amer: 6.2%
White: 76.3%	International: 0.0%
Unknown: 5.1%	

Attrition rates for 2004-2005 full-time students

Percent of students discontinuing law school:

Men: 5%	Women: 3%
First-year students: 9%	Second-year students: 4%
Third-year students: 1%	

LIBRARY RESOURCES

The library holds 76,493 and receives 5,297 current subscriptions.
Total volumes: 378,715
Percentage of the titles in the online catalog: 100%
Total seats available for library users: 465

INFORMATION TECHNOLOGY

Number of wired network connections available to students: 120 total (in the law library, excluding computer labs: 50; in classrooms: 0; in computer labs: 30; elsewhere in the law school: 40)
Law school has a wireless network.
Approximate number of simultaneous users that can be accommodated on wireless network: 800
Students are not required to own a computer.

EMPLOYMENT AND SALARIES

Proportion of 2004 graduates employed at graduation: 81%
Employed 9 months later, as of February 15, 2005: 94%
Salaries in the private sector (law firms, business, industry): $45,000–$70,000 (25th-75th percentile)
Median salary in the private sector: $57,000
Percentage in the private sector who reported salary information: 80%
Median salary in public service (government, judicial clerkships, academic posts, non-profits): $43,423

Percentage of 2004 graduates in:

Law firms: 63%	Bus./industry (legal): 7%
Bus./industry (nonlegal): 10%	Government: 10%
Public interest: 4%	Judicial clerkship: 3%
Academia : 2%	Unknown: 0%

2004 graduates employed in-state: 87%
2004 graduates employed in foreign countries: 0%
Number of states where graduates are employed: 19
Percentage of 2004 graduates working in: New England: 1%, Middle Atlantic: 2%, East North Central: 90%, West North Central: 0%, South Atlantic: 4%, East South Central: 0%, West South Central: 1%, Mountain: 0%, Pacific: 2%, Unknown: 0%

BAR PASSAGE RATES

Based on 2004 graduates taking Summer 2004 or Winter 2005 exams. Most of the school's first-time test takers took the bar in Illinois.

84%
School's bar passage rate for first-time test takers

85%
Statewide bar passage rate for first-time test takers

Drake University

- 2507 University Avenue, Des Moines, IA, 50311
- http://www.law.drake.edu/
- Private
- Year founded: 1881
- 2005-2006 tuition: full-time: $24,256; part-time: $830/credit hour
- Enrollment 2005-06 academic year: full-time: 462; part-time: 9
- U.S. News 2007 law specialty ranking: N/A

3.14-3.69 GPA, 25TH-75TH PERCENTILE

153-156 LSAT, 25TH-75TH PERCENTILE

42% ACCEPTANCE RATE

Tier 3 2007 U.S. NEWS LAW SCHOOL RANKING

ADMISSIONS
Admissions phone number: (515) 271-2782
Admissions email address: lawadmit@drake.edu
Application website: http://www.law.drake.edu/admissions/
Application deadline for Fall 2007 admission: 4/01

Admissions statistics:
Number of applicants for Fall 2005: 1,158
Number of acceptances: 490
Number enrolled: 143
Acceptance rate: 42%
GPA, 25th-75th percentile, entering class Fall 2005: 3.14-3.69
LSAT, 25th-75th percentile, entering class Fall 2005: 153-156

Part-time program:
Number of applicants for Fall 2005: 28
Number of acceptances: 3
Number enrolled: 2
Acceptance rate: 11%
GPA, 25th-75th percentile, entering class Fall 2005: N/A
LSAT, 25th-75th percentile, entering class Fall 2005: N/A

FINANCIAL AID
Financial aid phone number: (515) 271-2905
Financial aid application deadline: 3/01
Tuition 2005-2006 academic year: full-time: $24,256; part-time: $830/credit hour
Room and board: $7,125; books: $1,125; miscellaneous expenses: $3,900
Total of room/board/books/miscellaneous expenses: $12,150
University does not offer graduate student housing for which law students are eligible.

Financial aid profile
Percent of students that received grants for the 2004-2005 academic year: full-time: 54%
Median grant amount: full-time: $9,000

The average law-school debt of those in the Class of 2005 who borrowed: $70,441. Proportion who borrowed: 95%

ACADEMIC PROGRAMS
Calendar: semester
Joint degrees awarded: J.D./M.B.A.; J.D./M.P.A.; J.D./M.A. Poli Sci; J.D./M.A. Ag Econ; J.D./M.A. Social Work; J.D./Ph.D.
Typical first-year section size: Full-time: 72
Is there typically a "small section" of the first year class, other than Legal Writing, taught by full-time faculty?: Full-time: no; Part-time: no
Number of course titles, beyond the first year curriculum, offered last year: 140
Percentages of upper division course sections, excluding seminars, with an enrollment of:

Under 25: 72%	25 to 49: 13%
50 to 74: 5%	75 to 99: 9%
100+: 1%	

Areas of specialization: appellate advocacy, clinical training, dispute resolution, environmental law, healthcare law, intellectual property law, international law, tax law, trial advocacy

Fall 2005 faculty profile
Total teaching faculty: 47. Full-time: 47%; 55% men, 45% women, 9% minorities. Part-time: 53%; 68% men, 32% women, 8% minorities
Student-to-faculty ratio: 17.8

SPECIAL PROGRAMS *(as provided by law school)*:
At Drake Law School learning extends far beyond the classroom. The law school's "Lawyering from Day One" mission is reflected in its experiential education pyramid: observation-simulation-participation. Experiential learning begins with our unique First-Year Trial Practicum, where every member of the first-year class observes an actual jury trial—from jury selection through jury verdict—in an educational setting that includes small-group discussions led by faculty, seasoned judges, and veteran attorneys with lectures and practice panels that focus on

the key legal and procedural issues and on the litigation strategies and techniques of the lawyers trying the case.

Drake's lawyering skills courses range from pretrial and trial advocacy to individual alternative dispute resolution courses. Drake's nationally recognized Legal Clinic offers capstone clinical experiences in civil practice, children's rights, and criminal defense. Every student wanting to enroll in a live-client clinical course—about half of each class—has been able to take advantage of our clinical programs.

The Children's Rights Center cooperates with the Legislative Practice Center to forge a legislative agenda and lobby for its adoption.

The law school's constitutional law and agricultural law centers have national prominence. The director of the Constitutional Law Center teaches courses, hosts distinguished speakers, and arranges annual symposia. The Agricultural Law Center is in its twenty-first year. It offers six courses for students; sponsors the annual Summer Agricultural Law Institute; arranges student internships with federal and state agencies; and supports the Drake Journal of Agricultural Law.

The Center for Legislative Practice is a vehicle for courses in the J.D. program that focus on topics involving the structure, operation, and workings of government.

The American Judicature Society has just this past year moved its headquarters from Chicago to Des Moines and the Drake University campus, and the society and the law school are cooperating in research and programming.

Drake Law School draws on other colleges in the university and at Iowa State University to offer joint degree programs. It also has a popular program of summer study in Nantes, France, and faculty and student exchanges with Robert Gordon University in Aberdeen, Scotland, and Clermont-Ferrand in France.

Drake Law School is the only law school in Iowa's state capital, and a plethora of internships are available to our students. Drake also makes possible from 12 to 20 summer public-interest fellowships.

STUDENT BODY

Fall 2005 full-time enrollment: 462

Men: 51%	Women: 49%
African-American: 3.9%	American Indian: 0.4%
Asian-American: 3.0%	Mexican-American: 1.3%
Puerto Rican: 0.2%	Other Hisp-Amer: 1.1%
White: 85.1%	International: 1.7%
Unknown: 3.2%	

Fall 2005 part-time enrollment: 9

Men: 44%	Women: 56%
African-American: 0.0%	American Indian: 11.1%
Asian-American: 0.0%	Mexican-American: 0.0%
Puerto Rican: 0.0%	Other Hisp-Amer: 0.0%
White: 88.9%	International: 0.0%
Unknown: 0.0%	

Attrition rates for 2004-2005 full-time students

Percent of students discontinuing law school:

Men: 5%	Women: 4%

First-year students: 9%   Second-year students: 3%
Third-year students: N/A

LIBRARY RESOURCES

The library holds 43,991 and receives 3,241 current subscriptions.
Total volumes: 319,959
Percentage of the titles in the online catalog: 96%
Total seats available for library users: 705

INFORMATION TECHNOLOGY

Number of wired network connections available to students: 160 total (in the law library, excluding computer labs: 160; in classrooms: 0; in computer labs: 0; elsewhere in the law school: 0)
Law school has a wireless network.
Approximate number of simultaneous users that can be accommodated on wireless network: 640
Students are not required to own a computer.

EMPLOYMENT AND SALARIES

Proportion of 2004 graduates employed at graduation: N/A
Employed 9 months later, as of February 15, 2005: 95%
Salaries in the private sector (law firms, business, industry): $40,000–$65,000 (25th-75th percentile)
Median salary in the private sector: $56,750
Percentage in the private sector who reported salary information: 25%
Median salary in public service (government, judicial clerkships, academic posts, non-profits): $61,250

Percentage of 2004 graduates in:

Law firms: 63%	Bus./industry (legal): 7%
Bus./industry (nonlegal): 5%	Government: 11%
Public interest: 3%	Judicial clerkship: 7%
Academia : 2%	Unknown: 1%

2004 graduates employed in-state: 71%
2004 graduates employed in foreign countries: 1%
Number of states where graduates are employed: 20
Percentage of 2004 graduates working in: New England: 0%, Middle Atlantic: 1%, East North Central: 8%, West North Central: 73%, South Atlantic: 7%, East South Central: 0%, West South Central: 2%, Mountain: 6%, Pacific: 2%, Unknown: 0%

BAR PASSAGE RATES

Based on 2004 graduates taking Summer 2004 or Winter 2005 exams. Most of the school's first-time test takers took the bar in Iowa.

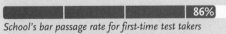

86%

School's bar passage rate for first-time test takers

86%

Statewide bar passage rate for first-time test takers

Duke University

■ Towerview and Science Drive, Box 90362, Durham, NC, 27708-0362
■ http://www.law.duke.edu
■ Private
■ Year founded: 1930
■ 2005-2006 tuition: full-time: $36,574; part-time: N/A
■ Enrollment 2005-06 academic year: full-time: 617; part-time: 31
■ U.S. News 2007 law specialty ranking: environmental law: 8, intelle-cutal property law: 7, international law: 13, tax law: 22

3.54-3.86 GPA, 25TH-75TH PERCENTILE

165-169 LSAT, 25TH-75TH PERCENTILE

21% ACCEPTANCE RATE

11 2007 U.S. NEWS LAW SCHOOL RANKING

ADMISSIONS
Admissions phone number: **(919) 613-7020**
Admissions email address: **admissions@law.duke.edu**
Application website:
  http://admissions.law.duke.edu/admis/appform.html
Application deadline for Fall 2007 admission: **1/01**

Admissions statistics:
Number of applicants for Fall 2005: **4,486**
Number of acceptances: **960**
Number enrolled: **199**
Acceptance rate: **21%**
GPA, 25th-75th percentile, entering class Fall 2005:
3.54-3.86
LSAT, 25th-75th percentile, entering class Fall 2005:
165-169

FINANCIAL AID
Financial aid phone number: **(919) 613-7026**
Financial aid application deadline: **3/15**
Tuition 2005-2006 academic year: full-time: **$36,574**; part-time: **N/A**
Room and board: **$9,000**; books: **$1,030**; miscellaneous expenses: **$5,509**
Total of room/board/books/miscellaneous expenses:
$15,539
University does not offer graduate student housing for which law students are eligible.

Financial aid profile
Percent of students that received grants for the 2004-2005 academic year: full-time: **72%**
Median grant amount: full-time: **$8,000**
The average law-school debt of those in the Class of 2005 who borrowed: **$90,903**. Proportion who borrowed: **98%**

ACADEMIC PROGRAMS
Calendar: **semester**
Joint degrees awarded: **J.D./M.A. Cultural Anthropology; J.D./M.A. East Asian Studies; J.D./M.S. Electronics/Comp. Engineering; J.D./M.A.**

Environmental Sci./Policy; J.D./M.A. Economics; J.D./M.A. History; J.D./M.A. Humanities; J.D./LL.M Inerntl. and Comparative Lang.; J.D/.M.B.A.; J.D./M.D.; J.D./M.S. Mechanical Engineering; J.D./M.E.M. Environmental Management; J.D./M.P.P. Public Policy; J.D./M.T.S. Theological Studies; J.D./M.A. Philosophy; J.D./M.A. Political Science; J.D./M.A. Public Policy Studies; J.D./M.A. Psychology; J.D./M.S. Biomedical Engineering; J.D./M.A. Classical Studies; J.D./M.A. Romance Studies; J.D./M.A. Sociology; J.D./M.A. Religion
Typical first-year section size: Full-time: **72**
Is there typically a "small section" of the first year class, other than Legal Writing, taught by full-time faculty?: Full-time: **yes**
Number of course titles, beyond the first year curriculum, offered last year: **135**
Percentages of upper division course sections, excluding seminars, with an enrollment of:

Under 25: **62%**		25 to 49: **19%**	
50 to 74: **11%**		75 to 99: **5%**	
100+: **3%**			

Areas of specialization: appellate advocacy, clinical training, dispute resolution, environmental law, healthcare law, intellectual property law, international law, tax law, trial advocacy

Fall 2005 faculty profile
Total teaching faculty: **106**. Full-time: **47%**; **78%** men, **22%** women, **8%** minorities. Part-time: **53%**; **70%** men, **30%** women, **9%** minorities
Student-to-faculty ratio: **12.6**

SPECIAL PROGRAMS (as provided by law school):
Joint degree Programs: Approximately 25 percent of Duke Law students pursue a joint degree. The J.D./LL.M. program offers concurrently a J.D. and a Master of Laws in International and Comparative Law. Duke students may earn both a J.D. and a master's degree in three years plus a summer. Duke also offers J.D./M.D., J.D./M.B.A., J.D./M.P.P., J.D./M.E.M. and J.D./M.T.S programs.

Clinics: Duke is a leader in clinical education. The Guantanamo Defense Clinic assists the Chief Defense Counsel for Guantanamo detainees with trial preparation. Students in the AIDS Legal Assistance Project help clients with HIV/AIDS prepare wills, apply for government benefits, and handle other issues. The Children's Education Law Clinic represents low income children in special education, school discipline and disability benefits cases. The Community Enterprise Law Clinic helps students develop transactional skills in a community development law setting. The Low Income Tax Payer Clinic helps clients in disputes with the IRS. In Wrongful Convictions, students investigate prisoners' claims of innocence. In Animal Law, students pursue animal protection issues. An Environmental Law Clinic is anticipated in 2006.

Capstone Projects: 3L students may develop projects integrating advanced substantive knowledge with a hands-on practice component, such as writing an appellate brief, or preparing congressional testimony.

Centers/Institutes: Duke facilitates interdisciplinary research and teaching through centers with partners across the campus. The Center on Law, Ethics and National Security provides unmatched opportunities for students in national security law and terrorism; The Program in Public Law fosters understanding of U.S. public institutions. The Center for the Study of the Public Domain studies the relationship between intellectual property law and innovation. The Global Capital Markets Center studies international business and finance. The Nicholas Institute for Environmental Policy Solutions focuses science, business, law and policy on solving environmental problems. The Center for Genome Ethics, Law, and Policy examines legal and policy implications of genomic discoveries.

International Programs: In addition to the J.D./LL.M. program, Duke offers an LL.M. in American Law for approximately 75 foreign lawyers. Duke's Summer Institutes in Geneva and Hong Kong offer instruction in international and transnational legal practice. Duke has an international externship program and dozens of exchange opportunities.

STUDENT BODY
Fall 2005 full-time enrollment: 617
Men: 54%	Women: 46%
African-American: 10.4%	American Indian: 0.6%
Asian-American: 7.1%	Mexican-American: 0.0%
Puerto Rican: 0.0%	Other Hisp-Amer: 4.1%
White: 59.0%	International: 5.3%
Unknown: 13.5%	

Fall 2005 part-time enrollment: 31
Men: 65%	Women: 35%
African-American: 16.1%	American Indian: 0.0%
Asian-American: 0.0%	Mexican-American: 0.0%
Puerto Rican: 0.0%	Other Hisp-Amer: 0.0%
White: 64.5%	International: 0.0%
Unknown: 19.4%	

Attrition rates for 2004-2005 full-time students
Percent of students discontinuing law school:
Men: 1%	Women: 1%

First-year students: 2%   Second-year students: N/A
Third-year students: N/A

LIBRARY RESOURCES
The library holds 215,550 and receives 7,016 current subscriptions.
Total volumes: 622,400
Percentage of the titles in the online catalog: 100%
Total seats available for library users: 503

INFORMATION TECHNOLOGY
Number of wired network connections available to students: 847 total (in the law library, excluding computer labs: 138; in classrooms: 679; in computer labs: 0; elsewhere in the law school: 30)
Law school has a wireless network.
Approximate number of simultaneous users that can be accommodated on wireless network: 500
Students are required to own a computer.

EMPLOYMENT AND SALARIES
Proportion of 2004 graduates employed at graduation: 95%
Employed 9 months later, as of February 15, 2005: 100%
Salaries in the private sector (law firms, business, industry): $100,000–$125,000 (25th-75th percentile)
Median salary in the private sector: $110,000
Percentage in the private sector who reported salary information: 84%
Median salary in public service (government, judicial clerkships, academic posts, non-profits): $45,000

Percentage of 2004 graduates in:
Law firms: 72%	Bus./industry (legal): 0%
Bus./industry (nonlegal): 3%	Government: 4%
Public interest: 3%	Judicial clerkship: 16%
Academia : 0%	Unknown: 2%

2004 graduates employed in-state: 10%
2004 graduates employed in foreign countries: 3%
Number of states where graduates are employed: 34
Percentage of 2004 graduates working in: New England: 2%, Middle Atlantic: 21%, East North Central: 5%, West North Central: 4%, South Atlantic: 42%, East South Central: 3%, West South Central: 5%, Mountain: 3%, Pacific: 13%, Unknown: 0%

BAR PASSAGE RATES
Based on 2004 graduates taking Summer 2004 or Winter 2005 exams. Most of the school's first-time test takers took the bar in New York.

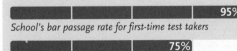

95%
School's bar passage rate for first-time test takers

75%
Statewide bar passage rate for first-time test takers

Duquesne University

- 600 Forbes Avenue, Pittsburgh, PA, 15282
- http://www.duq.edu/law
- Private
- Year founded: 1911
- 2005-2006 tuition: full-time: $23,759; part-time: $18,258
- Enrollment 2005-06 academic year: full-time: 422; part-time: 143
- U.S. News 2007 law specialty ranking: N/A

3.23-3.61 GPA, 25TH-75TH PERCENTILE

153-156 LSAT, 25TH-75TH PERCENTILE

44% ACCEPTANCE RATE

Tier 3 2007 U.S. NEWS LAW SCHOOL RANKING

ADMISSIONS

Admissions phone number: **(412) 396-6296**
Admissions email address: **ricci@duq.edu**
Application website: **N/A**
Application deadline for Fall 2007 admission: **4/01**

Admissions statistics:
Number of applicants for Fall 2005: **915**
Number of acceptances: **406**
Number enrolled: **162**
Acceptance rate: **44%**
GPA, 25th-75th percentile, entering class Fall 2005: **3.23-3.61**
LSAT, 25th-75th percentile, entering class Fall 2005: **153-156**

Part-time program:
Number of applicants for Fall 2005: **181**
Number of acceptances: **35**
Number enrolled: **31**
Acceptance rate: **19%**
GPA, 25th-75th percentile, entering class Fall 2005: **3.11-3.66**
LSAT, 25th-75th percentile, entering class Fall 2005: **153-157**

FINANCIAL AID

Financial aid phone number: **(412) 396-6607**
Financial aid application deadline: **5/31**
Tuition 2005-2006 academic year: full-time: **$23,759**; part-time: **$18,258**
Room and board: **$10,532**; books: **$1,200**; miscellaneous expenses: **$2,000**
Total of room/board/books/miscellaneous expenses: **$13,732**
University offers graduate student housing for which law students are eligible.

Financial aid profile
Percent of students that received grants for the 2004-2005 academic year: full-time: **31%**; part-time **8%**
Median grant amount: full-time: **$12,298**; part-time: **$7,719**
The average law-school debt of those in the Class of 2005 who borrowed: **$78,000**. Proportion who borrowed: **93%**

ACADEMIC PROGRAMS

Calendar: **semester**
Joint degrees awarded: **J.D./M.B.A.; J.D./M.S.-E.S.M; J.D./M.Div; J.D./M.A.Comm; J.D./M.S.T.**
Typical first-year section size: Full-time: **86**; Part-time: **29**
Is there typically a "small section" of the first year class, other than Legal Writing, taught by full-time faculty?: Full-time: **yes**; Part-time: **no**
Number of course titles, beyond the first year curriculum, offered last year: **108**
Percentages of upper division course sections, excluding seminars, with an enrollment of:
Under 25: **56%**   25 to 49: **22%**
50 to 74: **20%**   75 to 99: **2%**
100+: **0%**
Areas of specialization: appellate advocacy, clinical training, dispute resolution, environmental law, healthcare law, intellectual property law, international law, tax law, trial advocacy

Fall 2005 faculty profile
Total teaching faculty: **46**. Full-time: **57%**; **73%** men, **27%** women, **15%** minorities. Part-time: **43%**; **80%** men, **20%** women, **N/A** minorities
Student-to-faculty ratio: **16.3**

SPECIAL PROGRAMS *(as provided by law school):*

Now more than five years ago, the Duquesne University Law School created the Cyril H. Wecht Institute of Forensic Science and Law. It is the first such institute of its kind (and remains the only such kind) among the nation's law schools. The Institute's program consists of a highly interdisciplinary and lively curriculum that brings scholars, academics and professionals together from the social, applied, and natural sciences.

STUDENT BODY

Fall 2005 full-time enrollment: **422**
Men: **55%**   Women: **45%**
African-American: **2.1%**   American Indian: **0.0%**
Asian-American: **0.5%**   Mexican-American: **0.0%**
Puerto Rican: **0.0%**   Other Hisp-Amer: **0.7%**

White: **96.4%**   International: **0.2%**
Unknown: **0.0%**

Fall 2005 part-time enrollment: **143**
Men: **56%**   Women: **44%**
African-American: **5.6%**   American Indian: **0.0%**
Asian-American: **1.4%**   Mexican-American: **0.0%**
Puerto Rican: **0.0%**   Other Hisp-Amer: **0.7%**
White: **92.3%**   International: **0.0%**
Unknown: **0.0%**

Attrition rates for 2004-2005 full-time students
Percent of students discontinuing law school:
Men: **2%**   Women: **4%**
First-year students: **7%**   Second-year students: **3%**
Third-year students: **N/A**

LIBRARY RESOURCES
The library holds **81,030** and receives **3,942** current
    subscriptions.
Total volumes: **294,108**
Percentage of the titles in the online catalog: **99%**
Total seats available for library users: **386**

INFORMATION TECHNOLOGY
Number of wired network connections available to stu-
    dents: **50** total (in the law library, excluding computer
    labs: **50**; in classrooms: **0**; in computer labs: **0**; else-
    where in the law school: **0**)
Law school has a wireless network.
Approximate number of simultaneous users that can be
    accommodated on wireless network: **500**
Students are not required to own a computer.

EMPLOYMENT AND SALARIES
Proportion of 2004 graduates employed at graduation: **79%**
Employed 9 months later, as of February 15, 2005: **86%**

Salaries in the private sector (law firms, business, indus-
    try): **N/A–N/A** (25th-75th percentile)
Median salary in the private sector: **N/A**
Percentage in the private sector who reported salary
    information: **N/A**
Median salary in public service (government, judicial clerk-
    ships, academic posts, non-profits): **N/A**

Percentage of 2004 graduates in:
Law firms: **55%**   Bus./industry (legal): **14%**
Bus./industry (nonlegal): **1%**   Government: **12%**
Public interest: **0%**   Judicial clerkship: **12%**
Academia : **1%**   Unknown: **5%**

2004 graduates employed in-state: **79%**
2004 graduates employed in foreign countries: **0%**
Number of states where graduates are employed: **14**
Percentage of 2004 graduates working in: New England:
    2%, Middle Atlantic: **85%**, East North Central: **3%**, West
    North Central: **N/A**, South Atlantic: **7%**, East South
    Central: **1%**, West South Central: **1%**, Mountain: **1%**,
    Pacific: **N/A**, Unknown: **0%**

BAR PASSAGE RATES
Based on 2004 graduates taking Summer 2004 or
Winter 2005 exams. Most of the school's first-time test
takers took the bar in Pennsylvania.

| **80%** |
School's bar passage rate for first-time test takers

| **81%** |
Statewide bar passage rate for first-time test takers

Emory University

- 1301 Clifton Road, Atlanta, GA, 30322-2770
- http://www.law.emory.edu
- Private
- Year founded: 1916
- 2005-2006 tuition: full-time: $35,034; part-time: N/A
- Enrollment 2005-06 academic year: full-time: 680
- U.S. News 2007 law specialty ranking: tax law: 25, trial advocacy: 11

3.28-3.63	GPA, 25TH-75TH PERCENTILE
161-165	LSAT, 25TH-75TH PERCENTILE
29%	ACCEPTANCE RATE
26	2007 U.S. NEWS LAW SCHOOL RANKING

ADMISSIONS

Admissions phone number: **(404) 727-6802**
Admissions email address: **lawinfo@law.emory.edu**
Application website: **http://www.law.emory.edu/admissions/application.html**
Application deadline for Fall 2007 admission: **3/01**

Admissions statistics:

Number of applicants for Fall 2005: **3,659**
Number of acceptances: **1,064**
Number enrolled: **235**
Acceptance rate: **29%**
GPA, 25th-75th percentile, entering class Fall 2005: **3.28-3.63**
LSAT, 25th-75th percentile, entering class Fall 2005: **161-165**

FINANCIAL AID

Financial aid phone number: **(404) 727-6039**
Financial aid application deadline: **3/01**
Tuition 2005-2006 academic year: full-time: **$35,034**; part-time: **N/A**
Room and board: **$13,176**; books: **$1,852**; miscellaneous expenses: **$1,094**
Total of room/board/books/miscellaneous expenses: **$16,122**
University offers graduate student housing for which law students are eligible.

Financial aid profile

Percent of students that received grants for the 2004-2005 academic year: full-time: **31%**
Median grant amount: full-time: **$20,726**
The average law-school debt of those in the Class of 2005 who borrowed: **$95,161**. Proportion who borrowed: **81%**

ACADEMIC PROGRAMS

Calendar: **semester**
Joint degrees awarded: **J.D./M.B.A.; J.D./M.DIV.; J.D./MTS; J.D./MPH; J.D./REES; J.D./PH.D.; J.D./MA**
Typical first-year section size: Full-time: **71**

Is there typically a "small section" of the first year class, other than Legal Writing, taught by full-time faculty?: Full-time: **yes**
Number of course titles, beyond the first year curriculum, offered last year: **124**
Percentages of upper division course sections, excluding seminars, with an enrollment of:

Under 25: **60%**	25 to 49: **22%**
50 to 74: **6%**	75 to 99: **10%**
100+: **2%**	

Areas of specialization: appellate advocacy, clinical training, dispute resolution, environmental law, healthcare law, intellectual property law, international law, tax law, trial advocacy

Fall 2005 faculty profile

Total teaching faculty: **80**. Full-time: **53%**; **74%** men, **26%** women, **14%** minorities. Part-time: **48%**; **79%** men, **21%** women, **8%** minorities
Student-to-faculty ratio: **13.3**

SPECIAL PROGRAMS *(as provided by law school):*

Emory Law School is committed to the legal profession as a service profession, to teaching the practice of law as well as the study of law, and to our premier centers of excellence. We teach the practice of law through our outstanding programs in Trial Techniques, Intellectual Property, Child Advocacy and Environmental. Our centers of excellence in Law and Religion, International Law, Feminist Jurisprudence and Legal Theory, and Health Law and Policy are interdisciplinary, integrative and international in approach. We benefit from our location on the Emory University campus by combining with other strong campus programs (such as the Graduate School, the Candler School of Theology, the Business School, and the health science units of the Medical, Nursing and Public Health Schools), to create unique programs of study. We capitalize on our location in Atlanta with a talented cadre of adjunct professors.

These important elements combine synergistically to create Emory's unique community, work and mission. We train lawyers to make a seamless transition from study to practice with our eminent Kessler/Eidson Program for Trial Techniques.

Many students participate in Emory's field placement program by clerking for a federal judge, researching intellectual property issues for corporations such as Coca-Cola, representing clients on behalf of Atlanta Legal Aid, assisting the Securities and Exchange Commission in enforcement actions, mediating a landlord-tenant dispute, appearing in court on behalf of a client of a public defender or for a victim of domestic violence, or working on the prosecution of white collar criminals for the U.S. Department of Justice. Students gain practical experience in intellectual property and corporate/commercial law by participating in TI:GER (Technological Innovation: Generating Economic Results), a program of technology law and business law co-sponsored by Emory University's School of Law and Economics Department and Georgia Tech's Dupree School of Management.

STUDENT BODY

Fall 2005 full-time enrollment: 680

Men: 50%	Women: 50%
African-American: 9.7%	American Indian: 0.0%
Asian-American: 9.4%	Mexican-American: 0.0%
Puerto Rican: 0.0%	Other Hisp-Amer: 6.9%
White: 70.7%	International: 1.8%
Unknown: 1.5%	

Attrition rates for 2004-2005 full-time students

Percent of students discontinuing law school:

Men: 2%	Women: 2%
First-year students: 1%	Second-year students: 5%
Third-year students: N/A	

LIBRARY RESOURCES

The library holds 139,577 and receives 4,053 current subscriptions.
Total volumes: 400,929
Percentage of the titles in the online catalog: 96%
Total seats available for library users: 488

INFORMATION TECHNOLOGY

Number of wired network connections available to students: 123 total (in the law library, excluding computer labs: 37; in classrooms: 86; in computer labs: 0; elsewhere in the law school: 0)

Law school has a wireless network.
Approximate number of simultaneous users that can be accommodated on wireless network: 450
Students are not required to own a computer.

EMPLOYMENT AND SALARIES

Proportion of 2004 graduates employed at graduation: 81%
Employed 9 months later, as of February 15, 2005: 99%
Salaries in the private sector (law firms, business, industry): $60,000–$102,500 (25th-75th percentile)
Median salary in the private sector: $89,500
Percentage in the private sector who reported salary information: 94%
Median salary in public service (government, judicial clerkships, academic posts, non-profits): $45,000

Percentage of 2004 graduates in:

Law firms: 68%	Bus./industry (legal): 4%
Bus./industry (nonlegal): 5%	Government: 11%
Public interest: 4%	Judicial clerkship: 7%
Academia : 2%	Unknown: 0%

2004 graduates employed in-state: 47%
2004 graduates employed in foreign countries: 1%
Number of states where graduates are employed: 24
Percentage of 2004 graduates working in: New England: 2%, Middle Atlantic: 17%, East North Central: 4%, West North Central: 0%, South Atlantic: 65%, East South Central: 4%, West South Central: 3%, Mountain: 1%, Pacific: 3%, Unknown: 0%

BAR PASSAGE RATES

Based on 2004 graduates taking Summer 2004 or Winter 2005 exams. Most of the school's first-time test takers took the bar in Georgia.

90%
School's bar passage rate for first-time test takers

85%
Statewide bar passage rate for first-time test takers

Florida A&M University

- 1 N. Orange Avenue, Orlando, FL, 32801
- http://www.famu.edu/acad/colleges/law
- Public
- **2005-2006 tuition:** In-state: full-time: $7,158, part-time: $5,249; Out-of-state: full-time: $26,580
- **Enrollment 2005-06 academic year:** full-time: 231; part-time: 162
- **U.S. News 2007 law specialty ranking:** N/A

2.76-3.26 GPA, 25TH-75TH PERCENTILE

142-149 LSAT, 25TH-75TH PERCENTILE

26% ACCEPTANCE RATE

Unranked 2007 U.S. NEWS LAW SCHOOL RANKING

ADMISSIONS
Admissions phone number: **(407) 254-3263**
Admissions email address:
famulaw.admissions@famu.edu
Application website: **N/A**
Application deadline for Fall 2007 admission: **4/01**

Admissions statistics:
Number of applicants for Fall 2005: **670**
Number of acceptances: **175**
Number enrolled: **91**
Acceptance rate: **26%**
GPA, 25th-75th percentile, entering class Fall 2005: **2.76-3.26**
LSAT, 25th-75th percentile, entering class Fall 2005: **142-149**

Part-time program:
Number of applicants for Fall 2005: **367**
Number of acceptances: **120**
Number enrolled: **81**
Acceptance rate: **33%**
GPA, 25th-75th percentile, entering class Fall 2005: **2.66-3.34**
LSAT, 25th-75th percentile, entering class Fall 2005: **143-150**

FINANCIAL AID
Financial aid phone number: **() -**
Financial aid application deadline: **3/01**
Tuition 2005-2006 academic year: In-state: full-time: **$7,158**, part-time: **$5,249**; Out-of-state: full-time: **$26,580**
Room and board: **N/A**; books: **N/A**; miscellaneous expenses: **N/A**
Total of room/board/books/miscellaneous expenses: **$14,964**
University does not offer graduate student housing for which law students are eligible.

Financial aid profile
Percent of students that received grants for the 2004-2005 academic year: full-time: **10%**; part-time **6%**
Median grant amount: full-time: **$1,575**; part-time: **$1,575**
The average law-school debt of those in the Class of 2005 who borrowed: **$49,523**. Proportion who borrowed: **84%**

ACADEMIC PROGRAMS
Calendar: **semester**
Joint degrees awarded: **N/A**
Typical first-year section size: Full-time: **35**; Part-time: **31**
Is there typically a "small section" of the first year class, other than Legal Writing, taught by full-time faculty?:
Full-time: **no**; Part-time: **no**
Number of course titles, beyond the first year curriculum, offered last year: **45**
Percentages of upper division course sections, excluding seminars, with an enrollment of:

Under 25: **67%**	25 to 49: **17%**
50 to 74: **16%**	75 to 99: **0%**
100+: **0%**	

Areas of specialization: clinical training, dispute resolution, environmental law, healthcare law, intellectual property law, international law, tax law, trial advocacy

Fall 2005 faculty profile
Total teaching faculty: **23**. Full-time: **70%**; **56%** men, **44%** women, **75%** minorities. Part-time: **30%**; **86%** men, **14%** women, **71%** minorities
Student-to-faculty ratio: **15.0**

SPECIAL PROGRAMS *(as provided by law school):*
The clinical program offers third-year law students an opportunity to serve traditionally underserved clients under the supervision of the faculty, the bench and the bar. The clinics afford students the valuable learning experience of being able to internalize the law and legal theory through practical experiences of assisting real clients with real legal issues and providing them quality legal representation. Students participating in the clinics have the unique opportunity to handle problems that arise from poverty, inequality and other social ills. The students gain first-

hand insight into the strategic and ethical dimensions of the profession, and acquire valuable legal skills. Additionally, the clinical program helps students explore career potential by exposing them to a broad spectrum of legal opportunities. Students are able to make more informed selections about their career options and the legal settings in which they feel most comfortable. Frequently, the clinical placement and experience leads to a job offer upon graduation.

The clinical program offers externships, in-house clinics and judicial internships.

The externships provide students the opportunity to work in a legal setting, such as a government agency, a court program or a nonprofit legal services provider. Students handle significant legal tasks, such as mediation, legal drafting, research, fact investigation, negotiating and client interviewing while under the direct supervision of lawyers at the agency or nonprofit. The clinical program includes externships in mediation, criminal defense, criminal prosecution, appellate practice, and real estate.

The in-house clinics provide students with even more in-depth hands-on experience working as a lawyer. While the students work under the direct supervision of experienced clinical faculty, the students have an opportunity to interact with clients, opposing parties, opposing counsel and court personnel who can provide other valuable learning experiences. The clinical program includes in-house clinics in community economic development, housing, homelessness and legal advocacy, and guardian ad litem.

The judicial internships provide students with the unique opportunity to work with local judges. The experience affords students the ability to peer into the inner-workings behind judicial rulings and how juries decide cases. Students research and write on a broad variety of legal topics, enabling them to hone their research and writing skills under the direct supervision of members of the bench. Many judges also offer observation of court proceedings.

STUDENT BODY

Fall 2005 full-time enrollment: 231

Men: 42%	Women: 58%
African-American: 45.9%	American Indian: 1.7%
Asian-American: 1.7%	Mexican-American: 0.0%
Puerto Rican: 0.0%	Other Hisp-Amer: 13.0%
White: 36.4%	International: 0.0%
Unknown: 1.3%	

Fall 2005 part-time enrollment: 162

Men: 40%	Women: 60%
African-American: 34.0%	American Indian: 0.6%
Asian-American: 3.7%	Mexican-American: 0.0%
Puerto Rican: 0.0%	Other Hisp-Amer: 17.9%
White: 41.4%	International: 0.0%
Unknown: 2.5%	

Attrition rates for 2004-2005 full-time students
Percent of students discontinuing law school:
Men: **N/A**   Women: **N/A**

First-year students: **N/A**   Second-year students: **N/A**
Third-year students: **N/A**

LIBRARY RESOURCES

The library holds 13,354 and receives 795 current subscriptions.
Total volumes: 298,956
Percentage of the titles in the online catalog: **N/A**
Total seats available for library users: 185

INFORMATION TECHNOLOGY

Number of wired network connections available to students: 79 total (in the law library, excluding computer labs: 30; in classrooms: 12; in computer labs: 6; elsewhere in the law school: 31)
Law school has a wireless network.
Approximate number of simultaneous users that can be accommodated on wireless network: 1,500
Students are not required to own a computer.

EMPLOYMENT AND SALARIES

Proportion of 2004 graduates employed at graduation: **N/A**
Employed 9 months later, as of February 15, 2005: **N/A**
Salaries in the private sector (law firms, business, industry): **N/A–N/A** (25th-75th percentile)
Median salary in the private sector: **N/A**
Percentage in the private sector who reported salary information: **N/A**
Median salary in public service (government, judicial clerkships, academic posts, non-profits): **N/A**

Percentage of 2004 graduates in:

Law firms: **N/A**	Bus./industry (legal): **N/A**
Bus./industry (nonlegal): **N/A**	Government: **N/A**
Public interest: **N/A**	Judicial clerkship: **N/A**
Academia : **N/A**	Unknown: **N/A**

2004 graduates employed in-state: **N/A**
2004 graduates employed in foreign countries: **N/A**
Number of states where graduates are employed: **N/A**
Percentage of 2004 graduates working in: New England: **N/A**, Middle Atlantic: **N/A**, East North Central: **N/A**, West North Central: **N/A**, South Atlantic: **N/A**, East South Central: **N/A**, West South Central: **N/A**, Mountain: **N/A**, Pacific: **N/A**, Unknown: **N/A**

BAR PASSAGE RATES
Based on 2004 graduates taking Summer 2004 or Winter 2005 exams. Most of the school's first-time test takers took the bar in N/A.

N/A

School's bar passage rate for first-time test takers

N/A

Statewide bar passage rate for first-time test takers

Florida Coastal School of Law

- 7555 Beach Boulevard, Jacksonville, FL, 32216
- http://www.fcsl.edu
- Private
- **Year founded:** 1996
- **2005-2006 tuition:** full-time: $25,050; part-time: $20,240
- **Enrollment 2005-06 academic year:** full-time: 834; part-time: 214
- **U.S. News 2007 law specialty ranking:** N/A

2.88-3.49	GPA, 25TH-75TH PERCENTILE
150-154	LSAT, 25TH-75TH PERCENTILE
37%	ACCEPTANCE RATE
Tier 4	2007 U.S. NEWS LAW SCHOOL RANKING

ADMISSIONS

Admissions phone number: **(904) 680-7710**
Admissions email address: **admissions@fcsl.edu**
Application website: **N/A**
Application deadline for Fall 2007 admission: **rolling**

Admissions statistics:
Number of applicants for Fall 2005: **4,659**
Number of acceptances: **1,715**
Number enrolled: **431**
Acceptance rate: **37%**
GPA, 25th-75th percentile, entering class Fall 2005:
2.88-3.49
LSAT, 25th-75th percentile, entering class Fall 2005:
150-154

Part-time program:
Number of applicants for Fall 2005: **60**
Number of acceptances: **40**
Number enrolled: **18**
Acceptance rate: **67%**
GPA, 25th-75th percentile, entering class Fall 2005:
2.71-3.43
LSAT, 25th-75th percentile, entering class Fall 2005: **147-153**

FINANCIAL AID

Financial aid phone number: **(904) 680-7717**
Financial aid application deadline: N/A
Tuition 2005-2006 academic year: full-time: **$25,050**; part-time: **$20,240**
Room and board: **$8,316**; books: **$1,100**; miscellaneous expenses: **$7,605**
Total of room/board/books/miscellaneous expenses: **$17,021**
University does not offer graduate student housing for which law students are eligible.

Financial aid profile
Percent of students that received grants for the 2004-2005 academic year: full-time: **47%**; part-time **14%**
Median grant amount: full-time: **$5,000**; part-time: **$5,000**

The average law-school debt of those in the Class of 2005 who borrowed: **$86,193**. Proportion who borrowed: **93%**

ACADEMIC PROGRAMS

Calendar: **semester**
Joint degrees awarded: **N/A**
Typical first-year section size: Full-time: **75**; Part-time: **40**
Is there typically a "small section" of the first year class, other than Legal Writing, taught by full-time faculty?:
Full-time: **no**; Part-time: **no**
Number of course titles, beyond the first year curriculum, offered last year: **140**
Percentages of upper division course sections, excluding seminars, with an enrollment of:

Under 25: **50%**	25 to 49: **28%**
50 to 74: **18%**	75 to 99: **4%**
100+: **0%**	

Areas of specialization: appellate advocacy, clinical training, dispute resolution, environmental law, healthcare law, intellectual property law, international law, tax law, trial advocacy

Fall 2005 faculty profile
Total teaching faculty: **102**. Full-time: **48%**; **43%** men, **57%** women, **20%** minorities. Part-time: **52%**; **75%** men, **25%** women, **2%** minorities
Student-to-faculty ratio: **17.8**

SPECIAL PROGRAMS *(as provided by law school)*:

Florida Coastal School of Law (FCSL) offers live client clinics and placement clinics to upper class students. FCSL is a participant in the American Caribbean Law Initiative, which includes clinical experiences as well as classroom components. The school has also developed and regularly offers a General Practice Institute which prepares students for law office management and other business and practical aspects of law practice. Finally, the school has the Center for Law and Sports, which offers a certificate program.

STUDENT BODY

Fall 2005 full-time enrollment: 834

Men: 55%	Women: 45%
African-American: 5.4%	American Indian: 1.2%
Asian-American: 1.9%	Mexican-American: 0.1%
Puerto Rican: 0.8%	Other Hisp-Amer: 3.0%
White: 61.3%	International: 0.0%
Unknown: 26.3%	

Fall 2005 part-time enrollment: 214

Men: 47%	Women: 53%
African-American: 12.1%	American Indian: 0.9%
Asian-American: 3.3%	Mexican-American: 0.0%
Puerto Rican: 1.4%	Other Hisp-Amer: 3.7%
White: 53.3%	International: 0.0%
Unknown: 25.2%	

Attrition rates for 2004-2005 full-time students
Percent of students discontinuing law school:

Men: 10%	Women: 10%
First-year students: 16%	Second-year students: 4%
Third-year students: N/A	

LIBRARY RESOURCES

The library holds 103,667 and receives 3,175 current subscriptions.
Total volumes: 220,091
Percentage of the titles in the online catalog: 98%
Total seats available for library users: 479

INFORMATION TECHNOLOGY

Number of wired network connections available to students: 151 total (in the law library, excluding computer labs: 150; in classrooms: 1; in computer labs: 0; elsewhere in the law school: 0)
Law school has a wireless network.
Approximate number of simultaneous users that can be accommodated on wireless network: 500
Students are not required to own a computer.

EMPLOYMENT AND SALARIES

Proportion of 2004 graduates employed at graduation: **N/A**
Employed 9 months later, as of February 15, 2005: **92%**
Salaries in the private sector (law firms, business, industry): **$38,000–$60,000** (25th-75th percentile)
Median salary in the private sector: **$45,000**
Percentage in the private sector who reported salary information: **63%**
Median salary in public service (government, judicial clerkships, academic posts, non-profits): **$38,000**

Percentage of 2004 graduates in:

Law firms: 49%	Bus./industry (legal): 14%
Bus./industry (nonlegal): 0%	Government: 19%
Public interest: 11%	Judicial clerkship: 1%
Academia : 2%	Unknown: 4%

2004 graduates employed in-state: 81%
2004 graduates employed in foreign countries: 1%
Number of states where graduates are employed: 15
Percentage of 2004 graduates working in: New England: 2%, Middle Atlantic: 2%, East North Central: 0%, West North Central: 0%, South Atlantic: 92%, East South Central: 2%, West South Central: 1%, Mountain: 1%, Pacific: 1%, Unknown: 0%

BAR PASSAGE RATES

Based on 2004 graduates taking Summer 2004 or Winter 2005 exams. Most of the school's first-time test takers took the bar in Florida.

71%
School's bar passage rate for first-time test takers

73%
Statewide bar passage rate for first-time test takers

Florida International University

- University Park, GL 485, Miami, FL, 33199
- http://www.fiu.edu/law
- Public
- **Year founded:** 2002
- **2005-2006 tuition:** In-state: $267/credit hour; Out-of-state: $726/credit hour
- **Enrollment 2005-06 academic year:** full-time: 176; part-time: 156
- **U.S. News 2007 law specialty ranking:** N/A

3.11-3.65 GPA, 25TH-75TH PERCENTILE

153-157 LSAT, 25TH-75TH PERCENTILE

14% ACCEPTANCE RATE

Unranked 2007 U.S. NEWS LAW SCHOOL RANKING

ADMISSIONS

Admissions phone number: **(305) 348-8006**
Admissions email address: **lawadmit@fiu.edu**
Application website:
http://law.fiu.edu/admissions/apply.htm
Application deadline for Fall 2007 admission: 5/01

Admissions statistics:

Number of applicants for Fall 2005: **1,064**
Number of acceptances: **150**
Number enrolled: **64**
Acceptance rate: **14%**
GPA, 25th-75th percentile, entering class Fall 2005: **3.11-3.65**
LSAT, 25th-75th percentile, entering class Fall 2005: **153-157**

Part-time program:

Number of applicants for Fall 2005: **432**
Number of acceptances: **88**
Number enrolled: **56**
Acceptance rate: **20%**
GPA, 25th-75th percentile, entering class Fall 2005: **2.98-3.51**
LSAT, 25th-75th percentile, entering class Fall 2005: **151-155**

FINANCIAL AID

Financial aid phone number: **(305) 348-8006**
Financial aid application deadline: 3/01
Tuition 2005-2006 academic year: In-state: **$267/credit hour**; Out-of-state: **$726/credit hour**
Room and board: **$9,672**; books: **$2,160**; miscellaneous expenses: **$2,008**
Total of room/board/books/miscellaneous expenses: **$13,840**
University offers graduate student housing for which law students are eligible.

Financial aid profile

Percent of students that received grants for the 2004-2005 academic year: full-time: **60%**; part-time **17%**
Median grant amount: full-time: **$4,000**; part-time: **$3,000**
The average law-school debt of those in the Class of 2005 who borrowed: **$16,308**. Proportion who borrowed: **83%**

ACADEMIC PROGRAMS

Calendar: **semester**
Joint degrees awarded: **J.D./M.B.A.; J.D./M.S.W.; J.D./MA Latin American/Caribbean Studies; J.D./M.A. International Business; J.S./M.A. Public Administration; J.D./M.S. Psychology; J.D./M.S. Criminal Justice**
Typical first-year section size: Full-time: **64**; Part-time: **56**
Is there typically a "small section" of the first year class, other than Legal Writing, taught by full-time faculty?: Full-time: **no**; Part-time: **no**
Number of course titles, beyond the first year curriculum, offered last year: **52**
Percentages of upper division course sections, excluding seminars, with an enrollment of:
   Under 25: **74%**   25 to 49: **12%**
   50 to 74: **15%**   75 to 99: **N/A**
   100+: **N/A**
Areas of specialization: appellate advocacy, clinical training, dispute resolution, environmental law, healthcare law, intellectual property law, international law, tax law, trial advocacy

Fall 2005 faculty profile

Total teaching faculty: **43**. Full-time: **58%**; 60% men, 40% women, 52% minorities. Part-time: **42%**; 72% men, 28% women, 33% minorities
Student-to-faculty ratio: **13.3**

SPECIAL PROGRAMS *(as provided by law school):*

Located in Miami, the Florida International University College of Law is the first and only public law school in South Florida. The College of Law enrolled its first class in fall 2002, and attained provisional approval by the American Bar Association at the earliest possible time, in August 2004, qualifying its graduates to sit for the bar examination in all states. Reflecting the ethnic, cultural, and racial diversity of South Florida, the College of Law is among the most diverse in the nation. Its student body is "majority minority"; the most recent entering class included more than 39 percent of Hispanic students and more than 12 percent African American and other black students. The student body is among the most qualified of any law school in Florida; with more than 10 applications for each seat in the most recent entering class, admission to the College of Law is highly competitive. The FIU College of Law's academic program emphasizes international and comparative law. The required curriculum includes a three-hour first-year course, Introduction to International and Comparative Law. All domestic law courses include an international or comparative law dimension. This pervasive approach to international and comparative law encourages students to analyze legal systemic, political, economic, social, and other cultural differences which may contribute to different legal treatment of comparable problems in different countries. In addition, the College of Law will offer a rich array of upper level electives in the International and Comparative Law areas. The College of Law offers foreign summer programs in Seville, Spain, and Rio de Janeiro, Brazil. The curriculum also emphasizes instruction in legal skills and values of the profession. The Legal Skills and Values Program combines demanding traditional instruction in legal research and writing with an introduction to other lawyering skills, like interviewing, counseling, and issues of professionalism. It is a required three-semester curriculum. The Clinical Program advances the law school's goals of educating lawyers for ethical and effective practice of law and of promoting community service through the representation of real clients. The first clinics at the College of Law are an immigration/human rights clinic, a criminal law clinic, and a community development clinic. Students assume responsibility for matters of great importance to real clients. As a public, urban law school, the College of Law is committed to serving the community of which it is a part by educating future lawyers who will understand the value to the community and to them personally of helping those in need. In recognition of this, students must satisfy a community service requirement through the law school's Community Service Program. As the state of Florida's public research university in South Florida, FIU offers a broad range of high quality graduate level degree programs. Law students interested in interdisciplinary study may take advantage of these curricula through one of the following joint degree programs: J.D./M.B.A., J.D./master of international business, J.D./master of Latin American and Caribbean studies, J.D./M.P.A., J.D./M.S. in psychology, J.D./master of social work, J.D./M.S. in criminal justice. In addition, the University will work with students who wish to formulate an individualized joint degree program with another academic unit within the University.

STUDENT BODY

Fall 2005 full-time enrollment: 176

Men: 47%	Women: 53%
African-American: 9.1%	American Indian: 0.0%
Asian-American: 3.4%	Mexican-American: 0.0%
Puerto Rican: 0.0%	Other Hisp-Amer: 36.4%
White: 43.2%	International: 0.0%
Unknown: 8.0%	

Fall 2005 part-time enrollment: 156

Men: 60%	Women: 40%
African-American: 11.5%	American Indian: 1.3%
Asian-American: 1.9%	Mexican-American: 0.0%
Puerto Rican: 0.0%	Other Hisp-Amer: 45.5%
White: 37.8%	International: 0.0%
Unknown: 1.9%	

Attrition rates for 2004-2005 full-time students
Percent of students discontinuing law school:

Men: 11%	Women: 19%
First-year students: 34%	Second-year students: 4%
Third-year students: N/A	

LIBRARY RESOURCES
The library holds 77,567 and receives 1,135 current subscriptions.
Total volumes: 190,649
Percentage of the titles in the online catalog: 100%
Total seats available for library users: 196

INFORMATION TECHNOLOGY
Number of wired network connections available to students: 2 total (in the law library, excluding computer labs: 0; in classrooms: 1; in computer labs: 1; elsewhere in the law school: 0)
Law school has a wireless network.
Approximate number of simultaneous users that can be accommodated on wireless network: 1,000
Students are not required to own a computer.

EMPLOYMENT AND SALARIES
Proportion of 2004 graduates employed at graduation: N/A
Employed 9 months later, as of February 15, 2005: N/A
Salaries in the private sector (law firms, business, industry): N/A–N/A (25th-75th percentile)
Median salary in the private sector: N/A
Percentage in the private sector who reported salary information: N/A
Median salary in public service (government, judicial clerkships, academic posts, non-profits): N/A

Percentage of 2004 graduates in:

Law firms: N/A	Bus./industry (legal): N/A
Bus./industry (nonlegal): N/A	Government: N/A
Public interest: N/A	Judicial clerkship: N/A
Academia : N/A	Unknown: N/A

2004 graduates employed in-state: N/A
2004 graduates employed in foreign countries: N/A
Number of states where graduates are employed: N/A
Percentage of 2004 graduates working in: New England: N/A, Middle Atlantic: N/A, East North Central: N/A, West North Central: N/A, South Atlantic: N/A, East South Central: N/A, West South Central: N/A, Mountain: N/A, Pacific: N/A, Unknown: N/A

BAR PASSAGE RATES
Based on 2004 graduates taking Summer 2004 or Winter 2005 exams. Most of the school's first-time test takers took the bar in Florida.

N/A
School's bar passage rate for first-time test takers

N/A
Statewide bar passage rate for first-time test takers

Florida State University

- 425 W. Jefferson Street, Tallahassee, FL, 32306-1601
- http://www.law.fsu.edu
- Public
- Year founded: 1966
- 2005-2006 tuition: In-state: $300/credit hour; Out-of-state: $930/credit hour
- Enrollment 2005-06 academic year: full-time: 772
- U.S. News 2007 law specialty ranking: environmental law: 14, tax law: 25

3.21-3.67	GPA, 25TH-75TH PERCENTILE
158-161	LSAT, 25TH-75TH PERCENTILE
23%	ACCEPTANCE RATE
53	2007 U.S. NEWS LAW SCHOOL RANKING

ADMISSIONS

Admissions phone number: **(850) 644-3787**
Admissions email address: **admissions@law.fsu.edu**
Application website:
https://www.law.fsu.edu/prospective_students/admissions/onlineapp.php
Application deadline for Fall 2007 admission: **2/15**

Admissions statistics:

Number of applicants for Fall 2005: **3,877**
Number of acceptances: **873**
Number enrolled: **284**
Acceptance rate: **23%**
GPA, 25th-75th percentile, entering class Fall 2005: **3.21-3.67**
LSAT, 25th-75th percentile, entering class Fall 2005: **158-161**

FINANCIAL AID

Financial aid phone number: **(850) 644-5716**
Financial aid application deadline: **2/15**
Tuition 2005-2006 academic year: In-state: **$300/credit hour**; Out-of-state: **$930/credit hour**
Room and board: **$9,510**; books: **$1,000**; miscellaneous expenses: **$4,000**
Total of room/board/books/miscellaneous expenses: **$14,510**
University offers graduate student housing for which law students are eligible.

Financial aid profile

Percent of students that received grants for the 2004-2005 academic year: full-time: **33%**
Median grant amount: full-time: **$1,000**
The average law-school debt of those in the Class of 2005 who borrowed: **$46,486**. Proportion who borrowed: **92%**

ACADEMIC PROGRAMS

Calendar: **semester**

Joint degrees awarded: **J.D./M.B.A.; J.D./M.S. International Affairs; J.D./M.P.A.; J.D./M.S. Economics; J.D./M.S. URP; J.D./M.S.W.; J.D./L.I.S.**
Typical first-year section size: Full-time: **74**
Is there typically a "small section" of the first year class, other than Legal Writing, taught by full-time faculty?: Full-time: **no**
Number of course titles, beyond the first year curriculum, offered last year: **108**
Percentages of upper division course sections, excluding seminars, with an enrollment of:

Under 25: **49%**	25 to 49: **28%**
50 to 74: **11%**	75 to 99: **6%**
100+: **6%**	

Areas of specialization: appellate advocacy, clinical training, dispute resolution, environmental law, healthcare law, intellectual property law, international law, tax law, trial advocacy

Fall 2005 faculty profile

Total teaching faculty: **114**. Full-time: **47%**; **56%** men, **44%** women, **11%** minorities. Part-time: **53%**; **70%** men, **30%** women, **3%** minorities
Student-to-faculty ratio: **13.8**

SPECIAL PROGRAMS *(as provided by law school)*:

The College of Law offers seven joint-degree programs and two certificate programs. The following joint degrees are available: J.D./M.B.A., J.D./M.P.A., J.D./M.S.W., J.D./M.I.S., J.D./masters in economics, J.D./masters in international affairs, and J.D./masters in urban and regional planning. The college also offers certificate programs in Environmental, Natural Resources and Land Use Law, and International Law. The certificate programs are rigorous, focused courses of study, that, when coupled with experience gained through externships and other opportunities, are designed to prepare graduates to work in highly specialized areas of law.

The college offers one of the most extensive clinical externship programs in the United States. Students earn academic credit while learning to assume the role of attorney or judicial clerk in the litigation and adjudication of real cases. Judicial externships are available with state trial and appellate courts, including the Florida Supreme Court and the federal courts. Externship opportunities with government agencies and commissions, the state attorney, the public defender, and legal services offices are also provided, as well as opportunities abroad with the International Bar Association in London. The college is also home to the internationally recognized Children's Advocacy Center, which trains law students in legal advocacy with an emphasis on intensive one-on-one and small group instruction. The Center is unique among law school clinical programs for providing a broad range of legal services. With approximately 80 on-going cases, it represents children, persons with disabilities, and victims of domestic violence. It also handles special education, Medicaid, foster care, delinquency, criminal, school expulsions, developmental services, and supplemental security income (SSI) cases.

The college also sponsors a summer program at Oxford University in England. As the oldest on-going program in Oxford sponsored by a U.S. law school, it provides students with a unique opportunity to study comparative law and the history of the common law and its institutions in their original setting.

STUDENT BODY

Fall 2005 full-time enrollment: 772

Men: 54%	Women: 46%
African-American: 5.3%	American Indian: 1.0%
Asian-American: 4.1%	Mexican-American: 0.1%
Puerto Rican: 1.8%	Other Hisp-Amer: 6.3%
White: 77.1%	International: 1.6%
Unknown: 2.6%	

Attrition rates for 2004-2005 full-time students
Percent of students discontinuing law school:

Men: 2%	Women: 1%
First-year students: 4%	Second-year students: 1%
Third-year students: 0%	

LIBRARY RESOURCES

The library holds 163,328 and receives 3,602 current subscriptions.
Total volumes: 485,342
Percentage of the titles in the online catalog: 100%
Total seats available for library users: 410

INFORMATION TECHNOLOGY

Number of wired network connections available to students: 0 total (in the law library, excluding computer labs: 0; in classrooms: 0; in computer labs: 0; elsewhere in the law school: 0)

Law school has a wireless network.
Approximate number of simultaneous users that can be accommodated on wireless network: 2,700
Students are required to own a computer.

EMPLOYMENT AND SALARIES

Proportion of 2004 graduates employed at graduation: 85%
Employed 9 months later, as of February 15, 2005: 99%
Salaries in the private sector (law firms, business, industry): $48,000–$75,000 (25th-75th percentile)
Median salary in the private sector: $60,000
Percentage in the private sector who reported salary information: 47%
Median salary in public service (government, judicial clerkships, academic posts, non-profits): $37,500

Percentage of 2004 graduates in:

Law firms: 44%	Bus./industry (legal): 1%
Bus./industry (nonlegal): 5%	Government: 32%
Public interest: 5%	Judicial clerkship: 8%
Academia : 2%	Unknown: 4%

2004 graduates employed in-state: 81%
2004 graduates employed in foreign countries: 0%
Number of states where graduates are employed: 17
Percentage of 2004 graduates working in: New England: 0%, Middle Atlantic: 1%, East North Central: 1%, West North Central: 1%, South Atlantic: 92%, East South Central: 1%, West South Central: 2%, Mountain: 2%, Pacific: 1%, Unknown: 1%

BAR PASSAGE RATES

Based on 2004 graduates taking Summer 2004 or Winter 2005 exams. Most of the school's first-time test takers took the bar in Florida.

77%
School's bar passage rate for first-time test takers

73%
Statewide bar passage rate for first-time test takers

Fordham University

- 140 W. 62nd Street, New York, NY, 10023-7485
- http://law.fordham.edu/index.htm
- Private
- Year founded: 1905
- 2005-2006 tuition: full-time: $35,141; part-time: $26,398
- Enrollment 2005-06 academic year: full-time: 1,170; part-time: 346
- U.S. News 2007 law specialty ranking: clinical training: 12, dispute resolution: 13, intellecutal property law: 19

3.37-3.76 GPA, 25TH-75TH PERCENTILE

164-167 LSAT, 25TH-75TH PERCENTILE

21% ACCEPTANCE RATE

32 2007 U.S. NEWS LAW SCHOOL RANKING

ADMISSIONS

Admissions phone number: **(212) 636-6810**
Admissions email address:
lawadmissions@law.fordham.edu
Application website:
http://law.fordham.edu/admissions.htm
Application deadline for Fall 2007 admission: **3/01**

Admissions statistics:

Number of applicants for Fall 2005: **5,823**
Number of acceptances: **1,244**
Number enrolled: **323**
Acceptance rate: **21%**
GPA, 25th-75th percentile, entering class Fall 2005:
3.37-3.76
LSAT, 25th-75th percentile, entering class Fall 2005:
164-167

Part-time program:

Number of applicants for Fall 2005: **1,043**
Number of acceptances: **249**
Number enrolled: **160**
Acceptance rate: **24%**
GPA, 25th-75th percentile, entering class Fall 2005:
3.24-3.65
LSAT, 25th-75th percentile, entering class Fall 2005:
160-163

FINANCIAL AID

Financial aid phone number: **(212) 636-6815**
Financial aid application deadline: **4/01**
Tuition 2005-2006 academic year: full-time: **$35,141**; part-time: **$26,398**
Room and board: **N/A**; books: **N/A**; miscellaneous expenses: **N/A**
Total of room/board/books/miscellaneous expenses:
$20,424
University offers graduate student housing for which law students are eligible.

Financial aid profile

Percent of students that received grants for the 2004-2005 academic year: full-time: **29%**; part-time **22%**
Median grant amount: full-time: **$6,300**; part-time: **$5,000**
The average law-school debt of those in the Class of 2005 who borrowed: **$94,004**. Proportion who borrowed: **79%**

ACADEMIC PROGRAMS

Calendar: **semester**
Joint degrees awarded: **J.D./M.B.A.; J.D./M.S.W.; J.D./M.A.**
Typical first-year section size: Full-time: **80**; Part-time: **80**
Is there typically a "small section" of the first year class, other than Legal Writing, taught by full-time faculty?:
Full-time: **yes**; Part-time: **yes**
Number of course titles, beyond the first year curriculum, offered last year: **205**
Percentages of upper division course sections, excluding seminars, with an enrollment of:

Under 25: **63%**	25 to 49: **21%**
50 to 74: **9%**	75 to 99: **3%**
100+: **3%**	

Areas of specialization: appellate advocacy, clinical training, dispute resolution, environmental law, healthcare law, intellectual property law, international law, tax law, trial advocacy

Fall 2005 faculty profile

Total teaching faculty: **300**. Full-time: **24%**; **64%** men, **36%** women, **23%** minorities. Part-time: **76%**; **67%** men, **33%** women, **11%** minorities
Student-to-faculty ratio: **15.9**

SPECIAL PROGRAMS (as provided by law school):

Fordham offers a full range of specialized academic programs that further promote the art and science of legal analysis and the cultivation of a vigorous ongoing dialogue between students and professors in and out of the classroom. The following programs give students the opportunity to work closely with professors who are nationally recognized for advancing scholarship in their respective fields:

The Brendan Moore Advocacy Center fosters the study of lawyers as advocates, with special emphasis on client representation at the trial level. Moore Advocates are selected from among first-year day and second-year evening students and participate in a two-year program of sequenced class offerings, externships, and special programs.

The school's clinical program gives students opportunities to integrate theory and analysis with lawyering skills in problem-solving settings. With 17 full-time faculty, three part-time professors, one adjunct, and one full-time social worker, Fordham's clinical program is one of the largest in the nation. The program engages students in live-client clinics and simulation courses in 13 practice areas, including an innovative interdisciplinary Child and Family Litigation Clinic, where students from Fordham's schools of law, graduate social work, and applied psychology work on teams. Fordham also offers a large externship placement program: More than 250 students participate annually at nonprofit and governmental organizations.

The Fordham Center for Corporate, Securities, and Financial Law sponsors both roundtable discussions with business leaders in the business community and public programs.

The Joseph R. Crowley Program in International Human Rights is one of the nation's premier academic organizations dealing with the rights of individuals throughout the world. Students in the Crowley program plan and participate in an annual fact-finding human-rights mission to a designated host country, which is unprecedented in American legal education. Other international programs include the Center on European Law and Fordham's unique Belfast/Dublin summer program.

The Louis Stein Center for Law and Ethics promotes the integration of ethical perspectives in legal practice and legal institutions and the development of the law generally. It received the American Bar Association's 2001 E. Smythe Gambrell Professionalism Award for developing national legal ethics conferences. The center oversees the Stein Scholars Program, a three-year program for approximately 20 selected first-year law students.

STUDENT BODY

Fall 2005 full-time enrollment: 1,170

Men: 52%	Women: 48%
African-American: 5.0%	American Indian: 0.8%
Asian-American: 9.7%	Mexican-American: 0.3%
Puerto Rican: 1.4%	Other Hisp-Amer: 6.3%
White: 61.3%	International: 0.0%
Unknown: 15.4%	

Fall 2005 part-time enrollment: 346

Men: 58%	Women: 42%
African-American: 7.5%	American Indian: 0.3%
Asian-American: 14.5%	Mexican-American: 0.9%
Puerto Rican: 0.6%	Other Hisp-Amer: 6.9%
White: 52.9%	International: 0.0%
Unknown: 16.5%	

Attrition rates for 2004-2005 full-time students

Percent of students discontinuing law school:

Men: 0%	Women: 0%
First-year students: 0%	Second-year students: N/A
Third-year students: 0%	

LIBRARY RESOURCES

The library holds 272,679 and receives 4,880 current subscriptions.
Total volumes: 626,231
Percentage of the titles in the online catalog: 100%
Total seats available for library users: 473

INFORMATION TECHNOLOGY

Number of wired network connections available to students: 448 total (in the law library, excluding computer labs: 258; in classrooms: 160; in computer labs: 0; elsewhere in the law school: 30)
Law school has a wireless network.
Approximate number of simultaneous users that can be accommodated on wireless network: 600
Students are not required to own a computer.

EMPLOYMENT AND SALARIES

Proportion of 2004 graduates employed at graduation: 86%
Employed 9 months later, as of February 15, 2005: 98%
Salaries in the private sector (law firms, business, industry): $96,250–$125,000 (25th-75th percentile)
Median salary in the private sector: $125,000
Percentage in the private sector who reported salary information: 77%
Median salary in public service (government, judicial clerkships, academic posts, non-profits): $47,500

Percentage of 2004 graduates in:

Law firms: 72%	Bus./industry (legal): 1%
Bus./industry (nonlegal): 6%	Government: 10%
Public interest: 3%	Judicial clerkship: 4%
Academia : 2%	Unknown: 2%

2004 graduates employed in-state: 75%
2004 graduates employed in foreign countries: 1%
Number of states where graduates are employed: 18
Percentage of 2004 graduates working in: New England: 2%, Middle Atlantic: 83%, East North Central: 1%, West North Central: 1%, South Atlantic: 2%, East South Central: N/A, West South Central: N/A, Mountain: N/A, Pacific: 2%, Unknown: 8%

BAR PASSAGE RATES

Based on 2004 graduates taking Summer 2004 or Winter 2005 exams. Most of the school's first-time test takers took the bar in New York.

87%
School's bar passage rate for first-time test takers

75%
Statewide bar passage rate for first-time test takers

Franklin Pierce Law Center

- Two White Street, Concord, NH, 03301
- http://www.piercelaw.edu
- Private
- Year founded: 1973
- 2005-2006 tuition: full-time: $27,300; part-time: N/A
- Enrollment 2005-06 academic year: full-time: 437; part-time: 3
- U.S. News 2007 law specialty ranking: intellecutal property law: 7

3.00-3.60 GPA, 25TH-75TH PERCENTILE

150-156 LSAT, 25TH-75TH PERCENTILE

38% ACCEPTANCE RATE

Tier 4 2007 U.S. NEWS LAW SCHOOL RANKING

ADMISSIONS

Admissions phone number: **(603) 228-9217**
Admissions email address: **admissions@piercelaw.edu**
Application website:
http://www.piercelaw.edu/bulletin/bulletin.htm
Application deadline for Fall 2007 admission: **4/01**

Admissions statistics:

Number of applicants for Fall 2005: **1,536**
Number of acceptances: **577**
Number enrolled: **142**
Acceptance rate: **38%**
GPA, 25th-75th percentile, entering class Fall 2005: **3.00-3.60**
LSAT, 25th-75th percentile, entering class Fall 2005: **150-156**

Part-time program:

Number of applicants for Fall 2005: **1**
Number of acceptances: **1**
Number enrolled: **1**
Acceptance rate: **100%**
GPA, 25th-75th percentile, entering class Fall 2005: **N/A**
LSAT, 25th-75th percentile, entering class Fall 2005: **N/A**

FINANCIAL AID

Financial aid phone number: **(603) 228-1541**
Financial aid application deadline: 3/15
Tuition 2005-2006 academic year: full-time: **$27,300**; part-time: **N/A**
Room and board: **$8,814**; books: **$1,000**; miscellaneous expenses: **$5,030**
Total of room/board/books/miscellaneous expenses: **$14,844**
University offers graduate student housing for which law students are eligible.

Financial aid profile

Percent of students that received grants for the 2004-2005 academic year: full-time: **60%**; part-time **33%**
Median grant amount: full-time: **$3,000**; part-time: **$1,400**
The average law-school debt of those in the Class of 2005 who borrowed: **$86,766**. Proportion who borrowed: **82%**

ACADEMIC PROGRAMS

Calendar: **semester**
Joint degrees awarded: **J.D./MIP; J.D./MEL**
Typical first-year section size: Full-time: **70**
Is there typically a "small section" of the first year class, other than Legal Writing, taught by full-time faculty?: Full-time: **yes**
Number of course titles, beyond the first year curriculum, offered last year: **85**
Percentages of upper division course sections, excluding seminars, with an enrollment of:

Under 25: **64%**	25 to 49: **21%**
50 to 74: **11%**	75 to 99: **4%**
100+: **1%**	

Areas of specialization: appellate advocacy, clinical training, dispute resolution, environmental law, healthcare law, intellectual property law, international law, tax law, trial advocacy

Fall 2005 faculty profile

Total teaching faculty: **63**. Full-time: **30%**; **74%** men, **26%** women, **11%** minorities. Part-time: **70%**; **64%** men, **36%** women, **0%** minorities
Student-to-faculty ratio: **18.5**

SPECIAL PROGRAMS *(as provided by law school):*

Pierce Law students may work in a wide variety of civil, criminal or IP clinics. Opportunities for semester long externship placements are available locally and around the country. Pierce Law also offers summer programs in Beijing and Cork, Ireland.

STUDENT BODY

Fall 2005 full-time enrollment: 437

Men: **60%**	Women: **40%**
African-American: **4.3%**	American Indian: **0.0%**
Asian-American: **10.5%**	Mexican-American: **0.9%**
Puerto Rican: **0.0%**	Other Hisp-Amer: **2.7%**
White: **69.8%**	International: **3.7%**
Unknown: **8.0%**	

Fall 2005 part-time enrollment: 3

Men: **33%**	Women: **67%**
African-American: **0.0%**	American Indian: **0.0%**
Asian-American: **0.0%**	Mexican-American: **0.0%**
Puerto Rican: **0.0%**	Other Hisp-Amer: **0.0%**
White: **66.7%**	International: **33.3%**
Unknown: **0.0%**	

Attrition rates for 2004-2005 full-time students
Percent of students discontinuing law school:

Men: **6%**	Women: **4%**
First-year students: **10%**	Second-year students: **2%**
Third-year students: **4%**	

LIBRARY RESOURCES
The library holds **69,820** and receives **4,593** current subscriptions.
Total volumes: **260,165**
Percentage of the titles in the online catalog: **92%**
Total seats available for library users: **243**

INFORMATION TECHNOLOGY
Number of wired network connections available to students: **338** total (in the law library, excluding computer labs: **108**; in classrooms: **158**; in computer labs: **31**; elsewhere in the law school: **41**)
Law school has a wireless network.
Approximate number of simultaneous users that can be accommodated on wireless network: **540**
Students are not required to own a computer.

EMPLOYMENT AND SALARIES
Proportion of 2004 graduates employed at graduation: **N/A**
Employed 9 months later, as of February 15, 2005: **86%**

Salaries in the private sector (law firms, business, industry): **$48,000–$120,000** (25th-75th percentile)
Median salary in the private sector: **$75,000**
Percentage in the private sector who reported salary information: **69%**
Median salary in public service (government, judicial clerkships, academic posts, non-profits): **$41,000**

Percentage of 2004 graduates in:

Law firms: **58%**	Bus./industry (legal): **10%**
Bus./industry (nonlegal): **10%**	Government: **9%**
Public interest: **6%**	Judicial clerkship: **5%**
Academia : **2%**	Unknown: **N/A**

2004 graduates employed in-state: **28%**
2004 graduates employed in foreign countries: **8%**
Number of states where graduates are employed: **20**
Percentage of 2004 graduates working in: New England: **48%**, Middle Atlantic: **9%**, East North Central: **3%**, West North Central: **3%**, South Atlantic: **17%**, East South Central: **1%**, West South Central: **1%**, Mountain: **5%**, Pacific: **5%**, Unknown: **0%**

BAR PASSAGE RATES
Based on 2004 graduates taking Summer 2004 or Winter 2005 exams. Most of the school's first-time test takers took the bar in New Hampshire.

62%
School's bar passage rate for first-time test takers

64%
Statewide bar passage rate for first-time test takers

George Mason University

- 3301 Fairfax Drive, Arlington, VA, 22201-4426
- http://www.law.gmu.edu
- Public
- **Year founded:** 1980
- **2005-2006 tuition:** In-state: full-time: $12,936, part-time: $462/credit hour; Out-of-state: full-time: $24,500
- **Enrollment 2005-06 academic year:** full-time: 414; part-time: 303
- **U.S. News 2007 law specialty ranking:** intellecutal property law: 24

3.15-3.83 GPA, 25TH-75TH PERCENTILE

158-166 LSAT, 25TH-75TH PERCENTILE

15% ACCEPTANCE RATE

37 2007 U.S. NEWS LAW SCHOOL RANKING

ADMISSIONS

Admissions phone number: **(703) 993-8010**
Admissions email address: **arichar5@gmu.edu**
Application website:
http://www.law.gmu.edu/admission/onlineapp.html
Application deadline for Fall 2007 admission: **4/01**

Admissions statistics:

Number of applicants for Fall 2005: **5,199**
Number of acceptances: **787**
Number enrolled: **140**
Acceptance rate: **15%**
GPA, 25th-75th percentile, entering class Fall 2005: **3.15-3.83**
LSAT, 25th-75th percentile, entering class Fall 2005: **158-166**

Part-time program:

Number of applicants for Fall 2005: **751**
Number of acceptances: **127**
Number enrolled: **76**
Acceptance rate: **17%**
GPA, 25th-75th percentile, entering class Fall 2005: **2.94-3.68**
LSAT, 25th-75th percentile, entering class Fall 2005: **158-165**

FINANCIAL AID

Financial aid phone number: **(703) 993-4350**
Financial aid application deadline: **4/01**
Tuition 2005-2006 academic year: In-state: full-time: **$12,936**, part-time: **$462/credit hour**; Out-of-state: full-time: **$24,500**
Room and board: **$10,570**; books: **$940**; miscellaneous expenses: **$4,558**
Total of room/board/books/miscellaneous expenses: **$16,068**
University does not offer graduate student housing for which law students are eligible.

Financial aid profile

Percent of students that received grants for the 2004-2005 academic year: full-time: **14%**; part-time **2%**
Median grant amount: full-time: **$5,000**; part-time: **$5,000**
The average law-school debt of those in the Class of 2005 who borrowed: **$55,908**. Proportion who borrowed: **77%**

ACADEMIC PROGRAMS

Calendar: **semester**
Joint degrees awarded: **J.D./M.A. Economics; J.D./Ph.D. Economics; J.D./M.P.P**
Typical first-year section size: Full-time: **94**; Part-time: **91**
Is there typically a "small section" of the first year class, other than Legal Writing, taught by full-time faculty?: Full-time: **yes**; Part-time: **no**
Number of course titles, beyond the first year curriculum, offered last year: **145**
Percentages of upper division course sections, excluding seminars, with an enrollment of:

Under 25: **78%**	25 to 49: **15%**
50 to 74: **4%**	75 to 99: **2%**
100+: **1%**	

Areas of specialization: appellate advocacy, clinical training, dispute resolution, environmental law, intellecual property law, international law, tax law, trial advocacy

Fall 2005 faculty profile

Total teaching faculty: **174**. Full-time: **23%**; **93%** men, **8%** women, **10%** minorities. Part-time: **77%**; **75%** men, **25%** women, **4%** minorities
Student-to-faculty ratio: **16.5**

SPECIAL PROGRAMS (as provided by law school):

George Mason has long integrated economic and quantitative methods into its curriculum. A unique course required of all students, Economic Foundations of Legal Studies, introduces legal methods along with economic and quantitative tools, stressing the application of nonlegal methods in legal contexts. The school reinforces this approach in most courses, where almost every professor is an expert in some area of economics and quantitative methods. Economic analysis does not replace the traditional methodology that has proven successful in training generations of lawyers. The school teaches the wide range of traditional topics that form the bulk of modern practice, but in most courses, a focus on quantitative and economic aspects of legal problems enhances the traditional methodology. In addition, students who have earned a Ph.D. in economics, finance, or political science, may apply for the Robert A. Levy Fellowship in Law & Liberty. This Fellowship, which covers tuition and provides a substantial stipend, was established to encourage scholars to enter the academic field of law and economics. Second, George Mason provides a three-year legal research and writing program that emphasizes continual practice of research and writing skills through the development of actual transactions and cases, the effective use of technology, and personalized evaluation of writing skills. Students take four, small-group research and writing courses, participate in two oral argument competitions, and complete at least two upperclass writing seminars of their choice. George Mason clinical programs include the Clinic for Legal Assistance to Service Members, the Law and Mental Illness Clinic, and the Immigration Clinic, among others. Additionally, George Mason's proximity to Washington, D.C., offers a wealth of supervised externship possibilities. The externship program allows students to work outside of the law school, for academic credit, under the supervision of an attorney. Finally, students may elect to focus their legal studies in a particular area of law by completing a specialty track program or sequence. George Mason's largest track is Intellectual Property Law, which includes over 30 credit hours of courses devoted to patent, trademark, and copyright law. Other programs focus on litigation, technology law, corporate law, and regulatory law. George Mason also houses several academic centers, including the Law & Economics Center and the National Center for Technology & Law, and offers two LL.M. programs in Law and Economics and Intellectual Property, which provide students with more opportunities to develop expertise in particular areas of the law.

STUDENT BODY

Fall 2005 full-time enrollment: 414

Men: 61%	Women: 39%
African-American: 3.1%	American Indian: 0.7%
Asian-American: 6.5%	Mexican-American: 0.0%
Puerto Rican: 0.0%	Other Hisp-Amer: 5.6%
White: 81.6%	International: 2.4%
Unknown: 0.0%	

Fall 2005 part-time enrollment: 303

Men: 63%	Women: 37%
African-American: 3.6%	American Indian: 1.0%
Asian-American: 9.2%	Mexican-American: 0.0%
Puerto Rican: 0.0%	Other Hisp-Amer: 3.6%
White: 79.5%	International: 3.0%
Unknown: 0.0%	

Attrition rates for 2004-2005 full-time students
Percent of students discontinuing law school:
Men: 4%   Women: 2%

First-year students: 10%   Second-year students: N/A
Third-year students: N/A

LIBRARY RESOURCES
The library holds 164,097 and receives 5,585 current subscriptions.
Total volumes: 447,746
Percentage of the titles in the online catalog: 100%
Total seats available for library users: 320

INFORMATION TECHNOLOGY
Number of wired network connections available to students: 888 total (in the law library, excluding computer labs: 216; in classrooms: 637; in computer labs: 0; elsewhere in the law school: 35)
Law school has a wireless network.
Approximate number of simultaneous users that can be accommodated on wireless network: 800
Students are not required to own a computer.

EMPLOYMENT AND SALARIES
Proportion of 2004 graduates employed at graduation: 98%
Employed 9 months later, as of February 15, 2005: 100%
Salaries in the private sector (law firms, business, industry): $60,000–$120,000 (25th-75th percentile)
Median salary in the private sector: $84,750
Percentage in the private sector who reported salary information: 70%
Median salary in public service (government, judicial clerkships, academic posts, non-profits): $48,947

Percentage of 2004 graduates in:

Law firms: 44%	Bus./industry (legal): 10%
Bus./industry (nonlegal): 4%	Government: 19%
Public interest: 6%	Judicial clerkship: 13%
Academia : 4%	Unknown: 0%

2004 graduates employed in-state: 47%
2004 graduates employed in foreign countries: 1%
Number of states where graduates are employed: 20
Percentage of 2004 graduates working in: New England: 0%, Middle Atlantic: 3%, East North Central: 2%, West North Central: 0%, South Atlantic: 89%, East South Central: 0%, West South Central: 0%, Mountain: 3%, Pacific: 2%, Unknown: 0%

BAR PASSAGE RATES
Based on 2004 graduates taking Summer 2004 or Winter 2005 exams. Most of the school's first-time test takers took the bar in Virginia.

80%
School's bar passage rate for first-time test takers

74%
Statewide bar passage rate for first-time test takers

George Washington University

■ 2000 H Street NW, Washington, D.C., 20052
■ http://www.law.gwu.edu
■ Private
■ Year founded: 1865
■ 2005-2006 tuition: full-time: $34,500; part-time: $24,260
■ Enrollment 2005-06 academic year: full-time: 1,366; part-time: 270
■ U.S. News 2007 law specialty ranking: clinical training: 15, environmental law: 12, intellecutal property law: 3, international law: 6

3.45-3.80	GPA, 25TH-75TH PERCENTILE
163-166	LSAT, 25TH-75TH PERCENTILE
19%	ACCEPTANCE RATE
19	2007 U.S. NEWS LAW SCHOOL RANKING

ADMISSIONS

Admissions phone number: **(202) 739-0648**
Admissions email address: **jdadmit@law.gwu.edu**
Application website: **N/A**
Application deadline for Fall 2007 admission: **3/01**

Admissions statistics:

Number of applicants for Fall 2005: **9,812**
Number of acceptances: **1,888**
Number enrolled: **413**
Acceptance rate: **19%**
GPA, 25th-75th percentile, entering class Fall 2005: **3.45-3.80**
LSAT, 25th-75th percentile, entering class Fall 2005: **163-166**

Part-time program:

Number of applicants for Fall 2005: **1,260**
Number of acceptances: **225**
Number enrolled: **122**
Acceptance rate: **18%**
GPA, 25th-75th percentile, entering class Fall 2005: **3.29-3.65**
LSAT, 25th-75th percentile, entering class Fall 2005: **160-164**

FINANCIAL AID

Financial aid phone number: **(202) 994-7230**
Financial aid application deadline: **3/01**
Tuition 2005-2006 academic year: full-time: **$34,500**; part-time: **$24,260**
Room and board: **$10,700**; books: **$890**; miscellaneous expenses: **$5,450**
Total of room/board/books/miscellaneous expenses: **$17,040**
University does not offer graduate student housing for which law students are eligible.

Financial aid profile

Percent of students that received grants for the 2004-2005 academic year: full-time: **41%**; part-time **13%**

Median grant amount: full-time: **$10,000**; part-time: **$7,000**
The average law-school debt of those in the Class of 2005 who borrowed: **$88,673**. Proportion who borrowed: **91%**

ACADEMIC PROGRAMS

Calendar: **semester**
Joint degrees awarded: **J.D./M.A.; J.D./M.B.A.; J.D./M.P.H.; J.D./M.P.A.; J.D./M.P.H.; J.D./M.A.**
Typical first-year section size: Full-time: **100**; Part-time: **120**
Is there typically a "small section" of the first year class, other than Legal Writing, taught by full-time faculty?: Full-time: **yes**; Part-time: **no**
Number of course titles, beyond the first year curriculum, offered last year: **189**
Percentages of upper division course sections, excluding seminars, with an enrollment of:

Under 25: **61%**	25 to 49: **22%**
50 to 74: **7%**	75 to 99: **6%**
100+: **4%**	

Areas of specialization: appellate advocacy, clinical training, dispute resolution, environmental law, healthcare law, intellectual property law, international law, tax law, trial advocacy

Fall 2005 faculty profile

Total teaching faculty: **439**. Full-time: **22%**; **65%** men, **35%** women, **14%** minorities. Part-time: **78%**; **65%** men, **35%** women, **13%** minorities
Student-to-faculty ratio: **15.1**

SPECIAL PROGRAMS (as provided by law school):

Clinical programs:

Civil Litigation Clinic: Students counsel clients, draft pleadings, prepare cases for hearings, conduct examinations of witnesses, and argue cases.

Consumer Mediation Clinic: Students act as neutral third-party mediators who assist local consumers and businesses in resolving disputes.

Federal, Criminal, and Appellate Clinic: Students represent indigent clients and litigate direct appeals from criminal convictions.

Health Law Rights Clinic: Students assist in providing legal representation to older D.C. residents with Medicare, Medicaid, and other issues.

Immigration Clinic: Students handle immigration law matters and represent clients in removal proceedings.

International Human Rights Clinic: Students work on cases before international tribunals and treaty bodies, and in U.S. courts.

The J. B. and Maurice C. Shapiro Environmental Law Clinic: Students represent clients in both the federal and state systems.

Law Students in Court: Students represent indigent persons in the D.C. Superior Court.

The Project for Older Prisoners: Students assist low-risk prisoners over the age of 55 to help them obtain paroles, pardons, or alternative forms of incarceration.

Public Justice Advocacy Clinic: Students are assigned significant and direct responsibility in civil public-interest litigation.

Small Business Clinic: Students guide local entrepreneurs through the legal requirements to start a new business.

Vaccine Injury Clinic: Students represent individuals who suffered serious vaccine-related injuries, before the U.S. Court of Federal Claims.

Summer and exchange programs: GW summer programs are offered in intellectual property law in Munich, international human rights law in Oxford, and European and international economic law in Augsburg, Germany. Through the North American Consortium on Legal Education students may spend a semester at a Canadian or Mexican member school.

Internships: The Outside Placement Program provides students with a wide variety of opportunities to earn academic credit for work in public-interest, government, and nonprofit organizations. Recent student placements have included the U.S. Patent and Trademark Office, the Department of Justice, House and Senate judiciary committees, the Department of State, the Securities and Exchange Commission, the National Gay and Lesbian Task Force, the White House Office of Legal Counsel, Human Rights Watch, the World Bank, Public Defender Services, and judges from D.C. Superior Court, D.C. Court of Appeals, U.S. District Court for D.C., U.S. Court of Appeals for the Federal Circuit, and the Court of Federal Claims.

STUDENT BODY

Fall 2005 full-time enrollment: 1,366

Men: 54%	Women: 46%
African-American: 9.2%	American Indian: 0.7%
Asian-American: 9.0%	Mexican-American: 0.0%
Puerto Rican: 0.0%	Other Hisp-Amer: 8.2%
White: 63.0%	International: 0.7%
Unknown: 9.2%	

Fall 2005 part-time enrollment: 270

Men: 63%	Women: 37%
African-American: 6.7%	American Indian: 0.4%
Asian-American: 14.4%	Mexican-American: 0.0%
Puerto Rican: 0.0%	Other Hisp-Amer: 4.1%
White: 59.6%	International: 0.4%
Unknown: 14.4%	

Attrition rates for 2004-2005 full-time students
Percent of students discontinuing law school:

Men: 3%	Women: 2%
First-year students: 5%	Second-year students: 1%
Third-year students: 0%	

LIBRARY RESOURCES

The library holds 138,359 and receives 4,304 current subscriptions.

Total volumes: 591,863

Percentage of the titles in the online catalog: 100%

Total seats available for library users: 643

INFORMATION TECHNOLOGY

Number of wired network connections available to students: 54 total (in the law library, excluding computer labs: 54; in classrooms: 0; in computer labs: 0; elsewhere in the law school: 0)

Law school has a wireless network.

Approximate number of simultaneous users that can be accommodated on wireless network: 3,000

Students are required to own a computer.

EMPLOYMENT AND SALARIES

Proportion of 2004 graduates employed at graduation: 94%

Employed 9 months later, as of February 15, 2005: 98%

Salaries in the private sector (law firms, business, industry): $90,000–$125,000 (25th-75th percentile)

Median salary in the private sector: $125,000

Percentage in the private sector who reported salary information: 65%

Median salary in public service (government, judicial clerkships, academic posts, non-profits): $49,000

Percentage of 2004 graduates in:

Law firms: 51%	Bus./industry (legal): 5%
Bus./industry (nonlegal): N/A	Government: 17%
Public interest: 4%	Judicial clerkship: 11%
Academia : 1%	Unknown: 11%

2004 graduates employed in-state: 42%

2004 graduates employed in foreign countries: 2%

Number of states where graduates are employed: 29

Percentage of 2004 graduates working in: New England: 3%, Middle Atlantic: 17%, East North Central: 3%, West North Central: 0%, South Atlantic: 67%, East South Central: 1%, West South Central: 1%, Mountain: 2%, Pacific: 4%, Unknown: 0%

BAR PASSAGE RATES

Based on 2004 graduates taking Summer 2004 or Winter 2005 exams. Most of the school's first-time test takers took the bar in New York.

87%

School's bar passage rate for first-time test takers

75%

Statewide bar passage rate for first-time test takers

Georgetown University

- 600 New Jersey Avenue NW, Washington, DC, 20001-2075
- http://www.law.georgetown.edu
- Private
- Year founded: 1870
- 2005-2006 tuition: full-time: $35,080; part-time: $1,285/credit hour
- Enrollment 2005-06 academic year: full-time: 1,580; part-time: 360
- U.S. News 2007 law specialty ranking: clinical training: 1, dispute resolution: 7, environmental law: 5, intellecutal property law: 15, international law: 4, tax law: 3, trial advocacy: 7

3.42-3.80 GPA, 25TH-75TH PERCENTILE

167-170 LSAT, 25TH-75TH PERCENTILE

19% ACCEPTANCE RATE

14 2007 U.S. NEWS LAW SCHOOL RANKING

ADMISSIONS

Admissions phone number: **(202) 662-9015**
Admissions email address: **admis@law.georgetown.edu**
Application website:
http://www.law.georgetown.edu/admissions
Application deadline for Fall 2007 admission: **2/01**

Admissions statistics:
Number of applicants for Fall 2005: **10,700**
Number of acceptances: **2,064**
Number enrolled: **454**
Acceptance rate: **19%**
GPA, 25th-75th percentile, entering class Fall 2005: **3.42-3.80**
LSAT, 25th-75th percentile, entering class Fall 2005: **167-170**

Part-time program:
Number of applicants for Fall 2005: **1,002**
Number of acceptances: **171**
Number enrolled: **129**
Acceptance rate: **17%**
GPA, 25th-75th percentile, entering class Fall 2005: **3.34-3.72**
LSAT, 25th-75th percentile, entering class Fall 2005: **160-166**

FINANCIAL AID

Financial aid phone number: **(202) 662-9210**
Financial aid application deadline: **3/11**
Tuition 2005-2006 academic year: full-time: **$35,080**; part-time: **$1,285/credit hour**
Room and board: **$13,710**; books: **$875**; miscellaneous expenses: **$4,235**
Total of room/board/books/miscellaneous expenses: **$18,820**
University offers graduate student housing for which law students are eligible.

Financial aid profile
Percent of students that received grants for the 2004-2005 academic year: full-time: **28%**; part-time **2%**
Median grant amount: full-time: **$12,100**; part-time: **$7,500**
The average law-school debt of those in the Class of 2005 who borrowed: **$92,675**. Proportion who borrowed: **80%**

ACADEMIC PROGRAMS

Calendar: **semester**
Joint degrees awarded: **J.D./M.S.F.S.; J.D./M.B.A.; J.D./M.P.H.; J.D./M.P.P.; J.D./GOVT; J.D./PHIL; J.D./M.A. Arab Studies; J.D./M.A. Russian & E. European Studies; J.D./M.A. Latin American Studies; J.D./M.A. Security Studies; J.D./M.A. German & European Studies**
Typical first-year section size: Full-time: **112**; Part-time: **125**
Is there typically a "small section" of the first year class, other than Legal Writing, taught by full-time faculty?: Full-time: **yes**; Part-time: **yes**
Number of course titles, beyond the first year curriculum, offered last year: **307**
Percentages of upper division course sections, excluding seminars, with an enrollment of:
Under 25: **61%**   25 to 49: **22%**
50 to 74: **8%**   75 to 99: **4%**
100+: **5%**
Areas of specialization: appellate advocacy, clinical training, dispute resolution, environmental law, healthcare law, intellectual property law, international law, tax law, trial advocacy

Fall 2005 faculty profile
Total teaching faculty: **336**. Full-time: **38%**; **68%** men, **32%** women, **12%** minorities. Part-time: **62%**; **80%** men, **20%** women, **4%** minorities
Student-to-faculty ratio: **14.7**

SPECIAL PROGRAMS (as provided by law school):
First Year students have a choice between two curricula. Curriculum A includes civil procedure, contracts, constitutional law, constitutional criminal procedure, property, and torts.

Curriculum B offers a comparable grounding in the subjects studied in Curriculum A, along with a greater emphasis on the interdisciplinary sources of law, an introduction to public law and the administrative state, and a seminar in modern legal theory. With more than 100 full time faculty, Georgetown is able to offer a comprehensive legal curriculum with more than 350 courses and seminars.

Georgetown's 14 clinics, with nearly 300 students participating each year, constitute the largest in-house clinical program of any law school in the nation. The clinical program offers students an opportunity to serve the public and interact with real clients, while they explore career possibilities in various areas of legal practice. Clinical students practice in a wide range of legal settings.

Eleven Joint Degree Programs enable students to gain J.D. and master's degrees in several different areas of studies as well as J.D./Ph.D.s in government and philosophy.

The Office of Public Interest and Community Service advises students on public interest careers and supports a vast array of public interest activities, courses and programs. The Public Interest Law Scholars program provides financial and other support to students who demonstrate a commitment to spend most of their careers in public service.

Two-credit externships are available.

The Law Center is home to several major institutes. For example, the Supreme Court Institute moots more than half the cases argued before the court and allows some student participation.

The Law Center is widely recognized as one of the foremost institutions of international and comparative law scholarship and teaching in the world, with more than 100 courses and seminars in this area.

The Global Law Scholars program prepares students for transnational practice in which they regularly encounter problems that involve multiple legal systems.

A Summer Study Abroad program, focused on comparative legal issues, is held in London, England. The International Summer Internship program provides opportunities for students to work abroad with practicing lawyers in law firms, corporations, and government organizations.

STUDENT BODY

Fall 2005 full-time enrollment: 1,580

Men: 55%	Women: 45%
African-American: 8.9%	American Indian: 0.1%
Asian-American: 9.0%	Mexican-American: 0.7%
Puerto Rican: 0.3%	Other Hisp-Amer: 3.4%
White: 73.3%	International: 3.7%
Unknown: 0.7%	

Fall 2005 part-time enrollment: 360

Men: 61%	Women: 39%
African-American: 9.2%	American Indian: 0.8%
Asian-American: 12.2%	Mexican-American: 1.4%
Puerto Rican: 0.8%	Other Hisp-Amer: 3.9%
White: 65.8%	International: 4.7%
Unknown: 1.1%	

Attrition rates for 2004-2005 full-time students

Percent of students discontinuing law school:
Men: 1%   Women: 1%

First-year students: 2%   Second-year students: 0%
Third-year students: 0%

LIBRARY RESOURCES

The library holds 355,075 and receives 9,640 current subscriptions.
Total volumes: 1,123,199
Percentage of the titles in the online catalog: 100%
Total seats available for library users: 1,169

INFORMATION TECHNOLOGY

Number of wired network connections available to students: 1,455 total (in the law library, excluding computer labs: 465; in classrooms: 650; in computer labs: 20; elsewhere in the law school: 320)
Law school has a wireless network.
Approximate number of simultaneous users that can be accommodated on wireless network: 3,000
Students are not required to own a computer.

EMPLOYMENT AND SALARIES

Proportion of 2004 graduates employed at graduation: 90%
Employed 9 months later, as of February 15, 2005: 98%
Salaries in the private sector (law firms, business, industry): $125,000–$125,000 (25th-75th percentile)
Median salary in the private sector: $125,000
Percentage in the private sector who reported salary information: 83%
Median salary in public service (government, judicial clerkships, academic posts, non-profits): $48,947

Percentage of 2004 graduates in:

Law firms: 61%	Bus./industry (legal): 1%
Bus./industry (nonlegal): 4%	Government: 7%
Public interest: 5%	Judicial clerkship: 9%
Academia : 2%	Unknown: 11%

2004 graduates employed in-state: 41%
2004 graduates employed in foreign countries: 2%
Number of states where graduates are employed: 35
Percentage of 2004 graduates working in: New England: 4%, Middle Atlantic: 21%, East North Central: 5%, West North Central: 1%, South Atlantic: 45%, East South Central: 1%, West South Central: 3%, Mountain: 1%, Pacific: 7%, Unknown: 10%

BAR PASSAGE RATES

Based on 2004 graduates taking Summer 2004 or Winter 2005 exams. Most of the school's first-time test takers took the bar in New York.

93%
School's bar passage rate for first-time test takers

75%
Statewide bar passage rate for first-time test takers

Georgia State University

- PO Box 4049, Atlanta, GA, 30302-4049
- http://law.gsu.edu
- Public
- Year founded: 1982
- 2005-2006 tuition: In-state: full-time: $6,484, part-time: $6,020; Out-of-state: full-time: $21,644
- Enrollment 2005-06 academic year: full-time: 494; part-time: 191
- U.S. News 2007 law specialty ranking: N/A

3.16-3.66 GPA, 25TH-75TH PERCENTILE

156-161 LSAT, 25TH-75TH PERCENTILE

21% ACCEPTANCE RATE

97 2007 U.S. NEWS LAW SCHOOL RANKING

ADMISSIONS

Admissions phone number: **(404) 651-2048**
Admissions email address: **admissions@gsulaw.gsu.edu**
Application website: **https://www.applyweb.com/aw?gsu-law**
Application deadline for Fall 2007 admission: 3/13

Admissions statistics:

Number of applicants for Fall 2005: **2,359**
Number of acceptances: **499**
Number enrolled: **151**
Acceptance rate: **21%**
GPA, 25th-75th percentile, entering class Fall 2005: **3.16-3.66**
LSAT, 25th-75th percentile, entering class Fall 2005: **156-161**

Part-time program:

Number of applicants for Fall 2005: **424**
Number of acceptances: **86**
Number enrolled: **68**
Acceptance rate: **20%**
GPA, 25th-75th percentile, entering class Fall 2005: **2.95-3.65**
LSAT, 25th-75th percentile, entering class Fall 2005: **155-161**

FINANCIAL AID

Financial aid phone number: **(404) 651-2227**
Financial aid application deadline: **4/01**
Tuition 2005-2006 academic year: In-state: full-time: **$6,484**, part-time: **$6,020**; Out-of-state: full-time: **$21,644**
Room and board: **$9,000**; books: **$1,500**; miscellaneous expenses: **$4,474**
Total of room/board/books/miscellaneous expenses: **$14,974**
University offers graduate student housing for which law students are eligible.

Financial aid profile

Percent of students that received grants for the 2004-2005 academic year: full-time: **9%**; part-time **16%**

Median grant amount: full-time: **$6,022**; part-time: **$6,022**
The average law-school debt of those in the Class of 2005 who borrowed: **$52,975**. Proportion who borrowed: **68%**

ACADEMIC PROGRAMS

Calendar: **semester**
Joint degrees awarded: **J.D./MSHA; J.D./M.B.A./M.H.A.; M.B.A./J.D.; M.P.A./J.D.; M.A./J.D. (Philosophy); MCRP/J.D.**
Typical first-year section size: Full-time: **70**; Part-time: **70**
Is there typically a "small section" of the first year class, other than Legal Writing, taught by full-time faculty?: Full-time: **no**; Part-time: **no**
Number of course titles, beyond the first year curriculum, offered last year: **101**
Percentages of upper division course sections, excluding seminars, with an enrollment of:

Under 25: **57%**	25 to 49: **28%**
50 to 74: **13%**	75 to 99: **2%**
100+: **0%**	

Areas of specialization: appellate advocacy, clinical training, dispute resolution, environmental law, healthcare law, intellectual property law, international law, tax law, trial advocacy

Fall 2005 faculty profile

Total teaching faculty: **94**. Full-time: **45%**; **55%** men, **45%** women, **14%** minorities. Part-time: **55%**; **71%** men, **29%** women, **15%** minorities
Student-to-faculty ratio: **16.2**

SPECIAL PROGRAMS *(as provided by law school)*:

Through work with government, nonprofit public-interest organizations and county, state and federal judges, the Externship Program exposes students to a broad range of legal fields. The College of Law collaborates with three Georgia State University units—the J. Mack Robinson College of Business, the Andrew Young School of Policy Studies and the Department of Philosophy—and the Georgia Institute of Technology's College of Architecture, to offer joint degree programs. The Consortium on Negotiation and Conflict Resolution is an inter-institutional, interdisciplinary program supporting theory building and practice in conflict resolution. Each semester, CNCR employs law students as graduate research assistants to support programming. The College of Law offers three international programs, two for American law students to study abroad and the other for law students of former communist countries to participate in a one-semester certificate program at the college. One program, co-sponsored by the University of Warsaw-Poland and Georgia State University, is conducted in Europe and includes visits to arbitral institutions in Warsaw, Vienna, Budapest, Prague and Venice. A second program, called the Comparative Environmental Law Program, is held in Rio de Janeiro, Brazil and allows students to explore comparative issues in environmental and public health law. A third program, called the International Connection, is a cooperative effort of the College of Law and members of the Atlanta legal and business communities to enable individual law students from former communist counties to attend the college for one semester on funded fellowships. Our required Litigation Workshop offers second-year students intensive skills training. Through involvement in the Student Trial Lawyers Association and the National Association of Criminal Defense Lawyers Student Association, our students compete annually in mock trial competitions held at locations throughout the country. The Law School also offers students the opportunity to develop skills in appellate advocacy. Under the auspices of the College's Moot Court Program, teams of students compete annually in the most challenging and prestigious moot court competitions in the country. The Tax Clinic provides a live-client component of the college's Lawyers Skills Development Program. Students who take the clinic course serve low-income individuals who are involved in disputes with the Internal Revenue Service. The College also offers specialized programs of study through its centers. Centers include the Capitol City Center for State Law and Legislation; the Center for Law, Health and Society; and the Center for the Comparative Study of Metropolitan Growth.

STUDENT BODY

Fall 2005 full-time enrollment: 494

Men: 51%	Women: 49%
African-American: 9.9%	American Indian: 0.4%
Asian-American: 7.3%	Mexican-American: 0.0%
Puerto Rican: 0.0%	Other Hisp-Amer: 2.6%
White: 66.0%	International: 0.0%
Unknown: 13.8%	

Fall 2005 part-time enrollment: 191

Men: 54%	Women: 46%
African-American: 13.6%	American Indian: 0.5%
Asian-American: 3.7%	Mexican-American: 0.0%
Puerto Rican: 0.0%	Other Hisp-Amer: 1.6%
White: 67.0%	International: 0.0%
Unknown: 13.6%	

Attrition rates for 2004-2005 full-time students
Percent of students discontinuing law school:
Men: 6%   Women: 5%

First-year students: 12%   Second-year students: 4%
Third-year students: 1%

LIBRARY RESOURCES

The library holds 65,212 and receives 2,408 current subscriptions.
Total volumes: 342,894
Percentage of the titles in the online catalog: 99%
Total seats available for library users: 354

INFORMATION TECHNOLOGY

Number of wired network connections available to students: 778 total (in the law library, excluding computer labs: 191; in classrooms: 561; in computer labs: 6; elsewhere in the law school: 20)
Law school has a wireless network.
Approximate number of simultaneous users that can be accommodated on wireless network: 240
Students are not required to own a computer.

EMPLOYMENT AND SALARIES

Proportion of 2004 graduates employed at graduation: N/A
Employed 9 months later, as of February 15, 2005: 92%
Salaries in the private sector (law firms, business, industry): $52,000–$100,000 (25th-75th percentile)
Median salary in the private sector: $65,000
Percentage in the private sector who reported salary information: 73%
Median salary in public service (government, judicial clerkships, academic posts, non-profits): $45,500

Percentage of 2004 graduates in:

Law firms: 62%	Bus./industry (legal): 2%
Bus./industry (nonlegal): 9%	Government: 13%
Public interest: 6%	Judicial clerkship: 7%
Academia : 0%	Unknown: 1%

2004 graduates employed in-state: 95%
2004 graduates employed in foreign countries: 0%
Number of states where graduates are employed: 5
Percentage of 2004 graduates working in: New England: 0%, Middle Atlantic: 0%, East North Central: 0%, West North Central: 0%, South Atlantic: 99%, East South Central: 0%, West South Central: 0%, Mountain: 0%, Pacific: 1%, Unknown: 0%

BAR PASSAGE RATES

Based on 2004 graduates taking Summer 2004 or Winter 2005 exams. Most of the school's first-time test takers took the bar in Georgia.

92%
School's bar passage rate for first-time test takers

85%
Statewide bar passage rate for first-time test takers

Golden Gate University

- 536 Mission Street, San Francisco, CA, 94105
- http://www.ggu.edu/law/
- Private
- Year founded: 1901
- 2005-2006 tuition: full-time: $29,100; part-time: $20,370
- Enrollment 2005-06 academic year: full-time: 669; part-time: 182
- U.S. News 2007 law specialty ranking: environmental law: 20

3.00-3.47 GPA, 25TH-75TH PERCENTILE

150-155 LSAT, 25TH-75TH PERCENTILE

36% ACCEPTANCE RATE

Tier 4 2007 U.S. NEWS LAW SCHOOL RANKING

ADMISSIONS

Admissions phone number: (415) 442-6630
Admissions email address: lawadmit@ggu.edu
Application website: N/A
Application deadline for Fall 2007 admission: 3/01

Admissions statistics:

Number of applicants for Fall 2005: 3,016
Number of acceptances: 1,077
Number enrolled: 268
Acceptance rate: 36%
GPA, 25th-75th percentile, entering class Fall 2005:
3.00-3.47
LSAT, 25th-75th percentile, entering class Fall 2005: 150-155

Part-time program:

Number of applicants for Fall 2005: 282
Number of acceptances: 107
Number enrolled: 53
Acceptance rate: 38%
GPA, 25th-75th percentile, entering class Fall 2005:
2.85-3.35
LSAT, 25th-75th percentile, entering class Fall 2005:
149-155

FINANCIAL AID

Financial aid phone number: (415) 442-6630
Financial aid application deadline: 3/01
Tuition 2005-2006 academic year: full-time: $29,100; part-time: $20,370
Room and board: $13,500; books: $1,000; miscellaneous expenses: $6,300
Total of room/board/books/miscellaneous expenses:
$20,800
University does not offer graduate student housing for which law students are eligible.

Financial aid profile

Percent of students that received grants for the 2004-2005 academic year: full-time: 35%; part-time 23%

Median grant amount: full-time: $10,000; part-time:
$6,500
The average law-school debt of those in the Class of 2005 who borrowed: $89,337. Proportion who borrowed: 77%

ACADEMIC PROGRAMS

Calendar: semester
Joint degrees awarded: J.D./M.B.A.; J.D./Ph.D.
Typical first-year section size: Full-time: 59; Part-time: 49
Is there typically a "small section" of the first year class, other than Legal Writing, taught by full-time faculty?:
Full-time: yes; Part-time: no
Number of course titles, beyond the first year curriculum, offered last year: 181
Percentages of upper division course sections, excluding seminars, with an enrollment of:

Under 25: **74%**   25 to 49: **13%**
50 to 74: **10%**   75 to 99: **3%**
100+: **0%**

Areas of specialization: appellate advocacy, clinical training, dispute resolution, environmental law, intellectual property law, international law, tax law, trial advocacy

Fall 2005 faculty profile

Total teaching faculty: 92. Full-time: 33%; 67% men, 33% women, 23% minorities. Part-time: 67%; 55% men, 45% women, 24% minorities
Student-to-faculty ratio: 22.4

SPECIAL PROGRAMS (as provided by law school):

Practice-oriented legal education: Golden Gate University law students study a practice-oriented curriculum designed to help them hit the ground running as effective legal advocates. Through simulation classes, in-house law clinics, outplacement clinics, judicial externships, trial and appellate practice teams, certificate programs, and our highly competitive Honors Lawyering Program, Golden Gate students start thinking and working like lawyers from the day they arrive.

Clinics: Golden Gate University has two award-winning in-house clinical programs, where four full-time faculty and several law fellows supervise students representing real clients.

The Environmental Law and Justice Clinic represents individuals and community groups in poor communities fighting environmental hazards. The Women's Employment Rights Clinic represents women in employment cases. Students may also work under faculty supervision in private, public-interest, and government law offices in the fields of family law, real-estate law, landlord-tenant law, environmental law, criminal law (prosecution or defense), business law, and public-interest law, or may work for local courts and judges as judicial externs.

Honors Lawyering Program: Students who qualify for the program spend their summers in small, simulated law firms studying required courses through a practice-oriented, integrated curriculum. Then, each fall semester they work in law offices or judges' chambers as full-time apprentices. Admission is highly competitive, based on the applicant's college record or first-semester law school performance.

Certificate programs: After the first year, students may concentrate in specific fields of study and earn certificates in business law, criminal law, intellectual property law, international law, labor and employment law, litigation, public-interest law, or real estate law.

Study abroad programs: Students may spend a summer studying international and comparative law at GGU's summer session in Bangkok, Thailand, or at our summer program at the University of Paris X in Paris, France.

Extensive summer school in San Francisco: Extensive summer classes are available over the summer for GGU students, or visiting students, who wish to accelerate their studies.

Joint degree programs: Joint degree programs are available in business (J.D./M.B.A. from GGU) and psychology (J.D./Ph.D. from GGU and the Pacific Graduate School of Psychology).

Midyear or fall admission: Students may enroll in August or January.

STUDENT BODY

Fall 2005 full-time enrollment: 669

Men: 43%	Women: 57%
African-American: 1.9%	American Indian: 0.9%
Asian-American: 16.7%	Mexican-American: 2.7%
Puerto Rican: 0.1%	Other Hisp-Amer: 2.4%
White: 59.9%	International: 0.6%
Unknown: 14.6%	

Fall 2005 part-time enrollment: 182

Men: 45%	Women: 55%
African-American: 4.4%	American Indian: 0.5%
Asian-American: 14.3%	Mexican-American: 2.2%
Puerto Rican: 0.0%	Other Hisp-Amer: 4.9%
White: 31.3%	International: 1.6%
Unknown: 40.7%	

Attrition rates for 2004-2005 full-time students
Percent of students discontinuing law school:

Men: 17%	Women: 14%
First-year students: 29%	Second-year students: 8%
Third-year students: 2%	

LIBRARY RESOURCES
The library holds 48,778 and receives 4,259 current subscriptions.
Total volumes: 353,479
Percentage of the titles in the online catalog: 100%
Total seats available for library users: 300

INFORMATION TECHNOLOGY
Number of wired network connections available to students: 553 total (in the law library, excluding computer labs: 126; in classrooms: 427; in computer labs: 0; elsewhere in the law school: 0)
Law school has a wireless network.
Approximate number of simultaneous users that can be accommodated on wireless network: 600
Students are not required to own a computer.

EMPLOYMENT AND SALARIES
Proportion of 2004 graduates employed at graduation: N/A
Employed 9 months later, as of February 15, 2005: 68%
Salaries in the private sector (law firms, business, industry): $47,000–$65,000 (25th-75th percentile)
Median salary in the private sector: $60,000
Percentage in the private sector who reported salary information: 65%
Median salary in public service (government, judicial clerkships, academic posts, non-profits): $48,102

Percentage of 2004 graduates in:

Law firms: 48%	Bus./industry (legal): 18%
Bus./industry (nonlegal): 0%	Government: 7%
Public interest: 8%	Judicial clerkship: 3%
Academia : 5%	Unknown: 12%

2004 graduates employed in-state: 63%
2004 graduates employed in foreign countries: 1%
Number of states where graduates are employed: 5
Percentage of 2004 graduates working in: New England: 0%, Middle Atlantic: 1%, East North Central: 0%, West North Central: 0%, South Atlantic: 3%, East South Central: 0%, West South Central: 0%, Mountain: 1%, Pacific: 63%, Unknown: 31%

BAR PASSAGE RATES
Based on 2004 graduates taking Summer 2004 or Winter 2005 exams. Most of the school's first-time test takers took the bar in California.

35%
School's bar passage rate for first-time test takers

61%
Statewide bar passage rate for first-time test takers

Gonzaga University

- PO Box 3528, Spokane, WA, 99220-3528
- http://law.gonzaga.edu
- Private
- Year founded: 1912
- 2005-2006 tuition: full-time: $26,388; part-time: $15,858
- Enrollment 2005-06 academic year: full-time: 556; part-time: 22
- U.S. News 2007 law specialty ranking: N/A

3.13-3.56	GPA, 25TH-75TH PERCENTILE
152-156	LSAT, 25TH-75TH PERCENTILE
37%	ACCEPTANCE RATE
Tier 3	2007 U.S. NEWS LAW SCHOOL RANKING

ADMISSIONS

Admissions phone number: **(800) 793-1710**
Admissions email address: **admissions@lawschool.gon-zaga.edu**
Application website: **N/A**
Application deadline for Fall 2007 admission: **2/01**

Admissions statistics:

Number of applicants for Fall 2005: **1,485**
Number of acceptances: **546**
Number enrolled: **192**
Acceptance rate: **37%**
GPA, 25th-75th percentile, entering class Fall 2005: **3.13-3.56**
LSAT, 25th-75th percentile, entering class Fall 2005: **152-156**

FINANCIAL AID

Financial aid phone number: **(800) 448-2138**
Financial aid application deadline: **2/01**
Tuition 2005-2006 academic year: full-time: **$26,388**; part-time: **$15,858**
Room and board: **$3,375**; books: **$1,000**; miscellaneous expenses: **$4,740**
Total of room/board/books/miscellaneous expenses: **$9,115**
University does not offer graduate student housing for which law students are eligible.

Financial aid profile

Percent of students that received grants for the 2004-2005 academic year: full-time: **91%**
Median grant amount: full-time: **$8,000**
The average law-school debt of those in the Class of 2005 who borrowed: **$80,996**. Proportion who borrowed: **92%**

ACADEMIC PROGRAMS

Calendar: **semester**
Joint degrees awarded: **J.D./M.B.A.; J.D./MACC; J.D./MSW**
Typical first-year section size: Full-time: **80**

Is there typically a "small section" of the first year class, other than Legal Writing, taught by full-time faculty?: Full-time: **no**
Number of course titles, beyond the first year curriculum, offered last year: **81**
Percentages of upper division course sections, excluding seminars, with an enrollment of:

Under 25: **60%**	25 to 49: **17%**
50 to 74: **17%**	75 to 99: **5%**
100+: **1%**	

Areas of specialization: appellate advocacy, clinical training, dispute resolution, environmental law, healthcare law, intellectual property law, international law, tax law, trial advocacy

Fall 2005 faculty profile

Total teaching faculty: **87**. Full-time: **43%**; **57%** men, **43%** women, **11%** minorities. Part-time: **57%**; **76%** men, **24%** women, **0%** minorities
Student-to-faculty ratio: **18.0**

SPECIAL PROGRAMS *(as provided by law school)*:

Gonzaga's curriculum is firmly rooted in the theory and practice of law. Classes emphasize the link between legal doctrine and practice application, text and experience. Students engage in a rigorous study of written law and immediately put the law to work: They write contracts, draft complaints, and present closing arguments.

The School of Law emphasizes social justice in and out of the classroom. Gonzaga students complete 30 hours of mandatory, not-for-credit public service as a condition of graduation. This requirement may be satisfied by the completion of a service-learning class, an externship, a clinical placement, or a volunteer community activity.

Gonzaga requires two years of legal research and writing, the cornerstone of legal work. Courses provide an exceptional grounding in the most practical and essential skills the law demands.

The School of Law and the School of Business Administration offer joint programs leading to the J.D./master of business administration and J.D./master of accountancy degrees. These programs prepare attorneys to deal with business problems.

Gonzaga offers summer sessions. Most courses are taught in the evening to accommodate the many students who work as legal interns and clerks during the break. In addition, a summer study abroad program is offered in Florence.

The Clinical Law Program—an on-campus public-service law office and off-campus externships—afford upper-division students the opportunity to practice law under the close supervision of veteran attorneys. The clinic, known as University Legal Assistance, acts as a medium-sized public-service law firm. It is staffed by 40 to 50 law students, five faculty members, and support personnel. Students represent clients and handle cases at the trial and appellate levels of the state, federal, and tribal court systems. Areas of clinical practice include elder law, family law, civil rights, environmental law, consumer protection, criminal defense, Indian law, administrative law, disability law, international criminal law, and tax laws.

The School of Law's externship program offers approximately 70 students each year an opportunity to practice in a wide variety of locations. Depending on the externship, the student will have client contact, case management including trial, and legal research and consultation with decision makers.

STUDENT BODY

Fall 2005 full-time enrollment: 556

Men: 56%	Women: 44%
African-American: 0.4%	American Indian: 1.3%
Asian-American: 7.0%	Mexican-American: 0.0%
Puerto Rican: 0.0%	Other Hisp-Amer: 3.4%
White: 87.9%	International: 0.0%
Unknown: 0.0%	

Fall 2005 part-time enrollment: 22

Men: 32%	Women: 68%
African-American: 0.0%	American Indian: 0.0%
Asian-American: 0.0%	Mexican-American: 0.0%
Puerto Rican: 0.0%	Other Hisp-Amer: 0.0%
White: 100.0%	International: 0.0%
Unknown: 0.0%	

Attrition rates for 2004-2005 full-time students

Percent of students discontinuing law school:

Men: 5%	Women: 9%
First-year students: 18%	Second-year students: 1%
Third-year students: N/A	

LIBRARY RESOURCES

The library holds **63,469** and receives **2,579** current subscriptions.

Total volumes: **283,999**
Percentage of the titles in the online catalog: **100%**
Total seats available for library users: **428**

INFORMATION TECHNOLOGY

Number of wired network connections available to students: **140** total (in the law library, excluding computer labs: **87**; in classrooms: **18**; in computer labs: **10**; elsewhere in the law school: **25**)

Law school has a wireless network.

Approximate number of simultaneous users that can be accommodated on wireless network: **800**

Students are not required to own a computer.

EMPLOYMENT AND SALARIES

Proportion of 2004 graduates employed at graduation: **N/A**
Employed 9 months later, as of February 15, 2005: **93%**
Salaries in the private sector (law firms, business, industry): **$40,000–$60,000** (25th-75th percentile)
Median salary in the private sector: **$46,000**
Percentage in the private sector who reported salary information: **52%**
Median salary in public service (government, judicial clerkships, academic posts, non-profits): **$45,000**

Percentage of 2004 graduates in:

Law firms: 51%	Bus./industry (legal): 2%
Bus./industry (nonlegal): 12%	Government: 16%
Public interest: 4%	Judicial clerkship: 11%
Academia : 4%	Unknown: 0%

2004 graduates employed in-state: **62%**
2004 graduates employed in foreign countries: **0%**
Number of states where graduates are employed: **17**
Percentage of 2004 graduates working in: New England: **0%**, Middle Atlantic: **0%**, East North Central: **2%**, West North Central: **1%**, South Atlantic: **3%**, East South Central: **2%**, West South Central: **2%**, Mountain: **17%**, Pacific: **67%**, Unknown: **6%**

BAR PASSAGE RATES

Based on 2004 graduates taking Summer 2004 or Winter 2005 exams. Most of the school's first-time test takers took the bar in Washington.

76%
School's bar passage rate for first-time test takers

79%
Statewide bar passage rate for first-time test takers

Hamline University

- 1536 Hewitt Avenue, St. Paul, MN, 55104-1284
- http://www.hamline.edu/law
- Private
- Year founded: 1973
- 2005-2006 tuition: full-time: $25,484; part-time: $18,375
- Enrollment 2005-06 academic year: full-time: 516; part-time: 194
- U.S. News 2007 law specialty ranking: dispute resolution: 5

3.16-3.61 GPA, 25TH-75TH PERCENTILE

153-159 LSAT, 25TH-75TH PERCENTILE

40% ACCEPTANCE RATE

Tier 4 2007 U.S. NEWS LAW SCHOOL RANKING

ADMISSIONS

Admissions phone number: **(651) 523-2461**
Admissions email address: **lawadm@hamline.edu**
Application website:
　http://www.hamline.edu/law/apply.htm
Application deadline for Fall 2007 admission: **4/01**

Admissions statistics:
Number of applicants for Fall 2005: **1,362**
Number of acceptances: **550**
Number enrolled: **157**
Acceptance rate: **40%**
GPA, 25th-75th percentile, entering class Fall 2005:
　3.16-3.61
LSAT, 25th-75th percentile, entering class Fall 2005: **153-159**

Part-time program:
Number of applicants for Fall 2005: **248**
Number of acceptances: **138**
Number enrolled: **69**
Acceptance rate: **56%**
GPA, 25th-75th percentile, entering class Fall 2005:
　2.88-3.48
LSAT, 25th-75th percentile, entering class Fall 2005:
　148-154

FINANCIAL AID

Financial aid phone number: **(651) 523-3000**
Financial aid application deadline: **N/A**
Tuition 2005-2006 academic year: full-time: **$25,484**; part-time: **$18,375**
Room and board: **$12,430**; books: **$1,300**; miscellaneous expenses: **N/A**
Total of room/board/books/miscellaneous expenses:
　$13,730
University offers graduate student housing for which law students are eligible.

Financial aid profile
Percent of students that received grants for the 2004-2005 academic year: full-time: **43%**; part-time **38%**

Median grant amount: full-time: **$17,490**; part-time: **$8,575**
The average law-school debt of those in the Class of 2005 who borrowed: **$79,034**. Proportion who borrowed: **83%**

ACADEMIC PROGRAMS

Calendar: **semester**
Joint degrees awarded: **J.D./M.A.P.A.; J.D./M.A.O.L.; J.D./M.L.I.S.; J.D./M.A.M.; J.D./M.A.N.M.**
Typical first-year section size: Full-time: **60**; Part-time: **50**
Is there typically a "small section" of the first year class, other than Legal Writing, taught by full-time faculty?:
　Full-time: **no**; Part-time: **no**
Number of course titles, beyond the first year curriculum, offered last year: **109**
Percentages of upper division course sections, excluding seminars, with an enrollment of:
　Under 25: **63%**　　　25 to 49: **26%**
　50 to 74: **6%**　　　　75 to 99: **4%**
　100+: **0%**
Areas of specialization: appellate advocacy, clinical training, dispute resolution, environmental law, healthcare law, intellectual property law, international law, tax law, trial advocacy

Fall 2005 faculty profile
Total teaching faculty: **111**. Full-time: **33%**; **62%** men, **38%** women, **14%** minorities. Part-time: **67%**; **68%** men, **32%** women, **4%** minorities
Student-to-faculty ratio: **18.5**

SPECIAL PROGRAMS *(as provided by law school):*
Hamline has been a pioneer in hands-on, practice experience for its students. Students at Hamline are encouraged to participate in 19 Moot Court competitions (www.hamline.edu/law/curriculum/competitions); one of 11 clinics: Alternative Dispute Resolution, Child Advocacy, Education Law, Health Law, Immigration, Innocence, Mediation, Small Business/Nonprofit, State Public Defender, Trial Practice, and Student Director (www.hamline.edu/law/curriculum/clinics); six study abroad programs located in Norway, Israel, Italy, London, Paris/Budapest, and Puerto Rico (www.hamline.edu/law/cur-

riculum/global); a practicum (externship) program in seven substantive fields (www.hamline.edu/law/curriculum/practicum_program); and three law journals: Hamline Law Review, Journal of Public Law and Policy, and the Journal of Law and Religion (www.hamline.edu/law/journals).

Hamline is home to the nationally recognized Dispute Resolution Institute (www.hamline.edu/law/adr/dispute_resolution) which offers certificate programs in Alternative Dispute Resolution and Arbitration Law as well as international moot court competitions. Through a unique grant funded by FIPSE, students from six European and U.S. universities, including Hamline, may travel to and study alternative dispute resolution for a semester abroad at another participating institution.

Hamline now features a new Health Law Center (www.hamline.edu/law/health) which offers courses and clinical experience, research opportunities, speakers and symposia, and other programming for students and members of the community to bring legal education to the forefront of biotech development, administrative health practices, children's health issues, pharmaceutical policy, and other cutting-edge issues in law, health, and public policy.

Joint degree/dual degree options are available in business, management, and library science. Students may opt to pursue one of five dual degrees offered. Three master's degrees are offered in collaboration with Hamline's Graduate School of Management in business management, public administration, and nonprofit management. Additionally, the law school offers joint degree programs in organizational management and library and information sciences with the College of St. Catherine.

STUDENT BODY

Fall 2005 full-time enrollment: 516

Men: 44%	Women: 56%
African-American: 3.7%	American Indian: 0.6%
Asian-American: 4.7%	Mexican-American: 0.0%
Puerto Rican: 0.0%	Other Hisp-Amer: 3.9%
White: 86.0%	International: 1.2%
Unknown: 0.0%	

Fall 2005 part-time enrollment: 194

Men: 53%	Women: 47%
African-American: 3.1%	American Indian: 0.5%
Asian-American: 3.6%	Mexican-American: 0.0%
Puerto Rican: 0.0%	Other Hisp-Amer: 4.1%
White: 88.7%	International: 0.0%
Unknown: 0.0%	

Attrition rates for 2004-2005 full-time students

Percent of students discontinuing law school:

Men: 5%	Women: 2%
First-year students: 5%	Second-year students: 5%
Third-year students: N/A	

LIBRARY RESOURCES

The library holds 131,620 and receives 3,865 current subscriptions.
Total volumes: 268,009
Percentage of the titles in the online catalog: 99%
Total seats available for library users: 354

INFORMATION TECHNOLOGY

Number of wired network connections available to students: 319 total (in the law library, excluding computer labs: 42; in classrooms: 270; in computer labs: 0; elsewhere in the law school: 7)
Law school has a wireless network.
Approximate number of simultaneous users that can be accommodated on wireless network: 250
Students are required to own a computer.

EMPLOYMENT AND SALARIES

Proportion of 2004 graduates employed at graduation: 47%
Employed 9 months later, as of February 15, 2005: 81%
Salaries in the private sector (law firms, business, industry): $45,000–$62,500 (25th-75th percentile)
Median salary in the private sector: $50,000
Percentage in the private sector who reported salary information: 52%
Median salary in public service (government, judicial clerkships, academic posts, non-profits): $39,715

Percentage of 2004 graduates in:

Law firms: 48%	Bus./industry (legal): 4%
Bus./industry (nonlegal): 15%	Government: 8%
Public interest: 5%	Judicial clerkship: 18%
Academia : 1%	Unknown: 0%

2004 graduates employed in-state: 82%
2004 graduates employed in foreign countries: 1%
Number of states where graduates are employed: 12
Percentage of 2004 graduates working in: New England: 0%, Middle Atlantic: 0%, East North Central: 8%, West North Central: 84%, South Atlantic: 2%, East South Central: 0%, West South Central: 1%, Mountain: 3%, Pacific: 3%, Unknown: 0%

BAR PASSAGE RATES

Based on 2004 graduates taking Summer 2004 or Winter 2005 exams. Most of the school's first-time test takers took the bar in Minnesota.

86%
School's bar passage rate for first-time test takers

91%
Statewide bar passage rate for first-time test takers

Harvard University

- 1563 Massachusetts Avenue, Cambridge, MA, 02138
- http://www.law.harvard.edu
- Private
- Year founded: 1817
- 2005-2006 tuition: full-time: $35,100; part-time: N/A
- Enrollment 2005-06 academic year: full-time: 1,712
- U.S. News 2007 law specialty ranking: clinical training: 16, dispute resolution: 4, intellecutal property law: 16, international law: 3, tax law: 5

3.68-3.92 GPA, 25TH-75TH PERCENTILE

170-176 LSAT, 25TH-75TH PERCENTILE

12% ACCEPTANCE RATE

3 2007 U.S. NEWS LAW SCHOOL RANKING

ADMISSIONS

Admissions phone number: **(617) 495-3109**
Admissions email address: **jdadmiss@law.harvard.edu**
Application website:
   http://www.law.harvard.edu/Admissions/JD/apply.php
Application deadline for Fall 2007 admission: **2/01**

Admissions statistics:

Number of applicants for Fall 2005: **7,046**
Number of acceptances: **811**
Number enrolled: **557**
Acceptance rate: **12%**
GPA, 25th-75th percentile, entering class Fall 2005: **3.68-3.92**
LSAT, 25th-75th percentile, entering class Fall 2005: **170-176**

FINANCIAL AID

Financial aid phone number: **(617) 495-4606**
Financial aid application deadline: **3/01**
Tuition 2005-2006 academic year: full-time: **$35,100**; part-time: **N/A**
Room and board: **$16,469**; books: **$1,050**; miscellaneous expenses: **$4,081**
Total of room/board/books/miscellaneous expenses: **$21,600**
University offers graduate student housing for which law students are eligible.

Financial aid profile

Percent of students that received grants for the 2004-2005 academic year: full-time: **37%**
Median grant amount: full-time: **$14,755**
The average law-school debt of those in the Class of 2005 who borrowed: **$92,573**. Proportion who borrowed: **83%**

ACADEMIC PROGRAMS

Calendar: **semester**
Joint degrees awarded: **J.D./M.B.A.; J.D./M.P.P.; J.D./M.A.L.D.; J.D./M.P.A.; J.D./M.Div.; J.D./Ed.M.; J.D./Ph.D.; J.D./M.P.H.**

Typical first-year section size: Full-time: **80**
Is there typically a "small section" of the first year class, other than Legal Writing, taught by full-time faculty?: Full-time: **no**
Number of course titles, beyond the first year curriculum, offered last year: **267**
Percentages of upper division course sections, excluding seminars, with an enrollment of:
   Under 25: **45%**   25 to 49: **19%**
   50 to 74: **19%**   75 to 99: **5%**
   100+: **11%**
Areas of specialization: appellate advocacy, clinical training, dispute resolution, environmental law, healthcare law, intellectual property law, international law, tax law, trial advocacy

Fall 2005 faculty profile

Total teaching faculty: **122**. Full-time: **66%**; **81%** men, **19%** women, **11%** minorities. Part-time: **34%**; **63%** men, **37%** women, **5%** minorities
Student-to-faculty ratio: **11.0**

SPECIAL PROGRAMS *(as provided by law school):*

Harvard Law School combines the resources of the world's premier center for legal education and research with individualized and interactive instruction.

   HLS students engage directly with teachers who shape the legal landscape both in the United States and abroad. First-year sections have fewer than 80 students; 100 courses have enrollments of under 25. The First-Year Legal Research and Writing Program offers an intensive small-group experience geared to prepare students for legal practice; small first-year reading groups provide a forum for intimate discussion. Upper-level students choose from among more than 300 courses and seminars.

   HLS strongly promotes public service. HLS provides one of the most extensive clinical programs in the nation, with offerings in fields ranging from international human rights to Supreme Court practice to child advocacy to Internet law. The school guarantees funding for summer public interest work, and last year, 364 J.D. students received funding to work in 29 states and 29 countries. A special Office of Public Interest Advising provides comprehensive services to students pursuing public service careers, and the Low Income Protection Plan assists graduates who opt for lower-paying employment. Fellowship programs provide additional support to graduates entering public service.

The Law School offers special assistance to students preparing to become law teachers. Popular student-faculty workshops in fields such as public law, technology and the law, and international law give students a chance to read and critique works in progress presented by leading legal scholars, just as legal academics do.

The Law School provides many opportunities for interdisciplinary study. There are joint degree programs with other Harvard schools including the Business School, the School of Public Health, the Kennedy School of Government, the Design School, and the Graduate School of Arts and Sciences. Students may also design individualized concurrent degree programs with other graduate schools at Harvard, MIT, or the Fletcher School of Law & Diplomacy at Tufts University. Law students may propose a one-semester course of study at a foreign institution, and HLS offers a J.D./LL.M. with the University of Cambridge, England.

STUDENT BODY

Fall 2005 full-time enrollment: 1,712

Men: 56%	Women: 44%
African-American: 10.3%	American Indian: 0.6%
Asian-American: 12.4%	Mexican-American: 1.6%
Puerto Rican: 0.7%	Other Hisp-Amer: 3.4%
White: 53.6%	International: 3.7%
Unknown: 13.8%	

Attrition rates for 2004-2005 full-time students
Percent of students discontinuing law school:

Men: 0%	Women: 1%
First-year students: 0%	Second-year students: 1%
Third-year students: 0%	

LIBRARY RESOURCES

The library holds 828,559 and receives 15,303 current subscriptions.
Total volumes: 2,192,726
Percentage of the titles in the online catalog: 100%
Total seats available for library users: 802

INFORMATION TECHNOLOGY

Number of wired network connections available to students: 2,750 total (in the law library, excluding computer labs: 1,000; in classrooms: 800; in computer labs: 100; elsewhere in the law school: 850)
Law school has a wireless network.
Approximate number of simultaneous users that can be accommodated on wireless network: 1,800
Students are not required to own a computer.

EMPLOYMENT AND SALARIES

Proportion of 2004 graduates employed at graduation: 97%
Employed 9 months later, as of February 15, 2005: 100%
Salaries in the private sector (law firms, business, industry): $125,000–$125,000 (25th-75th percentile)
Median salary in the private sector: $125,000
Percentage in the private sector who reported salary information: 88%
Median salary in public service (government, judicial clerkships, academic posts, non-profits): $50,000

Percentage of 2004 graduates in:

Law firms: 60%	Bus./industry (legal): N/A
Bus./industry (nonlegal): 3%	Government: 3%
Public interest: 4%	Judicial clerkship: 29%
Academia : 1%	Unknown: N/A

2004 graduates employed in-state: 11%
2004 graduates employed in foreign countries: 2%
Number of states where graduates are employed: 40
Percentage of 2004 graduates working in: New England: 12%, Middle Atlantic: 28%, East North Central: 9%, West North Central: 1%, South Atlantic: 23%, East South Central: 2%, West South Central: 5%, Mountain: 2%, Pacific: 17%, Unknown: 0%

BAR PASSAGE RATES

Based on 2004 graduates taking Summer 2004 or Winter 2005 exams. Most of the school's first-time test takers took the bar in New York.

96%
School's bar passage rate for first-time test takers

75%
Statewide bar passage rate for first-time test takers

Hofstra University

- 121 Hofstra University, Hempstead, NY, 11549
- http://www.hofstra.edu/law
- Private
- **Year founded:** 1970
- **2005-2006 tuition:** full-time: $33,160; part-time: $1,160/credit hour
- **Enrollment 2005-06 academic year:** full-time: 835; part-time: 203
- **U.S. News 2007 law specialty ranking:** N/A

3.03-3.64 GPA, 25TH-75TH PERCENTILE

155-160 LSAT, 25TH-75TH PERCENTILE

38% ACCEPTANCE RATE

Tier 3 2007 U.S. NEWS LAW SCHOOL RANKING

ADMISSIONS
Admissions phone number: **(516) 463-5916**
Admissions email address: **lawadmissions@hofstra.edu**
Application website:
  https://www4.lsac.org/school/Hofstra.htm
Application deadline for Fall 2007 admission: **4/15**

Admissions statistics:
Number of applicants for Fall 2005: **4,535**
Number of acceptances: **1,724**
Number enrolled: **269**
Acceptance rate: **38%**
GPA, 25th-75th percentile, entering class Fall 2005:
  3.03-3.64
LSAT, 25th-75th percentile, entering class Fall 2005:
  155-160

Part-time program:
Number of applicants for Fall 2005: **696**
Number of acceptances: **267**
Number enrolled: **117**
Acceptance rate: **38%**
GPA, 25th-75th percentile, entering class Fall 2005:
  2.91-3.52
LSAT, 25th-75th percentile, entering class Fall 2005:
  152-156

FINANCIAL AID
Financial aid phone number: **(516) 463-5929**
Financial aid application deadline: **4/01**
Tuition 2005-2006 academic year: full-time: **$33,160**; part-time: **$1,160/credit hour**
Room and board: **$9,616**; books: **$900**; miscellaneous expenses: **$2,795**
Total of room/board/books/miscellaneous expenses: **$13,311**
University offers graduate student housing for which law students are eligible.

Financial aid profile
Percent of students that received grants for the 2004-2005 academic year: full-time: **52%**; part-time **10%**
Median grant amount: full-time: **$10,000**; part-time: **$6,000**
The average law-school debt of those in the Class of 2005 who borrowed: **$88,040**. Proportion who borrowed: **87%**

ACADEMIC PROGRAMS
Calendar: **semester**
Joint degrees awarded: **J.D./M.B.A.**
Typical first-year section size: Full-time: **115**; Part-time: **92**
Is there typically a "small section" of the first year class, other than Legal Writing, taught by full-time faculty?:
  Full-time: **yes**; Part-time: **yes**
Number of course titles, beyond the first year curriculum, offered last year: **123**
Percentages of upper division course sections, excluding seminars, with an enrollment of:
  Under 25: **45%**   25 to 49: **29%**
  50 to 74: **7%**   75 to 99: **10%**
  100+: **10%**
Areas of specialization: appellate advocacy, clinical training, dispute resolution, environmental law, healthcare law, intellectual property law, international law, tax law, trial advocacy

Fall 2005 faculty profile
Total teaching faculty: **110**. Full-time: **42%**; **61%** men, **39%** women, **9%** minorities. Part-time: **58%**; **92%** men, **8%** women, **0%** minorities
Student-to-faculty ratio: **17.7**

SPECIAL PROGRAMS (as provided by law school):
Each entering student is placed in a small section in one substantive course during the fall of the first year, enabling close interactions between students and faculty in a seminar-like environment. The first year curriculum includes a course on International and Comparative Law, introducing students to the realities of legal practice in a global environment.

The law school prides itself on an extensive array of courses designed to develop lawyering skills, including a wide menu of simulation-based courses, externships, and clinics. Seven clinics (criminal justice, housing rights, child advocacy, nonprofit business, political asylum, securities arbitration and mediation) focus on a wide range of subject matter and client representation skills, as do three externship programs tailored to the needs of students with different goals.

Other special programs include:

Center for Children, Families, and the Law: This is an interdisciplinary center for education, research, and public service.

Child and Family Advocacy Fellowships: Up to six Child and Family Fellows from the entering class receive scholarship assistance and internship experience, and pursue an interdisciplinary course of study.

Fellowships for the Advocacy for the Equality of Lesbian, Gay, Bisexual, and Transgendered People: The fellowships provide financial support for up to three students (of any sexual orientation) from each entering class.

Pro Bono Student Lawyers Project: The project places students with a variety of existing agencies, service organizations, law firms, and private practitioners. Students in the program volunteer their time without compensation or credit.

Unemployment Action Center: This prizewinning, student-run nonprofit corporation offers free advice and representation to persons denied unemployment benefits.

Study abroad programs: Hofstra offers four study abroad programs in international and comparative law. Three are offered during the summer, one in Sorrento, Italy, one in Nice, France, and the other in Sydney. The fourth is a unique program, conducted over the winter break in Curacao, Dutch Antilles. Classes in all the programs are conducted in English.

STUDENT BODY

Fall 2005 full-time enrollment: 835

Men: 53%	Women: 47%
African-American: 7.3%	American Indian: 0.4%
Asian-American: 6.0%	Mexican-American: 0.0%
Puerto Rican: 0.0%	Other Hisp-Amer: 6.5%
White: 65.1%	International: 2.5%
Unknown: 12.2%	

Fall 2005 part-time enrollment: 203

Men: 49%	Women: 51%
African-American: 7.9%	American Indian: 0.5%
Asian-American: 7.9%	Mexican-American: 0.0%
Puerto Rican: 0.0%	Other Hisp-Amer: 3.0%
White: 61.6%	International: 0.5%
Unknown: 18.7%	

Attrition rates for 2004-2005 full-time students

Percent of students discontinuing law school:

Men: 5%	Women: 4%
First-year students: 12%	Second-year students: 1%
Third-year students: 0%	

LIBRARY RESOURCES

The library holds 145,766 and receives 5,952 current subscriptions.

Total volumes: 550,765

Percentage of the titles in the online catalog: 100%

Total seats available for library users: 546

INFORMATION TECHNOLOGY

Number of wired network connections available to students: 166 total (in the law library, excluding computer labs: 120; in classrooms: 36; in computer labs: 0; elsewhere in the law school: 10)

Law school has a wireless network.

Approximate number of simultaneous users that can be accommodated on wireless network: 1,050

Students are not required to own a computer.

EMPLOYMENT AND SALARIES

Proportion of 2004 graduates employed at graduation: N/A

Employed 9 months later, as of February 15, 2005: 92%

Salaries in the private sector (law firms, business, industry): N/A–N/A (25th-75th percentile)

Median salary in the private sector: $77,000

Percentage in the private sector who reported salary information: 32%

Median salary in public service (government, judicial clerkships, academic posts, non-profits): $48,538

Percentage of 2004 graduates in:

Law firms: 64%	Bus./industry (legal): 14%
Bus./industry (nonlegal): N/A	Government: 13%
Public interest: 1%	Judicial clerkship: 4%
Academia : 2%	Unknown: 2%

2004 graduates employed in-state: 85%

2004 graduates employed in foreign countries: 0%

Number of states where graduates are employed: 20

Percentage of 2004 graduates working in: New England: 3%, Middle Atlantic: 86%, East North Central: 1%, West North Central: N/A, South Atlantic: 4%, East South Central: 1%, West South Central: 1%, Mountain: 2%, Pacific: 1%, Unknown: 2%

BAR PASSAGE RATES

Based on 2004 graduates taking Summer 2004 or Winter 2005 exams. Most of the school's first-time test takers took the bar in New York.

69%

School's bar passage rate for first-time test takers

75%

Statewide bar passage rate for first-time test takers

Howard University

■ 2900 Van Ness Street NW, Washington, D.C., 20008
■ http://www.law.howard.edu
■ Private
■ Year founded: 1869
■ 2005-2006 tuition: full-time: $17,855; part-time: N/A
■ Enrollment 2005-06 academic year: full-time: 451
■ U.S. News 2007 law specialty ranking: N/A

2.93-3.57 GPA, 25TH-75TH PERCENTILE

148-155 LSAT, 25TH-75TH PERCENTILE

23% ACCEPTANCE RATE

Tier 3 2007 U.S. NEWS LAW SCHOOL RANKING

ADMISSIONS

Admissions phone number: **(202) 806-8009**
Admissions email address: **admissions@law.howard.edu**
Application website:
  http://www4.lsac.org/school/howard.htm
Application deadline for Fall 2007 admission: **3/31**

Admissions statistics:
Number of applicants for Fall 2005: **2,373**
Number of acceptances: **551**
Number enrolled: **159**
Acceptance rate: **23%**
GPA, 25th-75th percentile, entering class Fall 2005:
  2.93-3.57
LSAT, 25th-75th percentile, entering class Fall 2005:
  148-155

FINANCIAL AID

Financial aid phone number: **(202) 806-8005**
Financial aid application deadline: **2/15**
Tuition 2005-2006 academic year: full-time: **$17,855**; part-time: **N/A**
Room and board: **$11,855**; books: **$1,351**; miscellaneous expenses: **$3,038**
Total of room/board/books/miscellaneous expenses: **$16,244**
University offers graduate student housing for which law students are eligible.

Financial aid profile
Percent of students that received grants for the 2004-2005 academic year: full-time: **69%**
Median grant amount: full-time: **$10,000**
The average law-school debt of those in the Class of 2005 who borrowed: **$9,055**. Proportion who borrowed: **95%**

ACADEMIC PROGRAMS

Calendar: **semester**
Joint degrees awarded: **J.D./M.B.A.**
Typical first-year section size: Full-time: **54**

Is there typically a "small section" of the first year class, other than Legal Writing, taught by full-time faculty?: Full-time: **no**
Number of course titles, beyond the first year curriculum, offered last year: **N/A**
Percentages of upper division course sections, excluding seminars, with an enrollment of:

Under 25: **N/A**	25 to 49: **N/A**
50 to 74: **N/A**	75 to 99: **N/A**
100+: **N/A**	

Areas of specialization: appellate advocacy, clinical training, dispute resolution, environmental law, healthcare law, intellectual property law, international law, tax law, trial advocacy

Fall 2005 faculty profile
Total teaching faculty: **66**. Full-time: **45%**; **63%** men, **37%** women, **87%** minorities. Part-time: **55%**; **61%** men, **39%** women, **75%** minorities
Student-to-faculty ratio: **13.0**

SPECIAL PROGRAMS (as provided by law school):

The law school's Clinical Law Center (CLC) offers students the opportunity to gain professional skills training and practical lawyering experiences that are generally deemed important to the effective practice of law. The CLC employs a model of learning through service and experience, with an ancillary benefit of providing pro bono legal assistance to the poor and underrepresented citizenry of the metropolitan District of Columbia area.

The CLC consists of the Criminal Justice Clinic, the Alternative Dispute Resolution Clinic, the Fair Housing Clinic and the Civil Rights Clinic.

We also offer an externship program, which allows second- and third-year students to work pro bono for course credit.

Howard students also participate in D.C. Law Students in Court, a clinic composed of a consortium of area law schools.

Howard University awards a combined J.D. and master of business administration degree through a four-year program offered by the law school and the university's School of Business.

Since 1965, Howard University School of Law has offered a master of law graduate degree program for foreign lawyers and graduates of foreign law schools.

Since 1996, the law school has conducted a South Africa summer abroad program at the University of the Western Cape in Cape Town. Participants in the program include 60 to 70 law students from South Africa and the United States. The program is open to law graduates and students enrolled in an American Bar Association-approved law school. Students from the United States must have completed one academic year of law school and be in good academic standing. The South African students are selected by the host institution.

STUDENT BODY

Fall 2005 full-time enrollment: 451

Men: **40%**	Women: **60%**
African-American: **79.8%**	American Indian: **0.7%**
Asian-American: **3.8%**	Mexican-American: **0.0%**
Puerto Rican: **0.0%**	Other Hisp-Amer: **2.7%**
White: **4.0%**	International: **6.9%**
Unknown: **2.2%**	

Attrition rates for 2004-2005 full-time students
Percent of students discontinuing law school:

Men: **2%**	Women: **1%**
First-year students: **3%**	Second-year students: **1%**
Third-year students: **N/A**	

LIBRARY RESOURCES

The library holds **30,657** and receives **2,656** current subscriptions.
Total volumes: **620,633**
Percentage of the titles in the online catalog: **100%**
Total seats available for library users: **374**

INFORMATION TECHNOLOGY

Number of wired network connections available to students: **568** total (in the law library, excluding computer labs: **319**; in classrooms: **145**; in computer labs: **62**; elsewhere in the law school: **42**)
Law school has a wireless network.

Approximate number of simultaneous users that can be accommodated on wireless network: **1,000**
Students are required to own a computer.

EMPLOYMENT AND SALARIES

Proportion of 2004 graduates employed at graduation: **80%**
Employed 9 months later, as of February 15, 2005: **86%**
Salaries in the private sector (law firms, business, industry): **$80,000–$125,000** (25th-75th percentile)
Median salary in the private sector: **$105,500**
Percentage in the private sector who reported salary information: **57%**
Median salary in public service (government, judicial clerkships, academic posts, non-profits): **$42,000**

Percentage of 2004 graduates in:

Law firms: **46%**	Bus./industry (legal): **5%**
Bus./industry (nonlegal): **5%**	Government: **12%**
Public interest: **9%**	Judicial clerkship: **16%**
Academia : **4%**	Unknown: **3%**

2004 graduates employed in-state: **42%**
2004 graduates employed in foreign countries: **3%**
Number of states where graduates are employed: **26**
Percentage of 2004 graduates working in: New England: **2%**, Middle Atlantic: **15%**, East North Central: **4%**, West North Central: **2%**, South Atlantic: **61%**, East South Central: **4%**, West South Central: **2%**, Mountain: **5%**, Pacific: **4%**, Unknown: **0%**

BAR PASSAGE RATES

Based on 2004 graduates taking Summer 2004 or Winter 2005 exams. Most of the school's first-time test takers took the bar in Maryland.

52%
School's bar passage rate for first-time test takers

72%
Statewide bar passage rate for first-time test takers

Ill. Institute of Tech. (Chicago-Kent)

- 565 W. Adams Street, Chicago, IL, 60661-3691
- http://www.kentlaw.edu/
- Private
- Year founded: 1888
- 2005-2006 tuition: full-time: $30,237; part-time: $22,091
- Enrollment 2005-06 academic year: full-time: 800; part-time: 247
- U.S. News 2007 law specialty ranking: intellecutal property law: 9

3.29-3.70	GPA, 25TH-75TH PERCENTILE
159-163	LSAT, 25TH-75TH PERCENTILE
26%	ACCEPTANCE RATE
60	2007 U.S. NEWS LAW SCHOOL RANKING

ADMISSIONS

Admissions phone number: **(312) 906-5020**
Admissions email address: **admit@kentlaw.edu**
Application website: **https://www.kentlaw.edu/admissions/jd_application.html**
Application deadline for Fall 2007 admission: **3/01**

Admissions statistics:
Number of applicants for Fall 2005: **3,085**
Number of acceptances: **813**
Number enrolled: **232**
Acceptance rate: **26%**
GPA, 25th-75th percentile, entering class Fall 2005: **3.29-3.70**
LSAT, 25th-75th percentile, entering class Fall 2005: **159-163**

Part-time program:
Number of applicants for Fall 2005: **841**
Number of acceptances: **227**
Number enrolled: **103**
Acceptance rate: **27%**
GPA, 25th-75th percentile, entering class Fall 2005: **3.03-3.56**
LSAT, 25th-75th percentile, entering class Fall 2005: **155-159**

FINANCIAL AID

Financial aid phone number: **(312) 906-5180**
Financial aid application deadline: **3/15**
Tuition 2005-2006 academic year: full-time: **$30,237**; part-time: **$22,091**
Room and board: **$13,860**; books: **$890**; miscellaneous expenses: **$3,015**
Total of room/board/books/miscellaneous expenses: **$17,765**
University offers graduate student housing for which law students are eligible.

Financial aid profile
Percent of students that received grants for the 2004-2005 academic year: full-time: **53%**; part-time **42%**

Median grant amount: full-time: **$7,000**; part-time: **$4,000**
The average law-school debt of those in the Class of 2005 who borrowed: **$94,272**. Proportion who borrowed: **85%**

ACADEMIC PROGRAMS
Calendar: **semester**
Joint degrees awarded: **J.D./M.B.A.; J.D./LL.M. Tax; J.D./M.S. FinMk; J.D./LL.M. FinSv; J.D./M.S. EnvMgt; J.D./M.P.A.; J.D./M.P.H.**
Typical first-year section size: Full-time: **52**; Part-time: **56**
Is there typically a "small section" of the first year class, other than Legal Writing, taught by full-time faculty?: Full-time: **no**; Part-time: **no**
Number of course titles, beyond the first year curriculum, offered last year: **126**
Percentages of upper division course sections, excluding seminars, with an enrollment of:

Under 25: **74%**	25 to 49: **16%**
50 to 74: **4%**	75 to 99: **3%**
100+: **2%**	

Areas of specialization: appellate advocacy, clinical training, dispute resolution, environmental law, healthcare law, intellectual property law, international law, tax law, trial advocacy

Fall 2005 faculty profile
Total teaching faculty: **150**. Full-time: **43%**; **66%** men, **34%** women, **8%** minorities. Part-time: **57%**; **72%** men, **28%** women, **5%** minorities
Student-to-faculty ratio: **12.4**

SPECIAL PROGRAMS (as provided by law school):
Chicago-Kent offers in-house clinical programs in the following areas: criminal defense, employment/general litigation, family law, health law, intellectual property/patent law, low-income tax-payer, mediation and other alternative dispute resolution procedures, interviewing and counseling practice (advice desk), and advanced clinic. We also offer the following externship programs: legal externship, judicial externship, Justice Web Collaboratory, international rule of law, and refugee and asylum

law. All clinical and externship programs are either three or four credit hours (except for advice desk, which is two credit hours).

Chicago-Kent houses the following centers and institutes: the Global Law and Policy Initiative, the Institute for Law and the Humanities, the Institute for Law and the Workplace, and the Institute for Science, Law, and Technology.

Chicago-Kent offers a summer abroad program in Mexico City in partnership with Mexico's Instituto Tecnologico y de Estudios de Monterrey. Chicago-Kent also offers students the opportunity to study in London in the spring semester through the London Law Consortium program, a program with six other law schools.

STUDENT BODY

Fall 2005 full-time enrollment: 800

Men: **54%**	Women: **46%**
African-American: **5.0%**	American Indian: **0.6%**
Asian-American: **10.4%**	Mexican-American: **1.5%**
Puerto Rican: **0.4%**	Other Hisp-Amer: **3.4%**
White: **69.6%**	International: **1.4%**
Unknown: **7.8%**	

Fall 2005 part-time enrollment: 247

Men: **58%**	Women: **42%**
African-American: **7.3%**	American Indian: **0.0%**
Asian-American: **9.3%**	Mexican-American: **3.6%**
Puerto Rican: **0.4%**	Other Hisp-Amer: **2.4%**
White: **69.6%**	International: **0.4%**
Unknown: **6.9%**	

Attrition rates for 2004-2005 full-time students
Percent of students discontinuing law school:

Men: **3%**	Women: **4%**
First-year students: **8%**	Second-year students: **2%**
Third-year students: **N/A**	

LIBRARY RESOURCES

The library holds **176,499** and receives **2,313** current subscriptions.
Total volumes: **547,378**
Percentage of the titles in the online catalog: **100%**
Total seats available for library users: **463**

INFORMATION TECHNOLOGY

Number of wired network connections available to students: **1,800** total (in the law library, excluding computer labs: **175**; in classrooms: **1,048**; in computer labs: **62**; elsewhere in the law school: **515**)

Law school has a wireless network.
Approximate number of simultaneous users that can be accommodated on wireless network: **250**
Students are required to own a computer.

EMPLOYMENT AND SALARIES

Proportion of 2004 graduates employed at graduation: **72%**
Employed 9 months later, as of February 15, 2005: **92%**
Salaries in the private sector (law firms, business, industry): **$55,000–$96,000** (25th-75th percentile)
Median salary in the private sector: **$69,000**
Percentage in the private sector who reported salary information: **47%**
Median salary in public service (government, judicial clerkships, academic posts, non-profits): **$43,222**

Percentage of 2004 graduates in:

Law firms: **59%**	Bus./industry (legal): **9%**
Bus./industry (nonlegal): **8%**	Government: **14%**
Public interest: **5%**	Judicial clerkship: **4%**
Academia : **2%**	Unknown: **N/A**

2004 graduates employed in-state: **84%**
2004 graduates employed in foreign countries: **2%**
Number of states where graduates are employed: **21**
Percentage of 2004 graduates working in: New England: **0%**, Middle Atlantic: **1%**, East North Central: **87%**, West North Central: **2%**, South Atlantic: **5%**, East South Central: **0%**, West South Central: **1%**, Mountain: **0%**, Pacific: **3%**, Unknown: **0%**

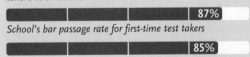

BAR PASSAGE RATES

Based on 2004 graduates taking Summer 2004 or Winter 2005 exams. Most of the school's first-time test takers took the bar in Illinois.

87%
School's bar passage rate for first-time test takers

85%
Statewide bar passage rate for first-time test takers

Indiana University–Bloomington

- 211 S. Indiana Avenue, Bloomington, IN, 47405-1001
- http://www.law.indiana.edu
- Public
- Year founded: 1842
- 2005-2006 tuition: In-state: full-time: $14,348, part-time: N/A; Out-of-state: full-time: $28,398
- Enrollment 2005-06 academic year: full-time: 662; part-time: 1
- U.S. News 2007 law specialty ranking: N/A

3.03-3.72 GPA, 25TH-75TH PERCENTILE

158-164 LSAT, 25TH-75TH PERCENTILE

38% ACCEPTANCE RATE

37 2007 U.S. NEWS LAW SCHOOL RANKING

ADMISSIONS
Admissions phone number: (812) 855-4765
Admissions email address: lawadmis@indiana.edu
Application website:
   https://app.applyyourself.com/?id=iu-bla
Application deadline for Fall 2007 admission: rolling

Admissions statistics:
Number of applicants for Fall 2005: 2,405
Number of acceptances: 916
Number enrolled: 228
Acceptance rate: 38%
GPA, 25th-75th percentile, entering class Fall 2005:
   3.03-3.72
LSAT, 25th-75th percentile, entering class Fall 2005:
   158-164

FINANCIAL AID
Financial aid phone number: (812) 855-7746
Financial aid application deadline: 3/01
Tuition 2005-2006 academic year: In-state: full-time:
   $14,349, part-time: N/A; Out-of-state: full-time: $28,398
Room and board: $8,316; books: $1,416; miscellaneous
   expenses: $4,284
Total of room/board/books/miscellaneous expenses:
   $14,016
University offers graduate student housing for which law
   students are eligible.

Financial aid profile
Percent of students that received grants for the 2004-2005
   academic year: full-time: 67%
Median grant amount: full-time: $5,650
The average law-school debt of those in the Class of 2005
   who borrowed: $68,732. Proportion who borrowed: 98%

ACADEMIC PROGRAMS
Calendar: semester
Joint degrees awarded: J.D./MPA (public/environmental
   affairs); J.D./MPA (accounting); J.D./MSES; J.D./MA
   (telecommunications); J.D./MA (music); JD/MA (Central

Eurasian/Uraltic Studies); J.D./MBA; J.D./MLS; J.D./MA
(social work); J.D./MA (history); Ph.D. (law & social science)
Typical first-year section size: Full-time: 75
Is there typically a "small section" of the first year class,
   other than Legal Writing, taught by full-time faculty?:
   Full-time: no
Number of course titles, beyond the first year curriculum,
   offered last year: 110
Percentages of upper division course sections, excluding
   seminars, with an enrollment of:
   Under 25: 61%   25 to 49: 25%
   50 to 74: 7%   75 to 99: 4%
   100+: 4%
Areas of specialization: appellate advocacy, clinical training,
   dispute resolution, environmental law, healthcare law,
   intellectual property law, international law, tax law, trial
   advocacy

Fall 2005 faculty profile
Total teaching faculty: 61. Full-time: 66%; 70% men, 30%
   women, 10% minorities. Part-time: 34%; 67% men, 33%
   women, 0% minorities
Student-to-faculty ratio: 14.1

SPECIAL PROGRAMS *(as provided by law school):*
Formal joint-degree programs combine award of a J.D.
degree and a masters degree in business, accounting, public
affairs, environmental science, journalism, telecommunications, or library science. The duration of most joint-degree
programs is four years. However, the School of Law and the
Kelley School of Business have recently established a three-
year J.D./M.B.A. program. Informal concurrent-degree programs with other disciplines, pursuing a J.D. and a masters
or doctoral degree, are frequently designed to meet students'
learning and career goals.
   The School offers opportunities to learn in real-life settings
through clinics, externships, and projects. Students in clinics
receive intensive instruction from faculty members; externships
offer academic credit and are supervised by practicing lawyers
in an off-site setting, with secondary supervision from full-time

faculty members. Clinical projects do not offer academic credit, but provide an opportunity for valuable experience. Clinics include the Community Legal Clinic; the Family and Children Mediation Clinic; the Entrepreneurship Law Clinic; the Federal Courts Clinic; the Conservation Law Clinic; and the Elder Law Clinic. Externships include the Public Interest Internship Program, Indiana Legal Services, and Student Legal Services. Extracurricular projects include the Inmate Legal Assistance Project, the Protective Order Project, and the Tenant Assistance Project.

There are numerous opportunities for students to study abroad for a semester or a summer. The School is a member of the London Law Consortium. Students may also participate in semester exchange programs at partner universities in France, Germany, Spain, Poland, New Zealand, China and Hong Kong. The School also offers eight summer programs in Europe and Latin America.

Many students also participate in the work of the Center for Constitutional Democracy, which is assisting democratic reform movements from Burma, Liberia, Kazakhstan, and Azerbaijan in the drafting of constitutions, the establishment of supporting institutions and related training and outreach.

STUDENT BODY

Fall 2005 full-time enrollment: 662

Men: 61%	Women: 39%
African-American: 6.2%	American Indian: 0.2%
Asian-American: 6.2%	Mexican-American: 3.6%
Puerto Rican: 0.0%	Other Hisp-Amer: 0.0%
White: 79.6%	International: 0.2%
Unknown: 4.1%	

Fall 2005 part-time enrollment: 1

Men: 100%	Women: 0%
African-American: 0.0%	American Indian: 0.0%
Asian-American: 0.0%	Mexican-American: 0.0%
Puerto Rican: 0.0%	Other Hisp-Amer: 0.0%
White: 100.0%	International: 0.0%
Unknown: 0.0%	

Attrition rates for 2004-2005 full-time students

Percent of students discontinuing law school:

Men: 1%	Women: 2%
First-year students: N/A	Second-year students: 3%
Third-year students: N/A	

LIBRARY RESOURCES

The library holds 240,154 and receives 9,060 current subscriptions.
Total volumes: 739,258

Percentage of the titles in the online catalog: 100%
Total seats available for library users: 673

INFORMATION TECHNOLOGY

Number of wired network connections available to students: 307 total (in the law library, excluding computer labs: 300; in classrooms: 7; in computer labs: 0; elsewhere in the law school: 0)
Law school has a wireless network.
Approximate number of simultaneous users that can be accommodated on wireless network: 900
Students are required to own a computer.

EMPLOYMENT AND SALARIES

Proportion of 2004 graduates employed at graduation: 87%
Employed 9 months later, as of February 15, 2005: 96%
Salaries in the private sector (law firms, business, industry): $58,000–$115,000 (25th-75th percentile)
Median salary in the private sector: $79,000
Percentage in the private sector who reported salary information: 68%
Median salary in public service (government, judicial clerkships, academic posts, non-profits): $46,450

Percentage of 2004 graduates in:

Law firms: 55%	Bus./industry (legal): 14%
Bus./industry (nonlegal): 0%	Government: 14%
Public interest: 3%	Judicial clerkship: 9%
Academia : 4%	Unknown: 2%

2004 graduates employed in-state: 39%
2004 graduates employed in foreign countries: 1%
Number of states where graduates are employed: 21
Percentage of 2004 graduates working in: New England: 2%, Middle Atlantic: 7%, East North Central: 65%, West North Central: 2%, South Atlantic: 15%, East South Central: 1%, West South Central: 4%, Mountain: 2%, Pacific: 3%, Unknown: 0%

BAR PASSAGE RATES

Based on 2004 graduates taking Summer 2004 or Winter 2005 exams. Most of the school's first-time test takers took the bar in Indiana.

92%
School's bar passage rate for first-time test takers

84%
Statewide bar passage rate for first-time test takers

Indiana University–Indianapolis

- 530 W. New York Street, Indianapolis, IN, 46202-3225
- http://www.indylaw.indiana.edu
- Public
- Year founded: 1894
- 2005-2006 tuition: In-state: full-time: $12,758, part-time: $8,823; Out-of-state: full-time: $26,852
- Enrollment 2005-06 academic year: full-time: 642; part-time: 271
- U.S. News 2007 law specialty ranking: healthcare law: 8

3.32-3.76 GPA, 25TH-75TH PERCENTILE

152-158 LSAT, 25TH-75TH PERCENTILE

30% ACCEPTANCE RATE

77 2007 U.S. NEWS LAW SCHOOL RANKING

ADMISSIONS

Admissions phone number: (317) 274-2459
Admissions email address: pkkinney@iupui.edu
Application website:
   http://www.indylaw.indiana.edu/admissions/app.htm
Application deadline for Fall 2007 admission: 3/01

Admissions statistics:
Number of applicants for Fall 2005: 1,537
Number of acceptances: 464
Number enrolled: 196
Acceptance rate: 30%
GPA, 25th-75th percentile, entering class Fall 2005:
   3.32-3.76
LSAT, 25th-75th percentile, entering class Fall 2005: 152-158

Part-time program:
Number of applicants for Fall 2005: 401
Number of acceptances: 134
Number enrolled: 81
Acceptance rate: 33%
GPA, 25th-75th percentile, entering class Fall 2005:
   3.12-3.59
LSAT, 25th-75th percentile, entering class Fall 2005:
   149-157

FINANCIAL AID

Financial aid phone number: (317) 278-2862
Financial aid application deadline: 3/01
Tuition 2005-2006 academic year: In-state: full-time: $12,758, part-time: $8,823; Out-of-state: full-time: $26,852
Room and board: $8,700; books: $1,600; miscellaneous expenses: $9,168
Total of room/board/books/miscellaneous expenses: $19,468
University offers graduate student housing for which law students are eligible.

Financial aid profile
Percent of students that received grants for the 2004-2005 academic year: full-time: 47%; part-time 7%

Median grant amount: full-time: $6,000; part-time: $2,500
The average law-school debt of those in the Class of 2005 who borrowed: $51,676. Proportion who borrowed: 69%

ACADEMIC PROGRAMS

Calendar: **semester**
Joint degrees awarded: **J.D./M.B.A.; J.D./M.P.A.; J.D./M.H.A.; J.D./M.P.H.; J.D./M.L.S.; J.D./MPhil**
Typical first-year section size: Full-time: **100**; Part-time: **86**
Is there typically a "small section" of the first year class, other than Legal Writing, taught by full-time faculty?: Full-time: **no**; Part-time: **no**
Number of course titles, beyond the first year curriculum, offered last year: **131**
Percentages of upper division course sections, excluding seminars, with an enrollment of:

Under 25: **47%**	25 to 49: **31%**
50 to 74: **16%**	75 to 99: **5%**
100+: **1%**	

Areas of specialization: appellate advocacy, clinical training, dispute resolution, environmental law, healthcare law, intellectual property law, international law, tax law, trial advocacy

Fall 2005 faculty profile
Total teaching faculty: **68**. Full-time: **54%; 59%** men, **41%** women, **11%** minorities. Part-time: **46%; 74%** men, **26%** women, **3%** minorities
Student-to-faculty ratio: **18.0**

SPECIAL PROGRAMS *(as provided by law school):*
Indiana University School of Law—Indianapolis has three in-house clinics, including the Civil Clinic, Disability Clinic and Criminal Clinic, providing students with real-world experience under the supervision of faculty. Our school facilitates a range of internship programs, such as placements in the Homeless Legal Assistance Project; Hospital Legal Department; Indiana Civil Liberties Union; Indiana Department of Revenue, just to name a few. Other internship opportunities include the Court Internship Program (students serve as law clerks in the federal and state trial courts and in the state appellate courts), the Law and State

Government Internship Program (placing student interns in a wide range of state and local government offices, such as the Governor's Office, the Attorney General's Office, and approximately thirty other offices), and internships with the Program in International Human Rights Law (students assist governments and non-governmental organizations on international human rights projects in countries on all six continents). We have the nationally recognized William S. and Christine S. Hall Center for Law and Health, which focuses on the important area of health law by engaging in a program of interdisciplinary research and scholarship in the health law and policy field. Located on the same campus as the Indiana University Medical Center, Indiana University's health professions schools, and the Indiana University Bioethics Center, the Center has excellent opportunities for interdisciplinary research on health law and policy issues. The Center for Intellectual Property Law and Innovation is a resource for education and research in intellectual property law, particularly as it applies to the life sciences. The Center for International and Comparative Law provides direction and administrative guidance for the summer study programs in China, Western Europe, Central and Eastern Europe as well as Latin America; the Program in International Human Rights Law; and other international activities and internships. The Center is the point of contact for students and faculty with interests in international and comparative law. The Program on Law and State Government serves as a vehicle to bring students, the law school, and the community of state government policy makers together in an academic forum for public debate and analysis of the legal issues facing state governments. Students in our Program in International Human Rights Law have helped people in nearly every corner of the world. Interns are placed according to interests, special skills, and experience.

STUDENT BODY

Fall 2005 full-time enrollment: 642

Men: 50%	Women: 50%
African-American: 5.1%	American Indian: 0.3%
Asian-American: 3.9%	Mexican-American: 2.3%
Puerto Rican: 0.5%	Other Hisp-Amer: 2.2%
White: 83.0%	International: 2.6%
Unknown: 0.0%	

Fall 2005 part-time enrollment: 271

Men: 55%	Women: 45%
African-American: 10.3%	American Indian: 0.4%
Asian-American: 4.1%	Mexican-American: 1.5%
Puerto Rican: 0.7%	Other Hisp-Amer: 1.1%
White: 80.8%	International: 1.1%
Unknown: 0.0%	

Attrition rates for 2004-2005 full-time students

Percent of students discontinuing law school:

Men: 2%	Women: 2%
First-year students: 3%	Second-year students: 3%
Third-year students: 0%	

LIBRARY RESOURCES

The library holds 192,454 and receives 3,137 current subscriptions.

Total volumes: 590,230

Percentage of the titles in the online catalog: 99%

Total seats available for library users: 498

INFORMATION TECHNOLOGY

Number of wired network connections available to students: 1,140 total (in the law library, excluding computer labs: 325; in classrooms: 686; in computer labs: 0; elsewhere in the law school: 129)

Law school has a wireless network.

Approximate number of simultaneous users that can be accommodated on wireless network: 1,500

Students are not required to own a computer.

EMPLOYMENT AND SALARIES

Proportion of 2004 graduates employed at graduation: 83%

Employed 9 months later, as of February 15, 2005: 94%

Salaries in the private sector (law firms, business, industry): $55,200–$80,200 (25th-75th percentile)

Median salary in the private sector: $65,280

Percentage in the private sector who reported salary information: 49%

Median salary in public service (government, judicial clerkships, academic posts, non-profits): $46,736

Percentage of 2004 graduates in:

Law firms: 50%	Bus./industry (legal): 3%
Bus./industry (nonlegal): 13%	Government: 11%
Public interest: 3%	Judicial clerkship: 4%
Academia : 4%	Unknown: 12%

2004 graduates employed in-state: 88%

2004 graduates employed in foreign countries: 0%

Number of states where graduates are employed: 15

Percentage of 2004 graduates working in: New England: 0%, Middle Atlantic: 1%, East North Central: 91%, West North Central: 1%, South Atlantic: 4%, East South Central: 0%, West South Central: 1%, Mountain: 0%, Pacific: 2%, Unknown: 0%

BAR PASSAGE RATES

Based on 2004 graduates taking Summer 2004 or Winter 2005 exams. Most of the school's first-time test takers took the bar in Indiana.

80%
School's bar passage rate for first-time test takers

84%
Statewide bar passage rate for first-time test takers

John Marshall Law School

- 315 S. Plymouth Court, Chicago, IL, 60604
- http://www.jmls.edu
- Private
- **Year founded:** 1899
- **2005-2006 tuition:** full-time: $27,540; part-time: $19,700
- **Enrollment 2005-06 academic year:** full-time: 1,133; part-time: 352
- **U.S. News 2007 law specialty ranking:** intellecutal property law: 14, trial advocacy: 14

2.80-3.38	GPA, 25TH-75TH PERCENTILE
152-156	LSAT, 25TH-75TH PERCENTILE
36%	ACCEPTANCE RATE
Tier 4	2007 U.S. NEWS LAW SCHOOL RANKING

ADMISSIONS

Admissions phone number: **(800) 537-4280**
Admissions email address: **admission@jmls.edu**
Application website:
　http://www.jmls.edu/supportdata/webviewbookapp.pdf
Application deadline for Fall 2007 admission: **4/01**

Admissions statistics:

Number of applicants for Fall 2005: **3,141**
Number of acceptances: **1,136**
Number enrolled: **419**
Acceptance rate: **36%**
GPA, 25th-75th percentile, entering class Fall 2005:
　2.80-3.38
LSAT, 25th-75th percentile, entering class Fall 2005:
　152-156

Part-time program:

Number of applicants for Fall 2005: **562**
Number of acceptances: **214**
Number enrolled: **122**
Acceptance rate: **38%**
GPA, 25th-75th percentile, entering class Fall 2005:
　2.63-3.31
LSAT, 25th-75th percentile, entering class Fall 2005: **151-155**

FINANCIAL AID

Financial aid phone number: **(800) 537-4280**
Financial aid application deadline: **N/A**
Tuition 2005-2006 academic year: full-time: **$27,540**; part-time: **$19,700**
Room and board: **$12,932**; books: **$1,400**; miscellaneous expenses: **$6,562**
Total of room/board/books/miscellaneous expenses: **$20,894**
University does not offer graduate student housing for which law students are eligible.

Financial aid profile

Percent of students that received grants for the 2004-2005 academic year: full-time: **30%**; part-time **28%**

Median grant amount: full-time: **$6,000**; part-time: **$4,500**
The average law-school debt of those in the Class of 2005 who borrowed: **$109,862**. Proportion who borrowed: **66%**

ACADEMIC PROGRAMS

Calendar: **semester**
Joint degrees awarded: **J.D./M.B.A.; J.D./MPA; J.D./MA; J.D./LLM Employee Benefits Law; J.D./LLM Intellectual property Law; J.D./LLM Information Technology Law; J.D./LLM International Business & Trade ; J.D./LLM Real Estate Law; J.D./LLM Tax Law**
Typical first-year section size: Full-time: **85**; Part-time: **60**
Is there typically a "small section" of the first year class, other than Legal Writing, taught by full-time faculty?:
　Full-time: **no**; Part-time: **no**
Number of course titles, beyond the first year curriculum, offered last year: **201**
Percentages of upper division course sections, excluding seminars, with an enrollment of:
　Under 25: **68%**　　　25 to 49: **15%**
　50 to 74: **11%**　　　75 to 99: **6%**
　100+: **0%**
Areas of specialization: appellate advocacy, clinical training, dispute resolution, environmental law, healthcare law, intellectual property law, international law, tax law, trial advocacy

Fall 2005 faculty profile

Total teaching faculty: **129**. Full-time: **39%**; **68%** men, **32%** women, **12%** minorities. Part-time: **61%**; **80%** men, **20%** women, **10%** minorities
Student-to-faculty ratio: **21.8**

SPECIAL PROGRAMS *(as provided by law school)*:

The John Marshall Law School provides its students the opportunity to gain an understanding of the basic competencies expected of attorneys. In addition, the law school has established a clinical legal education program, an academic program for which credit may be received. The program has two divisions: the Fair Housing Legal Clinic and the general externship program.

Fair Housing Legal Clinic: The law school operates the clinic, where students represent clients who have been denied housing because of race, color, national origin, sex, disability, familial status, marital status, age, source of income, or sexual orientation. The clinic offers an opportunity to participate in federal and state court litigation and administrative proceedings. Students draft pleadings, prepare motions, participate in hearings for temporary restraining orders and preliminary injunctions, conduct discovery, and assist in trials and hearings or possibly appeals.

Immigration Law Clinic: Students work with attorneys at the Midwest Immigrant and Human Rights Center, as well as with other attorneys approved by the law school. The educational objectives of the course include the development of case preparation and litigation skills in the administrative law context and the development of professional values through exposure to clients in a multicultural setting.

Externship programs: The law school offers several programs that permit students to learn important lawyering skills while working as externs with various members of the bench and bar. Students may enroll in the following externship programs: IRS Externship Program, the Lawyering Process, the Real Estate Legal Practicum, the Litigation Practicum, the Judicial Extern Program, and Clinical Legal Education in Intellectual Property.

STUDENT BODY

Fall 2005 full-time enrollment: 1,133
Men: 57%	Women: 43%
African-American: 3.9%	American Indian: 0.7%
Asian-American: 6.4%	Mexican-American: 2.0%
Puerto Rican: 0.1%	Other Hisp-Amer: 1.9%
White: 78.8%	International: 1.4%
Unknown: 4.8%	

Fall 2005 part-time enrollment: 352
Men: 59%	Women: 41%
African-American: 7.4%	American Indian: 0.9%
Asian-American: 3.7%	Mexican-American: 1.7%
Puerto Rican: 0.6%	Other Hisp-Amer: 2.8%
White: 79.3%	International: 1.1%
Unknown: 2.6%	

Attrition rates for 2004-2005 full-time students
Percent of students discontinuing law school:
Men: 14%	Women: 11%
First-year students: 19%	Second-year students: 17%
Third-year students: 4%	

LIBRARY RESOURCES
The library holds 91,884 and receives 5,514 current subscriptions.

Total volumes: 388,179
Percentage of the titles in the online catalog: 100%
Total seats available for library users: 624

INFORMATION TECHNOLOGY
Number of wired network connections available to students: 67 total (in the law library, excluding computer labs: 24; in classrooms: 0; in computer labs: 37; elsewhere in the law school: 6)
Law school has a wireless network.
Approximate number of simultaneous users that can be accommodated on wireless network: 2,000
Students are not required to own a computer.

EMPLOYMENT AND SALARIES
Proportion of 2004 graduates employed at graduation: 56%
Employed 9 months later, as of February 15, 2005: 89%
Salaries in the private sector (law firms, business, industry): $52,250–$90,000 (25th-75th percentile)
Median salary in the private sector: $65,000
Percentage in the private sector who reported salary information: 42%
Median salary in public service (government, judicial clerkships, academic posts, non-profits): $43,700

Percentage of 2004 graduates in:
Law firms: 57%	Bus./industry (legal): 14%
Bus./industry (nonlegal): 7%	Government: 17%
Public interest: 2%	Judicial clerkship: 2%
Academia : 2%	Unknown: 0%

2004 graduates employed in-state: 90%
2004 graduates employed in foreign countries: 0%
Number of states where graduates are employed: 17
Percentage of 2004 graduates working in: New England: 0%, Middle Atlantic: 1%, East North Central: 93%, West North Central: 1%, South Atlantic: 2%, East South Central: 1%, West South Central: 1%, Mountain: 0%, Pacific: 0%, Unknown: 0%

BAR PASSAGE RATES
Based on 2004 graduates taking Summer 2004 or Winter 2005 exams. Most of the school's first-time test takers took the bar in Illinois.

74%
School's bar passage rate for first-time test takers

85%
Statewide bar passage rate for first-time test takers

...wis and Clark Coll. (Northwestern)

■ 10015 S.W. Terwilliger Boulevard, Portland, OR, 97219
■ http://law.lclark.edu
■ Private
■ Year founded: 1884
■ 2005-2006 tuition: full-time: $26,348; part-time: $19,764
■ Enrollment 2005-06 academic year: full-time: 549; part-time: 199
■ U.S. News 2007 law specialty ranking: environmental law: 1

3.04-3.65	GPA, 25TH-75TH PERCENTILE
158-164	LSAT, 25TH-75TH PERCENTILE
38%	ACCEPTANCE RATE
77	2007 U.S. NEWS LAW SCHOOL RANKING

ADMISSIONS
Admissions phone number: **(503) 768-6613**
Admissions email address: **lawadmss@lclark.edu**
Application website:
https://www4.lsac.org/LSACD_on_the_Web/login/open.aspx
Application deadline for Fall 2007 admission: **3/01**

Admissions statistics:
Number of applicants for Fall 2005: **2,190**
Number of acceptances: **828**
Number enrolled: **191**
Acceptance rate: **38%**
GPA, 25th-75th percentile, entering class Fall 2005: **3.04-3.65**
LSAT, 25th-75th percentile, entering class Fall 2005: **158-164**

Part-time program:
Number of applicants for Fall 2005: **205**
Number of acceptances: **79**
Number enrolled: **41**
Acceptance rate: **39%**
GPA, 25th-75th percentile, entering class Fall 2005: **3.10-3.60**
LSAT, 25th-75th percentile, entering class Fall 2005: **155-163**

FINANCIAL AID
Financial aid phone number: **(503) 768-7090**
Financial aid application deadline: **3/01**
Tuition 2005-2006 academic year: full-time: **$26,348**; part-time: **$19,764**
Room and board: **$9,774**; books: **$1,006**; miscellaneous expenses: **$3,872**
Total of room/board/books/miscellaneous expenses: **$14,652**
University does not offer graduate student housing for which law students are eligible.

Financial aid profile
Percent of students that received grants for the 2004-2005 academic year: full-time: **45%**; part-time **25%**
Median grant amount: full-time: **$9,000**; part-time: **$7,000**
The average law-school debt of those in the Class of 2005 who borrowed: **$79,769**. Proportion who borrowed: **100%**

ACADEMIC PROGRAMS
Calendar: **semester**
Joint degrees awarded: **N/A**
Typical first-year section size: Full-time: **76**; Part-time: **73**
Is there typically a "small section" of the first year class, other than Legal Writing, taught by full-time faculty?: Full-time: **yes**; Part-time: **yes**
Number of course titles, beyond the first year curriculum, offered last year: **119**
Percentages of upper division course sections, excluding seminars, with an enrollment of:
Under 25: **53%**   25 to 49: **29%**
50 to 74: **13%**   75 to 99: **4%**
100+: **1%**
Areas of specialization: appellate advocacy, clinical training, dispute resolution, environmental law, healthcare law, intellectual property law, international law, tax law, trial advocacy

Fall 2005 faculty profile
Total teaching faculty: **63**. Full-time: **46%**; **76%** men, **24%** women, **3%** minorities. Part-time: **54%**; **65%** men, **35%** women, **6%** minorities
Student-to-faculty ratio: **14.1**

SPECIAL PROGRAMS *(as provided by law school):*
Students have many opportunities to test out theory in practice. The school offers clinical experience, where students work with law professors on cases, and the school allows students to get credit for experience earned in approved externships and internships, where students work with practicing attorneys in public agencies and nonprofit organizations.

Clinical experience is available through the Lewis and Clark Legal Clinic, operating in downtown Portland; the Pacific Environmental Advocacy Center; the International Environmental Law Project; and the Crime Victim Law Institute.

The Lewis and Clark Legal Clinic allows students to serve low-income clients in civil and administrative cases. Students interview and counsel clients, prepare cases and conduct trials, negotiate settlements, and prepare appeals. Students represent clients in matters of consumer law, employment law, business law, family law, and tenant and housing issues.

The Pacific Environmental Advocacy Center is a resource for public-interest organizations that need legal representation to protect the environment, and through working on these cases students are trained and educated.

The International Environmental Law Project is an on-campus clinic that gives law students the opportunity to work on real-life global environmental issues. Past student work has focused on trade and environment issues as well as protection of threatened and endangered species.

The Crime Victim Law Institute allows students to gain appellate experience serving as an expert resource on victim laws. The institute is a federally funded project dedicated to the study and enhancement of the crime victim's role in the criminal justice system. It is the only such academic institute in the United States.

Through a semester-long or summer externship, a student can satisfy personal interests and meet individual career goals. An externship involves full-time work, a substantial research paper, and a special seminar. Students have done externships all over the world.

Clinical internship seminars place students locally in law firms, with public agencies, or with the judiciary. Internships are available in criminal law, in-house corporate counsel, intellectual property, environmental or natural resources law, and disability law.

Students may become certified to appear in court. Many of our upper-division students make regular court appearances, both in school-approved courses, such as clinic, or working part-time in clerking positions.

STUDENT BODY

Fall 2005 full-time enrollment: 549

Men: 50%	Women: 50%
African-American: 1.6%	American Indian: 1.6%
Asian-American: 8.9%	Mexican-American: 2.0%
Puerto Rican: 0.7%	Other Hisp-Amer: 2.0%
White: 73.4%	International: 2.2%
Unknown: 7.5%	

Fall 2005 part-time enrollment: 199

Men: 51%	Women: 49%
African-American: 3.0%	American Indian: 2.5%
Asian-American: 9.0%	Mexican-American: 3.0%
Puerto Rican: 0.0%	Other Hisp-Amer: 4.0%
White: 65.8%	International: 0.5%
Unknown: 12.1%	

Attrition rates for 2004-2005 full-time students
Percent of students discontinuing law school:

Men: 3%	Women: 7%
First-year students: 9%	Second-year students: 5%
Third-year students: 1%	

LIBRARY RESOURCES

The library holds 96,171 and receives 3,975 current subscriptions.
Total volumes: 506,527
Percentage of the titles in the online catalog: 100%
Total seats available for library users: 385

INFORMATION TECHNOLOGY

Number of wired network connections available to students: 948 total (in the law library, excluding computer labs: 269; in classrooms: 292; in computer labs: 20; elsewhere in the law school: 367)
Law school has a wireless network.
Approximate number of simultaneous users that can be accommodated on wireless network: 500
Students are not required to own a computer.

EMPLOYMENT AND SALARIES

Proportion of 2004 graduates employed at graduation: N/A
Employed 9 months later, as of February 15, 2005: 94%
Salaries in the private sector (law firms, business, industry): $42,000–$60,000 (25th-75th percentile)
Median salary in the private sector: $48,000
Percentage in the private sector who reported salary information: 58%
Median salary in public service (government, judicial clerkships, academic posts, non-profits): $41,000

Percentage of 2004 graduates in:

Law firms: 46%	Bus./industry (legal): 11%
Bus./industry (nonlegal): N/A	Government: 17%
Public interest: 11%	Judicial clerkship: 14%
Academia : 1%	Unknown: 0%

2004 graduates employed in-state: 61%
2004 graduates employed in foreign countries: 1%
Number of states where graduates are employed: 21
Percentage of 2004 graduates working in: New England: 1%, Middle Atlantic: 2%, East North Central: 1%, West North Central: 2%, South Atlantic: 3%, East South Central: N/A, West South Central: 2%, Mountain: 5%, Pacific: 82%, Unknown: 0%

BAR PASSAGE RATES

Based on 2004 graduates taking Summer 2004 or Winter 2005 exams. Most of the school's first-time test takers took the bar in Oregon.

68%
School's bar passage rate for first-time test takers

72%
Statewide bar passage rate for first-time test takers

Louisiana State Univ.–Baton Rouge

- 400 Paul M. Hebert Law Center, Baton Rouge, LA, 70803
- http://www.law.lsu.edu
- Public
- Year founded: 1906
- 2005-2006 tuition: In-state: full-time: $12,022, part-time: N/A; Out-of-state: full-time: $21,118
- Enrollment 2005-06 academic year: full-time: 630; part-time: 17
- U.S. News 2007 law specialty ranking: N/A

3.23-3.77	GPA, 25TH-75TH PERCENTILE
154-159	LSAT, 25TH-75TH PERCENTILE
28%	ACCEPTANCE RATE
87	2007 U.S. NEWS LAW SCHOOL RANKING

ADMISSIONS

Admissions phone number: **(225) 578-8646**
Admissions email address: **admissions@law.lsu.edu**
Application website:
https://appl008.lsu.edu/admissions/lawappl.nsf/admissionapplication?OpenForm
Application deadline for Fall 2007 admission: 2/01

Admissions statistics:

Number of applicants for Fall 2005: **1,682**
Number of acceptances: **467**
Number enrolled: **218**
Acceptance rate: **28%**
GPA, 25th-75th percentile, entering class Fall 2005: **3.23-3.77**
LSAT, 25th-75th percentile, entering class Fall 2005: **154-159**

FINANCIAL AID

Financial aid phone number: **(225) 578-3103**
Financial aid application deadline: 3/01
Tuition 2005-2006 academic year: In-state: full-time: **$12,022**, part-time: N/A; Out-of-state: full-time: **$21,118**
Room and board: **$10,084**; books: **$2,000**; miscellaneous expenses: **$2,942**
Total of room/board/books/miscellaneous expenses: **$15,026**
University does not offer graduate student housing for which law students are eligible.

Financial aid profile

Percent of students that received grants for the 2004-2005 academic year: full-time: **41%**
Median grant amount: full-time: **$2,926**
The average law-school debt of those in the Class of 2005 who borrowed: **$53,544**. Proportion who borrowed: **81%**

ACADEMIC PROGRAMS

Calendar: **semester**
Joint degrees awarded: **N/A**
Typical first-year section size: Full-time: **72**

Is there typically a "small section" of the first year class, other than Legal Writing, taught by full-time faculty?: Full-time: **yes**; Part-time: **no**
Number of course titles, beyond the first year curriculum, offered last year: **98**
Percentages of upper division course sections, excluding seminars, with an enrollment of:
Under 25: **39%**   25 to 49: **30%**
50 to 74: **17%**   75 to 99: **13%**
100+: **1%**
Areas of specialization: appellate advocacy, clinical training, dispute resolution, environmental law, healthcare law, intellectual property law, international law, tax law, trial advocacy

Fall 2005 faculty profile

Total teaching faculty: **66**. Full-time: **56%**; **78%** men, **22%** women, **11%** minorities. Part-time: **44%**; **93%** men, **7%** women, **3%** minorities
Student-to-faculty ratio: **16.6**

SPECIAL PROGRAMS (as provided by law school):

The law center conducts a summer program in France. All classes in the six-week summer program are conducted in English and are designed to meet the requirements of the American Bar Association and the Association of American Law Schools. In summer 2003, the program was held in Lyon, France.

Full-time Louisiana State University law students may apply to participate in the LSU-Southern Co-op Program. All credit is transferred on a pass/fail basis.

In some law courses, students may earn externship credit. The Faculty Committee on Externships has the responsibility of approving courses in which students are given the opportunity to earn externship credits and the agencies and attorneys with which law student externs may be placed.
Students have worked with government agencies, local prosecutors and public defenders, and state and federal revenue offices.

The law center's graduate program is expanding to include students from Latin America as well as those from Europe. The law center has taken initial steps to formulate a Latin American trade program and has offered seminars and other programs in Costa Rica, Argentina, and Chile.

STUDENT BODY

Fall 2005 full-time enrollment: 630

Men: 50%	Women: 50%
African-American: 7.8%	American Indian: 0.2%
Asian-American: 1.4%	Mexican-American: 0.0%
Puerto Rican: 0.0%	Other Hisp-Amer: 1.1%
White: 81.0%	International: 0.3%
Unknown: 8.3%	

Fall 2005 part-time enrollment: 17

Men: 65%	Women: 35%
African-American: 35.3%	American Indian: 0.0%
Asian-American: 0.0%	Mexican-American: 0.0%
Puerto Rican: 0.0%	Other Hisp-Amer: 0.0%
White: 47.1%	International: 0.0%
Unknown: 17.6%	

Attrition rates for 2004-2005 full-time students

Percent of students discontinuing law school:

Men: 4%	Women: 4%
First-year students: 14%	Second-year students: N/A
Third-year students: N/A	

LIBRARY RESOURCES

The library holds 203,668 and receives 10,231 current subscriptions.
Total volumes: 836,843
Percentage of the titles in the online catalog: 100%
Total seats available for library users: 478

INFORMATION TECHNOLOGY

Number of wired network connections available to students: 61 total (in the law library, excluding computer labs: 61; in classrooms: 0; in computer labs: 0; elsewhere in the law school: 0)
Law school has a wireless network.

Approximate number of simultaneous users that can be accommodated on wireless network: 1,250
Students are not required to own a computer.

EMPLOYMENT AND SALARIES

Proportion of 2004 graduates employed at graduation: 78%
Employed 9 months later, as of February 15, 2005: 91%
Salaries in the private sector (law firms, business, industry): $40,000–$66,000 (25th-75th percentile)
Median salary in the private sector: $50,000
Percentage in the private sector who reported salary information: 62%
Median salary in public service (government, judicial clerkships, academic posts, non-profits): N/A

Percentage of 2004 graduates in:

Law firms: 59%	Bus./industry (legal): 3%
Bus./industry (nonlegal): 0%	Government: 9%
Public interest: 1%	Judicial clerkship: 21%
Academia : 2%	Unknown: 6%

2004 graduates employed in-state: 89%
2004 graduates employed in foreign countries: 0%
Number of states where graduates are employed: 11
Percentage of 2004 graduates working in: New England: N/A, Middle Atlantic: 1%, East North Central: N/A, West North Central: N/A, South Atlantic: 2%, East South Central: 1%, West South Central: 93%, Mountain: 1%, Pacific: 1%, Unknown: 0%

BAR PASSAGE RATES

Based on 2004 graduates taking Summer 2004 or Winter 2005 exams. Most of the school's first-time test takers took the bar in Louisiana.

78%
School's bar passage rate for first-time test takers

67%
Statewide bar passage rate for first-time test takers

Loyola Law School

■ 919 Albany Street, Los Angeles, CA, 90015-1211
■ http://www.lls.edu
■ Private
■ Year founded: 1920
■ 2005-2006 tuition: full-time: $31,454; part-time: $21,110
■ Enrollment 2005-06 academic year: full-time: 994; part-time: 325
■ U.S. News 2007 law specialty ranking: tax law: 19, trial advocacy: 4

3.05-3.50 GPA, 25TH-75TH PERCENTILE

160-163 LSAT, 25TH-75TH PERCENTILE

23% ACCEPTANCE RATE

65 2007 U.S. NEWS LAW SCHOOL RANKING

ADMISSIONS
Admissions phone number: (213) 736-1074
Admissions email address: Admissions@lls.edu
Application website: http://www.lls.edu/admissions
Application deadline for Fall 2007 admission: 2/02

Admissions statistics:
Number of applicants for Fall 2005: 4,213
Number of acceptances: 984
Number enrolled: 342
Acceptance rate: 23%
GPA, 25th-75th percentile, entering class Fall 2005: 3.05-3.50
LSAT, 25th-75th percentile, entering class Fall 2005: 160-163

Part-time program:
Number of applicants for Fall 2005: 622
Number of acceptances: 121
Number enrolled: 68
Acceptance rate: 19%
GPA, 25th-75th percentile, entering class Fall 2005: 2.93-3.52
LSAT, 25th-75th percentile, entering class Fall 2005: 158-161

FINANCIAL AID
Financial aid phone number: (213) 736-1140
Financial aid application deadline: 3/02
Tuition 2005-2006 academic year: full-time: $31,454; part-time: $21,110
Room and board: $10,826; books: $1,080; miscellaneous expenses: $6,366
Total of room/board/books/miscellaneous expenses: $18,272
University does not offer graduate student housing for which law students are eligible.

Financial aid profile
Percent of students that received grants for the 2004-2005 academic year: full-time: 20%; part-time 9%

Median grant amount: full-time: $30,254; part-time: $16,400
The average law-school debt of those in the Class of 2005 who borrowed: $94,800. Proportion who borrowed: 85%

ACADEMIC PROGRAMS
Calendar: semester
Joint degrees awarded: J.D./M.B.A.
Typical first-year section size: Full-time: 89; Part-time: 90
Is there typically a "small section" of the first year class, other than Legal Writing, taught by full-time faculty?: Full-time: no; Part-time: no
Number of course titles, beyond the first year curriculum, offered last year: 136
Percentages of upper division course sections, excluding seminars, with an enrollment of:
Under 25: 67%   25 to 49: 18%
50 to 74: 6%   75 to 99: 4%
100+: 5%
Areas of specialization: appellate advocacy, clinical training, dispute resolution, environmental law, healthcare law, intellectual property law, international law, tax law, trial advocacy

Fall 2005 faculty profile
Total teaching faculty: 162. Full-time: 41%; 58% men, 42% women, 21% minorities. Part-time: 59%; 75% men, 25% women, 7% minorities
Student-to-faculty ratio: 16.1

SPECIAL PROGRAMS (as provided by law school):
Academic support: Academic support includes programs designed to help students successfully complete law school. The Summer Institute provides students with an intensive introduction to legal reasoning skills. Legal Method I and II introduce first-year students to briefing cases, taking notes, preparing outlines, and taking exams. Center for Ethical Advocacy: This program includes basic and advanced trial advocacy instruction, masters courses in specialized areas, and a litigator-in-residence to provide mentoring for future civil litigators, all with an

emphasis on developing practical skills and sensitivity to ethical issues.

Entertainment law practicum: This program gives students a hands-on experience in the entertainment industry while earning units towards their degree.

Externships: Loyola offers a wide range of externship opportunities, providing over 350 students each year a chance to gain hands-on legal experience at many organizations.

Public-interest law department: One of the first schools in the nation to require students to perform pro bono work, Loyola has a strong commitment to public-interest law. Specialized public-interest programs and job opportunities with legal services organizations are provided in conjunction with student organizations, including the student-run Public Interest Law Foundation. The department also administers the Public Interest Scholars Program, Pro Bono Graduation Requirement, Summer Public Interest Employment Program, Public-Interest Postgraduate Fellowships, and Public Interest Loan Assistance Program.

Law and Technology at Caltech and Loyola law school: The Program is designed to promote study of the intersections between these disciplines.

Disability Rights Legal Center: This on-campus legal clinic provides free legal services to people with disabilities who have faced discrimination. Law student externs work with staff attorneys.

Disability Mediation Center: This is an on-campus mediation and conciliation project.

The Center for Conflict Resolution: The center provides mediation, conciliation, and facilitation services and conflict resolution training to the communities adjacent to the law school. The center is a public-interest externship that is offered year-round.

Cancer Legal Resource Center: The center is an on-campus, community-based resource program working with a pro bono panel of attorneys.

Study abroad: Summer programs in Beijing; San Jose, Costa Rica; and Bologna, Italy, offer students an opportunity to study international, comparative, or environmental law.

STUDENT BODY

Fall 2005 full-time enrollment: 994

Men: 51%	Women: 49%
African-American: 3.6%	American Indian: 0.5%
Asian-American: 25.4%	Mexican-American: 5.8%
Puerto Rican: 0.2%	Other Hisp-Amer: 5.0%
White: 51.2%	International: 0.5%
Unknown: 7.7%	

Fall 2005 part-time enrollment: 325

Men: 56%	Women: 44%
African-American: 4.0%	American Indian: 1.2%
Asian-American: 22.2%	Mexican-American: 5.5%
Puerto Rican: 0.0%	Other Hisp-Amer: 3.1%
White: 58.2%	International: 0.0%
Unknown: 5.8%	

Attrition rates for 2004-2005 full-time students

Percent of students discontinuing law school:
Men: 5%   Women: 5%

First-year students: 11%   Second-year students: 3%
Third-year students: 2%

LIBRARY RESOURCES

The library holds 251,533 and receives 7,336 current subscriptions.
Total volumes: 576,330
Percentage of the titles in the online catalog: 100%
Total seats available for library users: 549

INFORMATION TECHNOLOGY

Number of wired network connections available to students: 1,118 total (in the law library, excluding computer labs: 690; in classrooms: 132; in computer labs: 96; elsewhere in the law school: 200)
Law school has a wireless network.
Approximate number of simultaneous users that can be accommodated on wireless network: 1,200
Students are not required to own a computer.

EMPLOYMENT AND SALARIES

Proportion of 2004 graduates employed at graduation: 74%
Employed 9 months later, as of February 15, 2005: 97%
Salaries in the private sector (law firms, business, industry): $60,000–$110,000 (25th-75th percentile)
Median salary in the private sector: $70,000
Percentage in the private sector who reported salary information: 82%
Median salary in public service (government, judicial clerkships, academic posts, non-profits): $54,000

Percentage of 2004 graduates in:

Law firms: 61%	Bus./industry (legal): 3%
Bus./industry (nonlegal): 18%	Government: 4%
Public interest: 10%	Judicial clerkship: 3%
Academia : 1%	Unknown: 0%

2004 graduates employed in-state: 95%
2004 graduates employed in foreign countries: 1%
Number of states where graduates are employed: 14
Percentage of 2004 graduates working in: New England: 0%, Middle Atlantic: 1%, East North Central: 0%, West North Central: 1%, South Atlantic: 1%, East South Central: 0%, West South Central: 0%, Mountain: 1%, Pacific: 96%, Unknown: 0%

BAR PASSAGE RATES

Based on 2004 graduates taking Summer 2004 or Winter 2005 exams. Most of the school's first-time test takers took the bar in California.

66%
School's bar passage rate for first-time test takers

61%
Statewide bar passage rate for first-time test takers

Loyola University Chicago

- 1 E. Pearson Street, Chicago, IL, 60611
- http://www.luc.edu/schools/law
- Private
- Year founded: 1908
- 2005-2006 tuition: full-time: $29,900; part-time: $22,430
- Enrollment 2005-06 academic year: full-time: 602; part-time: 241
- U.S. News 2007 law specialty ranking: healthcare law: 7

3.15-3.68 GPA, 25TH-75TH PERCENTILE

159-163 LSAT, 25TH-75TH PERCENTILE

26% ACCEPTANCE RATE

70 2007 U.S. NEWS LAW SCHOOL RANKING

ADMISSIONS
Admissions phone number: **(312) 915-7170**
Admissions email address: **law-admissions@luc.edu**
Application website:
   http://www.luc.edu/schools/law/admissions/index.html
Application deadline for Fall 2007 admission: **4/01**

Admissions statistics:
Number of applicants for Fall 2005: **2,180**
Number of acceptances: **558**
Number enrolled: **169**
Acceptance rate: **26%**
GPA, 25th-75th percentile, entering class Fall 2005:
   3.15-3.68
LSAT, 25th-75th percentile, entering class Fall 2005:
   159-163

Part-time program:
Number of applicants for Fall 2005: **407**
Number of acceptances: **134**
Number enrolled: **90**
Acceptance rate: **33%**
GPA, 25th-75th percentile, entering class Fall 2005:
   2.99-3.56
LSAT, 25th-75th percentile, entering class Fall 2005: **153-158**

FINANCIAL AID
Financial aid phone number: **(312) 915-7170**
Financial aid application deadline: **3/01**
Tuition 2005-2006 academic year: full-time: **$29,900**;
   part-time: **$22,430**
Room and board: **$12,900**; books: **$950**; miscellaneous
   expenses: **$5,030**
Total of room/board/books/miscellaneous expenses:
   $18,880
University does not offer graduate student housing for
   which law students are eligible.

Financial aid profile
Percent of students that received grants for the 2004-2005
   academic year: full-time: **67%**; part-time **30%**

Median grant amount: full-time: **$14,200**; part-time:
   $10,500
The average law-school debt of those in the Class of 2005
   who borrowed: **N/A**. Proportion who borrowed: **N/A**

ACADEMIC PROGRAMS
Calendar: **semester**
Joint degrees awarded: **J.D./M.S.W.; J.D./M.B.A.;
   J.D./M.S.H.R.; J.D./M.A.**
Typical first-year section size: Full-time: **62**; Part-time: **62**
Is there typically a "small section" of the first year class,
   other than Legal Writing, taught by full-time faculty?:
   Full-time: **no**; Part-time: **no**
Number of course titles, beyond the first year curriculum,
   offered last year: **136**
Percentages of upper division course sections, excluding
   seminars, with an enrollment of:

Under 25: **49%**	25 to 49: **33%**
50 to 74: **18%**	75 to 99: **0%**
100+: **0%**	

Areas of specialization: appellate advocacy, clinical training,
   dispute resolution, environmental law, healthcare law,
   intellectual property law, international law, tax law, trial
   advocacy

Fall 2005 faculty profile
Total teaching faculty: **184**. Full-time: **20%**; **57%** men, **43%**
   women, **11%** minorities. Part-time: **80%**; **52%** men, **48%**
   women, **4%** minorities
Student-to-faculty ratio: **16.8**

SPECIAL PROGRAMS *(as provided by law school):*
Loyola Chicago offers five clinics: general poverty law (housing,
governmental benefits, etc.); child and family matters; federal
income tax disputes; elder law; and small business counseling
(transactional matters). It offers externships in six areas: child
law, business law, health law, criminal law, government agencies, and judicial.
   There are 10 institutes, centers, and special programs focusing on different areas: advocacy, antitrust/consumer law, business and tax law, Catholic healthcare and sponsorship, child and

family law, elder law, health law, intellectual property, international and comparative law, and public service. There are student fellowships in four areas: advocacy, antitrust, intellectual property and technology, and international.

We offer two summer abroad programs (Rome, Europe/Oxford) as well as other opportunities for students to study abroad (comparative advocacy in London and Chile during spring break).

There are eight regular lecture series and many ad hoc lectures and programs. A Great Books program brings interested students, faculty, and staff together to discuss great works of literature.

First-year students can take advantage of the instructional assistance program, one of an array of academic services for students. Public service is promoted; grants are funded by student activities to enable students to accept public-interest summer jobs, and a loan repayment assistance program is available for alums in public service.

STUDENT BODY

Fall 2005 full-time enrollment: 602

Men: 46%	Women: 54%
African-American: 2.8%	American Indian: 0.0%
Asian-American: 8.8%	Mexican-American: 1.8%
Puerto Rican: 0.3%	Other Hisp-Amer: 2.0%
White: 72.6%	International: 1.3%
Unknown: 10.3%	

Fall 2005 part-time enrollment: 241

Men: 49%	Women: 51%
African-American: 5.8%	American Indian: 0.4%
Asian-American: 9.1%	Mexican-American: 1.2%
Puerto Rican: 0.0%	Other Hisp-Amer: 1.7%
White: 71.8%	International: 2.1%
Unknown: 7.9%	

Attrition rates for 2004-2005 full-time students

Percent of students discontinuing law school:

Men: 1%	Women: 1%
First-year students: 0%	Second-year students: 2%
Third-year students: N/A	

LIBRARY RESOURCES

The library holds 60,747 and receives 4,516 current subscriptions.
Total volumes: 408,901
Percentage of the titles in the online catalog: 100%
Total seats available for library users: 456

INFORMATION TECHNOLOGY

Number of wired network connections available to students: 328 total (in the law library, excluding computer labs: 180; in classrooms: 148; in computer labs: 0; elsewhere in the law school: 0)
Law school has a wireless network.
Approximate number of simultaneous users that can be accommodated on wireless network: 660
Students are not required to own a computer.

EMPLOYMENT AND SALARIES

Proportion of 2004 graduates employed at graduation: 78%
Employed 9 months later, as of February 15, 2005: 98%
Salaries in the private sector (law firms, business, industry): $57,500-$125,000 (25th-75th percentile)
Median salary in the private sector: $83,000
Percentage in the private sector who reported salary information: 56%
Median salary in public service (government, judicial clerkships, academic posts, non-profits): $43,222

Percentage of 2004 graduates in:

Law firms: 55%	Bus./industry (legal): 1%
Bus./industry (nonlegal): 16%	Government: 13%
Public interest: 6%	Judicial clerkship: 8%
Academia : 2%	Unknown: 0%

2004 graduates employed in-state: 88%
2004 graduates employed in foreign countries: 0%
Number of states where graduates are employed: 17
Percentage of 2004 graduates working in: New England: 0%, Middle Atlantic: 1%, East North Central: 92%, West North Central: 1%, South Atlantic: 4%, East South Central: 0%, West South Central: 0%, Mountain: 1%, Pacific: 1%, Unknown: 0%

BAR PASSAGE RATES

Based on 2004 graduates taking Summer 2004 or Winter 2005 exams. Most of the school's first-time test takers took the bar in Illinois.

	92%

School's bar passage rate for first-time test takers

	85%

Statewide bar passage rate for first-time test takers

Loyola University New Orleans

- 7214 St. Charles Avenue, Box 901, New Orleans, LA, 70118
- http://law.loyno.edu/
- Private
- Year founded: 1931
- 2005-2006 tuition: full-time: N/A; part-time: N/A
- Enrollment 2005-06 academic year: full-time: 633; part-time: 170
- U.S. News 2007 law specialty ranking: N/A

3.16-3.63 GPA, 25TH-75TH PERCENTILE

151-156 LSAT, 25TH-75TH PERCENTILE

34% ACCEPTANCE RATE

Tier 3 2007 U.S. NEWS LAW SCHOOL RANKING

ADMISSIONS

Admissions phone number: **(504) 861-5575**
Admissions email address: **ladmit@loyno.edu**
Application website:
   http://law.loyno.edu/admissions/application.php
Application deadline for Fall 2007 admission: **rolling**

Admissions statistics:
Number of applicants for Fall 2005: **1,746**
Number of acceptances: **593**
Number enrolled: **215**
Acceptance rate: **34%**
GPA, 25th-75th percentile, entering class Fall 2005:
   3.16-3.63
LSAT, 25th-75th percentile, entering class Fall 2005: **151-156**

FINANCIAL AID

Financial aid phone number: **(504) 865-3231**
Financial aid application deadline: **N/A**
Tuition 2005-2006 academic year: full-time: **N/A**; part-
   time: **N/A**
Room and board: **N/A**; books: **N/A**; miscellaneous
   expenses: **N/A**
Total of room/board/books/miscellaneous expenses: **N/A**
University offers graduate student housing for which law
   students are eligible.

Financial aid profile
Percent of students that received grants for the 2004-2005
   academic year: full-time: **N/A**
Median grant amount: full-time: **N/A**
The average law-school debt of those in the Class of 2005
   who borrowed: **N/A**. Proportion who borrowed: **N/A**

ACADEMIC PROGRAMS

Calendar: **semester**
Joint degrees awarded: **N/A**
Typical first-year section size: Full-time:**N/A**
Is there typically a "small section" of the first year class,
   other than Legal Writing, taught by full-time faculty?:
   Full-time: **no**; Part-time: **no**

Number of course titles, beyond the first year curriculum,
   offered last year: **N/A**
Percentages of upper division course sections, excluding
   seminars, with an enrollment of:
   Under 25: **N/A**   25 to 49: **N/A**
   50 to 74: **N/A**   75 to 99: **N/A**
   100+: **N/A**
Areas of specialization: appellate advocacy, clinical training,
   dispute resolution, environmental law, intellectual property law, international law, tax law, trial advocacy

Fall 2005 faculty profile
Total teaching faculty: **N/A**. Full-time: **N/A**; **N/A** men, **N/A**
   women, **N/A** minorities. Part-time: **N/A**; **N/A** men, **N/A**
   women, **N/A** minorities
Student-to-faculty ratio: **17.6**

SPECIAL PROGRAMS *(as provided by law school):*
Loyola University New Orleans School of Law is only one of two
law schools in the United States to offer complete programs in
both civil law and common law. In addition, students may
obtain a certificate in the program in which they are not major-
ing. Loyola also offers a certificate in international legal studies.
   Loyola sponsors international summer programs in Vienna;
Moscow; Budapest, Hungary; and Cuernavaca, Mexico, with
additional programs in alternate years in Sao Paulo, Brazil, and
San Jose, Costa Rica. Each December Loyola has a program in
Brussels to study the European Union. In cooperation with other
colleges of the university, the law school has joint degree programs leading to a J.D./M.B.A., a J.D./M.A. in religious studies,
and a J.D./M.A. in mass communications. In cooperation with
the University of New Orleans, the law school also offers a
J.D./master of urban and regional planning and a J.D./M.P.A.
   Loyola has an extensive live clinic where students may represent clients in civil, criminal, and administrative cases. The
clinic also places students in the local district attorney's and city
attorney's offices. It is one of a handful of clinics where students represent criminal defendants facing serious felonies.
   The Gillis Long Poverty Law Center supports numerous programs to deliver legal services to the poor and supports a loan forgiveness program for graduates doing public-service work. Loyola

and Tulane jointly sponsor the Public Law Center, where students learn legislative and administrative drafting and lobbying. Loyola provides externships with federal and state courts and agencies.

Loyola has a long history of success in moot court programs. In the current year, the law school is sending teams to seven different competitions. In addition to these domestic successes, for the past three years Loyola is the only U.S. law school to have advanced to the final eight in the Willem C. Vis International Arbitration Commercial Law Moot Court competition, held annually in Vienna. This international event draws competitors from 128 schools in 40 countries around the world.

STUDENT BODY

Fall 2005 full-time enrollment: 633

Men: 46%	Women: 54%
African-American: 8.2%	American Indian: 1.1%
Asian-American: 3.9%	Mexican-American: 0.0%
Puerto Rican: 4.7%	Other Hisp-Amer: 1.7%
White: 72.7%	International: 0.3%
Unknown: 7.3%	

Fall 2005 part-time enrollment: 170

Men: 54%	Women: 46%
African-American: 12.9%	American Indian: 1.2%
Asian-American: 0.6%	Mexican-American: 0.0%
Puerto Rican: 5.3%	Other Hisp-Amer: 2.4%
White: 65.3%	International: 0.0%
Unknown: 12.4%	

Attrition rates for 2004-2005 full-time students
Percent of students discontinuing law school:

Men: N/A	Women: N/A
First-year students: N/A	Second-year students: N/A
Third-year students: N/A	

LIBRARY RESOURCES

The library holds 113,890 and receives N/A current subscriptions.
Total volumes: 338,150
Percentage of the titles in the online catalog: N/A
Total seats available for library users: 448

INFORMATION TECHNOLOGY

Number of wired network connections available to students: 142 total (in the law library, excluding computer labs: 57; in classrooms: 0; in computer labs: 73; elsewhere in the law school: 12)

Law school has a wireless network.
Approximate number of simultaneous users that can be accommodated on wireless network: 200
Students are not required to own a computer.

EMPLOYMENT AND SALARIES

Proportion of 2004 graduates employed at graduation: 80%
Employed 9 months later, as of February 15, 2005: 99%
Salaries in the private sector (law firms, business, industry): N/A–N/A (25th-75th percentile)
Median salary in the private sector: N/A
Percentage in the private sector who reported salary information: N/A
Median salary in public service (government, judicial clerkships, academic posts, non-profits): N/A

Percentage of 2004 graduates in:

Law firms: N/A	Bus./industry (legal): N/A
Bus./industry (nonlegal): N/A	Government: N/A
Public interest: N/A	Judicial clerkship: N/A
Academia : N/A	Unknown: N/A

2004 graduates employed in-state: N/A
2004 graduates employed in foreign countries: N/A
Number of states where graduates are employed: N/A
Percentage of 2004 graduates working in: New England: N/A, Middle Atlantic: N/A, East North Central: N/A, West North Central: N/A, South Atlantic: N/A, East South Central: N/A, West South Central: N/A, Mountain: N/A, Pacific: N/A, Unknown: N/A

BAR PASSAGE RATES

Based on 2004 graduates taking Summer 2004 or Winter 2005 exams. Most of the school's first-time test takers took the bar in Louisiana.

60%

School's bar passage rate for first-time test takers

67%

Statewide bar passage rate for first-time test takers

Marquette University

- **Sensenbrenner Hall, PO Box 1881, Milwaukee, WI, 53201-1881**
- **http://law.marquette.edu**
- **Private**
- **Year founded:** 1892
- **2005-2006 tuition:** full-time: $26,176; part-time: $15,675
- **Enrollment 2005-06 academic year:** full-time: 569; part-time: 146
- **U.S. News 2007 law specialty ranking:** dispute resolution: 11

3.14-3.62	GPA, 25TH-75TH PERCENTILE
155-159	LSAT, 25TH-75TH PERCENTILE
40%	ACCEPTANCE RATE
Tier 3	2007 U.S. NEWS LAW SCHOOL RANKING

ADMISSIONS
Admissions phone number: **(414) 288-6767**
Admissions email address: **law.admission@marquette.edu**
Application website: **N/A**
Application deadline for Fall 2007 admission: **4/01**

Admissions statistics:
Number of applicants for Fall 2005: **1,649**
Number of acceptances: **652**
Number enrolled: **166**
Acceptance rate: **40%**
GPA, 25th-75th percentile, entering class Fall 2005:
3.14-3.62
LSAT, 25th-75th percentile, entering class Fall 2005: **155-159**

Part-time program:
Number of applicants for Fall 2005: **202**
Number of acceptances: **67**
Number enrolled: **49**
Acceptance rate: **33%**
GPA, 25th-75th percentile, entering class Fall 2005:
2.96-3.76
LSAT, 25th-75th percentile, entering class Fall 2005:
155-160

FINANCIAL AID
Financial aid phone number: **(414) 288-7390**
Financial aid application deadline: **3/01**
Tuition 2005-2006 academic year: full-time: **$26,176**; part-time: **$15,675**
Room and board: **$9,782**; books: **$1,113**; miscellaneous expenses: **$5,011**
Total of room/board/books/miscellaneous expenses: **$15,906**
University does not offer graduate student housing for which law students are eligible.

Financial aid profile
Percent of students that received grants for the 2004-2005 academic year: full-time: **39%**; part-time **49%**
Median grant amount: full-time: **$6,000**; part-time: **$3,500**

The average law-school debt of those in the Class of 2005 who borrowed: **$76,686**. Proportion who borrowed: **90%**

ACADEMIC PROGRAMS
Calendar: **semester**
Joint degrees awarded: **J.D./M.B.A.; J.D./MA in Political Science; J.D./MA in International Affairs; J.D./MA in History of Philosophy; J.D./MA in Philosophy; J.D./Certificate in Dispute Resolution; J.D./M.B.A. in Sports Business**
Typical first-year section size: Full-time: **80**; Part-time: **50**
Is there typically a "small section" of the first year class, other than Legal Writing, taught by full-time faculty?:
Full-time: **yes**; Part-time: **yes**
Number of course titles, beyond the first year curriculum, offered last year: **132**
Percentages of upper division course sections, excluding seminars, with an enrollment of:

Under 25: **60%**	25 to 49: **21%**
50 to 74: **12%**	75 to 99: **7%**
100+: **0%**	

Areas of specialization: appellate advocacy, clinical training, dispute resolution, environmental law, healthcare law, intellectual property law, international law, tax law, trial advocacy

Fall 2005 faculty profile
Total teaching faculty: **151**. Full-time: **21%**; **45%** men, **55%** women, **10%** minorities. Part-time: **79%**; **68%** men, **33%** women, **3%** minorities
Student-to-faculty ratio: **17.3**

SPECIAL PROGRAMS *(as provided by law school):*
For more than 30 years, Marquette students have had the opportunity to begin transitioning from law school to law practice in one of the school's clinical programs.

Students may participate in internships with the Milwaukee County district attorney's office, the Office of the State Public Defender, trial and appellate judges, and a variety of governmental and nonprofit legal services agencies.

Students may also concentrate in specific doctrinal areas, such as alternative dispute resolution, intellectual property, international law, and sports law.

Marquette law students may take part in a cooperative program with the University of Queensland in Brisbane, Australia. This summer program alternates between Australia and the United States, and the program is taught by a combination of Marquette and University of Queensland faculty.

STUDENT BODY

Fall 2005 full-time enrollment: 569

Men: 57%	Women: 43%
African-American: 3.3%	American Indian: 0.4%
Asian-American: 2.8%	Mexican-American: 0.9%
Puerto Rican: 0.2%	Other Hisp-Amer: 2.1%
White: 88.4%	International: 1.8%
Unknown: 0.2%	

Fall 2005 part-time enrollment: 146

Men: 57%	Women: 43%
African-American: 0.0%	American Indian: 1.4%
Asian-American: 2.1%	Mexican-American: 0.0%
Puerto Rican: 0.0%	Other Hisp-Amer: 0.7%
White: 93.8%	International: 0.7%
Unknown: 1.4%	

Attrition rates for 2004-2005 full-time students
Percent of students discontinuing law school:

Men: 2%	Women: 0%
First-year students: 1%	Second-year students: 2%
Third-year students: 1%	

LIBRARY RESOURCES

The library holds 158,264 and receives 3,238 current subscriptions.
Total volumes: 328,048
Percentage of the titles in the online catalog: 100%
Total seats available for library users: 371

INFORMATION TECHNOLOGY

Number of wired network connections available to students: 154 total (in the law library, excluding computer labs: 75; in classrooms: 65; in computer labs: 0; elsewhere in the law school: 14)

Law school has a wireless network.
Approximate number of simultaneous users that can be accommodated on wireless network: 540
Students are not required to own a computer.

EMPLOYMENT AND SALARIES

Proportion of 2004 graduates employed at graduation: 62%
Employed 9 months later, as of February 15, 2005: 94%
Salaries in the private sector (law firms, business, industry): $42,000–$83,200 (25th-75th percentile)
Median salary in the private sector: $52,000
Percentage in the private sector who reported salary information: 70%
Median salary in public service (government, judicial clerkships, academic posts, non-profits): $41,148

Percentage of 2004 graduates in:

Law firms: 62%	Bus./industry (legal): 10%
Bus./industry (nonlegal): 11%	Government: 7%
Public interest: 5%	Judicial clerkship: 5%
Academia : 1%	Unknown: 0%

2004 graduates employed in-state: 78%
2004 graduates employed in foreign countries: 1%
Number of states where graduates are employed: 18
Percentage of 2004 graduates working in: New England: 1%, Middle Atlantic: 2%, East North Central: 84%, West North Central: 4%, South Atlantic: 3%, East South Central: 0%, West South Central: 0%, Mountain: 3%, Pacific: 3%, Unknown: 0%

BAR PASSAGE RATES

Based on 2004 graduates taking Summer 2004 or Winter 2005 exams. Most of the school's first-time test takers took the bar in Wisconsin.

100%
School's bar passage rate for first-time test takers

84%
Statewide bar passage rate for first-time test takers

Mercer University

- 1021 Georgia Avenue, Macon, GA, 31207-0001
- http://www.law.mercer.edu
- Private
- Year founded: 1873
- 2005-2006 tuition: full-time: $27,600; part-time: N/A
- Enrollment 2005-06 academic year: full-time: 407; part-time: 1
- U.S. News 2007 law specialty ranking: N/A

3.02-3.67	GPA, 25TH-75TH PERCENTILE
153-158	LSAT, 25TH-75TH PERCENTILE
30%	ACCEPTANCE RATE
87	2007 U.S. NEWS LAW SCHOOL RANKING

ADMISSIONS

Admissions phone number: **(478) 301-2605**
Admissions email address: **martin_sv@mercer.edu**
Application website: **http://www.law.mercer.edu/admissions/apply.cfm**
Application deadline for Fall 2007 admission: **3/15**

Admissions statistics:

Number of applicants for Fall 2005: **1,489**
Number of acceptances: **450**
Number enrolled: **155**
Acceptance rate: **30%**
GPA, 25th-75th percentile, entering class Fall 2005: **3.02-3.67**
LSAT, 25th-75th percentile, entering class Fall 2005: **153-158**

FINANCIAL AID

Financial aid phone number: **(478) 301-2064**
Financial aid application deadline: **4/01**
Tuition 2005-2006 academic year: full-time: **$27,600**; part-time: **N/A**
Room and board: **$7,200**; books: **$1,000**; miscellaneous expenses: **$4,800**
Total of room/board/books/miscellaneous expenses: **$13,000**
University offers graduate student housing for which law students are eligible.

Financial aid profile

Percent of students that received grants for the 2004-2005 academic year: full-time: **33%**
Median grant amount: full-time: **$16,000**
The average law-school debt of those in the Class of 2005 who borrowed: **$74,208**. Proportion who borrowed: **87%**

ACADEMIC PROGRAMS

Calendar: **semester**
Joint degrees awarded: **J.D./M.B.A.**
Typical first-year section size: Full-time: **72**

Is there typically a "small section" of the first year class, other than Legal Writing, taught by full-time faculty?:
Full-time: **yes**
Number of course titles, beyond the first year curriculum, offered last year: **95**
Percentages of upper division course sections, excluding seminars, with an enrollment of:

Under 25: **73%**	25 to 49: **16%**
50 to 74: **9%**	75 to 99: **3%**
100+: **0%**	

Areas of specialization: appellate advocacy, clinical training, dispute resolution, environmental law, healthcare law, intellectual property law, international law, tax law, trial advocacy

Fall 2005 faculty profile

Total teaching faculty: **55**. Full-time: **47%**; **69%** men, **31%** women, **12%** minorities. Part-time: **53%**; **83%** men, **17%** women, **3%** minorities
Student-to-faculty ratio: **13.5**

SPECIAL PROGRAMS (as provided by law school):

Mercer Law School is the home of the Legal Writing Institute and is the first and only law school in the country to offer a legal writing certificate program. The Certificate in Advanced Legal Writing, Research, and Drafting is awarded to students who complete a program that requires intensive, advanced-level writing workshops, as well as advanced training in legal research and drafting.

The school also hosts the Mercer Center for Legal Ethics and Professionalism, which engages in a variety of in-house and outreach educational activities with the purpose of improving the professionalism of students, lawyers, and judges. Further, students have ample opportunities to gain practical experience in government or public-interest externships through the school's Public Interest Practicum program, a Public Defender Clinic, and a Death Penalty Clinic. The law school also hosts an annual John James Lecture Series, which focuses on comparative law issues. Finally, although a law school's curriculum is rarely considered a "special program," Mercer's curriculum, which focuses on ethics and practical skills, was honored with the Gambrell Professionalism Award from the American Bar Association for its "depth and excellence" and "obvious commitment to professionalism."

STUDENT BODY

Fall 2005 full-time enrollment: 407

Men: 56%	Women: 44%
African-American: 9.1%	American Indian: 0.7%
Asian-American: 3.2%	Mexican-American: 0.2%
Puerto Rican: 0.2%	Other Hisp-Amer: 0.5%
White: 76.7%	International: 0.0%
Unknown: 9.3%	

Fall 2005 part-time enrollment: 1

Men: 0%	Women: 100%
African-American: 0.0%	American Indian: 0.0%
Asian-American: 0.0%	Mexican-American: 0.0%
Puerto Rican: 0.0%	Other Hisp-Amer: 0.0%
White: 100.0%	International: 0.0%
Unknown: 0.0%	

Attrition rates for 2004-2005 full-time students
Percent of students discontinuing law school:

Men: 2%	Women: 5%
First-year students: 9%	Second-year students: N/A
Third-year students: N/A	

LIBRARY RESOURCES

The library holds 57,064 and receives 3,300 current subscriptions.
Total volumes: 333,658
Percentage of the titles in the online catalog: 100%
Total seats available for library users: 388

INFORMATION TECHNOLOGY

Number of wired network connections available to students: 689 total (in the law library, excluding computer labs: 61; in classrooms: 604; in computer labs: 16; elsewhere in the law school: 8)

Law school has a wireless network.
Approximate number of simultaneous users that can be accommodated on wireless network: 80
Students are required to own a computer.

EMPLOYMENT AND SALARIES

Proportion of 2004 graduates employed at graduation: 59%
Employed 9 months later, as of February 15, 2005: 98%
Salaries in the private sector (law firms, business, industry): $47,500–$70,000 (25th-75th percentile)
Median salary in the private sector: $53,500
Percentage in the private sector who reported salary information: 75%
Median salary in public service (government, judicial clerkships, academic posts, non-profits): $39,250

Percentage of 2004 graduates in:

Law firms: 64%	Bus./industry (legal): 0%
Bus./industry (nonlegal): 5%	Government: 13%
Public interest: 7%	Judicial clerkship: 10%
Academia : 1%	Unknown: 0%

2004 graduates employed in-state: 78%
2004 graduates employed in foreign countries: 1%
Number of states where graduates are employed: 10
Percentage of 2004 graduates working in: New England: 0%, Middle Atlantic: 1%, East North Central: 0%, West North Central: 0%, South Atlantic: 94%, East South Central: 2%, West South Central: 2%, Mountain: 1%, Pacific: 0%, Unknown: 0%

BAR PASSAGE RATES

Based on 2004 graduates taking Summer 2004 or Winter 2005 exams. Most of the school's first-time test takers took the bar in Georgia.

93%
School's bar passage rate for first-time test takers

85%
Statewide bar passage rate for first-time test takers

Michigan State University

■ 368 Law College Building, East Lansing, MI, 48824-1300
■ http://www.law.msu.edu
■ Private
■ Year founded: 1891
■ 2005-2006 tuition: full-time: $26,097; part-time: $21,652
■ Enrollment 2005-06 academic year: full-time: 825; part-time: 219
■ U.S. News 2007 law specialty ranking: intellecutal property law: 17

3.04-3.66 GPA, 25TH-75TH PERCENTILE

155-161 LSAT, 25TH-75TH PERCENTILE

35% ACCEPTANCE RATE

Tier 4 2007 U.S. NEWS LAW SCHOOL RANKING

ADMISSIONS

Admissions phone number: **(517) 432-0222**
Admissions email address: **law@msu.edu**
Application website: **http://www.law.msu.edu/admissions/app.html**
Application deadline for Fall 2007 admission: **3/01**

Admissions statistics:
Number of applicants for Fall 2005: **2,473**
Number of acceptances: **876**
Number enrolled: **197**
Acceptance rate: **35%**
GPA, 25th-75th percentile, entering class Fall 2005: **3.04-3.66**
LSAT, 25th-75th percentile, entering class Fall 2005: **155-161**

Part-time program:
Number of applicants for Fall 2005: **268**
Number of acceptances: **134**
Number enrolled: **83**
Acceptance rate: **50%**
GPA, 25th-75th percentile, entering class Fall 2005: **3.07-3.56**
LSAT, 25th-75th percentile, entering class Fall 2005: **150-153**

FINANCIAL AID

Financial aid phone number: **(517) 432-6810**
Financial aid application deadline: **3/01**
Tuition 2005-2006 academic year: full-time: **$26,097**; part-time: **$21,652**
Room and board: **$7,828**; books: **$1,230**; miscellaneous expenses: **$3,600**
Total of room/board/books/miscellaneous expenses: **$12,658**
University offers graduate student housing for which law students are eligible.

Financial aid profile
Percent of students that received grants for the 2004-2005 academic year: full-time: **38%**; part-time **14%**
Median grant amount: full-time: **$26,664**; part-time: **$11,992**
The average law-school debt of those in the Class of 2005 who borrowed: **$73,230**. Proportion who borrowed: **83%**

ACADEMIC PROGRAMS

Calendar: **semester**
Joint degrees awarded: **J.D./M.B.A Eli Broad College of Business; J.D./M.S. in Urban Planning; J.D./M.P.A.; J.D./M.A. - English; J.D./M.A. Interdisciplinary Studies; J.D./M.A. Communications; J.D./M.A. Political Science; J.D/MA Labor Relations & Human Resources; J.D./M.A. Forestry; J.D./M.S. Fisheries & Wildlife; JD/MS Park, Recreation & Tourism Resourc; JD/MS/Ph.D Park, Recreation & Tourism Re; J.D./M.A. Urban & Regional Planning; J.D./M.B.A. Seidman School of Business; J.D./Ph.D. Political Science; J.D./M.S. in Forestry - Urban Studies; J.D./LL.B. w/University of Ottawa**
Typical first-year section size: Full-time: **73**; Part-time: **63**
Is there typically a "small section" of the first year class, other than Legal Writing, taught by full-time faculty?: Full-time: **no**; Part-time: **no**
Number of course titles, beyond the first year curriculum, offered last year: **154**
Percentages of upper division course sections, excluding seminars, with an enrollment of:

Under 25: **58%**	25 to 49: **26%**	
50 to 74: **9%**	75 to 99: **6%**	
100+: **1%**		

Areas of specialization: appellate advocacy, clinical training, dispute resolution, environmental law, healthcare law, intellectual property law, international law, tax law, trial advocacy

Fall 2005 faculty profile
Total teaching faculty: **90**. Full-time: **47%**; **64%** men, **36%** women, **10%** minorities. Part-time: **53%**; **73%** men, **27%** women, **4%** minorities
Student-to-faculty ratio: **20.7**

SPECIAL PROGRAMS *(as provided by law school)*:
Our rigorous and intellectually challenging juris doctor program offers concentrations in alternative dispute resolution, corporate law, criminal law, environmental and natural resource law, family law, health law, intellectual property and communications law, international and comparative law, public law and

regulation, and taxation law. The law building provides the latest classroom and library technology.

We offer two certificate programs: Trial Practice and Child and Family Advocacy. MSU Law offers a U.S.-Canadian joint degree program with the University of Ottawa Faculty of Law. Both MSU Law and University of Ottawa law students can earn two degrees, the J.D. and LL.B., in four years. The Law College also offers an LL.M. degree in American Law and in Intellectual Property and Communications Law as well as a Masters in Jurisprudence degree in Intellectual Property.

The Geoffrey Fieger Trial Practice Institute at MSU Law offers selected students the opportunity to practice real trial lawyering skills in a courtroom in front of judges, witnesses, and juries. Through this two-year program, each student participates in a complete civil and criminal trial.

Extensive opportunities for an interdisciplinary education exist at MSU Law. Even though MSU Law remains a private law college in the midst of a public university, the two institutions are integrated academically. The law college offers 14 dual degrees with other graduate programs at Michigan State University. In addition, the law college offers the Chance at Childhood Certificate Program and the Law and Social Work Clinic with the School of Social Work.

MSU Law is located only minutes from Michigan's capital city of Lansing. Externships are widely available in state governmental agencies and in the many public-service agencies located nearby. The law college offers a semester-long externship program in Washington, D.C.

In addition to those mentioned above, MSU Law is home to the following programs: Alternative Dispute Resolution Program; Business and Tax Law Center of West Michigan; Canadian Study Abroad Program; Canadian Summer Externship Program; Center for U.S.-Canadian Law; Institute for Legal Education of West Michigan; National Trial Advocacy Competition; Rental Housing Clinic; Small Business/Nonprofit Law Clinic; Study Abroad in Mexico Program; and Taxation Clinic.

MSU Law is an international center for the exchange of legal knowledge through conferences and symposia. During this year, the law college hosts programs on alternative dispute resolution, contract law, intellectual property, international trade, and indigenous law and policy.

STUDENT BODY

Fall 2005 full-time enrollment: 825

Men: 57%	Women: 43%
African-American: 3.6%	American Indian: 1.2%
Asian-American: 3.6%	Mexican-American: 0.0%
Puerto Rican: 0.0%	Other Hisp-Amer: 1.9%
White: 83.6%	International: 4.8%
Unknown: 1.1%	

Fall 2005 part-time enrollment: 219

Men: 47%	Women: 53%
African-American: 7.3%	American Indian: 0.5%
Asian-American: 4.6%	Mexican-American: 0.0%
Puerto Rican: 0.0%	Other Hisp-Amer: 3.2%
White: 82.6%	International: 0.9%
Unknown: 0.9%	

Attrition rates for 2004-2005 full-time students
Percent of students discontinuing law school:

Men: 4%	Women: 3%
First-year students: 10%	Second-year students: 2%
Third-year students: N/A	

LIBRARY RESOURCES

The library holds 138,492 and receives 3,960 current subscriptions.
Total volumes: 271,426
Percentage of the titles in the online catalog: 100%
Total seats available for library users: 455

INFORMATION TECHNOLOGY

Number of wired network connections available to students: 1,239 total (in the law library, excluding computer labs: 339; in classrooms: 800; in computer labs: 50; elsewhere in the law school: 50)
Law school has a wireless network.
Approximate number of simultaneous users that can be accommodated on wireless network: 5,865
Students are required to own a computer.

EMPLOYMENT AND SALARIES

Proportion of 2004 graduates employed at graduation: N/A
Employed 9 months later, as of February 15, 2005: 79%
Salaries in the private sector (law firms, business, industry): $42,500–$67,000 (25th-75th percentile)
Median salary in the private sector: $52,000
Percentage in the private sector who reported salary information: 46%
Median salary in public service (government, judicial clerkships, academic posts, non-profits): $46,249

Percentage of 2004 graduates in:

Law firms: 49%	Bus./industry (legal): 17%
Bus./industry (nonlegal): 0%	Government: 12%
Public interest: 4%	Judicial clerkship: 10%
Academia : 6%	Unknown: 3%

2004 graduates employed in-state: 55%
2004 graduates employed in foreign countries: 3%
Number of states where graduates are employed: 15
Percentage of 2004 graduates working in: New England: 0%, Middle Atlantic: 5%, East North Central: 58%, West North Central: 0%, South Atlantic: 8%, East South Central: 0%, West South Central: 1%, Mountain: 4%, Pacific: 1%, Unknown: 22%

BAR PASSAGE RATES

Based on 2004 graduates taking Summer 2004 or Winter 2005 exams. Most of the school's first-time test takers took the bar in Michigan.

68%
School's bar passage rate for first-time test takers

74%
Statewide bar passage rate for first-time test takers

Mississippi College

- 151 E. Griffith Street, Jackson, MS, 39201
- http://www.law.mc.edu
- Private
- Year founded: 1975
- 2005-2006 tuition: full-time: $19,514; part-time: N/A
- Enrollment 2005-06 academic year: full-time: 490
- U.S. News 2007 law specialty ranking: N/A

2.99-3.51 GPA, 25TH-75TH PERCENTILE

149-153 LSAT, 25TH-75TH PERCENTILE

39% ACCEPTANCE RATE

Tier 4 2007 U.S. NEWS LAW SCHOOL RANKING

ADMISSIONS

Admissions phone number: **(601) 925-7151**
Admissions email address: **hweaver@mc.edu**
Application website:
  http://www.law.mc.edu/admissions/apply_options.htm
Application deadline for Fall 2007 admission: **5/01**

Admissions statistics:

Number of applicants for Fall 2005: **1,274**
Number of acceptances: **491**
Number enrolled: **199**
Acceptance rate: **39%**
GPA, 25th-75th percentile, entering class Fall 2005:
  2.99-3.51
LSAT, 25th-75th percentile, entering class Fall 2005:
  149-153

FINANCIAL AID

Financial aid phone number: **(601) 925-7110**
Financial aid application deadline: **6/01**
Tuition 2005-2006 academic year: full-time: **$19,514**; part-time: **N/A**
Room and board: **$9,000**; books: **$900**; miscellaneous expenses: **$7,373**
Total of room/board/books/miscellaneous expenses: **$17,273**
University offers graduate student housing for which law students are eligible.

Financial aid profile

Percent of students that received grants for the 2004-2005 academic year: full-time: **32%**
Median grant amount: full-time: **$4,000**
The average law-school debt of those in the Class of 2005 who borrowed: **$66,115**. Proportion who borrowed: **89%**

ACADEMIC PROGRAMS

Calendar: **semester**
Joint degrees awarded: **J.D./M.B.A.**
Typical first-year section size: Full-time: **92**

Is there typically a "small section" of the first year class, other than Legal Writing, taught by full-time faculty?: Full-time: **no**
Number of course titles, beyond the first year curriculum, offered last year: **63**
Percentages of upper division course sections, excluding seminars, with an enrollment of:
  Under 25: **54%**   25 to 49: **26%**
  50 to 74: **18%**   75 to 99: **2%**
  100+: **0%**
Areas of specialization: appellate advocacy, clinical training, dispute resolution, environmental law, healthcare law, intellectual property law, international law, tax law, trial advocacy

Fall 2005 faculty profile

Total teaching faculty: **64**. Full-time: **28%**; **67%** men, **33%** women, **11%** minorities. Part-time: **72%**; **74%** men, **26%** women, **2%** minorities
Student-to-faculty ratio: **21.4**

SPECIAL PROGRAMS (as provided by law school):

The students at Mississippi College School of Law have a variety of study opportunities to add to their legal expertise and to permit them to apply their classroom learning in a practical setting. The Child Advocacy Program permits third-year students to appear in court on behalf of a child in a domestic relations case. The student is responsible for working up the case file, interviewing parties, and making a court appearance. A legal aid office is also being planned that will provide law students an opportunity to work with the public and acquire expertise in basic consumer issues, interact with members of the private bar, and gain experience in client interviewing. An active externship program places students with agencies to work side by side with practicing attorneys while earning credits. Our downtown location affords students the opportunity to perform paid or volunteer work with law firms, legal organizations, and public service groups to acquire practical skills. Our trial practice classes are taught by experienced trial attorneys who take our students through each stage of an actual trial.

STUDENT BODY

Fall 2005 full-time enrollment: 490

Men: **61%**	Women: **39%**
African-American: **7.3%**	American Indian: **0.2%**
Asian-American: **0.4%**	Mexican-American: **0.6%**
Puerto Rican: **0.0%**	Other Hisp-Amer: **0.0%**
White: **89.8%**	International: **0.0%**
Unknown: **1.6%**	

Attrition rates for 2004-2005 full-time students
Percent of students discontinuing law school:

Men: **2%**	Women: **1%**
First-year students: **4%**	Second-year students: **1%**
Third-year students: **N/A**	

LIBRARY RESOURCES

The library holds **174,091** and receives **3,491** current subscriptions.
Total volumes: **330,590**
Percentage of the titles in the online catalog: **98%**
Total seats available for library users: **396**

INFORMATION TECHNOLOGY

Number of wired network connections available to students: **72** total (in the law library, excluding computer labs: **72**; in classrooms: **0**; in computer labs: **0**; elsewhere in the law school: **0**)
Law school has a wireless network.
Approximate number of simultaneous users that can be accommodated on wireless network: **120**
Students are not required to own a computer.

EMPLOYMENT AND SALARIES

Proportion of 2004 graduates employed at graduation: **60%**

Employed 9 months later, as of February 15, 2005: **96%**
Salaries in the private sector (law firms, business, industry): **$45,000–$75,000** (25th-75th percentile)
Median salary in the private sector: **$57,500**
Percentage in the private sector who reported salary information: **40%**
Median salary in public service (government, judicial clerkships, academic posts, non-profits): **$38,000**

Percentage of 2004 graduates in:

Law firms: **72%**	Bus./industry (legal): **5%**
Bus./industry (nonlegal): **N/A**	Government: **9%**
Public interest: **1%**	Judicial clerkship: **11%**
Academia : **2%**	Unknown: **0%**

2004 graduates employed in-state: **76%**
2004 graduates employed in foreign countries: **0%**
Number of states where graduates are employed: **6**
Percentage of 2004 graduates working in: New England: **N/A**, Middle Atlantic: **N/A**, East North Central: **N/A**, West North Central: **1%**, South Atlantic: **4%**, East South Central: **87%**, West South Central: **7%**, Mountain: **1%**, Pacific: **N/A**, Unknown: **0%**

BAR PASSAGE RATES

Based on 2004 graduates taking Summer 2004 or Winter 2005 exams. Most of the school's first-time test takers took the bar in Mississippi.

84%
School's bar passage rate for first-time test takers

90%
Statewide bar passage rate for first-time test takers

New England School of Law

- 154 Stuart Street, Boston, MA, 02116
- http://www.nesl.edu
- Private
- **Year founded:** 1908
- **2005-2006 tuition:** full-time: $24,075; part-time: $18,075
- **Enrollment 2005-06 academic year:** full-time: 699; part-time: 396
- **U.S. News 2007 law specialty ranking:** N/A

3.12-3.56 GPA, 25TH-75TH PERCENTILE

150-153 LSAT, 25TH-75TH PERCENTILE

37% ACCEPTANCE RATE

Tier 4 2007 U.S. NEWS LAW SCHOOL RANKING

ADMISSIONS

Admissions phone number: **(617) 422-7210**
Admissions email address: **admit@admin.nesl.edu**
Application website: **N/A**
Application deadline for Fall 2007 admission: **3/15**

Admissions statistics:

Number of applicants for Fall 2005: **2,803**
Number of acceptances: **1,044**
Number enrolled: **253**
Acceptance rate: **37%**
GPA, 25th-75th percentile, entering class Fall 2005: **3.12-3.56**
LSAT, 25th-75th percentile, entering class Fall 2005: **150-153**

Part-time program:

Number of applicants for Fall 2005: **580**
Number of acceptances: **261**
Number enrolled: **129**
Acceptance rate: **45%**
GPA, 25th-75th percentile, entering class Fall 2005: **2.92-3.36**
LSAT, 25th-75th percentile, entering class Fall 2005: **148-152**

FINANCIAL AID

Financial aid phone number: **(617) 422-7298**
Financial aid application deadline: **4/20**
Tuition 2005-2006 academic year: full-time: **$24,075**; part-time: **$18,075**
Room and board: **$9,750**; books: **$1,150**; miscellaneous expenses: **$4,430**
Total of room/board/books/miscellaneous expenses: **$15,330**
University does not offer graduate student housing for which law students are eligible.

Financial aid profile

Percent of students that received grants for the 2004-2005 academic year: full-time: **47%**; part-time **29%**
Median grant amount: full-time: **$3,600**; part-time: **$4,200**

The average law-school debt of those in the Class of 2005 who borrowed: **$81,212**. Proportion who borrowed: **83%**

ACADEMIC PROGRAMS

Calendar: **semester**
Joint degrees awarded: **N/A**
Typical first-year section size: Full-time: **135**; Part-time: **130**
Is there typically a "small section" of the first year class, other than Legal Writing, taught by full-time faculty?: Full-time: **no**; Part-time: **no**
Number of course titles, beyond the first year curriculum, offered last year: **125**
Percentages of upper division course sections, excluding seminars, with an enrollment of:

Under 25: **43%**	25 to 49: **30%**
50 to 74: **15%**	75 to 99: **7%**
100+: **4%**	

Areas of specialization: appellate advocacy, clinical training, dispute resolution, environmental law, intellectual property law, international law, tax law, trial advocacy

Fall 2005 faculty profile

Total teaching faculty: **204**. Full-time: **30%**; **58%** men, **42%** women, **5%** minorities. Part-time: **70%**; **61%** men, **39%** women, **3%** minorities
Student-to-faculty ratio: **25.2**

SPECIAL PROGRAMS (as provided by law school):

New England School of Law offers a full-time day division, a part-time day and a part-time evening division, and the Special Part-time Program, a unique arrangement for parents with primary child-rearing responsibilities.

The school has an extensive clinical program that allows students to combine fieldwork with classroom study in 18 subject areas and includes a fully equipped clinical law office. About 60 percent of the students take a clinical course while in law school.

The law school is also a pioneer in incorporating relevant international law into domestic law courses throughout the curriculum. The law school is home to three academic centers that support a variety of projects involving students and faculty. The

Center for International Law and Policy sponsors an annual conference on a current issue in international law, as well as the International War Crimes Prosecution Project, through which students provide research and analysis to the prosecutor of the International Criminal Tribunals for the Former Yugoslavia and Rwanda. The Center for Law and Social Responsibility supports projects in criminal justice, domestic violence, environmental justice, law and science, and public service. The Center for Business Law organizes activities in the areas of intellectual property law, tax law, and corporate governance and ethics.

Three programs provide different types of judicial clerkship opportunities, and the school's Academic Skills Program offers optional academic support and supervised skills practice for first-year students.

Students who wish to study abroad can choose among summer programs in Galway, Ireland; London; Malta; or Prague, Czech Republic, or between-semester programs in the Netherlands or Denmark. The school also sponsors an exchange program for a semester at the University of Paris X-Nanterre.

STUDENT BODY

Fall 2005 full-time enrollment: 699

Men: 46%	Women: 54%
African-American: 2.4%	American Indian: 0.1%
Asian-American: 3.4%	Mexican-American: 0.6%
Puerto Rican: 0.7%	Other Hisp-Amer: 1.6%
White: 84.0%	International: 0.0%
Unknown: 7.2%	

Fall 2005 part-time enrollment: 396

Men: 53%	Women: 47%
African-American: 2.0%	American Indian: 0.0%
Asian-American: 4.0%	Mexican-American: 1.0%
Puerto Rican: 0.5%	Other Hisp-Amer: 2.8%
White: 83.1%	International: 0.0%
Unknown: 6.6%	

Attrition rates for 2004-2005 full-time students
Percent of students discontinuing law school:

Men: N/A	Women: N/A
First-year students: N/A	Second-year students: N/A
Third-year students: N/A	

LIBRARY RESOURCES

The library holds 55,098 and receives 3,056 current subscriptions.
Total volumes: 351,030
Percentage of the titles in the online catalog: 100%
Total seats available for library users: 374

INFORMATION TECHNOLOGY

Number of wired network connections available to students: 416 total (in the law library, excluding computer labs: 90; in classrooms: 250; in computer labs: 41; elsewhere in the law school: 35)
Law school has a wireless network.
Approximate number of simultaneous users that can be accommodated on wireless network: 600
Students are not required to own a computer.

EMPLOYMENT AND SALARIES

Proportion of 2004 graduates employed at graduation: 28%
Employed 9 months later, as of February 15, 2005: 81%
Salaries in the private sector (law firms, business, industry): $40,000–$60,000 (25th-75th percentile)
Median salary in the private sector: $45,500
Percentage in the private sector who reported salary information: 60%
Median salary in public service (government, judicial clerkships, academic posts, non-profits): $43,000

Percentage of 2004 graduates in:

Law firms: 40%	Bus./industry (legal): 10%
Bus./industry (nonlegal): 12%	Government: 11%
Public interest: 1%	Judicial clerkship: 6%
Academia : 0%	Unknown: 20%

2004 graduates employed in-state: 60%
2004 graduates employed in foreign countries: 1%
Number of states where graduates are employed: 25
Percentage of 2004 graduates working in: New England: 65%, Middle Atlantic: 11%, East North Central: 2%, West North Central: 1%, South Atlantic: 5%, East South Central: 1%, West South Central: 1%, Mountain: 3%, Pacific: 5%, Unknown: 7%

BAR PASSAGE RATES

Based on 2004 graduates taking Summer 2004 or Winter 2005 exams. Most of the school's first-time test takers took the bar in Massachusetts.

74%
School's bar passage rate for first-time test takers

84%
Statewide bar passage rate for first-time test takers

New York Law School

- 57 Worth Street, New York, NY, 10013-2960
- http://www.nyls.edu
- Private
- **Year founded:** 1891
- **2005-2006 tuition:** full-time: $38,600; part-time: $29,680
- **Enrollment 2005-06 academic year:** full-time: 1,106; part-time: 374
- **U.S. News 2007 law specialty ranking:** tax law: 25

3.12-3.61 GPA, 25TH-75TH PERCENTILE

153-157 LSAT, 25TH-75TH PERCENTILE

39% ACCEPTANCE RATE

Tier 3 2007 U.S. NEWS LAW SCHOOL RANKING

ADMISSIONS
Admissions phone number: **(212) 431-2888**
Admissions email address: **admissions@nyls.edu**
Application website: **N/A**
Application deadline for Fall 2007 admission: **4/01**

Admissions statistics:
Number of applicants for Fall 2005: **4,606**
Number of acceptances: **1,782**
Number enrolled: **403**
Acceptance rate: **39%**
GPA, 25th-75th percentile, entering class Fall 2005:
3.12-3.61
LSAT, 25th-75th percentile, entering class Fall 2005: **153-157**

Part-time program:
Number of applicants for Fall 2005: **1,008**
Number of acceptances: **331**
Number enrolled: **135**
Acceptance rate: **33%**
GPA, 25th-75th percentile, entering class Fall 2005:
2.91-3.38
LSAT, 25th-75th percentile, entering class Fall 2005: **151-155**

FINANCIAL AID
Financial aid phone number: **(212) 431-2828**
Financial aid application deadline: **4/01**
Tuition 2005-2006 academic year: full-time: **$38,600**; part-time: **$29,680**
Room and board: **$14,455**; books: **$850**; miscellaneous expenses: **$3,935**
Total of room/board/books/miscellaneous expenses:
$19,240
University offers graduate student housing for which law students are eligible.

Financial aid profile
Percent of students that received grants for the 2004-2005 academic year: full-time: **48%**; part-time **21%**
Median grant amount: full-time: **$7,500**; part-time: **$4,875**

The average law-school debt of those in the Class of 2005 who borrowed: **$84,325.** Proportion who borrowed: **87%**

ACADEMIC PROGRAMS
Calendar: **semester**
Joint degrees awarded: **J.D./M.B.A.**
Typical first-year section size: Full-time: **120**; Part-time: **120**
Is there typically a "small section" of the first year class, other than Legal Writing, taught by full-time faculty?:
Full-time: **yes**; Part-time: **yes**
Number of course titles, beyond the first year curriculum, offered last year: **190**
Percentages of upper division course sections, excluding seminars, with an enrollment of:

Under 25: **48%**	25 to 49: **32%**
50 to 74: **8%**	75 to 99: **5%**
100+: **7%**	

Areas of specialization: appellate advocacy, clinical training, dispute resolution, environmental law, healthcare law, intellectual property law, international law, tax law, trial advocacy

Fall 2005 faculty profile
Total teaching faculty: **154**. Full-time: **40%**; **66%** men, **34%** women, **15%** minorities. Part-time: **60%**; **61%** men, **39%** women, **5%** minorities
Student-to-faculty ratio: **20.3**

SPECIAL PROGRAMS *(as provided by law school):*
New York Law School gives each student a solid foundation in the law—the substantive knowledge and professional skills necessary to represent clients responsibly, effectively, and creatively. But what distinguishes our law school from most is an emphasis on meeting students' individual needs: A liaison program links students to senior administrators and upper-division students; a faculty advising system encourages faculty-to-student mentoring; and an alumni mentor program engages hundreds of graduates in career counseling of our students.

In addition to a rigorous moot court program, opportunities for study abroad, and an individualized professional development portfolio program, special programs include:

John Marshall Harlan Scholars: Named for the New York Law School alumnus and U.S. Supreme Court justice who served on the court from 1955 to 1971, this merit scholarship and rigorous academic honors program is designed for students with the strongest academic credentials. Students selected for the program may pursue in-depth study in various fields of law through affiliation with one of the law school's five academic research centers. In their second and third years, Harlan scholars are named to the New York Law School Law Review.

Lawyering Skills Center: The center offers several experiential learning programs, including the externship program (second- and third-year students work in selected law offices and complete related assignments at the law school), judicial externships (upperclass students work with judges and their law clerks in New York City and surrounding jurisdictions), and clinics (under faculty supervision, upperclass students work on real cases in the discrimination law enforcement, criminal law, mediation, poverty law, and elder law clinics).

Centers: The law school is home to five academic centers and an institute engaged in research, scholarship, and advocacy. They are the Center for International Law (which derives strength from interaction with New York City's business, financial, and legal communities); the Center for New York City Law (whose goal is to make the city's government and decisions more fair, comprehensible, and open to the public); the Center for Professional Values and Practice (which examines the many roles lawyers play); the Justice Action Center (which seeks to evaluate the efficacy of law as an agent of change and social betterment); the Media Center (which promotes education, discussion, research, and writing about mass-communication law); and the Institute for Information Law and Policy (which promotes the study of information, communication, and law in the global digital age).

In addition to the J.D. degree, the law school offers the joint J.D./M.B.A., and an LL.M. in taxation.

STUDENT BODY

Fall 2005 full-time enrollment: 1,106

Men: 46%	Women: 54%
African-American: 4.6%	American Indian: 0.5%
Asian-American: 6.6%	Mexican-American: 0.9%
Puerto Rican: 0.9%	Other Hisp-Amer: 4.9%
White: 55.2%	International: 1.4%
Unknown: 25.0%	

Fall 2005 part-time enrollment: 374

Men: 47%	Women: 53%
African-American: 10.2%	American Indian: 0.0%
Asian-American: 11.0%	Mexican-American: 0.3%
Puerto Rican: 1.6%	Other Hisp-Amer: 5.6%
White: 50.8%	International: 0.0%
Unknown: 20.6%	

Attrition rates for 2004-2005 full-time students
Percent of students discontinuing law school:

Men: 8%	Women: 5%
First-year students: 18%	Second-year students: 0%
Third-year students: 0%	

LIBRARY RESOURCES

The library holds 252,031 and receives 5,504 current subscriptions.
Total volumes: 513,597
Percentage of the titles in the online catalog: 99%
Total seats available for library users: 616

INFORMATION TECHNOLOGY

Number of wired network connections available to students: 360 total (in the law library, excluding computer labs: 200; in classrooms: 60; in computer labs: 0; elsewhere in the law school: 100)
Law school has a wireless network.
Approximate number of simultaneous users that can be accommodated on wireless network: 1,500
Students are not required to own a computer.

EMPLOYMENT AND SALARIES

Proportion of 2004 graduates employed at graduation: **N/A**
Employed 9 months later, as of February 15, 2005: **90%**
Salaries in the private sector (law firms, business, industry): **$52,500–$125,000** (25th-75th percentile)
Median salary in the private sector: **$100,000**
Percentage in the private sector who reported salary information: **15%**
Median salary in public service (government, judicial clerkships, academic posts, non-profits): **$43,340**

Percentage of 2004 graduates in:

Law firms: 39%	Bus./industry (legal): 13%
Bus./industry (nonlegal): 4%	Government: 13%
Public interest: 4%	Judicial clerkship: 7%
Academia : 1%	Unknown: 18%

2004 graduates employed in-state: 71%
2004 graduates employed in foreign countries: 1%
Number of states where graduates are employed: 13
Percentage of 2004 graduates working in: New England: 1%, Middle Atlantic: 83%, East North Central: 0%, West North Central: 0%, South Atlantic: 2%, East South Central: 1%, West South Central: 0%, Mountain: 1%, Pacific: 0%, Unknown: 11%

BAR PASSAGE RATES

Based on 2004 graduates taking Summer 2004 or Winter 2005 exams. Most of the school's first-time test takers took the bar in New York.

64%
School's bar passage rate for first-time test takers

75%
Statewide bar passage rate for first-time test takers

New York University

- 40 Washington Square S, New York, NY, 10012
- http://www.law.nyu.edu
- Private
- Year founded: 1835
- 2005-2006 tuition: full-time: $37,150; part-time: N/A
- Enrollment 2005-06 academic year: full-time: 1,424
- U.S. News 2007 law specialty ranking: clinical training: 3, environmental law: 14, intellectual property law: 12, international law: 1, tax law: 1, trial advocacy: 14

3.60-3.89 GPA, 25TH-75TH PERCENTILE

168-172 LSAT, 25TH-75TH PERCENTILE

21% ACCEPTANCE RATE

4 2007 U.S. NEWS LAW SCHOOL RANKING

ADMISSIONS

Admissions phone number: **(212) 998-6060**
Admissions email address: **law.moreinfo@nyu.edu**
Application website: **http://www.law.nyu.edu/depts/admissions/applications/online/jd.html**
Application deadline for Fall 2007 admission: **2/01**

Admissions statistics:

Number of applicants for Fall 2005: **7,872**
Number of acceptances: **1,655**
Number enrolled: **448**
Acceptance rate: **21%**
GPA, 25th-75th percentile, entering class Fall 2005: **3.60-3.89**
LSAT, 25th-75th percentile, entering class Fall 2005: **168-172**

FINANCIAL AID

Financial aid phone number: **(212) 998-6050**
Financial aid application deadline: **4/15**
Tuition 2005-2006 academic year: full-time: **$37,150**; part-time: N/A
Room and board: **$18,400**; books: **$925**; miscellaneous expenses: **$2,720**
Total of room/board/books/miscellaneous expenses: **$22,045**
University does not offer graduate student housing for which law students are eligible.

Financial aid profile

Percent of students that received grants for the 2004-2005 academic year: full-time: **28%**
Median grant amount: full-time: **$17,000**
The average law-school debt of those in the Class of 2005 who borrowed: **$111,850**. Proportion who borrowed: **86%**

ACADEMIC PROGRAMS

Calendar: **semester**
Joint degrees awarded: **J.D./M.A.; J.D./M.B.A.; J.D./M.P.A.; J.D./M.U.P.; J.D./M.S.W.; J.D./Ph.D.; J.D./M.P.A.K.S.**
Typical first-year section size: Full-time: **112**

Is there typically a "small section" of the first year class, other than Legal Writing, taught by full-time faculty?: Full-time: **yes**
Number of course titles, beyond the first year curriculum, offered last year: **253**
Percentages of upper division course sections, excluding seminars, with an enrollment of:

Under 25: **43%**   25 to 49: **24%**
50 to 74: **14%**   75 to 99: **10%**
100+: **8%**

Areas of specialization: appellate advocacy, clinical training, dispute resolution, environmental law, healthcare law, intellectual property law, international law, tax law, trial advocacy

Fall 2005 faculty profile

Total teaching faculty: **232**. Full-time: **58%**; **70%** men, **30%** women, **9%** minorities. Part-time: **42%**; **72%** men, **28%** women, **9%** minorities
Student-to-faculty ratio: **11.1**

SPECIAL PROGRAMS (as provided by law school):

New York University School of Law's curriculum is distinguished by its strength in traditional areas of legal study, interdisciplinary study, and clinical education, its enhanced commitment to students wishing to pursue careers in academia, and its longstanding dedication to educating lawyers to serve the public. Students enjoy the pedagogical diversity of the law school by mixing traditional courses with colloquia, global courses, clinics, independent research, journal work, study abroad, fellowships and more.

The J.D. program is enriched by the graduate program, which offers advanced degrees. Attorneys, law teachers, and judges from over 50 countries enroll each year in degree programs in corporation law, general studies, international legal studies, international taxation, labor and employment law, taxation, and trade regulation.

The curriculum is complemented by several institutes and centers, which include, but are not limited to, the Brennan Center for Justice, the Hauser Global Law School Program, the Institute for International Law and Justice, the Center for

Research in Crime and Justice, the Center for Environmental and Land Use Law, the Center for Law and Business, the Institute for Judicial Administration, and the Jean Monnet Center for International and Regional Economic Law and Justice.

STUDENT BODY

Fall 2005 full-time enrollment: 1,424

Men: 54%	Women: 46%
African-American: 8.6%	American Indian: 0.0%
Asian-American: 10.3%	Mexican-American: 0.5%
Puerto Rican: 0.5%	Other Hisp-Amer: 4.6%
White: 44.8%	International: 3.3%
Unknown: 27.4%	

Attrition rates for 2004-2005 full-time students
Percent of students discontinuing law school:

Men: 1%	Women: 1%
First-year students: 0%	Second-year students: 1%
Third-year students: 0%	

LIBRARY RESOURCES

The library holds 292,848 and receives 7,025 current subscriptions.
Total volumes: 1,082,282
Percentage of the titles in the online catalog: 100%
Total seats available for library users: 850

INFORMATION TECHNOLOGY

Number of wired network connections available to students: 1,810 total (in the law library, excluding computer labs: 35; in classrooms: 700; in computer labs: 25; elsewhere in the law school: 1,050)
Law school has a wireless network.
Approximate number of simultaneous users that can be accommodated on wireless network: 1,200
Students are required to own a computer.

EMPLOYMENT AND SALARIES

Proportion of 2004 graduates employed at graduation: 96%
Employed 9 months later, as of February 15, 2005: 99%
Salaries in the private sector (law firms, business, industry): $125,000–$125,000 (25th-75th percentile)
Median salary in the private sector: $125,000
Percentage in the private sector who reported salary information: 96%
Median salary in public service (government, judicial clerkships, academic posts, non-profits): $48,000

Percentage of 2004 graduates in:

Law firms: 69%	Bus./industry (legal): 0%
Bus./industry (nonlegal): 3%	Government: 4%
Public interest: 10%	Judicial clerkship: 14%
Academia : 0%	Unknown: 0%

2004 graduates employed in-state: 66%
2004 graduates employed in foreign countries: 0%
Number of states where graduates are employed: 32
Percentage of 2004 graduates working in: New England: 3%, Middle Atlantic: 69%, East North Central: 3%, West North Central: 0%, South Atlantic: 10%, East South Central: 1%, West South Central: 2%, Mountain: 1%, Pacific: 11%, Unknown: 0%

BAR PASSAGE RATES

Based on 2004 graduates taking Summer 2004 or Winter 2005 exams. Most of the school's first-time test takers took the bar in New York.

97%
School's bar passage rate for first-time test takers

75%
Statewide bar passage rate for first-time test takers

North Carolina Central University

- 1512 S. Alston Avenue, Durham, NC, 27707
- http://www.acc.nccu.edu/law
- Public
- Year founded: 1939
- 2005-2006 tuition: In-state: full-time: $4,291, part-time: $4,291; Out-of-state: full-time: $16,151
- Enrollment 2005-06 academic year: full-time: 372; part-time: 104
- U.S. News 2007 law specialty ranking: N/A

2.80-3.50	GPA, 25TH-75TH PERCENTILE
143-152	LSAT, 25TH-75TH PERCENTILE
20%	ACCEPTANCE RATE
Tier 4	2007 U.S. NEWS LAW SCHOOL RANKING

ADMISSIONS

Admissions phone number: (919) 530-5243
Admissions email address: recruiter@nccu.edu
Application website: N/A
Application deadline for Fall 2007 admission: 4/15

Admissions statistics:

Number of applicants for Fall 2005: 1,747
Number of acceptances: 350
Number enrolled: 171
Acceptance rate: 20%
GPA, 25th-75th percentile, entering class Fall 2005: 2.80-3.50
LSAT, 25th-75th percentile, entering class Fall 2005: 143-152

Part-time program:

Number of applicants for Fall 2005: 693
Number of acceptances: 131
Number enrolled: 30
Acceptance rate: 19%
GPA, 25th-75th percentile, entering class Fall 2005: 2.90-3.40
LSAT, 25th-75th percentile, entering class Fall 2005: 149-159

FINANCIAL AID

Financial aid phone number: (919) 530-6409
Financial aid application deadline: 7/01
Tuition 2005-2006 academic year: In-state: full-time: $4,291, part-time: $4,291; Out-of-state: full-time: $16,151
Room and board: $7,500; books: $700; miscellaneous expenses: $3,100
Total of room/board/books/miscellaneous expenses: $11,300
University offers graduate student housing for which law students are eligible.

Financial aid profile

Percent of students that received grants for the 2004-2005 academic year: full-time: 20%
Median grant amount: full-time: $3,175

The average law-school debt of those in the Class of 2005 who borrowed: $17,215. Proportion who borrowed: 70%

ACADEMIC PROGRAMS

Calendar: semester
Joint degrees awarded: J.D./M.B.A.; J.D./MLS
Typical first-year section size: Full-time: 84; Part-time: 60
Is there typically a "small section" of the first year class, other than Legal Writing, taught by full-time faculty?: Full-time: no; Part-time: no
Number of course titles, beyond the first year curriculum, offered last year: 58
Percentages of upper division course sections, excluding seminars, with an enrollment of:

Under 25: 64%	25 to 49: 15%
50 to 74: 8%	75 to 99: 9%
100+: 3%	

Areas of specialization: appellate advocacy, clinical training, dispute resolution, environmental law, healthcare law, intellectual property law, international law, tax law, trial advocacy

Fall 2005 faculty profile

Total teaching faculty: 33. Full-time: 52%; 53% men, 47% women, 47% minorities. Part-time: 48%; 50% men, 50% women, 38% minorities
Student-to-faculty ratio: 18.8

SPECIAL PROGRAMS (as provided by law school):

NCCU School of Law offers top notch clinics and joint master's degree programs with the Business and Library schools. Starting in Fall 2006, NCCU School of Law will open a Biotechnology and Pharmaceutical Law Institute and offer a certificate to J.D. graduates who complete related courses.

The clinical legal education program of NCCU School of Law is a central feature of the school and is committed to producing excellent attorneys who are sensitive to addressing the needs of people and communities that are traditionally underserved and underrepresented by the legal profession. Students have an opportunity to pursue justice in a variety of legal disciplines since NCCU School of Law offers seven clinical programs: Pro Bono,

Alternative Dispute Resolution, Criminal Litigation, Civil Litigation, Family, Small Business, and Domestic Violence Advocacy. Students also can work with local attorneys through externship opportunities in the clinic. Summer school is a continuation of the Evening Program, with part-time students enrolling in selected elective courses from May through August. Full-time students often take these classes in addition to their summer employment in the Triangle area. Additionally, numerous clinical courses are offered in the daytime hours throughout the summer.

STUDENT BODY

Fall 2005 full-time enrollment: 372

Men: 36%	Women: 64%
African-American: 53.2%	American Indian: 0.5%
Asian-American: 3.2%	Mexican-American: 0.0%
Puerto Rican: 0.5%	Other Hisp-Amer: 1.6%
White: 36.3%	International: 0.0%
Unknown: 4.6%	

Fall 2005 part-time enrollment: 104

Men: 50%	Women: 50%
African-American: 18.3%	American Indian: 2.9%
Asian-American: 4.8%	Mexican-American: 0.0%
Puerto Rican: 1.9%	Other Hisp-Amer: 1.9%
White: 69.2%	International: 0.0%
Unknown: 1.0%	

Attrition rates for 2004-2005 full-time students
Percent of students discontinuing law school:

Men: 5%	Women: 6%
First-year students: 13%	Second-year students: 2%
Third-year students: N/A	

LIBRARY RESOURCES

The library holds 63,509 and receives 4,250 current subscriptions.
Total volumes: 340,040
Percentage of the titles in the online catalog: 99%
Total seats available for library users: 256

INFORMATION TECHNOLOGY

Number of wired network connections available to students: 51 total (in the law library, excluding computer labs: 4; in classrooms: 11; in computer labs: 30; elsewhere in the law school: 6)

Law school has a wireless network.
Approximate number of simultaneous users that can be accommodated on wireless network: 500
Students are not required to own a computer.

EMPLOYMENT AND SALARIES

Proportion of 2004 graduates employed at graduation: **N/A**
Employed 9 months later, as of February 15, 2005: **83%**
Salaries in the private sector (law firms, business, industry): **N/A–N/A** (25th-75th percentile)
Median salary in the private sector: **N/A**
Percentage in the private sector who reported salary information: **0%**
Median salary in public service (government, judicial clerkships, academic posts, non-profits): **N/A**

Percentage of 2004 graduates in:

Law firms: 62%	Bus./industry (legal): 9%
Bus./industry (nonlegal): N/A	Government: 12%
Public interest: 12%	Judicial clerkship: 4%
Academia : 1%	Unknown: 0%

2004 graduates employed in-state: 86%
2004 graduates employed in foreign countries: 0%
Number of states where graduates are employed: 7
Percentage of 2004 graduates working in: New England: 1%, Middle Atlantic: 1%, East North Central: 5%, West North Central: 1%, South Atlantic: 88%, East South Central: 2%, West South Central: 1%, Mountain: 2%, Pacific: 1%, Unknown: 0%

BAR PASSAGE RATES

Based on 2004 graduates taking Summer 2004 or Winter 2005 exams. Most of the school's first-time test takers took the bar in North Carolina.

72%
School's bar passage rate for first-time test takers

75%
Statewide bar passage rate for first-time test takers

Northeastern University

■ 400 Huntington Avenue, Boston, MA, 02115
■ http://www.slaw.neu.edu
■ Private
■ **Year founded:** 1898
■ **2005-2006 tuition:** full-time: $32,811; part-time: N/A
■ **Enrollment 2005-06 academic year:** full-time: 623
■ **U.S. News 2007 law specialty ranking:** clinical training: 24

3.10-3.58	GPA, 25TH-75TH PERCENTILE
159-163	LSAT, 25TH-75TH PERCENTILE
27%	ACCEPTANCE RATE
87	2007 U.S. NEWS LAW SCHOOL RANKING

ADMISSIONS

Admissions phone number: **(617) 373-2395**
Admissions email address: **lawadmissions@nunet.neu.edu**
Application website:
   http://www.slaw.neu.edu/admiss/appadmis.htm
Application deadline for Fall 2007 admission: **3/01**

Admissions statistics:
Number of applicants for Fall 2005: **3,708**
Number of acceptances: **986**
Number enrolled: **212**
Acceptance rate: **27%**
GPA, 25th-75th percentile, entering class Fall 2005:
   3.10-3.58
LSAT, 25th-75th percentile, entering class Fall 2005:
   159-163

FINANCIAL AID

Financial aid phone number: **(617) 373-4620**
Financial aid application deadline: **2/15**
Tuition 2005-2006 academic year: full-time: **$32,811**; part-time: N/A
Room and board: **$13,275**; books: **$1,200**; miscellaneous
   expenses: **$1,323**
Total of room/board/books/miscellaneous expenses:
   $15,798
University offers graduate student housing for which law
   students are eligible.

Financial aid profile
Percent of students that received grants for the 2004-2005
   academic year: full-time: **73%**
Median grant amount: full-time: **$7,000**
The average law-school debt of those in the Class of 2005
   who borrowed: **$80,484**. Proportion who borrowed: **91%**

ACADEMIC PROGRAMS

Calendar: **quarter**
Joint degrees awarded: **J.D./M.P.H.; J.D./M.B.A.;**
   J.D./M.S./M.B.A.; J.D./M.S./PH.D.
Typical first-year section size: Full-time: **72**

Is there typically a "small section" of the first year class,
   other than Legal Writing, taught by full-time faculty?:
   Full-time: **no**
Number of course titles, beyond the first year curriculum,
   offered last year: **72**
Percentages of upper division course sections, excluding
   seminars, with an enrollment of:
   Under 25: **60%**   25 to 49: **29%**
   50 to 74: **6%**   75 to 99: **4%**
   100+: **1%**
Areas of specialization: appellate advocacy, clinical training,
   dispute resolution, environmental law, healthcare law,
   intellectual property law, international law, tax law, trial
   advocacy

Fall 2005 faculty profile
Total teaching faculty: **56**. Full-time: **54%**; 47% men, 53%
   women, 30% minorities. Part-time: **46%**; 38% men,
   62% women, 4% minorities
Student-to-faculty ratio: **17.0**

SPECIAL PROGRAMS *(as provided by law school):*

Northeastern University School of Law offers the nation's only
Cooperative Legal Education Program. This innovative approach
provides all students with a full year of hands-on legal experience
gained through four, three-month internships in law offices,
judges' chambers and other organizations throughout the world.
By participating in co-op placements with four different legal
employers, students have an extraordinary opportunity to experience the actual practice of law and to integrate practical experience with an excellent theoretical foundation of in-depth
classroom study. The Co-op Program also contributes to students' postgraduate success. On average, 40 percent of
Northeastern law students accept postgraduate employment with
one of their former co-op employers. The School of Law is a
national leader in education, research and service initiatives
addressing the most pressing challenges facing society. Through
its clinics, institutes and research centers, faculty and students
advocate together for those too-often underrepresented in the
justice system. By crafting interdisciplinary approaches to complex problems, the clinics, institutes and research centers reflect

a commitment to social and economic justice that distinguishes Northeastern as the nation's foremost public interest law school. The law school offers six upper-level courses in clinical legal education: Certiorari, Criminal Advocacy, Domestic Violence, Poverty Law and Practice, Prisoners' Rights, and Public Health. A variety of institutes, projects and special programs reflect the law school's commitment to interdisciplinary research and action: Domestic Violence Institute, Public Health Advocacy Institute, Tobacco Products Liability Project/ Tobacco Control Resource Center, Program on Human Rights and the Global Economy and the Partnering for Prevention and Community Safety Initiative.

STUDENT BODY

Fall 2005 full-time enrollment: 623

Men: 39%	Women: 61%
African-American: 7.4%	American Indian: 1.3%
Asian-American: 12.4%	Mexican-American: 0.0%
Puerto Rican: 0.0%	Other Hisp-Amer: 8.2%
White: 61.6%	International: 0.2%
Unknown: 9.0%	

Attrition rates for 2004-2005 full-time students
Percent of students discontinuing law school:

Men: 3%	Women: 2%
First-year students: 5%	Second-year students: 2%
Third-year students: N/A	

LIBRARY RESOURCES

The library holds 42,806 and receives 3,057 current subscriptions.
Total volumes: 275,908
Percentage of the titles in the online catalog: 100%
Total seats available for library users: 422

INFORMATION TECHNOLOGY

Number of wired network connections available to students: 139 total (in the law library, excluding computer labs: 57; in classrooms: 10; in computer labs: 50; elsewhere in the law school: 22)
Law school has a wireless network.

Approximate number of simultaneous users that can be accommodated on wireless network: 60
Students are not required to own a computer.

EMPLOYMENT AND SALARIES

Proportion of 2004 graduates employed at graduation: **N/A**
Employed 9 months later, as of February 15, 2005: **95%**
Salaries in the private sector (law firms, business, industry): **$45,000–$110,000** (25th-75th percentile)
Median salary in the private sector: **$70,000**
Percentage in the private sector who reported salary information: **58%**
Median salary in public service (government, judicial clerkships, academic posts, non-profits): **$42,000**

Percentage of 2004 graduates in:

Law firms: 37%	Bus./industry (legal): 8%
Bus./industry (nonlegal): 0%	Government: 17%
Public interest: 18%	Judicial clerkship: 18%
Academia : 2%	Unknown: 0%

2004 graduates employed in-state: 66%
2004 graduates employed in foreign countries: 1%
Number of states where graduates are employed: 18
Percentage of 2004 graduates working in: New England: 66%, Middle Atlantic: 12%, East North Central: 1%, West North Central: 1%, South Atlantic: 8%, East South Central: 0%, West South Central: 0%, Mountain: 1%, Pacific: 10%, Unknown: 0%

BAR PASSAGE RATES

Based on 2004 graduates taking Summer 2004 or Winter 2005 exams. Most of the school's first-time test takers took the bar in Massachusetts.

82%
School's bar passage rate for first-time test takers

84%
Statewide bar passage rate for first-time test takers

Northern Illinois University

- De Kalb, IL, 60115
- http://law.niu.edu
- Public
- **Year founded:** 1975
- **2005-2006 tuition:** In-state: full-time: $11,228, part-time: $468/ credit hour; Out-of-state: full-time: $20,138
- **Enrollment 2005-06 academic year:** full-time: 320; part-time: 14
- **U.S. News 2007 law specialty ranking:** N/A

3.05-3.63 GPA, 25TH-75TH PERCENTILE

154-158 LSAT, 25TH-75TH PERCENTILE

35% ACCEPTANCE RATE

Tier 3 2007 U.S. NEWS LAW SCHOOL RANKING

ADMISSIONS

Admissions phone number: **(815) 753-9485**
Admissions email address: **lawadm@niu.edu**
Application website: **http://law.niu.edu**
Application deadline for Fall 2007 admission: **5/15**

Admissions statistics:

Number of applicants for Fall 2005: **1,452**
Number of acceptances: **506**
Number enrolled: **128**
Acceptance rate: **35%**
GPA, 25th-75th percentile, entering class Fall 2005: **3.05-3.63**
LSAT, 25th-75th percentile, entering class Fall 2005: **154-158**

Part-time program:

Number of applicants for Fall 2005: **28**
Number of acceptances: **8**
Number enrolled: **4**
Acceptance rate: **29%**
GPA, 25th-75th percentile, entering class Fall 2005: **2.59-3.61**
LSAT, 25th-75th percentile, entering class Fall 2005: **156-161**

FINANCIAL AID

Financial aid phone number: **(815) 753-9485**
Financial aid application deadline: **3/01**
Tuition 2005-2006 academic year: In-state: full-time: **$11,228,** part-time: **$468/credit hour;** Out-of-state: full-time: **$20,138**
Room and board: **$7,850;** books: **$1,500;** miscellaneous expenses: **$2,862**
Total of room/board/books/miscellaneous expenses: **$12,212**
University offers graduate student housing for which law students are eligible.

Financial aid profile

Percent of students that received grants for the 2004-2005 academic year: full-time: **21%**

Median grant amount: full-time: **$8,346**
The average law-school debt of those in the Class of 2005 who borrowed: **$41,900.** Proportion who borrowed: **81%**

ACADEMIC PROGRAMS

Calendar: **semester**
Joint degrees awarded: **J.D./M.B.A.; J.D./MPA**
Typical first-year section size: Full-time: **53**
Is there typically a "small section" of the first year class, other than Legal Writing, taught by full-time faculty?: Full-time: **no**
Number of course titles, beyond the first year curriculum, offered last year: **53**
Percentages of upper division course sections, excluding seminars, with an enrollment of:

Under 25: **49%**   25 to 49: **16%**
50 to 74: **29%**   75 to 99: **6%**
100+: **0%**

Areas of specialization: appellate advocacy, clinical training, dispute resolution, environmental law, healthcare law, intellectual property law, international law, tax law, trial advocacy

Fall 2005 faculty profile

Total teaching faculty: **26.** Full-time: **62%; 56%** men, **44%** women, **44%** minorities. Part-time: **38%; 100%** men, **0%** women, **10%** minorities
Student-to-faculty ratio: **18.4**

SPECIAL PROGRAMS *(as provided by law school):*

Zeke Giorgi Legal Clinic: Located in downtown Rockford, Illinois, the clinic provides legal services to persons who might not otherwise have access to legal representation. Users of the clinic include victims of domestic abuse, the elderly, and parties involved in mediation services. The clinic also provides general information and referral services. Legal representation is provided by qualified College of Law students under the supervision of a licensed attorney.

The Zeke Giorgi Legal Clinic provides students an opportunity to complement classroom education with practical experience. This promotes both an understanding of and appreciation for professional responsibility in the context of the practice of law and the development of lawyering skills. Through the clinical experience, students participate in an educational process where legal theory and law practice interact through direct representation of and advocacy for individuals who might not otherwise have access to the judicial system.

Summer study: The College of Law offers upper-level courses during the summer.

Foreign study: The College of Law offers a summer program abroad in Agen, France. Courses are taught by members of the Northern Illinois University faculty in cooperation with members of the law faculty of the University of Bordeaux-Montesquieu IV.

Civil and criminal externships: Students in the civil externship work in the offices of Prairie State Legal Services, the regional provider of legal services to indigent persons and senior citizens. In the criminal externship, students experience the practice of criminal law either as prosecutors in the offices of the state's attorney or as defense counsel in the offices of the public defender.

Judicial externship program: Students receive academic credit for working for one semester as a law clerk for a state or federal judge.

Appellate Defender Clinic: Students work under the supervision of the same attorneys who assist in teaching the appellate advocacy course and are given the opportunity in a practice setting to work on active cases.

Pro bono service opportunities: Pro bono service is defined as work done for the benefit of underserved populations in public agencies, public-interest or pro bono organizations, or charitable or other nonprofit groups or corporations. Various forms of scholarships, stipends, or other grants are designated for the support of students performing voluntary service.

STUDENT BODY

Fall 2005 full-time enrollment: 320

Men: 49%	Women: 51%
African-American: 8.4%	American Indian: 0.3%
Asian-American: 6.9%	Mexican-American: 6.6%
Puerto Rican: 0.0%	Other Hisp-Amer: 0.0%
White: 77.2%	International: 0.3%
Unknown: 0.3%	

Fall 2005 part-time enrollment: 14

Men: 36%	Women: 64%
African-American: 7.1%	American Indian: 7.1%
Asian-American: 0.0%	Mexican-American: 0.0%
Puerto Rican: 0.0%	Other Hisp-Amer: 14.3%
White: 64.3%	International: 0.0%
Unknown: 7.1%	

Attrition rates for 2004-2005 full-time students

Percent of students discontinuing law school:

Men: 5%	Women: 3%
First-year students: 10%	Second-year students: 2%
Third-year students: N/A	

LIBRARY RESOURCES

The library holds 39,673 and receives 3,264 current subscriptions.

Total volumes: 242,270

Percentage of the titles in the online catalog: 100%

Total seats available for library users: 215

INFORMATION TECHNOLOGY

Number of wired network connections available to students: 16 total (in the law library, excluding computer labs: 14; in classrooms: 2; in computer labs: 0; elsewhere in the law school: 0)

Law school has a wireless network.

Approximate number of simultaneous users that can be accommodated on wireless network: 150

Students are not required to own a computer.

EMPLOYMENT AND SALARIES

Proportion of 2004 graduates employed at graduation: 52%

Employed 9 months later, as of February 15, 2005: 90%

Salaries in the private sector (law firms, business, industry): $40,000–$50,000 (25th-75th percentile)

Median salary in the private sector: $44,000

Percentage in the private sector who reported salary information: 73%

Median salary in public service (government, judicial clerkships, academic posts, non-profits): $42,000

Percentage of 2004 graduates in:

Law firms: 55%	Bus./industry (legal): 10%
Bus./industry (nonlegal): N/A	Government: 24%
Public interest: 4%	Judicial clerkship: 4%
Academia : 3%	Unknown: 0%

2004 graduates employed in-state: 81%

2004 graduates employed in foreign countries: 0%

Number of states where graduates are employed: 12

Percentage of 2004 graduates working in: New England: 0%, Middle Atlantic: 0%, East North Central: 87%, West North Central: 1%, South Atlantic: 1%, East South Central: 0%, West South Central: 4%, Mountain: 0%, Pacific: 1%, Unknown: 5%

BAR PASSAGE RATES

Based on 2004 graduates taking Summer 2004 or Winter 2005 exams. Most of the school's first-time test takers took the bar in Illinois.

86%

School's bar passage rate for first-time test takers

85%

Statewide bar passage rate for first-time test takers

Northern Kentucky University (Chase)

- Nunn Hall, Highland Heights, KY, 41099-6031
- http://www.nku.edu/~chase
- Public
- Year founded: 1893
- 2005-2006 tuition: In-state: full-time: $10,128, part-time: $7,596; Out-of-state: full-time: $22,104
- Enrollment 2005-06 academic year: full-time: 296; part-time: 283
- U.S. News 2007 law specialty ranking: N/A

3.01-3.57 GPA, 25TH-75TH PERCENTILE

152-158 LSAT, 25TH-75TH PERCENTILE

25% ACCEPTANCE RATE

Tier 4 2007 U.S. NEWS LAW SCHOOL RANKING

ADMISSIONS
Admissions phone number: **(859) 572-5384**
Admissions email address: **beersk@nku.edu**
Application website: **N/A**
Application deadline for Fall 2007 admission: **3/01**

Admissions statistics:
Number of applicants for Fall 2005: **858**
Number of acceptances: **213**
Number enrolled: **110**
Acceptance rate: **25%**
GPA, 25th-75th percentile, entering class Fall 2005: **3.01-3.57**
LSAT, 25th-75th percentile, entering class Fall 2005: **152-158**

Part-time program:
Number of applicants for Fall 2005: **187**
Number of acceptances: **100**
Number enrolled: **78**
Acceptance rate: **53%**
GPA, 25th-75th percentile, entering class Fall 2005: **3.03-3.56**
LSAT, 25th-75th percentile, entering class Fall 2005: **150-154**

FINANCIAL AID
Financial aid phone number: **(859) 572-6437**
Financial aid application deadline: **3/01**
Tuition 2005-2006 academic year: In-state: full-time: **$10,128**, part-time: **$7,596**; Out-of-state: full-time: **$22,104**
Room and board: **$13,604**; books: **$1,000**; miscellaneous expenses: **$0**
Total of room/board/books/miscellaneous expenses: **$14,604**
University offers graduate student housing for which law students are eligible.

Financial aid profile
Percent of students that received grants for the 2004-2005 academic year: full-time: **37%**; part-time **12%**
Median grant amount: full-time: **$9,240**; part-time: **$6,930**

The average law-school debt of those in the Class of 2005 who borrowed: **$56,736**. Proportion who borrowed: **71%**

ACADEMIC PROGRAMS
Calendar: **semester**
Joint degrees awarded: **J.D./M.B.A.**
Typical first-year section size: Full-time: **108**; Part-time: **113**
Is there typically a "small section" of the first year class, other than Legal Writing, taught by full-time faculty?: Full-time: **yes**; Part-time: **yes**
Number of course titles, beyond the first year curriculum, offered last year: **62**
Percentages of upper division course sections, excluding seminars, with an enrollment of:

Under 25: **57%**	25 to 49: **27%**
50 to 74: **12%**	75 to 99: **2%**
100+: **1%**	

Areas of specialization: appellate advocacy, clinical training, dispute resolution, environmental law, healthcare law, intellectual property law, international law, tax law, trial advocacy

Fall 2005 faculty profile
Total teaching faculty: **32**. Full-time: **72%**; **74%** men, **26%** women, **13%** minorities. Part-time: **28%**; **56%** men, **44%** women, **0%** minorities
Student-to-faculty ratio: **17.4**

SPECIAL PROGRAMS (as provided by law school):
Special programs include internships through the Local Government Law Center and externships at the Innocence Project of the Kentucky Department of Public Advocacy, Internal Revenue Service, U.S. Court of Appeals for the Sixth Circuit, Children's Law Center, and numerous courts and agencies in Kentucky and Ohio. Interest on Lawyer Trust Account (IOLTA) fellowships are also awarded for student placement in Northern Kentucky Legal Aid. Scholarships are available for students participating in trial advocacy courses that include competition.

STUDENT BODY

Fall 2005 full-time enrollment: 296

Men: 55%	Women: 45%
African-American: 4.4%	American Indian: 1.4%
Asian-American: 1.0%	Mexican-American: 0.0%
Puerto Rican: 0.0%	Other Hisp-Amer: 1.7%
White: 91.6%	International: 0.0%
Unknown: 0.0%	

Fall 2005 part-time enrollment: 283

Men: 53%	Women: 47%
African-American: 4.6%	American Indian: 0.4%
Asian-American: 0.7%	Mexican-American: 0.0%
Puerto Rican: 0.0%	Other Hisp-Amer: 2.1%
White: 92.2%	International: 0.0%
Unknown: 0.0%	

Attrition rates for 2004-2005 full-time students
Percent of students discontinuing law school:

Men: 13%	Women: 9%
First-year students: 16%	Second-year students: 16%
Third-year students: 3%	

LIBRARY RESOURCES

The library holds 65,465 and receives 2,290 current subscriptions.
Total volumes: 317,855
Percentage of the titles in the online catalog: 100%
Total seats available for library users: 222

INFORMATION TECHNOLOGY

Number of wired network connections available to students: 23 total (in the law library, excluding computer labs: 19; in classrooms: 0; in computer labs: 0; elsewhere in the law school: 4)
Law school has a wireless network.
Approximate number of simultaneous users that can be accommodated on wireless network: 600
Students are not required to own a computer.

EMPLOYMENT AND SALARIES

Proportion of 2004 graduates employed at graduation: 65%
Employed 9 months later, as of February 15, 2005: 92%
Salaries in the private sector (law firms, business, industry): $50,000–$81,000 (25th-75th percentile)
Median salary in the private sector: $60,000
Percentage in the private sector who reported salary information: 49%
Median salary in public service (government, judicial clerkships, academic posts, non-profits): $41,557

Percentage of 2004 graduates in:

Law firms: 45%	Bus./industry (legal): 24%
Bus./industry (nonlegal): 0%	Government: 13%
Public interest: 9%	Judicial clerkship: 6%
Academia : 3%	Unknown: 0%

2004 graduates employed in-state: 41%
2004 graduates employed in foreign countries: 0%
Number of states where graduates are employed: 6
Percentage of 2004 graduates working in: New England: 0%, Middle Atlantic: 0%, East North Central: 55%, West North Central: 0%, South Atlantic: 3%, East South Central: 41%, West South Central: 0%, Mountain: 0%, Pacific: 1%, Unknown: 0%

BAR PASSAGE RATES

Based on 2004 graduates taking Summer 2004 or Winter 2005 exams. Most of the school's first-time test takers took the bar in Kentucky.

79%
School's bar passage rate for first-time test takers

78%
Statewide bar passage rate for first-time test takers

Northwestern University

- 357 E. Chicago Avenue, Chicago, IL, 60611
- http://www.law.northwestern.edu
- Private
- Year founded: 1859
- 2005-2006 tuition: full-time: $38,372; part-time: N/A
- Enrollment 2005-06 academic year: full-time: 772
- U.S. News 2007 law specialty ranking: clinical training: 9, dispute resolution: 11, tax law: 4, trial advocacy: 7

3.46-3.78	GPA, 25TH-75TH PERCENTILE
167-171	LSAT, 25TH-75TH PERCENTILE
17%	ACCEPTANCE RATE
12	2007 U.S. NEWS LAW SCHOOL RANKING

ADMISSIONS

Admissions phone number: (312) 503-8465
Admissions email address:
   nulawadm@law.northwestern.edu
Application website: http://www.law.nwu.edu/depts/admissions/index.htm
Application deadline for Fall 2007 admission: 2/15

Admissions statistics:
Number of applicants for Fall 2005: 4,678
Number of acceptances: 781
Number enrolled: 243
Acceptance rate: 17%
GPA, 25th-75th percentile, entering class Fall 2005:
   3.46-3.78
LSAT, 25th-75th percentile, entering class Fall 2005:
   167-171

FINANCIAL AID

Financial aid phone number: (312) 503-8465
Financial aid application deadline: 2/15
Tuition 2005-2006 academic year: full-time: $38,372; part-time: N/A
Room and board: $12,078; books: $1,382; miscellaneous expenses: $6,616
Total of room/board/books/miscellaneous expenses:
   $20,076
University offers graduate student housing for which law students are eligible.

Financial aid profile
Percent of students that received grants for the 2004-2005 academic year: full-time: 36%
Median grant amount: full-time: $16,000
The average law-school debt of those in the Class of 2005 who borrowed: $110,868. Proportion who borrowed: 76%

ACADEMIC PROGRAMS

Calendar: **semester**
Joint degrees awarded: **JD/MBA; JD/PhD; MSL-MSJ**
Typical first-year section size: Full-time: **65**

Is there typically a "small section" of the first year class, other than Legal Writing, taught by full-time faculty?:
   Full-time: **no**
Number of course titles, beyond the first year curriculum, offered last year: **198**
Percentages of upper division course sections, excluding seminars, with an enrollment of:

Under 25: **43%**	25 to 49: **33%**
50 to 74: **20%**	75 to 99: **3%**
100+: **1%**	

Areas of specialization: appellate advocacy, clinical training, dispute resolution, environmental law, healthcare law, intellectual property law, international law, tax law, trial advocacy

Fall 2005 faculty profile
Total teaching faculty: 115. Full-time: 50%; 67% men, 33% women, 11% minorities. Part-time: 50%; 83% men, 17% women, 7% minorities
Student-to-faculty ratio: 11.9

SPECIAL PROGRAMS *(as provided by law school):*

Northwestern provides a superior foundation in legal reasoning, analysis, and writing as well as a thorough understanding of the structures and policies of the law. But communication, collaborative learning, teamwork, and cross-training in business are hallmarks of Northwestern, and students' interpersonal skills grow along with their legal skills.

Emphasis on communication and interpersonal skills begins during the admissions process, in which every applicant is urged to interview. We also place a heavy emphasis on work experience, which contributes to students learning a great deal from not only faculty but also one another.

Team building begins at orientation, and it continues throughout the curriculum. Second- and third-year students may participate in an international team project, in which they research a foreign country and then travel to that country for two weeks in the spring to conduct fieldwork.

Courses are offered in cooperation with the Kellogg School of Management in areas such as finance, accounting, statistics, business law, mergers and acquisitions, and negotiations.

Northwestern offers the largest and most integrated three-year J.D./M.B.A. program in the country.

In our comprehensive clinical program, students learn strong litigation and negotiation skills and gain experience representing clients and reforming laws and legal institutions.

Our innovative simulation-based curriculum, including the Program on Advocacy and Professionalism and the Program on Negotiations and Mediation, both part of the Bartlit Center for Trial Strategy, gives students the skills they need to negotiate and communicate effectively, solve problems, prepare briefs, examine witnesses, present evidence, and argue cases.

After learning these skills, students gain real-world training working in public-interest organizations, businesses, judges' chambers, and criminal and defense law offices through our extensive externship program.

Students work with clinical faculty to represent impoverished clients. Working in teams, they prepare cases in juvenile justice, immigration and asylum, and criminal matters. Bluhm Legal Clinic centers—on children and family justice, small-business opportunity, international human rights, wrongful convictions, and investor protection—are nationally recognized.

Finally, through the Owen L. Coon/James A. Rahl Senior Research Program, third-year students have the opportunity to work closely with Northwestern's renowned faculty, exploring answers to challenging questions of doctrine and policy.

STUDENT BODY

Fall 2005 full-time enrollment: 772

Men: 53%	Women: 47%
African-American: 7.1%	American Indian: 0.3%
Asian-American: 15.5%	Mexican-American: 0.3%
Puerto Rican: 0.5%	Other Hisp-Amer: 7.1%
White: 58.3%	International: 0.0%
Unknown: 10.9%	

Attrition rates for 2004-2005 full-time students

Percent of students discontinuing law school:

Men: N/A	Women: N/A
First-year students: N/A	Second-year students: N/A
Third-year students: N/A	

LIBRARY RESOURCES

The library holds 333,211 and receives 5,452 current subscriptions.

Total volumes: 733,026

Percentage of the titles in the online catalog: 99%

Total seats available for library users: 651

INFORMATION TECHNOLOGY

Number of wired network connections available to students: 218 total (in the law library, excluding computer labs: 73; in classrooms: 64; in computer labs: 2; elsewhere in the law school: 79)

Law school has a wireless network.

Approximate number of simultaneous users that can be accommodated on wireless network: 800

Students are required to own a computer.

EMPLOYMENT AND SALARIES

Proportion of 2004 graduates employed at graduation: 97%

Employed 9 months later, as of February 15, 2005: 99%

Salaries in the private sector (law firms, business, industry): $125,000–$125,000 (25th-75th percentile)

Median salary in the private sector: $125,000

Percentage in the private sector who reported salary information: 100%

Median salary in public service (government, judicial clerkships, academic posts, non-profits): $50,000

Percentage of 2004 graduates in:

Law firms: 79%	Bus./industry (legal): 4%
Bus./industry (nonlegal): N/A	Government: 5%
Public interest: 1%	Judicial clerkship: 11%
Academia : 0%	Unknown: 0%

2004 graduates employed in-state: 46%

2004 graduates employed in foreign countries: 1%

Number of states where graduates are employed: 24

Percentage of 2004 graduates working in: New England: 1%, Middle Atlantic: 17%, East North Central: 52%, West North Central: 2%, South Atlantic: 10%, East South Central: 1%, West South Central: 3%, Mountain: 2%, Pacific: 11%, Unknown: 0%

BAR PASSAGE RATES

Based on 2004 graduates taking Summer 2004 or Winter 2005 exams. Most of the school's first-time test takers took the bar in Illinois.

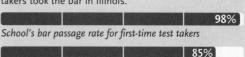

98%

School's bar passage rate for first-time test takers

85%

Statewide bar passage rate for first-time test takers

Nova Southeastern University (Broad)

- 3305 College Avenue, Fort Lauderdale, FL, 33314-7721
- http://www.nsulaw.nova.edu/
- Private
- Year founded: 1974
- 2005-2006 tuition: full-time: $25,780; part-time: $19,460
- Enrollment 2005-06 academic year: full-time: 744; part-time: 199
- U.S. News 2007 law specialty ranking: N/A

2.93-3.37	GPA, 25TH-75TH PERCENTILE
148-152	LSAT, 25TH-75TH PERCENTILE
28%	ACCEPTANCE RATE
Tier 4	2007 U.S. NEWS LAW SCHOOL RANKING

ADMISSIONS

Admissions phone number: **(954) 262-6117**
Admissions email address: **admission@nsu.law.nova.edu**
Application website: **http://www.nsulaw.nova.edu/admissions/index.cfm**
Application deadline for Fall 2007 admission: **3/01**

Admissions statistics:

Number of applicants for Fall 2005: **2,442**
Number of acceptances: **680**
Number enrolled: **270**
Acceptance rate: **28%**
GPA, 25th-75th percentile, entering class Fall 2005: **2.93-3.37**
LSAT, 25th-75th percentile, entering class Fall 2005: **148-152**

Part-time program:

Number of applicants for Fall 2005: **371**
Number of acceptances: **95**
Number enrolled: **66**
Acceptance rate: **26%**
GPA, 25th-75th percentile, entering class Fall 2005: **2.68-3.38**
LSAT, 25th-75th percentile, entering class Fall 2005: **148-153**

FINANCIAL AID

Financial aid phone number: **(954) 262-7412**
Financial aid application deadline: **4/15**
Tuition 2005-2006 academic year: full-time: **$25,780**; part-time: **$19,460**
Room and board: **$10,431**; books: **$1,200**; miscellaneous expenses: **$4,895**
Total of room/board/books/miscellaneous expenses: **$16,526**
University does not offer graduate student housing for which law students are eligible.

Financial aid profile

Percent of students that received grants for the 2004-2005 academic year: full-time: **19%**; part-time **20%**
Median grant amount: full-time: **$7,000**; part-time: **$5,000**
The average law-school debt of those in the Class of 2005 who borrowed: **$84,536**. Proportion who borrowed: **82%**

ACADEMIC PROGRAMS

Calendar: **semester**
Joint degrees awarded: **J.D./M.B.A.; J.D./MS (Computers); J.D./MS (Psychology); J.D./MS (Dispute Resolution); J.D./MURP (Urban & Regional Planning)**
Typical first-year section size: Full-time: **59**; Part-time: **62**
Is there typically a "small section" of the first year class, other than Legal Writing, taught by full-time faculty?: Full-time: **no**; Part-time: **no**
Number of course titles, beyond the first year curriculum, offered last year: **129**
Percentages of upper division course sections, excluding seminars, with an enrollment of:

Under 25: **71%**	25 to 49: **15%**
50 to 74: **7%**	75 to 99: **7%**
100+: **0%**	

Areas of specialization: appellate advocacy, clinical training, dispute resolution, environmental law, healthcare law, intellectual property law, international law, tax law, trial advocacy

Fall 2005 faculty profile

Total teaching faculty: **131**. Full-time: **42%**; **51%** men, **49%** women, **18%** minorities. Part-time: **58%**; **75%** men, **25%** women, **14%** minorities
Student-to-faculty ratio: **13.4**

SPECIAL PROGRAMS (as provided by law school):

Every student is guaranteed a seat in a full-semester, in-house or externship clinic (alternative dispute resolution, business, children/family, criminal, environmental/land use, international, or personal injury).

Students may also earn credit for judicial clerkships and serving as a guardian ad litem.

Bilingual students can participate in a dual-degree program with the University of Barcelona and be prepared for admission to the bar in Spain and Latin American countries.

STUDENT BODY

Fall 2005 full-time enrollment: 744

Men: 50%	Women: 50%
African-American: 5.0%	American Indian: 0.1%
Asian-American: 3.0%	Mexican-American: 0.9%
Puerto Rican: 1.3%	Other Hisp-Amer: 15.6%
White: 67.7%	International: 2.0%
Unknown: 4.3%	

Fall 2005 part-time enrollment: 199

Men: 47%	Women: 53%
African-American: 9.0%	American Indian: 0.5%
Asian-American: 3.0%	Mexican-American: 0.0%
Puerto Rican: 2.5%	Other Hisp-Amer: 22.6%
White: 59.8%	International: 0.0%
Unknown: 2.5%	

Attrition rates for 2004-2005 full-time students

Percent of students discontinuing law school:

Men: 10%	Women: 7%
First-year students: 21%	Second-year students: 2%
Third-year students: N/A	

LIBRARY RESOURCES

The library holds 149,755 and receives 5,467 current subscriptions.

Total volumes: 359,673

Percentage of the titles in the online catalog: 100%

Total seats available for library users: 524

INFORMATION TECHNOLOGY

Number of wired network connections available to students: 0 total (in the law library, excluding computer labs: 0; in classrooms: 0; in computer labs: 0; elsewhere in the law school: 0)

Law school has a wireless network.

Approximate number of simultaneous users that can be accommodated on wireless network: 1,200

Students are required to own a computer.

EMPLOYMENT AND SALARIES

Proportion of 2004 graduates employed at graduation: N/A

Employed 9 months later, as of February 15, 2005: 77%

Salaries in the private sector (law firms, business, industry): $45,000–$65,000 (25th-75th percentile)

Median salary in the private sector: $51,000

Percentage in the private sector who reported salary information: 58%

Median salary in public service (government, judicial clerkships, academic posts, non-profits): $38,000

Percentage of 2004 graduates in:

Law firms: 56%	Bus./industry (legal): 12%
Bus./industry (nonlegal): N/A	Government: 17%
Public interest: 6%	Judicial clerkship: 3%
Academia : 2%	Unknown: 3%

2004 graduates employed in-state: 88%

2004 graduates employed in foreign countries: 0%

Number of states where graduates are employed: 11

Percentage of 2004 graduates working in: New England: 0%, Middle Atlantic: 1%, East North Central: 1%, West North Central: 0%, South Atlantic: 91%, East South Central: 0%, West South Central: 0%, Mountain: 0%, Pacific: 0%, Unknown: 6%

BAR PASSAGE RATES

Based on 2004 graduates taking Summer 2004 or Winter 2005 exams. Most of the school's first-time test takers took the bar in Florida.

62%

School's bar passage rate for first-time test takers

73%

Statewide bar passage rate for first-time test takers

Ohio Northern University (Pettit)

- 525 S. Main Street, Ada, OH, 45810-1599
- http://www.law.onu.edu
- Private
- Year founded: 1885
- 2005-2006 tuition: full-time: $23,980; part-time: N/A
- Enrollment 2005-06 academic year: full-time: 324
- U.S. News 2007 law specialty ranking: N/A

3.15-3.69 GPA, 25TH-75TH PERCENTILE

150-155 LSAT, 25TH-75TH PERCENTILE

27% ACCEPTANCE RATE

Tier 4 2007 U.S. NEWS LAW SCHOOL RANKING

ADMISSIONS

Admissions phone number: (877) 452-9668
Admissions email address: **admissions@eugene.onu.edu**
Application website: **N/A**
Application deadline for Fall 2007 admission: **rolling**

Admissions statistics:

Number of applicants for Fall 2005: **1,553**
Number of acceptances: **421**
Number enrolled: **116**
Acceptance rate: **27%**
GPA, 25th-75th percentile, entering class Fall 2005:
3.15-3.69
LSAT, 25th-75th percentile, entering class Fall 2005: **150-155**

FINANCIAL AID

Financial aid phone number: **(419) 772-2272**
Financial aid application deadline: **6/01**
Tuition 2005-2006 academic year: full-time: **$23,980**; part-time: **N/A**
Room and board: **$7,290**; books: **$1,000**; miscellaneous expenses: **$1,600**
Total of room/board/books/miscellaneous expenses: **$9,890**
University offers graduate student housing for which law students are eligible.

Financial aid profile

Percent of students that received grants for the 2004-2005 academic year: full-time: **50%**
Median grant amount: full-time: **$12,500**
The average law-school debt of those in the Class of 2005 who borrowed: **$78,146**. Proportion who borrowed: **98%**

ACADEMIC PROGRAMS

Calendar: **semester**
Joint degrees awarded: **N/A**
Typical first-year section size: Full-time: **65**
Is there typically a "small section" of the first year class, other than Legal Writing, taught by full-time faculty?:
Full-time: **no**

Number of course titles, beyond the first year curriculum, offered last year: **60**
Percentages of upper division course sections, excluding seminars, with an enrollment of:

Under 25: **70%**	25 to 49: **16%**
50 to 74: **13%**	75 to 99: **1%**
100+: **0%**	

Areas of specialization: appellate advocacy, clinical training, dispute resolution, environmental law, intellectual property law, international law, tax law, trial advocacy

Fall 2005 faculty profile

Total teaching faculty: **24**. Full-time: **75%**; **61%** men, **39%** women, **6%** minorities. Part-time: **25%**; **83%** men, **17%** women, **N/A** minorities
Student-to-faculty ratio: **14.8**

SPECIAL PROGRAMS *(as provided by law school):*

The Ohio Northern University Law College offers a number of clinical programs, the purpose of which is to provide practical and educational experience to students in the context of actually representing clients, while at the same time providing a service to the public. One mechanism for providing service to the community is the use of specially trained and certified students who work under the close supervision of a practicing attorney.

Located in Lima, Ohio, the ONU Legal Clinic provides legal services to over 200 individuals per year. Other clinics include: bankruptcy, corporate transactional, environmental, governmental, litigation, nonprofit litigation, prosecution, and public defender.

Additional opportunities for students include judicial externship, alternative dispute resolution, and the Innocence Project.

STUDENT BODY

Fall 2005 full-time enrollment: 324

Men: **51%**	Women: **49%**
African-American: **6.5%**	American Indian: **0.0%**
Asian-American: **2.8%**	Mexican-American: **0.0%**
Puerto Rican: **0.0%**	Other Hisp-Amer: **1.2%**
White: **89.5%**	International: **0.0%**
Unknown: **0.0%**	

Percent of students discontinuing law school:
Men: **11%**   Women: **8%**
First-year students: **19%**   Second-year students: **6%**
Third-year students: **N/A**

LIBRARY RESOURCES

The library holds **129,517** and receives **2,296** current subscriptions.
Total volumes: **378,086**
Percentage of the titles in the online catalog: **96%**
Total seats available for library users: **325**

INFORMATION TECHNOLOGY

Number of wired network connections available to students: **218** total (in the law library, excluding computer labs: **176**; in classrooms: **38**; in computer labs: **4**; elsewhere in the law school: **0**)
Law school has a wireless network.
Approximate number of simultaneous users that can be accommodated on wireless network: **800**
Students are not required to own a computer.

EMPLOYMENT AND SALARIES

Proportion of 2004 graduates employed at graduation: **N/A**
Employed 9 months later, as of February 15, 2005: **86%**
Salaries in the private sector (law firms, business, industry): **$46,000–$51,000** (25th-75th percentile)
Median salary in the private sector: **$48,500**

Percentage in the private sector who reported salary information: **42%**
Median salary in public service (government, judicial clerkships, academic posts, non-profits): **$40,000**

Percentage of 2004 graduates in:

Law firms: **55%**	Bus./industry (legal): **0%**
Bus./industry (nonlegal): **11%**	Government: **17%**
Public interest: **2%**	Judicial clerkship: **6%**
Academia : **4%**	Unknown: **5%**

2004 graduates employed in-state: **40%**
2004 graduates employed in foreign countries: **0%**
Number of states where graduates are employed: **18**
Percentage of 2004 graduates working in: New England: **0%**, Middle Atlantic: **21%**, East North Central: **51%**, West North Central: **0%**, South Atlantic: **17%**, East South Central: **3%**, West South Central: **0%**, Mountain: **3%**, Pacific: **3%**, Unknown: **2%**

BAR PASSAGE RATES

Based on 2004 graduates taking Summer 2004 or Winter 2005 exams. Most of the school's first-time test takers took the bar in Ohio.

72%
School's bar passage rate for first-time test takers

81%
Statewide bar passage rate for first-time test takers

Ohio State University (Moritz)

- 55 W. 12th Avenue, Columbus, OH, 43210
- http://www.moritzlaw.osu.edu
- Public
- **Year founded:** 1891
- **2005-2006 tuition:** In-state: full-time: $15,909, part-time: N/A;
  Out-of-state: full-time: $29,511
- **Enrollment 2005-06 academic year:** full-time: 723
- **U.S. News 2007 law specialty ranking:** dispute resolution: 3

3.33-3.72 GPA, 25TH-75TH PERCENTILE

158-164 LSAT, 25TH-75TH PERCENTILE

28% ACCEPTANCE RATE

39 2007 U.S. NEWS LAW SCHOOL RANKING

ADMISSIONS

Admissions phone number: **(614) 292-8810**
Admissions email address: **lawadmit@osu.edu**
Application website: **N/A**
Application deadline for Fall 2007 admission: **3/01**

Admissions statistics:

Number of applicants for Fall 2005: **2,282**
Number of acceptances: **629**
Number enrolled: **217**
Acceptance rate: **28%**
GPA, 25th-75th percentile, entering class Fall 2005:
3.33-3.72
LSAT, 25th-75th percentile, entering class Fall 2005:
158-164

FINANCIAL AID

Financial aid phone number: **(614) 292-8807**
Financial aid application deadline: **3/01**
Tuition 2005-2006 academic year: In-state: full-time:
$15,909, part-time: **N/A**; Out-of-state: full-time: **$29,511**
Room and board: **$6,372**; books: **$2,500**; miscellaneous
expenses: **$6,112**
Total of room/board/books/miscellaneous expenses:
$14,984
University offers graduate student housing for which law
students are eligible.

Financial aid profile

Percent of students that received grants for the 2004-2005
academic year: full-time: **85%**
Median grant amount: full-time: **$4,000**
The average law-school debt of those in the Class of 2005
who borrowed: **$48,573.** Proportion who borrowed: **87%**

ACADEMIC PROGRAMS

Calendar: **semester**
Joint degrees awarded: **M.B.A.; HSMP; PP&M; MHA;
AFAM&AST; SOCWK; PH.D.; MPH; MD; EDU P&L;
M.A.**
Typical first-year section size: Full-time: **75**

Is there typically a "small section" of the first year class,
other than Legal Writing, taught by full-time faculty?:
Full-time: **yes**
Number of course titles, beyond the first year curriculum,
offered last year: **80**
Percentages of upper division course sections, excluding
seminars, with an enrollment of:

Under 25: **41%**	25 to 49: **32%**
50 to 74: **23%**	75 to 99: **3%**
100+: **2%**	

Areas of specialization: appellate advocacy, clinical training,
dispute resolution, environmental law, healthcare law,
intellectual property law, international law, tax law, trial
advocacy

Fall 2005 faculty profile

Total teaching faculty: **N/A**. Full-time: **N/A**; **N/A** men, **N/A**
women, **N/A** minorities. Part-time: **N/A**; **N/A** men, **N/A**
women, **N/A** minorities
Student-to-faculty ratio: **14.1**

SPECIAL PROGRAMS *(as provided by law school):*

The college offers a rigorous academic program, encompassing
both a traditional law school curriculum and electives in a wide
range of topics. First-year students enroll in at least one small-
section class in the fall semester, and they experience an intensive writing and analysis course taught by a full-time faculty
member in the spring semester.

The college's clinical program, among the oldest and finest
in the country, offers an extensive selection of clinics in civil,
criminal, children's issues, housing, mediation, and legislation.
The college is widely regarded as having one of the nation's
finest programs in the area of alternative dispute resolution.

Ohio State law students have the opportunity to gain firsthand insight into the judicial system through the college's judicial externship program, and engage in problem-based business
law courses through the Distinguished Practitioner class series.

Students with an interest in international law may select
from a menu of approximately 12 courses that have an international law or comparative law focus, including a summer and
semester-long study abroad programs in Oxford, England.

The college offers joint degree programs with many other colleges and departments at the university, including business administration and health administration. Students can receive credit for a government or nonprofit legal internship and related courses in the college's Washington, D.C., summer program.

STUDENT BODY

Fall 2005 full-time enrollment: 723

Men: 59%	Women: 41%
African-American: 8.3%	American Indian: 0.4%
Asian-American: 10.2%	Mexican-American: 0.8%
Puerto Rican: 0.4%	Other Hisp-Amer: 2.4%
White: 75.8%	International: 1.7%
Unknown: 0.0%	

Attrition rates for 2004-2005 full-time students
Percent of students discontinuing law school:

Men: 2%	Women: 2%
First-year students: 5%	Second-year students: 1%
Third-year students: N/A	

LIBRARY RESOURCES

The library holds 178,176 and receives 7,876 current subscriptions.
Total volumes: 789,615
Percentage of the titles in the online catalog: 82%
Total seats available for library users: 689

INFORMATION TECHNOLOGY

Number of wired network connections available to students: 0 total (in the law library, excluding computer labs: 0; in classrooms: 0; in computer labs: 0; elsewhere in the law school: 0)
Law school has a wireless network.
Approximate number of simultaneous users that can be accommodated on wireless network: 512
Students are not required to own a computer.

EMPLOYMENT AND SALARIES

Proportion of 2004 graduates employed at graduation: 74%
Employed 9 months later, as of February 15, 2005: 97%
Salaries in the private sector (law firms, business, industry): $50,000–$90,000 (25th-75th percentile)
Median salary in the private sector: $82,000
Percentage in the private sector who reported salary information: 57%
Median salary in public service (government, judicial clerkships, academic posts, non-profits): $42,000

Percentage of 2004 graduates in:

Law firms: 52%	Bus./industry (legal): 8%
Bus./industry (nonlegal): 6%	Government: 15%
Public interest: 3%	Judicial clerkship: 12%
Academia : 4%	Unknown: 0%

2004 graduates employed in-state: 71%
2004 graduates employed in foreign countries: 1%
Number of states where graduates are employed: 26
Percentage of 2004 graduates working in: New England: 1%, Middle Atlantic: 3%, East North Central: 79%, West North Central: 0%, South Atlantic: 8%, East South Central: 1%, West South Central: 3%, Mountain: 3%, Pacific: 1%, Unknown: 1%

BAR PASSAGE RATES

Based on 2004 graduates taking Summer 2004 or Winter 2005 exams. Most of the school's first-time test takers took the bar in Ohio.

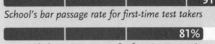

91%
School's bar passage rate for first-time test takers

81%
Statewide bar passage rate for first-time test takers

Oklahoma City University

■ **2501 N. Blackwelder, Oklahoma City, OK, 73106-1493**
■ **http://www.okcu.edu/law**
■ **Private**
■ **Year founded:** 1907
■ **2005-2006 tuition:** full-time: $825/credit hour; part-time: $825/credit hour
■ **Enrollment 2005-06 academic year:** full-time: 546; part-time: 138
■ **U.S. News 2007 law specialty ranking:** N/A

2.78-3.43 GPA, 25TH-75TH PERCENTILE

148-152 LSAT, 25TH-75TH PERCENTILE

41% ACCEPTANCE RATE

Tier 4 2007 U.S. NEWS LAW SCHOOL RANKING

ADMISSIONS

Admissions phone number: **(800) 633-7242**
Admissions email address: **lawadmit@okcu.edu**
Application website: **http://www.okcu.edu/law/admissions/admissions_applynow.php**
Application deadline for Fall 2007 admission: **4/01**

Admissions statistics:
Number of applicants for Fall 2005: **1,241**
Number of acceptances: **505**
Number enrolled: **184**
Acceptance rate: **41%**
GPA, 25th-75th percentile, entering class Fall 2005: **2.78-3.43**
LSAT, 25th-75th percentile, entering class Fall 2005: **148-152**

Part-time program:
Number of applicants for Fall 2005: **136**
Number of acceptances: **62**
Number enrolled: **33**
Acceptance rate: **46%**
GPA, 25th-75th percentile, entering class Fall 2005: **2.54-3.36**
LSAT, 25th-75th percentile, entering class Fall 2005: **146-152**

FINANCIAL AID

Financial aid phone number: **(800) 633-7242**
Financial aid application deadline: **3/01**
Tuition 2005-2006 academic year: full-time: **$825/credit hour**; part-time: **$825/credit hour**
Room and board: **$6,250**; books: **$1,600**; miscellaneous expenses: **$7,890**
Total of room/board/books/miscellaneous expenses: **$15,740**
University offers graduate student housing for which law students are eligible.

Financial aid profile
Percent of students that received grants for the 2004-2005 academic year: full-time: **19%**; part-time **29%**
Median grant amount: full-time: **$12,000**; part-time: **$3,350**
The average law-school debt of those in the Class of 2005 who borrowed: **$92,750**. Proportion who borrowed: **81%**

ACADEMIC PROGRAMS

Calendar: **semester**
Joint degrees awarded: **J.D./M.B.A.**
Typical first-year section size: Full-time: **84**; Part-time: **45**
Is there typically a "small section" of the first year class, other than Legal Writing, taught by full-time faculty?: Full-time: **yes**; Part-time: **no**
Number of course titles, beyond the first year curriculum, offered last year: **85**
Percentages of upper division course sections, excluding seminars, with an enrollment of:

Under 25: **54%**	25 to 49: **20%**
50 to 74: **13%**	75 to 99: **12%**
100+: **0%**	

Areas of specialization: appellate advocacy, clinical training, dispute resolution, environmental law, healthcare law, intellectual property law, international law, tax law, trial advocacy

Fall 2005 faculty profile
Total teaching faculty: **48**. Full-time: **60%**; **66%** men, **34%** women, **14%** minorities. Part-time: **40%**; **79%** men, **21%** women, **5%** minorities
Student-to-faculty ratio: **18.6**

SPECIAL PROGRAMS *(as provided by law school):*
Oklahoma City University (OCU) co-sponsors (with Stetson University) three summer international programs in Granada, Spain; Freiburg, Germany and The Hague, the Netherlands; and Buenos Aires, Argentina. OCU LAW is seeking ABA approval of a fourth summer program in Tianjin, China, to begin in the summer of 2006. OCU Law is also part of a student exchange program with Bucerius Law School, located in Hamburg, Germany. Taking advantage of our location in a state capital and

our close proximity to federal and state government agencies and courts, OCU Law offers a range of externship opportunities. In an externship, a student earns academic credit in practice placements with field supervisors, operating under the guidance of a full-time director of externship programs. Our numerous placement sites include the U.S. Attorney for the Western District of Oklahoma, the United States Court of Appeals for the Tenth Circuit, the United States District Court for the Western District of Oklahoma, the Oklahoma Supreme Court, the Oklahoma Court of Criminal Appeals, the Oklahoma Corporation Commission, the Child Support Enforcement Division of the Oklahoma Department of Human Services, the Oklahoma County Public Defender's office, Oklahoma Indian Legal Services, Inc., and Legal Aid Services of Oklahoma. The externship program is complemented by Oklahoma's liberal student intern license policy. Students who have completed 50 course hours are eligible to apply for a license for law students, allowing them to appear in court under certain circumstances. The Certificate in Business Law is obtained with either an Electronic Commerce Concentration or a Financial Services and Commercial Law Concentration. Students may also earn a certificate in Public Law or a certificate in Client Representation in Alternative Dispute Resolution. OCU Law operates three legal centers that provide curricular and other programs for students, the bench and bar, and the wider community. First, the Native American Legal Resource Center provides legal services in many areas of Native American law, including representation of victims of domestic violence in conjunction with the Apache Tribe of Oklahoma, drafting constitutions and codes, and assisting tribal courts. Second, the Center on Alternative Dispute Resolution trains students to represent clients in mediation, arbitration, and negotiation, and conducts research on issues related to dispute resolution. Third, the Center for the Study of State Constitutional Law and Government promotes scholarship and discussion on important issues relating to state government, hosting prominent speakers and important conferences.

STUDENT BODY

Fall 2005 full-time enrollment: 546

Men: 60%	Women: 40%
African-American: 2.6%	American Indian: 6.6%
Asian-American: 4.4%	Mexican-American: 3.7%
Puerto Rican: 0.2%	Other Hisp-Amer: 0.0%
White: 80.8%	International: 0.9%
Unknown: 0.9%	

Fall 2005 part-time enrollment: 138

Men: 62%	Women: 38%
African-American: 5.1%	American Indian: 8.7%
Asian-American: 1.4%	Mexican-American: 7.2%
Puerto Rican: 0.0%	Other Hisp-Amer: 0.0%
White: 76.1%	International: 0.0%
Unknown: 1.4%	

Attrition rates for 2004-2005 full-time students
Percent of students discontinuing law school:
Men: 8%   Women: 5%

First-year students: 18%   Second-year students: 2%
Third-year students: N/A

LIBRARY RESOURCES
The library holds 93,805 and receives 4,354 current subscriptions.
Total volumes: 311,643
Percentage of the titles in the online catalog: 99%
Total seats available for library users: 364

INFORMATION TECHNOLOGY
Number of wired network connections available to students: 147 total (in the law library, excluding computer labs: 104; in classrooms: 26; in computer labs: 4; elsewhere in the law school: 13)
Law school has a wireless network.
Approximate number of simultaneous users that can be accommodated on wireless network: 2,400
Students are not required to own a computer.

EMPLOYMENT AND SALARIES
Proportion of 2004 graduates employed at graduation: N/A
Employed 9 months later, as of February 15, 2005: 77%
Salaries in the private sector (law firms, business, industry): $38,000–$65,000 (25th-75th percentile)
Median salary in the private sector: $48,526
Percentage in the private sector who reported salary information: 65%
Median salary in public service (government, judicial clerkships, academic posts, non-profits): $39,125

Percentage of 2004 graduates in:

Law firms: 50%	Bus./industry (legal): 17%
Bus./industry (nonlegal): N/A	Government: 22%
Public interest: 0%	Judicial clerkship: 1%
Academia : 1%	Unknown: 9%

2004 graduates employed in-state: 56%
2004 graduates employed in foreign countries: 0%
Number of states where graduates are employed: 19
Percentage of 2004 graduates working in: New England: N/A, Middle Atlantic: N/A, East North Central: N/A, West North Central: 6%, South Atlantic: 4%, East South Central: 4%, West South Central: 83%, Mountain: 3%, Pacific: N/A, Unknown: 1%

BAR PASSAGE RATES
Based on 2004 graduates taking Summer 2004 or Winter 2005 exams. Most of the school's first-time test takers took the bar in Oklahoma.

72%
School's bar passage rate for first-time test takers

83%
Statewide bar passage rate for first-time test takers

Pace University

■ 78 N. Broadway, White Plains, NY, 10603
■ http://www.law.pace.edu
■ Private
■ Year founded: 1976
■ 2005-2006 tuition: full-time: $33,782; part-time: $25,350
■ Enrollment 2005-06 academic year: full-time: 495; part-time: 248
■ U.S. News 2007 law specialty ranking: environmental law: 3

3.09-3.50 GPA, 25TH-75TH PERCENTILE

153-156 LSAT, 25TH-75TH PERCENTILE

33% ACCEPTANCE RATE

Tier 3 2007 U.S. NEWS LAW SCHOOL RANKING

ADMISSIONS
Admissions phone number: **(914) 422-4210**
Admissions email address: **admissions@law.pace.edu**
Application website:
   http://www.law.pace.edu/adm/apply/jd.html
Application deadline for Fall 2007 admission: **3/01**

Admissions statistics:
Number of applicants for Fall 2005: **2,708**
Number of acceptances: **889**
Number enrolled: **172**
Acceptance rate: **33%**
GPA, 25th-75th percentile, entering class Fall 2005:
   3.09-3.50
LSAT, 25th-75th percentile, entering class Fall 2005: **153-156**

Part-time program:
Number of applicants for Fall 2005: **509**
Number of acceptances: **161**
Number enrolled: **88**
Acceptance rate: **32%**
GPA, 25th-75th percentile, entering class Fall 2005:
   2.91-3.49
LSAT, 25th-75th percentile, entering class Fall 2005: **151-154**

FINANCIAL AID
Financial aid phone number: **(914) 422-4048**
Financial aid application deadline: **2/01**
Tuition 2005-2006 academic year: full-time: **$33,782**; part-time: **$25,350**
Room and board: **$12,442**; books: **$1,120**; miscellaneous expenses: **$2,900**
Total of room/board/books/miscellaneous expenses: **$16,462**
University offers graduate student housing for which law students are eligible.

Financial aid profile
Percent of students that received grants for the 2004-2005 academic year: full-time: **56%**; part-time **27%**

Median grant amount: full-time: **$10,000**; part-time: **$4,000**
The average law-school debt of those in the Class of 2005 who borrowed: **$75,000**. Proportion who borrowed: **90%**

ACADEMIC PROGRAMS
Calendar: **semester**
Joint degrees awarded: **J.D./M.B.A.; J.D./M.P.A.; J.D./M.E.M.; J.D./M.S.**
Typical first-year section size: Full-time: **53**; Part-time: **56**
Is there typically a "small section" of the first year class, other than Legal Writing, taught by full-time faculty?:
   Full-time: **yes**; Part-time: **yes**
Number of course titles, beyond the first year curriculum, offered last year: **137**
Percentages of upper division course sections, excluding seminars, with an enrollment of:

Under 25: **71%**	25 to 49: **17%**
50 to 74: **9%**	75 to 99: **3%**
100+: **1%**	

Areas of specialization: appellate advocacy, clinical training, dispute resolution, environmental law, healthcare law, intellectual property law, international law, tax law, trial advocacy

Fall 2005 faculty profile
Total teaching faculty: **73**. Full-time: **49%**; **61%** men, **39%** women, **11%** minorities. Part-time: **51%**; **59%** men, **41%** women, **5%** minorities
Student-to-faculty ratio: **15.4**

SPECIAL PROGRAMS (as provided by law school):
The Pace Women's Justice Center is a domestic violence training center and resource for the judiciary, law enforcement, law students and attorneys. Law students participate in the Center's Teen Dating Violence Institute and Elder Law Division as well as provide direct representation under supervising attorneys in the Family Court Externship to clients seeking protective orders, child custody/visitation orders.
   Pace Law School has one of the top-ranked environmental programs in the country. The program offers over 20 classes

in environmental law, opportunities to conduct research in energy and land use law, externships in Washington, D.C., at the United Nations and in New York, and international environmental law classes taught in Brazil. The Land Use Law Center teaches students to understand how best to develop and conserve the land through research and publications, outreach and community service, and project management and technology.

The Federal Judicial Extern Honors Program allows selected students to hone their writing skills, first in a mentoring program with a faculty member and then as judicial externs in a U.S. district or circuit judge's chambers.

Direct-representation clinics enable students to take their extensive classroom training and make the transition to representing clients or prosecuting charges. Students take full responsibility for their own caseloads under the close supervision of a full-time faculty member. Externship programs are also available and are clinical courses in which fieldwork is conducted under the supervision of practicing attorneys who are not full-time members of the faculty.

Simulation courses give students the opportunity to learn specific components of lawyering work, such as written and oral advocacy, interviewing and counseling clients, negotiation, analyzing a trial record, developing strategy, opening and closing arguments, selecting a jury and drafting jury instructions, witness preparation, and examination.

Pace's London Law Program, offered in the spring semester, is the only one affiliated with a European law faculty that allows for all internationally oriented courses to be taught by distinguished senior members of the University College Faculty of Laws, University of London. The London Law Program offers students extensive externship opportunities with British barristers and solicitors, members of Parliament, international human-rights organizations, or environmental organizations.

STUDENT BODY
Fall 2005 full-time enrollment: 495
Men: 41%	Women: 59%
African-American: 1.6%	American Indian: 0.2%
Asian-American: 7.9%	Mexican-American: 0.4%
Puerto Rican: 0.8%	Other Hisp-Amer: 2.8%
White: 71.5%	International: 2.0%
Unknown: 12.7%	

Fall 2005 part-time enrollment: 248
Men: 48%	Women: 52%
African-American: 5.2%	American Indian: 0.0%
Asian-American: 8.1%	Mexican-American: 0.4%
Puerto Rican: 0.4%	Other Hisp-Amer: 5.2%
White: 66.1%	International: 0.0%
Unknown: 14.5%	

Attrition rates for 2004-2005 full-time students
Percent of students discontinuing law school:
Men: 6%   Women: 7%

First-year students: 14%   Second-year students: 5%
Third-year students: 1%

LIBRARY RESOURCES
The library holds 129,724 and receives 4,014 current subscriptions.
Total volumes: 382,538
Percentage of the titles in the online catalog: 100%
Total seats available for library users: 380

INFORMATION TECHNOLOGY
Number of wired network connections available to students: 278 total (in the law library, excluding computer labs: 60; in classrooms: 100; in computer labs: 76; elsewhere in the law school: 42)
Law school has a wireless network.
Approximate number of simultaneous users that can be accommodated on wireless network: 5,632
Students are not required to own a computer.

EMPLOYMENT AND SALARIES
Proportion of 2004 graduates employed at graduation: N/A
Employed 9 months later, as of February 15, 2005: 90%
Salaries in the private sector (law firms, business, industry): $47,941–$66,471 (25th-75th percentile)
Median salary in the private sector: $55,412
Percentage in the private sector who reported salary information: 67%
Median salary in public service (government, judicial clerkships, academic posts, non-profits): $48,000

Percentage of 2004 graduates in:
Law firms: 52%	Bus./industry (legal): 26%
Bus./industry (nonlegal): 0%	Government: 13%
Public interest: 2%	Judicial clerkship: 5%
Academia : 2%	Unknown: 0%

2004 graduates employed in-state: 78%
2004 graduates employed in foreign countries: 2%
Number of states where graduates are employed: 8
Percentage of 2004 graduates working in: New England: 5%, Middle Atlantic: 88%, East North Central: 0%, West North Central: 0%, South Atlantic: 2%, East South Central: 0%, West South Central: 0%, Mountain: 0%, Pacific: 1%, Unknown: 2%

BAR PASSAGE RATES
Based on 2004 graduates taking Summer 2004 or Winter 2005 exams. Most of the school's first-time test takers took the bar in New York.

73%
School's bar passage rate for first-time test takers

75%
Statewide bar passage rate for first-time test takers

Penn. State University (Dickinson)

- 150 S. College Street, Carlisle, PA, 17013-2899
- http://www.dsl.psu.edu
- Private
- Year founded: 1834
- 2005-2006 tuition: full-time: $26,680; part-time: N/A
- Enrollment 2005-06 academic year: full-time: 580
- U.S. News 2007 law specialty ranking: dispute resolution: 9

3.11-3.67	GPA, 25TH-75TH PERCENTILE
154-157	LSAT, 25TH-75TH PERCENTILE
29%	ACCEPTANCE RATE
87	2007 U.S. NEWS LAW SCHOOL RANKING

ADMISSIONS

Admissions phone number: **(717) 240-5207**
Admissions email address: **dsladmit@psu.edu**
Application website:
  http://www.dsl.psu.edu/admissions/applyjd.cfm
Application deadline for Fall 2007 admission: **3/02**

Admissions statistics:

Number of applicants for Fall 2005: **2,491**
Number of acceptances: **732**
Number enrolled: **205**
Acceptance rate: **29%**
GPA, 25th-75th percentile, entering class Fall 2005:
  3.11-3.67
LSAT, 25th-75th percentile, entering class Fall 2005: **154-157**

FINANCIAL AID

Financial aid phone number: **(800) 840-1122**
Financial aid application deadline: **3/01**
Tuition 2005-2006 academic year: full-time: **$26,680**;
  part-time: **N/A**
Room and board: **$8,460**; books: **$1,100**; miscellaneous
  expenses: **$5,418**
Total of room/board/books/miscellaneous expenses:
  $14,978
University does not offer graduate student housing for
  which law students are eligible.

Financial aid profile

Percent of students that received grants for the 2004-2005
  academic year: full-time: **49%**
Median grant amount: full-time: **$7,913**
The average law-school debt of those in the Class of 2005
  who borrowed: **$69,943**. Proportion who borrowed: **88%**

ACADEMIC PROGRAMS

Calendar: **semester**
Joint degrees awarded: **J.D./M.P.A.; J.D./M.B.A.;
  J.D./MEPC; J.D./M.ENG.PC; J.D./MSPC; J.D./MSIS;
  J.D./M.S.; J.D./M.Ed.; J.D./M.F.R.; J.D./MAgr;
  J.D./Ph.D.**

Typical first-year section size: Full-time: **60**
Is there typically a "small section" of the first year class,
  other than Legal Writing, taught by full-time faculty?:
  Full-time: **no**
Number of course titles, beyond the first year curriculum,
  offered last year: **131**
Percentages of upper division course sections, excluding
  seminars, with an enrollment of:

Under 25: **52%**		25 to 49: **27%**
50 to 74: **10%**		75 to 99: **10%**
100+: **1%**		

Areas of specialization: appellate advocacy, clinical training,
  dispute resolution, environmental law, healthcare law,
  intellectual property law, international law, tax law, trial
  advocacy

Fall 2005 faculty profile

Total teaching faculty: **101**. Full-time: **42%**; **62%** men, **38%**
  women, **17%** minorities. Part-time: **58%**; **76%** men, **24%**
  women, **5%** minorities
Student-to-faculty ratio: **13.8**

SPECIAL PROGRAMS (as provided by law school):

Penn State University is undertaking a $110 million capital
investment in new signature facilities for The Dickinson School
of Law, uniquely designed to ensure the law school's deep pro-
grammatic integration with other top graduate departments at
Penn State's University Park campus.

The University also is allocating an additional several million
dollars annually to the law school in order to support curricular
enhancements and to sustain a remarkably successful program
of recruiting world-renowned scholars. Additionally, Penn State
intends to establish a new school of international affairs and it
is the University's intention that this new school be administered within the law school.

Penn State Dickinson students have the opportunity to engage
in a rich array of interdisciplinary programs and activities. For
example, students interested in pursing a joint degree program
can choose a J.D./M.B.A. in collaboration with the Smeal College
of Business Administration, a J.D./M.P.A. in collaboration with
the School of Public Affairs, a J.D./M.D. in collaboration with the

College of Medicine, and other joint degrees across the full range of Penn State graduate disciplines. Additionally, students interested in studying international and domestic dispute resolution will be studying in one of the nation's 10 best alternative dispute resolution programs. The cornerstone of the program is the Penn State Institute of Arbitration Law and Practice, which publishes two of the world's leading scholarly journals on arbitration. Penn State Dickinson also boasts a superior trial advocacy program and a full range of in-house clinics, including a Political Asylum Clinic, Family Law Clinic, Disability Law Clinic, Elder Law Clinic, Child Advocacy Clinic, Sports and Entertainment Law Clinic, and a planned new Environmental Law Clinic. Penn State also offers externships with state and federal judges, public interest law firms, and a variety of state and federal agencies, including a semester-long Washington, D.C., program. Penn State offers an innovative L.L.M program for foreign lawyers and study abroad opportunities for students in Europe, Asia, Africa, the Middle East, and Canada.

STUDENT BODY

Fall 2005 full-time enrollment: 580

Men: 54%	Women: 46%
African-American: 7.4%	American Indian: 0.2%
Asian-American: 7.2%	Mexican-American: 0.0%
Puerto Rican: 0.3%	Other Hisp-Amer: 6.9%
White: 77.4%	International: 0.5%
Unknown: 0.0%	

Attrition rates for 2004-2005 full-time students
Percent of students discontinuing law school:

Men: 4%	Women: 3%
First-year students: 11%	Second-year students: 1%
Third-year students: N/A	

LIBRARY RESOURCES

The library holds 90,578 and receives 6,730 current subscriptions.
Total volumes: 506,566
Percentage of the titles in the online catalog: 100%
Total seats available for library users: 425

INFORMATION TECHNOLOGY

Number of wired network connections available to students: 50 total (in the law library, excluding computer labs: 0; in classrooms: 12; in computer labs: 0; elsewhere in the law school: 38)

Law school has a wireless network.
Approximate number of simultaneous users that can be accommodated on wireless network: 480
Students are not required to own a computer.

EMPLOYMENT AND SALARIES

Proportion of 2004 graduates employed at graduation: 69%
Employed 9 months later, as of February 15, 2005: 93%
Salaries in the private sector (law firms, business, industry): $40,000–$70,000 (25th-75th percentile)
Median salary in the private sector: $50,000
Percentage in the private sector who reported salary information: 63%
Median salary in public service (government, judicial clerkships, academic posts, non-profits): $40,000

Percentage of 2004 graduates in:

Law firms: 39%	Bus./industry (legal): 12%
Bus./industry (nonlegal): 0%	Government: 17%
Public interest: 5%	Judicial clerkship: 23%
Academia : 0%	Unknown: 3%

2004 graduates employed in-state: 51%
2004 graduates employed in foreign countries: 0%
Number of states where graduates are employed: 23
Percentage of 2004 graduates working in: New England: 1%, Middle Atlantic: 58%, East North Central: 1%, West North Central: 1%, South Atlantic: 16%, East South Central: 3%, West South Central: 1%, Mountain: 1%, Pacific: 3%, Unknown: 16%

BAR PASSAGE RATES

Based on 2004 graduates taking Summer 2004 or Winter 2005 exams. Most of the school's first-time test takers took the bar in Pennsylvania.

78%
School's bar passage rate for first-time test takers

81%
Statewide bar passage rate for first-time test takers

Pepperdine University (McConnell)

- 24255 Pacific Coast Highway, Malibu, CA, 90263
- http://law.pepperdine.edu
- Private
- Year founded: 1969
- 2005-2006 tuition: full-time: $31,860; part-time: N/A
- Enrollment 2005-06 academic year: full-time: 704
- U.S. News 2007 law specialty ranking: dispute resolution: 1

3.38-3.71 GPA, 25TH-75TH PERCENTILE

157-161 LSAT, 25TH-75TH PERCENTILE

25% ACCEPTANCE RATE

87 2007 U.S. NEWS LAW SCHOOL RANKING

ADMISSIONS

Admissions phone number: **(310) 506-4631**
Admissions email address: **soladmis@pepperdine.edu**
Application website: **http://law.pepperdine.edu/admissions/applications**
Application deadline for Fall 2007 admission: **3/01**

Admissions statistics:

Number of applicants for Fall 2005: **3,314**
Number of acceptances: **839**
Number enrolled: **243**
Acceptance rate: **25%**
GPA, 25th-75th percentile, entering class Fall 2005: **3.38-3.71**
LSAT, 25th-75th percentile, entering class Fall 2005: **157-161**

FINANCIAL AID

Financial aid phone number: **(310) 506-4633**
Financial aid application deadline: **4/01**
Tuition 2005-2006 academic year: full-time: **$31,860**; part-time: **N/A**
Room and board: **$14,098**; books: **$700**; miscellaneous expenses: **$4,910**
Total of room/board/books/miscellaneous expenses: **$19,708**
University offers graduate student housing for which law students are eligible.

Financial aid profile

Percent of students that received grants for the 2004-2005 academic year: full-time: **83%**
Median grant amount: full-time: **$1,500**
The average law-school debt of those in the Class of 2005 who borrowed: **$101,130**. Proportion who borrowed: **52%**

ACADEMIC PROGRAMS

Calendar: **semester**
Joint degrees awarded: **J.D./MBA; J.D./MDR; J.D./MPP; J.D./MDIV**
Typical first-year section size: Full-time: **80**

Is there typically a "small section" of the first year class, other than Legal Writing, taught by full-time faculty?: Full-time: **no**
Number of course titles, beyond the first year curriculum, offered last year: **109**
Percentages of upper division course sections, excluding seminars, with an enrollment of:
Under 25: **60%**   25 to 49: **24%**
50 to 74: **8%**   75 to 99: **5%**
100+: **2%**
Areas of specialization: appellate advocacy, clinical training, dispute resolution, environmental law, intellectual property law, international law, tax law, trial advocacy

Fall 2005 faculty profile

Total teaching faculty: **76**. Full-time: **37%**; **75%** men, **25%** women, **18%** minorities. Part-time: **63%**; **60%** men, **40%** women, **2%** minorities
Student-to-faculty ratio: **19.8**

SPECIAL PROGRAMS *(as provided by law school)*:

The law school operates an international study program in London during both the summer session and fall semester. We operate a legal aid clinic at the Union Rescue Mission in Los Angeles and a special education advocacy clinic from the Malibu campus. We offer the Center for Entrepreneurship and Technology Law, to train students in the business side of technology companies; the Straus Institute for Dispute Resolution, to train students in mediation, negotiation, arbitration, and other means of settling disputes; and the Institute on Law, Religion, and Ethics, to explore the influence of religion upon the development of the law and ethical standards. We have exchange programs with the University of Copenhagen, the University of Augsburg in Germany, and the Universidad Peruana de Ciencias y Aplicadas in Lima, Peru.

STUDENT BODY

Fall 2005 full-time enrollment: **704**

Men: **48%**   Women: **52%**
African-American: **4.7%**   American Indian: **0.3%**
Asian-American: **9.9%**   Mexican-American: **2.1%**

Puerto Rican: 0.0% Other Hisp-Amer: 1.7%
White: 57.5% International: 0.0%
Unknown: 23.7%

Attrition rates for 2004-2005 full-time students
Percent of students discontinuing law school:
Men: 4% Women: 5%
First-year students: 13% Second-year students: 0%
Third-year students: N/A

LIBRARY RESOURCES
The library holds 117,956 and receives 3,603 current
subscriptions.
Total volumes: 375,160
Percentage of the titles in the online catalog: 82%
Total seats available for library users: 508

INFORMATION TECHNOLOGY
Number of wired network connections available to students: 80 total (in the law library, excluding computer
labs: 70; in classrooms: 10; in computer labs: 0; elsewhere in the law school: 0)
Law school has a wireless network.
Approximate number of simultaneous users that can be
accommodated on wireless network: 700
Students are not required to own a computer.

EMPLOYMENT AND SALARIES
Proportion of 2004 graduates employed at graduation: 58%
Employed 9 months later, as of February 15, 2005: 91%
Salaries in the private sector (law firms, business, indus-
try): $61,000–$105,000 (25th-75th percentile)

Median salary in the private sector: $80,000
Percentage in the private sector who reported salary
information: 48%
Median salary in public service (government, judicial clerkships, academic posts, non-profits): $56,000

Percentage of 2004 graduates in:
Law firms: 66% Bus./industry (legal): 6%
Bus./industry (nonlegal): 10% Government: 10%
Public interest: 1% Judicial clerkship: 4%
Academia : 1% Unknown: 2%

2004 graduates employed in-state: 75%
2004 graduates employed in foreign countries: 1%
Number of states where graduates are employed: 18
Percentage of 2004 graduates working in: New England:
0%, Middle Atlantic: 1%, East North Central: 1%, West
North Central: 3%, South Atlantic: 4%, East South
Central: 3%, West South Central: 4%, Mountain: 8%,
Pacific: 75%, Unknown: 0%

BAR PASSAGE RATES
Based on 2004 graduates taking Summer 2004 or
Winter 2005 exams. Most of the school's first-time test
takers took the bar in California.

74%
School's bar passage rate for first-time test takers

61%
Statewide bar passage rate for first-time test takers

Quinnipiac University

- 275 Mount Carmel Avenue, Hamden, CT, 06518
- http://law.quinnipiac.edu
- Private
- Year founded: 1977
- 2005-2006 tuition: full-time: $32,040; part-time: $22,540
- Enrollment 2005-06 academic year: full-time: 383; part-time: 165
- U.S. News 2007 law specialty ranking: dispute resolution: 13

3.08-3.53 GPA, 25TH-75TH PERCENTILE

155-159 LSAT, 25TH-75TH PERCENTILE

23% ACCEPTANCE RATE

Tier 3 2007 U.S. NEWS LAW SCHOOL RANKING

ADMISSIONS

Admissions phone number: **(203) 582-3400**
Admissions email address: **ladm@quinnipiac.edu**
Application website: **http://law.quinnipiac.edu/x37.xml**
Application deadline for Fall 2007 admission: **3/01**

Admissions statistics:

Number of applicants for Fall 2005: **2,225**
Number of acceptances: **515**
Number enrolled: **82**
Acceptance rate: **23%**
GPA, 25th-75th percentile, entering class Fall 2005:
3.08-3.53
LSAT, 25th-75th percentile, entering class Fall 2005: **155-159**

Part-time program:

Number of applicants for Fall 2005: **355**
Number of acceptances: **103**
Number enrolled: **50**
Acceptance rate: **29%**
GPA, 25th-75th percentile, entering class Fall 2005:
2.95-3.50
LSAT, 25th-75th percentile, entering class Fall 2005: **152-155**

FINANCIAL AID

Financial aid phone number: **(203) 582-3405**
Financial aid application deadline: **N/A**
Tuition 2005-2006 academic year: full-time: **$32,040**; part-time: **$22,540**
Room and board: **$8,480**; books: **$1,200**; miscellaneous expenses: **$6,938**
Total of room/board/books/miscellaneous expenses: **$16,618**
University does not offer graduate student housing for which law students are eligible.

Financial aid profile

Percent of students that received grants for the 2004-2005 academic year: full-time: **85%**; part-time **52%**
Median grant amount: full-time: **$10,000**; part-time: **$6,000**

The average law-school debt of those in the Class of 2005 who borrowed: **$81,046**. Proportion who borrowed: **81%**

ACADEMIC PROGRAMS

Calendar: **semester**
Joint degrees awarded: **J.D./M.B.A.; J.D./M.H.A.**
Typical first-year section size: Full-time: **44**; Part-time: **42**
Is there typically a "small section" of the first year class, other than Legal Writing, taught by full-time faculty?:
Full-time: **no**; Part-time: **no**
Number of course titles, beyond the first year curriculum, offered last year: **105**
Percentages of upper division course sections, excluding seminars, with an enrollment of:

Under 25: **69%**	25 to 49: **21%**
50 to 74: **7%**	75 to 99: **4%**
100+: **0%**	

Areas of specialization: appellate advocacy, clinical training, dispute resolution, environmental law, healthcare law, intellectual property law, international law, tax law, trial advocacy

Fall 2005 faculty profile

Total teaching faculty: **64**. Full-time: **42%**; **63%** men, **37%** women, **11%** minorities. Part-time: **58%**; **73%** men, **27%** women, **3%** minorities
Student-to-faculty ratio: **14.5**

SPECIAL PROGRAMS *(as provided by law school):*

The law school offers five in-house clinics: the Civil Clinic, in which students represent low-income clients in a variety of general practice matters, including family, bankruptcy, foreclosure, and consumer cases in state and federal courts, as well as some transactional matters; the Health Law Clinic, in which students represent clients in health-related matters, including mental health and patients' rights cases, access to healthcare, advanced healthcare directives, public benefits, and disability cases; the Tax Clinic, in which students represent clients in tax controversies before the IRS at the audit, appeals, and collection level, as well as before the U.S. tax and district courts; the Defense Appellate Clinic, in which students represent defendants in appeals of their convictions under the supervision of attorneys from the public defenders' appellate unit; and the Prosecution Appellate Clinic, in which students represent the state of Connecticut in appeals of criminal convictions under the supervision of an attorney from the chief state's attorney's appellate unit.

The law school offers externships in which students are placed with attorneys in eight practice areas: criminal justice (prosecution and public defenders' offices), corporate counsel (legal departments of corporations), family and juvenile (legal services and private law offices), judicial (federal and state trial and appellate judges), legal services (legal services offices), legislative (Connecticut state legislature), mediation, and public interest (government and private organizations).

There are two centers: the Center on Dispute Resolution and the Center for Health Law and Policy.

The law school has a summer program at Trinity College in Dublin.

STUDENT BODY

Fall 2005 full-time enrollment: 383

Men: 47%	Women: 53%
African-American: 1.8%	American Indian: 0.3%
Asian-American: 4.2%	Mexican-American: 0.0%
Puerto Rican: 0.0%	Other Hisp-Amer: 1.8%
White: 91.1%	International: 0.8%
Unknown: 0.0%	

Fall 2005 part-time enrollment: 165

Men: 51%	Women: 49%
African-American: 1.8%	American Indian: 0.6%
Asian-American: 4.8%	Mexican-American: 0.0%
Puerto Rican: 0.0%	Other Hisp-Amer: 1.2%
White: 91.5%	International: 0.0%
Unknown: 0.0%	

Attrition rates for 2004-2005 full-time students

Percent of students discontinuing law school:

Men: 6%	Women: 5%
First-year students: 15%	Second-year students: N/A
Third-year students: 2%	

LIBRARY RESOURCES

The library holds 155,334 and receives 2,601 current subscriptions.
Total volumes: 401,505
Percentage of the titles in the online catalog: 99%
Total seats available for library users: 400

INFORMATION TECHNOLOGY

Number of wired network connections available to students: 395 total (in the law library, excluding computer labs: 273; in classrooms: 22; in computer labs: 32; elsewhere in the law school: 68)
Law school has a wireless network.
Approximate number of simultaneous users that can be accommodated on wireless network: 500
Students are not required to own a computer.

EMPLOYMENT AND SALARIES

Proportion of 2004 graduates employed at graduation: N/A
Employed 9 months later, as of February 15, 2005: 92%
Salaries in the private sector (law firms, business, industry): $41,500–$78,077 (25th-75th percentile)
Median salary in the private sector: $60,000
Percentage in the private sector who reported salary information: 63%
Median salary in public service (government, judicial clerkships, academic posts, non-profits): $48,000

Percentage of 2004 graduates in:

Law firms: 41%	Bus./industry (legal): 13%
Bus./industry (nonlegal): 8%	Government: 19%
Public interest: 1%	Judicial clerkship: 7%
Academia : 3%	Unknown: 8%

2004 graduates employed in-state: 78%
2004 graduates employed in foreign countries: 0%
Number of states where graduates are employed: 12
Percentage of 2004 graduates working in: New England: 79%, Middle Atlantic: 12%, East North Central: 0%, West North Central: 0%, South Atlantic: 5%, East South Central: 1%, West South Central: 0%, Mountain: 1%, Pacific: 1%, Unknown: 2%

BAR PASSAGE RATES

Based on 2004 graduates taking Summer 2004 or Winter 2005 exams. Most of the school's first-time test takers took the bar in Connecticut.

74%

School's bar passage rate for first-time test takers

82%

Statewide bar passage rate for first-time test takers

Regent University

- 1000 Regent University Drive, Virginia Beach, VA, 23464-9880
- http://www.regent.edu/law/admissions
- Private
- Year founded: 1986
- 2005-2006 tuition: full-time: $23,870; part-time: $17,710
- Enrollment 2005-06 academic year: full-time: 444; part-time: 45
- U.S. News 2007 law specialty ranking: N/A

3.08-3.72 GPA, 25TH-75TH PERCENTILE

150-156 LSAT, 25TH-75TH PERCENTILE

45% ACCEPTANCE RATE

Tier 4 2007 U.S. NEWS LAW SCHOOL RANKING

ADMISSIONS

Admissions phone number: **(757) 226-4584**
Admissions email address: **lawschool@regent.edu**
Application website:
http://www.regent.edu/acad/schlaw/admissions/apply.cfm
Application deadline for Fall 2007 admission: **6/01**

Admissions statistics:

Number of applicants for Fall 2005: **720**
Number of acceptances: **322**
Number enrolled: **156**
Acceptance rate: **45%**
GPA, 25th-75th percentile, entering class Fall 2005: **3.08-3.72**
LSAT, 25th-75th percentile, entering class Fall 2005: **150-156**

Part-time program:

Number of applicants for Fall 2005: **25**
Number of acceptances: **11**
Number enrolled: **5**
Acceptance rate: **44%**
GPA, 25th-75th percentile, entering class Fall 2005: **3.30-3.51**
LSAT, 25th-75th percentile, entering class Fall 2005: **149-155**

FINANCIAL AID

Financial aid phone number: **(757) 226-4559**
Financial aid application deadline: **4/01**
Tuition 2005-2006 academic year: full-time: **$23,870**; part-time: **$17,710**
Room and board: **$6,138**; books: **$1,372**; miscellaneous expenses: **$7,483**
Total of room/board/books/miscellaneous expenses: **$14,993**
University offers graduate student housing for which law students are eligible.

Financial aid profile

Percent of students that received grants for the 2004-2005 academic year: full-time: **85%**; part-time **82%**
Median grant amount: full-time: **$4,300**; part-time: **$3,160**
The average law-school debt of those in the Class of 2005 who borrowed: **$71,645**. Proportion who borrowed: **96%**

ACADEMIC PROGRAMS

Calendar: **semester**
Joint degrees awarded: **J.D. / M.A. Communications; J.D. / M.A. Management; J.D. / M.A. Journalism; J.D. / M.A. Counseling; J.D. / Masters Business Administration; J.D. / M.A. Divinity; J.D / M.A. Government; J.D. / M.D.V**
Typical first-year section size: Full-time: **80**; Part-time: **40**
Is there typically a "small section" of the first year class, other than Legal Writing, taught by full-time faculty?: Full-time: **no**; Part-time: **no**
Number of course titles, beyond the first year curriculum, offered last year: **71**
Percentages of upper division course sections, excluding seminars, with an enrollment of:

Under 25: **69%**   25 to 49: **19%**
50 to 74: **9%**   75 to 99: **3%**
100+: **0%**

Areas of specialization: appellate advocacy, clinical training, dispute resolution, environmental law, healthcare law, intellectual property law, international law, tax law, trial advocacy

Fall 2005 faculty profile

Total teaching faculty: **43**. Full-time: **53%**; **78%** men, **22%** women, **22%** minorities. Part-time: **47%**; **70%** men, **30%** women, **5%** minorities
Student-to-faculty ratio: **18.3**

SPECIAL PROGRAMS (as provided by law school):

In addition to classes such as appellate advocacy, Regent Law students may further develop their law skills through clinical opportunities, externships and co-curricular activities. Each program provides students with the opportunity to earn academic credit through independent studies while honing their skills in areas such as legal writing, oral advocacy, client counseling, interviewing and negotiation. Law students who have completed the first year of classes have the opportunity to earn academic credit for work performed in a variety of nonprofit practice settings, including public-interest organizations, municipal and state government agencies, and courts. Externs typically work 8 to 10 hours per week and perform legal research, draft legal documents, interview witnesses and assist in court. Externships provide students an avenue to explore one or more areas of the law. Each summer Regent Law hosts a program in Strasbourg, France, focusing on international law and human rights. Strasbourg is the home of the European Court of Human Rights, the Council of Europe, and the European Parliament, offering international law study at its best. Strasbourg students enroll in courses on comparative law, international human rights and the origins of western legal tradition. Regent faculty and other distinguished scholars and practicing attorneys teach in the Strasbourg program. Biblical perspectives are incorporated into the Strasbourg program classes, as are courses taught on the Virginia Beach campus. The School of Law also provides opportunities for hands-on, student-client contact through its litigation and family mediation clinics, which are open to second- and third-year students. The law school values the clinical experience, through which students learn transferable skills to enhance their professional law capabilities. In addition, Regent Law students have the unique opportunity to observe and participate in one of our country's foremost public-interest law firms, the American Center for Law and Justice. The ACLJ engages in litigation, provides legal services, renders advice, counsels clients and supports attorneys who are involved in defending Americans' religious and civil liberties. One of its primary offices is located on the Virginia Beach campus of Regent University; law students may obtain volunteer and paid positions to assist ACLJ staff attorneys.

STUDENT BODY

Fall 2005 full-time enrollment: 444

Men: 53%	Women: 47%
African-American: 5.0%	American Indian: 0.7%
Asian-American: 3.8%	Mexican-American: 0.0%
Puerto Rican: 0.0%	Other Hisp-Amer: 2.0%
White: 84.7%	International: 0.7%
Unknown: 3.2%	

Fall 2005 part-time enrollment: 45

Men: 42%	Women: 58%
African-American: 15.6%	American Indian: 0.0%
Asian-American: 2.2%	Mexican-American: 0.0%
Puerto Rican: 0.0%	Other Hisp-Amer: 2.2%
White: 75.6%	International: 0.0%
Unknown: 4.4%	

Attrition rates for 2004-2005 full-time students
Percent of students discontinuing law school:

Men: 5%	Women: 8%
First-year students: 8%	Second-year students: 13%
Third-year students: 1%	

LIBRARY RESOURCES

The library holds 66,988 and receives 2,242 current subscriptions.
Total volumes: 387,451
Percentage of the titles in the online catalog: 98%
Total seats available for library users: 358

INFORMATION TECHNOLOGY

Number of wired network connections available to students: 246 total (in the law library, excluding computer labs: 223; in classrooms: 10; in computer labs: 0; elsewhere in the law school: 13)
Law school has a wireless network.
Approximate number of simultaneous users that can be accommodated on wireless network: 120
Students are not required to own a computer.

EMPLOYMENT AND SALARIES

Proportion of 2004 graduates employed at graduation: 46%
Employed 9 months later, as of February 15, 2005: 89%
Salaries in the private sector (law firms, business, industry): $35,000–$53,000 (25th-75th percentile)
Median salary in the private sector: $42,500
Percentage in the private sector who reported salary information: 63%
Median salary in public service (government, judicial clerkships, academic posts, non-profits): $38,000

Percentage of 2004 graduates in:

Law firms: 41%	Bus./industry (legal): 0%
Bus./industry (nonlegal): 20%	Government: 17%
Public interest: 9%	Judicial clerkship: 7%
Academia : 6%	Unknown: 0%

2004 graduates employed in-state: 61%
2004 graduates employed in foreign countries: 0%
Number of states where graduates are employed: 18
Percentage of 2004 graduates working in: New England: 0%, Middle Atlantic: 2%, East North Central: 4%, West North Central: 0%, South Atlantic: 80%, East South Central: 1%, West South Central: 6%, Mountain: 1%, Pacific: 6%, Unknown: 0%

BAR PASSAGE RATES

Based on 2004 graduates taking Summer 2004 or Winter 2005 exams. Most of the school's first-time test takers took the bar in Virginia.

61%
School's bar passage rate for first-time test takers

74%
Statewide bar passage rate for first-time test takers

Roger Williams University (Papitto)

■ 10 Metacom Avenue, Bristol, RI, 02809-5171
■ http://law.rwu.edu
■ Private
■ Year founded: 1992
■ 2005-2006 tuition: full-time: $910/credit hour; part-time: $910/credit hour
■ Enrollment 2005-06 academic year: full-time: 511; part-time: 97
■ U.S. News 2007 law specialty ranking: N/A

2.94-3.54	GPA, 25TH-75TH PERCENTILE
151-155	LSAT, 25TH-75TH PERCENTILE
41%	ACCEPTANCE RATE
Tier 4	2007 U.S. NEWS LAW SCHOOL RANKING

ADMISSIONS

Admissions phone number: **(401) 254-4555**
Admissions email address: **Admissions@rwu.edu**
Application website:
    http://law.rwu.edu/Admission/Apply.htm
Application deadline for Fall 2007 admission: **4/15**

Admissions statistics:

Number of applicants for Fall 2005: **1,743**
Number of acceptances: **716**
Number enrolled: **198**
Acceptance rate: **41%**
GPA, 25th-75th percentile, entering class Fall 2005:
    2.94-3.54
LSAT, 25th-75th percentile, entering class Fall 2005: **151-155**

FINANCIAL AID

Financial aid phone number: **(401) 254-4641**
Financial aid application deadline: **N/A**
Tuition 2005-2006 academic year: full-time: **$910/credit hour;** part-time: **$910/credit hour**
Room and board: **N/A**; books: **N/A**; miscellaneous expenses: **N/A**
Total of room/board/books/miscellaneous expenses: **$15,234**
University does not offer graduate student housing for which law students are eligible.

Financial aid profile

Percent of students that received grants for the 2004-2005 academic year: full-time: **41%**; part-time **48%**
Median grant amount: full-time: **$10,000**; part-time: **$7,500**
The average law-school debt of those in the Class of 2005 who borrowed: **$86,714.** Proportion who borrowed: **84%**

ACADEMIC PROGRAMS

Calendar: **semester**
Joint degrees awarded: **J.D./M.M.A.; J.D./MLRHR; J.D./M.S.C.J.**
Typical first-year section size: Full-time: **92**; Part-time: **42**

Is there typically a "small section" of the first year class, other than Legal Writing, taught by full-time faculty?:
    Full-time: **no**; Part-time: **no**
Number of course titles, beyond the first year curriculum, offered last year: **130**
Percentages of upper division course sections, excluding seminars, with an enrollment of:
    Under 25: **52%**   25 to 49: **24%**
    50 to 74: **18%**   75 to 99: **5%**
    100+: **0%**
Areas of specialization: appellate advocacy, clinical training, dispute resolution, environmental law, healthcare law, intellectual property law, international law, tax law, trial advocacy

Fall 2005 faculty profile

Total teaching faculty: **N/A**. Full-time: **N/A**; **N/A** men, **N/A** women, **N/A** minorities. Part-time: **N/A**; **N/A** men, **N/A** women, **N/A** minorities
Student-to-faculty ratio: **19.9**

SPECIAL PROGRAMS *(as provided by law school):*

Joint degree programs: Roger Williams University offers a J.D./M.S. in criminal justice. This program is designed to prepare graduates to formulate system policy and serve effectively as administrators of U.S. justice system agencies. The School of Law also offers two joint degree programs in conjunction with the University of Rhode Island. The J.D./master of marine affairs program is geared toward students interested in maritime, admiralty, and environmental law. The J.D./M.S. in labor relations and human resources program prepares students for those fields. Other special programs include: Marine Affairs Institute: The institute is a distinguished focal point for the exploration of legal, economic, and policy issues raised by the development of the oceans and coastal zone. Students take elective courses in traditional admiralty law and practice, pollution and environmental regulation, coastal zoning, fisheries, and the international law of the sea. Feinstein Institute for Legal Service: The school believes that lawyers should serve the communities that support them and requires students to complete 20 hours of community service. The institute promotes public service. Honors program: This is a three-year program of seminars, clinics, and externships. Scholarships of half to full tuition are awarded to students selected for the Honors College by the admissions committee. Practical experience: The School of Law operates clinics in criminal defense, and community justice and legal assistance. These clinics serve the community by helping indigent clients and provide an excellent opportunity for students to represent clients before courts and agencies under faculty supervision. Students may also engage in a semester-long supervised clerkship in a judge's chambers or in a public-interest or governmental law office for academic credit. Study abroad: The London Program on Comparative Advocacy provides a unique opportunity to participate in a mini-pupilage with a barrister. The program in Lisbon, Portugal, is the only study abroad law program there. The classes are taught in English by professors from the Catholic University of Portugal and the Roger Williams University School of Law.

STUDENT BODY

Fall 2005 full-time enrollment: 511

Men: 50%	Women: 50%
African-American: 3.5%	American Indian: 0.8%
Asian-American: 5.1%	Mexican-American: 0.2%
Puerto Rican: 0.6%	Other Hisp-Amer: 2.5%
White: 70.8%	International: 0.6%
Unknown: 15.9%	

Fall 2005 part-time enrollment: 97

Men: 53%	Women: 47%
African-American: 2.1%	American Indian: 0.0%
Asian-American: 3.1%	Mexican-American: 0.0%
Puerto Rican: 0.0%	Other Hisp-Amer: 3.1%
White: 78.4%	International: 0.0%
Unknown: 13.4%	

Attrition rates for 2004-2005 full-time students
Percent of students discontinuing law school:

Men: 6%	Women: 10%
First-year students: 18%	Second-year students: 2%
Third-year students: 1%	

LIBRARY RESOURCES

The library holds 128,349 and receives 3,657 current subscriptions.
Total volumes: 287,384
Percentage of the titles in the online catalog: 100%
Total seats available for library users: 389

INFORMATION TECHNOLOGY

Number of wired network connections available to students: 196 total (in the law library, excluding computer labs: 120; in classrooms: 0; in computer labs: 44; elsewhere in the law school: 32)
Law school has a wireless network.
Approximate number of simultaneous users that can be accommodated on wireless network: 240
Students are not required to own a computer.

EMPLOYMENT AND SALARIES

Proportion of 2004 graduates employed at graduation: N/A
Employed 9 months later, as of February 15, 2005: 69%
Salaries in the private sector (law firms, business, industry): $36,500–$70,000 (25th-75th percentile)
Median salary in the private sector: $42,500
Percentage in the private sector who reported salary information: 62%
Median salary in public service (government, judicial clerkships, academic posts, non-profits): $41,000

Percentage of 2004 graduates in:

Law firms: 52%	Bus./industry (legal): 11%
Bus./industry (nonlegal): N/A	Government: 11%
Public interest: 9%	Judicial clerkship: 14%
Academia : 3%	Unknown: 1%

2004 graduates employed in-state: 46%
2004 graduates employed in foreign countries: 3%
Number of states where graduates are employed: 17
Percentage of 2004 graduates working in: New England: 74%, Middle Atlantic: 10%, East North Central: 2%, West North Central: 1%, South Atlantic: 7%, East South Central: 0%, West South Central: 1%, Mountain: 2%, Pacific: 0%, Unknown: 0%

BAR PASSAGE RATES

Based on 2004 graduates taking Summer 2004 or Winter 2005 exams. Most of the school's first-time test takers took the bar in Rhode Island.

71%
School's bar passage rate for first-time test takers

77%
Statewide bar passage rate for first-time test takers

Rutgers State University–Camden

- 217 N. Fifth Street, Camden, NJ, 08102-1203
- http://www-camlaw.rutgers.edu
- Public
- Year founded: 1926
- 2005-2006 tuition: In-state: full-time: $18,016, part-time: $14,348; Out-of-state: full-time: $25,609
- Enrollment 2005-06 academic year: full-time: 571; part-time: 216
- U.S. News 2007 law specialty ranking: N/A

3.10-3.65 GPA, 25TH-75TH PERCENTILE

159-163 LSAT, 25TH-75TH PERCENTILE

14% ACCEPTANCE RATE

65 2007 U.S. NEWS LAW SCHOOL RANKING

ADMISSIONS
Admissions phone number: (800) 466-7561
Admissions email address:
admissions@camlaw.rutgers.edu
Application website: **http://www-camlaw.rutgers.edu/admissions/**
Application deadline for Fall 2007 admission: 4/01

Admissions statistics:
Number of applicants for Fall 2005: **2,481**
Number of acceptances: **344**
Number enrolled: **140**
Acceptance rate: **14%**
GPA, 25th-75th percentile, entering class Fall 2005: **3.10-3.65**
LSAT, 25th-75th percentile, entering class Fall 2005: **159-163**

Part-time program:
Number of applicants for Fall 2005: **2,481**
Number of acceptances: **230**
Number enrolled: **121**
Acceptance rate: **9%**
GPA, 25th-75th percentile, entering class Fall 2005: **3.10-3.61**
LSAT, 25th-75th percentile, entering class Fall 2005: **154-161**

FINANCIAL AID
Financial aid phone number: (856) 225-6039
Financial aid application deadline: 3/03
Tuition 2005-2006 academic year: In-state: full-time: $18,016, part-time: $14,348; Out-of-state: full-time: $25,609
Room and board: $9,583; books: $1,200; miscellaneous expenses: $2,302
Total of room/board/books/miscellaneous expenses: $13,085
University offers graduate student housing for which law students are eligible.

Financial aid profile
Percent of students that received grants for the 2004-2005 academic year: full-time: 40%; part-time 8%
Median grant amount: full-time: $4,000; part-time: $1,500
The average law-school debt of those in the Class of 2005 who borrowed: $60,959. Proportion who borrowed: 83%

ACADEMIC PROGRAMS
Calendar: **semester**
Joint degrees awarded: **J.D./M.B.A.; J.D./M.P.A.; J.D./M.P.A.P.; J.D./M.S.W.; J.D./M.A.**
Typical first-year section size: Full-time: **85**; Part-time: **50**
Is there typically a "small section" of the first year class, other than Legal Writing, taught by full-time faculty?: Full-time: **yes**; Part-time: **yes**
Number of course titles, beyond the first year curriculum, offered last year: **102**
Percentages of upper division course sections, excluding seminars, with an enrollment of:

Under 25: **61%**	25 to 49: **25%**	
50 to 74: **10%**	75 to 99: **3%**	
100+: **2%**		

Areas of specialization: appellate advocacy, clinical training, dispute resolution, environmental law, healthcare law, intellectual property law, international law, tax law, trial advocacy

Fall 2005 faculty profile
Total teaching faculty: **110**. Full-time: **39%**; **74%** men, **26%** women, **12%** minorities. Part-time: **61%**; **69%** men, **31%** women, **6%** minorities
Student-to-faculty ratio: **15.7**

SPECIAL PROGRAMS *(as provided by law school)*:
Rutgers University School of Law at Camden offers students a rich and robust array of programs ranging from business concentrations to public-interest activities to an outstanding externship program. Students are encouraged to pursue their interests intensively as they progress from basic courses to advanced programs that provide practical applications of the law through both simulated and clinical lawyering experiences.

The unique legal writing program provides the communications skills and training that young lawyers need to succeed. After completing the first-year legal research and writing program, students must take an average of one course every semester that includes an intensive writing component.

The law school's clinical program enables students to learn both litigation and counseling skills in a wide variety of practice areas, including domestic violence, immigration, and elder law. Our pro bono program includes bankruptcy, mediation, tax assistance, immigration, and research opportunities, among others. In the Civil Practice Clinic, students interview and represent clients, make strategic decisions, draft documents, conduct negotiations, and make court appearances.

The Rutgers Community Development Clinic provides legal representation and related technical assistance to nonprofit organizations and small businesses in Camden and is assisting in the city's revitalization.

The Rutgers/LEAP Legal Project, a partnership between the Civil Practice Clinic and the LEAP Academy charter school, provides legal advice, representation, and community education to students and their parents.

In the Marshall-Brennan Fellows program, second- and third-year students teach a course on constitutional rights and responsibilities in Camden public high schools.

The externship program enables students to experience the law in many varied settings. Students work in trial judges' chambers, hospital legal departments, and legal services agencies, among other settings.

Many students earn specialized degrees simultaneously with their J.D. degrees, including the J.D./M.B.A./M.S.W./M.P.A. A joint degree program is also offered with the University of Medicine and Dentistry of New Jersey.

The law school has one of the highest percentages of students who accept clerkships with federal and state judges upon graduation. These positions are highly regarded by employers and serve as springboards to outstanding careers in both the public and private sectors.

STUDENT BODY

Fall 2005 full-time enrollment: 571

Men: 60%	Women: 40%
African-American: 5.4%	American Indian: 0.0%
Asian-American: 10.2%	Mexican-American: 0.7%
Puerto Rican: 1.1%	Other Hisp-Amer: 3.3%
White: 78.1%	International: 1.2%
Unknown: 0.0%	

Fall 2005 part-time enrollment: 216

Men: 58%	Women: 42%
African-American: 8.8%	American Indian: 0.5%
Asian-American: 2.8%	Mexican-American: 1.9%
Puerto Rican: 2.8%	Other Hisp-Amer: 7.9%
White: 75.0%	International: 0.5%
Unknown: 0.0%	

Attrition rates for 2004-2005 full-time students
Percent of students discontinuing law school:

Men: 2%	Women: 2%

First-year students: **6%** Second-year students: **0%**
Third-year students: **N/A**

LIBRARY RESOURCES
The library holds **90,428** and receives **4,457** current subscriptions.
Total volumes: **439,801**
Percentage of the titles in the online catalog: **100%**
Total seats available for library users: **403**

INFORMATION TECHNOLOGY
Number of wired network connections available to students: **166** total (in the law library, excluding computer labs: **60**; in classrooms: **6**; in computer labs: **50**; elsewhere in the law school: **50**)
Law school has a wireless network.
Approximate number of simultaneous users that can be accommodated on wireless network: **512**
Students are not required to own a computer.

EMPLOYMENT AND SALARIES
Proportion of 2004 graduates employed at graduation: **87%**
Employed 9 months later, as of February 15, 2005: **93%**
Salaries in the private sector (law firms, business, industry): **$52,000–$100,000** (25th-75th percentile)
Median salary in the private sector: **$72,000**
Percentage in the private sector who reported salary information: **48%**
Median salary in public service (government, judicial clerkships, academic posts, non-profits): **$37,000**

Percentage of 2004 graduates in:

Law firms: **33%**	Bus./industry (legal): **7%**
Bus./industry (nonlegal): **6%**	Government: **6%**
Public interest: **2%**	Judicial clerkship: **40%**
Academia : **1%**	Unknown: **5%**

2004 graduates employed in-state: **56%**
2004 graduates employed in foreign countries: **0%**
Number of states where graduates are employed: **18**
Percentage of 2004 graduates working in: New England: **1%**, Middle Atlantic: **86%**, East North Central: **2%**, West North Central: **1%**, South Atlantic: **6%**, East South Central: **0%**, West South Central: **1%**, Mountain: **1%**, Pacific: **1%**, Unknown: **2%**

BAR PASSAGE RATES
Based on 2004 graduates taking Summer 2004 or Winter 2005 exams. Most of the school's first-time test takers took the bar in New Jersey.

81%
School's bar passage rate for first-time test takers

80%
Statewide bar passage rate for first-time test takers

Rutgers State University—Newark

- 123 Washington Street, Newark, NJ, 07102
- http://law.newark.rutgers.edu
- Public
- **Year founded:** 1908
- **2005-2006 tuition:** In-state: full-time: $17,789, part-time: $14,191; Out-of-state: full-time: $25,382
- **Enrollment 2005-06 academic year:** full-time: 564; part-time: 240
- **U.S. News 2007 law specialty ranking:** clinical training: 27

3.06-3.55 GPA, 25TH-75TH PERCENTILE

154-161 LSAT, 25TH-75TH PERCENTILE

24% ACCEPTANCE RATE

80 2007 U.S. NEWS LAW SCHOOL RANKING

ADMISSIONS

Admissions phone number: **(973) 353-5554**
Admissions email address:
awalton@andromeda.rutgers.edu
Application website: **http://law.newark.rutgers.edu/admissions.html**
Application deadline for Fall 2007 admission: **3/15**

Admissions statistics:
Number of applicants for Fall 2005: **2,886**
Number of acceptances: **690**
Number enrolled: **181**
Acceptance rate: **24%**
GPA, 25th-75th percentile, entering class Fall 2005: **3.06-3.55**
LSAT, 25th-75th percentile, entering class Fall 2005: **154-161**

Part-time program:
Number of applicants for Fall 2005: **606**
Number of acceptances: **121**
Number enrolled: **68**
Acceptance rate: **20%**
GPA, 25th-75th percentile, entering class Fall 2005: **3.02-3.51**
LSAT, 25th-75th percentile, entering class Fall 2005: **153-159**

FINANCIAL AID

Financial aid phone number: **(973) 353-1702**
Financial aid application deadline: **3/01**
Tuition 2005-2006 academic year: In-state: full-time: **$17,789,** part-time: **$14,191;** Out-of-state: full-time: **$25,382**
Room and board: **$13,081;** books: **$1,200;** miscellaneous expenses: **$3,230**
Total of room/board/books/miscellaneous expenses: **$17,511**
University offers graduate student housing for which law students are eligible.

Financial aid profile
Percent of students that received grants for the 2004-2005 academic year: full-time: **45%**; part-time **22%**
Median grant amount: full-time: **$4,000**; part-time: **$3,000**
The average law-school debt of those in the Class of 2005 who borrowed: **$58,940.** Proportion who borrowed: **86%**

ACADEMIC PROGRAMS

Calendar: **semester**
Joint degrees awarded: **N/A**
Typical first-year section size: Full-time: **60**; Part-time: **70**
Is there typically a "small section" of the first year class, other than Legal Writing, taught by full-time faculty?: Full-time: **yes**; Part-time: **yes**
Number of course titles, beyond the first year curriculum, offered last year: **115**
Percentages of upper division course sections, excluding seminars, with an enrollment of:

Under 25: **55%**	25 to 49: **29%**
50 to 74: **13%**	75 to 99: **2%**
100+: **1%**	

Areas of specialization: appellate advocacy, clinical training, dispute resolution, environmental law, healthcare law, intellectual property law, international law, tax law, trial advocacy

Fall 2005 faculty profile
Total teaching faculty: **78.** Full-time: **60%**; **57%** men, **43%** women, **21%** minorities. Part-time: **40%**; **71%** men, **29%** women, **10%** minorities
Student-to-faculty ratio: **15.4**

SPECIAL PROGRAMS *(as provided by law school):*
The School of Law-Newark has been a pioneer in the commitment to increasing diversity in the legal profession. The embodiment of that commitment is the Minority Student Program (MSP). The MSP was established in 1968, when the faculty determined to pursue aggressively a policy of diversity and equal opportunity for those who had been historically under-represented in law schools and in the legal profession. Since 1968, more than 1,800 students of color, and students

from disadvantaged backgrounds of all races, have participated in the MSP and have graduated from the law school to
become leaders at the Bar. The school's strong and historic
commitment to public service is evident throughout the curriculum, particularly in our eight legal clinics, where students are exposed to the legal issues facing the poor and
underrepresented. Noncurricular public interest opportunities and activities, carried out under the Eric R. Neisser
Public Interest Program, include pro bono work, internships,
fellowships, summer placements, and loan repayment assistance, as well as regular programming about public issues.
With nearly 35 years of pacesetting experience, Rutgers Law
School offers students rich opportunities for hands-on legal
experience in real cases involving underrepresented clients,
communities or causes. This fall, 20 professors are supervising more than 100 second- and third-year law students
enrolled in one of our clinics: Child Advocacy Clinic,
Constitutional Litigation Clinic, Community Law Clinic,
Environmental Law Clinic, Federal Tax Law Clinic, Special
Education Clinic, Urban Legal Clinic, and Women's Rights
Litigation Clinic. Under intensive faculty oversight, students
handle a myriad of litigation and transactional matters,
including civil rights and liberties, child custody and
guardianship, consumer protection, human health and environmental protection, Social Security disability, welfare, intellectual property, housing, community development, business
formation, mergers and asset purchases, federal taxation,
women's rights, special education and criminal defense.
Rutgers School of Law–Newark offers judicial externships, as
well as externships in intellectual property law with the
United States Patent and Trademark Office, in immigration
law with the Department of Homeland Security, United
States Immigration & Customs Enforcement Services, Office
of the Chief Counsel, New York District (USICE) or the
American Friends Service Committee, Immigration Rights
Program (AFSC), and in labor law, with the National Labor
Relations Board. The objectives of the externship program
are to improve legal analysis, writing, and practice skills, and
heighten awareness of ethical issues by affording students
close contact with practicing public servants and judges who
have agreed to supervise.

STUDENT BODY

Fall 2005 full-time enrollment: 564

Men: 54%	Women: 46%
African-American: 14.7%	American Indian: 0.5%
Asian-American: 14.4%	Mexican-American: 1.4%
Puerto Rican: 5.1%	Other Hisp-Amer: 5.0%
White: 57.3%	International: 1.6%
Unknown: 0.0%	

Fall 2005 part-time enrollment: 240

Men: 62%	Women: 38%
African-American: 12.5%	American Indian: 0.0%
Asian-American: 10.0%	Mexican-American: 0.8%
Puerto Rican: 3.8%	Other Hisp-Amer: 7.9%
White: 60.4%	International: 4.6%
Unknown: 0.0%	

Attrition rates for 2004-2005 full-time students
Percent of students discontinuing law school:

Men: 7%	Women: 5%
First-year students: 12%	Second-year students: 3%
Third-year students: 2%	

LIBRARY RESOURCES

The library holds 188,600 and receives 3,160 current
   subscriptions.
Total volumes: 522,600
Percentage of the titles in the online catalog: 44%
Total seats available for library users: 522

INFORMATION TECHNOLOGY

Number of wired network connections available to students: 540 total (in the law library, excluding computer
   labs: 160; in classrooms: 350; in computer labs: 0; elsewhere in the law school: 30)
Law school has a wireless network.
Approximate number of simultaneous users that can be
   accommodated on wireless network: 600
Students are not required to own a computer.

EMPLOYMENT AND SALARIES

Proportion of 2004 graduates employed at graduation: 67%
Employed 9 months later, as of February 15, 2005: 95%
Salaries in the private sector (law firms, business, indus-
   try): $85,000–$125,000 (25th-75th percentile)
Median salary in the private sector: N/A
Percentage in the private sector who reported salary
   information: 59%
Median salary in public service (government, judicial clerk-
   ships, academic posts, non-profits): $38,500

Percentage of 2004 graduates in:

Law firms: 44%	Bus./industry (legal): 3%
Bus./industry (nonlegal): 10%	Government: 4%
Public interest: 4%	Judicial clerkship: 33%
Academia : 2%	Unknown: 1%

2004 graduates employed in-state: 70%
2004 graduates employed in foreign countries: 1%
Number of states where graduates are employed: 12
Percentage of 2004 graduates working in: New England:
   2%, Middle Atlantic: 92%, East North Central: 1%, West
   North Central: 0%, South Atlantic: 3%, East South
   Central: 0%, West South Central: 1%, Mountain: 0%,
   Pacific: 1%, Unknown: 1%

BAR PASSAGE RATES

Based on 2004 graduates taking Summer 2004 or
Winter 2005 exams. Most of the school's first-time test
takers took the bar in New Jersey.

73%

School's bar passage rate for first-time test takers

80%

Statewide bar passage rate for first-time test takers

Samford University (Cumberland)

- 800 Lakeshore Drive, Birmingham, AL, 35229
- http://cumberland.samford.edu
- Private
- **Year founded:** 1847
- **2005-2006 tuition:** full-time: $24,708; part-time: $14,832
- **Enrollment 2005-06 academic year:** full-time: 527; part-time: 5
- **U.S. News 2007 law specialty ranking:** trial advocacy: 11

2.98-3.52	GPA, 25TH-75TH PERCENTILE
154-158	LSAT, 25TH-75TH PERCENTILE
32%	ACCEPTANCE RATE
Tier 3	2007 U.S. NEWS LAW SCHOOL RANKING

ADMISSIONS

Admissions phone number: **(205) 726-2702**
Admissions email address: **law.admissions@samford.edu**
Application website: **http://cumberland.samford.edu/application**
Application deadline for Fall 2007 admission: **5/01**

Admissions statistics:

Number of applicants for Fall 2005: **1,420**
Number of acceptances: **450**
Number enrolled: **173**
Acceptance rate: **32%**
GPA, 25th-75th percentile, entering class Fall 2005: **2.98-3.52**
LSAT, 25th-75th percentile, entering class Fall 2005: **154-158**

Part-time program:

Number of applicants for Fall 2005: **5**
Number of acceptances: **5**
Number enrolled: **2**
Acceptance rate: **100%**
GPA, 25th-75th percentile, entering class Fall 2005: **2.39-3.76**
LSAT, 25th-75th percentile, entering class Fall 2005: **144-144**

FINANCIAL AID

Financial aid phone number: **(205) 726-2905**
Financial aid application deadline: **3/01**
Tuition 2005-2006 academic year: full-time: **$24,708**; part-time: **$14,832**
Room and board: **$11,418**; books: **$1,380**; miscellaneous expenses: **$4,494**
Total of room/board/books/miscellaneous expenses: **$17,292**
University does not offer graduate student housing for which law students are eligible.

Financial aid profile

Percent of students that received grants for the 2004-2005 academic year: full-time: **31%**
Median grant amount: full-time: **$15,000**
The average law-school debt of those in the Class of 2005 who borrowed: **$76,624**. Proportion who borrowed: **85%**

ACADEMIC PROGRAMS

Calendar: **semester**
Joint degrees awarded: **J.D./M.P.H.; J.D./M.B.A.; J.D./M.A.cc; J.D./M.Div; J.D./M.S. in Environmental Management; J.D./M.P.A.**
Typical first-year section size: Full-time: **58**
Is there typically a "small section" of the first year class, other than Legal Writing, taught by full-time faculty?: Full-time: **no**; Part-time: **no**
Number of course titles, beyond the first year curriculum, offered last year: **94**
Percentages of upper division course sections, excluding seminars, with an enrollment of:

Under 25: **50%**	25 to 49: **27%**
50 to 74: **13%**	75 to 99: **11%**
100+: **0%**	

Areas of specialization: appellate advocacy, clinical training, dispute resolution, environmental law, healthcare law, intellectual property law, international law, tax law, trial advocacy

Fall 2005 faculty profile

Total teaching faculty: **45**. Full-time: **51%**; **74%** men, **26%** women, **9%** minorities. Part-time: **49%**; **73%** men, **27%** women, **14%** minorities
Student-to-faculty ratio: **18.2**

SPECIAL PROGRAMS (as provided by law school):

Cumberland law students may take advantage of several special programs to enhance their classroom education. They begin with our clinical programs, which are a logical extension of our nationally recognized advocacy program.

Cumberland's clinical education program is in the form of semester-long and summer externships. These externships offer students placements in corporate, government, public-interest, and litigation areas. Judicial externships involve placements with federal and state judges. These externships give students an opportunity to apply in a real setting what they have learned in the classroom, to observe experienced lawyers in action, and to practice their skills under the supervision of an experienced lawyer.

Cumberland offers a certificate in trial advocacy to students who excel in our advocacy program. To obtain the certificate, students must successfully complete the core advocacy courses.

Because of Cumberland's location in a biotechnology center, the law school has created the Center for Biotechnology, Law, and Ethics to place the law school on the cutting edge of this rapidly growing field. The center is the only one of its kind in the United States and focuses on the rigorous analysis of the legal, ethical, and public-policy issues created by biotechnology. The center also focuses on practical training in the legal disciplines related to biotechnology.

Cumberland sponsors three international study programs in the summer. The first program is an International and Comparative Law Program offered at Sidney-Sussex College in Cambridge, England. The second program is the Cumberland-at-Victoria, British Columbia International and Environmental Law program. The program is located at the University of Victoria on Vancouver Island and offers courses focusing on the environment, maritime and international trade issues. The third program is at the Federal University of Ceara in Fortaleza, Brazil. The program features Comparative Law and also focuses on Alternative Dispute Resolution.

The Cumberland Public Interest Project seeks to develop in students a sensitivity to people's needs and concerns, an understanding of a lawyer's duty to serve, and the will to be responsible community leaders, by providing volunteer placements with organizations that serve underrepresented or economically disadvantaged groups.

Finally, thanks to the breadth of resources made available by Samford University and augmented by the University of Alabama-Birmingham, with its world-renowned medical center, Cumberland is able to offer joint degree programs in accountancy, business, divinity, environmental management, public administration, and public health.

STUDENT BODY

Fall 2005 full-time enrollment: 527
Men: 60%   Women: 40%
African-American: 6.8%   American Indian: 1.1%
Asian-American: 0.9%   Mexican-American: 0.2%
Puerto Rican: 0.0%   Other Hisp-Amer: 1.7%
White: 79.9%   International: 0.0%
Unknown: 9.3%

Fall 2005 part-time enrollment: 5
Men: 40%   Women: 60%
African-American: 40.0%   American Indian: 0.0%
Asian-American: 0.0%   Mexican-American: 0.0%
Puerto Rican: 0.0%   Other Hisp-Amer: 20.0%
White: 40.0%   International: 0.0%
Unknown: 0.0%

Attrition rates for 2004-2005 full-time students
Percent of students discontinuing law school:
Men: 4%   Women: 3%
First-year students: 6%   Second-year students: 5%
Third-year students: N/A

LIBRARY RESOURCES
The library holds 37,092 and receives 2,029 current subscriptions.
Total volumes: 290,954
Percentage of the titles in the online catalog: 100%
Total seats available for library users: 474

INFORMATION TECHNOLOGY
Number of wired network connections available to students: 231 total (in the law library, excluding computer labs: 200; in classrooms: 0; in computer labs: 6; elsewhere in the law school: 25)
Law school doesn't have a wireless network.
Approximate number of simultaneous users that can be accommodated on wireless network: N/A
Students are not required to own a computer.

EMPLOYMENT AND SALARIES
Proportion of 2004 graduates employed at graduation: 60%
Employed 9 months later, as of February 15, 2005: 97%
Salaries in the private sector (law firms, business, industry): $45,000–$70,000 (25th-75th percentile)
Median salary in the private sector: $55,000
Percentage in the private sector who reported salary information: 69%
Median salary in public service (government, judicial clerkships, academic posts, non-profits): $44,200

Percentage of 2004 graduates in:
Law firms: 74%   Bus./industry (legal): 1%
Bus./industry (nonlegal): 5%   Government: 11%
Public interest: 1%   Judicial clerkship: 6%
Academia : 1%   Unknown: 1%

2004 graduates employed in-state: 65%
2004 graduates employed in foreign countries: 0%
Number of states where graduates are employed: 10
Percentage of 2004 graduates working in: New England: 0%, Middle Atlantic: 0%, East North Central: 0%, West North Central: 0%, South Atlantic: 21%, East South Central: 78%, West South Central: 1%, Mountain: 0%, Pacific: 0%, Unknown: 1%

BAR PASSAGE RATES
Based on 2004 graduates taking Summer 2004 or Winter 2005 exams. Most of the school's first-time test takers took the bar in Alabama.

85%

School's bar passage rate for first-time test takers

81%

Statewide bar passage rate for first-time test takers

Santa Clara University

- 500 El Camino Real, Santa Clara, CA, 95053-0421
- http://www.scu.edu/law
- Private
- Year founded: 1851
- 2005-2006 tuition: full-time: $1,066/credit hour; part-time: $1,066/credit hour
- Enrollment 2005-06 academic year: full-time: 721; part-time: 234
- U.S. News 2007 law specialty ranking: intellecutal property law: 4

3.21-3.60 GPA, 25TH-75TH PERCENTILE

157-161 LSAT, 25TH-75TH PERCENTILE

37% ACCEPTANCE RATE

87 2007 U.S. NEWS LAW SCHOOL RANKING

ADMISSIONS

Admissions phone number: (408) 554-4800
Admissions email address: **lawadmissions@scu.edu**
Application website:
http://https://www.scu.edu/apply/law/handler.cfm?event =home
Application deadline for Fall 2007 admission: **6/30**

Admissions statistics:
Number of applicants for Fall 2005: **4,112**
Number of acceptances: **1,539**
Number enrolled: **247**
Acceptance rate: **37%**
GPA, 25th-75th percentile, entering class Fall 2005: **3.21-3.60**
LSAT, 25th-75th percentile, entering class Fall 2005: **157-161**

Part-time program:
Number of applicants for Fall 2005: **375**
Number of acceptances: **126**
Number enrolled: **63**
Acceptance rate: **34%**
GPA, 25th-75th percentile, entering class Fall 2005: **2.94-3.37**
LSAT, 25th-75th percentile, entering class Fall 2005: **156-161**

FINANCIAL AID

Financial aid phone number: (408) 554-4447
Financial aid application deadline: **3/01**
Tuition 2005-2006 academic year: full-time: **$1,066/credit hour**; part-time: **$1,066/credit hour**
Room and board: **$12,042**; books: **$654**; miscellaneous expenses: **$6,119**
Total of room/board/books/miscellaneous expenses: **$18,815**
University offers graduate student housing for which law students are eligible.

Financial aid profile
Percent of students that received grants for the 2004-2005 academic year: full-time: **30%**; part-time **20%**
Median grant amount: full-time: **$12,000**; part-time: **$10,000**
The average law-school debt of those in the Class of 2005 who borrowed: **$88,792**. Proportion who borrowed: **78%**

ACADEMIC PROGRAMS

Calendar: **semester**
Joint degrees awarded: **J.D./M.B.A.; J.D./M.S.T.**
Typical first-year section size: Full-time: **82**; Part-time: **64**
Is there typically a "small section" of the first year class, other than Legal Writing, taught by full-time faculty?: Full-time: **yes**; Part-time: **no**
Number of course titles, beyond the first year curriculum, offered last year: **244**
Percentages of upper division course sections, excluding seminars, with an enrollment of:
Under 25: **64%**   25 to 49: **20%**
50 to 74: **9%**   75 to 99: **8%**
100+: **0%**
Areas of specialization: appellate advocacy, clinical training, dispute resolution, environmental law, healthcare law, intellectual property law, international law, tax law, trial advocacy

Fall 2005 faculty profile
Total teaching faculty: **105**. Full-time: **49%**; **59%** men, **41%** women, **27%** minorities. Part-time: **51%**; **65%** men, **35%** women, **4%** minorities
Student-to-faculty ratio: **18.5**

SPECIAL PROGRAMS *(as provided by law school):*
Combined-degree programs: The J.D./M.B.A. program is a powerful union of Santa Clara's nationally recognized School of Law and Leavey School of Business. The J.D./M.S.T. is done in conjunction with San Jose State University. Students would take sufficient courses to satisfy both SJSU's M.S. in taxation degree and SCU's J.D. degree.

International law certificate: A specialized curriculum allows students to earn a certificate in international law. The Institute of International and Comparative Law sponsors summer law study programs in Munich, Germany; Strasbourg, France; Geneva; Oxford, England; Hong Kong; Singapore; Seoul; Bangkok, Thailand; Ho Chi Minh City, Vietnam; Beijing; Kuala Lumpur, Malaysia; Tokyo; and Sydney, Australia. All of the programs, with the exception of Oxford, offer internships.

Computer and high-technology law certificate: Santa Clara has capitalized on its Silicon Valley location by establishing a specialized curriculum that emphasizes computer and high-technology law. Students seeking an emphasis on high-technology issues can enroll in courses such as patent law, copyright, biotechnology law, and technology licensing. They may also intern with a leading high-tech firm and earn a certificate in high-technology law.

Public-interest and social justice law certificate: Students can earn a certificate in public interest and social justice. Santa Clara's Center for Social Justice and Public Service offers an impressive array of resources for students. Santa Clara University is distinctive in making explicit its intention to evoke from students a commitment to fashioning a more humane and just world.

Clinical programs: The Katharine and George Community Law Center allows students to practice law under the supervision of an experienced attorney. Students work in the areas of immigration, workers' rights, employment law, small-business development, and consumer protection. Students may earn credit for work as law clerks with public agencies such as the district attorney or public defender, with legal aid offices, or with private law offices. Students may also work as judges' clerks in appellate courts, including the California Supreme Court, or trial courts, including the U.S. District Court and local superior court. Santa Clara hosts the Northern California Innocence Project, in which law students investigate, evaluate, and, where possible, pursue relief for claims of wrongful conviction.

STUDENT BODY
Fall 2005 full-time enrollment: 721

Men: 50%	Women: 50%
African-American: 4.3%	American Indian: 0.4%
Asian-American: 26.9%	Mexican-American: 0.0%
Puerto Rican: 0.0%	Other Hisp-Amer: 11.2%
White: 56.2%	International: 0.3%
Unknown: 0.7%	

Fall 2005 part-time enrollment: 234

Men: 54%	Women: 46%
African-American: 3.0%	American Indian: 0.4%
Asian-American: 26.1%	Mexican-American: 0.0%
Puerto Rican: 0.0%	Other Hisp-Amer: 8.5%
White: 61.5%	International: 0.0%
Unknown: 0.4%	

Attrition rates for 2004-2005 full-time students
Percent of students discontinuing law school:
Men: 4%   Women: 4%

First-year students: 12%   Second-year students: 1%
Third-year students: N/A

LIBRARY RESOURCES
The library holds 143,375 and receives 4,183 current subscriptions.
Total volumes: 351,098
Percentage of the titles in the online catalog: 100%
Total seats available for library users: 483

INFORMATION TECHNOLOGY
Number of wired network connections available to students: 799 total (in the law library, excluding computer labs: 205; in classrooms: 552; in computer labs: 36; elsewhere in the law school: 6)
Law school has a wireless network.
Approximate number of simultaneous users that can be accommodated on wireless network: 160
Students are not required to own a computer.

EMPLOYMENT AND SALARIES
Proportion of 2004 graduates employed at graduation: 74%
Employed 9 months later, as of February 15, 2005: 95%
Salaries in the private sector (law firms, business, industry): $75,000–$125,000 (25th-75th percentile)
Median salary in the private sector: $125,000
Percentage in the private sector who reported salary information: 42%
Median salary in public service (government, judicial clerkships, academic posts, non-profits): $51,000

Percentage of 2004 graduates in:

Law firms: 55%	Bus./industry (legal): 11%
Bus./industry (nonlegal): 7%	Government: 9%
Public interest: 2%	Judicial clerkship: 2%
Academia : 0%	Unknown: 14%

2004 graduates employed in-state: 79%
2004 graduates employed in foreign countries: 0%
Number of states where graduates are employed: 11
Percentage of 2004 graduates working in: New England: 0%, Middle Atlantic: 1%, East North Central: 1%, West North Central: 1%, South Atlantic: 1%, East South Central: 0%, West South Central: 0%, Mountain: 2%, Pacific: 79%, Unknown: 16%

BAR PASSAGE RATES
Based on 2004 graduates taking Summer 2004 or Winter 2005 exams. Most of the school's first-time test takers took the bar in California.

68%
School's bar passage rate for first-time test takers

61%
Statewide bar passage rate for first-time test takers

Seattle University

- 901 12th Avenue, Seattle, WA, 98122-1090
- http://www.law.seattleu.edu
- Private
- Year founded: 1972
- 2005-2006 tuition: full-time: $26,026; part-time: $17,352
- Enrollment 2005-06 academic year: full-time: 874; part-time: 235
- U.S. News 2007 law specialty ranking: clinical training: 27

3.17-3.63 GPA, 25TH-75TH PERCENTILE

152-159 LSAT, 25TH-75TH PERCENTILE

26% ACCEPTANCE RATE

93 2007 U.S. NEWS LAW SCHOOL RANKING

ADMISSIONS
Admissions phone number: **(206) 398-4200**
Admissions email address: **lawadmin@seattleu.edu**
Application website: **http://www.law.seattleu.edu/admission/admissionapp.asp**
Application deadline for Fall 2007 admission: **4/01**

Admissions statistics:
Number of applicants for Fall 2005: **2,857**
Number of acceptances: **743**
Number enrolled: **297**
Acceptance rate: **26%**
GPA, 25th-75th percentile, entering class Fall 2005: **3.17-3.63**
LSAT, 25th-75th percentile, entering class Fall 2005: **152-159**

Part-time program:
Number of applicants for Fall 2005: **267**
Number of acceptances: **102**
Number enrolled: **68**
Acceptance rate: **38%**
GPA, 25th-75th percentile, entering class Fall 2005: **2.90-3.48**
LSAT, 25th-75th percentile, entering class Fall 2005: **153-160**

FINANCIAL AID
Financial aid phone number: **(206) 398-4250**
Financial aid application deadline: **N/A**
Tuition 2005-2006 academic year: full-time: **$26,026**; part-time: **$17,352**
Room and board: **$9,918**; books: **$1,258**; miscellaneous expenses: **$3,969**
Total of room/board/books/miscellaneous expenses: **$15,145**
University offers graduate student housing for which law students are eligible.

Financial aid profile
Percent of students that received grants for the 2004-2005 academic year: full-time: **48%**; part-time **38%**
Median grant amount: full-time: **$6,000**; part-time: **$5,000**
The average law-school debt of those in the Class of 2005 who borrowed: **$81,751**. Proportion who borrowed: **91%**

ACADEMIC PROGRAMS
Calendar: **semester**
Joint degrees awarded: **J.D./M.B.A.; J.D./M.I.B.; J.D./M.S.F.**
Typical first-year section size: Full-time: **86**; Part-time: **70**
Is there typically a "small section" of the first year class, other than Legal Writing, taught by full-time faculty?: Full-time: **no**; Part-time: **no**
Number of course titles, beyond the first year curriculum, offered last year: **145**
Percentages of upper division course sections, excluding seminars, with an enrollment of:

Under 25: **55%**	25 to 49: **26%**
50 to 74: **11%**	75 to 99: **6%**
100+: **1%**	

Areas of specialization: appellate advocacy, clinical training, dispute resolution, environmental law, healthcare law, intellectual property law, international law, tax law, trial advocacy

Fall 2005 faculty profile
Total teaching faculty: **92**. Full-time: **57%**; **56%** men, **44%** women, **25%** minorities. Part-time: **43%**; **78%** men, **23%** women, **8%** minorities
Student-to-faculty ratio: **15.6**

SPECIAL PROGRAMS *(as provided by law school)*:
A Jesuit, Catholic institution, Seattle University School of Law provides students with a very strong part-time and full-time academic program leading to the juris doctor degree, joint degree programs in business and law, and an LL.M. program in American law for graduates of foreign law schools.

The school provides an individualized learning experience, with an emphasis on values and issues of social justice. The faculty consists of an outstanding group of legal educators, committed to quality teaching and academic research. The School of Law has an award-winning legal writing program, staffed with 12 faculty members teaching courses in small group sessions. There is an on-site, full-service clinical program, with six full-time and eight part-time faculty members supervising students in both live-client and externship settings. The Access to Justice Institute coordinates the pro bono volunteer activities of our students and involves them in a variety of local, national, and international activities.

In addition to a number of focus areas within the curriculum, which include networking groups of faculty, students, graduates, and other practicing lawyers and judges, the school has established the Center on Corporations, Law, and Society. Its aim is to foster interdisciplinary scholarship and dialogue about the extent to which corporate institutions operate in a manner that maximizes their positive contributions, while simultaneously protecting the interests of consumers, shareholders, employees, the environment, and other public-interest values.

The school operates a very active program of continuing legal education, which is open to students, and a summer program in Anchorage, Alaska. It has developed international programs and activities in Canada, Mexico, Nicaragua, Russia, and South Korea.

The school has established a nationally recognized program of academic support for students, providing the skills necessary for success in the law school program. The school proudly contains a very diverse community of students, faculty, and staff.

STUDENT BODY

Fall 2005 full-time enrollment: 874

Men: 44%	Women: 56%
African-American: 3.8%	American Indian: 1.6%
Asian-American: 13.3%	Mexican-American: 3.9%
Puerto Rican: 0.7%	Other Hisp-Amer: 0.7%
White: 70.4%	International: 1.4%
Unknown: 4.3%	

Fall 2005 part-time enrollment: 235

Men: 45%	Women: 55%
African-American: 5.5%	American Indian: 1.3%
Asian-American: 14.0%	Mexican-American: 2.6%
Puerto Rican: 0.4%	Other Hisp-Amer: 2.6%
White: 70.6%	International: 0.0%
Unknown: 3.0%	

Attrition rates for 2004-2005 full-time students
Percent of students discontinuing law school:

Men: 3%	Women: 1%
First-year students: 6%	Second-year students: 1%
Third-year students: N/A	

LIBRARY RESOURCES
The library holds 73,907 and receives 3,143 current subscriptions.

Total volumes: 356,028
Percentage of the titles in the online catalog: 100%
Total seats available for library users: 369

INFORMATION TECHNOLOGY
Number of wired network connections available to students: 2,140 total (in the law library, excluding computer labs: 367; in classrooms: 665; in computer labs: 24; elsewhere in the law school: 1,084)
Law school has a wireless network.
Approximate number of simultaneous users that can be accommodated on wireless network: 25,000
Students are required to own a computer.

EMPLOYMENT AND SALARIES
Proportion of 2004 graduates employed at graduation: 60%
Employed 9 months later, as of February 15, 2005: 100%
Salaries in the private sector (law firms, business, industry): $67,500–$90,000 (25th-75th percentile)
Median salary in the private sector: $80,000
Percentage in the private sector who reported salary information: 10%
Median salary in public service (government, judicial clerkships, academic posts, non-profits): $40,000

Percentage of 2004 graduates in:

Law firms: 50%	Bus./industry (legal): 26%
Bus./industry (nonlegal): 0%	Government: 11%
Public interest: 6%	Judicial clerkship: 4%
Academia : 3%	Unknown: 0%

2004 graduates employed in-state: 90%
2004 graduates employed in foreign countries: 1%
Number of states where graduates are employed: 18
Percentage of 2004 graduates working in: New England: 0%, Middle Atlantic: 0%, East North Central: 1%, West North Central: 0%, South Atlantic: 2%, East South Central: 0%, West South Central: 0%, Mountain: 3%, Pacific: 93%, Unknown: 0%

BAR PASSAGE RATES
Based on 2004 graduates taking Summer 2004 or Winter 2005 exams. Most of the school's first-time test takers took the bar in Washington.

80%
School's bar passage rate for first-time test takers

79%
Statewide bar passage rate for first-time test takers

Seton Hall University

■ 1 Newark Center, Newark, NJ, 07102-5210
■ http://law.shu.edu
■ Private
■ Year founded: 1951
■ 2005-2006 tuition: full-time: $32,620; part-time: $23,872
■ Enrollment 2005-06 academic year: full-time: 766; part-time: 376
■ U.S. News 2007 law specialty ranking: healthcare law: 4

3.00-3.60 GPA, 25TH-75TH PERCENTILE

158-162 LSAT, 25TH-75TH PERCENTILE

25% ACCEPTANCE RATE

70 2007 U.S. NEWS LAW SCHOOL RANKING

ADMISSIONS

Admissions phone number: (888) 415-7271
Admissions email address: admitme@shu.edu
Application website:
   http://www4.lsac.org/school/setonHall.htm
Application deadline for Fall 2007 admission: 4/01

Admissions statistics:

Number of applicants for Fall 2005: 2,498
Number of acceptances: 627
Number enrolled: 205
Acceptance rate: 25%
GPA, 25th-75th percentile, entering class Fall 2005:
   3.00-3.60
LSAT, 25th-75th percentile, entering class Fall 2005:
   158-162

Part-time program:

Number of applicants for Fall 2005: 582
Number of acceptances: 357
Number enrolled: 162
Acceptance rate: 61%
GPA, 25th-75th percentile, entering class Fall 2005:
   3.00-3.50
LSAT, 25th-75th percentile, entering class Fall 2005:
   152-156

FINANCIAL AID

Financial aid phone number: (973) 642-8850
Financial aid application deadline: 4/01
Tuition 2005-2006 academic year: full-time: $32,620; part-time: $23,872
Room and board: $11,700; books: $1,100; miscellaneous expenses: $4,470
Total of room/board/books/miscellaneous expenses: $17,270
University offers graduate student housing for which law students are eligible.

Financial aid profile

Percent of students that received grants for the 2004-2005 academic year: full-time: 52%; part-time 12%
Median grant amount: full-time: $14,000; part-time: $3,000
The average law-school debt of those in the Class of 2005 who borrowed: $83,500. Proportion who borrowed: 83%

ACADEMIC PROGRAMS

Calendar: semester
Joint degrees awarded: M.B.A./J.D.; M.D./J.D.; M.D./M.S.J.; MADIR/J.D.; B.S./J.D.
Typical first-year section size: Full-time: 80; Part-time: 110
Is there typically a "small section" of the first year class, other than Legal Writing, taught by full-time faculty?: Full-time: no; Part-time: no
Number of course titles, beyond the first year curriculum, offered last year: 140
Percentages of upper division course sections, excluding seminars, with an enrollment of:

Under 25: 43%	25 to 49: 25%
50 to 74: 22%	75 to 99: 10%
100+: 0%	

Areas of specialization: appellate advocacy, clinical training, dispute resolution, environmental law, healthcare law, intellectual property law, international law, tax law, trial advocacy

Fall 2005 faculty profile

Total teaching faculty: 187. Full-time: 28%; 67% men, 33% women, 21% minorities. Part-time: 72%; 71% men, 29% women, 13% minorities
Student-to-faculty ratio: 14.9

SPECIAL PROGRAMS (as provided by law school):

Seton Hall Law School's commitment to public interest pervades its curriculum. The Center for Social Justice is a clinical education center that serves as a national model. The school's litigation clinics represent over 3,000 disadvantaged and under-represented clients annually in litigation such as housing, consumer protection, family law, juvenile justice, and immigration. Students in the appellate clinic appear in the Second Circuit.

The Institute of Law, Science and Technology, which provides resources and support to public and private sectors, prepares future lawyers to meet emerging challenges in the complex areas of Intellectual Property and new technology law. The institute offers a Juris Doctorate (J.D.) with a concentration in Intellectual Property and, in conjunction with the Health Law & Policy Program, a master of science in jurisprudence (M.S.J.).

The Health Law & Policy Program is dedicated to education, scholarship and reform in the field of health law and policy, and offers students the opportunity to pursue a J.D. with a concentration in Health Law, the M.S.J., or the master's of law (LL.M.) in health law. The program serves the community at large through frequent lectures and symposia.

The Health Care Compliance Certification Program is a multi-day educational program for compliance professionals and lawyers in the pharmaceutical and medical device industries. The program addresses the compliance issues, statutes, regulations, and other guidance in the areas of fraud and abuse law and FDA law, to enable professionals to understand the legal underpinnings of the compliance programs that they enforce.

Seton Hall Law School offers judicial internships in the state and Federal Courts in the New York metropolitan area. Externship programs are extensive, including the Environmental Protection Agency, the Office of the U.S. Trustee for Bankruptcy, the Internal Revenue Service, the European Court of Justice or Court of First Instance, Securities and Exchange, the National Labor Relations Board and the Office of the U.S. Attorney.

STUDENT BODY

Fall 2005 full-time enrollment: 766

Men: 57%	Women: 43%
African-American: 2.7%	American Indian: 0.1%
Asian-American: 7.7%	Mexican-American: 0.3%
Puerto Rican: 1.0%	Other Hisp-Amer: 3.4%
White: 82.8%	International: 2.0%
Unknown: 0.0%	

Fall 2005 part-time enrollment: 376

Men: 54%	Women: 46%
African-American: 6.6%	American Indian: 0.5%
Asian-American: 10.1%	Mexican-American: 0.0%
Puerto Rican: 2.9%	Other Hisp-Amer: 6.4%
White: 71.3%	International: 2.1%
Unknown: 0.0%	

Attrition rates for 2004-2005 full-time students
Percent of students discontinuing law school:

Men: 4%	Women: 4%
First-year students: 12%	Second-year students: 2%
Third-year students: N/A	

LIBRARY RESOURCES
The library holds 93,614 and receives 10,011 current subscriptions.
Total volumes: 446,916
Percentage of the titles in the online catalog: 100%
Total seats available for library users: 540

INFORMATION TECHNOLOGY
Number of wired network connections available to students: 236 total (in the law library, excluding computer labs: 50; in classrooms: 16; in computer labs: 90; elsewhere in the law school: 80)
Law school has a wireless network.
Approximate number of simultaneous users that can be accommodated on wireless network: 2,000
Students are required to own a computer.

EMPLOYMENT AND SALARIES
Proportion of 2004 graduates employed at graduation: 92%
Employed 9 months later, as of February 15, 2005: 97%
Salaries in the private sector (law firms, business, industry): $45,000–$90,000 (25th-75th percentile)
Median salary in the private sector: $60,000
Percentage in the private sector who reported salary information: 54%
Median salary in public service (government, judicial clerkships, academic posts, non-profits): $35,000

Percentage of 2004 graduates in:

Law firms: 40%	Bus./industry (legal): 13%
Bus./industry (nonlegal): 1%	Government: 5%
Public interest: 1%	Judicial clerkship: 40%
Academia : 0%	Unknown: 0%

2004 graduates employed in-state: 80%
2004 graduates employed in foreign countries: 0%
Number of states where graduates are employed: 10
Percentage of 2004 graduates working in: New England: 1%, Middle Atlantic: 97%, East North Central: 0%, West North Central: 0%, South Atlantic: 3%, East South Central: 0%, West South Central: 0%, Mountain: 0%, Pacific: 1%, Unknown: 0%

BAR PASSAGE RATES
Based on 2004 graduates taking Summer 2004 or Winter 2005 exams. Most of the school's first-time test takers took the bar in New Jersey.

82%
School's bar passage rate for first-time test takers

80%
Statewide bar passage rate for first-time test takers

South Texas College of Law

■ 1303 San Jacinto Street, Houston, TX, 77002-7000
■ http://www.stcl.edu
■ Private
■ Year founded: 1923
■ 2005-2006 tuition: full-time: $20,850; part-time: $14,100
■ Enrollment 2005-06 academic year: full-time: 959; part-time: 303
■ U.S. News 2007 law specialty ranking: trial advocacy: 3

2.98-3.50 GPA, 25TH-75TH PERCENTILE

151-156 LSAT, 25TH-75TH PERCENTILE

37% ACCEPTANCE RATE

Tier 4 2007 U.S. NEWS LAW SCHOOL RANKING

ADMISSIONS

Admissions phone number: **(713) 646-1810**
Admissions email address: **admissions@stcl.edu**
Application website: **http://www.stcl.edu**
Application deadline for Fall 2007 admission: 2/15

Admissions statistics:

Number of applicants for Fall 2005: **2,524**
Number of acceptances: **932**
Number enrolled: **344**
Acceptance rate: **37%**
GPA, 25th-75th percentile, entering class Fall 2005:
2.98-3.50
LSAT, 25th-75th percentile, entering class Fall 2005: **151-156**

Part-time program:

Number of applicants for Fall 2005: **428**
Number of acceptances: **154**
Number enrolled: **109**
Acceptance rate: **36%**
GPA, 25th-75th percentile, entering class Fall 2005:
2.84-3.46
LSAT, 25th-75th percentile, entering class Fall 2005:
150-156

FINANCIAL AID

Financial aid phone number: **(713) 646-1820**
Financial aid application deadline: 5/01
Tuition 2005-2006 academic year: full-time: **$20,850**; part-time: **$14,100**
Room and board: **$7,912**; books: **$1,200**; miscellaneous expenses: **$5,642**
Total of room/board/books/miscellaneous expenses: **$14,754**
University does not offer graduate student housing for which law students are eligible.

Financial aid profile

Percent of students that received grants for the 2004-2005 academic year: full-time: **40%**; part-time **29%**
Median grant amount: full-time: **$1,461**; part-time: **$961**

The average law-school debt of those in the Class of 2005 who borrowed: **$76,282**. Proportion who borrowed: **78%**

ACADEMIC PROGRAMS

Calendar: **semester**
Joint degrees awarded: **N/A**
Typical first-year section size: Full-time: **90**; Part-time: **60**
Is there typically a "small section" of the first year class, other than Legal Writing, taught by full-time faculty?: Full-time: **no**; Part-time: **no**
Number of course titles, beyond the first year curriculum, offered last year: **127**
Percentages of upper division course sections, excluding seminars, with an enrollment of:

Under 25: **50%**	25 to 49: **18%**
50 to 74: **15%**	75 to 99: **17%**
100+: **0%**	

Areas of specialization: appellate advocacy, clinical training, dispute resolution, environmental law, healthcare law, intellectual property law, international law, tax law, trial advocacy

Fall 2005 faculty profile

Total teaching faculty: **104**. Full-time: **52%**; **67%** men, **33%** women, **9%** minorities. Part-time: **48%**; **78%** men, **22%** women, **12%** minorities
Student-to-faculty ratio: **19.7**

SPECIAL PROGRAMS (as provided by law school):

Development of strong legal and advocacy skills is important at South Texas, as evidenced by its five Centers of Excellence and its skills and clinical programs. Since 1980, the Advocacy Program has outperformed all other law school teams in the nation by winning an array of state, regional, and national championship victories. The Frank Evans Center for Conflict Resolution allows students to learn from and interact with practicing attorneys who specialize in mediation and arbitration. The Law Institute for Medical Studies focuses on legal issues facing the medical profession and provides students the opportunity to work with those in the field. The Corporate Compliance Center attracts students interested in working in corporate counsel and business environments. The Center explores issues on how companies promote policies and procedures that ensure legal and ethical behavior, and how they detect and deter wrongdoing. The Transactional Practice Center is designed to teach students the fundamental elements of completing a business transaction, such as a real estate purchase or development, buying or selling a corporation, or creating a partnership. South Texas also offers five off-site clinics that place students in the real world of lawyering, including state and federal trial and appellate court chambers, prosecutors' and defenders' offices, public interest legal service providers, and state and federal government agencies. In the International Criminal Process Clinic, students work with defenders at The Hague involved with the United Nations' Ad Hoc International Tribunal for the Former Yugoslavia. In the General Civil Clinic, students work in an on-site clinic while providing direct representation for clients in a variety of administrative and state court settings. The Langdell Scholar Program, conducted by course-proficient upperclassmen, continues to benefit eligible students in mastering legal analysis, while garnering an aptitude in effective outlining, study skills, and exam-taking techniques. For students interested in the increased globalization of law, South Texas offers a variety of foreign programs throughout the year. Two ABA-approved cooperative exchange programs allow students to study for a semester in the Netherlands or Denmark. Summer study abroad opportunities are offered in Malta, Turkey, Ireland, England, Czech Republic, and Mexico.

STUDENT BODY

Fall 2005 full-time enrollment: 959

Men: 53%	Women: 47%
African-American: 1.7%	American Indian: 0.4%
Asian-American: 9.8%	Mexican-American: 2.6%
Puerto Rican: 0.4%	Other Hisp-Amer: 4.2%
White: 80.7%	International: 0.2%
Unknown: 0.0%	

Fall 2005 part-time enrollment: 303

Men: 57%	Women: 43%
African-American: 8.9%	American Indian: 1.7%
Asian-American: 7.9%	Mexican-American: 4.6%
Puerto Rican: 0.3%	Other Hisp-Amer: 4.6%
White: 71.9%	International: 0.0%
Unknown: 0.0%	

Attrition rates for 2004-2005 full-time students

Percent of students discontinuing law school:

Men: 7%	Women: 7%
First-year students: 11%	Second-year students: 4%
Third-year students: 1%	

LIBRARY RESOURCES

The library holds 82,188 and receives 4,325 current subscriptions.
Total volumes: 504,656
Percentage of the titles in the online catalog: 100%
Total seats available for library users: 849

INFORMATION TECHNOLOGY

Number of wired network connections available to students: 1,017 total (in the law library, excluding computer labs: 996; in classrooms: 0; in computer labs: 0; elsewhere in the law school: 21)
Law school has a wireless network.
Approximate number of simultaneous users that can be accommodated on wireless network: 100
Students are not required to own a computer.

EMPLOYMENT AND SALARIES

Proportion of 2004 graduates employed at graduation: N/A
Employed 9 months later, as of February 15, 2005: 80%
Salaries in the private sector (law firms, business, industry): $68,000–$105,000 (25th-75th percentile)
Median salary in the private sector: $80,000
Percentage in the private sector who reported salary information: 20%
Median salary in public service (government, judicial clerkships, academic posts, non-profits): $48,000

Percentage of 2004 graduates in:

Law firms: 71%	Bus./industry (legal): 9%
Bus./industry (nonlegal): 0%	Government: 11%
Public interest: 1%	Judicial clerkship: 5%
Academia : 2%	Unknown: 1%

2004 graduates employed in-state: 98%
2004 graduates employed in foreign countries: 0%
Number of states where graduates are employed: 6
Percentage of 2004 graduates working in: New England: 0%, Middle Atlantic: 0%, East North Central: 0%, West North Central: 0%, South Atlantic: 1%, East South Central: 0%, West South Central: 98%, Mountain: 0%, Pacific: 0%, Unknown: 1%

BAR PASSAGE RATES

Based on 2004 graduates taking Summer 2004 or Winter 2005 exams. Most of the school's first-time test takers took the bar in Texas.

70%
School's bar passage rate for first-time test takers

79%
Statewide bar passage rate for first-time test takers

Southern Illinois Univ.—Carbondale

- Lesar Law Building, Carbondale, IL, 62901
- http://www.law.siu.edu
- Public
- Year founded: 1973
- 2005-2006 tuition: In-state: full-time: $9,705, part-time: N/A; Out-of-state: full-time: $26,085
- Enrollment 2005-06 academic year: full-time: 377
- U.S. News 2007 law specialty ranking: N/A

3.13-3.67 GPA, 25TH-75TH PERCENTILE

152-157 LSAT, 25TH-75TH PERCENTILE

37% ACCEPTANCE RATE

Tier 3 2007 U.S. NEWS LAW SCHOOL RANKING

ADMISSIONS

Admissions phone number: **(800) 739-9187**
Admissions email address: **lawadmit@siu.edu**
Application website: **http://www.law.siu.edu**
Application deadline for Fall 2007 admission: **3/01**

Admissions statistics:

Number of applicants for Fall 2005: **713**
Number of acceptances: **262**
Number enrolled: **122**
Acceptance rate: **37%**
GPA, 25th-75th percentile, entering class Fall 2005: **3.13-3.67**
LSAT, 25th-75th percentile, entering class Fall 2005: **152-157**

FINANCIAL AID

Financial aid phone number: **(618) 453-4334**
Financial aid application deadline: **4/01**
Tuition 2005-2006 academic year: In-state: full-time: **$9,705**, part-time: **N/A**; Out-of-state: full-time: **$26,085**
Room and board: **$7,370**; books: **$1,080**; miscellaneous expenses: **$2,399**
Total of room/board/books/miscellaneous expenses: **$10,849**
University offers graduate student housing for which law students are eligible.

Financial aid profile

Percent of students that received grants for the 2004-2005 academic year: full-time: **58%**
Median grant amount: full-time: **$3,100**
The average law-school debt of those in the Class of 2005 who borrowed: **$50,558**. Proportion who borrowed: **100%**

ACADEMIC PROGRAMS

Calendar: **semester**
Joint degrees awarded: **J.D./M.B.A.; J.D./M.A.CC; J.D./M.P.A.; J.D./M.D.; J.D./Ph.D; J.D./M.S.W.; J.D./MS.Ed.**
Typical first-year section size: Full-time: **65**

Is there typically a "small section" of the first year class, other than Legal Writing, taught by full-time faculty?: Full-time: **no**
Number of course titles, beyond the first year curriculum, offered last year: **75**
Percentages of upper division course sections, excluding seminars, with an enrollment of:
Under 25: **64%** 25 to 49: **20%**
50 to 74: **13%** 75 to 99: **3%**
100+: **0%**
Areas of specialization: appellate advocacy, clinical training, dispute resolution, environmental law, healthcare law, intellectual property law, international law, tax law, trial advocacy

Fall 2005 faculty profile

Total teaching faculty: **35**. Full-time: **60%; 62%** men, **38%** women, **0%** minorities. Part-time: **40%; 64%** men, **36%** women, **14%** minorities
Student-to-faculty ratio: **12.6**

SPECIAL PROGRAMS (as provided by law school):

Three in-house clinics are offered to senior law students for up to six hours of credit: the Elder Law Clinic, the Alternative Dispute Resolution Clinic, and the Domestic Violence Clinic. Senior law students may also enroll in externships: credit is earned by working in a public-interest or legal services agency; with local prosecutors, public defenders, and local judges; or for local and state government agencies. Centers include: Self Help Legal Center and the Center for Health Law and Policy.

STUDENT BODY

Fall 2005 full-time enrollment: 377

Men: **62%** Women: **38%**
African-American: **2.4%** American Indian: **0.8%**
Asian-American: **3.2%** Mexican-American: **0.3%**
Puerto Rican: **0.3%** Other Hisp-Amer: **1.1%**
White: **82.5%** International: **0.0%**
Unknown: **9.5%**

Attrition rates for 2004-2005 full-time students
Percent of students discontinuing law school:
Men: 5%   Women: 6%
First-year students: 15%   Second-year students: 1%
Third-year students: 1%

LIBRARY RESOURCES
The library holds 74,481 and receives 3,960 current
subscriptions.
Total volumes: 393,131
Percentage of the titles in the online catalog: 100%
Total seats available for library users: 355

INFORMATION TECHNOLOGY
Number of wired network connections available to students: 14 total (in the law library, excluding computer
labs: 3; in classrooms: 0; in computer labs: 0; elsewhere
in the law school: 11)
Law school has a wireless network.
Approximate number of simultaneous users that can be
accommodated on wireless network: 600
Students are not required to own a computer.

EMPLOYMENT AND SALARIES
Proportion of 2004 graduates employed at graduation:
N/A
Employed 9 months later, as of February 15, 2005: 82%
Salaries in the private sector (law firms, business, indus-
try): $40,000–$50,000 (25th-75th percentile)
Median salary in the private sector: $41,500

Percentage in the private sector who reported salary
information: 61%
Median salary in public service (government, judicial clerkships, academic posts, non-profits): $39,600

Percentage of 2004 graduates in:
Law firms: 56%   Bus./industry (legal): 2%
Bus./industry (nonlegal): 4%   Government: 27%
Public interest: 10%   Judicial clerkship: 0%
Academia : 1%   Unknown: 0%

2004 graduates employed in-state: 77%
2004 graduates employed in foreign countries: 0%
Number of states where graduates are employed: 11
Percentage of 2004 graduates working in: New England:
0%, Middle Atlantic: 0%, East North Central: 78%, West
North Central: 10%, South Atlantic: 3%, East South
Central: 5%, West South Central: 0%, Mountain: 3%,
Pacific: 1%, Unknown: 0%

BAR PASSAGE RATES
Based on 2004 graduates taking Summer 2004 or
Winter 2005 exams. Most of the school's first-time test
takers took the bar in Illinois.

83%
School's bar passage rate for first-time test takers

85%
Statewide bar passage rate for first-time test takers

Southern Methodist University

- PO Box 750116, Dallas, TX, 75275-0116
- http://www.law.smu.edu
- Private
- Year founded: 1911
- 2005-2006 tuition: full-time: $31,238; part-time: $23,429
- Enrollment 2005-06 academic year: full-time: 618; part-time: 211
- U.S. News 2007 law specialty ranking: tax law: 17

3.31-3.86 GPA, 25TH-75TH PERCENTILE

155-164 LSAT, 25TH-75TH PERCENTILE

23% ACCEPTANCE RATE

43 2007 U.S. NEWS LAW SCHOOL RANKING

ADMISSIONS

Admissions phone number: (214) 768-2550
Admissions email address: lawadmit@mail.smu.edu
Application website: N/A
Application deadline for Fall 2007 admission: 2/15

Admissions statistics:

Number of applicants for Fall 2005: 2,399
Number of acceptances: 545
Number enrolled: 181
Acceptance rate: 23%
GPA, 25th-75th percentile, entering class Fall 2005:
3.31-3.86
LSAT, 25th-75th percentile, entering class Fall 2005:
155-164

Part-time program:

Number of applicants for Fall 2005: 578
Number of acceptances: 169
Number enrolled: 109
Acceptance rate: 29%
GPA, 25th-75th percentile, entering class Fall 2005:
2.98-3.61
LSAT, 25th-75th percentile, entering class Fall 2005:
153-160

FINANCIAL AID

Financial aid phone number: (214) 768-1588
Financial aid application deadline: 2/15
Tuition 2005-2006 academic year: full-time: $31,238; part-time: $23,429
Room and board: $14,000; books: $1,800; miscellaneous expenses: $2,600
Total of room/board/books/miscellaneous expenses: $18,400
University offers graduate student housing for which law students are eligible.

Financial aid profile

Percent of students that received grants for the 2004-2005 academic year: full-time: 75%; part-time 17%

Median grant amount: full-time: $10,000; part-time: $5,000
The average law-school debt of those in the Class of 2005 who borrowed: $27,529. Proportion who borrowed: N/A

ACADEMIC PROGRAMS

Calendar: semester
Joint degrees awarded: J.D./M.B.A.
Typical first-year section size: Full-time: 95; Part-time: 90
Is there typically a "small section" of the first year class, other than Legal Writing, taught by full-time faculty?:
Full-time: no; Part-time: no
Number of course titles, beyond the first year curriculum, offered last year: 123
Percentages of upper division course sections, excluding seminars, with an enrollment of:

Under 25: 43%	25 to 49: 35%
50 to 74: 11%	75 to 99: 10%
100+: 2%	

Areas of specialization: appellate advocacy, clinical training, dispute resolution, environmental law, healthcare law, intellectual property law, international law, tax law, trial advocacy

Fall 2005 faculty profile

Total teaching faculty: 72. Full-time: 57%; 59% men, 41% women, 15% minorities. Part-time: 43%; 77% men, 23% women, 10% minorities
Student-to-faculty ratio: 15.4

SPECIAL PROGRAMS (as provided by law school):

Clinical education has been part of the law school's curriculum for over 50 years. Currently, SMU has four in-house clinics: Criminal Justice Clinic; Civil Clinic; Child Advocacy Clinic; and Federal Taxpayers Clinic. In addition, SMU has one partnership clinic: the Criminal Prosecution Clinic is jointly run with the Dallas County District Attorney's Office. All of the in-house clinics provide legal services to indigent individuals who might otherwise be without competent legal representation. Students may choose from an array of faculty-approved externship placements in state and federal courts; local, state, and federal agencies; and various legal departments. Classes are offered during a seven-week summer session; in addition, a limited number of students may elect to enroll in the Summer Program in Oxford.

STUDENT BODY

Fall 2005 full-time enrollment: 618

Men: 50%	Women: 50%
African-American: 4.2%	American Indian: 1.0%
Asian-American: 7.9%	Mexican-American: 1.1%
Puerto Rican: 0.0%	Other Hisp-Amer: 7.0%
White: 73.3%	International: 0.8%
Unknown: 4.7%	

Fall 2005 part-time enrollment: 211

Men: 61%	Women: 39%
African-American: 5.2%	American Indian: 0.5%
Asian-American: 8.5%	Mexican-American: 0.9%
Puerto Rican: 0.0%	Other Hisp-Amer: 4.3%
White: 70.6%	International: 0.0%
Unknown: 10.0%	

Attrition rates for 2004-2005 full-time students
Percent of students discontinuing law school:

Men: 0%	Women: 0%
First-year students: 0%	Second-year students: N/A
Third-year students: 0%	

LIBRARY RESOURCES

The library holds 219,391 and receives N/A current subscriptions.
Total volumes: 601,946
Percentage of the titles in the online catalog: N/A
Total seats available for library users: 737

INFORMATION TECHNOLOGY

Number of wired network connections available to students: 0 total (in the law library, excluding computer labs: 0; in classrooms: 0; in computer labs: 0; elsewhere in the law school: 0)
Law school has a wireless network.

Approximate number of simultaneous users that can be accommodated on wireless network: 1,053
Students are not required to own a computer.

EMPLOYMENT AND SALARIES

Proportion of 2004 graduates employed at graduation: **N/A**
Employed 9 months later, as of February 15, 2005: **96%**
Salaries in the private sector (law firms, business, industry): **$52,000–$123,500** (25th-75th percentile)
Median salary in the private sector: **$77,000**
Percentage in the private sector who reported salary information: **68%**
Median salary in public service (government, judicial clerkships, academic posts, non-profits): **$43,000**

Percentage of 2004 graduates in:

Law firms: 67%	Bus./industry (legal): 12%
Bus./industry (nonlegal): 0%	Government: 9%
Public interest: 5%	Judicial clerkship: 5%
Academia : 2%	Unknown: 0%

2004 graduates employed in-state: 86%
2004 graduates employed in foreign countries: 0%
Number of states where graduates are employed: 20
Percentage of 2004 graduates working in: New England: 1%, Middle Atlantic: 2%, East North Central: 1%, West North Central: 2%, South Atlantic: 3%, East South Central: 1%, West South Central: 88%, Mountain: 1%, Pacific: 2%, Unknown: 0%

BAR PASSAGE RATES

Based on 2004 graduates taking Summer 2004 or Winter 2005 exams. Most of the school's first-time test takers took the bar in Texas.

88%
School's bar passage rate for first-time test takers

79%
Statewide bar passage rate for first-time test takers

Southwestern Univ. School of Law

■ 675 S. Westmoreland Avenue, Los Angeles, CA, 90005-3992
■ http://www.swlaw.edu
■ Private
■ Year founded: 1911
■ 2005-2006 tuition: full-time: $29,950; part-time: $19,005
■ Enrollment 2005-06 academic year: full-time: 658; part-time: 273
■ U.S. News 2007 law specialty ranking: N/A

3.11-3.60 GPA, 25TH-75TH PERCENTILE

154-158 LSAT, 25TH-75TH PERCENTILE

26% ACCEPTANCE RATE

Tier 3 2007 U.S. NEWS LAW SCHOOL RANKING

ADMISSIONS

Admissions phone number: **(213) 738-6717**
Admissions email address: **admissions@swlaw.edu**
Application website:
  http://www.swlaw.edu/prospective/admissions.html
Application deadline for Fall 2007 admission: 6/30

Admissions statistics:

Number of applicants for Fall 2005: **3,332**
Number of acceptances: **857**
Number enrolled: **248**
Acceptance rate: **26%**
GPA, 25th-75th percentile, entering class Fall 2005:
  3.11-3.60
LSAT, 25th-75th percentile, entering class Fall 2005:
  154-158

Part-time program:

Number of applicants for Fall 2005: **583**
Number of acceptances: **146**
Number enrolled: **86**
Acceptance rate: **25%**
GPA, 25th-75th percentile, entering class Fall 2005:
  3.10-3.51
LSAT, 25th-75th percentile, entering class Fall 2005: **151-156**

FINANCIAL AID

Financial aid phone number: **(213) 738-6719**
Financial aid application deadline: 6/01
Tuition 2005-2006 academic year: full-time: **$29,950**; part-time: **$19,005**
Room and board: **N/A**; books: **N/A**; miscellaneous expenses: **N/A**
Total of room/board/books/miscellaneous expenses: **$15,600**
University does not offer graduate student housing for which law students are eligible.

Financial aid profile

Percent of students that received grants for the 2004-2005 academic year: full-time: **33%**; part-time **14%**

Median grant amount: full-time: **$8,000**; part-time: **$5,000**
The average law-school debt of those in the Class of 2005 who borrowed: **$93,716**. Proportion who borrowed: **78%**

ACADEMIC PROGRAMS

Calendar: **semester**
Joint degrees awarded: **N/A**
Typical first-year section size: Full-time: **71**; Part-time: **78**
Is there typically a "small section" of the first year class, other than Legal Writing, taught by full-time faculty?:
  Full-time: **no**; Part-time: **no**
Number of course titles, beyond the first year curriculum, offered last year: **141**
Percentages of upper division course sections, excluding seminars, with an enrollment of:

Under 25: **53%**	25 to 49: **24%**
50 to 74: **16%**	75 to 99: **7%**
100+: **1%**	

Areas of specialization: appellate advocacy, clinical training, dispute resolution, environmental law, healthcare law, intellectual property law, international law, tax law, trial advocacy

Fall 2005 faculty profile

Total teaching faculty: **85**. Full-time: **55%**; **70%** men, **30%** women, **15%** minorities. Part-time: **45%**; **76%** men, **24%** women, **16%** minorities
Student-to-faculty ratio: **15.7**

SPECIAL PROGRAMS *(as provided by law school)*:

The Donald E. Biederman Entertainment and Media Law Institute: Taking advantage of its position in the heart of the entertainment capital of the world and the Digital Coast, Southwestern established the Biederman Institute. With the largest contingent of full-time entertainment and media law faculty at any law school, Southwestern also boasts a deep pool of alumni and adjunct faculty who hold prominent positions in these industries. The institute oversees more than 40 entertainment, media, intellectual property, and sports law courses; 50 externship placements; a special law firm practicum; an international entertainment law journal; and summer entertainment law programs in London and Los Angeles. The Institute also maintains ongoing relationships with law firms and companies operating in these industries; co-sponsors major entertainment- and media-related symposia with other professional organizations; and offers the only LL.M. degree in entertainment and media law.

SCALE two-year alternative J.D. program: In addition to the three traditional J.D. programs offered—full-time day, part-time evening, and part-time day (for students with child-care responsibilities)—SCALE, introduced in 1974, is an alternative, innovative J.D. course of study offered exclusively at Southwestern. Its two calendar years of instruction are equivalent to three full academic years in the traditional curriculum. The program presents the law as an integrated whole rather than as a series of discrete courses and often utilizes simulated client files. Development of practical lawyering skills and externship opportunities are also emphasized.

Foreign summer programs: London, England (emphasis on international entertainment and media law); Vancouver, British Columbia, Canada (emphasis on comparative criminal law and urban planning law); Buenos Aires (emphasis on international law and institutions, particularly in Latin America); and Guanajuato, Mexico (as part of a consortium with other law schools).

STUDENT BODY

Fall 2005 full-time enrollment: 658

Men: 47%	Women: 53%
African-American: 2.7%	American Indian: 0.9%
Asian-American: 19.9%	Mexican-American: 6.1%
Puerto Rican: 0.5%	Other Hisp-Amer: 4.0%
White: 51.2%	International: 1.8%
Unknown: 12.9%	

Fall 2005 part-time enrollment: 273

Men: 54%	Women: 46%
African-American: 7.0%	American Indian: 1.1%
Asian-American: 18.7%	Mexican-American: 7.3%
Puerto Rican: 0.4%	Other Hisp-Amer: 3.3%
White: 50.5%	International: 1.1%
Unknown: 10.6%	

Attrition rates for 2004-2005 full-time students
Percent of students discontinuing law school:

Men: 7%	Women: 7%
First-year students: 18%	Second-year students: 3%
Third-year students: 1%	

LIBRARY RESOURCES

The library holds 131,737 and receives 4,500 current subscriptions.
Total volumes: 467,579

Percentage of the titles in the online catalog: 100%
Total seats available for library users: 610

INFORMATION TECHNOLOGY

Number of wired network connections available to students: 782 total (in the law library, excluding computer labs: 442; in classrooms: 340; in computer labs: 0; elsewhere in the law school: 0)
Law school has a wireless network.
Approximate number of simultaneous users that can be accommodated on wireless network: 400
Students are not required to own a computer.

EMPLOYMENT AND SALARIES

Proportion of 2004 graduates employed at graduation: 80%
Employed 9 months later, as of February 15, 2005: 91%
Salaries in the private sector (law firms, business, industry): $60,000–$91,000 (25th-75th percentile)
Median salary in the private sector: $82,500
Percentage in the private sector who reported salary information: 52%
Median salary in public service (government, judicial clerkships, academic posts, non-profits): $45,500

Percentage of 2004 graduates in:

Law firms: 51%	Bus./industry (legal): 21%
Bus./industry (nonlegal): N/A	Government: 6%
Public interest: 4%	Judicial clerkship: 2%
Academia : 2%	Unknown: 15%

2004 graduates employed in-state: 84%
2004 graduates employed in foreign countries: 0%
Number of states where graduates are employed: 8
Percentage of 2004 graduates working in: New England: N/A, Middle Atlantic: 2%, East North Central: N/A, West North Central: 1%, South Atlantic: 1%, East South Central: N/A, West South Central: N/A, Mountain: 1%, Pacific: 84%, Unknown: 12%

BAR PASSAGE RATES

Based on 2004 graduates taking Summer 2004 or Winter 2005 exams. Most of the school's first-time test takers took the bar in California.

58%
School's bar passage rate for first-time test takers

61%
Statewide bar passage rate for first-time test takers

St. John's University

- 8000 Utopia Parkway, Jamaica, NY, 11439
- http://www.law.stjohns.edu/
- Private
- Year founded: 1925
- 2005-2006 tuition: full-time: $32,700; part-time: $24,525
- Enrollment 2005-06 academic year: full-time: 756; part-time: 196
- U.S. News 2007 law specialty ranking: N/A

3.18-3.72 GPA, 25TH-75TH PERCENTILE

158-163 LSAT, 25TH-75TH PERCENTILE

31% ACCEPTANCE RATE

80 2007 U.S. NEWS LAW SCHOOL RANKING

ADMISSIONS
Admissions phone number: (718) 990-6474
Admissions email address: lawinfo@stjohns.edu
Application website: http://www.law.stjohns.edu/
Application deadline for Fall 2007 admission: 4/01

Admissions statistics:
Number of applicants for Fall 2005: 3,314
Number of acceptances: 1,035
Number enrolled: 236
Acceptance rate: 31%
GPA, 25th-75th percentile, entering class Fall 2005: 3.18-3.72
LSAT, 25th-75th percentile, entering class Fall 2005: 158-163

Part-time program:
Number of applicants for Fall 2005: 756
Number of acceptances: 249
Number enrolled: 89
Acceptance rate: 33%
GPA, 25th-75th percentile, entering class Fall 2005: 3.07-3.54
LSAT, 25th-75th percentile, entering class Fall 2005: 152-156

FINANCIAL AID
Financial aid phone number: (718) 990-1485
Financial aid application deadline: 3/01
Tuition 2005-2006 academic year: full-time: $32,700; part-time: $24,525
Room and board: $12,400; books: $1,000; miscellaneous expenses: $4,140
Total of room/board/books/miscellaneous expenses: $17,540
University offers graduate student housing for which law students are eligible.

Financial aid profile
Percent of students that received grants for the 2004-2005 academic year: full-time: 49%; part-time 23%

Median grant amount: full-time: $15,000; part-time: $9,000
The average law-school debt of those in the Class of 2005 who borrowed: $81,362. Proportion who borrowed: 85%

ACADEMIC PROGRAMS
Calendar: semester
Joint degrees awarded: M.A./J.D.; M.B.A./J.D.; J.D./LL.M.
Typical first-year section size: Full-time: 79; Part-time: 55
Is there typically a "small section" of the first year class, other than Legal Writing, taught by full-time faculty?: Full-time: yes; Part-time: no
Number of course titles, beyond the first year curriculum, offered last year: 102
Percentages of upper division course sections, excluding seminars, with an enrollment of:

Under 25: 65%	25 to 49: 16%
50 to 74: 11%	75 to 99: 6%
100+: 2%	

Areas of specialization: appellate advocacy, clinical training, dispute resolution, environmental law, healthcare law, intellectual property law, international law, tax law, trial advocacy

Fall 2005 faculty profile
Total teaching faculty: 138. Full-time: 41%; 59% men, 41% women, 18% minorities. Part-time: 59%; 77% men, 23% women, 7% minorities
Student-to-faculty ratio: 17.2

SPECIAL PROGRAMS (as provided by law school):
The mission of the Frank S. Polestino Trial Advocacy Institute is to promote criminal and civil trial practice. The Institute sponsors the National Civil Rights Trial Competition, the Polestino Advocates (a select group of students who represent the school in external trial competitions), the Advocate in the Spotlight series, a trial skills training series, internal trial competitions, and the McKenna Forum panel debate on topics in criminal practice. Among the school's six clinics, the Elder Law Clinic students represent low-income Queens seniors in the areas of consumer law, debtor-creditor law, and benefit entitlements.

The clinic has developed an expertise in predatory lending cases. In the Securities Arbitration Clinic, students assist underserved small investors with securities disputes, in arbitrations before The National Association of Securities Dealers and The New York Stock Exchange. Students in the Child Advocacy Clinic appear in Queens and Nassau County Family Court proceedings and are appointed to represent children who have been abused or neglected. The Domestic Violence Litigation Clinic partners the law school with the nonprofit New York Legal Assistance Group to provide hands-on clinical experience for students who represent victims of domestic violence. The Immigration Rights Clinic, co-sponsored by New York Catholic Charities, provides students with the opportunity to represent immigrants, refugees, and asylum-seekers in a wide range of cases. The Prosecution Clinic is a partnership between St. John's and the Queens County and Bronx County District Attorney's Offices. The goals are two-fold: training students to develop the skills necessary to be a prosecutor and prompting students to think critically about the role of the prosecutor in the criminal justice system. In addition, seven externship programs are offered (general, civil, criminal justice, judicial, environmental, international human rights, and summer externships), which provide students with the opportunity to observe and participate in a wide variety of lawyering experiences. Placements are generally in public-interest, public-service, and not-for-profit agencies.

STUDENT BODY

Fall 2005 full-time enrollment: 756

Men: 54%	Women: 46%
African-American: 5.0%	American Indian: 0.0%
Asian-American: 8.5%	Mexican-American: 0.7%
Puerto Rican: 0.8%	Other Hisp-Amer: 5.2%
White: 63.9%	International: 3.8%
Unknown: 12.2%	

Fall 2005 part-time enrollment: 196

Men: 49%	Women: 51%
African-American: 15.3%	American Indian: 0.5%
Asian-American: 12.2%	Mexican-American: 1.5%
Puerto Rican: 0.5%	Other Hisp-Amer: 9.7%
White: 49.0%	International: 3.1%
Unknown: 8.2%	

Attrition rates for 2004-2005 full-time students
Percent of students discontinuing law school:

Men: 6%	Women: 3%
First-year students: 7%	Second-year students: 7%
Third-year students: 2%	

LIBRARY RESOURCES

The library holds 153,219 and receives 4,805 current subscriptions.

Total volumes: 487,264
Percentage of the titles in the online catalog: 100%
Total seats available for library users: 571

INFORMATION TECHNOLOGY

Number of wired network connections available to students: 141 total (in the law library, excluding computer labs: 9; in classrooms: 13; in computer labs: 52; elsewhere in the law school: 67)
Law school has a wireless network.
Approximate number of simultaneous users that can be accommodated on wireless network: 1,120
Students are not required to own a computer.

EMPLOYMENT AND SALARIES

Proportion of 2004 graduates employed at graduation: 69%
Employed 9 months later, as of February 15, 2005: 93%
Salaries in the private sector (law firms, business, industry): $52,000–$125,000 (25th-75th percentile)
Median salary in the private sector: $70,000
Percentage in the private sector who reported salary information: 60%
Median salary in public service (government, judicial clerkships, academic posts, non-profits): $47,000

Percentage of 2004 graduates in:

Law firms: 64%	Bus./industry (legal): 5%
Bus./industry (nonlegal): 6%	Government: 13%
Public interest: 2%	Judicial clerkship: 6%
Academia : 4%	Unknown: 0%

2004 graduates employed in-state: 90%
2004 graduates employed in foreign countries: 0%
Number of states where graduates are employed: 12
Percentage of 2004 graduates working in: New England: 2%, Middle Atlantic: 93%, East North Central: 0%, West North Central: 0%, South Atlantic: 3%, East South Central: 0%, West South Central: 0%, Mountain: 0%, Pacific: 0%, Unknown: 0%

BAR PASSAGE RATES

Based on 2004 graduates taking Summer 2004 or Winter 2005 exams. Most of the school's first-time test takers took the bar in New York.

86%
School's bar passage rate for first-time test takers

75%
Statewide bar passage rate for first-time test takers

St. Louis University

- 3700 Lindell Boulevard, St. Louis, MO, 63108
- http://law.slu.edu
- Private
- Year founded: 1843
- 2005-2006 tuition: full-time: $28,610; part-time: $20,880
- Enrollment 2005-06 academic year: full-time: 664; part-time: 216
- U.S. News 2007 law specialty ranking: healthcare law: 1

3.35-3.77 GPA, 25TH-75TH PERCENTILE

154-160 LSAT, 25TH-75TH PERCENTILE

40% ACCEPTANCE RATE

80 2007 U.S. NEWS LAW SCHOOL RANKING

ADMISSIONS

Admissions phone number: (314) 977-2800
Admissions email address: **admissions@law.slu.edu**
Application website:
  http://law.slu.edu/admissions/index.html
Application deadline for Fall 2007 admission: 3/01

Admissions statistics:
Number of applicants for Fall 2005: **1,845**
Number of acceptances: **734**
Number enrolled: **225**
Acceptance rate: **40%**
GPA, 25th-75th percentile, entering class Fall 2005:
  3.35-3.77
LSAT, 25th-75th percentile, entering class Fall 2005:
  154-160

Part-time program:
Number of applicants for Fall 2005: **487**
Number of acceptances: **135**
Number enrolled: **75**
Acceptance rate: **28%**
GPA, 25th-75th percentile, entering class Fall 2005:
  3.12-3.69
LSAT, 25th-75th percentile, entering class Fall 2005: **151-156**

FINANCIAL AID

Financial aid phone number: (314) 977-3369
Financial aid application deadline: 3/01
Tuition 2005-2006 academic year: full-time: **$28,610**; part-time: **$20,880**
Room and board: **$8,250**; books: **$1,250**; miscellaneous expenses: **$2,500**
Total of room/board/books/miscellaneous expenses:
  $12,000
University does not offer graduate student housing for which law students are eligible.

Financial aid profile
Percent of students that received grants for the 2004-2005 academic year: full-time: **48%**; part-time **20%**

Median grant amount: full-time: **$14,000**; part-time: **$3,000**
The average law-school debt of those in the Class of 2005 who borrowed: **$81,612**. Proportion who borrowed: **88%**

ACADEMIC PROGRAMS

Calendar: **semester**
Joint degrees awarded: **J.D./M.H.A.; J.D./M.B.A.; J.D./M.A.UA; J.D./M.P.A.; J.D./M.P.H.; J.D./Ph.D.**
Typical first-year section size: Full-time: **0**; Part-time: **75**
Is there typically a "small section" of the first year class, other than Legal Writing, taught by full-time faculty?:
  Full-time: **yes**; Part-time: **no**
Number of course titles, beyond the first year curriculum, offered last year: **96**
Percentages of upper division course sections, excluding seminars, with an enrollment of:

Under 25: **44%**	25 to 49: **27%**
50 to 74: **10%**	75 to 99: **11%**
100+: **8%**	

Areas of specialization: appellate advocacy, clinical training, dispute resolution, environmental law, healthcare law, intellectual property law, international law, tax law, trial advocacy

Fall 2005 faculty profile
Total teaching faculty: **73**. Full-time: **51%**; **65%** men, **35%** women, **8%** minorities. Part-time: **49%**; **67%** men, **33%** women, **3%** minorities
Student-to-faculty ratio: **17.6**

SPECIAL PROGRAMS *(as provided by law school)*:
Saint Louis University School of Law prepares students to achieve professional success through focused study and research in specialized areas of law. Founded more than 20 years ago, the nationally-recognized Center for Health Law Studies offers a robust selection of 22 courses and seminars in bioethics, access to health care, provider liability and health care finance. The Center draws on a strong national base of students, and places its graduates nationally in a variety of health care practice settings, including government and public service.

The William C. Wefel Center for Employment Law and the Center for International and Comparative Law offer rich curricula leading to certification for placement in these expanding practice areas.

Concentration programs are offered in Civil and Criminal Litigation, Taxation, Business Transactional Law, and Urban Development, Land Use and Environmental Law.

Students study abroad at a five-week summer program at the University's campus in Madrid, and at programs in Ireland, Belgium, Germany and France.

Live-client clinical learning opportunities and externships enrich the academic experience. Housed in a stand-alone building a block from the law school and working under the supervision of clinical faculty, clinic students gain valuable practical experience representing clients in cases in the federal and state courts in Missouri and Illinois. Clinic students, in collaboration with private civil rights attorneys and other public service organizations, have been involved in complex public interest litigation impacting hundreds of thousands of persons. Access to judicial, governmental, nonprofit and in-house corporate counsel externships is one of the benefits of attending law school in a thriving hub of legal and governmental activity. Placements include the EEOC, IRS, U.S. Attorney's Office, Missouri Attorney General, and corporate legal departments of *Fortune* 500 corporations headquartered in the St. Louis metropolitan area.

The Part-Time Evening Program provides working adults an opportunity to earn a law degree by attending classes three nights a week for four years with summer attendance, or five years without summer attendance.

Interdisciplinary study opportunities include joint J.D./masters degree programs in business administration, health care administration, public administration, urban affairs and public health.

STUDENT BODY

Fall 2005 full-time enrollment: 664

Men: 47%	Women: 53%
African-American: 3.2%	American Indian: 0.6%
Asian-American: 3.3%	Mexican-American: 0.0%
Puerto Rican: 0.0%	Other Hisp-Amer: 2.6%
White: 84.2%	International: 0.5%
Unknown: 5.7%	

Fall 2005 part-time enrollment: 216

Men: 56%	Women: 44%
African-American: 8.3%	American Indian: 0.5%
Asian-American: 2.3%	Mexican-American: 0.5%
Puerto Rican: 0.0%	Other Hisp-Amer: 0.5%
White: 87.0%	International: 0.0%
Unknown: 0.9%	

Attrition rates for 2004-2005 full-time students
Percent of students discontinuing law school:

Men: 7%	Women: 5%
First-year students: 13%	Second-year students: 4%
Third-year students: 2%	

LIBRARY RESOURCES

The library holds 298,349 and receives 3,637 current subscriptions.
Total volumes: 639,517
Percentage of the titles in the online catalog: 88%
Total seats available for library users: 460

INFORMATION TECHNOLOGY

Number of wired network connections available to students: 705 total (in the law library, excluding computer labs: 201; in classrooms: 399; in computer labs: 4; elsewhere in the law school: 101)
Law school has a wireless network.
Approximate number of simultaneous users that can be accommodated on wireless network: 900
Students are not required to own a computer.

EMPLOYMENT AND SALARIES

Proportion of 2004 graduates employed at graduation: 71%
Employed 9 months later, as of February 15, 2005: 93%
Salaries in the private sector (law firms, business, industry): $49,000–$67,500 (25th-75th percentile)
Median salary in the private sector: $56,000
Percentage in the private sector who reported salary information: 55%
Median salary in public service (government, judicial clerkships, academic posts, non-profits): $33,972

Percentage of 2004 graduates in:

Law firms: 61%	Bus./industry (legal): 18%
Bus./industry (nonlegal): N/A	Government: 10%
Public interest: 5%	Judicial clerkship: 5%
Academia : 1%	Unknown: 0%

2004 graduates employed in-state: 67%
2004 graduates employed in foreign countries: N/A
Number of states where graduates are employed: 18
Percentage of 2004 graduates working in: New England: N/A, Middle Atlantic: N/A, East North Central: N/A, West North Central: N/A, South Atlantic: N/A, East South Central: N/A, West South Central: N/A, Mountain: N/A, Pacific: N/A, Unknown: N/A

BAR PASSAGE RATES

Based on 2004 graduates taking Summer 2004 or Winter 2005 exams. Most of the school's first-time test takers took the bar in Missouri.

86%

School's bar passage rate for first-time test takers

88%

Statewide bar passage rate for first-time test takers

St. Mary's University

■ 1 Camino Santa Maria, San Antonio, TX, 78228-8602
■ http://law.stmarytx.edu
■ Private
■ Year founded: 1927
■ 2005-2006 tuition: full-time: $21,410; part-time: N/A
■ Enrollment 2005-06 academic year: full-time: 762
■ U.S. News 2007 law specialty ranking: N/A

2.81-3.42 GPA, 25TH-75TH PERCENTILE

151-156 LSAT, 25TH-75TH PERCENTILE

37% ACCEPTANCE RATE

Tier 4 2007 U.S. NEWS LAW SCHOOL RANKING

ADMISSIONS

Admissions phone number: **(210) 436-3523**
Admissions email address: **lawadmissions@stmarytx.edu**
Application website: **N/A**
Application deadline for Fall 2007 admission: **3/31**

Admissions statistics:

Number of applicants for Fall 2005: **2,069**
Number of acceptances: **769**
Number enrolled: **267**
Acceptance rate: **37%**
GPA, 25th-75th percentile, entering class Fall 2005:
2.81-3.42
LSAT, 25th-75th percentile, entering class Fall 2005: **151-156**

FINANCIAL AID

Financial aid phone number: **(210) 431-6743**
Financial aid application deadline: **3/24**
Tuition 2005-2006 academic year: full-time: **$21,410**; part-time: **N/A**
Room and board: **$7,230**; books: **$1,300**; miscellaneous expenses: **$4,852**
Total of room/board/books/miscellaneous expenses: **$13,382**
University offers graduate student housing for which law students are eligible.

Financial aid profile

Percent of students that received grants for the 2004-2005 academic year: full-time: **41%**
Median grant amount: full-time: **$3,288**
The average law-school debt of those in the Class of 2005 who borrowed: **$83,104**. Proportion who borrowed: **82%**

ACADEMIC PROGRAMS

Calendar: **semester**
Joint degrees awarded: **J.D./M.B.A.; J.D./International Relations; J.D./Masters of Public Administration; J.D./Masters of Accounting**
Typical first-year section size: Full-time: **67**

Is there typically a "small section" of the first year class, other than Legal Writing, taught by full-time faculty?: Full-time: **no**
Number of course titles, beyond the first year curriculum, offered last year: **115**
Percentages of upper division course sections, excluding seminars, with an enrollment of:

Under 25: **45%**	25 to 49: **23%**
50 to 74: **20%**	75 to 99: **12%**
100+: **0%**	

Areas of specialization: appellate advocacy, clinical training, dispute resolution, environmental law, healthcare law, intellectual property law, international law, tax law, trial advocacy

Fall 2005 faculty profile

Total teaching faculty: **66**. Full-time: **42%**; **68%** men, **32%** women, **21%** minorities. Part-time: **58%**; **63%** men, **37%** women, **16%** minorities
Student-to-faculty ratio: **23.5**

SPECIAL PROGRAMS (as provided by law school):

The law school offers 10 joint degree programs in cooperation with the graduate school. These include accounting, business administration, communications studies, computer science, economics, English language and literature, industrial engineering, international relations, public administration, and theology.

Our nationally recognized Center for Legal and Social Justice provides opportunities for students to represent the underserved in the areas of civil justice, criminal justice, and immigration and human rights. Students gain invaluable, hands-on legal experience representing San Antonio's indigent and disadvantaged citizens in actual cases. Students have access to an expansive array of judicial settings for internships. Nine federal and state courts have internship programs available to our students.

The St. Mary's Institute on World Legal Problems, held each summer in Innsbruck, Austria, offers a U.S. Supreme Court justice or other judge as a visiting jurist, as well as visiting professors from countries such as Germany, Italy, China, Austria, and Russia. The late Chief Justice William Rehnquist and Supreme

Court justices Sandra Day O'Connor, John Paul Stevens, Antonin Scalia, and Ruth Bader Ginsburg have all taught in the program. This summer Professor Frank Hoepfel of the International Criminal Tuibunal for the former Yugoslavia will be our guest jurist. Students not only experience a fascinating cultural exchange but also participate in a superior educational exploration of intriguing legal and political systems on a global scale.

Our LL.M program offers students the opportunity for an advanced, expanded educational experience. Our LL.M. in American legal studies is designed for graduates of foreign law schools, to enhance their understanding of the U.S. legal system. The LL.M. in international and comparative law is designed for U.S. lawyers and law school graduates who wish to gain specialized training in international and comparative law, especially with a business focus.

STUDENT BODY

Fall 2005 full-time enrollment: 762

Men: 58%	Women: 42%
African-American: 2.5%	American Indian: 1.6%
Asian-American: 4.3%	Mexican-American: 14.4%
Puerto Rican: 0.3%	Other Hisp-Amer: 5.9%
White: 71.0%	International: 0.0%
Unknown: 0.0%	

Attrition rates for 2004-2005 full-time students
Percent of students discontinuing law school:

Men: 6%	Women: 6%
First-year students: 11%	Second-year students: 6%
Third-year students: N/A	

LIBRARY RESOURCES

The library holds 75,529 and receives 4,397 current subscriptions.
Total volumes: 411,734
Percentage of the titles in the online catalog: 100%
Total seats available for library users: 390

INFORMATION TECHNOLOGY

Number of wired network connections available to students: 603 total (in the law library, excluding computer labs: 173; in classrooms: 400; in computer labs: 30; elsewhere in the law school: N/A)

Law school has a wireless network.
Approximate number of simultaneous users that can be accommodated on wireless network: 740
Students are not required to own a computer.

EMPLOYMENT AND SALARIES

Proportion of 2004 graduates employed at graduation: N/A
Employed 9 months later, as of February 15, 2005: 86%
Salaries in the private sector (law firms, business, industry): $37,500–$61,080 (25th-75th percentile)
Median salary in the private sector: $48,540
Percentage in the private sector who reported salary information: 62%
Median salary in public service (government, judicial clerkships, academic posts, non-profits): $40,877

Percentage of 2004 graduates in:

Law firms: 63%	Bus./industry (legal): 1%
Bus./industry (nonlegal): 7%	Government: 14%
Public interest: 5%	Judicial clerkship: 5%
Academia : 4%	Unknown: 1%

2004 graduates employed in-state: 96%
2004 graduates employed in foreign countries: 0%
Number of states where graduates are employed: 6
Percentage of 2004 graduates working in: New England: N/A, Middle Atlantic: N/A, East North Central: N/A, West North Central: 1%, South Atlantic: 1%, East South Central: 1%, West South Central: 96%, Mountain: 1%, Pacific: N/A, Unknown: 1%

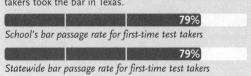

BAR PASSAGE RATES

Based on 2004 graduates taking Summer 2004 or Winter 2005 exams. Most of the school's first-time test takers took the bar in Texas.

79%
School's bar passage rate for first-time test takers

79%
Statewide bar passage rate for first-time test takers

St. Thomas University

- 16401 N.W. 37th Avenue, Miami Gardens, FL, 33054
- http://www.stu.edu
- Private
- **Year founded:** 1984
- **2005-2006 tuition:** full-time: $25,800; part-time: N/A
- **Enrollment 2005-06 academic year:** full-time: 806
- **U.S. News 2007 law specialty ranking:** N/A

2.58-3.33 GPA, 25TH-75TH PERCENTILE

147-152 LSAT, 25TH-75TH PERCENTILE

39% ACCEPTANCE RATE

Tier 4 2007 U.S. NEWS LAW SCHOOL RANKING

ADMISSIONS

Admissions phone number: **(305) 623-2311**
Admissions email address: **admitme@stu.edu**
Application website: **N/A**
Application deadline for Fall 2007 admission: **5/01**

Admissions statistics:

Number of applicants for Fall 2005: **2,379**
Number of acceptances: **925**
Number enrolled: **328**
Acceptance rate: **39%**
GPA, 25th-75th percentile, entering class Fall 2005:
2.58-3.33
LSAT, 25th-75th percentile, entering class Fall 2005:
147-152

FINANCIAL AID

Financial aid phone number: **(305) 628-6725**
Financial aid application deadline: **5/01**
Tuition 2005-2006 academic year: full-time: **$25,800**; part-time: **N/A**
Room and board: **$10,835**; books: **$1,000**; miscellaneous expenses: **$5,705**
Total of room/board/books/miscellaneous expenses: **$17,540**
University offers graduate student housing for which law students are eligible.

Financial aid profile

Percent of students that received grants for the 2004-2005 academic year: full-time: **34%**
Median grant amount: full-time: **$12,350**
The average law-school debt of those in the Class of 2005 who borrowed: **$82,000**. Proportion who borrowed: **82%**

ACADEMIC PROGRAMS

Calendar: **semester**
Joint degrees awarded: **J.D./M.B.A. - Accounting; J.D./M.B.A. - International Business; J.D./M.B.A. - Sports Administration; J.D./MS - Marriage & Family Counseling; J.D./BS - Ebvironmental Justice**

Typical first-year section size: Full-time: **70**
Is there typically a "small section" of the first year class, other than Legal Writing, taught by full-time faculty?: Full-time: **no**
Number of course titles, beyond the first year curriculum, offered last year: **97**
Percentages of upper division course sections, excluding seminars, with an enrollment of:
Under 25: **69%**   25 to 49: **19%**
50 to 74: **8%**   75 to 99: **4%**
100+: **1%**
Areas of specialization: appellate advocacy, clinical training, dispute resolution, environmental law, healthcare law, intellectual property law, international law, tax law, trial advocacy

Fall 2005 faculty profile

Total teaching faculty: **84**. Full-time: **37%**; **52%** men, **48%** women, **16%** minorities. Part-time: **63%**; **62%** men, **38%** women, **28%** minorities
Student-to-faculty ratio: **20.2**

SPECIAL PROGRAMS *(as provided by law school):*

As a requirement of graduation, students must have completed six credits of professional skills courses. The law school offers 10 clinical programs in the following subject matters that qualify as professional skills courses: Appellate Litigation, Bankruptcy, Civil Practice, Criminal Practice, Elder Law, Family Court, Florida Supreme Court, Immigration, Tax and Judicial Internships. All of the clinical offerings allow students an up-close and hands-on experience with top practitioners and Judges in their fields.

The law school offers four joint degree programs in cooperation with other graduate divisions of the university. A J.D./M.B.A. in accounting couples skills traditionally in great demand in the corporate tax and accounting worlds. The J.D./M.B.A. in international business opens that burgeoning field to the new attorney. The J.D./M.S. in marriage and family counseling is one of the only programs of its kind in the country. A joint J.D./M.S. in sports administration prepares participants for positions in the world of sport. St. Thomas University is a highly recognized leader in this field, having pioneered the first undergraduate sports management program in the nation in 1973.

Law students may study at the Royal College University Escorial Maria Cristina, a part of the University of Madrid. The program is designed to prepare students for practicing law in the globalized twenty-first century.

Additionally, the law school has a commitment to its students' success. The school has a comprehensive program of dean's fellows, tutors, practice examinations, lectures, and a dean for academic support, designed to assist students individually and in small groups. The law school also provides a program to assist graduates with the bar examination.

STUDENT BODY

Fall 2005 full-time enrollment: 806

Men: 57%	Women: 43%
African-American: 7.2%	American Indian: 0.4%
Asian-American: 4.7%	Mexican-American: 1.0%
Puerto Rican: 1.6%	Other Hisp-Amer: 24.8%
White: 54.0%	International: 2.0%
Unknown: 4.3%	

Attrition rates for 2004-2005 full-time students

Percent of students discontinuing law school:

Men: 8%	Women: 4%
First-year students: 14%	Second-year students: 2%
Third-year students: N/A	

LIBRARY RESOURCES

The library holds 114,453 and receives 3,071 current subscriptions.
Total volumes: 324,202
Percentage of the titles in the online catalog: 100%
Total seats available for library users: 472

INFORMATION TECHNOLOGY

Number of wired network connections available to students: 57 total (in the law library, excluding computer labs: 52; in classrooms: 0; in computer labs: 0; elsewhere in the law school: 5)

Law school has a wireless network.
Approximate number of simultaneous users that can be accommodated on wireless network: 1,652
Students are not required to own a computer.

EMPLOYMENT AND SALARIES

Proportion of 2004 graduates employed at graduation: N/A
Employed 9 months later, as of February 15, 2005: 58%
Salaries in the private sector (law firms, business, industry): $45,000–$60,000 (25th-75th percentile)
Median salary in the private sector: $50,000
Percentage in the private sector who reported salary information: 69%
Median salary in public service (government, judicial clerkships, academic posts, non-profits): $40,000

Percentage of 2004 graduates in:

Law firms: 64%	Bus./industry (legal): 6%
Bus./industry (nonlegal): 0%	Government: 9%
Public interest: 9%	Judicial clerkship: 7%
Academia : 5%	Unknown: 0%

2004 graduates employed in-state: 90%
2004 graduates employed in foreign countries: 0%
Number of states where graduates are employed: 2
Percentage of 2004 graduates working in: New England: N/A, Middle Atlantic: N/A, East North Central: N/A, West North Central: N/A, South Atlantic: 95%, East South Central: 5%, West South Central: N/A, Mountain: N/A, Pacific: N/A, Unknown: 0%

BAR PASSAGE RATES

Based on 2004 graduates taking Summer 2004 or Winter 2005 exams. Most of the school's first-time test takers took the bar in Florida.

62%
School's bar passage rate for first-time test takers

73%
Statewide bar passage rate for first-time test takers

Stanford University

■ Crown Quadrangle, 559 Nathan Abbott Way, Stanford, CA, 94305-8610
■ http://www.law.stanford.edu
■ Private
■ Year founded: 1893
■ 2005-2006 tuition: full-time: $35,780; part-time: N/A
■ Enrollment 2005-06 academic year: full-time: 527
■ U.S. News 2007 law specialty ranking: clinical training: 24, dispute resolution: 9, environmental law: 10, intellecutal property law: 2, international law: 13, tax law: 9

3.80-3.96 GPA, 25ᵀᴴ-75ᵀᴴ PERCENTILE

167-172 LSAT, 25ᵀᴴ-75ᵀᴴ PERCENTILE

8% ACCEPTANCE RATE

2 2007 U.S. NEWS LAW SCHOOL RANKING

ADMISSIONS

Admissions phone number: **(650) 723-4985**
Admissions email address: **admissions@law.stanford.edu**
Application website: **http://www.law.stanford.edu/admissions/**
Application deadline for Fall 2007 admission: **2/01**

Admissions statistics:
Number of applicants for Fall 2005: **4,863**
Number of acceptances: **379**
Number enrolled: **173**
Acceptance rate: **8%**
GPA, 25th-75th percentile, entering class Fall 2005: **3.80-3.96**
LSAT, 25th-75th percentile, entering class Fall 2005: **167-172**

FINANCIAL AID

Financial aid phone number: **(650) 723-9247**
Financial aid application deadline: **3/15**
Tuition 2005-2006 academic year: full-time: **$35,780**; part-time: **N/A**
Room and board: **$14,966**; books: **$1,546**; miscellaneous expenses: **$2,542**
Total of room/board/books/miscellaneous expenses: **$19,054**
University offers graduate student housing for which law students are eligible.

Financial aid profile
Percent of students that received grants for the 2004-2005 academic year: full-time: **43%**
Median grant amount: full-time: **$15,339**
The average law-school debt of those in the Class of 2005 who borrowed: **$100,687**. Proportion who borrowed: **86%**

ACADEMIC PROGRAMS

Calendar: **semester**
Joint degrees awarded: **J.D./M.B.A.; J.D./Ph.D.; J.D./M.D.; J.D./M.P.A.**

Typical first-year section size: Full-time: **60**
Is there typically a "small section" of the first year class, other than Legal Writing, taught by full-time faculty?: Full-time: **yes**
Number of course titles, beyond the first year curriculum, offered last year: **137**
Percentages of upper division course sections, excluding seminars, with an enrollment of:
Under 25: **61%**   25 to 49: **28%**
50 to 74: **10%**   75 to 99: **1%**
100+: **1%**
Areas of specialization: appellate advocacy, clinical training, dispute resolution, environmental law, healthcare law, intellectual property law, international law, tax law, trial advocacy

Fall 2005 faculty profile
Total teaching faculty: **N/A**. Full-time: **N/A**; **N/A** men, **N/A** women, **N/A** minorities. Part-time: **N/A**; **N/A** men, **N/A** women, **N/A** minorities
Student-to-faculty ratio: **9.2**

SPECIAL PROGRAMS *(as provided by law school):*

Stanford Law School offers students many opportunities to focus on a particular area of law through academic programs and centers that consolidate faculty scholarship, research, and course work. These include: Stanford Environmental and Natural Resources Law and Policy Program; Stanford Center on International Conflict and Negotiation; Gould Negotiation and Mediation Teaching Program; Stanford Program in International Law; Rule of Law Program; Stanford Program in Law, Economics, and Business, including the John M. Olin Program in Law and Economics and the George R. Roberts Program in Law, Business, and Corporate Governance; Stanford Criminal Justice Center; and the Stanford Program in Law, Science, and Technology, including the Center for Internet and Society, the Center for Law and the Biosciences, and the Center for E-Commerce. We offer joint study programs with several Stanford departments, including the Graduate School of Business, Department of Economics, Interdisciplinary Graduate Program in Environment and

Resources, and Department of Sociology. Joint degree programs are also available with the Woodrow Wilson School of Public and International Affairs at Princeton University and the School of Advanced International Studies at Johns Hopkins University. Stanford Law School was a pioneer of clinical education in the early 1970s, and we offer a rich array of in-house clinical courses to seamlessly combine academic instruction and practical training. These include clinics in community law, Supreme Court litigation, cyberlaw, immigrants' rights, capital defense, environmental law, criminal prosecution, international human rights, and youth and education law—with more slated to open in the near future. As part of their clinical training, students may work at the nearby Stanford Community Law Clinic, which provides legal assistance to low-income residents of local communities. Through the school's externship program, students may combine fieldwork with their studies, working at local organizations, as well as those in other parts of the nation or abroad. The law school established the Pro Bono Initiative to enrich the expertise of its renowned faculty, enhance the legal skills of our students, and simultaneously offer opportunities to serve the public. The school's Public Interest Program acts as a resource for students looking for meaningful volunteer opportunities.

STUDENT BODY

Fall 2005 full-time enrollment: 527

Men: 56%	Women: 44%
African-American: 7.8%	American Indian: 1.1%
Asian-American: 11.2%	Mexican-American: 11.2%
Puerto Rican: 0.8%	Other Hisp-Amer: 0.4%
White: 54.3%	International: 2.8%
Unknown: 10.4%	

Attrition rates for 2004-2005 full-time students
Percent of students discontinuing law school:

Men: 1%	Women: N/A
First-year students: 1%	Second-year students: 1%
Third-year students: 1%	

LIBRARY RESOURCES

The library holds 212,918 and receives 6,792 current subscriptions.
Total volumes: 539,300
Percentage of the titles in the online catalog: 97%
Total seats available for library users: 502

INFORMATION TECHNOLOGY

Number of wired network connections available to students: 274 total (in the law library, excluding computer labs: 63; in classrooms: 189; in computer labs: 22; elsewhere in the law school: 0)
Law school has a wireless network.
Approximate number of simultaneous users that can be accommodated on wireless network: 92,500
Students are required to own a computer.

EMPLOYMENT AND SALARIES

Proportion of 2004 graduates employed at graduation: 99%
Employed 9 months later, as of February 15, 2005: 99%
Salaries in the private sector (law firms, business, industry): $125,000–$125,000 (25th-75th percentile)
Median salary in the private sector: $125,000
Percentage in the private sector who reported salary information: 93%
Median salary in public service (government, judicial clerkships, academic posts, non-profits): $50,000

Percentage of 2004 graduates in:

Law firms: 58%	Bus./industry (legal): 0%
Bus./industry (nonlegal): 5%	Government: 2%
Public interest: 4%	Judicial clerkship: 30%
Academia : 1%	Unknown: 0%

2004 graduates employed in-state: 46%
2004 graduates employed in foreign countries: 1%
Number of states where graduates are employed: 27
Percentage of 2004 graduates working in: New England: 3%, Middle Atlantic: 16%, East North Central: 6%, West North Central: 2%, South Atlantic: 11%, East South Central: 1%, West South Central: 5%, Mountain: 6%, Pacific: 49%, Unknown: 0%

BAR PASSAGE RATES

Based on 2004 graduates taking Summer 2004 or Winter 2005 exams. Most of the school's first-time test takers took the bar in California.

92%
School's bar passage rate for first-time test takers

61%
Statewide bar passage rate for first-time test takers

Stetson University

- 1401 61st Street S, Gulfport, FL, 33707
- http://www.law.stetson.edu
- Private
- **Year founded:** 1900
- **2005-2006 tuition:** full-time: $26,280; part-time: $22,765
- **Enrollment 2005-06 academic year:** full-time: 757; part-time: 230
- **U.S. News 2007 law specialty ranking:** trial advocacy: 1

3.28-3.71 GPA, 25TH-75TH PERCENTILE

152-156 LSAT, 25TH-75TH PERCENTILE

23% ACCEPTANCE RATE

Tier 3 2007 U.S. NEWS LAW SCHOOL RANKING

ADMISSIONS

Admissions phone number: **(727) 562-7802**
Admissions email address: **lawadmit@law.stetson.edu**
Application website: **http://www.law.stetson.edu/admissions/**
Application deadline for Fall 2007 admission: 3/01

Admissions statistics:

Number of applicants for Fall 2005: **2,968**
Number of acceptances: **696**
Number enrolled: **276**
Acceptance rate: **23%**
GPA, 25th-75th percentile, entering class Fall 2005: **3.28-3.71**
LSAT, 25th-75th percentile, entering class Fall 2005: **152-156**

Part-time program:

Number of applicants for Fall 2005: **489**
Number of acceptances: **145**
Number enrolled: **69**
Acceptance rate: **30%**
GPA, 25th-75th percentile, entering class Fall 2005: **2.75-3.53**
LSAT, 25th-75th percentile, entering class Fall 2005: **149-156**

FINANCIAL AID

Financial aid phone number: **(727) 562-7813**
Financial aid application deadline: **N/A**
Tuition 2005-2006 academic year: full-time: **$26,280**; part-time: **$22,765**
Room and board: **$8,329**; books: **$1,200**; miscellaneous expenses: **$4,117**
Total of room/board/books/miscellaneous expenses: **$13,646**
University does not offer graduate student housing for which law students are eligible.

Financial aid profile

Percent of students that received grants for the 2004-2005 academic year: full-time: **24%**; part-time **10%**
Median grant amount: full-time: **$12,380**; part-time: **$9,612**
The average law-school debt of those in the Class of 2005 who borrowed: **$92,239**. Proportion who borrowed: **90%**

ACADEMIC PROGRAMS

Calendar: **semester**
Joint degrees awarded: **J.D./M.B.A.**
Typical first-year section size: Full-time: **68**; Part-time: **70**
Is there typically a "small section" of the first year class, other than Legal Writing, taught by full-time faculty?: Full-time: **no**; Part-time: **no**
Number of course titles, beyond the first year curriculum, offered last year: **129**
Percentages of upper division course sections, excluding seminars, with an enrollment of:

Under 25: **74%**	25 to 49: **19%**
50 to 74: **6%**	75 to 99: **1%**
100+: **0%**	

Areas of specialization: appellate advocacy, clinical training, dispute resolution, environmental law, healthcare law, intellectual property law, international law, tax law, trial advocacy

Fall 2005 faculty profile

Total teaching faculty: **93**. Full-time: **44%**; **59%** men, **41%** women, **12%** minorities. Part-time: **56%**; **69%** men, **31%** women, **10%** minorities
Student-to-faculty ratio: **17.5**

SPECIAL PROGRAMS *(as provided by law school):*

The College of Law is a vibrant place that holds many opportunities for students. We have many internships, clinics, and extracurricular opportunities. Please visit our website at www.law.stetson.edu for more information. Students may earn certificates of concentration in four areas: advocacy, elder law, higher education law and policy, and international law. The College of Law offers an honors program for top students. A

J.D./M.B.A. dual-degree program is available to law students with an interest in business.

Summer abroad programs are held in Granada, Spain; Buenos Aires, Argentina; Freiburg, Germany; and The Hague, the Netherlands. Stetson offers academic credit and practical experience in its clinics: Prosecution; Public Defender; Elder Law; Local Government Law; and Civil Poverty. The College of Law offers the following internships for academic credit: Bankruptcy Court; State Trial Court; State Appellate Court; Florida Supreme Court; Federal Court; In-House Counsel; Environmental; Health Law; Elder Law; Intellectual Property; Federal Litigation; State Litigation; and Labor Law. A comprehensive academic success program and leadership development program is available for all students. Other programs include the Teaching Fellows, Research Assistants, and Teaching Assistants (all paid positions).

STUDENT BODY

Fall 2005 full-time enrollment: 757

Men: 47%	Women: 53%
African-American: 4.4%	American Indian: 0.5%
Asian-American: 2.4%	Mexican-American: 0.4%
Puerto Rican: 2.0%	Other Hisp-Amer: 9.6%
White: 77.1%	International: 0.7%
Unknown: 2.9%	

Fall 2005 part-time enrollment: 230

Men: 45%	Women: 55%
African-American: 10.4%	American Indian: 0.4%
Asian-American: 2.2%	Mexican-American: 0.4%
Puerto Rican: 1.3%	Other Hisp-Amer: 7.4%
White: 75.7%	International: 0.0%
Unknown: 2.2%	

Attrition rates for 2004-2005 full-time students
Percent of students discontinuing law school:

Men: 0%	Women: 1%
First-year students: 0%	Second-year students: 1%
Third-year students: N/A	

LIBRARY RESOURCES

The library holds 121,993 and receives 3,854 current subscriptions.
Total volumes: 403,644
Percentage of the titles in the online catalog: 100%
Total seats available for library users: 609

INFORMATION TECHNOLOGY

Number of wired network connections available to students: 1,255 total (in the law library, excluding computer labs: 348; in classrooms: 729; in computer labs: 54; elsewhere in the law school: 124)
Law school has a wireless network.
Approximate number of simultaneous users that can be accommodated on wireless network: 2,600
Students are required to own a computer.

EMPLOYMENT AND SALARIES

Proportion of 2004 graduates employed at graduation: 49%
Employed 9 months later, as of February 15, 2005: 91%
Salaries in the private sector (law firms, business, industry): $50,000–$65,000 (25th-75th percentile)
Median salary in the private sector: $58,000
Percentage in the private sector who reported salary information: 64%
Median salary in public service (government, judicial clerkships, academic posts, non-profits): $38,000

Percentage of 2004 graduates in:

Law firms: 56%	Bus./industry (legal): 8%
Bus./industry (nonlegal): 0%	Government: 18%
Public interest: 11%	Judicial clerkship: 4%
Academia : 3%	Unknown: 0%

2004 graduates employed in-state: 85%
2004 graduates employed in foreign countries: 0%
Number of states where graduates are employed: 14
Percentage of 2004 graduates working in: New England: 0%, Middle Atlantic: 1%, East North Central: 1%, West North Central: 0%, South Atlantic: 94%, East South Central: 2%, West South Central: 1%, Mountain: 0%, Pacific: 0%, Unknown: 1%

BAR PASSAGE RATES

Based on 2004 graduates taking Summer 2004 or Winter 2005 exams. Most of the school's first-time test takers took the bar in Florida.

74%
School's bar passage rate for first-time test takers

73%
Statewide bar passage rate for first-time test takers

Suffolk University

■ 120 Tremont Street, Boston, MA, 02108
■ http://www.law.suffolk.edu/
■ Private
■ **Year founded:** 1906
■ **2005-2006 tuition:** full-time: $31,814; part-time: $23,860
■ **Enrollment 2005-06 academic year:** full-time: 1,058; part-time: 613
■ **U.S. News 2007 law specialty ranking:** N/A

3.10-3.60	GPA, 25TH-75TH PERCENTILE
154-158	LSAT, 25TH-75TH PERCENTILE
42%	ACCEPTANCE RATE
Tier 4	2007 U.S. NEWS LAW SCHOOL RANKING

ADMISSIONS

Admissions phone number: **(617) 573-8144**
Admissions email address: **lawadm@admin.suffolk.edu**
Application website: **http://www.law.suffolk.edu/admiss/**
Application deadline for Fall 2007 admission: **3/01**

Admissions statistics:
Number of applicants for Fall 2005: **2,623**
Number of acceptances: **1,112**
Number enrolled: **359**
Acceptance rate: **42%**
GPA, 25th-75th percentile, entering class Fall 2005:
3.10-3.60
LSAT, 25th-75th percentile, entering class Fall 2005:
154-158

Part-time program:
Number of applicants for Fall 2005: **578**
Number of acceptances: **299**
Number enrolled: **195**
Acceptance rate: **52%**
GPA, 25th-75th percentile, entering class Fall 2005:
3.00-3.60
LSAT, 25th-75th percentile, entering class Fall 2005: **151-156**

FINANCIAL AID

Financial aid phone number: **(617) 573-8147**
Financial aid application deadline: **3/01**
Tuition 2005-2006 academic year: full-time: **$31,814**; part-time: **$23,860**
Room and board: **$12,406**; books: **$900**; miscellaneous expenses: **$3,536**
Total of room/board/books/miscellaneous expenses: **$16,842**
University does not offer graduate student housing for which law students are eligible.

Financial aid profile
Percent of students that received grants for the 2004-2005 academic year: full-time: **54%**; part-time **22%**
Median grant amount: full-time: **$4,000**; part-time: **$3,485**

The average law-school debt of those in the Class of 2005 who borrowed: **$85,527**. Proportion who borrowed: **87%**

ACADEMIC PROGRAMS

Calendar: **semester**
Joint degrees awarded: **J.D./M.B.A.; J.D./M.P.A.; J.D./M.S.F.; J.D./M.S.I.E.; J.D./M.S.C.J.**
Typical first-year section size: Full-time: **91**; Part-time: **95**
Is there typically a "small section" of the first year class, other than Legal Writing, taught by full-time faculty?:
Full-time: **yes**; Part-time: **yes**
Number of course titles, beyond the first year curriculum, offered last year: **290**
Percentages of upper division course sections, excluding seminars, with an enrollment of:
Under 25: **56%**   25 to 49: **25%**
50 to 74: **8%**   75 to 99: **6%**
100+: **6%**
Areas of specialization: appellate advocacy, clinical training, dispute resolution, environmental law, healthcare law, intellectual property law, international law, tax law, trial advocacy

Fall 2005 faculty profile
Total teaching faculty: **197**. Full-time: **39%**; **70%** men, **30%** women, **11%** minorities. Part-time: **61%**; **76%** men, **24%** women, **6%** minorities
Student-to-faculty ratio: **17.1**

SPECIAL PROGRAMS *(as provided by law school):*

Our mission is to prepare students to practice law in an ethical and professional manner and to use their legal skills often in combination with other professional training in business and government.

Suffolk University Law School was one of the first schools in the country to develop academic concentrations. The law school offers concentrations in civil litigation, financial services, health and biomedical law, intellectual property law, and international law.

The law school, in collaboration with Suffolk University's Sawyer School of Management and College of Arts and

Sciences, offers five joint degree programs. The programs offer a juris doctor degree along with a master's degree in several disciplines: business administration, public administration, finance, international economics, and criminal justice.

The law school offers a variety of civil and criminal clinical programs, in which students represent clients under the direct supervision of experienced attorneys and law school faculty.

The Suffolk University Juvenile Justice Center aspires to meet the needs of juveniles involved with the courts. It is the center's goal to provide a demonstration model for advocates to address the legal needs of the child. The clinic serves local Boston juvenile courts.

The law school's internship program provides an opportunity for students to apply doctrinal legal knowledge to real-world challenges. Participants engage in professionally supervised settings, including government agencies, courts, nonprofit corporations, legal aid organizations, and private law firms.

The Rappaport Honors Program is a joint program offered at Suffolk University Law School and Harvard Law School that brings together a cadre of highly qualified law students from Boston-area law schools who demonstrate exceptional commitment toward public service.

The law school offers a summer program in Boston open to students who have completed the first year of law school in good standing at an American Bar Association law school.

Suffolk offers the Summer Law Program at Lund University in Sweden. A measure of integration of law students and law faculty from the University of Lund and other international law faculties distinguishes our program from other foreign-country programs.

We also offer international internship opportunities through the Center for International Study, located in Salzburg, Austria.

STUDENT BODY

Fall 2005 full-time enrollment: 1,058

Men: 51%	Women: 49%
African-American: 2.7%	American Indian: 0.4%
Asian-American: 5.8%	Mexican-American: 0.0%
Puerto Rican: 0.0%	Other Hisp-Amer: 2.0%
White: 79.8%	International: 1.1%
Unknown: 8.2%	

Fall 2005 part-time enrollment: 613

Men: 54%	Women: 46%
African-American: 2.3%	American Indian: 0.2%
Asian-American: 5.7%	Mexican-American: 0.0%
Puerto Rican: 0.0%	Other Hisp-Amer: 3.1%
White: 80.1%	International: 2.3%
Unknown: 6.4%	

Attrition rates for 2004-2005 full-time students

Percent of students discontinuing law school:

Men: 3%	Women: 4%
First-year students: 8%	Second-year students: 3%
Third-year students: 1%	

LIBRARY RESOURCES

The library holds 179,782 and receives 6,620 current subscriptions.

Total volumes: 360,624

Percentage of the titles in the online catalog: 100%

Total seats available for library users: 880

INFORMATION TECHNOLOGY

Number of wired network connections available to students: 2,675 total (in the law library, excluding computer labs: 1,125; in classrooms: 1,340; in computer labs: 100; elsewhere in the law school: 110)

Law school has a wireless network.

Approximate number of simultaneous users that can be accommodated on wireless network: 900

Students are not required to own a computer.

EMPLOYMENT AND SALARIES

Proportion of 2004 graduates employed at graduation: 58%

Employed 9 months later, as of February 15, 2005: 87%

Salaries in the private sector (law firms, business, industry): $42,000–$100,000 (25th-75th percentile)

Median salary in the private sector: $60,000

Percentage in the private sector who reported salary information: 75%

Median salary in public service (government, judicial clerkships, academic posts, non-profits): $43,000

Percentage of 2004 graduates in:

Law firms: 51%	Bus./industry (legal): 9%
Bus./industry (nonlegal): 12%	Government: 11%
Public interest: 2%	Judicial clerkship: 10%
Academia : 1%	Unknown: 4%

2004 graduates employed in-state: 71%

2004 graduates employed in foreign countries: 0%

Number of states where graduates are employed: 23

Percentage of 2004 graduates working in: New England: 79%, Middle Atlantic: 5%, East North Central: 1%, West North Central: 0%, South Atlantic: 2%, East South Central: 1%, West South Central: 1%, Mountain: 1%, Pacific: 1%, Unknown: 9%

BAR PASSAGE RATES

Based on 2004 graduates taking Summer 2004 or Winter 2005 exams. Most of the school's first-time test takers took the bar in Massachusetts.

80%

School's bar passage rate for first-time test takers

84%

Statewide bar passage rate for first-time test takers

ᴊyracuse University

- ■ Suite 340, Syracuse, NY, 13244-1030
- ■ http://www.law.syr.edu
- ■ Private
- ■ Year founded: 1895
- ■ 2005-2006 tuition: full-time: $33,462; part-time: $28,909
- ■ Enrollment 2005-06 academic year: full-time: 749; part-time: 7
- ■ U.S. News 2007 law specialty ranking: N/A

3.12-3.54 GPA, 25ᵀᴴ-75ᵀᴴ PERCENTILE

153-157 LSAT, 25ᵀᴴ-75ᵀᴴ PERCENTILE

34% ACCEPTANCE RATE

Tier 3 2007 U.S. NEWS LAW SCHOOL RANKING

ADMISSIONS

Admissions phone number: (315) 443-1962
Admissions email address: admissions@law.syr.edu
Application website: N/A
Application deadline for Fall 2007 admission: 4/01

Admissions statistics:
Number of applicants for Fall 2005: 2,719
Number of acceptances: 920
Number enrolled: 264
Acceptance rate: 34%
GPA, 25th-75th percentile, entering class Fall 2005:
3.12-3.54
LSAT, 25th-75th percentile, entering class Fall 2005: 153-157

Part-time program:
Number of applicants for Fall 2005: 46
Number of acceptances: 6
Number enrolled: 2
Acceptance rate: 13%
GPA, 25th-75th percentile, entering class Fall 2005: N/A
LSAT, 25th-75th percentile, entering class Fall 2005: N/A

FINANCIAL AID

Financial aid phone number: (315) 443-1963
Financial aid application deadline: 2/15
Tuition 2005-2006 academic year: full-time: $33,462; part-time: $28,909
Room and board: $11,268; books: $1,140; miscellaneous expenses: $3,580
Total of room/board/books/miscellaneous expenses: $15,988
University offers graduate student housing for which law students are eligible.

Financial aid profile
Percent of students that received grants for the 2004-2005 academic year: full-time: 86%
Median grant amount: full-time: $8,248
The average law-school debt of those in the Class of 2005 who borrowed: $80,181. Proportion who borrowed: 88%

ACADEMIC PROGRAMS

Calendar: semester
Joint degrees awarded: J.D./M.B.A.-BusA; J.D./MA-Econ; J.D./MA-IntRel; J.D./MPA-PubA; J.D./MS-InfoS; J.D./MA-TV, Radio & Film; J.D./MS-Engin-Neuroscience; J.D./MA-PoliSci; J.D/MA-Mag, newspaper, online journalism; J.D./MS-Culural Foundations of Educ; J.D./MS-Bioengineering; J.D./MS-Media Management; J.D./MS-Social Studies Education
Typical first-year section size: Full-time: 68
Is there typically a "small section" of the first year class, other than Legal Writing, taught by full-time faculty?: Full-time: yes
Number of course titles, beyond the first year curriculum, offered last year: 141
Percentages of upper division course sections, excluding seminars, with an enrollment of:
Under 25: 66%   25 to 49: 16%
50 to 74: 11%   75 to 99: 5%
100+: 2%
Areas of specialization: appellate advocacy, clinical training, dispute resolution, environmental law, intellectual property law, international law, tax law, trial advocacy

Fall 2005 faculty profile
Total teaching faculty: 69. Full-time: 61%; 64% men, 36% women, 14% minorities. Part-time: 39%; 81% men, 19% women, 11% minorities
Student-to-faculty ratio: 15.7

SPECIAL PROGRAMS *(as provided by law school):*
Syracuse University College of Law has six Centers and an Institute; a distinguished clinical legal education program with six distinct in-house clinics and an externship program; an extensive advocacy skills training program; and numerous joint degree and interdisciplinary opportunities. Our Syracuse University New Technology Law Center (SUNTEC) was selected by the New York State Office of Science, Technology and Academic Research (NYSTAR) to provide legal support services to university research centers and early-stage technology companies throughout New York State. Students in the

Global Law and Practice Center acted as research associates for the office of the prosecutor of the U.N.-created War Crimes Court in Sierra Leone. The Family Law and Social Policy Center offers students the opportunity to gain experience by representing clients in the Children's Rights Clinic and working with Family Court and governmental agencies. Students in the Center for Indigenous Law, Governance & Citizenship focus on issues relating to citizenship, rights and responsibilities, governance and the administrative laws of indigenous peoples and nations in the U.S. and Canada. Students collaborate with other schools on campus and Indigenous nations in the area. In the Institute for National Security and Counterterrorism, a joint enterprise with the Maxwell School of Citizenship and Public Affairs, students study and analyze matters related to national and international security. Under faculty supervision, students in the Clinical Legal Education Program draft pleadings and other documents, represent clients in court and before administrative bodies, take depositions and testimony, and work with clients to resolve legal problems. Students can participate in the Criminal Law Clinic; Community Development Clinic; Disability Law and Policy Clinic; Children's Rights and Family Law Clinic; Low Income Taxpayer Clinic; and Securities Arbitration Clinic. The new Disability Law and Policy Program, which began in Fall 2004, houses the nation's first joint degree program in law and education, with a concentration in disability studies. There are also opportunities within the University-based Burton Blatt Institute, which addresses issues related to disabilities and the law. The college's nationally recognized Advocacy Skills Programs provide numerous opportunities for students to learn and sharpen their advocacy skills. SU College of Law received the Emil Gumpert Award for best law school advocacy program in the U.S. by the American College of Trial Lawyers. The New York State Bar Association has cited Syracuse as the best trial skills law school in New York State 11 times in recent years, awarding the college its coveted Tiffany Cup.

STUDENT BODY

Fall 2005 full-time enrollment: 749

Men: 54%	Women: 46%
African-American: 4.8%	American Indian: 1.1%
Asian-American: 7.7%	Mexican-American: 0.5%
Puerto Rican: 0.4%	Other Hisp-Amer: 3.2%
White: 62.9%	International: 3.5%
Unknown: 15.9%	

Fall 2005 part-time enrollment: 7

Men: 43%	Women: 57%
African-American: 14.3%	American Indian: 0.0%
Asian-American: 14.3%	Mexican-American: 0.0%
Puerto Rican: 0.0%	Other Hisp-Amer: 14.3%
White: 57.1%	International: 0.0%
Unknown: 0.0%	

Attrition rates for 2004-2005 full-time students
Percent of students discontinuing law school:
Men: 3%   Women: 3%

First-year students: 10%   Second-year students: **N/A**
Third-year students: **N/A**

LIBRARY RESOURCES
The library holds 83,987 and receives 3,364 current subscriptions.
Total volumes: 453,680
Percentage of the titles in the online catalog: 95%
Total seats available for library users: 429

INFORMATION TECHNOLOGY
Number of wired network connections available to students: 24 total (in the law library, excluding computer labs: 15; in classrooms: 0; in computer labs: 0; elsewhere in the law school: 9)
Law school has a wireless network.
Approximate number of simultaneous users that can be accommodated on wireless network: 500
Students are required to own a computer.

EMPLOYMENT AND SALARIES
Proportion of 2004 graduates employed at graduation: 68%
Employed 9 months later, as of February 15, 2005: 93%
Salaries in the private sector (law firms, business, industry): $40,000–$73,000 (25th-75th percentile)
Median salary in the private sector: $50,000
Percentage in the private sector who reported salary information: 72%
Median salary in public service (government, judicial clerkships, academic posts, non-profits): $41,250

Percentage of 2004 graduates in:

Law firms: 49%	Bus./industry (legal): 6%
Bus./industry (nonlegal): 6%	Government: 14%
Public interest: 4%	Judicial clerkship: 18%
Academia : 2%	Unknown: 1%

2004 graduates employed in-state: 45%
2004 graduates employed in foreign countries: 3%
Number of states where graduates are employed: 27
Percentage of 2004 graduates working in: New England: 4%, Middle Atlantic: 59%, East North Central: 5%, West North Central: 2%, South Atlantic: 14%, East South Central: 1%, West South Central: 2%, Mountain: 4%, Pacific: 6%, Unknown: 0%

BAR PASSAGE RATES
Based on 2004 graduates taking Summer 2004 or Winter 2005 exams. Most of the school's first-time test takers took the bar in New York.

76%
School's bar passage rate for first-time test takers

75%
Statewide bar passage rate for first-time test takers

Temple University (Beasley)

- 1719 N. Broad Street, Philadelphia, PA, 19122
- http://www.temple.edu/lawschool
- Public
- **Year founded:** 1895
- **2005-2006 tuition:** In-state: full-time: $14,100, part-time: $11,386; Out-of-state: full-time: $24,158
- **Enrollment 2005-06 academic year:** full-time: 796; part-time: 248
- **U.S. News 2007 law specialty ranking:** tax law: 25, trial advocacy: 2

3.09-3.61 GPA, 25TH-75TH PERCENTILE

160-163 LSAT, 25TH-75TH PERCENTILE

29% ACCEPTANCE RATE

58 2007 U.S. NEWS LAW SCHOOL RANKING

ADMISSIONS

Admissions phone number: **(800) 560-1428**
Admissions email address: **lawadmis@temple.edu**
Application website: **N/A**
Application deadline for Fall 2007 admission: **3/01**

Admissions statistics:

Number of applicants for Fall 2005: **4,846**
Number of acceptances: **1,409**
Number enrolled: **250**
Acceptance rate: **29%**
GPA, 25th-75th percentile, entering class Fall 2005: **3.09-3.61**
LSAT, 25th-75th percentile, entering class Fall 2005: **160-163**

Part-time program:

Number of applicants for Fall 2005: **397**
Number of acceptances: **135**
Number enrolled: **73**
Acceptance rate: **34%**
GPA, 25th-75th percentile, entering class Fall 2005: **2.92-3.58**
LSAT, 25th-75th percentile, entering class Fall 2005: **156-161**

FINANCIAL AID

Financial aid phone number: **(800) 560-1428**
Financial aid application deadline: **3/01**
Tuition 2005-2006 academic year: In-state: full-time: **$14,100**, part-time: **$11,386**; Out-of-state: full-time: **$24,158**
Room and board: **$10,262**; books: **$1,500**; miscellaneous expenses: **$7,492**
Total of room/board/books/miscellaneous expenses: **$19,254**
University offers graduate student housing for which law students are eligible.

Financial aid profile

Percent of students that received grants for the 2004-2005 academic year: full-time: **45%**; part-time **16%**

Median grant amount: full-time: **$6,401**; part-time: **$5,121**
The average law-school debt of those in the Class of 2005 who borrowed: **$66,430**. Proportion who borrowed: **83%**

ACADEMIC PROGRAMS

Calendar: **semester**
Joint degrees awarded: **J.D./M.B.A.**
Typical first-year section size: Full-time: **64**; Part-time: **69**
Is there typically a "small section" of the first year class, other than Legal Writing, taught by full-time faculty?: Full-time: **no**; Part-time: **no**
Number of course titles, beyond the first year curriculum, offered last year: **174**
Percentages of upper division course sections, excluding seminars, with an enrollment of:

Under 25: **68%**	25 to 49: **19%**
50 to 74: **7%**	75 to 99: **5%**
100+: **1%**	

Areas of specialization: appellate advocacy, clinical training, dispute resolution, environmental law, healthcare law, intellectual property law, international law, tax law, trial advocacy

Fall 2005 faculty profile

Total teaching faculty: **N/A**. Full-time: **N/A**; **N/A** men, **N/A** women, **N/A** minorities. Part-time: **N/A**; **N/A** men, **N/A** women, **N/A** minorities
Student-to-faculty ratio: **14.7**

SPECIAL PROGRAMS *(as provided by law school)*:

Temple Law School has a unique student-centered curriculum that integrates both critical thinking and practical legal skills. Our innovative skills courses and our extensive clinical program are designed so that our students graduate ready to perform skillfully in the legal marketplace.

Temple has a national reputation for its prize-winning trial advocacy programs, including the distinction of being the only two-time winner of the American College of Trial Lawyers Emil Gumpert Award for Excellence in teaching trial advocacy. Similarly, our program for teaching transactional skills, such as interviewing, negotiating, counseling, and drafting, has received national awards for excellence. Prospective business lawyers can also pursue the J.D./M.B.A. dual-degree program, or the J.D./LL.M. in Taxation. Clinical opportunities range from those that emphasize transactional skills, such as the program at the Center for Community Non-Profit Organizations, to those that focus on criminal litigation skills in district attorneys' and public defenders' offices.

With excellent programs in Philadelphia and around the world, Temple Law School is uniquely situated to prepare its students to be leaders in the international marketplace. Through Temple's semester abroad program in Tokyo, Japan (the only ABA-accredited semester abroad program offered by an American law school in Asia), summer programs in Rome, Italy and Tel Aviv, Israel, and opportunities to study in Beijing, China and Cork, Ireland, our students can experience the culture and study the legal systems of other countries, as well as transnational organizations. Temple's strong reputation in international law is further enhanced by the J.D./LL.M. in Transnational Law and the faculty's Institute for International Law and Public Policy.

Temple's outstanding intellectual property and technology law program focuses not only on traditional patent, trademark and copyright law, but also encompasses legal issues involving new and emerging technologies such as electronic commerce, the Internet, and biotechnology.

Finally, public service is a Temple tradition. Students provide legal services in the Philadelphia community through the clinical program and many volunteer and community outreach programs. Public interest careers are supported by the Student Public Interest Network, the Public Interest Scholars Program, and the Barrack Public Interest Fellowships, a loan repayment assistance program.

STUDENT BODY

Fall 2005 full-time enrollment: 796

Men: 50%	Women: 50%
African-American: 8.3%	American Indian: 0.5%
Asian-American: 12.2%	Mexican-American: 0.8%
Puerto Rican: 1.1%	Other Hisp-Amer: 2.5%
White: 72.7%	International: 1.0%
Unknown: 0.9%	

Fall 2005 part-time enrollment: 248

Men: 57%	Women: 43%
African-American: 6.9%	American Indian: 0.0%
Asian-American: 8.9%	Mexican-American: 0.8%
Puerto Rican: 0.8%	Other Hisp-Amer: 2.0%
White: 79.4%	International: 0.8%
Unknown: 0.4%	

Attrition rates for 2004-2005 full-time students
Percent of students discontinuing law school:

Men: 2%	Women: 3%
First-year students: 3%	Second-year students: 4%
Third-year students: 1%	

LIBRARY RESOURCES

The library holds 110,550 and receives 3,048 current subscriptions.
Total volumes: 573,568
Percentage of the titles in the online catalog: 97%
Total seats available for library users: 700

INFORMATION TECHNOLOGY

Number of wired network connections available to students: 427 total (in the law library, excluding computer labs: 160; in classrooms: 145; in computer labs: 56; elsewhere in the law school: 66)
Law school has a wireless network.
Approximate number of simultaneous users that can be accommodated on wireless network: 1,024
Students are not required to own a computer.

EMPLOYMENT AND SALARIES

Proportion of 2004 graduates employed at graduation: 69%
Employed 9 months later, as of February 15, 2005: 96%
Salaries in the private sector (law firms, business, industry): $60,000–$107,000 (25th-75th percentile)
Median salary in the private sector: $83,000
Percentage in the private sector who reported salary information: 65%
Median salary in public service (government, judicial clerkships, academic posts, non-profits): $42,000

Percentage of 2004 graduates in:

Law firms: 48%	Bus./industry (legal): 6%
Bus./industry (nonlegal): 11%	Government: 14%
Public interest: 7%	Judicial clerkship: 9%
Academia : 2%	Unknown: 3%

2004 graduates employed in-state: 77%
2004 graduates employed in foreign countries: 1%
Number of states where graduates are employed: 20
Percentage of 2004 graduates working in: New England: 1%, Middle Atlantic: 84%, East North Central: 1%, West North Central: 0%, South Atlantic: 6%, East South Central: 1%, West South Central: 0%, Mountain: 1%, Pacific: 1%, Unknown: 4%

BAR PASSAGE RATES

Based on 2004 graduates taking Summer 2004 or Winter 2005 exams. Most of the school's first-time test takers took the bar in Pennsylvania.

88%
School's bar passage rate for first-time test takers

81%
Statewide bar passage rate for first-time test takers

Texas Southern University (Marshall)

- 3100 Cleburne Street, Houston, TX, 77004
- http://www.tsu.edu/academics/law/index.asp
- Public
- **Year founded:** 1947
- **2005-2006 tuition:** In-state: full-time: $10,268, part-time: N/A; Out-of-state: full-time: $13,688
- **Enrollment 2005-06 academic year:** full-time: 657
- **U.S. News 2007 law specialty ranking:** N/A

2.58-3.23	GPA, 25TH-75TH PERCENTILE
144-149	LSAT, 25TH-75TH PERCENTILE
22%	ACCEPTANCE RATE
Tier 4	2007 U.S. NEWS LAW SCHOOL RANKING

ADMISSIONS

Admissions phone number: **(713) 313-7114**
Admissions email address: **lawadmit@tsulaw.edu**
Application website: **N/A**
Application deadline for Fall 2007 admission: **4/01**

Admissions statistics:

Number of applicants for Fall 2005: **2,102**
Number of acceptances: **459**
Number enrolled: **236**
Acceptance rate: **22%**
GPA, 25th-75th percentile, entering class Fall 2005: **2.58-3.23**
LSAT, 25th-75th percentile, entering class Fall 2005: **144-149**

FINANCIAL AID

Financial aid phone number: **(713) 313-7243**
Financial aid application deadline: **4/01**
Tuition 2005-2006 academic year: In-state: full-time: **$10,268**, part-time: N/A; Out-of-state: full-time: **$13,688**
Room and board: **$6,526**; books: **$1,677**; miscellaneous expenses: **$3,381**
Total of room/board/books/miscellaneous expenses: **$11,584**
University offers graduate student housing for which law students are eligible.

Financial aid profile

Percent of students that received grants for the 2004-2005 academic year: full-time: **36%**
Median grant amount: full-time: **$3,000**
The average law-school debt of those in the Class of 2005 who borrowed: **$19,397**. Proportion who borrowed: **100%**

ACADEMIC PROGRAMS

Calendar: **semester**
Joint degrees awarded: **Public Affairs; M.B.A.**
Typical first-year section size: Full-time: **60**

Is there typically a "small section" of the first year class, other than Legal Writing, taught by full-time faculty?: Full-time: **no**
Number of course titles, beyond the first year curriculum, offered last year: **112**
Percentages of upper division course sections, excluding seminars, with an enrollment of:

Under 25: **55%**	25 to 49: **23%**
50 to 74: **16%**	75 to 99: **5%**
100+: **0%**	

Areas of specialization: appellate advocacy, clinical training, dispute resolution, environmental law, healthcare law, intellectual property law, international law, tax law, trial advocacy

Fall 2005 faculty profile

Total teaching faculty: **41**. Full-time: **78%**; **53%** men, **47%** women, **84%** minorities. Part-time: **22%**; **89%** men, **11%** women, **89%** minorities
Student-to-faculty ratio: **16.3**

SPECIAL PROGRAMS (as provided by law school):

The mission of the law school is to prepare a diverse group of students for leadership roles in legal, business, and governmental professions.

The Texas Southern University-Thurgood Marshall School of Law offers a legal clinical studies program, institutes, centers, internship/externships and other special programs. The legal clinic includes family law, housing law, immigration, and a legal aid clinic (Criminal Misdemeanor Defense). This program provides opportunities for students to work on existing cases as part of their legal education. The mission of the legal clinic studies program is to provide a real-life lawyering experience for the law student and high quality legal services to a community that has been historically underrepresented and to create positive awareness of the university and law school within the community. The law school offers three institutes that are geared toward specific concentrations: the Institute for International and Immigration Law, the Earl Carl Institute, and the Center for Government Law. The Earl Carl Institute expanded its advocacy initiative when it established the Institute for Trial Advocacy and created the drug defense and advocacy clinic. The institute's mission is to help solve legal and social problems facing the urban community. Institute publications and projects addressed are racially discriminatory effects of zoning, juvenile justice, potential impact of genetic technology on the criminal justice system in America, establishing small business development programs, and reviewing public school desegregation consent decrees.

The law school offers the Center for Legal Pedagogy. This center is dedicated to the study of instructional design for legal education and uses principles from the cognitive sciences about learning and discourse theory to study, implement, and evaluate law school teaching methodologies. Educational support to students in the form of mentoring and an advisory program is provided here.

Students can participate in both internship/externship programs. These programs are structured so participating students have the opportunity to have an internship and a classroom component. There are three externships: civil, criminal and judicial.

The law school also offers a special program called the academic support program that assists students in study skills, case briefing, organization and developing time management techniques to use in classes, class examinations, and the bar examination.

STUDENT BODY

Fall 2005 full-time enrollment: 657

Men: 44%	Women: 56%
African-American: 49.6%	American Indian: 0.3%
Asian-American: 7.5%	Mexican-American: 19.8%
Puerto Rican: 0.0%	Other Hisp-Amer: 2.7%
White: 19.8%	International: 0.0%
Unknown: 0.3%	

Attrition rates for 2004-2005 full-time students
Percent of students discontinuing law school:

Men: 8%	Women: 4%
First-year students: 13%	Second-year students: 1%
Third-year students: N/A	

LIBRARY RESOURCES

The library holds 149,708 and receives 2,734 current subscriptions.
Total volumes: 623,753
Percentage of the titles in the online catalog: 89%
Total seats available for library users: 372

INFORMATION TECHNOLOGY

Number of wired network connections available to students: 945 total (in the law library, excluding computer labs: 300; in classrooms: 560; in computer labs: 65; elsewhere in the law school: 20)
Law school has a wireless network.
Approximate number of simultaneous users that can be accommodated on wireless network: 300
Students are not required to own a computer.

EMPLOYMENT AND SALARIES

Proportion of 2004 graduates employed at graduation: 74%
Employed 9 months later, as of February 15, 2005: 75%
Salaries in the private sector (law firms, business, industry): N/A–N/A (25th-75th percentile)
Median salary in the private sector: N/A
Percentage in the private sector who reported salary information: N/A
Median salary in public service (government, judicial clerkships, academic posts, non-profits): N/A

Percentage of 2004 graduates in:

Law firms: 59%	Bus./industry (legal): 6%
Bus./industry (nonlegal): 13%	Government: 10%
Public interest: 1%	Judicial clerkship: 6%
Academia : 4%	Unknown: 2%

2004 graduates employed in-state: 72%
2004 graduates employed in foreign countries: 0%
Number of states where graduates are employed: 22
Percentage of 2004 graduates working in: New England: 0%, Middle Atlantic: 3%, East North Central: 1%, West North Central: 2%, South Atlantic: 7%, East South Central: 2%, West South Central: 76%, Mountain: 0%, Pacific: 4%, Unknown: 6%

BAR PASSAGE RATES

Based on 2004 graduates taking Summer 2004 or Winter 2005 exams. Most of the school's first-time test takers took the bar in Texas.

55%
School's bar passage rate for first-time test takers

79%
Statewide bar passage rate for first-time test takers

Texas Tech University

- 1802 Hartford Avenue, Lubbock, TX, 79409-0004
- http://www.law.ttu.edu
- Public
- **Year founded:** 1967
- **2005-2006 tuition:** In-state: full-time: $12,662, part-time: N/A; Out-of-state: full-time: $19,382
- **Enrollment 2005-06 academic year:** full-time: 701
- **U.S. News 2007 law specialty ranking:** trial advocacy: 14

3.28-3.75 GPA, 25ᵀᴴ-75ᵀᴴ PERCENTILE

151-158 LSAT, 25ᵀᴴ-75ᵀᴴ PERCENTILE

35% ACCEPTANCE RATE

Tier 3 2007 U.S. NEWS LAW SCHOOL RANKING

ADMISSIONS

Admissions phone number: **(806) 742-3791**
Admissions email address: **donna.williams@ttu.edu**
Application website: **N/A**
Application deadline for Fall 2007 admission: **2/01**

Admissions statistics:

Number of applicants for Fall 2005: **1,805**
Number of acceptances: **636**
Number enrolled: **270**
Acceptance rate: **35%**
GPA, 25th-75th percentile, entering class Fall 2005: **3.28-3.75**
LSAT, 25th-75th percentile, entering class Fall 2005: **151-158**

FINANCIAL AID

Financial aid phone number: **(806) 742-3681**
Financial aid application deadline: **N/A**
Tuition 2005-2006 academic year: In-state: full-time: **$12,622**, part-time: **N/A**; Out-of-state: full-time: **$19,382**
Room and board: **$7,097**; books: **$914**; miscellaneous expenses: **$4,185**
Total of room/board/books/miscellaneous expenses: **$12,196**
University offers graduate student housing for which law students are eligible.

Financial aid profile

Percent of students that received grants for the 2004-2005 academic year: full-time: **44%**
Median grant amount: full-time: **$5,000**
The average law-school debt of those in the Class of 2005 who borrowed: **$48,633**. Proportion who borrowed: **81%**

ACADEMIC PROGRAMS

Calendar: **semester**
Joint degrees awarded: **J.D./M.B.A.; J.D./M.P.A.; J.D./M.S. TAX; J.D./M.S. AAE; J.D./M.S. ET; J.D./M.S. PFP; J.D./M.S. BIOTECH; J.D./M.S. CS/H/SS/E**
Typical first-year section size: Full-time: **60**

Is there typically a "small section" of the first year class, other than Legal Writing, taught by full-time faculty?: Full-time: **no**
Number of course titles, beyond the first year curriculum, offered last year: **95**
Percentages of upper division course sections, excluding seminars, with an enrollment of:

Under 25: **51%** 25 to 49: **26%**
50 to 74: **10%** 75 to 99: **7%**
100+: **5%**

Areas of specialization: appellate advocacy, clinical training, dispute resolution, environmental law, healthcare law, intellectual property law, international law, tax law, trial advocacy

Fall 2005 faculty profile

Total teaching faculty: **53**. Full-time: **68%**; **69%** men, **31%** women, **19%** minorities. Part-time: **32%**; **82%** men, **18%** women, **18%** minorities
Student-to-faculty ratio: **16.6**

SPECIAL PROGRAMS *(as provided by law school):*

Summer Law Institute: University of Guanajuato, Guanajuato, Mexico. The School of Law at Texas Tech University is a partner in a consortium of three law schools that have developed a cooperative teaching program with the University of Guanajuato. The Institute offers a thorough introduction to Mexican and International Law subjects. The Institute has been approved by the Accreditation Committee of the ABA Section on Legal Education.

Semester Abroad Programs: Universidad Pablo de Olavide in Sevilla, Spain; Universite de Jean Moulin, Lyon III, Lyon, France; and La Trobe University School of Law, Melbourne, Australia.

Law and Science Certificate Program: The Law and Science Certificate Program offers students an opportunity to concentrate in an area of the law relating to science. Students may obtain a General Law and Science Certificate or choose one of the following specializations: Environmental Law, Oil and Gas Law, Health Law, Intellectual Property Law, and Biodefense Law.

Centers: Center for Biodefense, Law and Public Policy; Center for Water Law & Policy; Center for Military Law & Policy.

Clinical Programs: Third-year students have the opportunity to represent clients and participate in real cases through five clinical projects: Civil Practice Clinic, Criminal Justice Clinic, Tax Clinic, Advanced ADR Clinic, and Innocence Project Clinic. Full-time faculty members with extensive trial experience teach the clinical courses. Students in the Civil Practice Clinic represent clients in a wide range of civil matters. Students in the Criminal Justice Clinic represent indigent defendants accused of misdemeanors, felonies, and juvenile offenses in Lubbock County and the surrounding metropolitan area. Tax Clinic students represent low-income taxpayers in disputes with the Internal Revenue Service. The Advanced ADR Clinic provides students intensive mediation and conflict resolution skills training and qualifies as the 40 hour basic mediation training. The Innocence Project Clinic provides assistance to inmates wrongly convicted of crimes in Texas and who cannot afford counsel.

Career Services Center: The Center offers a wide range of employment-related services to students and alumni by providing a forum for interviewing prospective employers throughout the nation. The Center also conducts workshops on resume writing, interviewing skills, and individualized job search strategies.

STUDENT BODY

Fall 2005 full-time enrollment: 701

Men: 51%	Women: 49%
African-American: 2.9%	American Indian: 0.7%
Asian-American: 4.0%	Mexican-American: 10.1%
Puerto Rican: 0.0%	Other Hisp-Amer: 0.0%
White: 81.7%	International: 0.3%
Unknown: 0.3%	

Attrition rates for 2004-2005 full-time students
Percent of students discontinuing law school:

Men: 1%	Women: 2%
First-year students: 2%	Second-year students: 1%
Third-year students: 0%	

LIBRARY RESOURCES

The library holds 65,905 and receives 2,831 current subscriptions.
Total volumes: 297,238
Percentage of the titles in the online catalog: 100%
Total seats available for library users: 563

INFORMATION TECHNOLOGY

Number of wired network connections available to students: 824 total (in the law library, excluding computer labs: 418; in classrooms: 386; in computer labs: 2; elsewhere in the law school: 18)
Law school has a wireless network.
Approximate number of simultaneous users that can be accommodated on wireless network: 260
Students are required to own a computer.

EMPLOYMENT AND SALARIES

Proportion of 2004 graduates employed at graduation: 78%
Employed 9 months later, as of February 15, 2005: 96%
Salaries in the private sector (law firms, business, industry): $39,000–$118,000 (25th-75th percentile)
Median salary in the private sector: $68,800
Percentage in the private sector who reported salary information: 72%
Median salary in public service (government, judicial clerkships, academic posts, non-profits): $38,000

Percentage of 2004 graduates in:

Law firms: 77%	Bus./industry (legal): 3%
Bus./industry (nonlegal): 0%	Government: 13%
Public interest: 1%	Judicial clerkship: 6%
Academia : 1%	Unknown: 0%

2004 graduates employed in-state: 96%
2004 graduates employed in foreign countries: 0%
Number of states where graduates are employed: 4
Percentage of 2004 graduates working in: New England: 0%, Middle Atlantic: 0%, East North Central: 0%, West North Central: 0%, South Atlantic: 1%, East South Central: 0%, West South Central: 98%, Mountain: 1%, Pacific: 0%, Unknown: 0%

BAR PASSAGE RATES

Based on 2004 graduates taking Summer 2004 or Winter 2005 exams. Most of the school's first-time test takers took the bar in Texas.

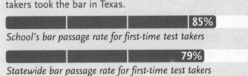

85%
School's bar passage rate for first-time test takers

79%
Statewide bar passage rate for first-time test takers

Texas Wesleyan University

- 1515 Commerce Street, Fort Worth, TX, 76102
- http://www.law.txwes.edu/
- Private
- **Year founded:** 1992
- **2005-2006 tuition:** full-time: $20,520; part-time: $14,834
- **Enrollment 2005-06 academic year:** full-time: 432; part-time: 238
- **U.S. News 2007 law specialty ranking:** N/A

2.89-3.50	GPA, 25TH-75TH PERCENTILE
153-157	LSAT, 25TH-75TH PERCENTILE
29%	ACCEPTANCE RATE
Tier 4	2007 U.S. NEWS LAW SCHOOL RANKING

ADMISSIONS

Admissions phone number: (817) 212-4040
Admissions email address: **lculver@law.txwes.edu**
Application website: **http://www.law.txwes.edu/application.htm**
Application deadline for Fall 2007 admission: **3/31**

Admissions statistics:
Number of applicants for Fall 2005: **1,671**
Number of acceptances: **484**
Number enrolled: **141**
Acceptance rate: **29%**
GPA, 25th-75th percentile, entering class Fall 2005: **2.89-3.50**
LSAT, 25th-75th percentile, entering class Fall 2005: **153-157**

Part-time program:
Number of applicants for Fall 2005: **417**
Number of acceptances: **223**
Number enrolled: **112**
Acceptance rate: **53%**
GPA, 25th-75th percentile, entering class Fall 2005: **2.82-3.38**
LSAT, 25th-75th percentile, entering class Fall 2005: **150-154**

FINANCIAL AID

Financial aid phone number: (817) 212-4090
Financial aid application deadline: 5/15
Tuition 2005-2006 academic year: full-time: **$20,520**; part-time: **$14,834**
Room and board: **$9,918**; books: **$1,650**; miscellaneous expenses: **$1,908**
Total of room/board/books/miscellaneous expenses: **$13,476**
University offers graduate student housing for which law students are eligible.

Financial aid profile
Percent of students that received grants for the 2004-2005 academic year: full-time: **36%**; part-time **17%**

Median grant amount: full-time: **$2,500**; part-time: **$2,500**
The average law-school debt of those in the Class of 2005 who borrowed: **$61,293**. Proportion who borrowed: **91%**

ACADEMIC PROGRAMS

Calendar: **semester**
Joint degrees awarded: **N/A**
Typical first-year section size: Full-time: **98**; Part-time: **76**
Is there typically a "small section" of the first year class, other than Legal Writing, taught by full-time faculty?: Full-time: **no**; Part-time: **no**
Number of course titles, beyond the first year curriculum, offered last year: **88**
Percentages of upper division course sections, excluding seminars, with an enrollment of:

Under 25: **59%**	25 to 49: **23%**
50 to 74: **12%**	75 to 99: **5%**
100+: **1%**	

Areas of specialization: appellate advocacy, clinical training, dispute resolution, environmental law, healthcare law, intellectual property law, international law, tax law, trial advocacy

Fall 2005 faculty profile
Total teaching faculty: **69**. Full-time: **54%**; **70%** men, **30%** women, **11%** minorities. Part-time: **46%**; **72%** men, **28%** women, **6%** minorities
Student-to-faculty ratio: **17.9**

SPECIAL PROGRAMS *(as provided by law school):*

In addition to offering a comprehensive array of traditional law school courses, Texas Wesleyan University School of Law provides its students with many opportunities to learn and exercise those skills that are essential in every lawyers practice. The three main venues for skills instruction in the school are the law clinic, the externship program, and our practicum courses. The law school's clinic is a law office in which students, under the supervision of a faculty member, represent real clients with real needs. The law clinic specializes in social security and SSI disability benefits cases, and in family law and domestic violence cases. Students interview and advise clients, prepare pleadings and legal briefs, and conduct hearings as the first chair lawyer. Texas Wesleyan School of Law offers an extensive and wide-ranging externship program that allows students to take what they have learned in their classes and apply it in the real world. This program enables students to work with practicing attorneys for academic credit in a variety of settings. Because the law school is located in a major metropolitan area, our students are able to have an externship experience in just about any area of the law or any type of practice. For many students, the externship experience proves to be so rewarding that they work a second placement into their law school careers. The law school's practicum curriculum is the final means by which we provide our students the opportunity to learn and exercise those skills that are essential in the practice of law. These courses involve the practical application of previously studied theory and they allow students to enhance their skills while focusing on discrete substantive areas of law. For example, students in our Estate Planning Practicum might spend a semester drafting and executing the documents necessary to organize a large private estate. Alternatively, in the law school's Business Planning Practicum the students might spend their time putting together a large public corporation. Texas Wesleyan University School of Law exists to train our students for the practice of law. To accomplish this mission we combine a comprehensive array of traditional law school courses with many opportunities for our students to take what they learn in the classroom and apply it in realist settings. Through our law clinic, the externship program, and our practicum curriculum, each student has ample opportunity to gain the experience he or she needs to hit the ground running after graduation.

STUDENT BODY

Fall 2005 full-time enrollment: 432

Men: 47%	Women: 53%
African-American: 3.0%	American Indian: 1.6%
Asian-American: 6.9%	Mexican-American: 5.3%
Puerto Rican: 0.2%	Other Hisp-Amer: 2.1%
White: 75.2%	International: 0.7%
Unknown: 4.9%	

Fall 2005 part-time enrollment: 238

Men: 54%	Women: 46%
African-American: 5.9%	American Indian: 0.0%
Asian-American: 8.0%	Mexican-American: 6.3%
Puerto Rican: 0.0%	Other Hisp-Amer: 2.1%
White: 71.8%	International: 0.4%
Unknown: 5.5%	

Attrition rates for 2004-2005 full-time students
Percent of students discontinuing law school:

Men: 9%	Women: 6%
First-year students: 18%	Second-year students: 3%
Third-year students: N/A	

LIBRARY RESOURCES

The library holds 150,727 and receives 4,836 current subscriptions.
Total volumes: 240,437
Percentage of the titles in the online catalog: 99%
Total seats available for library users: 383

INFORMATION TECHNOLOGY

Number of wired network connections available to students: 5 total (in the law library, excluding computer labs: 5; in classrooms: 0; in computer labs: 0; elsewhere in the law school: 0)
Law school has a wireless network.
Approximate number of simultaneous users that can be accommodated on wireless network: 180
Students are not required to own a computer.

EMPLOYMENT AND SALARIES

Proportion of 2004 graduates employed at graduation: 43%
Employed 9 months later, as of February 15, 2005: 83%
Salaries in the private sector (law firms, business, industry): $40,000–$65,000 (25th-75th percentile)
Median salary in the private sector: $55,000
Percentage in the private sector who reported salary information: 69%
Median salary in public service (government, judicial clerkships, academic posts, non-profits): $44,000

Percentage of 2004 graduates in:

Law firms: 52%	Bus./industry (legal): 17%
Bus./industry (nonlegal): 0%	Government: 14%
Public interest: 4%	Judicial clerkship: 2%
Academia : 5%	Unknown: 6%

2004 graduates employed in-state: N/A
2004 graduates employed in foreign countries: N/A
Number of states where graduates are employed: 11
Percentage of 2004 graduates working in: New England: 1%, Middle Atlantic: 0%, East North Central: 1%, West North Central: 0%, South Atlantic: 2%, East South Central: 1%, West South Central: 93%, Mountain: 1%, Pacific: 0%, Unknown: N/A

BAR PASSAGE RATES

Based on 2004 graduates taking Summer 2004 or Winter 2005 exams. Most of the school's first-time test takers took the bar in Texas.

66%
School's bar passage rate for first-time test takers

79%
Statewide bar passage rate for first-time test takers

Thomas Jefferson School of Law

- 2121 San Diego Avenue, San Diego, CA, 92110
- http://www.tjsl.edu
- Private
- Year founded: 1969
- 2005-2006 tuition: full-time: $28,550; part-time: $17,950
- Enrollment 2005-06 academic year: full-time: 609; part-time: 194
- U.S. News 2007 law specialty ranking: N/A

2.74-3.39 GPA, 25TH-75TH PERCENTILE

151-156 LSAT, 25TH-75TH PERCENTILE

24% ACCEPTANCE RATE

Tier 4 2007 U.S. NEWS LAW SCHOOL RANKING

ADMISSIONS

Admissions phone number: **(619) 297-9700**
Admissions email address: **info@tjsl.edu**
Application website: **N/A**
Application deadline for Fall 2007 admission: **4/30**

Admissions statistics:
Number of applicants for Fall 2005: **4,170**
Number of acceptances: **1,003**
Number enrolled: **232**
Acceptance rate: **24%**
GPA, 25th-75th percentile, entering class Fall 2005:
2.74-3.39
LSAT, 25th-75th percentile, entering class Fall 2005: **151-156**

Part-time program:
Number of applicants for Fall 2005: **406**
Number of acceptances: **98**
Number enrolled: **44**
Acceptance rate: **24%**
GPA, 25th-75th percentile, entering class Fall 2005:
2.65-3.29
LSAT, 25th-75th percentile, entering class Fall 2005:
150-154

FINANCIAL AID

Financial aid phone number: **(619) 297-9700**
Financial aid application deadline: **4/30**
Tuition 2005-2006 academic year: full-time: **$28,550**; part-time: **$17,950**
Room and board: **N/A**; books: **N/A**; miscellaneous expenses: **N/A**
Total of room/board/books/miscellaneous expenses: **$19,746**
University does not offer graduate student housing for which law students are eligible.

Financial aid profile
Percent of students that received grants for the 2004-2005 academic year: full-time: **64%**; part-time **49%**
Median grant amount: full-time: **$6,000**; part-time: **$3,400**

The average law-school debt of those in the Class of 2005 who borrowed: **$83,776**. Proportion who borrowed: **89%**

ACADEMIC PROGRAMS

Calendar: **semester**
Joint degrees awarded: **N/A**
Typical first-year section size: Full-time: **70**; Part-time: **30**
Is there typically a "small section" of the first year class, other than Legal Writing, taught by full-time faculty?: Full-time: **no**; Part-time: **no**
Number of course titles, beyond the first year curriculum, offered last year: **96**
Percentages of upper division course sections, excluding seminars, with an enrollment of:

Under 25: **25%**	25 to 49: **36%**
50 to 74: **18%**	75 to 99: **16%**
100+: **5%**	

Areas of specialization: appellate advocacy, clinical training, dispute resolution, environmental law, healthcare law, intellectual property law, international law, tax law, trial advocacy

Fall 2005 faculty profile
Total teaching faculty: **54**. Full-time: **52%**; **46%** men, **54%** women, **11%** minorities. Part-time: **48%**; **81%** men, **19%** women, **0%** minorities
Student-to-faculty ratio: **21.9**

STUDENT BODY

Fall 2005 full-time enrollment: **609**

Men: **56%**	Women: **44%**
African-American: **0.3%**	American Indian: **0.5%**
Asian-American: **7.6%**	Mexican-American: **4.1%**
Puerto Rican: **0.0%**	Other Hisp-Amer: **3.4%**
White: **84.1%**	International: **0.0%**
Unknown: **0.0%**	

Fall 2005 part-time enrollment: **194**

Men: **60%**	Women: **40%**
African-American: **5.7%**	American Indian: **0.0%**
Asian-American: **8.8%**	Mexican-American: **4.6%**

Puerto Rican: **0.0%** Other Hisp-Amer: **2.1%**
White: **78.9%** International: **0.0%**
Unknown: **0.0%**

Attrition rates for 2004-2005 full-time students
Percent of students discontinuing law school:
Men: **10%** Women: **7%**
First-year students: **13%** Second-year students: **6%**
Third-year students: **2%**

LIBRARY RESOURCES
The library holds **118,870** and receives **3,498** current
subscriptions.
Total volumes: **250,613**
Percentage of the titles in the online catalog: **100%**
Total seats available for library users: **385**

INFORMATION TECHNOLOGY
Number of wired network connections available to students: **50** total (in the law library, excluding computer
labs: **50**; in classrooms: **0**; in computer labs: **0**; elsewhere in the law school: **0**)
Law school has a wireless network.
Approximate number of simultaneous users that can be
accommodated on wireless network: **500**
Students are not required to own a computer.

EMPLOYMENT AND SALARIES
Proportion of 2004 graduates employed at graduation: **N/A**
Employed 9 months later, as of February 15, 2005: **83%**
Salaries in the private sector (law firms, business, indus-
try): **$45,000–$70,000** (25th-75th percentile)

Median salary in the private sector: **$50,000**
Percentage in the private sector who reported salary
information: **33%**
Median salary in public service (government, judicial clerkships, academic posts, non-profits): **$47,633**

Percentage of 2004 graduates in:
Law firms: **57%** Bus./industry (legal): **24%**
Bus./industry (nonlegal): **0%** Government: **9%**
Public interest: **3%** Judicial clerkship: **3%**
Academia : **3%** Unknown: **0%**

2004 graduates employed in-state: **70%**
2004 graduates employed in foreign countries: **1%**
Number of states where graduates are employed: **21**
Percentage of 2004 graduates working in: New England:
N/A, Middle Atlantic: **N/A**, East North Central: **N/A**,
West North Central: **N/A**, South Atlantic: **N/A**, East
South Central: **N/A**, West South Central: **N/A**, Mountain:
N/A, Pacific: **N/A**, Unknown: **N/A**

BAR PASSAGE RATES
Based on 2004 graduates taking Summer 2004 or
Winter 2005 exams. Most of the school's first-time test
takers took the bar in California.

| 36% |

School's bar passage rate for first-time test takers

| 61% |

Statewide bar passage rate for first-time test takers

Thomas M. Cooley Law School

- 300 S. Capitol Avenue, PO Box 13038, Lansing, MI, 48901
- http://www.cooley.edu
- Private
- Year founded: 1972
- 2005-2006 tuition: full-time: $23,140; part-time: $16,540
- Enrollment 2005-06 academic year: full-time: 503; part-time: 2,749
- U.S. News 2007 law specialty ranking: clinical training: 19

2.72-3.39 GPA, 25TH-75TH PERCENTILE

146-152 LSAT, 25TH-75TH PERCENTILE

69% ACCEPTANCE RATE

Tier 4 2007 U.S. NEWS LAW SCHOOL RANKING

ADMISSIONS

Admissions phone number: **(517) 371-5140**
Admissions email address: **admissions@cooley.edu**
Application website: **http://www.cooley.edu/admissions**
Application deadline for Fall 2007 admission: **rolling**

Admissions statistics:

Number of applicants for Fall 2005: **4,226**
Number of acceptances: **2,895**
Number enrolled: **385**
Acceptance rate: **69%**
GPA, 25th-75th percentile, entering class Fall 2005:
2.72-3.39
LSAT, 25th-75th percentile, entering class Fall 2005:
146-152

Part-time program:

Number of applicants for Fall 2005: **588**
Number of acceptances: **297**
Number enrolled: **1,129**
Acceptance rate: **51%**
GPA, 25th-75th percentile, entering class Fall 2005:
2.71-3.30
LSAT, 25th-75th percentile, entering class Fall 2005:
144-149

FINANCIAL AID

Financial aid phone number: **(517) 371-5140**
Financial aid application deadline: **N/A**
Tuition 2005-2006 academic year: full-time: **$23,140**; part-time: **$16,540**
Room and board: **$6,860**; books: **$800**; miscellaneous expenses: **$3,500**
Total of room/board/books/miscellaneous expenses: **$11,160**
University N/A graduate student housing for which law students are eligible.

Financial aid profile

Percent of students that received grants for the 2004-2005 academic year: full-time: **55%**; part-time **44%**

Median grant amount: full-time: **$7,507**; part-time: **$4,950**
The average law-school debt of those in the Class of 2005 who borrowed: **$75,762**. Proportion who borrowed: **89%**

ACADEMIC PROGRAMS

Calendar: **semester**
Joint degrees awarded: **J.D./M.P.A.**
Typical first-year section size: Full-time:**N/A**
Is there typically a "small section" of the first year class, other than Legal Writing, taught by full-time faculty?:
Full-time: **no**; Part-time: **no**
Number of course titles, beyond the first year curriculum, offered last year: **195**
Percentages of upper division course sections, excluding seminars, with an enrollment of:
Under 25: **67%**   25 to 49: **13%**
50 to 74: **6%**   75 to 99: **10%**
100+: **4%**
Areas of specialization: appellate advocacy, clinical training, dispute resolution, environmental law, healthcare law, intellectual property law, international law, tax law, trial advocacy

Fall 2005 faculty profile

Total teaching faculty: **204**. Full-time: **39%**; **65%** men, **35%** women, **9%** minorities. Part-time: **61%**; **66%** men, **34%** women, **5%** minorities
Student-to-faculty ratio: **23.6**

SPECIAL PROGRAMS *(as provided by law school):*

All special programs are designed to fulfill Cooley's mission, which is to provide all students with the knowledge, skills, and ethics needed to enter the practice of law and pass a bar exam. Flexible schedules provide full programs for day, evening, and weekend-only students, opening opportunities for midcareer students. Students may select concentrations in general practice, business transactions, litigation, and public and international law.

LL.M. programs in taxation and intellectual property are available for weekend post-J.D. study.

Cooley has led the law profession's movement to plain English. The required writing sequence, taught by tenured and tenure-track professors, explores all aspects of legal writing.

All students complete their choice of clinic or demonstrate comparable experience. Clinics include the 60-Plus Elder Law Clinic, Estate Planning Clinic (for night and weekend students), Innocence Project, Public Defender Clinic, and externships (judicial, corporate, general practice, and governmental agencies)—with externs at more than 900 sites across the United States.

Study abroad is offered in the winter term in Australia and New Zealand, and during the summer in Canada and seven European venues.

Special programs are offered by the Center for Ethics and Responsibility, the Indian Law Center, and the Forensics Science Institute. The Academic Resource Center offers all students seeking to improve academic performance the opportunity to work with lawyers and educators, at no charge to the student.

No- or low-cost bar exam preparation programs are available to all students.

Honors scholarships are given to the top 25 percent of each class.

STUDENT BODY

Fall 2005 full-time enrollment: 503

Men: 57%	Women: 43%
African-American: 5.2%	American Indian: 1.0%
Asian-American: 6.6%	Mexican-American: 0.8%
Puerto Rican: 0.8%	Other Hisp-Amer: 2.8%
White: 79.5%	International: 3.4%
Unknown: 0.0%	

Fall 2005 part-time enrollment: 2,749

Men: 52%	Women: 48%
African-American: 12.7%	American Indian: 0.3%
Asian-American: 6.3%	Mexican-American: 1.2%
Puerto Rican: 0.8%	Other Hisp-Amer: 3.0%
White: 73.0%	International: 2.8%
Unknown: 0.0%	

Attrition rates for 2004-2005 full-time students
Percent of students discontinuing law school:

Men: 18%	Women: 17%
First-year students: 24%	Second-year students: 11%
Third-year students: N/A	

LIBRARY RESOURCES

The library holds 183,786 and receives 6,281 current subscriptions.

Total volumes: 541,986
Percentage of the titles in the online catalog: 100%
Total seats available for library users: 937

INFORMATION TECHNOLOGY

Number of wired network connections available to students: 48 total (in the law library, excluding computer labs: 48; in classrooms: 0; in computer labs: 0; elsewhere in the law school: 0)
Law school has a wireless network.
Approximate number of simultaneous users that can be accommodated on wireless network: N/A
Students are not required to own a computer.

EMPLOYMENT AND SALARIES

Proportion of 2004 graduates employed at graduation: N/A
Employed 9 months later, as of February 15, 2005: 71%
Salaries in the private sector (law firms, business, industry): N/A–N/A (25th-75th percentile)
Median salary in the private sector: N/A
Percentage in the private sector who reported salary information: N/A
Median salary in public service (government, judicial clerkships, academic posts, non-profits): N/A

Percentage of 2004 graduates in:

Law firms: 45%	Bus./industry (legal): 16%
Bus./industry (nonlegal): N/A	Government: 18%
Public interest: 10%	Judicial clerkship: 8%
Academia : 3%	Unknown: 1%

2004 graduates employed in-state: N/A
2004 graduates employed in foreign countries: N/A
Number of states where graduates are employed: 33
Percentage of 2004 graduates working in: New England: N/A, Middle Atlantic: N/A, East North Central: N/A, West North Central: N/A, South Atlantic: N/A, East South Central: N/A, West South Central: N/A, Mountain: N/A, Pacific: N/A, Unknown: N/A

BAR PASSAGE RATES

Based on 2004 graduates taking Summer 2004 or Winter 2005 exams. Most of the school's first-time test takers took the bar in Michigan.

55%
School's bar passage rate for first-time test takers

74%
Statewide bar passage rate for first-time test takers

Touro College (Fuchsberg)

■ 300 Nassau Road, Huntington, NY, 11743
■ http://www.tourolaw.edu
■ Private
■ Year founded: 1980
■ 2005-2006 tuition: full-time: $27,120; part-time: $20,420
■ Enrollment 2005-06 academic year: full-time: 521; part-time: 240
■ U.S. News 2007 law specialty ranking: N/A

2.87-3.44 GPA, 25TH-75TH PERCENTILE

150-153 LSAT, 25TH-75TH PERCENTILE

35% ACCEPTANCE RATE

Tier 4 2007 U.S. NEWS LAW SCHOOL RANKING

ADMISSIONS
Admissions phone number: **(631) 421-2244**
Admissions email address: **admissions@tourolaw.edu**
Application website: **http://www.tourolaw.edu/admissions/app.asp**
Application deadline for Fall 2007 admission: **rolling**

Admissions statistics:
Number of applicants for Fall 2005: **1,976**
Number of acceptances: **683**
Number enrolled: **227**
Acceptance rate: **35%**
GPA, 25th-75th percentile, entering class Fall 2005: **2.87-3.44**
LSAT, 25th-75th percentile, entering class Fall 2005: **150-153**

Part-time program:
Number of applicants for Fall 2005: **496**
Number of acceptances: **158**
Number enrolled: **71**
Acceptance rate: **32%**
GPA, 25th-75th percentile, entering class Fall 2005: **2.69-3.34**
LSAT, 25th-75th percentile, entering class Fall 2005: **147-152**

FINANCIAL AID
Financial aid phone number: **(631) 421-2244**
Financial aid application deadline: **4/30**
Tuition 2005-2006 academic year: full-time: **$27,120**; part-time: **$20,420**
Room and board: **$15,964**; books: **$1,744**; miscellaneous expenses: **$3,706**
Total of room/board/books/miscellaneous expenses: **$21,414**
University does not offer graduate student housing for which law students are eligible.

Financial aid profile
Percent of students that received grants for the 2004-2005 academic year: full-time: **44%**; part-time **55%**

Median grant amount: full-time: **$4,000**; part-time: **$2,000**
The average law-school debt of those in the Class of 2005 who borrowed: **$78,149**. Proportion who borrowed: **83%**

ACADEMIC PROGRAMS
Calendar: **semester**
Joint degrees awarded: **J.D./M.P.A.; J.D./M.B.A. (C.W. Post); J.D./M.S.W.; J.D./M.B.A. (Dowling)**
Typical first-year section size: Full-time: **71**; Part-time: **65**
Is there typically a "small section" of the first year class, other than Legal Writing, taught by full-time faculty?: Full-time: **no**; Part-time: **no**
Number of course titles, beyond the first year curriculum, offered last year: **70**
Percentages of upper division course sections, excluding seminars, with an enrollment of:
Under 25: **56%**   25 to 49: **17%**
50 to 74: **24%**   75 to 99: **2%**
100+: **2%**
Areas of specialization: appellate advocacy, clinical training, dispute resolution, environmental law, healthcare law, intellectual property law, international law, tax law, trial advocacy

Fall 2005 faculty profile
Total teaching faculty: **57**. Full-time: **54%**; **65%** men, **35%** women, **13%** minorities. Part-time: **46%**; **62%** men, **38%** women, **12%** minorities
Student-to-faculty ratio: **17.4**

SPECIAL PROGRAMS *(as provided by law school):*
Touro Law Center's curriculum emphasizes law practice training through diverse course offerings, clinics, externships, and law institutes. Clinical offerings include five in-house clinics where clients bring real cases to on-campus offices: civil rights litigation, elder law, family law, international human rights/asylum litigation, and not-for-profit corporation law, with the last two designed for part-time evening students. There are four field-placement clinics: business, law, and technology; civil practice; criminal law; and judicial clerkship. And, mirroring the

medical-school model, there are two rotations, where students work intensively in practice groups on real cases in the U.S. Attorney's Office and a regional law services agency. The law center also offers externships in private law firms, corporate law departments, government agencies, the courts, and public-interest organizations. In addition to its on-site summer program, the law center offers four summer abroad programs: Moscow; Shimla and Dharamsala, India; Xiamen, China; and Potsdam, Germany; as well as summer internships in law firms, courts, and government offices in England, Ireland, France, Belgium, Portugal, and Israel.

The law center provides a unique program of outside-the-classroom assistance. The Writing Resources Center offers workshops and tutorials to assist students in producing a professional work product. Teaching assistants, assigned to most required courses, present weekly reviews on substantive material covered in class, as well as sessions on effective study methods, test-taking techniques, and writing skills. Touro also provides the Legal Education Access Program, designed to enhance the experience of students of color.

STUDENT BODY
Fall 2005 full-time enrollment: 521

Men: 56%	Women: 44%
African-American: 7.1%	American Indian: 0.4%
Asian-American: 9.8%	Mexican-American: 0.0%
Puerto Rican: 0.0%	Other Hisp-Amer: 6.0%
White: 75.2%	International: 1.2%
Unknown: 0.4%	

Fall 2005 part-time enrollment: 240

Men: 55%	Women: 45%
African-American: 14.2%	American Indian: 0.8%
Asian-American: 7.1%	Mexican-American: 0.0%
Puerto Rican: 0.0%	Other Hisp-Amer: 6.7%
White: 69.6%	International: 0.0%
Unknown: 1.7%	

Attrition rates for 2004-2005 full-time students
Percent of students discontinuing law school:

Men: 11%	Women: 9%
First-year students: 25%	Second-year students: 4%
Third-year students: 2%	

LIBRARY RESOURCES
The library holds 68,362 and receives 4,584 current subscriptions.
Total volumes: 423,805
Percentage of the titles in the online catalog: 100%

Total seats available for library users: 380

INFORMATION TECHNOLOGY
Number of wired network connections available to students: 0 total (in the law library, excluding computer labs: 0; in classrooms: 0; in computer labs: 0; elsewhere in the law school: 0)
Law school has a wireless network.
Approximate number of simultaneous users that can be accommodated on wireless network: 1,000
Students are not required to own a computer.

EMPLOYMENT AND SALARIES
Proportion of 2004 graduates employed at graduation: N/A
Employed 9 months later, as of February 15, 2005: 66%
Salaries in the private sector (law firms, business, industry): $47,000–$65,000 (25th-75th percentile)
Median salary in the private sector: $56,250
Percentage in the private sector who reported salary information: 63%
Median salary in public service (government, judicial clerkships, academic posts, non-profits): $45,000

Percentage of 2004 graduates in:

Law firms: 55%	Bus./industry (legal): 9%
Bus./industry (nonlegal): 11%	Government: 19%
Public interest: 1%	Judicial clerkship: 5%
Academia : 0%	Unknown: 0%

2004 graduates employed in-state: 89%
2004 graduates employed in foreign countries: 1%
Number of states where graduates are employed: 6
Percentage of 2004 graduates working in: New England: N/A, Middle Atlantic: 96%, East North Central: N/A, West North Central: N/A, South Atlantic: 3%, East South Central: N/A, West South Central: N/A, Mountain: N/A, Pacific: N/A, Unknown: 0%

BAR PASSAGE RATES
Based on 2004 graduates taking Summer 2004 or Winter 2005 exams. Most of the school's first-time test takers took the bar in New York.

65%
School's bar passage rate for first-time test takers

75%
Statewide bar passage rate for first-time test takers

Tulane University

■ 6329 Freret Street, John Giffen Weinmann Hall, New Orleans, LA, 70118-6231
■ http://www.law.tulane.edu
■ Private
■ Year founded: 1847
■ 2005-2006 tuition: full-time: N/A; part-time: N/A
■ Enrollment 2005-06 academic year: full-time: 970
■ U.S. News 2007 law specialty ranking: clinical training: 30, environmental law: 7

3.28-3.73	GPA, 25TH-75TH PERCENTILE
158-163	LSAT, 25TH-75TH PERCENTILE
26%	ACCEPTANCE RATE
43	2007 U.S. NEWS LAW SCHOOL RANKING

ADMISSIONS

Admissions phone number: **(504) 865-5930**
Admissions email address: **admissions@law.tulane.edu**
Application website:
  https://www4.lsac.org/school/Tulane.htm
Application deadline for Fall 2007 admission: **rolling**

Admissions statistics:
Number of applicants for Fall 2005: **4,126**
Number of acceptances: **1,055**
Number enrolled: **300**
Acceptance rate: **26%**
GPA, 25th-75th percentile, entering class Fall 2005:
  3.28-3.73
LSAT, 25th-75th percentile, entering class Fall 2005:
  158-163

FINANCIAL AID

Financial aid phone number: **(504) 865-5931**
Financial aid application deadline: **N/A**
Tuition 2005-2006 academic year: full-time: **N/A**; part-time: **N/A**
Room and board: **N/A**; books: **N/A**; miscellaneous expenses: **N/A**
Total of room/board/books/miscellaneous expenses: **N/A**
University offers graduate student housing for which law students are eligible.

Financial aid profile
Percent of students that received grants for the 2004-2005 academic year: full-time: **N/A**
Median grant amount: full-time: **N/A**
The average law-school debt of those in the Class of 2005 who borrowed: **N/A**. Proportion who borrowed: **N/A**

ACADEMIC PROGRAMS

Calendar: **semester**
Joint degrees awarded: **N/A**
Typical first-year section size: Full-time:**N/A**

Is there typically a "small section" of the first year class, other than Legal Writing, taught by full-time faculty?:
  Full-time: **no**
Number of course titles, beyond the first year curriculum, offered last year: **N/A**
Percentages of upper division course sections, excluding seminars, with an enrollment of:
  Under 25: **N/A**   25 to 49: **N/A**
  50 to 74: **N/A**   75 to 99: **N/A**
  100+: **N/A**
Areas of specialization: appellate advocacy, clinical training, dispute resolution, environmental law, healthcare law, intellectual property law, international law, tax law, trial advocacy

Fall 2005 faculty profile
Total teaching faculty: **N/A**. Full-time: **N/A**; **N/A** men, **N/A** women, **N/A** minorities. Part-time: **N/A**; **N/A** men, **N/A** women, **N/A** minorities
Student-to-faculty ratio: **18.8**

SPECIAL PROGRAMS *(as provided by law school):*

Clinics: Tulane has six law clinics in which student attorneys represent indigent clients under the supervision of licensed staff attorneys: civil litigation, domestic violence, criminal defense, environmental law, juvenile litigation, and legislative and administrative advocacy.
  Centers: The Maritime Law Center and the Eason-Weinmann Center for Comparative Law conduct activities and programs in which students participate.
  Institutes: The Institute for Environmental Law and Policy engages J.D. candidates through research positions and through project work with international institutions and nongovernmental organizations. The law school also offers programs through its Admiralty Law Institute, Latin American Law Institute, Tax Institute, and Estate Planning Institute.
  Summer study: Tulane offers nine foreign summer programs in: Rhodos, Greece, emphasis on maritime law; Spetses and Crete, Greece; Siena, Italy, emphasis on European Union law; Berlin, emphasis on intercultural negotiation and mediation; Amsterdam, emphasis on international criminal law and

human rights; Cambridge and London, England; and Paris, emphasis on comparative law.

Internships: J.D. students can undertake externships for credit during the course of the academic year in New Orleans with one of several federal District Court judges or Louisiana Supreme Court Justices, the office of the National Labor Relations Board, the U.S. Department of Labor's Office of Administrative Law Judges (dealing with maritime cases), and with organizations engaging in indigent capital defense.

Certificate programs: Tulane J.D. students may earn a certificate of specialization in one of five areas of concentration: environmental law, admiralty law, sports law, European legal studies, and civil law.

Study abroad programs: Tulane has formal international exchange programs with 11 law schools around the world. J.D. students may study for one semester at partner universities in: Buenos Aires, Argentina; Sydney, Australia; Hong Kong; Heidelberg, Germany; Bologna, Italy; Amsterdam, the Netherlands; Copenhagen, Denmark; Barcelona, Spain; and Paris, Lyon, and Strasbourg, France.

Pro Bono program: All Tulane students must complete 30 hours of supervised pro bono legal assistance as a condition of graduation. Tulane was the first law school in the nation to require such community service of its J.D. students.

STUDENT BODY

Fall 2005 full-time enrollment: 970

Men: **50%**	Women: **50%**
African-American: **7.9%**	American Indian: **0.7%**
Asian-American: **5.1%**	Mexican-American: **0.8%**
Puerto Rican: **0.7%**	Other Hisp-Amer: **2.7%**
White: **74.9%**	International: **2.2%**
Unknown: **4.9%**	

Attrition rates for 2004-2005 full-time students
Percent of students discontinuing law school:
Men: **N/A**   Women: **N/A**
First-year students: **N/A**   Second-year students: **N/A**
Third-year students: **N/A**

LIBRARY RESOURCES

The library holds **298,370** and receives **N/A** current subscriptions.
Total volumes: **553,972**
Percentage of the titles in the online catalog: **N/A**
Total seats available for library users: **557**

INFORMATION TECHNOLOGY

Number of wired network connections available to students: **295** total (in the law library, excluding computer labs: **295**; in classrooms: **0**; in computer labs: **0**; elsewhere in the law school: **0**)
Law school has a wireless network.
Approximate number of simultaneous users that can be accommodated on wireless network: **1,000**
Students are not required to own a computer.

EMPLOYMENT AND SALARIES

Proportion of 2004 graduates employed at graduation: **75%**
Employed 9 months later, as of February 15, 2005: **95%**
Salaries in the private sector (law firms, business, industry): **N/A–N/A** (25th-75th percentile)
Median salary in the private sector: **N/A**
Percentage in the private sector who reported salary information: **N/A**
Median salary in public service (government, judicial clerkships, academic posts, non-profits): **N/A**

Percentage of 2004 graduates in:

Law firms: **N/A**	Bus./industry (legal): **N/A**
Bus./industry (nonlegal): **N/A**	Government: **N/A**
Public interest: **N/A**	Judicial clerkship: **N/A**
Academia : **N/A**	Unknown: **N/A**

2004 graduates employed in-state: **N/A**
2004 graduates employed in foreign countries: **N/A**
Number of states where graduates are employed: **N/A**
Percentage of 2004 graduates working in: New England: **N/A**, Middle Atlantic: **N/A**, East North Central: **N/A**, West North Central: **N/A**, South Atlantic: **N/A**, East South Central: **N/A**, West South Central: **N/A**, Mountain: **N/A**, Pacific: **N/A**, Unknown: **N/A**

BAR PASSAGE RATES

Based on 2004 graduates taking Summer 2004 or Winter 2005 exams. Most of the school's first-time test takers took the bar in Louisiana.

70%
School's bar passage rate for first-time test takers

67%
Statewide bar passage rate for first-time test takers

University at Buffalo–SUNY

■ John Lord O'Brian Hall, Buffalo, NY, 14260
■ http://www.law.buffalo.edu
■ Public
■ Year founded: 1887
■ 2005-2006 tuition: In-state: full-time: $13,484, part-time: N/A; Out-of-state: full-time: $19,584
■ Enrollment 2005-06 academic year: full-time: 731
■ U.S. News 2007 law specialty ranking: N/A

3.15-3.64 GPA, 25TH-75TH PERCENTILE

152-157 LSAT, 25TH-75TH PERCENTILE

36% ACCEPTANCE RATE

80 2007 U.S. NEWS LAW SCHOOL RANKING

ADMISSIONS

Admissions phone number: **(716) 645-2907**
Admissions email address: **law-admissions@buffalo.edu**
Application website: **http://www.law.buffalo.edu/admissions**
Application deadline for Fall 2007 admission: **3/15**

Admissions statistics:

Number of applicants for Fall 2005: **1,544**
Number of acceptances: **560**
Number enrolled: **247**
Acceptance rate: **36%**
GPA, 25th-75th percentile, entering class Fall 2005: **3.15-3.64**
LSAT, 25th-75th percentile, entering class Fall 2005: **152-157**

FINANCIAL AID

Financial aid phone number: **(716) 645-7324**
Financial aid application deadline: **3/01**
Tuition 2005-2006 academic year: In-state: full-time: **$13,484**, part-time: N/A; Out-of-state: full-time: **$19,584**
Room and board: **$9,301**; books: **$1,025**; miscellaneous expenses: **$2,799**
Total of room/board/books/miscellaneous expenses: **$13,125**
University offers graduate student housing for which law students are eligible.

Financial aid profile

Percent of students that received grants for the 2004-2005 academic year: full-time: **76%**
Median grant amount: full-time: **$2,450**
The average law-school debt of those in the Class of 2005 who borrowed: **$50,873**. Proportion who borrowed: **88%**

ACADEMIC PROGRAMS

Calendar: **semester**
Joint degrees awarded: **N/A**
Typical first-year section size: Full-time: **83**

Is there typically a "small section" of the first year class, other than Legal Writing, taught by full-time faculty?: Full-time: **yes**
Number of course titles, beyond the first year curriculum, offered last year: **200**
Percentages of upper division course sections, excluding seminars, with an enrollment of:

Under 25: **68%**   25 to 49: **22%**
50 to 74: **6%**   75 to 99: **4%**
100+: **0%**

Areas of specialization: appellate advocacy, clinical training, dispute resolution, environmental law, healthcare law, intellectual property law, international law, tax law, trial advocacy

Fall 2005 faculty profile

Total teaching faculty: **131**. Full-time: **28%**; **70%** men, **30%** women, **16%** minorities. Part-time: **72%**; **67%** men, **33%** women, **11%** minorities
Student-to-faculty ratio: **13.2**

SPECIAL PROGRAMS (as provided by law school):

The University at Buffalo Law School provides a nurturing, innovative, and intellectually challenging environment.

Concentrations: Students may choose a concentration including: civil litigation; affordable-housing and community development law; criminal law; environmental law; family law; health law; international law; finance transactions; international law; labor and employment law; and technology and intellectual property.

Clinics: Our nationally renowned clinics offer sophisticated practice in affordable housing, community economic development, environment and development, family violence, elder law, and securities law. One example of extraordinary clinic work is a collaboration of the Affordable Housing, Community and Economic Development and Family Violence Clinics to build a residence for domestic violence victims including a day-care center and other supportive services.

Bridge courses: January bridge courses, taught primarily by accomplished attorneys and judges, link theory with practice.

Each January, students can select up to three one-credit courses for a practical view of law.

Interdisciplinary programs: UB law students can pursue both a J.D. and a second degree simultaneously: J.D./M.B.A. (management); J.D./M.S.W. (social work); J.D./M.U.P. (urban planning); J.D./PharmD. (pharmacy); J.D./M.A. in applied economics; J.D./M.L.S. (library science); and J.D./M.P.H. (public health).

Centers: The Baldy Center for Law and Social Policy is the focal point for interdisciplinary research and teaching. The Buffalo Criminal Law Center assists legislators, organizes conferences, publishes the Buffalo Criminal Law Journal, and offers an LL.M. The Buffalo Human Rights Center organizes international conferences, publishes Buffalo Human Rights Law Review and arranges student internships with international human-rights organizations. The Center for the Study of Business Transactions is a joint venture with the School of Management. The Edwin F. Jaeckle Center for State and Local Democracy supports a balanced academic program of theoretical study and education for public service.

Institutes: The law school and the UB School of Management collaborate to offer a New York City-based semester at the Levin Institute. The Institute offers classes taught by law school and management faculty, presentations by accomplished practitioners and real-time case-study projects from international banking, investment and law firms.

Programs: The Program for Excellence in Family Law integrates teaching, research, policy, and practice, including a child welfare sequence and practice opportunities in matrimonial mediation and law guardian work.

STUDENT BODY

Fall 2005 full-time enrollment: 731

Men: 50%	Women: 50%
African-American: 4.8%	American Indian: 0.5%
Asian-American: 7.7%	Mexican-American: 0.0%
Puerto Rican: 0.0%	Other Hisp-Amer: 3.6%
White: 70.6%	International: 0.0%
Unknown: 12.9%	

Attrition rates for 2004-2005 full-time students

Percent of students discontinuing law school:

Men: 3%	Women: 2%
First-year students: N/A	Second-year students: 9%
Third-year students: N/A	

LIBRARY RESOURCES

The library holds 109,747 and receives 6,651 current subscriptions.

Total volumes: 567,785

Percentage of the titles in the online catalog: 100%

Total seats available for library users: 526

INFORMATION TECHNOLOGY

Number of wired network connections available to students: 70 total (in the law library, excluding computer labs: 45; in classrooms: 0; in computer labs: 0; elsewhere in the law school: 25)

Law school has a wireless network.

Approximate number of simultaneous users that can be accommodated on wireless network: 490

Students are not required to own a computer.

EMPLOYMENT AND SALARIES

Proportion of 2004 graduates employed at graduation: 85%

Employed 9 months later, as of February 15, 2005: 95%

Salaries in the private sector (law firms, business, industry): $40,000–$65,000 (25th-75th percentile)

Median salary in the private sector: $47,750

Percentage in the private sector who reported salary information: 74%

Median salary in public service (government, judicial clerkships, academic posts, non-profits): $45,000

Percentage of 2004 graduates in:

Law firms: 60%	Bus./industry (legal): 11%
Bus./industry (nonlegal): 7%	Government: 10%
Public interest: 5%	Judicial clerkship: 3%
Academia : 3%	Unknown: 1%

2004 graduates employed in-state: 85%

2004 graduates employed in foreign countries: 2%

Number of states where graduates are employed: 16

Percentage of 2004 graduates working in: New England: 1%, Middle Atlantic: 86%, East North Central: 1%, West North Central: 0%, South Atlantic: 4%, East South Central: 0%, West South Central: 1%, Mountain: 1%, Pacific: 3%, Unknown: 1%

BAR PASSAGE RATES

Based on 2004 graduates taking Summer 2004 or Winter 2005 exams. Most of the school's first-time test takers took the bar in New York.

79%

School's bar passage rate for first-time test takers

75%

Statewide bar passage rate for first-time test takers

University of Akron

■ C. Blake McDowell Law Center, Akron, OH, 44325-2901
■ http://www.uakron.edu/law
■ Public
■ **Year founded:** 1921
■ **2005-2006 tuition:** In-state: full-time: $13,878, part-time: $10,185; Out-of-state: full-time: $21,871
■ **Enrollment 2005-06 academic year:** full-time: 309; part-time: 216
■ **U.S. News 2007 law specialty ranking:** intellecutal property law: 24, trial advocacy: 7

3.12-3.67 GPA, 25TH-75TH PERCENTILE

156-160 LSAT, 25TH-75TH PERCENTILE

31% ACCEPTANCE RATE

Tier 3 2007 U.S. NEWS LAW SCHOOL RANKING

ADMISSIONS

Admissions phone number: (800) 425-7668
Admissions email address: **lawadmissions@uakron.edu**
Application website: **http://www.uakron.edu/law/lawad-missions/application.php**
Application deadline for Fall 2007 admission: 3/30

Admissions statistics:

Number of applicants for Fall 2005: **1,564**
Number of acceptances: **489**
Number enrolled: **115**
Acceptance rate: **31%**
GPA, 25th-75th percentile, entering class Fall 2005: **3.12-3.67**
LSAT, 25th-75th percentile, entering class Fall 2005: **156-160**

Part-time program:

Number of applicants for Fall 2005: **400**
Number of acceptances: **193**
Number enrolled: **67**
Acceptance rate: **48%**
GPA, 25th-75th percentile, entering class Fall 2005: **3.00-3.57**
LSAT, 25th-75th percentile, entering class Fall 2005: **150-155**

FINANCIAL AID

Financial aid phone number: (800) 621-3847
Financial aid application deadline: 3/15
Tuition 2005-2006 academic year: In-state: full-time: **$13,878**, part-time: **$10,185**; Out-of-state: full-time: **$21,871**
Room and board: **$12,624**; books: **$1,024**; miscellaneous expenses: **$0**
Total of room/board/books/miscellaneous expenses: **$13,648**
University offers graduate student housing for which law students are eligible.

Financial aid profile

Percent of students that received grants for the 2004-2005 academic year: full-time: **65%**; part-time **12%**

Median grant amount: full-time: **$9,550**; part-time: **$3,000**
The average law-school debt of those in the Class of 2005 who borrowed: **$51,814**. Proportion who borrowed: **81%**

ACADEMIC PROGRAMS

Calendar: **semester**
Joint degrees awarded: **J.D./M.B.A.; J.D./MTAX; J.D./M.P.A.; J.D./M.B.A./HR; J.D./MAP**
Typical first-year section size: Full-time: **34**; Part-time: **68**
Is there typically a "small section" of the first year class, other than Legal Writing, taught by full-time faculty?: Full-time: **no**; Part-time: **no**
Number of course titles, beyond the first year curriculum, offered last year: **85**
Percentages of upper division course sections, excluding seminars, with an enrollment of:

Under 25: **59%**	25 to 49: **25%**
50 to 74: **10%**	75 to 99: **6%**
100+: **0%**	

Areas of specialization: appellate advocacy, clinical training, dispute resolution, environmental law, healthcare law, intellectual property law, international law, tax law, trial advocacy

Fall 2005 faculty profile

Total teaching faculty: **52**. Full-time: **56%**; 66% men, 34% women, 10% minorities. Part-time: **44%**; 48% men, 52% women, 4% minorities
Student-to-faculty ratio: **13.9**

SPECIAL PROGRAMS *(as provided by law school):*

Clinical programs: Students counsel clients in court, and may appear at trial and on appeal. Many clinic students have represented clients in federal District Court on prisoner civil rights cases. Clinic students write briefs that are argued before the Ohio Supreme Court, the U.S. Supreme Court, and the U.S. Court of Appeals for the Sixth Circuit. Clinical programs include appellate review; clinical seminar; Criminal External Placement Clinic; Jail Inmate Assistance Program; Judicial Placement Clinic; Prisoner Legal Assistance Clinic; Public External Placement Clinic; New Business Legal Clinic; part-time employment; Street Law Program; Trial Litigation Clinic; and Civil Litigation Clinic.

Certificate programs: Certificates may be earned in intellectual property and litigation.

Competition team programs: In the past 20 years, Akron trial teams have been champions or co-champions in 39 Association of Trial Lawyers of America or National Trial Competition district tournaments. At the national tournaments they placed first two times and second six times. The National Institute for Trial Advocacy has ranked UA teams among the top 16 trial programs nationally in 15 of its 17 years of rankings. Specialized studies: Students may specialize in the areas of business, criminal, intellectual property and technology (in any of four clusters), international, labor and employment, litigation, public interest, and taxation.

Writing program: Courses include the two-part legal analysis, research, and writing, as well as legal drafting and advanced legal research. There is a general writing requirement.

Full- and part-time programs: Both the full-time and part-time programs have early-graduation options.

Career programs: On campus interviews, practice interviews, career fairs, mentorships, internships, and pro bono fellowships help prepare students to enter the legal profession.

Joint degree programs: J.D./master in business administration; J.D./master of science and management in human resources; J.D./master in taxation; J.D./master in public administration; J.D./master of applied politics.

Centers: At the Center for Intellectual Property and Technology Law, we don't just teach IP; we create it. UA offers an LL.M in IP, one of only 17 programs nationally. Students may interact with inventors, scientists, and researchers who shape tomorrow's technology. Thanks in part to a world-renowned polymer science program, the University of Akron holds the second-largest intellectual property portfolio among public universities in Ohio. The Center for Constitutional Law promotes scholarship concerning the U.S. Constitution to help illuminate its application to modern times.

STUDENT BODY

Fall 2005 full-time enrollment: 309

Men: 62%	Women: 38%
African-American: 5.2%	American Indian: 0.0%
Asian-American: 1.9%	Mexican-American: 0.0%
Puerto Rican: 0.0%	Other Hisp-Amer: 1.9%
White: 77.3%	International: 0.6%
Unknown: 12.9%	

Fall 2005 part-time enrollment: 216

Men: 57%	Women: 43%
African-American: 5.1%	American Indian: 0.0%
Asian-American: 4.6%	Mexican-American: 0.0%
Puerto Rican: 0.0%	Other Hisp-Amer: 1.4%
White: 82.4%	International: 0.0%
Unknown: 6.5%	

Attrition rates for 2004-2005 full-time students
Percent of students discontinuing law school:

Men: 8%	Women: 5%

First-year students: 19%   Second-year students: 2%
Third-year students: 1%

LIBRARY RESOURCES
The library holds 62,585 and receives 3,328 current subscriptions.
Total volumes: 288,287
Percentage of the titles in the online catalog: 100%
Total seats available for library users: 293

INFORMATION TECHNOLOGY
Number of wired network connections available to students: 1 total (in the law library, excluding computer labs: 0; in classrooms: 0; in computer labs: 1; elsewhere in the law school: 0)
Law school has a wireless network.
Approximate number of simultaneous users that can be accommodated on wireless network: 840
Students are not required to own a computer.

EMPLOYMENT AND SALARIES
Proportion of 2004 graduates employed at graduation: 65%
Employed 9 months later, as of February 15, 2005: 89%
Salaries in the private sector (law firms, business, industry): $42,769–$79,077 (25th-75th percentile)
Median salary in the private sector: $61,154
Percentage in the private sector who reported salary information: 44%
Median salary in public service (government, judicial clerkships, academic posts, non-profits): $40,839

Percentage of 2004 graduates in:

Law firms: 44%	Bus./industry (legal): 2%
Bus./industry (nonlegal): 18%	Government: 17%
Public interest: 4%	Judicial clerkship: 6%
Academia : 8%	Unknown: 2%

2004 graduates employed in-state: 83%
2004 graduates employed in foreign countries: 0%
Number of states where graduates are employed: 13
Percentage of 2004 graduates working in: New England: 0%, Middle Atlantic: 6%, East North Central: 85%, West North Central: 0%, South Atlantic: 6%, East South Central: 1%, West South Central: 0%, Mountain: 3%, Pacific: 1%, Unknown: 0%

BAR PASSAGE RATES
Based on 2004 graduates taking Summer 2004 or Winter 2005 exams. Most of the school's first-time test takers took the bar in Ohio.

79%
School's bar passage rate for first-time test takers

81%
Statewide bar passage rate for first-time test takers

University of Alabama–Tuscaloosa

- Box 870382, Tuscaloosa, AL, 35487
- http://www.law.ua.edu
- Public
- Year founded: 1872
- 2005-2006 tuition: In-state: full-time: $8,660, part-time: N/A; Out-of-state: full-time: $18,028
- Enrollment 2005-06 academic year: full-time: 484
- U.S. News 2007 law specialty ranking: N/A

3.18-3.71 GPA, 25TH-75TH PERCENTILE

160-164 LSAT, 25TH-75TH PERCENTILE

26% ACCEPTANCE RATE

43 2007 U.S. NEWS LAW SCHOOL RANKING

ADMISSIONS

Admissions phone number: **(205) 348-5440**
Admissions email address: **admissions@law.ua.edu**
Application website:
http://www.law.ua.edu/admissions/info.php?re=onlineapp
Application deadline for Fall 2007 admission: **3/01**

Admissions statistics:
Number of applicants for Fall 2005: **1,071**
Number of acceptances: **283**
Number enrolled: **157**
Acceptance rate: **26%**
GPA, 25th-75th percentile, entering class Fall 2005: **3.18-3.71**
LSAT, 25th-75th percentile, entering class Fall 2005: **160-164**

FINANCIAL AID

Financial aid phone number: **(205) 348-6756**
Financial aid application deadline: **N/A**
Tuition 2005-2006 academic year: In-state: full-time: **$8,660**, part-time: **N/A**; Out-of-state: full-time: **$18,028**
Room and board: **$7,310**; books: **$1,168**; miscellaneous expenses: **$4,818**
Total of room/board/books/miscellaneous expenses: **$13,296**
University offers graduate student housing for which law students are eligible.

Financial aid profile
Percent of students that received grants for the 2004-2005 academic year: full-time: **41%**
Median grant amount: full-time: **$4,150**
The average law-school debt of those in the Class of 2005 who borrowed: **$48,597**. Proportion who borrowed: **71%**

ACADEMIC PROGRAMS

Calendar: **semester**
Joint degrees awarded: **J.D./M.B.A.**
Typical first-year section size: Full-time: **50**

Is there typically a "small section" of the first year class, other than Legal Writing, taught by full-time faculty?: Full-time: **no**
Number of course titles, beyond the first year curriculum, offered last year: **122**
Percentages of upper division course sections, excluding seminars, with an enrollment of:
Under 25: **71%**   25 to 49: **14%**
50 to 74: **12%**   75 to 99: **2%**
100+: **2%**
Areas of specialization: appellate advocacy, clinical training, dispute resolution, environmental law, healthcare law, intellectual property law, international law, tax law, trial advocacy

Fall 2005 faculty profile
Total teaching faculty: **84**. Full-time: **50%**; **71%** men, **29%** women, **14%** minorities. Part-time: **50%**; **95%** men, **5%** women, **N/A** minorities
Student-to-faculty ratio: **10.3**

SPECIAL PROGRAMS (as provided by law school):

Students need not attend law school in a large metropolis in order to receive an excellent clinical education. Skills training is an important mission of the University of Alabama School of Law. The law school's clinical program offers students an opportunity to represent real clients in areas including criminal law, domestic relations, consumer law, elder law, and housing law.

Clinical experiences help second- and third-year students develop the tools they need to serve clients, the profession, and society as a whole. They help students develop the self-confidence needed to practice effectively. Clinics also assist students in understanding and fulfilling their ethical obligations as attorneys. Most students describe their clinical experience at Alabama as one of the most significant components of their legal education.

Students may also receive law school credit for work in externship placements. Summer externships are available in district attorneys' offices in Alabama, the Alabama attorney general's office, public defenders' offices, U.S. attorneys' offices, the National Labor Relations Board, the Office of Prosecution Services, Legal Aid, Legal Services, and Alabama Governor's

Legal Counsel, as well as with judges in federal and state courts. Externships available during the academic year are with judges in the federal district courts in Alabama.

The law school's Public Interest Institute is dedicated to the idea that the privilege of being an attorney includes service to one's community. The Public Interest Institute enhances the possibilities for public service by making available up-to-date information on volunteer opportunities in Tuscaloosa and other Alabama communities; promoting public-interest programs at the law school; providing service programs and awards for law students; and working with the law school's career services office to promote public-interest jobs and externship opportunities, as well as offer funding options. Students who seek out public-interest summer opportunities also may qualify for grants to defray some out-of-pocket costs.

The law school provides a five-week summer program at the University of Fribourg in Switzerland. Alabama law students interested in summer study abroad also may attend a five-week program at the Australian National University in Canberra, Australia.

STUDENT BODY

Fall 2005 full-time enrollment: 484

Men: 63%	Women: 37%
African-American: 7.6%	American Indian: 0.8%
Asian-American: 1.0%	Mexican-American: 0.0%
Puerto Rican: 0.0%	Other Hisp-Amer: 1.0%
White: 89.5%	International: 0.0%
Unknown: 0.0%	

Attrition rates for 2004-2005 full-time students

Percent of students discontinuing law school:

Men: 2%	Women: 3%
First-year students: 7%	Second-year students: 1%
Third-year students: N/A	

LIBRARY RESOURCES

The library holds 136,194 and receives 3,368 current subscriptions.
Total volumes: 581,559
Percentage of the titles in the online catalog: 97%
Total seats available for library users: 535

INFORMATION TECHNOLOGY

Number of wired network connections available to students: 10 total (in the law library, excluding computer labs: 10; in classrooms: 0; in computer labs: 0; elsewhere in the law school: 0)

Law school has a wireless network.
Approximate number of simultaneous users that can be accommodated on wireless network: 254
Students are not required to own a computer.

EMPLOYMENT AND SALARIES

Proportion of 2004 graduates employed at graduation: 64%
Employed 9 months later, as of February 15, 2005: 98%
Salaries in the private sector (law firms, business, industry): $50,000–$80,000 (25th-75th percentile)
Median salary in the private sector: $71,250
Percentage in the private sector who reported salary information: 70%
Median salary in public service (government, judicial clerkships, academic posts, non-profits): $42,000

Percentage of 2004 graduates in:

Law firms: 63%	Bus./industry (legal): 8%
Bus./industry (nonlegal): N/A	Government: 11%
Public interest: 5%	Judicial clerkship: 10%
Academia : 1%	Unknown: 3%

2004 graduates employed in-state: 76%
2004 graduates employed in foreign countries: N/A
Number of states where graduates are employed: 12
Percentage of 2004 graduates working in: New England: 1%, Middle Atlantic: 1%, East North Central: 2%, West North Central: N/A, South Atlantic: 13%, East South Central: 81%, West South Central: 2%, Mountain: N/A, Pacific: 1%, Unknown: 0%

BAR PASSAGE RATES

Based on 2004 graduates taking Summer 2004 or Winter 2005 exams. Most of the school's first-time test takers took the bar in Alabama.

97%
School's bar passage rate for first-time test takers

81%
Statewide bar passage rate for first-time test takers

University of Arizona (Rogers)

- PO Box 210176, Tucson, AZ, 85721-0176
- http://www.law.arizona.edu
- Public
- Year founded: 1915
- 2005-2006 tuition: In-state: full-time: $13,202, part-time: N/A; Out-of-state: full-time: $22,182
- Enrollment 2005-06 academic year: full-time: 456
- U.S. News 2007 law specialty ranking: N/A

3.28-3.78 GPA, 25TH-75TH PERCENTILE

159-164 LSAT, 25TH-75TH PERCENTILE

24% ACCEPTANCE RATE

43 2007 U.S. NEWS LAW SCHOOL RANKING

ADMISSIONS

Admissions phone number: **(520) 621-3477**
Admissions email address: **admissions@law.arizona.edu**
Application website: **http://www.law.arizona.edu/admissions/application.htm**
Application deadline for Fall 2007 admission: **2/15**

Admissions statistics:

Number of applicants for Fall 2005: **2,194**
Number of acceptances: **517**
Number enrolled: **151**
Acceptance rate: **24%**
GPA, 25th-75th percentile, entering class Fall 2005: **3.28-3.78**
LSAT, 25th-75th percentile, entering class Fall 2005: **159-164**

FINANCIAL AID

Financial aid phone number: **(520) 626-8101**
Financial aid application deadline: **3/01**
Tuition 2005-2006 academic year: In-state: full-time: **$13,202**, part-time: **N/A**; Out-of-state: full-time: **$22,182**
Room and board: **$8,060**; books: **$1,000**; miscellaneous expenses: **$5,100**
Total of room/board/books/miscellaneous expenses: **$14,160**
University offers graduate student housing for which law students are eligible.

Financial aid profile

Percent of students that received grants for the 2004-2005 academic year: full-time: **88%**
Median grant amount: full-time: **$5,000**
The average law-school debt of those in the Class of 2005 who borrowed: **$48,594**. Proportion who borrowed: **85%**

ACADEMIC PROGRAMS

Calendar: **semester**
Joint degrees awarded: **J.D/Ph.D. Economics; J.D/Ph.D. Philosophy; J.D/Ph.D. Psychology; J.D./M.B.A.; J.D./M.P.A.; J.D./M.A. American Indian Studies;** J.D./M.A. Economics; J.D./M.A. Latin American Studies; J.D./M.A .Women's Studies; J.D./M.M.F. Finance
Typical first-year section size: Full-time: **84**
Is there typically a "small section" of the first year class, other than Legal Writing, taught by full-time faculty?: Full-time: **yes**
Number of course titles, beyond the first year curriculum, offered last year: **125**
Percentages of upper division course sections, excluding seminars, with an enrollment of:

Under 25: **81%**	25 to 49: **10%**
50 to 74: **6%**	75 to 99: **2%**
100+: **1%**	

Areas of specialization: appellate advocacy, clinical training, dispute resolution, environmental law, healthcare law, intellectual property law, international law, tax law, trial advocacy

Fall 2005 faculty profile

Total teaching faculty: **147**. Full-time: **41%**; **68%** men, **32%** women, **20%** minorities. Part-time: **59%**; **71%** men, **29%** women, **8%** minorities
Student-to-faculty ratio: **12.7**

SPECIAL PROGRAMS (as provided by law school):

Small Section Program: The heart of a student's first year at the Rogers College of Law, the small section serves as an academic and personal hub for the students. Typically in contracts, torts, or civil procedure, small sections consist of 25-30 students taught by full-time faculty assisted by second-year law students who serve as informal advisors.

Litigation and Trial Advocacy Program: Directed by a professor who is a national leader in the field, the trial advocacy program received the prestigious Emil Gumpert Award from the American College of Trial Lawyers in 2003. The program includes three courses (basic trial advocacy, advanced trial advocacy, and pretrial litigation), all based on the simulation method.

Intellectual Property Law and Science Program: An innovative program including a focus on the special intersections among law and business and science.

Criminal Justice and Security Program: An intensive weekly colloquium series investigating all aspects of criminal justice, from the streets to the forensics lab to the courtroom.

Environmental Law, Science and Policy Program: The curriculum bridges law and science, and introduces students to the work of six leading researchers in various aspects of environmental law, science and policy.

Indigenous Peoples Law and Policy Program: This outstanding program is interdisciplinary in focus and international in perspective, with high quality classroom offerings and unique clinical opportunities.

Law Clinics and Internships: Practical experience in law under the guidance and supervision of law faculty and practicing lawyers for a substantial number of our students who receive academic credit for participation in four in-house clinics (child advocacy law, domestic violence law, immigration law, and indigenous peoples law and policy), in prosecution and defense clinics, and in judicial, appellate practice and legislative internships.

Dual Degrees: The college offers 10 established dual-degree programs: the J.D./Ph.D. in philosophy, psychology, or economics; the J.D./M.B.A.; the J.D./M.P.A.; the J.D./M.A. in economics, American Indian studies, Latin American studies, or women's studies; and the J.D./M.M.F. in finance.

Graduate Degree Programs: The college also offers Master of Laws (LL.M.) degrees in international trade law and in indigenous peoples law and policy, and the Doctor of Juridical Sciences (S.J.D.) degree.

STUDENT BODY

Fall 2005 full-time enrollment: 456

Men: 50%	Women: 50%
African-American: 3.7%	American Indian: 5.3%
Asian-American: 10.5%	Mexican-American: 4.6%
Puerto Rican: 0.4%	Other Hisp-Amer: 5.7%
White: 64.5%	International: 0.9%
Unknown: 4.4%	

Attrition rates for 2004-2005 full-time students
Percent of students discontinuing law school:

Men: 1%	Women: 3%
First-year students: N/A	Second-year students: 4%
Third-year students: 1%	

LIBRARY RESOURCES

The library holds 94,112 and receives 4,435 current subscriptions.
Total volumes: 422,660
Percentage of the titles in the online catalog: 99%
Total seats available for library users: 368

INFORMATION TECHNOLOGY

Number of wired network connections available to students: 90 total (in the law library, excluding computer labs: 30; in classrooms: 60; in computer labs: 0; elsewhere in the law school: 0)
Law school has a wireless network.
Approximate number of simultaneous users that can be accommodated on wireless network: 750
Students are not required to own a computer.

EMPLOYMENT AND SALARIES

Proportion of 2004 graduates employed at graduation: 71%
Employed 9 months later, as of February 15, 2005: 93%
Salaries in the private sector (law firms, business, industry): $65,000–$95,000 (25th-75th percentile)
Median salary in the private sector: $80,000
Percentage in the private sector who reported salary information: 52%
Median salary in public service (government, judicial clerkships, academic posts, non-profits): $43,000

Percentage of 2004 graduates in:

Law firms: 44%	Bus./industry (legal): 4%
Bus./industry (nonlegal): 3%	Government: 28%
Public interest: 3%	Judicial clerkship: 20%
Academia : 1%	Unknown: 0%

2004 graduates employed in-state: 68%
2004 graduates employed in foreign countries: 0%
Number of states where graduates are employed: 17
Percentage of 2004 graduates working in: New England: 0%, Middle Atlantic: 2%, East North Central: 2%, West North Central: 3%, South Atlantic: 7%, East South Central: 0%, West South Central: 4%, Mountain: 76%, Pacific: 8%, Unknown: 0%

BAR PASSAGE RATES

Based on 2004 graduates taking Summer 2004 or Winter 2005 exams. Most of the school's first-time test takers took the bar in Arizona.

84%
School's bar passage rate for first-time test takers

74%
Statewide bar passage rate for first-time test takers

University of Arkansas–Fayetteville

■ 107 Waterman Hall, Fayetteville, AR, 72701
■ http://law.uark.edu/
■ Public
■ **Year founded:** 1928
■ **2005-2006 tuition:** In-state: $308/credit hour; Out-of-state: $617/credit hour
■ **Enrollment 2005-06 academic year:** full-time: 440
■ **U.S. News 2007 law specialty ranking:** N/A

3.09-3.69	GPA, 25TH-75TH PERCENTILE
152-159	LSAT, 25TH-75TH PERCENTILE
24%	ACCEPTANCE RATE
Tier 3	2007 U.S. NEWS LAW SCHOOL RANKING

ADMISSIONS

Admissions phone number: **(479) 575-3102**
Admissions email address: **jkmiller@uark.edu**
Application website: **N/A**
Application deadline for Fall 2007 admission: **4/01**

Admissions statistics:

Number of applicants for Fall 2005: **1,449**
Number of acceptances: **354**
Number enrolled: **143**
Acceptance rate: **24%**
GPA, 25th-75th percentile, entering class Fall 2005: **3.09-3.69**
LSAT, 25th-75th percentile, entering class Fall 2005: **152-159**

FINANCIAL AID

Financial aid phone number: **(479) 575-3806**
Financial aid application deadline: **4/01**
Tuition 2005-2006 academic year: In-state: **$308/credit hour**; Out-of-state: **$617/credit hour**
Room and board: **$5,189**; books: **$1,000**; miscellaneous expenses: **$5,346**
Total of room/board/books/miscellaneous expenses: **$11,535**
University offers graduate student housing for which law students are eligible.

Financial aid profile

Percent of students that received grants for the 2004-2005 academic year: full-time: **38%**
Median grant amount: full-time: **$6,000**
The average law-school debt of those in the Class of 2005 who borrowed: **$50,422.** Proportion who borrowed: **84%**

ACADEMIC PROGRAMS

Calendar: **semester**
Joint degrees awarded: **J.D./M.B.A.; J.D./M.P.A.; LL.M/M.S.C.**
Typical first-year section size: Full-time: **81**

Is there typically a "small section" of the first year class, other than Legal Writing, taught by full-time faculty?: Full-time: **no**
Number of course titles, beyond the first year curriculum, offered last year: **81**
Percentages of upper division course sections, excluding seminars, with an enrollment of:

Under 25: **60%**   25 to 49: **25%**
50 to 74: **7%**   75 to 99: **5%**
100+: **3%**

Areas of specialization: appellate advocacy, clinical training, dispute resolution, environmental law, healthcare law, intellectual property law, international law, tax law, trial advocacy

Fall 2005 faculty profile

Total teaching faculty: **38.** Full-time: **76%**; **59%** men, **41%** women, **21%** minorities. Part-time: **24%**; **78%** men, **22%** women, **0%** minorities
Student-to-faculty ratio: **13.2**

SPECIAL PROGRAMS *(as provided by law school):*

The University of Arkansas School of Law offers its students the opportunity to participate in several innovative and dynamic programs.

Summer abroad: We co-sponsor summer programs in Cambridge, England, and St. Petersburg, Russia. Both programs allow students to experience different cultures while participating in international and comparative law courses taught in English by well-qualified faculty from here and abroad.

Clinics: Students may choose from a wide range of clinical experiences, including civil practice, federal practice (focusing on bankruptcy), criminal prosecution, criminal defense, a mediation clinic, and a new transactional clinic that allows students to work for nonprofit organizations.

Skills classes: The innovative skills program offers students a range of courses that revolve around simulated client problems. While every student must take at least one skills class, many of our students take more than one. Skills offerings include alternative dispute resolution; ADR in the workplace; business planning; solo practice planning; mediation; interviewing, counseling, and negotiation; trial advocacy; pretrial practice; drafting legal documents; and conflict resolution.

Legal writing: This intensive and extensive program is taught by committed, full-time legal writing professionals. The legal writing faculty consists of four full-time faculty members who work with and under the leadership of a tenured, full-time member of the law faculty. The required first-year curriculum includes five hours of legal research and writing. Second-year students must take a two-credit, upper-level course in legal research and writing. We try to keep our first-year LRW classes at 30 students and limit the upper-level class to sections of no more than 15.

Small-class experience: Because of our excellent student-faculty ratio (13.7:1, one of the best in the country), we are able to offer a considerable array of upper-level seminars and courses with small to very small enrollments. Seminars are typically limited to 16 students, and in 2005-06 we offered 35 classes in addition to legal writing classes, clinical offerings, and externships—with enrollments of fewer than 20 students.

Agricultural law: We offer the only LL.M. program in agricultural law in the country. In addition, we are home to the National Center for Agricultural Law Research and Information.

STUDENT BODY
Fall 2005 full-time enrollment: **440**

Men: **56%**	Women: **44%**
African-American: **15.9%**	American Indian: **2.3%**
Asian-American: **2.7%**	Mexican-American: **0.2%**
Puerto Rican: **0.0%**	Other Hisp-Amer: **1.6%**
White: **76.6%**	International: **0.5%**
Unknown: **0.2%**	

Attrition rates for 2004-2005 full-time students
Percent of students discontinuing law school:

Men: **2%**	Women: **N/A**
First-year students: **2%**	Second-year students: **1%**
Third-year students: **N/A**	

LIBRARY RESOURCES
The library holds **187,946** and receives **3,574** current subscriptions.
Total volumes: **299,494**
Percentage of the titles in the online catalog: **97%**
Total seats available for library users: **343**

INFORMATION TECHNOLOGY
Number of wired network connections available to students: **18** total (in the law library, excluding computer labs: **0**; in classrooms: **0**; in computer labs: **0**; elsewhere in the law school: **18**)
Law school has a wireless network.
Approximate number of simultaneous users that can be accommodated on wireless network: **500**
Students are not required to own a computer.

EMPLOYMENT AND SALARIES
Proportion of 2004 graduates employed at graduation: **N/A**
Employed 9 months later, as of February 15, 2005: **92%**
Salaries in the private sector (law firms, business, industry): **N/A–N/A** (25th-75th percentile)
Median salary in the private sector: **N/A**
Percentage in the private sector who reported salary information: **N/A**
Median salary in public service (government, judicial clerkships, academic posts, non-profits): **N/A**

Percentage of 2004 graduates in:

Law firms: **65%**	Bus./industry (legal): **8%**
Bus./industry (nonlegal): **N/A**	Government: **14%**
Public interest: **3%**	Judicial clerkship: **10%**
Academia : **0%**	Unknown: **0%**

2004 graduates employed in-state: **63%**
2004 graduates employed in foreign countries: **0%**
Number of states where graduates are employed: **13**
Percentage of 2004 graduates working in: New England: **0%**, Middle Atlantic: **1%**, East North Central: **0%**, West North Central: **9%**, South Atlantic: **3%**, East South Central: **7%**, West South Central: **77%**, Mountain: **1%**, Pacific: **2%**, Unknown: **0%**

BAR PASSAGE RATES
Based on 2004 graduates taking Summer 2004 or Winter 2005 exams. Most of the school's first-time test takers took the bar in Arkansas.

85%
School's bar passage rate for first-time test takers

82%
Statewide bar passage rate for first-time test takers

University of Ark.–Little Rock (Bowen)

- 1201 McMath Avenue, Little Rock, AR, 72202-5142
- http://www.law.ualr.edu/
- Public
- **Year founded:** 1969
- **2005-2006 tuition:** In-state: full-time: $9,369, part-time: $6,559; Out-of-state: full-time: $18,819
- **Enrollment 2005-06 academic year:** full-time: 312; part-time: 160
- **U.S. News 2007 law specialty ranking:** N/A

3.20-3.73 GPA, 25TH-75TH PERCENTILE

151-158 LSAT, 25TH-75TH PERCENTILE

16% ACCEPTANCE RATE

Tier 3 2007 U.S. NEWS LAW SCHOOL RANKING

ADMISSIONS

Admissions phone number: (501) 324-9439
Admissions email address: **lawadm@ualr.edu**
Application website:
　http://www.law.ualr.edu/admissions.html
Application deadline for Fall 2007 admission: **4/15**

Admissions statistics:

Number of applicants for Fall 2005: **929**
Number of acceptances: **153**
Number enrolled: **89**
Acceptance rate: **16%**
GPA, 25th-75th percentile, entering class Fall 2005:
　3.20-3.73
LSAT, 25th-75th percentile, entering class Fall 2005: **151-158**

Part-time program:

Number of applicants for Fall 2005: **148**
Number of acceptances: **80**
Number enrolled: **54**
Acceptance rate: **54%**
GPA, 25th-75th percentile, entering class Fall 2005:
　2.90-3.59
LSAT, 25th-75th percentile, entering class Fall 2005:
　146-156

FINANCIAL AID

Financial aid phone number: (501) 569-3035
Financial aid application deadline: 3/01
Tuition 2005-2006 academic year: In-state: full-time: $9,369, part-time: $6,559; Out-of-state: full-time: $18,819
Room and board: $9,289; books: $1,400; miscellaneous expenses: $0
Total of room/board/books/miscellaneous expenses: $10,689
University does not offer graduate student housing for which law students are eligible.

Financial aid profile

Percent of students that received grants for the 2004-2005 academic year: full-time: **29%**; part-time **16%**

Median grant amount: full-time: **$4,000**; part-time: **$2,000**
The average law-school debt of those in the Class of 2005 who borrowed: **N/A**. Proportion who borrowed: **81%**

ACADEMIC PROGRAMS

Calendar: **semester**
Joint degrees awarded: **J.D./M.B.A.; J.D./M.P.A.; J.D./M.P.H.; J.D./M.D.**
Typical first-year section size: Full-time: **90**; Part-time: **60**
Is there typically a "small section" of the first year class, other than Legal Writing, taught by full-time faculty?:
　Full-time: **no**; Part-time: **no**
Number of course titles, beyond the first year curriculum, offered last year: **90**
Percentages of upper division course sections, excluding seminars, with an enrollment of:

Under 25: **71%**	25 to 49: **20%**
50 to 74: **5%**	75 to 99: **3%**
100+: **0%**	

Areas of specialization: appellate advocacy, clinical training, dispute resolution, environmental law, healthcare law, intellectual property law, international law, tax law, trial advocacy

Fall 2005 faculty profile

Total teaching faculty: **N/A**. Full-time: **N/A**; **N/A** men, **N/A** women, **N/A** minorities. Part-time: **N/A**; **N/A** men, **N/A** women, **N/A** minorities
Student-to-faculty ratio: **16.9**

SPECIAL PROGRAMS *(as provided by law school):*

We offer four joint degrees: J.D./M.B.A., J.D./M.P.A., J.D./M.P.H., and J.D./M.D. We also have two clinical programs: Litigation and Mediation.

STUDENT BODY

Fall 2005 full-time enrollment: 312

Men: **49%**	Women: **51%**
African-American: **6.4%**	American Indian: **1.6%**
Asian-American: **0.6%**	Mexican-American: **0.6%**

Puerto Rican: **0.0%**
White: **88.5%**
Unknown: **0.3%**

Other Hisp-Amer: **1.6%**
International: **0.3%**

Fall 2005 part-time enrollment: **160**

Men: **51%**
African-American: **10.6%**
Asian-American: **0.6%**
Puerto Rican: **0.0%**
White: **86.9%**
Unknown: **0.0%**

Women: **49%**
American Indian: **0.6%**
Mexican-American: **0.0%**
Other Hisp-Amer: **1.3%**
International: **0.0%**

Attrition rates for 2004-2005 full-time students
Percent of students discontinuing law school:
Men: **2%**
First-year students: **3%**
Third-year students: **1%**

Women: **2%**
Second-year students: **1%**

LIBRARY RESOURCES

The library holds **90,727** and receives **3,593** current
  subscriptions.
Total volumes: **289,993**
Percentage of the titles in the online catalog: **100%**
Total seats available for library users: **357**

INFORMATION TECHNOLOGY

Number of wired network connections available to students: **2** total (in the law library, excluding computer
  labs: **2**; in classrooms: **0**; in computer labs: **0**; elsewhere
  in the law school: **0**)
Law school has a wireless network.
Approximate number of simultaneous users that can be
  accommodated on wireless network: **300**
Students are not required to own a computer.

EMPLOYMENT AND SALARIES

Proportion of 2004 graduates employed at graduation: **N/A**
Employed 9 months later, as of February 15, 2005: **96%**

Salaries in the private sector (law firms, business, industry): **$40,000–$50,000** (25th-75th percentile)
Median salary in the private sector: **$45,000**
Percentage in the private sector who reported salary
  information: **50%**
Median salary in public service (government, judicial clerkships, academic posts, non-profits): **$40,000**

Percentage of 2004 graduates in:
Law firms: **63%**
Bus./industry (nonlegal): **N/A**
Public interest: **1%**
Academia : **6%**

Bus./industry (legal): **11%**
Government: **14%**
Judicial clerkship: **5%**
Unknown: **0%**

2004 graduates employed in-state: **85%**
2004 graduates employed in foreign countries: **0%**
Number of states where graduates are employed: **10**
Percentage of 2004 graduates working in: New England:
  0%, Middle Atlantic: **0%**, East North Central: **0%**, West
  North Central: **1%**, South Atlantic: **7%**, East South
  Central: **3%**, West South Central: **87%**, Mountain: **1%**,
  Pacific: **0%**, Unknown: **0%**

BAR PASSAGE RATES

Based on 2004 graduates taking Summer 2004 or
Winter 2005 exams. Most of the school's first-time test
takers took the bar in Arkansas.

77%
School's bar passage rate for first-time test takers

82%
Statewide bar passage rate for first-time test takers

University of Baltimore

- 1420 N. Charles Street, Baltimore, MD, 21201-5779
- http://www.law.ubalt.edu
- Public
- Year founded: 1925
- 2005-2006 tuition: In-state: full-time: $15,978, part-time: $662/credit hour; Out-of-state: full-time: $28,512
- Enrollment 2005-06 academic year: full-time: 674; part-time: 312
- U.S. News 2007 law specialty ranking: N/A

2.98-3.52 GPA, 25TH-75TH PERCENTILE

152-156 LSAT, 25TH-75TH PERCENTILE

30% ACCEPTANCE RATE

Tier 4 2007 U.S. NEWS LAW SCHOOL RANKING

ADMISSIONS

Admissions phone number: (410) 837-4459
Admissions email address: lwadmiss@ubmail.ubalt.edu
Application website: http://www.law.ubalt.edu/admissions/apply/online.html
Application deadline for Fall 2007 admission: 9/27

Admissions statistics:
Number of applicants for Fall 2005: 2,417
Number of acceptances: 727
Number enrolled: 229
Acceptance rate: 30%
GPA, 25th-75th percentile, entering class Fall 2005: 2.98-3.52
LSAT, 25th-75th percentile, entering class Fall 2005: 152-156

Part-time program:
Number of applicants for Fall 2005: 673
Number of acceptances: 146
Number enrolled: 94
Acceptance rate: 22%
GPA, 25th-75th percentile, entering class Fall 2005: 2.83-3.50
LSAT, 25th-75th percentile, entering class Fall 2005: 150-157

FINANCIAL AID

Financial aid phone number: (410) 837-4763
Financial aid application deadline: N/A
Tuition 2005-2006 academic year: In-state: full-time: $15,978, part-time: $662/credit hour; Out-of-state: full-time: $28,512
Room and board: N/A; books: N/A; miscellaneous expenses: N/A
Total of room/board/books/miscellaneous expenses: $15,394
University does not offer graduate student housing for which law students are eligible.

Financial aid profile
Percent of students that received grants for the 2004-2005 academic year: full-time: 14%; part-time 13%
Median grant amount: full-time: $6,000; part-time: $3,000
The average law-school debt of those in the Class of 2005 who borrowed: $57,983. Proportion who borrowed: 98%

ACADEMIC PROGRAMS

Calendar: **semester**
Joint degrees awarded: **J.D./M.S.; J.D./M.B.A.; J.D./M.P.A.; J.D./PH.D-PS; J.D./LL.M TAX; J.D./M.S.-DR**
Typical first-year section size: Full-time: **64**; Part-time: **80**
Is there typically a "small section" of the first year class, other than Legal Writing, taught by full-time faculty?: Full-time: **no**; Part-time: **no**
Number of course titles, beyond the first year curriculum, offered last year: **119**
Percentages of upper division course sections, excluding seminars, with an enrollment of:

Under 25: **73%**	25 to 49: **16%**
50 to 74: **8%**	75 to 99: **3%**
100+: **1%**	

Areas of specialization: appellate advocacy, clinical training, dispute resolution, environmental law, healthcare law, intellectual property law, international law, tax law, trial advocacy

Fall 2005 faculty profile
Total teaching faculty: 122. Full-time: 28%; 68% men, 32% women, 15% minorities. Part-time: 72%; 74% men, 26% women, 14% minorities
Student-to-faculty ratio: 21.9

SPECIAL PROGRAMS *(as provided by law school):*
The University of Baltimore School of Law offers the following programs:
Clinics: Family Law Clinic, Civil Advocacy Clinic, Community Development Clinic, Clinical Fellows Program, Enhanced Clinical Writing Program, Tax Clinic, and Criminal Law Clinic.

Centers: Center for International and Cooperative Law, Center for Litigation Skills, and Center for Children, Families, and the Courts.

Institutes: Summer Institute.

Internships: attorney practice, judicial, and EXPLOR program.

Summer study: Programs are offered in Aberdeen, Scotland, and Haifa, Israel, as well as in South America in the Critical Global Classroom Program.

STUDENT BODY

Fall 2005 full-time enrollment: 674

Men: 50%	Women: 50%
African-American: 8.9%	American Indian: 0.4%
Asian-American: 4.7%	Mexican-American: 0.0%
Puerto Rican: 0.0%	Other Hisp-Amer: 2.4%
White: 69.3%	International: 0.6%
Unknown: 13.6%	

Fall 2005 part-time enrollment: 312

Men: 52%	Women: 48%
African-American: 19.6%	American Indian: 0.6%
Asian-American: 5.1%	Mexican-American: 0.0%
Puerto Rican: 0.0%	Other Hisp-Amer: 2.2%
White: 59.9%	International: 1.0%
Unknown: 11.5%	

Attrition rates for 2004-2005 full-time students

Percent of students discontinuing law school:

Men: 4%	Women: 3%
First-year students: 9%	Second-year students: 0%
Third-year students: N/A	

LIBRARY RESOURCES

The library holds 33,202 and receives 3,377 current subscriptions.

Total volumes: 353,776

Percentage of the titles in the online catalog: 100%

Total seats available for library users: 349

INFORMATION TECHNOLOGY

Number of wired network connections available to students: 29 total (in the law library, excluding computer labs: 0; in classrooms: 0; in computer labs: 28; elsewhere in the law school: 1)

Law school has a wireless network.

Approximate number of simultaneous users that can be accommodated on wireless network: 700

Students are not required to own a computer.

EMPLOYMENT AND SALARIES

Proportion of 2004 graduates employed at graduation: N/A

Employed 9 months later, as of February 15, 2005: 85%

Salaries in the private sector (law firms, business, industry): $50,000–$80,000 (25th-75th percentile)

Median salary in the private sector: $70,000

Percentage in the private sector who reported salary information: 40%

Median salary in public service (government, judicial clerkships, academic posts, non-profits): $34,552

Percentage of 2004 graduates in:

Law firms: 43%	Bus./industry (legal): 15%
Bus./industry (nonlegal): N/A	Government: 16%
Public interest: 1%	Judicial clerkship: 23%
Academia : 2%	Unknown: N/A

2004 graduates employed in-state: N/A

2004 graduates employed in foreign countries: N/A

Number of states where graduates are employed: N/A

Percentage of 2004 graduates working in: New England: N/A, Middle Atlantic: N/A, East North Central: N/A, West North Central: N/A, South Atlantic: N/A, East South Central: N/A, West South Central: N/A, Mountain: N/A, Pacific: N/A, Unknown: N/A

BAR PASSAGE RATES

Based on 2004 graduates taking Summer 2004 or Winter 2005 exams. Most of the school's first-time test takers took the bar in Maryland.

57%
School's bar passage rate for first-time test takers

72%
Statewide bar passage rate for first-time test takers

University of California (Hastings)

- 200 McAllister Street, San Francisco, CA, 94102
- http://www.uchastings.edu
- Public
- Year founded: 1878
- 2005-2006 tuition: In-state: full-time: $22,297, part-time: N/A; Out-of-state: full-time: $33,522
- Enrollment 2005-06 academic year: full-time: 1,251
- U.S. News 2007 law specialty ranking: clinical training: 30, tax law: 22

3.38-3.69 GPA, 25TH-75TH PERCENTILE

160-164 LSAT, 25TH-75TH PERCENTILE

24% ACCEPTANCE RATE

43 2007 U.S. NEWS LAW SCHOOL RANKING

ADMISSIONS

Admissions phone number: (415) 565-4623
Admissions email address: admiss@uchastings.edu
Application website: http://www.uchastings.edu/admwelcome_01
Application deadline for Fall 2007 admission: 3/01

Admissions statistics:
Number of applicants for Fall 2005: 6,189
Number of acceptances: 1,470
Number enrolled: 419
Acceptance rate: 24%
GPA, 25th-75th percentile, entering class Fall 2005: 3.38-3.69
LSAT, 25th-75th percentile, entering class Fall 2005: 160-164

FINANCIAL AID

Financial aid phone number: (415) 565-4624
Financial aid application deadline: 3/01
Tuition 2005-2006 academic year: In-state: full-time: $22,297, part-time: N/A; Out-of-state: full-time: $33,522
Room and board: $14,031; books: $863; miscellaneous expenses: $4,506
Total of room/board/books/miscellaneous expenses: $19,400
University does not offer graduate student housing for which law students are eligible.

Financial aid profile
Percent of students that received grants for the 2004-2005 academic year: full-time: 72%
Median grant amount: full-time: $5,500
The average law-school debt of those in the Class of 2005 who borrowed: $69,998. Proportion who borrowed: 85%

ACADEMIC PROGRAMS

Calendar: **semester**
Joint degrees awarded: **J.D./MBA; J.D./MA Economics**
Typical first-year section size: Full-time: **85**

Is there typically a "small section" of the first year class, other than Legal Writing, taught by full-time faculty?: Full-time: **no**
Number of course titles, beyond the first year curriculum, offered last year: **131**
Percentages of upper division course sections, excluding seminars, with an enrollment of:

Under 25: **62%**	25 to 49: **14%**
50 to 74: **10%**	75 to 99: **13%**
100+: **1%**	

Areas of specialization: appellate advocacy, clinical training, dispute resolution, environmental law, healthcare law, intellectual property law, international law, tax law, trial advocacy

Fall 2005 faculty profile
Total teaching faculty: **217**. Full-time: **31%**; 67% men, 33% women, 21% minorities. Part-time: **69%**; 63% men, 37% women, 7% minorities
Student-to-faculty ratio: **20.4**

SPECIAL PROGRAMS *(as provided by law school):*

In clinical assignments, students interview clients and witnesses, prepare interrogatories, engage in discovery, investigate facts, draft and argue motions, brief witnesses, and participate in trials. Students can choose participation in clinics in civil justice, criminal practice, environmental law, immigrants' rights, legislation, local government, mediation, or workers' rights, usually on a semester-long basis.

As judicial externs, Hastings students research and prepare bench memoranda, review motions, screen petitions for review, draft opinions, and sit in on arguments and trials. Every semester some 60 students are externs for judges in the U.S. Court of Appeals, federal District Court, Bankruptcy Court, California Supreme Court, California Court of Appeal, and San Francisco Superior Court, and for U.S. magistrates.

Hastings has developed curricular depth in special areas of the law that lead to concentrations. Five upper-division concentrations are offered. Civil litigation, family law, international law, and tax require 20 credit hours to qualify for a concentrated-studies certificate, and public-interest law requires 25 credit hours.

Hastings has organized exchange programs with Leiden University in the Netherlands; the University of Heidelberg, Germany; the University of Copenhagen, and Vermont Law School.

Students may participate in a joint degree program between the college and another graduate program in a law-related discipline, such as public policy or business administration.

The Legal Education Opportunity Program offers academic assistance to students admitted under the LEOP admissions criteria. By establishing a cooperative learning environment, LEOP fosters academic excellence in a highly competitive legal studies program.

Hastings's centers coordinate the academic program in their areas, carry on major research efforts, and sponsor various conferences and activities. These are the State and Local Government Center, the Center of Negotiation and Mediation, the Center for Human Rights and International Justice, and the Center for WorkLife Law.

STUDENT BODY

Fall 2005 full-time enrollment: 1,251

Men: 46%	Women: 54%
African-American: 2.6%	American Indian: 0.3%
Asian-American: 23.7%	Mexican-American: 3.4%
Puerto Rican: 0.4%	Other Hisp-Amer: 3.1%
White: 45.2%	International: 1.2%
Unknown: 20.0%	

Attrition rates for 2004-2005 full-time students
Percent of students discontinuing law school:

Men: 1%	Women: 0%
First-year students: 1%	Second-year students: 0%
Third-year students: N/A	

LIBRARY RESOURCES

The library holds 214,487 and receives 7,961 current subscriptions.
Total volumes: 707,052
Percentage of the titles in the online catalog: 100%
Total seats available for library users: 376

INFORMATION TECHNOLOGY

Number of wired network connections available to students: 430 total (in the law library, excluding computer labs: 202; in classrooms: 170; in computer labs: 13; elsewhere in the law school: 45)

Law school has a wireless network.
Approximate number of simultaneous users that can be accommodated on wireless network: 1,040
Students are not required to own a computer.

EMPLOYMENT AND SALARIES

Proportion of 2004 graduates employed at graduation: 57%
Employed 9 months later, as of February 15, 2005: 92%
Salaries in the private sector (law firms, business, industry): $68,000–$125,000 (25th-75th percentile)
Median salary in the private sector: $94,500
Percentage in the private sector who reported salary information: 66%
Median salary in public service (government, judicial clerkships, academic posts, non-profits): $46,500

Percentage of 2004 graduates in:

Law firms: 60%	Bus./industry (legal): 8%
Bus./industry (nonlegal): 0%	Government: 12%
Public interest: 9%	Judicial clerkship: 6%
Academia : 1%	Unknown: 4%

2004 graduates employed in-state: 82%
2004 graduates employed in foreign countries: 1%
Number of states where graduates are employed: 25
Percentage of 2004 graduates working in: New England: N/A, Middle Atlantic: 3%, East North Central: 1%, West North Central: N/A, South Atlantic: 3%, East South Central: 1%, West South Central: 1%, Mountain: 2%, Pacific: 86%, Unknown: 2%

BAR PASSAGE RATES

Based on 2004 graduates taking Summer 2004 or Winter 2005 exams. Most of the school's first-time test takers took the bar in California.

81%
School's bar passage rate for first-time test takers

61%
Statewide bar passage rate for first-time test takers

University of California–Berkeley

- Boalt Hall, Berkeley, CA, 94720-7200
- http://www.law.berkeley.edu
- Public
- **Year founded:** 1894
- **2005-2006 tuition:** In-state: full-time: $24,340, part-time: N/A; Out-of-state: full-time: $36,585
- **Enrollment 2005-06 academic year:** full-time: 874
- **U.S. News 2007 law specialty ranking:** clinical training: 13, environmental law: 11, intellecutal property law: 1, international law: 9

3.67-3.90 GPA, 25TH-75TH PERCENTILE

164-169 LSAT, 25TH-75TH PERCENTILE

10% ACCEPTANCE RATE

8 2007 U.S. NEWS LAW SCHOOL RANKING

ADMISSIONS

Admissions phone number: **(510) 642-2274**
Admissions email address: **admissions@law.berkeley.edu**
Application website: **http://www.law.berkeley.edu/prospectives/admissions/**
Application deadline for Fall 2007 admission: **2/01**

Admissions statistics:

Number of applicants for Fall 2005: **7,535**
Number of acceptances: **778**
Number enrolled: **264**
Acceptance rate: **10%**
GPA, 25th-75th percentile, entering class Fall 2005: **3.67-3.90**
LSAT, 25th-75th percentile, entering class Fall 2005: **164-169**

FINANCIAL AID

Financial aid phone number: **(510) 642-1563**
Financial aid application deadline: **3/02**
Tuition 2005-2006 academic year: In-state: full-time: **$24,340**, part-time: N/A; Out-of-state: full-time: **$36,585**
Room and board: **$13,610**; books: **$1,300**; miscellaneous expenses: **$4,236**
Total of room/board/books/miscellaneous expenses: **$19,146**
University offers graduate student housing for which law students are eligible.

Financial aid profile

Percent of students that received grants for the 2004-2005 academic year: full-time: **74%**
Median grant amount: full-time: **$6,652**
The average law-school debt of those in the Class of 2005 who borrowed: **$59,620**. Proportion who borrowed: **73%**

ACADEMIC PROGRAMS

Calendar: **semester**
Joint degrees awarded: **JD/Ph.D. Jurisprudence and Social Policy; J.D./M.A. Public Policy; J.D./M.A. International & Area Studies; J.D./M.A. Social Welfare; J.D./M.A.** Economics; J.D./Ph.D. English; J.D./M.A. Journalism; J.D./Ph.D. Computer Science
Typical first-year section size: Full-time: **95**
Is there typically a "small section" of the first year class, other than Legal Writing, taught by full-time faculty?: Full-time: **yes**
Number of course titles, beyond the first year curriculum, offered last year: **207**
Percentages of upper division course sections, excluding seminars, with an enrollment of:

Under 25: **73%**   25 to 49: **13%**
50 to 74: **6%**   75 to 99: **4%**
100+: **3%**

Areas of specialization: appellate advocacy, clinical training, dispute resolution, environmental law, healthcare law, intellectual property law, international law, tax law, trial advocacy

Fall 2005 faculty profile

Total teaching faculty: **N/A**. Full-time: **N/A**; **N/A** men, **N/A** women, **N/A** minorities. Part-time: **N/A**; **N/A** men, **N/A** women, **N/A** minorities
Student-to-faculty ratio: **14.2**

SPECIAL PROGRAMS *(as provided by law school):*

Boalt's clinical program: The clinical program at UC-Berkeley School of Law (Boalt Hall) provides many opportunities for students to work on real cases. During their second and third years, students participate in a variety of clinical projects that provide legal services directly to individual clients or that involve close interaction with lawyers on large-scale cases or other legal matters. Whether they assist a victim of domestic violence, gain political asylum for a refugee, argue in a federal court, help an HIV-positive mother with her legal needs, or represent a child in a guardianship, most students describe their clinical experience as one of the most significant components of their legal education.

Boalt's clinical program includes the Death Penalty Clinic; the International Human Rights Law Clinic; the Samuelson Law, Technology, and Public Policy Clinic; the East Bay Community Law Center; faculty-supervised clinics; the Field

Placement Program; the Professional Skills Program; and student-initiated projects.

Centers at Boalt: Centers at Boalt Hall act as incubators for cutting-edge legal research in areas such as technology, public affairs, and tax policy. They give students a chance to work with leading scholars and practitioners, and they promote in-depth learning, advanced research, and extracurricular offerings such as lectures, conferences, and other events.

The centers include the Berkeley Center for Law and Technology; the Center for Clinical Education; the Center for Social Justice; the Center for the Study of Law and Society; the Earl Warren Legal Institute; the Kadish Center for Law, Morality, and Public Affairs; and the Robert D. Burch Center for Tax Policy and Public Finance.

Boalt's curriculum programs: Boalt Hall's curriculum gives students in the J.D. program the opportunity to study one subject in a sustained manner and at a more advanced level than is usually possible in general law school courses. When students elect this concentrated study, they may take two to four prerequisite courses during their second year and then spend a significant portion of their third year taking more specialized courses. Areas of concentration include business, law, and economics; comparative legal studies; environmental law; international legal studies; law and technology; and social justice.

STUDENT BODY

Fall 2005 full-time enrollment: 874

Men: 41%	Women: 59%
African-American: 4.5%	American Indian: 1.0%
Asian-American: 19.1%	Mexican-American: 6.2%
Puerto Rican: 0.0%	Other Hisp-Amer: 3.5%
White: 37.8%	International: 0.0%
Unknown: 27.9%	

Attrition rates for 2004-2005 full-time students

Percent of students discontinuing law school:

Men: 3%	Women: 4%
First-year students: 1%	Second-year students: 3%
Third-year students: 6%	

LIBRARY RESOURCES

The library holds 271,803 and receives 7,923 current subscriptions.

Total volumes: 865,801

Percentage of the titles in the online catalog: 100%

Total seats available for library users: 401

INFORMATION TECHNOLOGY

Number of wired network connections available to students: **109** total (in the law library, excluding computer labs: **96**; in classrooms: **0**; in computer labs: **3**; elsewhere in the law school: **10**)

Law school has a wireless network.

Approximate number of simultaneous users that can be accommodated on wireless network: **1,200**

Students are not required to own a computer.

EMPLOYMENT AND SALARIES

Proportion of 2004 graduates employed at graduation: 97%

Employed 9 months later, as of February 15, 2005: 100%

Salaries in the private sector (law firms, business, industry): **$125,000–$125,000** (25th-75th percentile)

Median salary in the private sector: **$125,000**

Percentage in the private sector who reported salary information: **66%**

Median salary in public service (government, judicial clerkships, academic posts, non-profits): **$54,282**

Percentage of 2004 graduates in:

Law firms: **64%**	Bus./industry (legal): **1%**
Bus./industry (nonlegal): **2%**	Government: **7%**
Public interest: **7%**	Judicial clerkship: **16%**
Academia : **2%**	Unknown: **1%**

2004 graduates employed in-state: **66%**

2004 graduates employed in foreign countries: **2%**

Number of states where graduates are employed: **22**

Percentage of 2004 graduates working in: New England: **2%**, Middle Atlantic: **10%**, East North Central: **3%**, West North Central: **1%**, South Atlantic: **8%**, East South Central: **0%**, West South Central: **2%**, Mountain: **1%**, Pacific: **71%**, Unknown: **1%**

BAR PASSAGE RATES

Based on 2004 graduates taking Summer 2004 or Winter 2005 exams. Most of the school's first-time test takers took the bar in California.

84%

School's bar passage rate for first-time test takers

61%

Statewide bar passage rate for first-time test takers

University of California–Davis

■ 400 Mrak Hall Drive, Davis, CA, 95616-5201
■ http://www.law.ucdavis.edu
■ Public
■ Year founded: 1965
■ 2005-2006 tuition: In-state: full-time: $23,524, part-time: N/A;
  Out-of-state: full-time: $35,769
■ Enrollment 2005-06 academic year: full-time: 571
■ U.S. News 2007 law specialty ranking: N/A

3.46-3.79 GPA, 25TH-75TH PERCENTILE

158-164 LSAT, 25TH-75TH PERCENTILE

23% ACCEPTANCE RATE

34 2007 U.S. NEWS LAW SCHOOL RANKING

ADMISSIONS

Admissions phone number: **(530) 752-6477**
Admissions email address: **lawadmissions@ucdavis.edu**
Application website:
  https://www4.lsac.org/school/Davis.htm
Application deadline for Fall 2007 admission: 2/01

Admissions statistics:
Number of applicants for Fall 2005: **3,768**
Number of acceptances: **877**
Number enrolled: **194**
Acceptance rate: **23%**
GPA, 25th-75th percentile, entering class Fall 2005:
  3.46-3.79
LSAT, 25th-75th percentile, entering class Fall 2005:
  158-164

FINANCIAL AID

Financial aid phone number: **(530) 752-6573**
Financial aid application deadline: **3/02**
Tuition 2005-2006 academic year: In-state: full-time:
  $23,524, part-time: **N/A**; Out-of-state: full-time: **$35,769**
Room and board: **$9,554**; books: **$987**; miscellaneous
  expenses: **$2,767**
Total of room/board/books/miscellaneous expenses:
  $13,308
University offers graduate student housing for which law
  students are eligible.

Financial aid profile
Percent of students that received grants for the 2004-2005
  academic year: full-time: **75%**
Median grant amount: full-time: **$8,200**
The average law-school debt of those in the Class of 2005
  who borrowed: **$57,057**. Proportion who borrowed: **90%**

ACADEMIC PROGRAMS

Calendar: **semester**
Joint degrees awarded: **J.D./M.B.A.; J.D./M.S.; J.D./M.A.;**
  J.D./M.C.P.
Typical first-year section size: Full-time: **65**

Is there typically a "small section" of the first year class,
  other than Legal Writing, taught by full-time faculty?:
  Full-time: **yes**
Number of course titles, beyond the first year curriculum,
  offered last year: **77**
Percentages of upper division course sections, excluding
  seminars, with an enrollment of:
  Under 25: **43%**   25 to 49: **24%**
  50 to 74: **14%**   75 to 99: **10%**
  100+: **9%**
Areas of specialization: appellate advocacy, clinical training,
  dispute resolution, environmental law, healthcare law,
  intellectual property law, international law, tax law, trial
  advocacy

Fall 2005 faculty profile
Total teaching faculty: **75**. Full-time: **56%**; **60%** men, **40%**
  women, **33%** minorities. Part-time: **44%**; **76%** men, **24%**
  women, **12%** minorities
Student-to-faculty ratio: **13.5**

SPECIAL PROGRAMS *(as provided by law school):*

The law school offers a three-year, full-time program in law
leading to the juris doctor degree. Students may also earn combined degrees, working simultaneously toward a J.D. degree
and a graduate degree in another field, including the M.B.A.
degree.

At King Hall, a faculty with a national reputation for excellent
scholarship and teaching is combined with an outstanding and
diverse student body. Each first-year section has fewer than 70
students. Each student is taught at least one of the required
first-year courses in small sections of 25 to 35 students. The first
year begins with a weeklong introductory course and includes
courses in legal research and writing. Upper-division courses
may be selected within broad areas of concentration such as
criminal justice, business and taxation, civil litigation, estate
planning and taxation, labor and employment law, environmental law, human-rights and civil liberties law, immigration law,
intellectual property, international law, land policy, and public
law.

King Hall is renowned for its clinical programs, in which students have the opportunity to develop lawyering skills under the supervision of practicing attorneys. Students work in clinics at the law school in the areas of immigration, prison law, family law, and civil rights litigation. Students may also work in separate externship programs at placements outside King Hall that are closely supervised by faculty: criminal justice, tax law, employment law, environmental law, legislative process, public-interest law, and judicial externships in trial and appellate courts.

The clinics are only one part of King Hall's effort to provide its students with an education that balances theory and practice. Skills courses, covering the major elements of both litigation and nonlitigation practice, include pretrial skills (interviewing, counseling, and document drafting), negotiation and alternative dispute resolution, and introductory and advanced trial practice courses. Virtually every King Hall student participates in one or more of the school's trial and appellate advocacy programs. These programs include appellate advocacy, the various moot court competitions, the trial practice classes, and the trial practice competition.

The Public Service Law Program provides services and support to students seeking public-interest or public-sector careers, including individualized academic and career counseling, speakers, and special events. Graduating students who complete the academic, service, and experiential program requirements are awarded a certificate.

STUDENT BODY

Fall 2005 full-time enrollment: **571**

Men: **40%**	Women: **60%**
African-American: **1.8%**	American Indian: **0.7%**
Asian-American: **23.5%**	Mexican-American: **7.9%**
Puerto Rican: **0.2%**	Other Hisp-Amer: **2.6%**
White: **48.9%**	International: **0.9%**
Unknown: **13.7%**	

Attrition rates for 2004-2005 full-time students
Percent of students discontinuing law school:

Men: **2%**	Women: **2%**
First-year students: **1%**	Second-year students: **4%**
Third-year students: **N/A**	

LIBRARY RESOURCES

The library holds **94,719** and receives **4,208** current subscriptions.
Total volumes: **437,445**
Percentage of the titles in the online catalog: **100%**
Total seats available for library users: **328**

INFORMATION TECHNOLOGY

Number of wired network connections available to students: **89** total (in the law library, excluding computer labs: **13**; in classrooms: **0**; in computer labs: **47**; elsewhere in the law school: **29**)
Law school has a wireless network.
Approximate number of simultaneous users that can be accommodated on wireless network: **400**
Students are not required to own a computer.

EMPLOYMENT AND SALARIES

Proportion of 2004 graduates employed at graduation: **81%**
Employed 9 months later, as of February 15, 2005: **92%**
Salaries in the private sector (law firms, business, industry): **$68,000–$125,000** (25th-75th percentile)
Median salary in the private sector: **$80,000**
Percentage in the private sector who reported salary information: **77%**
Median salary in public service (government, judicial clerkships, academic posts, non-profits): **$43,500**

Percentage of 2004 graduates in:

Law firms: **59%**	Bus./industry (legal): **8%**
Bus./industry (nonlegal): **0%**	Government: **7%**
Public interest: **14%**	Judicial clerkship: **10%**
Academia : **1%**	Unknown: **1%**

2004 graduates employed in-state: **81%**
2004 graduates employed in foreign countries: **1%**
Number of states where graduates are employed: **14**
Percentage of 2004 graduates working in: New England: **0%**, Middle Atlantic: **3%**, East North Central: **0%**, West North Central: **0%**, South Atlantic: **3%**, East South Central: **0%**, West South Central: **2%**, Mountain: **4%**, Pacific: **84%**, Unknown: **3%**

BAR PASSAGE RATES

Based on 2004 graduates taking Summer 2004 or Winter 2005 exams. Most of the school's first-time test takers took the bar in California.

76%
School's bar passage rate for first-time test takers

61%
Statewide bar passage rate for first-time test takers

University of California–Los Angeles

- 71 Dodd Hall, PO Box 951445, Los Angeles, CA, 90095-1445
- http://www.law.ucla.edu
- Public
- **Year founded:** 1949
- **2005-2006 tuition:** In-state: full-time: $24,581, part-time: N/A; Out-of-state: full-time: $35,545
- **Enrollment 2005-06 academic year:** full-time: 970
- **U.S. News 2007 law specialty ranking:** clinical training: 16, intellecutal property law: 28, international law: 13, tax law: 7

3.51-3.82 GPA, 25TH-75TH PERCENTILE

162-169 LSAT, 25TH-75TH PERCENTILE

16% ACCEPTANCE RATE

15 2007 U.S. NEWS LAW SCHOOL RANKING

ADMISSIONS

Admissions phone number: (310) 825-2080
Admissions email address: **admissions@law.ucla.edu**
Application website: **http://www1.law.ucla.edu/~admissions/**
Application deadline for Fall 2007 admission: 2/01

Admissions statistics:

Number of applicants for Fall 2005: **6,319**
Number of acceptances: **1,015**
Number enrolled: **317**
Acceptance rate: **16%**
GPA, 25th-75th percentile, entering class Fall 2005: **3.51-3.82**
LSAT, 25th-75th percentile, entering class Fall 2005: **162-169**

FINANCIAL AID

Financial aid phone number: (310) 825-2459
Financial aid application deadline: 3/01
Tuition 2005-2006 academic year: In-state: full-time: **$24,581**, part-time: N/A; Out-of-state: full-time: **$35,545**
Room and board: **$12,381**; books: **$1,800**; miscellaneous expenses: **$4,872**
Total of room/board/books/miscellaneous expenses: **$19,053**
University offers graduate student housing for which law students are eligible.

Financial aid profile

Percent of students that received grants for the 2004-2005 academic year: full-time: **61%**
Median grant amount: full-time: **$8,424**
The average law-school debt of those in the Class of 2005 who borrowed: **$61,000**. Proportion who borrowed: **98%**

ACADEMIC PROGRAMS

Calendar: **semester**
Joint degrees awarded: **J.D./M.B.A.; J.D./M.A. (Urban Planning); J.D./M.A. (American Indian Studies);** **J.D./M.S.W.; J.D./M.P.P.; J.D./M.A. (African American Studies); J.D./M.P.H.**
Typical first-year section size: Full-time: **80**
Is there typically a "small section" of the first year class, other than Legal Writing, taught by full-time faculty?: Full-time: **yes**
Number of course titles, beyond the first year curriculum, offered last year: **151**
Percentages of upper division course sections, excluding seminars, with an enrollment of:
Under 25: **54%**   25 to 49: **28%**
50 to 74: **6%**   75 to 99: **10%**
100+: **2%**
Areas of specialization: appellate advocacy, clinical training, dispute resolution, environmental law, healthcare law, intellectual property law, international law, tax law, trial advocacy

Fall 2005 faculty profile

Total teaching faculty: **91**. Full-time: **76%**; **75%** men, **25%** women, **10%** minorities. Part-time: **24%**; **73%** men, **27%** women, **5%** minorities
Student-to-faculty ratio: **11.8**

SPECIAL PROGRAMS *(as provided by law school):*

UCLA School of Law is the youngest top-tier law school in the nation and has established a tradition of innovation in its approach to teaching, research and scholarship. With approximately 100 faculty and nearly 1,000 students, UCLA Law brings leading legal scholars and practitioners together with bright and eager students to form a learning culture that values intellectual curiosity and encourages interdisciplinary pursuits. The school pioneered clinical teaching, is a leader in interdisciplinary research and training, and is at the forefront of efforts to link research to society and the legal profession.

Each year a talented and diverse law student population assembles within UCLA Law's rigorous yet collegial environment. Students pursue their interests from among a rich curriculum of courses and programs on numerous issues that impact all aspects of law in today's society. UCLA Law's curricular approach emphasizes both theoretical ability and transactional skills, making our graduates best prepared to meet the demands of practicing law in an ever-complex and competitive world.

In their academic endeavors, students can pursue concentrated courses of study in fields such as business law, entertainment and media law, critical race studies, environmental law and public interest law. UCLA Law also offers opportunities for interdisciplinary study through joint/concurrent degree programs in the areas of business, public policy, Afro-American studies, public health, American Indian studies, social welfare and urban planning.

UCLA Law also provides valuable opportunities to enhance student learning and preparation for professional pursuits. Students participate in intensive, supervised educational experiences in the school's noted clinical program and choose from among a variety of externships.

The majority of UCLA Law students are earning their juris doctor (J.D.) degree, a full-time only program that requires three years of study. A nine-month master of laws (LL.M.) program is designed to provide outstanding J.D. and bachelor of laws (LL.B.) graduates with the opportunity to gain advanced knowledge in law. UCLA Law's highly selective doctor of juridical science (S.J.D.) degree program is designed for those seeking to pursue careers as teachers and scholars of law.

STUDENT BODY

Fall 2005 full-time enrollment: 970

Men: 50%	Women: 50%
African-American: 4.3%	American Indian: 1.8%
Asian-American: 15.9%	Mexican-American: 6.8%
Puerto Rican: 0.1%	Other Hisp-Amer: 1.0%
White: 46.4%	International: 1.0%
Unknown: 22.7%	

Attrition rates for 2004-2005 full-time students
Percent of students discontinuing law school:

Men: 2%	Women: 1%
First-year students: 4%	Second-year students: 1%
Third-year students: N/A	

LIBRARY RESOURCES

The library holds 230,482 and receives 8,482 current subscriptions.
Total volumes: 630,825
Percentage of the titles in the online catalog: 100%
Total seats available for library users: 774

INFORMATION TECHNOLOGY

Number of wired network connections available to students: 1,610 total (in the law library, excluding computer labs: 400; in classrooms: 1,200; in computer labs: 10; elsewhere in the law school: 0)
Law school has a wireless network.
Approximate number of simultaneous users that can be accommodated on wireless network: 1,250
Students are not required to own a computer.

EMPLOYMENT AND SALARIES

Proportion of 2004 graduates employed at graduation: 93%
Employed 9 months later, as of February 15, 2005: 100%
Salaries in the private sector (law firms, business, industry): $75,000–$125,000 (25th-75th percentile)
Median salary in the private sector: $125,000
Percentage in the private sector who reported salary information: 76%
Median salary in public service (government, judicial clerkships, academic posts, non-profits): $52,261

Percentage of 2004 graduates in:

Law firms: 72%	Bus./industry (legal): 2%
Bus./industry (nonlegal): 2%	Government: 6%
Public interest: 7%	Judicial clerkship: 9%
Academia : 2%	Unknown: 0%

2004 graduates employed in-state: 85%
2004 graduates employed in foreign countries: 1%
Number of states where graduates are employed: 16
Percentage of 2004 graduates working in: New England: 0%, Middle Atlantic: 6%, East North Central: 1%, West North Central: 1%, South Atlantic: 3%, East South Central: 0%, West South Central: 1%, Mountain: 3%, Pacific: 85%, Unknown: 0%

BAR PASSAGE RATES

Based on 2004 graduates taking Summer 2004 or Winter 2005 exams. Most of the school's first-time test takers took the bar in California.

86%
School's bar passage rate for first-time test takers

61%
Statewide bar passage rate for first-time test takers

University of Chicago

- 1111 E. 60th Street, Chicago, IL, 60637
- http://www.law.uchicago.edu
- Private
- Year founded: 1902
- 2005-2006 tuition: full-time: $36,138; part-time: N/A
- Enrollment 2005-06 academic year: full-time: 589
- U.S. News 2007 law specialty ranking: clinical training: 19, tax law: 17

3.46-3.80 GPA, 25TH-75TH PERCENTILE

168-172 LSAT, 25TH-75TH PERCENTILE

15% ACCEPTANCE RATE

6 2007 U.S. NEWS LAW SCHOOL RANKING

ADMISSIONS

Admissions phone number: **(773) 702-9484**
Admissions email address: **admissions@law.uchicago.edu**
Application website: **https://grad-application.uchicago.edu/intro/law/intro1.cfm**
Application deadline for Fall 2007 admission: **2/01**

Admissions statistics:

Number of applicants for Fall 2005: **4,800**
Number of acceptances: **705**
Number enrolled: **192**
Acceptance rate: **15%**
GPA, 25th-75th percentile, entering class Fall 2005: **3.46-3.80**
LSAT, 25th-75th percentile, entering class Fall 2005: **168-172**

FINANCIAL AID

Financial aid phone number: **(773) 702-9484**
Financial aid application deadline: **3/01**
Tuition 2005-2006 academic year: full-time: **$36,138**; part-time: **N/A**
Room and board: **$12,825**; books: **$1,575**; miscellaneous expenses: **$5,937**
Total of room/board/books/miscellaneous expenses: **$20,337**
University offers graduate student housing for which law students are eligible.

Financial aid profile

Percent of students that received grants for the 2004-2005 academic year: full-time: **52%**
Median grant amount: full-time: **$9,900**
The average law-school debt of those in the Class of 2005 who borrowed: **$114,263**. Proportion who borrowed: **67%**

ACADEMIC PROGRAMS

Calendar: **quarter**
Joint degrees awarded: **J.D./M.B.A.; J.D./M.P.P.; J.D./Ph.D. History; J.D./Ph.D. Business; J.D./A.M. INR; J.D./Ph.D. Economics**

Typical first-year section size: Full-time: **96**
Is there typically a "small section" of the first year class, other than Legal Writing, taught by full-time faculty?: Full-time: **no**
Number of course titles, beyond the first year curriculum, offered last year: **155**
Percentages of upper division course sections, excluding seminars, with an enrollment of:
Under 25: **30%**   25 to 49: **39%**
50 to 74: **19%**   75 to 99: **6%**
100+: **6%**
Areas of specialization: appellate advocacy, clinical training, dispute resolution, environmental law, healthcare law, intellectual property law, international law, tax law, trial advocacy

Fall 2005 faculty profile

Total teaching faculty: **109**. Full-time: **49%**; 85% men, 15% women, 9% minorities. Part-time: **51%**; 80% men, 20% women, 7% minorities
Student-to-faculty ratio: **9.5**

SPECIAL PROGRAMS *(as provided by law school)*:

Housed in the Arthur Kane Center, Chicago's clinics give more than 100 students each year a chance to represent clients with real-world legal problems under the guidance of the clinical faculty.

The Mandel Legal Aid Clinic offers projects in criminal and juvenile justice, employment discrimination, civil rights, housing, appellate advocacy and mental health. Students interview clients, investigate facts, negotiate with adverse parties, conduct discovery, draft briefs, draft legislation, and appear on behalf of clients in state and federal courts.

The program focuses on cutting-edge advocacy that can change entire areas of the law. For example, students in the Criminal and Juvenile Justice Project, in addition to representing children and young adults accused of delinquent or criminal behavior, are often involved in policy reform and community education.

The clinic is also engaged in class action litigation that challenges the restrictions imposed on people confined at state-operated mental health facilities and the lack of procedural protections afforded people who have filed claims of employment discrimination with the state of Illinois. Finally, the clinic offers a social service component that allows graduate students from the university's School of Social Services Administration to collaborate with law students on selected cases.

The Institute for Justice Clinic on Entrepreneurship offers free legal services to low- to moderate-income entrepreneurs. Students provide a range of transactional legal services to entrepreneurs principally located in the inner city of Chicago. These services include business formation; assistance with license and permit applications; contract and lease negotiation; landlord, supplier, and lender negotiation; advice on intellectual property; and basic tax and regulatory compliance.

Chicago's clinical opportunities outside of the law school include our poverty and housing law clinic, offered in cooperation with the Legal Assistance Foundation of Chicago.

STUDENT BODY
Fall 2005 full-time enrollment: 589

Men: 55%	Women: 45%
African-American: 7.5%	American Indian: 0.3%
Asian-American: 13.1%	Mexican-American: 2.9%
Puerto Rican: 1.2%	Other Hisp-Amer: 6.3%
White: 56.2%	International: 0.5%
Unknown: 12.1%	

Attrition rates for 2004-2005 full-time students
Percent of students discontinuing law school:

Men: N/A	Women: N/A
First-year students: N/A	Second-year students: N/A
Third-year students: N/A	

LIBRARY RESOURCES
The library holds 292,898 and receives 8,878 current subscriptions.
Total volumes: 718,749
Percentage of the titles in the online catalog: 99%
Total seats available for library users: 450

INFORMATION TECHNOLOGY
Number of wired network connections available to students: 1,038 total (in the law library, excluding computer labs: 228; in classrooms: 800; in computer labs: 2; elsewhere in the law school: 8)

Law school has a wireless network.
Approximate number of simultaneous users that can be accommodated on wireless network: 500
Students are required to own a computer.

EMPLOYMENT AND SALARIES
Proportion of 2004 graduates employed at graduation: 99%
Employed 9 months later, as of February 15, 2005: 100%
Salaries in the private sector (law firms, business, industry): $125,000–$125,000 (25th-75th percentile)
Median salary in the private sector: $125,000
Percentage in the private sector who reported salary information: 95%
Median salary in public service (government, judicial clerkships, academic posts, non-profits): $50,593

Percentage of 2004 graduates in:

Law firms: 68%	Bus./industry (legal): 1%
Bus./industry (nonlegal): 1%	Government: 4%
Public interest: 4%	Judicial clerkship: 21%
Academia : 1%	Unknown: 0%

2004 graduates employed in-state: 36%
2004 graduates employed in foreign countries: 3%
Number of states where graduates are employed: 28
Percentage of 2004 graduates working in: New England: 4%, Middle Atlantic: 15%, East North Central: 39%, West North Central: 2%, South Atlantic: 10%, East South Central: 2%, West South Central: 8%, Mountain: 3%, Pacific: 14%, Unknown: 0%

BAR PASSAGE RATES
Based on 2004 graduates taking Summer 2004 or Winter 2005 exams. Most of the school's first-time test takers took the bar in Illinois.

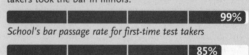

99%	
School's bar passage rate for first-time test takers	
85%	
Statewide bar passage rate for first-time test takers	

University of Cincinnati

■ PO Box 210040, Cincinnati, OH, 45221-0040
■ http://www.law.uc.edu
■ Public
■ Year founded: 1833
■ 2005-2006 tuition: In-state: full-time: $16,210, part-time: N/A;
   Out-of-state: full-time: $29,284
■ Enrollment 2005-06 academic year: full-time: 397
■ U.S. News 2007 law specialty ranking: N/A

3.29-3.83	GPA, 25TH-75TH PERCENTILE
156-162	LSAT, 25TH-75TH PERCENTILE
37%	ACCEPTANCE RATE
53	2007 U.S. NEWS LAW SCHOOL RANKING

ADMISSIONS

Admissions phone number: (513) 556-6805
Admissions email address: admissions@law.uc.edu
Application website: http://www.law.uc.edu/admissions
Application deadline for Fall 2007 admission: 4/01

Admissions statistics:

Number of applicants for Fall 2005: 1,186
Number of acceptances: 435
Number enrolled: 133
Acceptance rate: 37%
GPA, 25th-75th percentile, entering class Fall 2005:
   3.29-3.83
LSAT, 25th-75th percentile, entering class Fall 2005:
   156-162

FINANCIAL AID

Financial aid phone number: (513) 556-6805
Financial aid application deadline: 4/01
Tuition 2005-2006 academic year: In-state: full-time:
   $16,210, part-time: N/A; Out-of-state: full-time: $29,284
Room and board: $7,890; books: $1,143; miscellaneous
   expenses: $4,388
Total of room/board/books/miscellaneous expenses:
   $13,421
University offers graduate student housing for which law
   students are eligible.

Financial aid profile

Percent of students that received grants for the 2004-2005
   academic year: full-time: 64%
Median grant amount: full-time: $6,000
The average law-school debt of those in the Class of 2005
   who borrowed: $49,263. Proportion who borrowed: 70%

ACADEMIC PROGRAMS

Calendar: semester
Joint degrees awarded: J.D./M.B.A.; J.D./M.C.P.
   (Community Planning); J.D./M.A. (Women's Studies);
   J.D./M.S. (Political Science); J.D./Ph.D (Political

Science); J.D./M.S. (Economics); J.D./M.S.W. (Social
Work)
Typical first-year section size: Full-time: 76
Is there typically a "small section" of the first year class,
   other than Legal Writing, taught by full-time faculty?:
   Full-time: yes
Number of course titles, beyond the first year curriculum,
   offered last year: 113
Percentages of upper division course sections, excluding
   seminars, with an enrollment of:
   Under 25: 66%   25 to 49: 23%
   50 to 74: 3%   75 to 99: 3%
   100+: 5%
Areas of specialization: appellate advocacy, clinical training,
   dispute resolution, environmental law, healthcare law,
   intellectual property law, international law, tax law, trial
   advocacy

Fall 2005 faculty profile

Total teaching faculty: 89. Full-time: 33%; 48% men, 52%
women, 17% minorities. Part-time: 67%; 83% men, 17%
women, 8% minorities
Student-to-faculty ratio: 11.8

SPECIAL PROGRAMS (as provided by law school):

Urban Morgan Institute for Human Rights, established in 1979,
is one of the first major national centers to focus on human rights
law that have developed largely since WW II. Dedicated to draw-
ing the attention of the legal and scholarly communities to this
new area of the law, the Institute conducts seminars/conferences,
is building a major research library and edits the preeminent academic journal, the Human Rights Quarterly (Johns Hopkins
University Press). The Center for Corporate Law provides an outstanding opportunity for qualified applicants to focus their legal
studies in a Corporate Law Fellowship program. The Center is an
endowed teaching and research vehicle within the College.
Activities include monitoring and expansion of corporate law
course offerings at the College, maintenance of a Corporate Law
Fellowship program for outstanding students with an interest in
the study of corporate law, presentation of conferences, including
the annual Corporate Law Symposium, encouragement and sup-

port for faculty scholarly activities, and the maintenance of an outstanding library collection. Rosenthal Institute for Justice is involved in a variety of public interest activities at the college and sponsors summer fellowships for law students interested in working on public policy research; recent projects include capital punishment, search and seizure, and discrimination in housing. The Center also sponsors the Ohio Innocence Project, which allows students, under the supervision of professors and practicing attorneys, to investigate the cases of inmates in Ohio who were convicted of serious crimes and have steadfastly maintained their innocence. Weaver Institute for Law & Psychiatry, established in 1997 in conjunction with a generous gift from Glenn Weaver, MD, a long-time adjunct professor at the College, embraces a vision of the interrelationship between law and psychiatry, recognizing the need for effective advocacy for individuals with mental illnesses while respecting the collective expertise of medical and mental health professionals. Center for Practice in Negotiations & Problem Solving enables students to learn skills and theory for practice in negotiations, mediation and other dispute resolution processes, through coursework, practice placements, research, and participation in national competitions. The College and the University of Canterbury, Christchurch, New Zealand, participate in an exchange program that allows law students to take an academic semester of classes at the other institution. Tuition reciprocity exists between the two Universities allowing our law students to attend Canterbury under the same cost and financial aid terms as a regular law school semester.

STUDENT BODY

Fall 2005 full-time enrollment: 397

Men: 50%	Women: 50%
African-American: 7.6%	American Indian: 1.0%
Asian-American: 5.5%	Mexican-American: 0.0%
Puerto Rican: 1.0%	Other Hisp-Amer: 1.8%
White: 83.1%	International: 0.0%
Unknown: 0.0%	

Attrition rates for 2004-2005 full-time students
Percent of students discontinuing law school:

Men: 2%	Women: N/A
First-year students: 2%	Second-year students: N/A
Third-year students: N/A	

LIBRARY RESOURCES

The library holds 196,995 and receives 8,367 current subscriptions.
Total volumes: 422,146
Percentage of the titles in the online catalog: 100%
Total seats available for library users: 333

INFORMATION TECHNOLOGY

Number of wired network connections available to students: 6 total (in the law library, excluding computer labs: 6; in classrooms: 0; in computer labs: 0; elsewhere in the law school: 0)
Law school has a wireless network.
Approximate number of simultaneous users that can be accommodated on wireless network: 220
Students are not required to own a computer.

EMPLOYMENT AND SALARIES

Proportion of 2004 graduates employed at graduation: 71%
Employed 9 months later, as of February 15, 2005: 96%
Salaries in the private sector (law firms, business, industry): $52,000–$90,000 (25th-75th percentile)
Median salary in the private sector: $70,000
Percentage in the private sector who reported salary information: 53%
Median salary in public service (government, judicial clerkships, academic posts, non-profits): $45,000

Percentage of 2004 graduates in:

Law firms: 46%	Bus./industry (legal): 13%
Bus./industry (nonlegal): 0%	Government: 12%
Public interest: 6%	Judicial clerkship: 15%
Academia : 6%	Unknown: 2%

2004 graduates employed in-state: 64%
2004 graduates employed in foreign countries: 2%
Number of states where graduates are employed: 18
Percentage of 2004 graduates working in: New England: 2%, Middle Atlantic: 1%, East North Central: 70%, West North Central: 1%, South Atlantic: 5%, East South Central: 6%, West South Central: 4%, Mountain: 4%, Pacific: 4%, Unknown: 0%

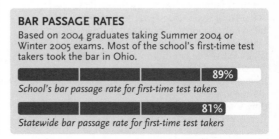

BAR PASSAGE RATES

Based on 2004 graduates taking Summer 2004 or Winter 2005 exams. Most of the school's first-time test takers took the bar in Ohio.

89%
School's bar passage rate for first-time test takers

81%
Statewide bar passage rate for first-time test takers

University of Colorado–Boulder

■ Box 401, Boulder, CO, 80309-0401
■ http://www.colorado.edu/law/
■ Public
■ Year founded: 1892
■ 2005-2006 tuition: In-state: full-time: $13,546, part-time: N/A;
  Out-of-state: full-time: $28,450
■ Enrollment 2005-06 academic year: full-time: 495; part-time: 4
■ U.S. News 2007 law specialty ranking: environmental law: 9

| **3.43-3.82** | GPA, 25TH-75TH PERCENTILE |

3.43-3.82 GPA, 25TH-75TH PERCENTILE

160-164 LSAT, 25TH-75TH PERCENTILE

25% ACCEPTANCE RATE

43 2007 U.S. NEWS LAW SCHOOL RANKING

ADMISSIONS

Admissions phone number: **(303) 492-7203**
Admissions email address: **lawadmin@colorado.edu**
Application website: **http://www.colorado.edu/law/admissions/request.htm**
Application deadline for Fall 2007 admission: **2/15**

Admissions statistics:

Number of applicants for Fall 2005: **2,537**
Number of acceptances: **646**
Number enrolled: **168**
Acceptance rate: **25%**
GPA, 25th-75th percentile, entering class Fall 2005:
3.43-3.82
LSAT, 25th-75th percentile, entering class Fall 2005:
160-164

FINANCIAL AID

Financial aid phone number: **(303) 492-8223**
Financial aid application deadline: **3/01**
Tuition 2005-2006 academic year: In-state: full-time:
$13,546, part-time: N/A; Out-of-state: full-time: **$28,450**
Room and board: **$7,236;** books: **$1,306;** miscellaneous
  expenses: **$3,528**
Total of room/board/books/miscellaneous expenses:
$12,070
University offers graduate student housing for which law
  students are eligible.

Financial aid profile

Percent of students that received grants for the 2004-2005
  academic year: full-time: **57%**
Median grant amount: full-time: **$2,500**
The average law-school debt of those in the Class of 2005
  who borrowed: **$53,623.** Proportion who borrowed: **80%**

ACADEMIC PROGRAMS

Calendar: **semester**
Joint degrees awarded: **J.D./M.B.A.; J.D./M.P.A.; J.D./M.A.
  International Affairs; J.D./M.S. Telecommunications;
  J.D./M.S. Environmental Law; J.D./M.D.**

Typical first-year section size: Full-time: **83**
Is there typically a "small section" of the first year class,
  other than Legal Writing, taught by full-time faculty?:
  Full-time: **yes**; Part-time: **no**
Number of course titles, beyond the first year curriculum,
  offered last year: **91**
Percentages of upper division course sections, excluding
  seminars, with an enrollment of:

Under 25: **57%**	25 to 49: **18%**
50 to 74: **18%**	75 to 99: **7%**
100+: **0%**	

Areas of specialization: appellate advocacy, clinical training,
  dispute resolution, environmental law, healthcare law,
  intellectual property law, international law, tax law, trial
  advocacy

Fall 2005 faculty profile

Total teaching faculty: **73.** Full-time: **49%; 67%** men, **33%**
  women, **19%** minorities. Part-time: **51%; 76%** men, **24%**
  women, **0%** minorities
Student-to-faculty ratio: **12.7**

SPECIAL PROGRAMS *(as provided by law school):*

The University of Colorado offers programs to enrich students'
educations, providing hands on legal experience. The Natural
Resources Law Center promotes sustainability in the American
West, informing and influencing policy and law. Students propose interdisciplinary research projects, and work with natural
resources experts through renowned conferences and workshops. The Byron White Center for the Study of American
Constitutional Law integrates practicing lawyers' and scholars'
perspectives on constitutional law issues. The Center's annual
conference allows students to listen to and meet with influential
speakers, such as Justice Ruth Bader Ginsburg. Entrepreneurial
Law Center students provide legal advice and transactional services to entrepreneurs and university faculty requiring assistance
with developing and financing new businesses. The Silicon
Flatirons Telecommunications Program holds seminars and
symposia that expose students, practitioners and industry leaders
to emerging issues in telecommunications law. Juvenile and
Family Law Program students represent clients in court as

guardians ad litem and as counsel in truancy and dependency and neglect cases. Externships are available, including those with family law magistrates. Certificate Programs are offered in many areas, including tax emphasis and environmental policy. Externships are available with government, nonprofits, public interest and private firms. Lend-a-Law Student Program students assist attorneys with pro bono or reduced fee work. In 1948, CU was one of the first to develop Clinics Programs. Legal Aid and Defender Program students represent indigent clients in civil and criminal cases. It is courtroom intensive, with rigorous classroom academic and professional skill building. Natural Resources Litigation Clinic students work as associates representing public interest clients before administrative agencies, courts and legislatures. American Indian Law Clinic students represent clients in a multitude of Indian law matters, including tribal constitution and code development, and provide programs for the Indian community. They may serve as externs with organizations, including the Native American Rights Fund. The Wrongful Convictions Clinic pairs students with the Colorado Innocence Project. Students interview clients, make recommendations and work on post-conviction briefs, and related legislation. Appellate Advocacy Clinic students complete appellate briefs for prosecution and defense cases on appeal, and conduct oral argument before an attorney panel.

STUDENT BODY

Fall 2005 full-time enrollment: 495

Men: 48%	Women: 52%
African-American: 3.2%	American Indian: 3.0%
Asian-American: 8.9%	Mexican-American: 3.0%
Puerto Rican: 0.6%	Other Hisp-Amer: 3.0%
White: 78.0%	International: 0.2%
Unknown: 0.0%	

Fall 2005 part-time enrollment: 4

Men: 0%	Women: 100%
African-American: 0.0%	American Indian: 0.0%
Asian-American: 0.0%	Mexican-American: 0.0%
Puerto Rican: 0.0%	Other Hisp-Amer: 0.0%
White: 100.0%	International: 0.0%
Unknown: 0.0%	

Attrition rates for 2004-2005 full-time students
Percent of students discontinuing law school:

Men: 2%	Women: 1%
First-year students: 2%	Second-year students: 2%
Third-year students: 1%	

LIBRARY RESOURCES

The library holds 171,464 and receives 4,037 current subscriptions.
Total volumes: 523,473
Percentage of the titles in the online catalog: 100%

Total seats available for library users: 340

INFORMATION TECHNOLOGY

Number of wired network connections available to students: 70 total (in the law library, excluding computer labs: 20; in classrooms: 0; in computer labs: 50; elsewhere in the law school: 0)
Law school has a wireless network.
Approximate number of simultaneous users that can be accommodated on wireless network: 400
Students are not required to own a computer.

EMPLOYMENT AND SALARIES

Proportion of 2004 graduates employed at graduation: 72%
Employed 9 months later, as of February 15, 2005: 90%
Salaries in the private sector (law firms, business, industry): $45,000–$90,000 (25th-75th percentile)
Median salary in the private sector: $60,000
Percentage in the private sector who reported salary information: 61%
Median salary in public service (government, judicial clerkships, academic posts, non-profits): $42,000

Percentage of 2004 graduates in:

Law firms: 52%	Bus./industry (legal): 10%
Bus./industry (nonlegal): 0%	Government: 12%
Public interest: 7%	Judicial clerkship: 16%
Academia : 4%	Unknown: 1%

2004 graduates employed in-state: 79%
2004 graduates employed in foreign countries: 0%
Number of states where graduates are employed: 18
Percentage of 2004 graduates working in: New England: 1%, Middle Atlantic: 1%, East North Central: 2%, West North Central: 1%, South Atlantic: 4%, East South Central: 2%, West South Central: 2%, Mountain: 81%, Pacific: 5%, Unknown: 3%

BAR PASSAGE RATES

Based on 2004 graduates taking Summer 2004 or Winter 2005 exams. Most of the school's first-time test takers took the bar in Colorado.

87%
School's bar passage rate for first-time test takers

74%
Statewide bar passage rate for first-time test takers

University of Connecticut

- 55 Elizabeth Street, Hartford, CT, 06105-2296
- http://www.law.uconn.edu
- Public
- **Year founded:** 1921
- **2005-2006 tuition:** In-state: full-time: $15,648, part-time: $10,920; Out-of-state: full-time: $33,024
- **Enrollment 2005-06 academic year:** full-time: 497; part-time: 174
- **U.S. News 2007 law specialty ranking:** N/A

3.23-3.63 GPA, 25ᵀᴴ-75ᵀᴴ PERCENTILE

159-163 LSAT, 25ᵀᴴ-75ᵀᴴ PERCENTILE

17% ACCEPTANCE RATE

50 2007 U.S. NEWS LAW SCHOOL RANKING

ADMISSIONS

Admissions phone number: **(860) 570-5100**
Admissions email address: **admit@law.uconn.edu**
Application website: **http://www.law.uconn.edu/admissions/admsfin/forms.html**
Application deadline for Fall 2007 admission: **3/01**

Admissions statistics:

Number of applicants for Fall 2005: **2,311**
Number of acceptances: **395**
Number enrolled: **126**
Acceptance rate: **17%**
GPA, 25th-75th percentile, entering class Fall 2005: **3.23-3.63**
LSAT, 25th-75th percentile, entering class Fall 2005: **159-163**

Part-time program:

Number of applicants for Fall 2005: **1,068**
Number of acceptances: **183**
Number enrolled: **73**
Acceptance rate: **17%**
GPA, 25th-75th percentile, entering class Fall 2005: **3.20-3.65**
LSAT, 25th-75th percentile, entering class Fall 2005: **155-160**

FINANCIAL AID

Financial aid phone number: **(860) 570-5147**
Financial aid application deadline: **3/01**
Tuition 2005-2006 academic year: In-state: full-time: **$15,648**, part-time: **$10,920**; Out-of-state: full-time: **$33,024**
Room and board: **$10,400**; books: **$1,090**; miscellaneous expenses: **$4,400**
Total of room/board/books/miscellaneous expenses: **$15,890**
University does not offer graduate student housing for which law students are eligible.

Financial aid profile

Percent of students that received grants for the 2004-2005 academic year: full-time: **80%**; part-time **12%**
Median grant amount: full-time: **$7,175**; part-time: **$3,000**
The average law-school debt of those in the Class of 2005 who borrowed: **$59,732**. Proportion who borrowed: **86%**

ACADEMIC PROGRAMS

Calendar: **semester**
Joint degrees awarded: **J.D./MA; J.D./MSW; J.D./M.B.A.; J.D./MLS; J.D./MPA; J.D./MPH**
Typical first-year section size: Full-time: **64**; Part-time: **66**
Is there typically a "small section" of the first year class, other than Legal Writing, taught by full-time faculty?: Full-time: **yes**; Part-time: **yes**
Number of course titles, beyond the first year curriculum, offered last year: **115**
Percentages of upper division course sections, excluding seminars, with an enrollment of:

Under 25: **57%**   25 to 49: **30%**
50 to 74: **13%**   75 to 99: **0%**
100+: **0%**

Areas of specialization: appellate advocacy, clinical training, dispute resolution, environmental law, healthcare law, intellectual property law, international law, tax law, trial advocacy

Fall 2005 faculty profile

Total teaching faculty: **91**. Full-time: **53%**; **67%** men, **33%** women, **10%** minorities. Part-time: **47%**; **81%** men, **19%** women, **7%** minorities
Student-to-faculty ratio: **11.8**

SPECIAL PROGRAMS (as provided by law school):

Connecticut provides an array of in-house clinical programs in which students receive academic credit for representing actual clients in a variety of legal settings. (Asylum and Human Rights Clinic, the Tax Clinic, the Mediation Clinic, and the Trial and Appellate Divisions of the Criminal Clinic.) The Asylum and Human Rights Clinic, has a success rate of nearly 80 percent more than three times the national average in obtaining political asylum for refugees who have fled severe persecution in their native lands.

The Law School supports two independent, nonprofit advocacy organizations in which students intern for academic credit. The Center for Children's Advocacy has received national recognition for its innovative, holistic model of legal representation of children, while the Connecticut Urban Legal Initiative provides high-quality transactional representation to a wide variety of nonprofit organizations in pursuit of the broad goal of neighborhood revitalization. The Law School offers numerous externship clinics in which students are placed at government agencies or public-interest organizations while participating in weekly seminars conducted by faculty.

The Law School sponsors certificate programs in Intellectual Property and Tax Studies. The Certificate Program in Intellectual Property draws on local leading technology firms and pharmaceutical companies to prepare students to participate in the new information economy. The Certificate Program in Tax Studies provides students with a rich array of tax offerings, including the award-winning Tax Clinic as well as courses including Insurance Tax and Taxation of American Indians.

Exchange programs with institutions in other countries include France, Germany, Ireland, England, Holland, and Italy, as well as Puerto Rico. Students also may arrange exchanges in other countries upon approval.

The Phoenix Masters Program in Insurance Law, the nation's only LL.M. program in insurance law, offers 20 specialized insurance-law courses, most of which are open to J.D. students. The program also sponsors a journal, staffed and operated exclusively by J.D. students, and is the world's only academic law review dedicated exclusively to the publication of original research on the law relating to insurance, risk and responsibility.

The Law School currently offers the following dual degree programs: J.D./M.P.A., J.D./M.A.-Public Policy, J.D./M.S.W., J.D./M.L.S., J.D./M.P.H. and J.D./M.B.A.

STUDENT BODY

Fall 2005 full-time enrollment: 497

Men: 49%	Women: 51%
African-American: 6.4%	American Indian: 0.6%
Asian-American: 5.8%	Mexican-American: 1.0%
Puerto Rican: 3.2%	Other Hisp-Amer: 5.2%
White: 69.8%	International: 0.8%
Unknown: 7.0%	

Fall 2005 part-time enrollment: 174

Men: 51%	Women: 49%
African-American: 4.6%	American Indian: 0.6%
Asian-American: 5.7%	Mexican-American: 0.6%
Puerto Rican: 1.7%	Other Hisp-Amer: 4.0%
White: 74.7%	International: 0.0%
Unknown: 8.0%	

Attrition rates for 2004-2005 full-time students

Percent of students discontinuing law school:

Men: 0%	Women: N/A
First-year students: 1%	Second-year students: N/A
Third-year students: N/A	

LIBRARY RESOURCES

The library holds 154,903 and receives 5,006 current subscriptions.

Total volumes: 527,337

Percentage of the titles in the online catalog: 100%

Total seats available for library users: 718

INFORMATION TECHNOLOGY

Number of wired network connections available to students: 822 total (in the law library, excluding computer labs: 427; in classrooms: 379; in computer labs: 0; elsewhere in the law school: 16)

Law school doesn't have a wireless network.

Approximate number of simultaneous users that can be accommodated on wireless network: 0

Students are not required to own a computer.

EMPLOYMENT AND SALARIES

Proportion of 2004 graduates employed at graduation: 62%

Employed 9 months later, as of February 15, 2005: 96%

Salaries in the private sector (law firms, business, industry): $50,000–$87,000 (25th-75th percentile)

Median salary in the private sector: $75,000

Percentage in the private sector who reported salary information: 72%

Median salary in public service (government, judicial clerkships, academic posts, non-profits): $46,680

Percentage of 2004 graduates in:

Law firms: 50%	Bus./industry (legal): 3%
Bus./industry (nonlegal): 11%	Government: 11%
Public interest: 4%	Judicial clerkship: 18%
Academia : 3%	Unknown: 0%

2004 graduates employed in-state: 62%

2004 graduates employed in foreign countries: 1%

Number of states where graduates are employed: 17

Percentage of 2004 graduates working in: New England: 75%, Middle Atlantic: 14%, East North Central: 2%, West North Central: 0%, South Atlantic: 3%, East South Central: 1%, West South Central: 0%, Mountain: 1%, Pacific: 4%, Unknown: 0%

BAR PASSAGE RATES

Based on 2004 graduates taking Summer 2004 or Winter 2005 exams. Most of the school's first-time test takers took the bar in Connecticut.

94%

School's bar passage rate for first-time test takers

82%

Statewide bar passage rate for first-time test takers

University of Dayton

- 300 College Park, Dayton, OH, 45469-2772
- http://www.law.udayton.edu
- Private
- Year founded: 1974
- 2005-2006 tuition: full-time: $842/credit hour; part-time: N/A
- Enrollment 2005-06 academic year: full-time: 468; part-time: 1
- U.S. News 2007 law specialty ranking: N/A

2.87-3.45 GPA, 25TH-75TH PERCENTILE

152-156 LSAT, 25TH-75TH PERCENTILE

27% ACCEPTANCE RATE

Tier 4 2007 U.S. NEWS LAW SCHOOL RANKING

ADMISSIONS

Admissions phone number: **(937) 229-3555**
Admissions email address: **lawinfo@udayton.edu**
Application website: **N/A**
Application deadline for Fall 2007 admission: **5/01**

Admissions statistics:

Number of applicants for Fall 2005: **2,116**
Number of acceptances: **580**
Number enrolled: **119**
Acceptance rate: **27%**
GPA, 25th-75th percentile, entering class Fall 2005: **2.87-3.45**
LSAT, 25th-75th percentile, entering class Fall 2005: **152-156**

FINANCIAL AID

Financial aid phone number: **(937) 229-3555**
Financial aid application deadline: **5/01**
Tuition 2005-2006 academic year: full-time: **$842/credit hour**; part-time: **N/A**
Room and board: **$9,356**; books: **$1,200**; miscellaneous expenses: **$555**
Total of room/board/books/miscellaneous expenses: **$11,111**
University offers graduate student housing for which law students are eligible.

Financial aid profile

Percent of students that received grants for the 2004-2005 academic year: full-time: **60%**
Median grant amount: full-time: **$10,000**
The average law-school debt of those in the Class of 2005 who borrowed: **$74,930**. Proportion who borrowed: **92%**

ACADEMIC PROGRAMS

Calendar: **semester**
Joint degrees awarded: **J.D./M.B.A.; J.D./M.S. Education**
Typical first-year section size: Full-time: **80**
Is there typically a "small section" of the first year class, other than Legal Writing, taught by full-time faculty?: Full-time: **yes**

Number of course titles, beyond the first year curriculum, offered last year: **68**
Percentages of upper division course sections, excluding seminars, with an enrollment of:

Under 25: **66%**	25 to 49: **8%**
50 to 74: **12%**	75 to 99: **14%**
100+: **0%**	

Areas of specialization: appellate advocacy, clinical training, dispute resolution, environmental law, healthcare law, intellectual property law, international law, tax law, trial advocacy

Fall 2005 faculty profile

Total teaching faculty: **50**. Full-time: **56%**; **68%** men, **32%** women, **14%** minorities. Part-time: **44%**; **77%** men, **23%** women, **5%** minorities
Student-to-faculty ratio: **15.4**

SPECIAL PROGRAMS (as provided by law school):

The University of Dayton offers a curriculum designed to focus on the Lawyer as Problem-Solver. Under this program, students will select from three curricular tracks in Advocacy and Dispute Resolution (including both criminal and civil), Personal and Transactional Practice, and Intellectual Property, Innovation, and Creativity. Each track includes externships and capstone or clinical experiences designed to integrate theory and practice, and to better prepare students for the transition to the practice of law. The Program in Law and Technology and the related Law and Innovation track provide students with opportunities to study the traditional areas of patent, copyright and trademark, and the new areas of international technology transfer and commercialization, and cybersecurity. The school also is seeking approval of a new LL.M. program in Intellectual Property. The Legal Profession Program is a two-semester sequence designed to prepare University of Dayton graduates for the practice of law from the first semester. Going beyond the traditional courses in Legal Research and Writing, this program emphasizes the development of professional skills and the ethics of lawyering.

STUDENT BODY

Fall 2005 full-time enrollment: 468

Men: 55%	Women: 45%
African-American: 4.5%	American Indian: 0.9%
Asian-American: 5.8%	Mexican-American: 0.9%
Puerto Rican: 0.2%	Other Hisp-Amer: 1.9%
White: 85.9%	International: 0.0%
Unknown: 0.0%	

Fall 2005 part-time enrollment: 1

Men: 0%	Women: 100%
African-American: 100.0%	American Indian: 0.0%
Asian-American: 0.0%	Mexican-American: 0.0%
Puerto Rican: 0.0%	Other Hisp-Amer: 0.0%
White: 0.0%	International: 0.0%
Unknown: 0.0%	

Attrition rates for 2004-2005 full-time students
Percent of students discontinuing law school:

Men: 6%	Women: 4%
First-year students: 12%	Second-year students: 1%
Third-year students: N/A	

LIBRARY RESOURCES

The library holds 41,756 and receives 4,778 current subscriptions.
Total volumes: 307,600
Percentage of the titles in the online catalog: 100%
Total seats available for library users: 501

INFORMATION TECHNOLOGY

Number of wired network connections available to students: 37 total (in the law library, excluding computer labs: 0; in classrooms: 0; in computer labs: 30; elsewhere in the law school: 7)
Law school has a wireless network.
Approximate number of simultaneous users that can be accommodated on wireless network: 1,000
Students are not required to own a computer.

EMPLOYMENT AND SALARIES

Proportion of 2004 graduates employed at graduation: N/A
Employed 9 months later, as of February 15, 2005: 86%
Salaries in the private sector (law firms, business, industry): $40,375–$60,000 (25th-75th percentile)
Median salary in the private sector: $48,000
Percentage in the private sector who reported salary information: 93%
Median salary in public service (government, judicial clerkships, academic posts, non-profits): $40,500

Percentage of 2004 graduates in:

Law firms: 58%	Bus./industry (legal): 13%
Bus./industry (nonlegal): 3%	Government: 15%
Public interest: 2%	Judicial clerkship: 4%
Academia : 1%	Unknown: 4%

2004 graduates employed in-state: 54%
2004 graduates employed in foreign countries: 0%
Number of states where graduates are employed: 21
Percentage of 2004 graduates working in: New England: 2%, Middle Atlantic: 7%, East North Central: 62%, West North Central: 1%, South Atlantic: 9%, East South Central: 8%, West South Central: 2%, Mountain: 2%, Pacific: 2%, Unknown: 5%

BAR PASSAGE RATES

Based on 2004 graduates taking Summer 2004 or Winter 2005 exams. Most of the school's first-time test takers took the bar in Ohio.

75%
School's bar passage rate for first-time test takers

81%
Statewide bar passage rate for first-time test takers

iversity of Denver (Sturm)

■ 2255 E. Evans Avenue, Denver, CO, 80208
■ http://www.law.du.edu
■ Private
■ Year founded: 1864
■ 2005-2006 tuition: full-time: $29,388; part-time: $18,960
■ Enrollment 2005-06 academic year: full-time: 814; part-time: 428
■ U.S. News 2007 law specialty ranking: environmental law: 14, tax law: 19

3.10-3.60 GPA, 25TH-75TH PERCENTILE

155-162 LSAT, 25TH-75TH PERCENTILE

24% ACCEPTANCE RATE

70 2007 U.S. NEWS LAW SCHOOL RANKING

ADMISSIONS

Admissions phone number: **(303) 871-6135**
Admissions email address: **admissions@law.du.edu**
Application website: **http://www.law.du.edu/ad/**
Application deadline for Fall 2007 admission: **rolling**

Admissions statistics:
Number of applicants for Fall 2005: **3,115**
Number of acceptances: **749**
Number enrolled: **262**
Acceptance rate: **24%**
GPA, 25th-75th percentile, entering class Fall 2005: **3.10-3.60**
LSAT, 25th-75th percentile, entering class Fall 2005: **155-162**

Part-time program:
Number of applicants for Fall 2005: **440**
Number of acceptances: **123**
Number enrolled: **87**
Acceptance rate: **28%**
GPA, 25th-75th percentile, entering class Fall 2005: **2.80-3.40**
LSAT, 25th-75th percentile, entering class Fall 2005: **148-159**

FINANCIAL AID

Financial aid phone number: **(303) 871-6136**
Financial aid application deadline: **N/A**
Tuition 2005-2006 academic year: full-time: **$29,388**; part-time: **$18,960**
Room and board: **$8,622**; books: **$1,306**; miscellaneous expenses: **$4,094**
Total of room/board/books/miscellaneous expenses: **$14,022**
University offers graduate student housing for which law students are eligible.

Financial aid profile
Percent of students that received grants for the 2004-2005 academic year: full-time: **45%**; part-time **8%**

Median grant amount: full-time: **$9,600**; part-time: **$4,000**
The average law-school debt of those in the Class of 2005 who borrowed: **$82,077**. Proportion who borrowed: **83%**

ACADEMIC PROGRAMS

Calendar: **semester**
Joint degrees awarded: **M.B.A./J.D.; IS/J.D.; SWK/J.D.; PHIL/J.D.; ECON/J.D.; MIM/J.D.; MSLA/J.D.; PSY/J.D.; LLM TAX/J.D.; MMP/J.D.; MACOM/J.D.; COMP/J.D.; RECM/J.D.**
Typical first-year section size: Full-time: **90**; Part-time: **87**
Is there typically a "small section" of the first year class, other than Legal Writing, taught by full-time faculty?: Full-time: **yes**; Part-time: **no**
Number of course titles, beyond the first year curriculum, offered last year: **147**
Percentages of upper division course sections, excluding seminars, with an enrollment of:
Under 25: **71%**   25 to 49: **14%**
50 to 74: **10%**   75 to 99: **5%**
100+: **0%**
Areas of specialization: appellate advocacy, clinical training, dispute resolution, environmental law, healthcare law, intellectual property law, international law, tax law, trial advocacy

Fall 2005 faculty profile
Total teaching faculty: **109**. Full-time: **47%**; 53% men, 47% women, 20% minorities. Part-time: **53%**; 84% men, 16% women, 7% minorities
Student-to-faculty ratio: **14.1**

SPECIAL PROGRAMS *(as provided by law school):*
The University of Denver College of Law has a well-established internship program. These public internships include placement in government offices such as the SEC, U.S. Attorneys Offices, Attorney General Offices, the NLRB and District Attorneys and Public Defender Offices. There are also internships available with many state and federal trial and appellate courts. Other internships relating to public interest law involve

such organizations as Colorado Legal Services, Rocky Mountain Children's Law Center and the International Human Rights Clinic internship. Students may also do internships with private firms. Students are also permitted to do externships out of the state and even out of the country. The University of Denver also offers students a variety of practical legal experience through its clinical and affiliated programs. In 2004, the clinical program celebrated its one hundredth year of teaching law students in a clinical program, by which it offers practice skills and a commitment to the underrepresented in Colorado. In addition, in the Mediation/Arbitration clinic, clinical students learn how to settle disputes. The Environmental Law Clinical Partnership works on federal matters involving endangered species. The Rocky Mountain Child Advocacy Center teaches students to represent children. Our Federal Appellate Practicum develops appellate advocacy skills by representing clients in the United States Court of Appeals for the Tenth Circuit. To ensure that Sturm College of Law remains in the forefront of public service, every law student is required to perform a minimum of 50 hours of supervised, uncompensated, law-related public service work as a prerequisite to graduation. The Public Service Requirement can be satisfied through qualifying internships for credit, student law clinics, street law courses, Wills Lab or the Public Interest Practicum Program, the supervisor database of which includes with more than 160 attorneys and judges local, national and international, under whose auspices students can gain practical public service experience. To help prepare students for the internationalization of legal practice, the College of Law has developed innovative law courses taught exclusively in Spanish: International Business Transactions in Spanish, Employment Law in Spanish, Counseling and Negotiation in Spanish, and Immigration Law in Spanish. In addition, the College of Law offers internships in Latin America and Spain to provide students with real life experience in drafting legal documents, conducting business transactions, interviewing clients, doing research and analyzing legal problems in Spanish.

STUDENT BODY

Fall 2005 full-time enrollment: 814

Men: 54%	Women: 46%
African-American: 2.2%	American Indian: 4.3%
Asian-American: 5.4%	Mexican-American: 4.9%
Puerto Rican: 0.0%	Other Hisp-Amer: 0.0%
White: 79.6%	International: 0.0%
Unknown: 3.6%	

Fall 2005 part-time enrollment: 428

Men: 54%	Women: 46%
African-American: 8.9%	American Indian: 4.9%
Asian-American: 4.4%	Mexican-American: 4.0%
Puerto Rican: 0.0%	Other Hisp-Amer: 0.0%
White: 75.2%	International: 0.0%
Unknown: 2.6%	

Attrition rates for 2004-2005 full-time students
Percent of students discontinuing law school:

Men: 2%	Women: 2%
First-year students: 2%	Second-year students: 4%
Third-year students: N/A	

LIBRARY RESOURCES
The library holds 173,691 and receives 5,804 current subscriptions.
Total volumes: 358,464
Percentage of the titles in the online catalog: 100%
Total seats available for library users: 333

INFORMATION TECHNOLOGY
Number of wired network connections available to students: 1,575 total (in the law library, excluding computer labs: 167; in classrooms: 878; in computer labs: 40; elsewhere in the law school: 490)
Law school has a wireless network.
Approximate number of simultaneous users that can be accommodated on wireless network: 480
Students are required to own a computer.

EMPLOYMENT AND SALARIES
Proportion of 2004 graduates employed at graduation: 87%
Employed 9 months later, as of February 15, 2005: 97%
Salaries in the private sector (law firms, business, industry): $50,000–$90,000 (25th-75th percentile)
Median salary in the private sector: $65,000
Percentage in the private sector who reported salary information: 29%
Median salary in public service (government, judicial clerkships, academic posts, non-profits): $41,000

Percentage of 2004 graduates in:

Law firms: 50%	Bus./industry (legal): 4%
Bus./industry (nonlegal): 9%	Government: 17%
Public interest: 2%	Judicial clerkship: 11%
Academia : 1%	Unknown: 6%

2004 graduates employed in-state: 76%
2004 graduates employed in foreign countries: 1%
Number of states where graduates are employed: 26
Percentage of 2004 graduates working in: New England: 1%, Middle Atlantic: 1%, East North Central: 2%, West North Central: 3%, South Atlantic: 5%, East South Central: 0%, West South Central: 2%, Mountain: 81%, Pacific: 3%, Unknown: 1%

BAR PASSAGE RATES
Based on 2004 graduates taking Summer 2004 or Winter 2005 exams. Most of the school's first-time test takers took the bar in Colorado.

64%
School's bar passage rate for first-time test takers

74%
Statewide bar passage rate for first-time test takers

University of Detroit Mercy

- 651 E. Jefferson Avenue, Detroit, MI, 48226
- http://www.law.udmercy.edu
- Private
- Year founded: 1912
- 2005-2006 tuition: full-time: $845/credit hour; part-time: $845/credit hour
- Enrollment 2005-06 academic year: full-time: 519; part-time: 189
- U.S. News 2007 law specialty ranking: N/A

3.00-3.50 GPA, 25TH-75TH PERCENTILE

147-153 LSAT, 25TH-75TH PERCENTILE

46% ACCEPTANCE RATE

Tier 4 2007 U.S. NEWS LAW SCHOOL RANKING

ADMISSIONS
Admissions phone number: (313) 596-0264
Admissions email address: **udmlawao@udmercy.edu**
Application website:
https://www4.lsac.org/LSACD_on_the_Web/login/open.aspx
Application deadline for Fall 2007 admission: **4/15**

Admissions statistics:
Number of applicants for Fall 2005: **1,438**
Number of acceptances: **664**
Number enrolled: **196**
Acceptance rate: **46%**
GPA, 25th-75th percentile, entering class Fall 2005: **3.00-3.50**
LSAT, 25th-75th percentile, entering class Fall 2005: **147-153**

Part-time program:
Number of applicants for Fall 2005: **221**
Number of acceptances: **94**
Number enrolled: **58**
Acceptance rate: **43%**
GPA, 25th-75th percentile, entering class Fall 2005: **2.92-3.35**
LSAT, 25th-75th percentile, entering class Fall 2005: **145-150**

FINANCIAL AID
Financial aid phone number: (313) 596-0214
Financial aid application deadline: **4/01**
Tuition 2005-2006 academic year: full-time: **$845/credit hour**; part-time: **$845/credit hour**
Room and board: **$10,074**; books: **$1,620**; miscellaneous expenses: **$5,029**
Total of room/board/books/miscellaneous expenses: **$16,723**
University offers graduate student housing for which law students are eligible.

Financial aid profile
Percent of students that received grants for the 2004-2005 academic year: full-time: **13%**; part-time **8%**
Median grant amount: full-time: **$13,832**; part-time: **$3,631**
The average law-school debt of those in the Class of 2005 who borrowed: **$65,507**. Proportion who borrowed: **80%**

ACADEMIC PROGRAMS
Calendar: **semester**
Joint degrees awarded: **J.D./M.B.A.; J.D./LL.B**
Typical first-year section size: Full-time: **72**; Part-time: **57**
Is there typically a "small section" of the first year class, other than Legal Writing, taught by full-time faculty?: Full-time: **no**; Part-time: **no**
Number of course titles, beyond the first year curriculum, offered last year: **79**
Percentages of upper division course sections, excluding seminars, with an enrollment of:
Under 25: **49%**   25 to 49: **32%**
50 to 74: **17%**   75 to 99: **2%**
100+: **0%**
Areas of specialization: appellate advocacy, clinical training, dispute resolution, environmental law, healthcare law, intellectual property law, international law, tax law, trial advocacy

Fall 2005 faculty profile
Total teaching faculty: **N/A**. Full-time: **N/A**; **N/A** men, **N/A** women, **N/A** minorities. Part-time: **N/A**; **N/A** men, **N/A** women, **N/A** minorities
Student-to-faculty ratio: **17.8**

SPECIAL PROGRAMS *(as provided by law school):*
Mediation Training; Immigration Law Clinic; Mobile Law Office; Appellate Advocacy Clinic; Urban Law Clinic; NITA Intersession; American Inns of Court; Public Service Fellowships; Teaching Law in High School.

STUDENT BODY
Fall 2005 full-time enrollment: **519**
Men: **54%**   Women: **46%**

African-American: 1.9% American Indian: 0.0%
Asian-American: 1.9% Mexican-American: 0.0%
Puerto Rican: 0.0% Other Hisp-Amer: 1.2%
White: 55.3% International: 14.8%
Unknown: 24.9%

Fall 2005 part-time enrollment: 189

Men: 49% Women: 51%
African-American: 9.0% American Indian: 0.0%
Asian-American: 2.1% Mexican-American: 0.0%
Puerto Rican: 0.0% Other Hisp-Amer: 1.6%
White: 67.7% International: 1.1%
Unknown: 18.5%

Attrition rates for 2004-2005 full-time students
Percent of students discontinuing law school:
Men: 8% Women: 5%
First-year students: 16% Second-year students: 2%
Third-year students: N/A

LIBRARY RESOURCES

The library holds 155,933 and receives 3,000 current
subscriptions.
Total volumes: 356,891
Percentage of the titles in the online catalog: 90%
Total seats available for library users: 418

INFORMATION TECHNOLOGY

Number of wired network connections available to students: 30 total (in the law library, excluding computer
labs: 0; in classrooms: 0; in computer labs: 30; elsewhere in the law school: 0)
Law school has a wireless network.
Approximate number of simultaneous users that can be
accommodated on wireless network: 500
Students are not required to own a computer.

EMPLOYMENT AND SALARIES

Proportion of 2004 graduates employed at graduation: N/A
Employed 9 months later, as of February 15, 2005: 90%
Salaries in the private sector (law firms, business, indus-
try): $49,000–$80,000 (25th-75th percentile)
Median salary in the private sector: $65,000
Percentage in the private sector who reported salary
information: 83%
Median salary in public service (government, judicial clerk-
ships, academic posts, non-profits): $43,500

Percentage of 2004 graduates in:

Law firms: 60% Bus./industry (legal): 6%
Bus./industry (nonlegal): 17% Government: 7%
Public interest: 4% Judicial clerkship: 2%
Academia : 5% Unknown: 0%

2004 graduates employed in-state: 76%
2004 graduates employed in foreign countries: 20%
Number of states where graduates are employed: 3
Percentage of 2004 graduates working in: New England:
0%, Middle Atlantic: 0%, East North Central: 77%, West
North Central: 1%, South Atlantic: 1%, East South
Central: 1%, West South Central: 0%, Mountain: 0%,
Pacific: 0%, Unknown: 0%

BAR PASSAGE RATES

Based on 2004 graduates taking Summer 2004 or
Winter 2005 exams. Most of the school's first-time test
takers took the bar in Michigan.

69%
School's bar passage rate for first-time test takers

74%
Statewide bar passage rate for first-time test takers

University of Florida (Levin)

■ PO Box 117620, Gainesville, FL, 32611-7620
■ http://www.law.ufl.edu
■ Public
■ Year founded: 1909
■ 2005-2006 tuition: In-state: full-time: $7,786, part-time: N/A;
Out-of-state: full-time: $27,419
■ Enrollment 2005-06 academic year: full-time: 1,156
■ U.S. News 2007 law specialty ranking: environmental law: 12, tax law:
2

3.40-3.86	GPA, 25TH-75TH PERCENTILE
157-164	LSAT, 25TH-75TH PERCENTILE
24%	ACCEPTANCE RATE
41	2007 U.S. NEWS LAW SCHOOL RANKING

ADMISSIONS

Admissions phone number: (352) 392-0890
Admissions email address: patrick@law.ufl.edu
Application website: http://www.law.ufl.edu/admissions
Application deadline for Fall 2007 admission: 1/15

Admissions statistics:

Number of applicants for Fall 2005: 2,989
Number of acceptances: 704
Number enrolled: 207
Acceptance rate: 24%
GPA, 25th-75th percentile, entering class Fall 2005:
3.40-3.86
LSAT, 25th-75th percentile, entering class Fall 2005:
157-164

FINANCIAL AID

Financial aid phone number: (352) 392-0620
Financial aid application deadline: 3/15
Tuition 2005-2006 academic year: In-state: full-time:
$7,786, part-time: N/A; Out-of-state: full-time: $27,419
Room and board: N/A; books: N/A; miscellaneous
expenses: N/A
Total of room/board/books/miscellaneous expenses:
$11,930
University offers graduate student housing for which law
students are eligible.

Financial aid profile

Percent of students that received grants for the 2004-2005
academic year: full-time: 22%
Median grant amount: full-time: $2,100
The average law-school debt of those in the Class of 2005
who borrowed: $48,737. Proportion who borrowed: 65%

ACADEMIC PROGRAMS

Calendar: semester
Joint degrees awarded: J.D./M.S. Accounting; J.D./M.B.A.;
J.D./M.S. or Ph.D. Pol. Science; J.D./M.D.; J.D./M.S. or
Ph.D. Sociology; J.D./M.A. or Ph.D. Mass
Communication; J.D./M.A. or Ph.D. History; J.D./Ph.D.
Education Leadership; J.D./M.S. Urban Planning;
J.D./Ph.D. Psychology; J.D./M.A. Real Estate; J.D./M.A
.Finance; J.D./M.S. Sports Manag.; J.D./M.S. Forest
Conserv.; J.D./M.A .Women Studies; J.D./M.A. or Ph.D.
Anthrop; J.D./M.S. Envir. Engin; J.D./M.A. Latin
American Studies; J.D./M.A. or Ph.D. Medical Science;
J.D./M.A. Public Adminstration; J.D./D.V.M. Vet
Medicine
Typical first-year section size: Full-time: 100
Is there typically a "small section" of the first year class,
other than Legal Writing, taught by full-time faculty?:
Full-time: no
Number of course titles, beyond the first year curriculum,
offered last year: 192
Percentages of upper division course sections, excluding
seminars, with an enrollment of:

Under 25: 48%	25 to 49: 18%
50 to 74: 14%	75 to 99: 13%
100+: 7%	

Areas of specialization: appellate advocacy, clinical training,
dispute resolution, environmental law, healthcare law,
intellectual property law, international law, tax law, trial
advocacy

Fall 2005 faculty profile

Total teaching faculty: 100. Full-time: 63%; 52% men, 48%
women, 10% minorities. Part-time: 37%; 86% men, 14%
women, 5% minorities
Student-to-faculty ratio: 15.4

SPECIAL PROGRAMS *(as provided by law school):*

The University of Florida runs seven clinics: criminal, family
law full representation, family law pro se, juvenile, child welfare, mediation, and conservation. In addition to clinical opportunities, the college places over 125 students a year in
governmental agencies and not-for-profit organizations as a part
of its externship program.

Each summer the college offers courses at its Gainesville,
Florida, location and three study abroad programs in San Jose,
Costa Rica; Montpellier, France; and Cape Town, South Africa.
Students may also gain international experience in semester-

long, formal exchange programs with law schools in the Netherlands, France, Germany, Poland, and Australia.

Students wishing to specialize in certain areas of the law may obtain a certificate in that area. The college has five different certificate programs: children and family law, intellectual property, environmental and land use planning, estates and trusts planning, and international law.

STUDENT BODY
Fall 2005 full-time enrollment: 1,156

Men: 54%	Women: 46%
African-American: 6.6%	American Indian: 0.3%
Asian-American: 4.9%	Mexican-American: 0.0%
Puerto Rican: 0.0%	Other Hisp-Amer: 9.9%
White: 72.8%	International: 5.4%
Unknown: 0.0%	

Attrition rates for 2004-2005 full-time students
Percent of students discontinuing law school:

Men: 0%	Women: N/A
First-year students: N/A	Second-year students: 1%
Third-year students: 0%	

LIBRARY RESOURCES
The library holds 181,906 and receives 7,734 current subscriptions.
Total volumes: 620,792
Percentage of the titles in the online catalog: 99%
Total seats available for library users: 765

INFORMATION TECHNOLOGY
Number of wired network connections available to students: 16 total (in the law library, excluding computer labs: 0; in classrooms: 0; in computer labs: 12; elsewhere in the law school: 4)
Law school has a wireless network.
Approximate number of simultaneous users that can be accommodated on wireless network: 1,200
Students are required to own a computer.

EMPLOYMENT AND SALARIES
Proportion of 2004 graduates employed at graduation: 66%
Employed 9 months later, as of February 15, 2005: 96%
Salaries in the private sector (law firms, business, industry): $55,000–$80,000 (25th-75th percentile)
Median salary in the private sector: $65,000
Percentage in the private sector who reported salary information: 65%
Median salary in public service (government, judicial clerkships, academic posts, non-profits): $38,000

Percentage of 2004 graduates in:

Law firms: 58%	Bus./industry (legal): 0%
Bus./industry (nonlegal): 7%	Government: 19%
Public interest: 9%	Judicial clerkship: 4%
Academia : 1%	Unknown: 2%

2004 graduates employed in-state: 82%
2004 graduates employed in foreign countries: 1%
Number of states where graduates are employed: 18
Percentage of 2004 graduates working in: New England: 1%, Middle Atlantic: 1%, East North Central: 1%, West North Central: 2%, South Atlantic: 89%, East South Central: 1%, West South Central: 0%, Mountain: 1%, Pacific: 1%, Unknown: 2%

BAR PASSAGE RATES
Based on 2004 graduates taking Summer 2004 or Winter 2005 exams. Most of the school's first-time test takers took the bar in Florida.

80%

School's bar passage rate for first-time test takers

73%

Statewide bar passage rate for first-time test takers

University of Georgia

- Herty Drive, Athens, GA, 30602
- http://www.lawsch.uga.edu
- Public
- Year founded: 1859
- 2005-2006 tuition: In-state: full-time: $9,126, part-time: N/A; Out-of-state: full-time: $27,102
- Enrollment 2005-06 academic year: full-time: 694
- U.S. News 2007 law specialty ranking: N/A

3.28-3.80 GPA, 25TH-75TH PERCENTILE

158-164 LSAT, 25TH-75TH PERCENTILE

23% ACCEPTANCE RATE

34 2007 U.S. NEWS LAW SCHOOL RANKING

ADMISSIONS

Admissions phone number: **(706) 542-7060**
Admissions email address: **ugajd@uga.edu**
Application website:
http://www.law.uga.edu/admissions/jd/apply/lawapp.pdf
Application deadline for Fall 2007 admission: **2/01**

Admissions statistics:
Number of applicants for Fall 2005: **2,574**
Number of acceptances: **599**
Number enrolled: **210**
Acceptance rate: **23%**
GPA, 25th-75th percentile, entering class Fall 2005: **3.28-3.80**
LSAT, 25th-75th percentile, entering class Fall 2005: **158-164**

FINANCIAL AID

Financial aid phone number: **(706) 542-6147**
Financial aid application deadline: **8/27**
Tuition 2005-2006 academic year: In-state: full-time: **$9,126**, part-time: **N/A**; Out-of-state: full-time: **$27,102**
Room and board: **$5,000**; books: **$1,000**; miscellaneous expenses: **$4,400**
Total of room/board/books/miscellaneous expenses: **$10,400**
University offers graduate student housing for which law students are eligible.

Financial aid profile
Percent of students that received grants for the 2004-2005 academic year: full-time: **31%**
Median grant amount: full-time: **$2,000**
The average law-school debt of those in the Class of 2005 who borrowed: **$47,120**. Proportion who borrowed: **74%**

ACADEMIC PROGRAMS

Calendar: **semester**
Joint degrees awarded: **J.D./M.B.A.; J.D./M. Hist. Pres.; J.D./M.P.A.; J.D./M. Spts. Mgt.; J.D./M.S.W.**
Typical first-year section size: Full-time: **69**

Is there typically a "small section" of the first year class, other than Legal Writing, taught by full-time faculty?: Full-time: **no**
Number of course titles, beyond the first year curriculum, offered last year: **114**
Percentages of upper division course sections, excluding seminars, with an enrollment of:

Under 25: **55%**   25 to 49: **22%**
50 to 74: **8%**   75 to 99: **9%**
100+: **5%**

Areas of specialization: appellate advocacy, clinical training, dispute resolution, environmental law, healthcare law, intellectual property law, international law, tax law, trial advocacy

Fall 2005 faculty profile
Total teaching faculty: **N/A**. Full-time: **N/A**; **N/A** men, **N/A** women, **N/A** minorities. Part-time: **N/A**; **N/A** men, **N/A** women, **N/A** minorities
Student-to-faculty ratio: **15.3**

SPECIAL PROGRAMS (as provided by law school):

Eight separate programs currently provide hands-on legal experience to degree candidates at the law school. The state of Georgia's Third-Year Practice Act offers an opportunity for advanced students to represent clients under the supervision of clinical attorneys. The Criminal Defense Clinic gives students a chance to get experience in providing assistance to indigent criminal defendants in the office of the local Public Defender. The Prosecutorial Clinic provides externship experiences for students in state and federal offices in north Georgia.

The Capital Assistance Project is a resource for trial and appellate attorneys representing defendants in capital cases. The Land Use Clinic advises clients in dealing with growth and development issues. Students in the Public Interest Practicum counsel indigent and homeless clients. The Family Violence Clinic represents victims of domestic abuse. Students in the Environmental Law Practicum assist planners and developers in devising sustainable solutions to ecological problems. The Civil Externship Clinic offers an opportunity to work on behalf of public-interest organizations and governmental agencies.

The law school participates, with several other American law schools, in the London Law Consortium, in which students can earn a full semester's education in London in the spring. Beginning in 2006, the Law School operates, along with Ohio State College of Law, a spring semester program at Oxford University in England, utilizing faculty from Ohio State, Georgia and several of the Oxford colleges. An international summer clerkship program is administered by the Office of Career Services, and many students attend the Brussels Seminar on the Law and Institutions of the European Union (led by a Law School faculty member) each summer.

Joint degree programs exist in which law students may simultaneously earn degrees in business, historic preservation, public administration, social work and sports management. Concurrent degree programs can be arranged in any one of the university's 14 other schools and colleges.

STUDENT BODY

Fall 2005 full-time enrollment: 694

Men: 49%	Women: 51%
African-American: 14.1%	American Indian: 0.3%
Asian-American: 3.5%	Mexican-American: 0.0%
Puerto Rican: 0.0%	Other Hisp-Amer: 2.2%
White: 71.3%	International: 0.0%
Unknown: 8.6%	

Attrition rates for 2004-2005 full-time students
Percent of students discontinuing law school:

Men: 0%	Women: 0%
First-year students: 1%	Second-year students: N/A
Third-year students: N/A	

LIBRARY RESOURCES

The library holds 155,178 and receives 7,097 current subscriptions.
Total volumes: 512,418
Percentage of the titles in the online catalog: 90%
Total seats available for library users: 446

INFORMATION TECHNOLOGY

Number of wired network connections available to students: 0 total (in the law library, excluding computer labs: 0; in classrooms: 0; in computer labs: 0; elsewhere in the law school: 0)

Law school has a wireless network.
Approximate number of simultaneous users that can be accommodated on wireless network: 600
Students are not required to own a computer.

EMPLOYMENT AND SALARIES

Proportion of 2004 graduates employed at graduation: 76%
Employed 9 months later, as of February 15, 2005: 99%
Salaries in the private sector (law firms, business, industry): $61,000–$100,000 (25th-75th percentile)
Median salary in the private sector: $100,000
Percentage in the private sector who reported salary information: 38%
Median salary in public service (government, judicial clerkships, academic posts, non-profits): $48,000

Percentage of 2004 graduates in:

Law firms: 62%	Bus./industry (legal): 6%
Bus./industry (nonlegal): 1%	Government: 8%
Public interest: 4%	Judicial clerkship: 17%
Academia : 2%	Unknown: 0%

2004 graduates employed in-state: 76%
2004 graduates employed in foreign countries: 0%
Number of states where graduates are employed: 20
Percentage of 2004 graduates working in: New England: 1%, Middle Atlantic: 1%, East North Central: 1%, West North Central: 1%, South Atlantic: 88%, East South Central: 7%, West South Central: 1%, Mountain: 1%, Pacific: 1%, Unknown: 0%

BAR PASSAGE RATES

Based on 2004 graduates taking Summer 2004 or Winter 2005 exams. Most of the school's first-time test takers took the bar in Georgia.

93%

School's bar passage rate for first-time test takers

85%

Statewide bar passage rate for first-time test takers

University of Hawaii (Richardson)

■ 2515 Dole Street, Honolulu, HI, 96822
■ http://www.hawaii.edu/law
■ Public
■ Year founded: 1973
■ 2005-2006 tuition: In-state: full-time: $12,192, part-time: N/A; Out-of-state: full-time: $20,856
■ Enrollment 2005-06 academic year: full-time: 305
■ U.S. News 2007 law specialty ranking: environmental law: 21

3.03-3.66 GPA, 25TH-75TH PERCENTILE

156-161 LSAT, 25TH-75TH PERCENTILE

19% ACCEPTANCE RATE

93 2007 U.S. NEWS LAW SCHOOL RANKING

ADMISSIONS

Admissions phone number: **(808) 956-3000**
Admissions email address: **lawadm@hawaii.edu**
Application website: **http://www.hawaii.edu/law/admissions/forms**
Application deadline for Fall 2007 admission: **3/01**

Admissions statistics:

Number of applicants for Fall 2005: **1,091**
Number of acceptances: **203**
Number enrolled: **96**
Acceptance rate: **19%**
GPA, 25th-75th percentile, entering class Fall 2005: **3.03-3.66**
LSAT, 25th-75th percentile, entering class Fall 2005: **156-161**

FINANCIAL AID

Financial aid phone number: **(808) 956-7251**
Financial aid application deadline: **3/01**
Tuition 2005-2006 academic year: In-state: full-time: **$12,192**, part-time: **N/A**; Out-of-state: full-time: **$20,856**
Room and board: **$7,550**; books: **$900**; miscellaneous expenses: **$3,000**
Total of room/board/books/miscellaneous expenses: **$11,450**
University offers graduate student housing for which law students are eligible.

Financial aid profile

Percent of students that received grants for the 2004-2005 academic year: full-time: **40%**
Median grant amount: full-time: **$5,724**
The average law-school debt of those in the Class of 2005 who borrowed: **$46,512**. Proportion who borrowed: **69%**

ACADEMIC PROGRAMS

Calendar: **semester**
Joint degrees awarded: **JD/MBA; JD/MA**
Typical first-year section size: Full-time: **95**

Is there typically a "small section" of the first year class, other than Legal Writing, taught by full-time faculty?: Full-time: **no**
Number of course titles, beyond the first year curriculum, offered last year: **61**
Percentages of upper division course sections, excluding seminars, with an enrollment of:
Under 25: **72%**   25 to 49: **14%**
50 to 74: **7%**   75 to 99: **6%**
100+: **1%**
Areas of specialization: appellate advocacy, clinical training, dispute resolution, environmental law, healthcare law, intellectual property law, international law, tax law, trial advocacy

Fall 2005 faculty profile

Total teaching faculty: **36**. Full-time: **50%**; **67%** men, **33%** women, **28%** minorities. Part-time: **50%**; **50%** men, **50%** women, **50%** minorities
Student-to-faculty ratio: **13.6**

SPECIAL PROGRAMS (as provided by law school):

The law school offers the following clinics: trial practice, pretrial litigation, defense, prosecution, mediation, family law, environmental law, immigration, Native Hawaiian rights, elder law, and estate planning workshop.

Externships offer two-credit placements in the private, public, judicial, and legislative sectors. Students may take semester-long, 12-credit Pacific Asia externships; placements include American Samoa, Taiwan, Hong Kong, and Thailand.

The University of Hawaii offers opportunities for joint degrees and courses in a variety of centers and programs (including the East West Center, Center for Chinese Studies, Center for Japanese Studies, and Center for Korean Studies) and schools (including the School of Hawaiian, Asian, and Pacific Studies, School of Medicine, School of Ocean and Earth Science and Technology, and the College of Business Administration).

STUDENT BODY

Fall 2005 full-time enrollment: 305

Men: 53%	Women: 47%
African-American: 1.0%	American Indian: 1.3%
Asian-American: 55.4%	Mexican-American: 1.3%
Puerto Rican: 0.0%	Other Hisp-Amer: 0.7%
White: 19.0%	International: 2.3%
Unknown: 19.0%	

Attrition rates for 2004-2005 full-time students
Percent of students discontinuing law school:

Men: 1%	Women: N/A
First-year students: N/A	Second-year students: N/A
Third-year students: 1%	

LIBRARY RESOURCES

The library holds 41,941 and receives 4,313 current subscriptions.
Total volumes: 343,304
Percentage of the titles in the online catalog: 96%
Total seats available for library users: 417

INFORMATION TECHNOLOGY

Number of wired network connections available to students: 280 total (in the law library, excluding computer labs: 254; in classrooms: 11; in computer labs: 5; elsewhere in the law school: 10)
Law school has a wireless network.
Approximate number of simultaneous users that can be accommodated on wireless network: 500
Students are required to own a computer.

EMPLOYMENT AND SALARIES

Proportion of 2004 graduates employed at graduation: 68%

Employed 9 months later, as of February 15, 2005: 93%
Salaries in the private sector (law firms, business, industry): $65,000–$75,000 (25th-75th percentile)
Median salary in the private sector: $70,000
Percentage in the private sector who reported salary information: 68%
Median salary in public service (government, judicial clerkships, academic posts, non-profits): $45,000

Percentage of 2004 graduates in:

Law firms: 23%	Bus./industry (legal): 8%
Bus./industry (nonlegal): N/A	Government: 14%
Public interest: 9%	Judicial clerkship: 41%
Academia : 5%	Unknown: 0%

2004 graduates employed in-state: 87%
2004 graduates employed in foreign countries: 2%
Number of states where graduates are employed: 6
Percentage of 2004 graduates working in: New England: 2%, Middle Atlantic: 4%, East North Central: N/A, West North Central: N/A, South Atlantic: 2%, East South Central: N/A, West South Central: N/A, Mountain: N/A, Pacific: 92%, Unknown: 0%

BAR PASSAGE RATES

Based on 2004 graduates taking Summer 2004 or Winter 2005 exams. Most of the school's first-time test takers took the bar in Hawaii.

76%

School's bar passage rate for first-time test takers

77%

Statewide bar passage rate for first-time test takers

versity of Houston

- 100 Law Center, Houston, TX, 77204-6060
- http://www.law.uh.edu
- Public
- Year founded: 1947
- 2005-2006 tuition: In-state: full-time: $14,366, part-time: $8,204; Out-of-state: full-time: $21,296
- Enrollment 2005-06 academic year: full-time: 838; part-time: 199
- U.S. News 2007 law specialty ranking: healthcare law: 2, intellecutal property law: 5

3.22-3.73 GPA, 25TH-75TH PERCENTILE

157-162 LSAT, 25TH-75TH PERCENTILE

25% ACCEPTANCE RATE

70 2007 U.S. NEWS LAW SCHOOL RANKING

ADMISSIONS

Admissions phone number: (713) 743-2280
Admissions email address: lawadmissions@uh.edu
Application website: http://www.law.uh.edu/admissions/
Application deadline for Fall 2007 admission: 2/01

Admissions statistics:

Number of applicants for Fall 2005: 3,242
Number of acceptances: 813
Number enrolled: 261
Acceptance rate: 25%
GPA, 25th-75th percentile, entering class Fall 2005: 3.22-3.73
LSAT, 25th-75th percentile, entering class Fall 2005: 157-162

Part-time program:

Number of applicants for Fall 2005: 430
Number of acceptances: 83
Number enrolled: 57
Acceptance rate: 19%
GPA, 25th-75th percentile, entering class Fall 2005: 3.02-3.60
LSAT, 25th-75th percentile, entering class Fall 2005: 158-163

FINANCIAL AID

Financial aid phone number: (713) 743-2269
Financial aid application deadline: 4/01
Tuition 2005-2006 academic year: In-state: full-time: $14,366, part-time: $8,204; Out-of-state: full-time: $21,296
Room and board: $8,600; books: $3,300; miscellaneous expenses: $5,250
Total of room/board/books/miscellaneous expenses: $17,150
University offers graduate student housing for which law students are eligible.

Financial aid profile

Percent of students that received grants for the 2004-2005 academic year: full-time: 68%

Median grant amount: full-time: $6,696
The average law-school debt of those in the Class of 2005 who borrowed: $57,071. Proportion who borrowed: 84%

ACADEMIC PROGRAMS

Calendar: semester
Joint degrees awarded: J.D./M.B.A.; J.D./M.P.H.; J.D./PH.D. Crim.; J.D./M.A.-HIST; J.D./M.S.W.; J.D./PH.D. Med.
Typical first-year section size: Full-time: 80; Part-time: 60
Is there typically a "small section" of the first year class, other than Legal Writing, taught by full-time faculty?: Full-time: yes; Part-time: yes
Number of course titles, beyond the first year curriculum, offered last year: 204
Percentages of upper division course sections, excluding seminars, with an enrollment of:

Under 25: 53%	25 to 49: 29%
50 to 74: 13%	75 to 99: 5%
100+: 0%	

Areas of specialization: appellate advocacy, clinical training, dispute resolution, environmental law, healthcare law, intellectual property law, international law, tax law, trial advocacy

Fall 2005 faculty profile

Total teaching faculty: 235. Full-time: 34%; 71% men, 29% women, 13% minorities. Part-time: 66%; 73% men, 27% women, 6% minorities
Student-to-faculty ratio: 20.8

SPECIAL PROGRAMS *(as provided by law school):*

The UH Law Center offers seven programs that confer dual degrees: 1) J.D./M.P.H. with the University of Texas School of Public Health; 2) J.D./Ph.D. with The Institute for Medical Humanities at the University of Texas Medical Branch at Galveston; 3) J.D./M.B.A. with the UH Bauer College of Business; 4) J.D./M.A. in history with the UH Department of History; 5) J.D./M.S.W. with the UH Graduate School of Social Work; 6) J.D./Ph.D. in Criminal Justice with Sam Houston State University; and 7) J.D./M.D. with Baylor University.

Institutes and special programs enrich the J.D. experience at UH Law Center. With 38 courses, the Health Law & Policy Institute administers the largest and most comprehensive health law curriculum in the country, and sponsors the Houston Journal of Health Law and Policy.

The Institute for Intellectual Property & Information Law offers 15 courses taught by leading academics in the field, and sponsors two societies—the Intellectual Property Students Organization, and cyberlawsociety@UHLC. The Blakely Advocacy Institute provides litigation skills training and oversees special programs ranging from moot court and mock trial courses to the A.A. White Dispute Resolution and the Clinical Legal Education Program.

The Institute for Higher Education Law and Governance provides research opportunities through funded projects; a specialized library collection; and annual workshops, conferences, lectures, and speakers' series. The Center for Consumer Law is widely known for its high-profile People's Law School that provides free legal counseling to local residents. The Criminal Justice Institute includes the Texas Innocence Network, where J.D. students conduct research and advocate on behalf of inmates' claims of factual innocence.

Two programs deserve special note for the options they provide to J.D. students. International Law exposes students to a wide variety of international and comparative law courses, and qualifies graduating students to take the bar exam anywhere in the United States. Energy, Environment, and Natural Resources Law coordinates a substantial curriculum; schedules ongoing conferences; publishes a journal; and oversees sponsored research.

STUDENT BODY

Fall 2005 full-time enrollment: 838

Men: 53%	Women: 47%
African-American: 4.1%	American Indian: 0.8%
Asian-American: 13.1%	Mexican-American: 4.1%
Puerto Rican: 0.0%	Other Hisp-Amer: 4.7%
White: 70.4%	International: 0.2%
Unknown: 2.6%	

Fall 2005 part-time enrollment: 199

Men: 60%	Women: 40%
African-American: 3.0%	American Indian: 0.5%
Asian-American: 8.5%	Mexican-American: 3.0%
Puerto Rican: 0.0%	Other Hisp-Amer: 6.0%
White: 78.4%	International: 0.0%
Unknown: 0.5%	

Attrition rates for 2004-2005 full-time students
Percent of students discontinuing law school:

Men: 3%	Women: 2%
First-year students: 2%	Second-year students: 4%
Third-year students: 2%	

LIBRARY RESOURCES

The library holds 74,550 and receives 3,270 current subscriptions.
Total volumes: 488,931
Percentage of the titles in the online catalog: 100%
Total seats available for library users: 566

INFORMATION TECHNOLOGY

Number of wired network connections available to students: 0 total (in the law library, excluding computer labs: 0; in classrooms: 0; in computer labs: 0; elsewhere in the law school: 0)
Law school has a wireless network.
Approximate number of simultaneous users that can be accommodated on wireless network: 3,000
Students are required to own a computer.

EMPLOYMENT AND SALARIES

Proportion of 2004 graduates employed at graduation: 66%
Employed 9 months later, as of February 15, 2005: 96%
Salaries in the private sector (law firms, business, industry): $58,000–$110,000 (25th-75th percentile)
Median salary in the private sector: $90,000
Percentage in the private sector who reported salary information: 78%
Median salary in public service (government, judicial clerkships, academic posts, non-profits): $45,000

Percentage of 2004 graduates in:

Law firms: 70%	Bus./industry (legal): 4%
Bus./industry (nonlegal): 7%	Government: 7%
Public interest: 2%	Judicial clerkship: 6%
Academia : 4%	Unknown: 0%

2004 graduates employed in-state: 91%
2004 graduates employed in foreign countries: 0%
Number of states where graduates are employed: 10
Percentage of 2004 graduates working in: New England: 0%, Middle Atlantic: 2%, East North Central: 0%, West North Central: 0%, South Atlantic: 2%, East South Central: 0%, West South Central: 91%, Mountain: 1%, Pacific: 3%, Unknown: 1%

BAR PASSAGE RATES

Based on 2004 graduates taking Summer 2004 or Winter 2005 exams. Most of the school's first-time test takers took the bar in Texas.

85%
School's bar passage rate for first-time test takers

79%
Statewide bar passage rate for first-time test takers

University of Idaho

- PO Box 442321, Moscow, ID, 83844-2321
- http://www.law.uidaho.edu
- Public
- **Year founded:** 1909
- **2005-2006 tuition:** In-state: full-time: $8,908, part-time: N/A; Out-of-state: full-time: $17,678
- **Enrollment 2005-06 academic year:** full-time: 297
- **U.S. News 2007 law specialty ranking:** N/A

3.10-3.58	GPA, 25TH-75TH PERCENTILE
152-159	LSAT, 25TH-75TH PERCENTILE
31%	ACCEPTANCE RATE
Tier 3	2007 U.S. NEWS LAW SCHOOL RANKING

ADMISSIONS

Admissions phone number: **(208) 885-6423**
Admissions email address: **lawadmit@uidaho.edu**
Application website: **http://www.law.uidaho.edu/admissions/applynow**
Application deadline for Fall 2007 admission: **2/15**

Admissions statistics:
Number of applicants for Fall 2005: **828**
Number of acceptances: **260**
Number enrolled: **104**
Acceptance rate: **31%**
GPA, 25th-75th percentile, entering class Fall 2005: **3.10-3.58**
LSAT, 25th-75th percentile, entering class Fall 2005: **152-159**

FINANCIAL AID

Financial aid phone number: **(208) 885-6312**
Financial aid application deadline: **N/A**
Tuition 2005-2006 academic year: In-state: full-time: **$8,908**, part-time: **N/A**; Out-of-state: full-time: **$17,678**
Room and board: **$7,038**; books: **$1,336**; miscellaneous expenses: **$3,340**
Total of room/board/books/miscellaneous expenses: **$11,714**
University offers graduate student housing for which law students are eligible.

Financial aid profile
Percent of students that received grants for the 2004-2005 academic year: full-time: **38%**
Median grant amount: full-time: **$4,300**
The average law-school debt of those in the Class of 2005 who borrowed: **$50,719.** Proportion who borrowed: **93%**

ACADEMIC PROGRAMS

Calendar: **semester**
Joint degrees awarded: **J.D./M.S. Environmental Science; J.D./M.A. Accounting**
Typical first-year section size: Full-time: **52**

Is there typically a "small section" of the first year class, other than Legal Writing, taught by full-time faculty?: Full-time: **no**
Number of course titles, beyond the first year curriculum, offered last year: **53**
Percentages of upper division course sections, excluding seminars, with an enrollment of:
Under 25: **52%**   25 to 49: **17%**
50 to 74: **17%**   75 to 99: **13%**
100+: **0%**
Areas of specialization: appellate advocacy, clinical training, dispute resolution, environmental law, healthcare law, intellectual property law, international law, tax law, trial advocacy

Fall 2005 faculty profile
Total teaching faculty: **30.** Full-time: **37%; 64%** men, **36%** women, **0%** minorities. Part-time: **63%; 84%** men, **16%** women, **N/A** minorities
Student-to-faculty ratio: **16.8**

SPECIAL PROGRAMS *(as provided by law school):*

The University of Idaho College of Law has an impressive clinical program. Approximately 75 percent of the student body has a clinical experience before graduation.

The Legal Aid Clinic consists of seven in-house clinics. We are committed to our in-house clinics because they give students the opportunity to develop skills and acquire insights not available in a classroom.

Appellate students brief and argue cases before the Ninth Circuit Court of Appeals and the Idaho appellate courts. The courts have repeatedly praised the work of the Appellate Clinic in footnotes or in the body of a decision.

General Practice Clinic students represent clients who could not otherwise afford a lawyer in a variety of cases including criminal, domestic relations, and landlord-tenant law. There is also a limited legal clinic at the State prison in Orofino.

Tax Clinic students represent low-income taxpayers in issues before the IRS. The Tax Clinic also operates programs to advise non-English speaking residents of their Federal tax rights and responsibilities.

Tribal and Immigration Clinic students split time between criminal and juvenile delinquency proceedings in Nez Perce Tribal court and a variety of immigration cases.

The Small Business Legal Clinic gives students experience handling transactional legal problems and provides assistance to business owners and entrepreneurs in Idaho.

We have received new grants to start a Domestic Violence Clinic and a Victim's Rights clinic. Please visit our website for information on these recent additions.

Mini-Clinics

Pro-Se Clinic—Students assist self-representing litigants

Bankruptcy—Optional lab for students taking the Bankruptcy course

Externships

Semester-in-Practice—Eligible third-year students may spend a semester externing with an approved public agency or non-profit association in the Boise area.

Public Service or Private Externship—First- and second-year students are eligible to extern with an approved public agency, nonprofit association, or private law firm.

The Northwest Institute for Dispute Resolution offers two basic 40-hour mediation courses and two specialized courses each year. The Institute features nationally recognized faculty, and students enjoy a discounted rate.

The College of Law offers two concurrent degrees, a J.D./masters of environmental science and a J.D./masters of accounting.

STUDENT BODY

Fall 2005 full-time enrollment: 297

Men: 60%	Women: 40%
African-American: 1.0%	American Indian: 1.0%
Asian-American: 4.7%	Mexican-American: 0.3%
Puerto Rican: 0.0%	Other Hisp-Amer: 1.7%
White: 83.5%	International: 0.3%
Unknown: 7.4%	

Attrition rates for 2004-2005 full-time students
Percent of students discontinuing law school:

Men: 2%	Women: 6%
First-year students: 9%	Second-year students: 1%
Third-year students: N/A	

LIBRARY RESOURCES

The library holds 35,546 and receives 3,996 current subscriptions.

Total volumes: 235,205

Percentage of the titles in the online catalog: 99%

Total seats available for library users: 360

INFORMATION TECHNOLOGY

Number of wired network connections available to students: 302 total (in the law library, excluding computer labs: 225; in classrooms: 24; in computer labs: 0; elsewhere in the law school: 53)

Law school has a wireless network.

Approximate number of simultaneous users that can be accommodated on wireless network: 800

Students are not required to own a computer.

EMPLOYMENT AND SALARIES

Proportion of 2004 graduates employed at graduation: 46%

Employed 9 months later, as of February 15, 2005: 88%

Salaries in the private sector (law firms, business, industry): $27,600–$65,000 (25th-75th percentile)

Median salary in the private sector: $42,000

Percentage in the private sector who reported salary information: 55%

Median salary in public service (government, judicial clerkships, academic posts, non-profits): $40,850

Percentage of 2004 graduates in:

Law firms: 37%	Bus./industry (legal): 0%
Bus./industry (nonlegal): 5%	Government: 20%
Public interest: 8%	Judicial clerkship: 28%
Academia : 2%	Unknown: 0%

2004 graduates employed in-state: 53%

2004 graduates employed in foreign countries: 1%

Number of states where graduates are employed: 12

Percentage of 2004 graduates working in: New England: 0%, Middle Atlantic: 0%, East North Central: 0%, West North Central: 0%, South Atlantic: 2%, East South Central: 1%, West South Central: 0%, Mountain: 77%, Pacific: 19%, Unknown: 0%

BAR PASSAGE RATES

Based on 2004 graduates taking Summer 2004 or Winter 2005 exams. Most of the school's first-time test takers took the bar in Idaho.

76%
School's bar passage rate for first-time test takers

76%
Statewide bar passage rate for first-time test takers

Univ. of Illinois–Urbana-Champaign

- 504 E. Pennsylvania Avenue, Champaign, IL, 61820
- http://www.law.uiuc.edu/
- Public
- Year founded: 1897
- 2005-2006 tuition: In-state: full-time: $17,512, part-time: N/A; Out-of-state: full-time: $28,416
- Enrollment 2005-06 academic year: full-time: 640
- U.S. News 2007 law specialty ranking: N/A

3.04-3.66 GPA, 25TH-75TH PERCENTILE

162-167 LSAT, 25TH-75TH PERCENTILE

15% ACCEPTANCE RATE

27 2007 U.S. NEWS LAW SCHOOL RANKING

ADMISSIONS

Admissions phone number: (217) 244-6415
Admissions email address: admissions@law.uiuc.edu
Application website: http://www.law.uiuc.edu/admissions/apply.asp
Application deadline for Fall 2007 admission: 3/15

Admissions statistics:

Number of applicants for Fall 2005: 2,933
Number of acceptances: 446
Number enrolled: 188
Acceptance rate: 15%
GPA, 25th-75th percentile, entering class Fall 2005: 3.04-3.66
LSAT, 25th-75th percentile, entering class Fall 2005: 162-167

FINANCIAL AID

Financial aid phone number: (217) 244-6415
Financial aid application deadline: 3/15
Tuition 2005-2006 academic year: In-state: full-time: $17,512, part-time: N/A; Out-of-state: full-time: $28,416
Room and board: $9,120; books: $1,190; miscellaneous expenses: $2,861
Total of room/board/books/miscellaneous expenses: $13,171
University offers graduate student housing for which law students are eligible.

Financial aid profile

Percent of students that received grants for the 2004-2005 academic year: full-time: 51%
Median grant amount: full-time: $4,000
The average law-school debt of those in the Class of 2005 who borrowed: $62,223. Proportion who borrowed: 90%

ACADEMIC PROGRAMS

Calendar: semester
Joint degrees awarded: J.D./M.B.A.; J.D./MHRIR; J.D./M.Ed.; J.D./Ph.D.Ed.; J.D./M.D.; J.D./M.U.P.; J.D./D.V.M.; J.D./M.C.S.; J.D./M.S.Journ; J.D./MSNRES; J.D./M.S. Chem
Typical first-year section size: Full-time: 77
Is there typically a "small section" of the first year class, other than Legal Writing, taught by full-time faculty?: Full-time: yes
Number of course titles, beyond the first year curriculum, offered last year: 147
Percentages of upper division course sections, excluding seminars, with an enrollment of:
Under 25: 71%   25 to 49: 17%
50 to 74: 6%   75 to 99: 4%
100+: 2%
Areas of specialization: appellate advocacy, clinical training, dispute resolution, environmental law, healthcare law, intellectual property law, international law, tax law, trial advocacy

Fall 2005 faculty profile

Total teaching faculty: 96. Full-time: 51%; 63% men, 37% women, 12% minorities. Part-time: 49%; 72% men, 28% women, 17% minorities
Student-to-faculty ratio: 12.6

SPECIAL PROGRAMS (as provided by law school):

Course Offerings: Offering a perfect balance between traditional and progressive legal thinking, the College of Law provides a broad-based education that prepares students to enter today's fast-paced legal environment with exceptional communication skills and an unyielding ethical foundation. In the first year, students follow a curriculum that concentrates on fundamental legal areas. The College of Law ensures that first-year students are enrolled in numerous small sections, and a unique feature of the first-year curriculum, an elective course on statutory interpretation. During their second and third years, students must complete both an upper level writing requirement and a course in professional responsibility. Beyond these core requirements, students have complete flexibility in their scheduling and may choose from approximately 150 course offerings. Professional Skills Courses and Programs: The College of Law provides numerous opportunities for instruction in professional skills and other real-life practice experience. The list of simulation course offerings include, but are not limited to, Trial Advocacy, Advanced Trial Advocacy in Intellectual Property, Pre-Trial Litigation, Alternative Dispute Resolution, Negotiations, and CFI (Interviewing, Counseling, and Fact Investigation). The courses that involve interaction with live clients include externships, legislative projects, the appellate defender clinic, and four in-house clinics, including the Civil Litigation Clinic, the Transaction and Community Economic Development Clinic, the International Human Rights Clinic, and the Employee Justice Clinic. Summer Courses and Programs. The College conducts two summer sessions each year, and also offers a summer program in international intellectual property in conjunction with Oxford University in England and the University of Victoria in British Columbia. In addition to the IP program, the College encourages foreign study through several reciprocal exchange programs established with foreign universities. Students may also conduct foreign studies under the Individual Student Abroad for Academic Credit guidelines. Interdisciplinary Programs and Opportunities. Outside of the 11 formal joint degree programs, the College also offers numerous other methods by which students can pursue interdisciplinary study. The College cross-lists certain courses taught by other departments, and the College offers students up to six hours of law credit for courses taken in other University departments, subject to substantive requirements.

STUDENT BODY

Fall 2005 full-time enrollment: 640

Men: 61%	Women: 39%
African-American: 6.9%	American Indian: 0.6%
Asian-American: 18.0%	Mexican-American: 0.0%
Puerto Rican: 0.0%	Other Hisp-Amer: 8.0%
White: 55.9%	International: 1.9%
Unknown: 8.8%	

Attrition rates for 2004-2005 full-time students
Percent of students discontinuing law school:

Men: 4%	Women: 1%
First-year students: 1%	Second-year students: 7%
Third-year students: N/A	

LIBRARY RESOURCES

The library holds 267,487 and receives 9,006 current subscriptions.
Total volumes: 756,239
Percentage of the titles in the online catalog: 97%
Total seats available for library users: 366

INFORMATION TECHNOLOGY

Number of wired network connections available to students: 802 total (in the law library, excluding computer labs: 80; in classrooms: 574; in computer labs: 48; elsewhere in the law school: 100)
Law school has a wireless network.
Approximate number of simultaneous users that can be accommodated on wireless network: 500
Students are required to own a computer.

EMPLOYMENT AND SALARIES

Proportion of 2004 graduates employed at graduation: 72%
Employed 9 months later, as of February 15, 2005: 100%
Salaries in the private sector (law firms, business, industry): $60,000–$125,000 (25th-75th percentile)
Median salary in the private sector: $90,000
Percentage in the private sector who reported salary information: 68%
Median salary in public service (government, judicial clerkships, academic posts, non-profits): $45,000

Percentage of 2004 graduates in:

Law firms: 58%	Bus./industry (legal): 7%
Bus./industry (nonlegal): 5%	Government: 10%
Public interest: 3%	Judicial clerkship: 13%
Academia : 4%	Unknown: 0%

2004 graduates employed in-state: 66%
2004 graduates employed in foreign countries: 2%
Number of states where graduates are employed: 26
Percentage of 2004 graduates working in: New England: 2%, Middle Atlantic: 2%, East North Central: 72%, West North Central: 4%, South Atlantic: 9%, East South Central: 1%, West South Central: 3%, Mountain: 3%, Pacific: 2%, Unknown: 1%

BAR PASSAGE RATES

Based on 2004 graduates taking Summer 2004 or Winter 2005 exams. Most of the school's first-time test takers took the bar in Illinois.

90%
School's bar passage rate for first-time test takers

85%
Statewide bar passage rate for first-time test takers

University of Iowa

- 276 Boyd Law Building, Iowa City, IA, 52242
- http://www.uiowa.edu/~lawcoll
- Public
- **Year founded:** 1865
- **2005-2006 tuition:** In-state: full-time: $13,211, part-time: N/A; Out-of-state: full-time: $27,989
- **Enrollment 2005-06 academic year:** full-time: 656
- **U.S. News 2007 law specialty ranking:** international law: 12

3.39-3.77 GPA, 25TH-75TH PERCENTILE

158-163 LSAT, 25TH-75TH PERCENTILE

39% ACCEPTANCE RATE

22 2007 U.S. NEWS LAW SCHOOL RANKING

ADMISSIONS

Admissions phone number: **(319) 335-9133**
Admissions email address: **law-admissions@uiowa.edu**
Application website: **N/A**
Application deadline for Fall 2007 admission: **3/01**

Admissions statistics:

Number of applicants for Fall 2005: **1,339**
Number of acceptances: **519**
Number enrolled: **225**
Acceptance rate: **39%**
GPA, 25th-75th percentile, entering class Fall 2005: **3.39-3.77**
LSAT, 25th-75th percentile, entering class Fall 2005: **158-163**

FINANCIAL AID

Financial aid phone number: **(319) 335-9142**
Financial aid application deadline: **1/01**
Tuition 2005-2006 academic year: In-state: full-time: **$13,211**, part-time: **N/A**; Out-of-state: full-time: **$27,989**
Room and board: **$9,000**; books: **$2,300**; miscellaneous expenses: **$4,651**
Total of room/board/books/miscellaneous expenses: **$15,951**
University offers graduate student housing for which law students are eligible.

Financial aid profile

Percent of students that received grants for the 2004-2005 academic year: full-time: **43%**
Median grant amount: full-time: **$11,371**
The average law-school debt of those in the Class of 2005 who borrowed: **$59,665.** Proportion who borrowed: **84%**

ACADEMIC PROGRAMS

Calendar: **semester**
Joint degrees awarded: J.D./M.B.A; J.D./Biology; J.D./Health/Mgmt; J.D./Political Science; J.D./Sociology; J.D./Phiolosophy; J.D./Elec/Computer Engineering; J.D./Comm Studies; J.D./Urban/Reg Planning; J.D./History; J.D./Economics; J.D./Journalism; J.D./Social Work; J.D./Spanish; J.D./Lib/Information Systems; J.D./Higher Ed; J.D./Education Admin.; J.D./Accounting; J.D./Chemistry; J.D./MPH

Typical first-year section size: Full-time: **75**
Is there typically a "small section" of the first year class, other than Legal Writing, taught by full-time faculty?: Full-time: **yes**
Number of course titles, beyond the first year curriculum, offered last year: **108**
Percentages of upper division course sections, excluding seminars, with an enrollment of:

Under 25: **49%**	25 to 49: **27%**
50 to 74: **16%**	75 to 99: **8%**
100+: **0%**	

Areas of specialization: appellate advocacy, clinical training, dispute resolution, environmental law, healthcare law, intellectual property law, international law, tax law, trial advocacy

Fall 2005 faculty profile

Total teaching faculty: **85.** Full-time: **65%**; **62%** men, **38%** women, **11%** minorities. Part-time: **35%**; **67%** men, **33%** women, **N/A** minorities
Student-to-faculty ratio: **12.2**

SPECIAL PROGRAMS (as provided by law school):

Clinical law program: Students can gain experience in areas of substantive law including assistive technology, consumer rights, criminal defense, disability rights, domestic violence, general civil, immigration, nonprofit organizations, and workers' rights. Through the representation of real clients, students are able to develop and hone lawyering skills, from interviewing, counseling, and drafting court papers to trial practice, appellate advocacy, legislative lobbying, and policy development.

Study abroad programs: Iowa offers two study abroad programs. Iowa is the stateside home of the London Law Consortium, through which seven American law schools conduct a study abroad program for a spring semester of law school in London. The Iowa/Bordeaux Program offers up to six credits for one month of intensive coursework in the summer in Arcachon, France.

Summer entrant program: The College of Law offers two starting dates for entering students: mid-May or late August. These are separate applicant pools. Students who elect to enter law school in the fall also may attend summer school at any point during their academic career. Students entering in May complete nearly a full semester of work in the first summer term. A May entrant who completes two additional summer sessions in the following two years may graduate in 27 months.

Specialty programs: The College of Law offers one of the strongest programs for the study of international and comparative law. Over 40 percent of the faculty regularly teach or conduct research on international and comparative law subjects. Iowa's Innovation, Business and Law Program integrates antitrust, corporate and securities law, and intellectual property. Internationally recognized experts and award-winning professors teach intensive courses in each of these important areas of private law. Both programs draw upon Iowa's rich tradition of curricular innovation and interdisciplinary research.

STUDENT BODY

Fall 2005 full-time enrollment: 656

Men: 54%	Women: 46%
African-American: 4.7%	American Indian: 1.1%
Asian-American: 5.6%	Mexican-American: 4.6%
Puerto Rican: 0.0%	Other Hisp-Amer: 0.0%
White: 83.4%	International: 0.6%
Unknown: 0.0%	

Attrition rates for 2004-2005 full-time students

Percent of students discontinuing law school:

Men: 1%	Women: 0%
First-year students: 0%	Second-year students: N/A
Third-year students: 1%	

LIBRARY RESOURCES

The library holds 413,661 and receives 10,048 current subscriptions.

Total volumes: 1,154,749

Percentage of the titles in the online catalog: 100%

Total seats available for library users: 678

INFORMATION TECHNOLOGY

Number of wired network connections available to students: 420 total (in the law library, excluding computer labs: 380; in classrooms: 20; in computer labs: 0; elsewhere in the law school: 20)

Law school has a wireless network.

Approximate number of simultaneous users that can be accommodated on wireless network: 1,500

Students are not required to own a computer.

EMPLOYMENT AND SALARIES

Proportion of 2004 graduates employed at graduation: **88%**

Employed 9 months later, as of February 15, 2005: **99%**

Salaries in the private sector (law firms, business, industry): **$48,000–$90,000** (25th-75th percentile)

Median salary in the private sector: **$65,500**

Percentage in the private sector who reported salary information: **76%**

Median salary in public service (government, judicial clerkships, academic posts, non-profits): **$45,000**

Percentage of 2004 graduates in:

Law firms: 59%	Bus./industry (legal): 10%
Bus./industry (nonlegal): 5%	Government: 7%
Public interest: 3%	Judicial clerkship: 8%
Academia : 1%	Unknown: 7%

2004 graduates employed in-state: 38%

2004 graduates employed in foreign countries: 1%

Number of states where graduates are employed: 28

Percentage of 2004 graduates working in: New England: 0%, Middle Atlantic: 2%, East North Central: 20%, West North Central: 56%, South Atlantic: 8%, East South Central: 1%, West South Central: 2%, Mountain: 3%, Pacific: 5%, Unknown: 2%

BAR PASSAGE RATES

Based on 2004 graduates taking Summer 2004 or Winter 2005 exams. Most of the school's first-time test takers took the bar in Iowa.

89%
School's bar passage rate for first-time test takers

86%
Statewide bar passage rate for first-time test takers

iversity of Kansas

- Green Hall, 1535 W. 15th Street, Lawrence, KS, 66045-7577
- http://www.law.ku.edu
- Public
- **Year founded:** 1878
- **2005-2006 tuition:** In-state: full-time: $9,528, part-time: N/A; Out-of-state: full-time: $17,859
- **Enrollment 2005-06 academic year:** full-time: 497
- **U.S. News 2007 law specialty ranking:** N/A

3.27-3.77 GPA, 25TH-75TH PERCENTILE

154-160 LSAT, 25TH-75TH PERCENTILE

26% ACCEPTANCE RATE

70 2007 U.S. NEWS LAW SCHOOL RANKING

ADMISSIONS

Admissions phone number: **(866) 220-3654**
Admissions email address: **admitlaw@ku.edu**
Application website: **http://www.law.ku.edu/apply.shtml**
Application deadline for Fall 2007 admission: **3/15**

Admissions statistics:

Number of applicants for Fall 2005: **1,145**
Number of acceptances: **303**
Number enrolled: **157**
Acceptance rate: **26%**
GPA, 25th-75th percentile, entering class Fall 2005: **3.27-3.77**
LSAT, 25th-75th percentile, entering class Fall 2005: **154-160**

FINANCIAL AID

Financial aid phone number: **(785) 864-4700**
Financial aid application deadline: **3/01**
Tuition 2005-2006 academic year: In-state: full-time: **$9,528**, part-time: N/A; Out-of-state: full-time: **$17,859**
Room and board: **$8,270**; books: **$800**; miscellaneous expenses: **$4,230**
Total of room/board/books/miscellaneous expenses: **$13,300**
University offers graduate student housing for which law students are eligible.

Financial aid profile

Percent of students that received grants for the 2004-2005 academic year: full-time: **71%**
Median grant amount: full-time: **$3,304**
The average law-school debt of those in the Class of 2005 who borrowed: **$44,917**. Proportion who borrowed: **71%**

ACADEMIC PROGRAMS

Calendar: **semester**
Joint degrees awarded: **Business; Economics; Health Services Administration; Philosophy; Public Administration ; Social Welfare; Urban Planning;**
cal first-year section size: Full-time: **68**

Is there typically a "small section" of the first year class, other than Legal Writing, taught by full-time faculty?: Full-time: **yes**
Number of course titles, beyond the first year curriculum, offered last year: **87**
Percentages of upper division course sections, excluding seminars, with an enrollment of:
Under 25: **65%**   25 to 49: **22%**
50 to 74: **9%**   75 to 99: **2%**
100+: **1%**
Areas of specialization: appellate advocacy, clinical training, dispute resolution, environmental law, healthcare law, intellectual property law, international law, tax law, trial advocacy

Fall 2005 faculty profile

Total teaching faculty: **63**. Full-time: **52%**; **67%** men, **33%** women, **12%** minorities. Part-time: **48%**; **73%** men, **27%** women, **0%** minorities
Student-to-faculty ratio: **13.4**

SPECIAL PROGRAMS (as provided by law school):

The law school offers six certificate programs in areas including elder law; environmental and natural resources law; media, law, and policy; tax law; and tribal lawyering.

The final certificate program is offered through the Tribal Law and Government Center, which prepares students for careers representing indigenous nations and tribes.

The KU law school was a pioneer in clinical education and today has one of the strongest programs in the nation with eight clinical courses. KU offers both in-house clinical programs, which involve students in client representation under the supervision of full-time faculty attorneys, and externship programs, which allow students to work under the supervision of attorneys, judges, or legislators in the community.

The Legal Aid Clinic allows students to represent indigent citizens and serve as public defenders in municipal and juvenile courts. Students in the Defender Project represent state and federal prisoners in appellate and post-conviction litigation. The Criminal Justice Clinic gives students the opportunity to work with prosecutors in state district attorneys' offices and the office of the U.S. attorney. The Elder Law Clinic allows students to work in matters such as income maintenance, access to health-care, housing, and consumer protection. Students in the Judicial Clerkship Clinic serve as law clerks for state and federal trial judges. The Legislative Clinic assigns students as interns to state legislators. Students in the Media Law Clinic respond to questions from lawyers, policymakers, publishers, and others concerned with mass communications. The Public Policy Clinic allows students to undertake in-depth policy studies.

The law school offers seven joint degree programs: law and business, economics, health policy and management, philosophy, public administration, social welfare, and urban planning. Students receive a master's degree and a juris doctor degree.

KU's law school is a founding member of a consortium that sponsors a spring semester program in London. The school co-sponsors a summer program in Istanbul. The school also sponsors summer programs in Turkey and Ireland.

STUDENT BODY

Fall 2005 full-time enrollment: 497

Men: 57%	Women: 43%
African-American: 2.6%	American Indian: 3.0%
Asian-American: 6.2%	Mexican-American: 0.0%
Puerto Rican: 0.0%	Other Hisp-Amer: 6.0%
White: 73.6%	International: 2.8%
Unknown: 5.6%	

Attrition rates for 2004-2005 full-time students
Percent of students discontinuing law school:

Men: 1%	Women: 1%
First-year students: 1%	Second-year students: 2%
Third-year students: N/A	

LIBRARY RESOURCES

The library holds 134,285 and receives 5,891 current subscriptions.
Total volumes: 412,098
Percentage of the titles in the online catalog: 98%
Total seats available for library users: 383

INFORMATION TECHNOLOGY

Number of wired network connections available to students: 0 total (in the law library, excluding computer labs: 0; in classrooms: 0; in computer labs: 0; elsewhere in the law school: 0)

Law school has a wireless network.
Approximate number of simultaneous users that can be accommodated on wireless network: 245
Students are not required to own a computer.

EMPLOYMENT AND SALARIES

Proportion of 2004 graduates employed at graduation: 55%
Employed 9 months later, as of February 15, 2005: 89%
Salaries in the private sector (law firms, business, industry): $48,000–$80,000 (25th-75th percentile)
Median salary in the private sector: $53,000
Percentage in the private sector who reported salary information: 69%
Median salary in public service (government, judicial clerkships, academic posts, non-profits): $43,000

Percentage of 2004 graduates in:

Law firms: 51%	Bus./industry (legal): 8%
Bus./industry (nonlegal): 4%	Government: 20%
Public interest: 4%	Judicial clerkship: 9%
Academia : 3%	Unknown: 1%

2004 graduates employed in-state: 53%
2004 graduates employed in foreign countries: 1%
Number of states where graduates are employed: 20
Percentage of 2004 graduates working in: New England: 0%, Middle Atlantic: 1%, East North Central: 2%, West North Central: 78%, South Atlantic: 5%, East South Central: 1%, West South Central: 3%, Mountain: 7%, Pacific: 2%, Unknown: 0%

BAR PASSAGE RATES

Based on 2004 graduates taking Summer 2004 or Winter 2005 exams. Most of the school's first-time test takers took the bar in Kansas.

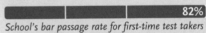

82%

School's bar passage rate for first-time test takers

81%

Statewide bar passage rate for first-time test takers

iversity of Kentucky

- 209 Law Building, Lexington, KY, 40506-0048
- http://www.uky.edu/law
- Public
- **Year founded:** 1908
- **2005-2006 tuition:** In-state: full-time: $11,540, part-time: N/A; Out-of-state: full-time: $21,242
- **Enrollment 2005-06 academic year:** full-time: 453
- **U.S. News 2007 law specialty ranking:** N/A

3.30-3.81 GPA, 25TH-75TH PERCENTILE

157-163 LSAT, 25TH-75TH PERCENTILE

35% ACCEPTANCE RATE

65 2007 U.S. NEWS LAW SCHOOL RANKING

ADMISSIONS

Admissions phone number: **(859) 257-6770**
Admissions email address: **lawadmissions@email.uky.edu**
Application website:
http://www.uky.edu/law/prospective_students
Application deadline for Fall 2007 admission: **3/01**

Admissions statistics:
Number of applicants for Fall 2005: **1,208**
Number of acceptances: **419**
Number enrolled: **172**
Acceptance rate: **35%**
GPA, 25th-75th percentile, entering class Fall 2005: **3.30-3.81**
LSAT, 25th-75th percentile, entering class Fall 2005: **157-163**

FINANCIAL AID

Financial aid phone number: **(859) 257-3172**
Financial aid application deadline: **4/01**
Tuition 2005-2006 academic year: In-state: full-time: **$11,540**, part-time: **N/A**; Out-of-state: full-time: **$21,242**
Room and board: **$9,300**; books: **$800**; miscellaneous expenses: **$2,960**
Total of room/board/books/miscellaneous expenses: **$13,060**
University offers graduate student housing for which law students are eligible.

Financial aid profile
Percent of students that received grants for the 2004-2005 academic year: full-time: **48%**
Median grant amount: full-time: **$4,440**
The average law-school debt of those in the Class of 2005 who borrowed: **$43,269.** Proportion who borrowed: **86%**

ACADEMIC PROGRAMS

Calendar: **semester**
Joint degrees awarded: **J.D./M.B.A.; J.D./MPA; J.D./MA**
Typical first-year section size: Full-time: **72**

Is there typically a "small section" of the first year class, other than Legal Writing, taught by full-time faculty?: Full-time: **yes**
Number of course titles, beyond the first year curriculum, offered last year: **56**
Percentages of upper division course sections, excluding seminars, with an enrollment of:

Under 25: **37%**   25 to 49: **39%**
50 to 74: **24%**   75 to 99: **0%**
100+: **0%**

Areas of specialization: appellate advocacy, clinical training, dispute resolution, environmental law, healthcare law, intellectual property law, international law, tax law, trial advocacy

Fall 2005 faculty profile
Total teaching faculty: **37.** Full-time: **57%**; **76%** men, **24%** women, **5%** minorities. Part-time: **43%**; **81%** men, **19%** women, **6%** minorities
Student-to-faculty ratio: **16.3**

SPECIAL PROGRAMS (as provided by law school):

UK Law's Civil Law Clinic, opened in 1998, provides third-year students with a unique opportunity to advise, counsel, and represent needy clients on a variety of legal matters. Students represent clients in negotiations with federal and state agencies, in administrative hearings, and in court proceedings.

In addition to the legal clinic, UK Law offers four externships in which students can obtain experience outside the college in applied research, fact gathering, interviewing, counseling, investigation, negotiation, working with outside experts, and trial advocacy. Those four programs are: the Kentucky Innocence Project externship, placing students with the Kentucky Department of Public Advocacy; the judicial clerkship externship, placing students with local, state and federal judges; the prison externship, a unique program at the Federal Correctional Institute-Lexington that is funded by a grant from the U.S. Department of Justice; and the prosecutorial externship, placing students with the Fayette County commonwealth's attorney.

STUDENT BODY

Fall 2005 full-time enrollment: 453

Men: 58%
African-American: 4.9%
Asian-American: 2.0%
Puerto Rican: 0.0%
White: 92.1%
Unknown: 0.0%

Women: 42%
American Indian: 0.0%
Mexican-American: 0.2%
Other Hisp-Amer: 0.9%
International: 0.0%

Attrition rates for 2004-2005 full-time students

Percent of students discontinuing law school:

Men: 1%
First-year students: 9%
Third-year students: N/A

Women: 5%
Second-year students: N/A

LIBRARY RESOURCES

The library holds 71,593 and receives 3,908 current subscriptions.

Total volumes: 465,187

Percentage of the titles in the online catalog: 100%

Total seats available for library users: 354

INFORMATION TECHNOLOGY

Number of wired network connections available to students: 68 total (in the law library, excluding computer labs: 48; in classrooms: 4; in computer labs: 0; elsewhere in the law school: 16)

Law school has a wireless network.

Approximate number of simultaneous users that can be accommodated on wireless network: 100

Students are not required to own a computer.

EMPLOYMENT AND SALARIES

Proportion of 2004 graduates employed at graduation: 64%

Employed 9 months later, as of February 15, 2005: 98%

Salaries in the private sector (law firms, business, industry): $40,000–$77,000 (25th-75th percentile)

Median salary in the private sector: $47,000

Percentage in the private sector who reported salary information: 60%

Median salary in public service (government, judicial clerkships, academic posts, non-profits): $36,500

Percentage of 2004 graduates in:

Law firms: 53%
Bus./industry (nonlegal): 1%
Public interest: 2%
Academia : 1%

Bus./industry (legal): 5%
Government: 16%
Judicial clerkship: 22%
Unknown: 0%

2004 graduates employed in-state: 75%

2004 graduates employed in foreign countries: 0%

Number of states where graduates are employed: 12

Percentage of 2004 graduates working in: New England: 0%, Middle Atlantic: 1%, East North Central: 6%, West North Central: 0%, South Atlantic: 12%, East South Central: 79%, West South Central: 0%, Mountain: 0%, Pacific: 2%, Unknown: 0%

BAR PASSAGE RATES

Based on 2004 graduates taking Summer 2004 or Winter 2005 exams. Most of the school's first-time test takers took the bar in Kentucky.

83%

School's bar passage rate for first-time test takers

78%

Statewide bar passage rate for first-time test takers

University of Louisville (Brandeis)

- Louisville, KY, 40292
- http://www.louisville.edu/brandeislaw/
- Public
- Year founded: 1846
- 2005-2006 tuition: In-state: full-time: $10,198, part-time: $8,520; Out-of-state: full-time: $22,320
- Enrollment 2005-06 academic year: full-time: 296; part-time: 100
- U.S. News 2007 law specialty ranking: N/A

3.43-3.68	GPA, 25TH-75TH PERCENTILE
155-159	LSAT, 25TH-75TH PERCENTILE
29%	ACCEPTANCE RATE
Tier 3	2007 U.S. NEWS LAW SCHOOL RANKING

ADMISSIONS

Admissions phone number: (502) 852-6365
Admissions email address: lawadmissions@louisville.edu
Application website: N/A
Application deadline for Fall 2007 admission: 5/15

Admissions statistics:

Number of applicants for Fall 2005: 1,066
Number of acceptances: 308
Number enrolled: 99
Acceptance rate: 29%
GPA, 25th-75th percentile, entering class Fall 2005:
3.43-3.68
LSAT, 25th-75th percentile, entering class Fall 2005: 155-159

Part-time program:

Number of applicants for Fall 2005: 171
Number of acceptances: 71
Number enrolled: 38
Acceptance rate: 42%
GPA, 25th-75th percentile, entering class Fall 2005:
3.24-3.65
LSAT, 25th-75th percentile, entering class Fall 2005:
150-157

FINANCIAL AID

Financial aid phone number: (502) 852-6391
Financial aid application deadline: 6/01
Tuition 2005-2006 academic year: In-state: full-time: $10,198, part-time: $8,520; Out-of-state: full-time: $22,320
Room and board: $5,800; books: $1,000; miscellaneous expenses: $8,216
Total of room/board/books/miscellaneous expenses: $15,016
University offers graduate student housing for which law students are eligible.

Financial aid profile

Percent of students that received grants for the 2004-2005 academic year: full-time: 42%; part-time 15%
Median grant amount: full-time: $5,000; part-time: $5,000

The average law-school debt of those in the Class of 2005 who borrowed: $46,213. Proportion who borrowed: 84%

ACADEMIC PROGRAMS

Calendar: **semester**
Joint degrees awarded: **M.B.A./J.D.; J.D./MDiv; J.D./MAPS; M.S.S.W./J.D.; J.D./M.A.H.**
Typical first-year section size: Full-time: **50**; Part-time: **36**
Is there typically a "small section" of the first year class, other than Legal Writing, taught by full-time faculty?: Full-time: **no**; Part-time: **no**
Number of course titles, beyond the first year curriculum, offered last year: **59**
Percentages of upper division course sections, excluding seminars, with an enrollment of:

Under 25: **50%**	25 to 49: **38%**
50 to 74: **12%**	75 to 99: **0%**
100+: **0%**	

Areas of specialization: appellate advocacy, dispute resolution, environmental law, healthcare law, intellectual property law, international law, tax law, trial advocacy

Fall 2005 faculty profile

Total teaching faculty: **34**. Full-time: **71%**; 67% men, 33% women, 13% minorities. Part-time: **29%**; 90% men, 10% women, 20% minorities
Student-to-faculty ratio: **15.0**

SPECIAL PROGRAMS (as provided by law school):

The law school offers a broad array of courses in general and specialized areas. Approximately 95 upper-division courses are offered each year, in addition to the required first-year courses. The emphasis on interdisciplinary study is represented in the five dual-degree programs J.D./M.B.A., J.D./master of divinity; J.D./master of arts in humanities; J.D./master of political science; and J.D./master of social work. Students may take up to six credits of preapproved graduate-level work in other disciplines. The law school's signature areas are in health policy and law; intellectual property law and technology transfer; and law and entrepreneurism.

Practice skills are developed through the numerous externships for credit (under the supervision of faculty members and members of the practicing bar). These include the judicial externship; Legal Aid; criminal justice (with the public defender, Jefferson County attorney, or commonwealth attorney); tax (with the Internal Revenue Service); domestic violence (at the Center for Women and Families); and technology externship (in the university's Office of Technology Transfer).

Students learn practical skills and service through the mandatory public-service program. All students must perform at least 30 hours of law-related public service before graduating. This is one of the first mandatory public-service programs to be implemented in the nation.

STUDENT BODY

Fall 2005 full-time enrollment: 296

Men: 52%	Women: 48%
African-American: 3.7%	American Indian: 0.3%
Asian-American: 3.0%	Mexican-American: 1.7%
Puerto Rican: 0.0%	Other Hisp-Amer: 0.0%
White: 87.2%	International: 0.3%
Unknown: 3.7%	

Fall 2005 part-time enrollment: 100

Men: 53%	Women: 47%
African-American: 2.0%	American Indian: 0.0%
Asian-American: 2.0%	Mexican-American: 2.0%
Puerto Rican: 0.0%	Other Hisp-Amer: 0.0%
White: 93.0%	International: 0.0%
Unknown: 1.0%	

Attrition rates for 2004-2005 full-time students
Percent of students discontinuing law school:

Men: 6%	Women: 4%
First-year students: 12%	Second-year students: 1%
Third-year students: N/A	

LIBRARY RESOURCES

The library holds 75,666 and receives 5,408 current subscriptions.
Total volumes: 415,986
Percentage of the titles in the online catalog: 100%
Total seats available for library users: 441

INFORMATION TECHNOLOGY

Number of wired network connections available to students: 6 total (in the law library, excluding computer labs: 6; in classrooms: 0; in computer labs: 0; elsewhere in the law school: 0)

Law school has a wireless network.
Approximate number of simultaneous users that can be accommodated on wireless network: 1,280
Students are not required to own a computer.

EMPLOYMENT AND SALARIES

Proportion of 2004 graduates employed at graduation: 62%
Employed 9 months later, as of February 15, 2005: 91%
Salaries in the private sector (law firms, business, industry): $40,000–$72,000 (25th-75th percentile)
Median salary in the private sector: $49,750
Percentage in the private sector who reported salary information: 63%
Median salary in public service (government, judicial clerkships, academic posts, non-profits): $35,250

Percentage of 2004 graduates in:

Law firms: 60%	Bus./industry (legal): 3%
Bus./industry (nonlegal): 10%	Government: 10%
Public interest: 6%	Judicial clerkship: 8%
Academia : 1%	Unknown: 3%

2004 graduates employed in-state: 86%
2004 graduates employed in foreign countries: 0%
Number of states where graduates are employed: 9
Percentage of 2004 graduates working in: New England: 0%, Middle Atlantic: 0%, East North Central: 5%, West North Central: 0%, South Atlantic: 3%, East South Central: 91%, West South Central: 0%, Mountain: 1%, Pacific: 1%, Unknown: 0%

BAR PASSAGE RATES

Based on 2004 graduates taking Summer 2004 or Winter 2005 exams. Most of the school's first-time test takers took the bar in Kentucky.

79%
School's bar passage rate for first-time test takers

78%
Statewide bar passage rate for first-time test takers

University of Maine

- 246 Deering Avenue, Portland, ME, 04102
- http://mainelaw.maine.edu/
- Public
- Year founded: 1961
- 2005-2006 tuition: In-state: full-time: $15,750, part-time: N/A; Out-of-state: full-time: $25,050
- Enrollment 2005-06 academic year: full-time: 249; part-time: 5
- U.S. News 2007 law specialty ranking: N/A

3.16-3.58	GPA, 25TH-75TH PERCENTILE
153-159	LSAT, 25TH-75TH PERCENTILE
40%	ACCEPTANCE RATE
Tier 3	2007 U.S. NEWS LAW SCHOOL RANKING

ADMISSIONS

Admissions phone number: **(207) 780-4341**
Admissions email address: **mainelaw@usm.maine.edu**
Application website:
  http://mainelaw.maine.edu/acrobat/MELawApp.pdf
Application deadline for Fall 2007 admission: **3/01**

Admissions statistics:

Number of applicants for Fall 2005: **694**
Number of acceptances: **280**
Number enrolled: **75**
Acceptance rate: **40%**
GPA, 25th-75th percentile, entering class Fall 2005:
  3.16-3.58
LSAT, 25th-75th percentile, entering class Fall 2005: **153-159**

FINANCIAL AID

Financial aid phone number: **(207) 780-5250**
Financial aid application deadline: **2/15**
Tuition 2005-2006 academic year: In-state: full-time:
  $15,750, part-time: N/A; Out-of-state: full-time: **$25,050**
Room and board: **$7,586**; books: **$900**; miscellaneous
  expenses: **$3,466**
Total of room/board/books/miscellaneous expenses:
  $11,952
University offers graduate student housing for which law
  students are eligible.

Financial aid profile

Percent of students that received grants for the 2004-2005
  academic year: full-time: **51%**
Median grant amount: full-time: **$4,000**
The average law-school debt of those in the Class of 2005
  who borrowed: **$62,420**. Proportion who borrowed: **84%**

ACADEMIC PROGRAMS

Calendar: **semester**
Joint degrees awarded: **J.D./Master of Business
  Administration; J.D./Masters of Public Policy & Mgmt;
  J.D/Master of Community Planning & Devel;
  J.D./Master of Health Policy & Mgmt**

Typical first-year section size: Full-time: **84**
Is there typically a "small section" of the first year class,
  other than Legal Writing, taught by full-time faculty?:
  Full-time: **yes**
Number of course titles, beyond the first year curriculum,
  offered last year: **48**
Percentages of upper division course sections, excluding
  seminars, with an enrollment of:

Under 25: **67%**	25 to 49: **22%**
50 to 74: **8%**	75 to 99: **3%**
100+: **0%**	

Areas of specialization: appellate advocacy, clinical training,
  dispute resolution, environmental law, healthcare law,
  intellectual property law, international law, tax law, trial
  advocacy

Fall 2005 faculty profile

Total teaching faculty: **46**. Full-time: **61%**; **68%** men, **32%**
  women, **0%** minorities. Part-time: **39%**; **56%** men, **44%**
  women, **6%** minorities
Student-to-faculty ratio: **15.5**

SPECIAL PROGRAMS *(as provided by law school):*

The University of Maine School of Law offers a wide variety of
special programs and opportunities for students. Ocean &
Coastal Law program: Maine Law is one of only a handful of
schools in the U.S. to provide a focus of study in ocean and
coastal law. In addition to environmental, natural resources, and
energy law courses, the school offers marine resources law, law
of the sea, and coastal zone law. Students supplement these curricular activities with research and scholarship for the Ocean
and Coastal Law Journal and as research assistants to the
school's Marine Law Institute and public agencies. Clinical programs: The Cumberland Legal Aid Clinic is an on-campus legal
services center serving economically disadvantaged people in
southern Maine. Clinic courses involve general practice, family
law, juvenile justice, prisoner assistance, domestic violence prevention, and intellectual property. Student attorneys provide all
of the legal work required for clients, including representation
in court, under the supervision of clinical faculty, and represent
domestic violence victims in obtaining protection-from-abuse

orders. Through a new intellectual property and technology clinic, students assist inventors and entrepreneurs in patent and transactional matters. The externship program provides another opportunity for law students to gain legal experience in public-service and nonprofit settings, such as Pine Tree Legal Assistance, Immigrant Legal Advocacy Project, the university counsel's office, U.S. attorney's office, Maine attorney general's office, Legal Services for the Elderly, and the Maine Patent Program. Intellectual property & technology law: Maine Law has a growing program in the area of technology and intellectual property law. The law school's Center for Law & Innovation supports Maine's investments in science and technology through educational programs and research projects. The center also administers the Intellectual Property Clinic and the Maine Patent Program, which provide education and assistance with the U.S. patent process to companies, inventors, and entrepreneurs. Public-inerest fellowships: The law school provides a substantial number of public-interest fellowships, which enable law students to do volunteer public-interest work during the summer months. Additionally, through the Bernstein District Court Fellowship Program, selected students work as summer law clerks to judges of the Maine District Courts.

STUDENT BODY

Fall 2005 full-time enrollment: 249

Men: 47%	Women: 53%
African-American: 2.0%	American Indian: 0.0%
Asian-American: 3.2%	Mexican-American: 0.0%
Puerto Rican: 0.4%	Other Hisp-Amer: 0.0%
White: 87.1%	International: 1.2%
Unknown: 6.0%	

Fall 2005 part-time enrollment: 5

Men: 60%	Women: 40%
African-American: 0.0%	American Indian: 0.0%
Asian-American: 0.0%	Mexican-American: 0.0%
Puerto Rican: 0.0%	Other Hisp-Amer: 0.0%
White: 80.0%	International: 0.0%
Unknown: 20.0%	

Attrition rates for 2004-2005 full-time students

Percent of students discontinuing law school:

Men: 3%	Women: 1%
First-year students: 4%	Second-year students: 3%
Third-year students: N/A	

LIBRARY RESOURCES

The library holds 72,359 and receives 2,974 current subscriptions.
Total volumes: 330,999

Percentage of the titles in the online catalog: 100%
Total seats available for library users: 209

INFORMATION TECHNOLOGY

Number of wired network connections available to students: 9 total (in the law library, excluding computer labs: 2; in classrooms: 5; in computer labs: 2; elsewhere in the law school: 0)
Law school has a wireless network.
Approximate number of simultaneous users that can be accommodated on wireless network: 200
Students are not required to own a computer.

EMPLOYMENT AND SALARIES

Proportion of 2004 graduates employed at graduation: N/A
Employed 9 months later, as of February 15, 2005: 90%
Salaries in the private sector (law firms, business, industry): $45,000–$60,000 (25th-75th percentile)
Median salary in the private sector: $52,000
Percentage in the private sector who reported salary information: 33%
Median salary in public service (government, judicial clerkships, academic posts, non-profits): $39,000

Percentage of 2004 graduates in:

Law firms: 45%	Bus./industry (legal): 3%
Bus./industry (nonlegal): 15%	Government: 15%
Public interest: 6%	Judicial clerkship: 15%
Academia : 1%	Unknown: 0%

2004 graduates employed in-state: 77%
2004 graduates employed in foreign countries: 0%
Number of states where graduates are employed: 11
Percentage of 2004 graduates working in: New England: 86%, Middle Atlantic: 1%, East North Central: 1%, West North Central: 0%, South Atlantic: 9%, East South Central: 0%, West South Central: 0%, Mountain: 1%, Pacific: 2%, Unknown: 0%

BAR PASSAGE RATES

Based on 2004 graduates taking Summer 2004 or Winter 2005 exams. Most of the school's first-time test takers took the bar in Maine.

69%
School's bar passage rate for first-time test takers

75%
Statewide bar passage rate for first-time test takers

University of Maryland

■ 500 W. Baltimore Street, Baltimore, MD, 21201-1786
■ http://www.law.umaryland.edu
■ Public
■ Year founded: 1870
■ 2005-2006 tuition: In-state: full-time: $17,701, part-time: $;13,274; Out-of-state: full-time: $28,980
■ Enrollment 2005-06 academic year: full-time: 666; part-time: 143
■ U.S. News 2007 law specialty ranking: clinical training: 5, environmental law: 4, healthcare law: 3

3.35-3.76 GPA, 25ᵀᴴ-75ᵀᴴ PERCENTILE

158-164 LSAT, 25ᵀᴴ-75ᵀᴴ PERCENTILE

16% ACCEPTANCE RATE

42 2007 U.S. NEWS LAW SCHOOL RANKING

ADMISSIONS
Admissions phone number: (410) 706-3492
Admissions email address:
admissions@law.umaryland.edu
Application website:
http://www.law.umaryland.edu/admiss_apply.asp
Application deadline for Fall 2007 admission: 3/01

Admissions statistics:
Number of applicants for Fall 2005: 3,587
Number of acceptances: 578
Number enrolled: 230
Acceptance rate: 16%
GPA, 25th-75th percentile, entering class Fall 2005: 3.35-3.76
LSAT, 25th-75th percentile, entering class Fall 2005: 158-164

Part-time program:
Number of applicants for Fall 2005: 527
Number of acceptances: 60
Number enrolled: 28
Acceptance rate: 11%
GPA, 25th-75th percentile, entering class Fall 2005: 3.30-3.68
LSAT, 25th-75th percentile, entering class Fall 2005: 157-162

FINANCIAL AID
Financial aid phone number: (410) 706-3492
Financial aid application deadline: 3/01
Tuition 2005-2006 academic year: In-state: full-time: $17,701, part-time: $13,274; Out-of-state: full-time: $28,980
Room and board: $14,985; books: $1,725; miscellaneous expenses: $6,632
Total of room/board/books/miscellaneous expenses: $23,342
University offers graduate student housing for which law students are eligible.

Financial aid profile
Percent of students that received grants for the 2004-2005 academic year: full-time: 54%; part-time 28%
Median grant amount: full-time: $4,800; part-time: $3,100
The average law-school debt of those in the Class of 2005 who borrowed: $68,259. Proportion who borrowed: 85%

ACADEMIC PROGRAMS
Calendar: semester
Joint degrees awarded: J.D./Ph.D. Public Policy; J.D./M.A. Public Policy; J.D./M.P.H.; J.D./M.B.A.; J.D./M.A.Criminal Justice; J.D./M.A. Liberal Arts; J.D./M.A. Public Management; J.D./M.S.W. Social Work; J.D./PharmD; J.D./M.A.Community Planning; J.D./M.S. Toxicology Risk Assessment; J.D./M.S. Nursing
Typical first-year section size: Full-time: 67; Part-time: 35
Is there typically a "small section" of the first year class, other than Legal Writing, taught by full-time faculty?: Full-time: yes; Part-time: yes
Number of course titles, beyond the first year curriculum, offered last year: 136
Percentages of upper division course sections, excluding seminars, with an enrollment of:
Under 25: 74%   25 to 49: 16%
50 to 74: 7%   75 to 99: 2%
100+: 1%
Areas of specialization: appellate advocacy, clinical training, dispute resolution, environmental law, healthcare law, intellectual property law, international law, tax law, trial advocacy

Fall 2005 faculty profile
Total teaching faculty: 150. Full-time: 37%; 60% men, 40% women, 18% minorities. Part-time: 63%; 64% men, 36% women, 8% minorities
Student-to-faculty ratio: 11.9

SPECIAL PROGRAMS *(as provided by law school):*
The Business Law Program provides innovative teaching, practical experience, research, and scholarship in the fields of busi-

ness organization law, securities regulation, intellectual property, tax, business transactions, and related areas.

The Center for Health and Homeland Security develops, coordinates and expands scientific research, policy development, training, and legal analysis, relating to the counterterrorism crisis and consequence management issues.

The Clinical Program teaches students to integrate the theory and practice of law. It has been ranked among the top clinical law programs in the country in the *U.S.News & World Report* annual survey.

The East Asian Legal Studies Program is a research and publishing institute that provides opportunities of advanced independent research for students and visiting scholars.

The Environmental Law Program combines regular course offerings in environmental law with special seminars taught by leading experts. The program has been ranked among the top such programs in the country in the *U.S.News & World Report* annual survey.

As part of its externship program, the School of Law offers placements in governmental and not-for-profit organizations dealing with legal issues. A limited number of externships are available with sponsoring organizations in South Africa.

The Intellectual Property Law Program provides a curriculum concentration and development support for students interested in pursuing careers practicing patent, copyright, trademark, and trade-secret law, as well as cyberspace, art, music, entertainment, sports, and media law. The Maryland Intellectual Property Legal Resource Center provides legal assistance to start-up technology companies.

The Law and Health Care Program prepares students to deal with increasingly complex health law issues. The program has been ranked among the top such programs in the country in the *U.S.News & World Report* annual survey.

The Legal Resource Center for Tobacco Regulation, Litigation, and Advocacy involves students in providing legal support to reduce the dangerous health effects of tobacco products.

The University of Maryland and the University of Baltimore law schools jointly sponsor a summer study abroad program at the University of Aberdeen (Scotland) Law School.

The Women, Leadership, and Equality Program supports faculty research and scholarship in the area of gender and leadership and offers students courses and field placements.

STUDENT BODY

Fall 2005 full-time enrollment: 666

Men: 41%	Women: 59%
African-American: 12.3%	American Indian: 0.5%
Asian-American: 11.4%	Mexican-American: 0.0%
Puerto Rican: 0.2%	Other Hisp-Amer: 4.8%
White: 67.3%	International: 1.2%
Unknown: 2.4%	

Fall 2005 part-time enrollment: 143

Men: 52%	Women: 48%
African-American: 24.5%	American Indian: 0.0%
Asian-American: 7.7%	Mexican-American: 0.7%
Puerto Rican: 0.0%	Other Hisp-Amer: 2.8%
White: 60.8%	International: 0.0%
Unknown: 3.5%	

Attrition rates for 2004-2005 full-time students
Percent of students discontinuing law school:

Men: 3%	Women: 1%
First-year students: 3%	Second-year students: 2%
Third-year students: 1%	

LIBRARY RESOURCES

The library holds 111,872 and receives 3,885 current subscriptions.
Total volumes: 468,320
Percentage of the titles in the online catalog: 100%
Total seats available for library users: 522

INFORMATION TECHNOLOGY

Number of wired network connections available to students: 1,208 total (in the law library, excluding computer labs: 385; in classrooms: 718; in computer labs: 15; elsewhere in the law school: 90)
Law school has a wireless network.
Approximate number of simultaneous users that can be accommodated on wireless network: 20
Students are required to own a computer.

EMPLOYMENT AND SALARIES

Proportion of 2004 graduates employed at graduation: 78%
Employed 9 months later, as of February 15, 2005: 97%
Salaries in the private sector (law firms, business, industry): $45,000–$95,000 (25th-75th percentile)
Median salary in the private sector: $60,000
Percentage in the private sector who reported salary information: 46%
Median salary in public service (government, judicial clerkships, academic posts, non-profits): $40,000

Percentage of 2004 graduates in:

Law firms: 32%	Bus./industry (legal): 9%
Bus./industry (nonlegal): 6%	Government: 22%
Public interest: 6%	Judicial clerkship: 19%
Academia : 7%	Unknown: 0%

2004 graduates employed in-state: 70%
2004 graduates employed in foreign countries: 1%
Number of states where graduates are employed: 22
Percentage of 2004 graduates working in: New England: 1%, Middle Atlantic: 4%, East North Central: 3%, West North Central: 0%, South Atlantic: 88%, East South Central: 1%, West South Central: 1%, Mountain: 1%, Pacific: 1%, Unknown: 0%

BAR PASSAGE RATES

Based on 2004 graduates taking Summer 2004 or Winter 2005 exams. Most of the school's first-time test takers took the bar in Maryland.

78%
School's bar passage rate for first-time test takers

72%
Statewide bar passage rate for first-time test takers

University of Memphis (Humphreys)

- 207 Humphreys Law School, Memphis, TN, 38152-3140
- http://www.law.memphis.edu
- Public
- Year founded: 1962
- 2005-2006 tuition: In-state: full-time: $9,352, part-time: $8,056; Out-of-state: full-time: $26,208
- Enrollment 2005-06 academic year: full-time: 368; part-time: 32
- U.S. News 2007 law specialty ranking: N/A

3.07-3.61 GPA, 25TH-75TH PERCENTILE

154-158 LSAT, 25TH-75TH PERCENTILE

23% ACCEPTANCE RATE

Tier 3 2007 U.S. NEWS LAW SCHOOL RANKING

ADMISSIONS

Admissions phone number: (901) 678-5403
Admissions email address: lawadmissions@mail.law.memphis.edu
Application website: http://www.law.memphis.edu/admissions
Application deadline for Fall 2007 admission: 3/01

Admissions statistics:

Number of applicants for Fall 2005: 1,166
Number of acceptances: 266
Number enrolled: 129
Acceptance rate: 23%
GPA, 25th-75th percentile, entering class Fall 2005: 3.07-3.61
LSAT, 25th-75th percentile, entering class Fall 2005: 154-158

Part-time program:

Number of applicants for Fall 2005: 42
Number of acceptances: 20
Number enrolled: 16
Acceptance rate: 48%
GPA, 25th-75th percentile, entering class Fall 2005: 3.06-3.44
LSAT, 25th-75th percentile, entering class Fall 2005: 144-150

FINANCIAL AID

Financial aid phone number: (901) 678-3687
Financial aid application deadline: 4/01
Tuition 2005-2006 academic year: In-state: full-time: $9,352, part-time: $8,056; Out-of-state: full-time: $26,208
Room and board: $7,084; books: $1,400; miscellaneous expenses: $3,777
Total of room/board/books/miscellaneous expenses: $12,261
University offers graduate student housing for which law students are eligible.

Financial aid profile

Percent of students that received grants for the 2004-2005 academic year: full-time: 25%; part-time 69%
Median grant amount: full-time: $3,500; part-time: $6,550
The average law-school debt of those in the Class of 2005 who borrowed: $55,673. Proportion who borrowed: 74%

ACADEMIC PROGRAMS

Calendar: semester
Joint degrees awarded: J.D./M.B.A.
Typical first-year section size: Full-time: 70
Is there typically a "small section" of the first year class, other than Legal Writing, taught by full-time faculty?: Full-time: no; Part-time: no
Number of course titles, beyond the first year curriculum, offered last year: 75
Percentages of upper division course sections, excluding seminars, with an enrollment of:

Under 25: 48%	25 to 49: 22%
50 to 74: 25%	75 to 99: 2%
100+: 2%	

Areas of specialization: appellate advocacy, clinical training, dispute resolution, environmental law, healthcare law, intellectual property law, international law, tax law, trial advocacy

Fall 2005 faculty profile

Total teaching faculty: 38. Full-time: 55%; 71% men, 29% women, 14% minorities. Part-time: 45%; 65% men, 35% women, 6% minorities
Student-to-faculty ratio: 14.2

SPECIAL PROGRAMS (as provided by law school):

The law school offers a full-time day program as well as a part-time day program for a limited number of students whose other responsibilities make full-time study difficult. The curriculum is designed to challenge students and prepare them for the modern practice of law. The curriculum reflects a commitment to traditional legal education, and academic emphasis is placed on fundamental lawyering skills and areas of knowledge.

In addition to the traditional fall and spring semesters, the University of Memphis offers a number of classes in the summer. The School of Law also offers advanced courses in lawyering skills, including trial advocacy, mediation, and alternative dispute resolution.

Several externships are available for students to work in administrative agencies, the court system, and other governmental entities under the supervision of a faculty instructor and a field supervisor. Students can also choose from one of four legal clinics operated by the School of Law: the General Sessions Courts Clinic, the Elder Law Clinic, the Domestic Violence Clinic, and the Child Advocacy Clinic. Students enrolled in the legal clinic courses work with indigent and elderly clients through Memphis Area Legal Services and with children in delinquency and dependency proceedings.

The School of Law, in conjunction with the Fogelman College of Business and Economics, offers a coordinated degree program leading to both the J.D. and M.B.A. degrees.

STUDENT BODY

Fall 2005 full-time enrollment: 368

Men: 57%	Women: 43%
African-American: 8.2%	American Indian: 0.0%
Asian-American: 1.1%	Mexican-American: 0.0%
Puerto Rican: 0.0%	Other Hisp-Amer: 0.8%
White: 89.9%	International: 0.0%
Unknown: 0.0%	

Fall 2005 part-time enrollment: 32

Men: 31%	Women: 69%
African-American: 75.0%	American Indian: 0.0%
Asian-American: 3.1%	Mexican-American: 0.0%
Puerto Rican: 0.0%	Other Hisp-Amer: 3.1%
White: 18.8%	International: 0.0%
Unknown: 0.0%	

Attrition rates for 2004-2005 full-time students
Percent of students discontinuing law school:

Men: 4%	Women: 2%
First-year students: 9%	Second-year students: 2%
Third-year students: N/A	

LIBRARY RESOURCES

The library holds 47,419 and receives 2,327 current subscriptions.
Total volumes: 268,179
Percentage of the titles in the online catalog: 100%
Total seats available for library users: 291

INFORMATION TECHNOLOGY

Number of wired network connections available to students: 30 total (in the law library, excluding computer labs: 30; in classrooms: 0; in computer labs: 0; elsewhere in the law school: 0)
Law school has a wireless network.
Approximate number of simultaneous users that can be accommodated on wireless network: 2,500
Students are not required to own a computer.

EMPLOYMENT AND SALARIES

Proportion of 2004 graduates employed at graduation: 53%
Employed 9 months later, as of February 15, 2005: 97%
Salaries in the private sector (law firms, business, industry): $50,000–$72,000 (25th-75th percentile)
Median salary in the private sector: $60,000
Percentage in the private sector who reported salary information: 34%
Median salary in public service (government, judicial clerkships, academic posts, non-profits): $44,000

Percentage of 2004 graduates in:

Law firms: 78%	Bus./industry (legal): 6%
Bus./industry (nonlegal): N/A	Government: 3%
Public interest: 4%	Judicial clerkship: 10%
Academia : N/A	Unknown: N/A

2004 graduates employed in-state: 90%
2004 graduates employed in foreign countries: N/A
Number of states where graduates are employed: 10
Percentage of 2004 graduates working in: New England: N/A, Middle Atlantic: 1%, East North Central: N/A, West North Central: 1%, South Atlantic: 4%, East South Central: 92%, West South Central: 1%, Mountain: 1%, Pacific: N/A, Unknown: N/A

BAR PASSAGE RATES

Based on 2004 graduates taking Summer 2004 or Winter 2005 exams. Most of the school's first-time test takers took the bar in Tennessee.

86%
School's bar passage rate for first-time test takers

82%
Statewide bar passage rate for first-time test takers

University of Miami

- PO Box 248087, Coral Gables, FL, 33124-8087
- http://www.law.miami.edu
- Private
- Year founded: 1926
- 2005-2006 tuition: full-time: $31,094; part-time: $23,030
- Enrollment 2005-06 academic year: full-time: 1,099; part-time: 52
- U.S. News 2007 law specialty ranking: international law: 19, tax law: 5

3.22-3.64 GPA, 25TH-75TH PERCENTILE

156-160 LSAT, 25TH-75TH PERCENTILE

37% ACCEPTANCE RATE

65 2007 U.S. NEWS LAW SCHOOL RANKING

ADMISSIONS

Admissions phone number: **(305) 284-2795**
Admissions email address: **admissions@law.miami.edu**
Application website: **http://www.law.miami.edu/admissions/forms**
Application deadline for Fall 2007 admission: **7/31**

Admissions statistics:

Number of applicants for Fall 2005: **4,946**
Number of acceptances: **1,838**
Number enrolled: **414**
Acceptance rate: **37%**
GPA, 25th-75th percentile, entering class Fall 2005: **3.22-3.64**
LSAT, 25th-75th percentile, entering class Fall 2005: **156-160**

Part-time program:

Number of applicants for Fall 2005: **114**
Number of acceptances: **11**
Number enrolled: **1**
Acceptance rate: **10%**
GPA, 25th-75th percentile, entering class Fall 2005: **N/A**
LSAT, 25th-75th percentile, entering class Fall 2005: **N/A**

FINANCIAL AID

Financial aid phone number: **(305) 284-3115**
Financial aid application deadline: **3/01**
Tuition 2005-2006 academic year: full-time: **$31,094**; part-time: **$23,030**
Room and board: **$10,130**; books: **$1,030**; miscellaneous expenses: **$5,170**
Total of room/board/books/miscellaneous expenses: **$16,330**
University does not offer graduate student housing for which law students are eligible.

Financial aid profile

Percent of students that received grants for the 2004-2005 academic year: full-time: **36%**
Median grant amount: full-time: **$14,500**

The average law-school debt of those in the Class of 2005 who borrowed: **$93,314**. Proportion who borrowed: **82%**

ACADEMIC PROGRAMS

Calendar: **semester**
Joint degrees awarded: **J.D./M.B.A.; J.D./M.P.H.; J.D./M.A.**
Typical first-year section size: Full-time: **100**
Is there typically a "small section" of the first year class, other than Legal Writing, taught by full-time faculty?: Full-time: **yes**; Part-time: **no**
Number of course titles, beyond the first year curriculum, offered last year: **156**
Percentages of upper division course sections, excluding seminars, with an enrollment of:
Under 25: **42%**   25 to 49: **28%**
50 to 74: **15%**   75 to 99: **6%**
100+: **10%**
Areas of specialization: appellate advocacy, clinical training, dispute resolution, environmental law, healthcare law, intellectual property law, international law, tax law, trial advocacy

Fall 2005 faculty profile

Total teaching faculty: **169**. Full-time: **34%**; **70%** men, **30%** women, **11%** minorities. Part-time: **66%**; **75%** men, **25%** women, **17%** minorities
Student-to-faculty ratio: **19.6**

SPECIAL PROGRAMS *(as provided by law school)*:

The University of Miami offers a remarkable array of special programs that enrich the first-rate education students receive. It offers one of the most sophisticated skills training programs in the nation, integrating trial, pretrial, and clinical experiences. Directed by a full-time faculty member, the program is greatly enhanced by distinguished trial attorneys and judges, who assist with the courses and help supervise clinical placements. The program places students with approximately 40 agencies in South Florida and elsewhere. UM also runs skills training in transactional law, alternative dispute resolution, mediation, and domestic and international legal research.

UM's joint degree programs include a J.D./LL.M. in tax, and also allow students to combine their J.D. studies with studies leading to master's degrees in business administration, public health, and marine affairs and policy.

The James Weldon Johnson/Robert H. Waters Summer Institute offers a select group of entering students an opportunity to participate in a unique learning experience before the beginning of fall classes. UM regularly offers four to five courses a year taught in Spanish, enabling students who are fluent in Spanish to refine their language skills while learning about civil and comparative law.

Clinics, centers, and other programs offer innumerable opportunities. The Center for Ethics and Public Service provides ethics training to businesses, schools, and lawyers. Students serving as Ethics Center Fellows take part in community service and training projects. The Children and Youth Law Clinic represents poor children in the foster care system. Under supervision by faculty members who are attorneys, students handle client interviews, hearings, motions, negotiations, discovery, mediations, and trials. The Center for Ecosystem Science and Policy, a university-wide body chaired by a member of the law faculty, studies the complex task of restoring damaged ecosystems such as the Everglades. The Center for the Study of Human Rights gives students the opportunity to become involved in a range of human rights issues.

The school offers three summer study abroad programs in international and comparative law in London, Spain, and the Mediterranean area. Selected UM students may spend a semester abroad at the University of Pompeu Fabra in Barcelona.

STUDENT BODY

Fall 2005 full-time enrollment: 1,099

Men: 56%	Women: 44%
African-American: 7.4%	American Indian: 0.5%
Asian-American: 4.0%	Mexican-American: 0.0%
Puerto Rican: 0.0%	Other Hisp-Amer: 11.9%
White: 67.6%	International: 1.5%
Unknown: 7.2%	

Fall 2005 part-time enrollment: 52

Men: 63%	Women: 37%
African-American: 3.8%	American Indian: 0.0%
Asian-American: 5.8%	Mexican-American: 0.0%
Puerto Rican: 0.0%	Other Hisp-Amer: 9.6%
White: 80.8%	International: 0.0%
Unknown: 0.0%	

Attrition rates for 2004-2005 full-time students

Percent of students discontinuing law school:

Men: 4%	Women: 2%
First-year students: 8%	Second-year students: 1%
Third-year students: N/A	

LIBRARY RESOURCES

The library holds 93,135 and receives 6,948 current subscriptions.
Total volumes: 596,242
Percentage of the titles in the online catalog: 100%
Total seats available for library users: 764

INFORMATION TECHNOLOGY

Number of wired network connections available to students: 253 total (in the law library, excluding computer labs: 102; in classrooms: 22; in computer labs: 82; elsewhere in the law school: 47)
Law school has a wireless network.
Approximate number of simultaneous users that can be accommodated on wireless network: 1,400
Students are not required to own a computer.

EMPLOYMENT AND SALARIES

Proportion of 2004 graduates employed at graduation: 73%
Employed 9 months later, as of February 15, 2005: 93%
Salaries in the private sector (law firms, business, industry): $63,800–$107,200 (25th-75th percentile)
Median salary in the private sector: $82,500
Percentage in the private sector who reported salary information: 25%
Median salary in public service (government, judicial clerkships, academic posts, non-profits): $39,100

Percentage of 2004 graduates in:

Law firms: 66%	Bus./industry (legal): 4%
Bus./industry (nonlegal): 4%	Government: 18%
Public interest: 3%	Judicial clerkship: 3%
Academia : 2%	Unknown: 0%

2004 graduates employed in-state: 82%
2004 graduates employed in foreign countries: 0%
Number of states where graduates are employed: 23
Percentage of 2004 graduates working in: New England: 1%, Middle Atlantic: 4%, East North Central: 4%, West North Central: 1%, South Atlantic: 84%, East South Central: 1%, West South Central: 1%, Mountain: 1%, Pacific: 2%, Unknown: 0%

BAR PASSAGE RATES

Based on 2004 graduates taking Summer 2004 or Winter 2005 exams. Most of the school's first-time test takers took the bar in Florida.

82%
School's bar passage rate for first-time test takers

73%
Statewide bar passage rate for first-time test takers

University of Michigan–Ann Arbor

- 625 S. State Street, Ann Arbor, MI, 48109-1215
- http://www.law.umich.edu/
- Public
- Year founded: 1859
- 2005-2006 tuition: In-state: full-time: $32,919, part-time: N/A; Out-of-state: full-time: $35,919
- Enrollment 2005-06 academic year: full-time: 1,179
- U.S. News 2007 law specialty ranking: clinical training: 10, international law: 8, tax law: 13

3.45-3.78 GPA, 25TH-75TH PERCENTILE

166-169 LSAT, 25TH-75TH PERCENTILE

19% ACCEPTANCE RATE

8 2007 U.S. NEWS LAW SCHOOL RANKING

ADMISSIONS

Admissions phone number: **(734) 764-0537**
Admissions email address: **law.jd.admissions@umich.edu**
Application website:
http://www.law.umich.edu/ProspectiveStudents/Admissions/applying.htm
Application deadline for Fall 2007 admission: 2/15

Admissions statistics:
Number of applicants for Fall 2005: **5,771**
Number of acceptances: **1,125**
Number enrolled: **366**
Acceptance rate: **19%**
GPA, 25th-75th percentile, entering class Fall 2005: **3.45-3.78**
LSAT, 25th-75th percentile, entering class Fall 2005: **166-169**

FINANCIAL AID

Financial aid phone number: **(734) 764-5289**
Financial aid application deadline: N/A
Tuition 2005-2006 academic year: In-state: full-time: **$32,919**, part-time: N/A; Out-of-state: full-time: **$35,919**
Room and board: **$9,722**; books: **$930**; miscellaneous expenses: **$4,788**
Total of room/board/books/miscellaneous expenses: **$15,440**
University offers graduate student housing for which law students are eligible.

Financial aid profile
Percent of students that received grants for the 2004-2005 academic year: full-time: **40%**
Median grant amount: full-time: **$10,100**
The average law-school debt of those in the Class of 2005 who borrowed: **$86,901**. Proportion who borrowed: **89%**

ACADEMIC PROGRAMS

Calendar: **semester**
Joint degrees awarded: **J.D./Phd Economics; J.D./MSI; J.D./Ms Natural Resources; J.D./MPH; J.D./MPP;**
J.D./MSW; J.D./MUP; J.D./M.B.A.; J.D./MA Economics; J.D./MS International Relations
Typical first-year section size: Full-time: **95**
Is there typically a "small section" of the first year class, other than Legal Writing, taught by full-time faculty?: Full-time: **yes**
Number of course titles, beyond the first year curriculum, offered last year: **130**
Percentages of upper division course sections, excluding seminars, with an enrollment of:

Under 25: **32%**	25 to 49: **27%**
50 to 74: **13%**	75 to 99: **14%**
100+: **13%**	

Areas of specialization: appellate advocacy, clinical training, dispute resolution, environmental law, healthcare law, intellectual property law, international law, tax law, trial advocacy

Fall 2005 faculty profile
Total teaching faculty: **116**. Full-time: **65%**; **72%** men, **28%** women, **9%** minorities. Part-time: **35%**; **56%** men, **44%** women, **12%** minorities
Student-to-faculty ratio: **16.9**

SPECIAL PROGRAMS *(as provided by law school):*

The University of Michigan Law School's clinical practice programs focus on developing expertise in client counseling, discovery, negotiation and mediation, legal writing, and trial skills. Clinical offerings include a general clinic in which students may be involved in civil and/or criminal work; the Child Advocacy Law Clinic; the Criminal Appellate Defense Clinic; a mediation clinic; a medico-legal Pediatric Advocacy Clinic; and the transactional Urban Communities Clinic. The nature of the local court dockets allow many students to handle cases from beginning to end, unlike large urban settings where caseload backlogs predominate. Michigan Law provides study abroad opportunities by allowing second- and third-year students to enroll for up to 12 credits of approved off-site study. Formal arrangements exist with the University of Leiden (the Netherlands), University of Paris II, University College London, Katholieke University (Belgium), Bucerius Law

School (Germany), Tel Aviv Law School, and European University Institute in Florence. Subject to approval, students may also create their own study abroad arrangements. Other off-site opportunities include our South Africa Externship Program, which allows students to work for a semester in South Africa for human rights organizations or other non-profit legal organizations. Because of the ABA's site visit requirements, externships are usually limited to New York, Washington, D.C., and Detroit. The Law School's Program in Refugee and Asylum Law allows in-depth study of international refugee law doctrine, its application in comparative jurisprudence, and direct engagement with the process of international refugee law reform. Michigan Law supports paid internships at the AIRE Centre in London and the International Law Commission of the UN in Geneva, as well as those offered through our Cambodian and refugee law programs. Michigan is one of a select group of U.S. law schools whose students are eligible to apply for paid traineeships on the International Court of Justice and to apply for clerkships at the European Court of Justice through the Dean Acheson Legal Stage Program. The Center for International and Comparative Law supports the internationally related endeavors of students and faculty and serves as a central information clearinghouse for international activities at the Law School and around the University.

STUDENT BODY

Fall 2005 full-time enrollment: 1,179

Men: 55%	Women: 45%
African-American: 6.3%	American Indian: 2.6%
Asian-American: 10.9%	Mexican-American: 0.0%
Puerto Rican: 0.0%	Other Hisp-Amer: 6.4%
White: 58.8%	International: 4.6%
Unknown: 10.4%	

Attrition rates for 2004-2005 full-time students

Percent of students discontinuing law school:

Men: 1%	Women: 1%
First-year students: N/A	Second-year students: 2%
Third-year students: 0%	

LIBRARY RESOURCES

The library holds 312,787 and receives 9,514 current subscriptions.
Total volumes: 965,069
Percentage of the titles in the online catalog: 99%
Total seats available for library users: 855

INFORMATION TECHNOLOGY

Number of wired network connections available to students: 375 total (in the law library, excluding computer labs: 10; in classrooms: 260; in computer labs: 62; elsewhere in the law school: 43)
Law school has a wireless network.
Approximate number of simultaneous users that can be accommodated on wireless network: 1,200
Students are not required to own a computer.

EMPLOYMENT AND SALARIES

Proportion of 2004 graduates employed at graduation: 95%
Employed 9 months later, as of February 15, 2005: 99%
Salaries in the private sector (law firms, business, industry): $120,000–$125,000 (25th-75th percentile)
Median salary in the private sector: $125,000
Percentage in the private sector who reported salary information: 78%
Median salary in public service (government, judicial clerkships, academic posts, non-profits): $50,598

Percentage of 2004 graduates in:

Law firms: 73%	Bus./industry (legal): 0%
Bus./industry (nonlegal): 3%	Government: 4%
Public interest: 5%	Judicial clerkship: 15%
Academia : 0%	Unknown: 0%

2004 graduates employed in-state: 15%
2004 graduates employed in foreign countries: 1%
Number of states where graduates are employed: 31
Percentage of 2004 graduates working in: New England: 3%, Middle Atlantic: 22%, East North Central: 35%, West North Central: 3%, South Atlantic: 12%, East South Central: 1%, West South Central: 4%, Mountain: 3%, Pacific: 15%, Unknown: 1%

BAR PASSAGE RATES

Based on 2004 graduates taking Summer 2004 or Winter 2005 exams. Most of the school's first-time test takers took the bar in New York.

96%
School's bar passage rate for first-time test takers

75%
Statewide bar passage rate for first-time test takers

University of Minnesota–Twin Cities

- 229 19th Avenue S, Minneapolis, MN, 55455
- http://www.law.umn.edu
- Public
- **Year founded:** 1888
- **2005-2006 tuition:** In-state: full-time: $19,969, part-time: N/A;
  Out-of-state: full-time: $30,353
- **Enrollment 2005-06 academic year:** full-time: 808
- **U.S. News 2007 law specialty ranking:** health care law: 10, intellecutal
  property law: 21

3.30-3.78	GPA, 25TH-75TH PERCENTILE
162-167	LSAT, 25TH-75TH PERCENTILE
28%	ACCEPTANCE RATE
19	2007 U.S. NEWS LAW SCHOOL RANKING

ADMISSIONS

Admissions phone number: **(612) 625-3487**
Admissions email address: **umnlsadm@umn.edu**
Application website: **https://www.law.umn.edu/admis-sions/online_application.htm**
Application deadline for Fall 2007 admission: **3/01**

Admissions statistics:
Number of applicants for Fall 2005: **3,068**
Number of acceptances: **866**
Number enrolled: **273**
Acceptance rate: **28%**
GPA, 25th-75th percentile, entering class Fall 2005:
  3.30-3.78
LSAT, 25th-75th percentile, entering class Fall 2005:
  162-167

FINANCIAL AID

Financial aid phone number: **(612) 625-3487**
Financial aid application deadline: **5/01**
Tuition 2005-2006 academic year: In-state: full-time:
  $19,969, part-time: **N/A**; Out-of-state: full-time: **$30,353**
Room and board: **N/A**; books: **N/A**; miscellaneous
  expenses: **N/A**
Total of room/board/books/miscellaneous expenses:
  $13,392
University offers graduate student housing for which law
  students are eligible.

Financial aid profile
Percent of students that received grants for the 2004-2005
  academic year: full-time: **56%**
Median grant amount: full-time: **$7,500**
The average law-school debt of those in the Class of 2005
  who borrowed: **$67,496**. Proportion who borrowed: **87%**

ACADEMIC PROGRAMS

Calendar: **semester**
Joint degrees awarded: **J.D./M.U.R.P.; J.D./M.B.S.;
  J.D./M.P.H.; J.D./Ph.D.; J.D./M.D.; J.D./M.B.A.;**
**J.D./M.S.; J.D./M.A.; J.D./M.P.A.; J.D./M.P.;
J.D./M.B.T.; J.D./M.P.P.**
Typical first-year section size: Full-time: **112**
Is there typically a "small section" of the first year class,
  other than Legal Writing, taught by full-time faculty?:
  Full-time: **yes**
Number of course titles, beyond the first year curriculum,
  offered last year: **193**
Percentages of upper division course sections, excluding
  seminars, with an enrollment of:
  Under 25: **58%**   25 to 49: **23%**
  50 to 74: **9%**   75 to 99: **7%**
  100+: **3%**
Areas of specialization: appellate advocacy, clinical training,
  dispute resolution, environmental law, healthcare law,
  intellectual property law, international law, tax law, trial
  advocacy

Fall 2005 faculty profile
Total teaching faculty: **157**. Full-time: **27%**; **69%** men, **31%**
  women, **14%** minorities. Part-time: **73%**; **57%** men, **43%**
  women, **6%** minorities
Student-to-faculty ratio: **12.5**

SPECIAL PROGRAMS *(as provided by law school)*:

Clinics: Over 55 percent of Minnesota's law students (compared
with only 25 percent nationwide) participate in a live-client
clinic, providing 18,000 hours of pro bono legal service in the
Twin Cities each year. In addition to its size, a hallmark of the
clinic program is its breadth, with clinics in diverse areas of
practice, including bankruptcy, immigration, criminal prosecution and defense, domestic violence, child advocacy, civil practice, and business law.

Public service: Through the Public Service Program, students
are asked to perform 50 hours of pro bono legal service. Those
who do so receive special recognition. Last year, University of
Minnesota law students served 2,351 clients through this program.

Judicial externships: An externship program with federal and
state courts allows students to serve as part-time law clerks
while receiving academic credit.

Foreign exchanges: Exchange programs in six countries enable students to study abroad for a semester or the summer. We also offer a Summer Study Abroad Program in Beijing, China.

Research institutes: The Human Rights Center's fellowship program awards grants to students to engage in human rights work; a Web library contains the largest collection of human rights materials in the world; and special partnership programs assist the United Nations and other human-rights organizations.

The Institute on Race and Poverty works to forge strategies to combat dilemmas like urban decay and racial segregation. Law student research assistants work with the institute's staff on research projects, community outreach, and national conferences.

The Kommerstad Center for Business Law and Entrepreneurship uses the Business Law Clinic, the Minnesota Journal of Business Law and Entrepreneurship, Student Entrepreneur Grants, and the Speaker Forum, to bring together members of the university community to consider issues faced by emerging businesses.

The Consortium on Law and Values in Health, Environment & the Life Sciences is a confederation of 13 university departments, including the Stem Cell Institute, the Center for Bioethics, and the Biomedical Genomics Institute. The consortium addresses legal, ethical, and policy issues raised by problems in health, environment, and the life sciences.

The Institute on Crime and Public Policy funds independent research and attracts top speakers and faculty to create an institutional focus for criminal law projects.

STUDENT BODY

Fall 2005 full-time enrollment: 808

Men: 57%	Women: 43%
African-American: 2.4%	American Indian: 0.6%
Asian-American: 9.2%	Mexican-American: 0.0%
Puerto Rican: 0.0%	Other Hisp-Amer: 4.1%
White: 76.6%	International: 2.5%
Unknown: 4.7%	

Attrition rates for 2004-2005 full-time students
Percent of students discontinuing law school:

Men: 3%	Women: 1%
First-year students: 5%	Second-year students: 1%
Third-year students: 1%	

LIBRARY RESOURCES
The library holds 285,280 and receives 10,574 current subscriptions.
Total volumes: 1,020,040

Percentage of the titles in the online catalog: 97%
Total seats available for library users: **866**

INFORMATION TECHNOLOGY
Number of wired network connections available to students: **0** total (in the law library, excluding computer labs: **0**; in classrooms: **0**; in computer labs: **0**; elsewhere in the law school: **0**)
Law school has a wireless network.
Approximate number of simultaneous users that can be accommodated on wireless network: **970**
Students are required to own a computer.

EMPLOYMENT AND SALARIES
Proportion of 2004 graduates employed at graduation: 97%
Employed 9 months later, as of February 15, 2005: 99%
Salaries in the private sector (law firms, business, industry): $55,000–$90,000 (25th-75th percentile)
Median salary in the private sector: $70,000
Percentage in the private sector who reported salary information: 83%
Median salary in public service (government, judicial clerkships, academic posts, non-profits): $47,300

Percentage of 2004 graduates in:

Law firms: 53%	Bus./industry (legal): 11%
Bus./industry (nonlegal): 0%	Government: 7%
Public interest: 4%	Judicial clerkship: 23%
Academia : 0%	Unknown: 2%

2004 graduates employed in-state: 59%
2004 graduates employed in foreign countries: 2%
Number of states where graduates are employed: 28
Percentage of 2004 graduates working in: New England: 1%, Middle Atlantic: 6%, East North Central: 11%, West North Central: 62%, South Atlantic: 6%, East South Central: 0%, West South Central: 1%, Mountain: 4%, Pacific: 6%, Unknown: 1%

BAR PASSAGE RATES
Based on 2004 graduates taking Summer 2004 or Winter 2005 exams. Most of the school's first-time test takers took the bar in Minnesota.

99%
School's bar passage rate for first-time test takers

91%
Statewide bar passage rate for first-time test takers

University of Mississippi

- PO Box 1848, University, MS, 38677
- http://www.olemiss.edu/depts/law_school/
- Public
- Year founded: 1854
- 2005-2006 tuition: In-state: full-time: $7,720, part-time: $386/credit hour; Out-of-state: full-time: $14,360
- Enrollment 2005-06 academic year: full-time: 553; part-time: 1
- U.S. News 2007 law specialty ranking: N/A

3.26-3.77	GPA, 25TH-75TH PERCENTILE
151-158	LSAT, 25TH-75TH PERCENTILE
27%	ACCEPTANCE RATE
97	2007 U.S. NEWS LAW SCHOOL RANKING

ADMISSIONS

Admissions phone number: **(662) 915-6910**
Admissions email address: **lawmiss@olemiss.edu**
Application website:
http://www.olemiss.edu/depts/law_school/admis_APPLICATION.html
Application deadline for Fall 2007 admission: **3/01**

Admissions statistics:
Number of applicants for Fall 2005: **1,678**
Number of acceptances: **456**
Number enrolled: **187**
Acceptance rate: **27%**
GPA, 25th-75th percentile, entering class Fall 2005: **3.26-3.77**
LSAT, 25th-75th percentile, entering class Fall 2005: **151-158**

FINANCIAL AID

Financial aid phone number: **(800) 891-4569**
Financial aid application deadline: **3/15**
Tuition 2005-2006 academic year: In-state: full-time: **$7,720**, part-time: **$386/credit hour**; Out-of-state: full-time: **$14,360**
Room and board: **$9,686**; books: **$1,300**; miscellaneous expenses: **$3,196**
Total of room/board/books/miscellaneous expenses: **$14,182**
University offers graduate student housing for which law students are eligible.

Financial aid profile
Percent of students that received grants for the 2004-2005 academic year: full-time: **30%**
Median grant amount: full-time: **$6,646**
The average law-school debt of those in the Class of 2005 who borrowed: **$37,566**. Proportion who borrowed: **78%**

ACADEMIC PROGRAMS

Calendar: **semester**
Joint degrees awarded: **N/A**
Typical first-year section size: Full-time: **57**

Is there typically a "small section" of the first year class, other than Legal Writing, taught by full-time faculty?: Full-time: **no**
Number of course titles, beyond the first year curriculum, offered last year: **67**
Percentages of upper division course sections, excluding seminars, with an enrollment of:
Under 25: **35%**   25 to 49: **35%**
50 to 74: **13%**   75 to 99: **14%**
100+: **3%**
Areas of specialization: appellate advocacy, clinical training, dispute resolution, environmental law, intellectual property law, international law, tax law, trial advocacy

Fall 2005 faculty profile
Total teaching faculty: **36**. Full-time: **72%**; **69%** men, **31%** women, **15%** minorities. Part-time: **28%**; **80%** men, **20%** women, **0%** minorities
Student-to-faculty ratio: **16.9**

SPECIAL PROGRAMS *(as provided by law school):*

Special programs include the Public Service Externship and Prosecutorial Externship, as well as the Criminal Appeals Clinic and Civil Law Clinic.
Summer sessions are available in Cambridge, England.

STUDENT BODY

Fall 2005 full-time enrollment: **553**
Men: **54%**	Women: **46%**
African-American: **8.9%**	American Indian: **0.5%**
Asian-American: **0.9%**	Mexican-American: **0.0%**
Puerto Rican: **0.0%**	Other Hisp-Amer: **0.2%**
White: **89.5%**	International: **0.0%**
Unknown: **0.0%**	

Fall 2005 part-time enrollment: **1**
Men: **0%**	Women: **100%**
African-American: **0.0%**	American Indian: **0.0%**
Asian-American: **0.0%**	Mexican-American: **0.0%**
Puerto Rican: **0.0%**	Other Hisp-Amer: **0.0%**

White: 0.0% International: 0.0%
Unknown: 100.0%

Attrition rates for 2004-2005 full-time students
Percent of students discontinuing law school:
Men: 4% Women: 2%
First-year students: 10% Second-year students: 0%
Third-year students: N/A

LIBRARY RESOURCES
The library holds 74,016 and receives 2,144 current subscriptions.
Total volumes: 328,134
Percentage of the titles in the online catalog: 99%
Total seats available for library users: 302

INFORMATION TECHNOLOGY
Number of wired network connections available to students: 715 total (in the law library, excluding computer labs: 121; in classrooms: 458; in computer labs: 4; elsewhere in the law school: 132)
Law school has a wireless network.
Approximate number of simultaneous users that can be accommodated on wireless network: 400
Students are not required to own a computer.

EMPLOYMENT AND SALARIES
Proportion of 2004 graduates employed at graduation: 73%
Employed 9 months later, as of February 15, 2005: 95%
Salaries in the private sector (law firms, business, industry): $49,000–$75,000 (25th-75th percentile)

Median salary in the private sector: $60,000
Percentage in the private sector who reported salary information: 78%
Median salary in public service (government, judicial clerkships, academic posts, non-profits): $37,733

Percentage of 2004 graduates in:
Law firms: 67% Bus./industry (legal): 3%
Bus./industry (nonlegal): 3% Government: 6%
Public interest: 3% Judicial clerkship: 13%
Academia : 3% Unknown: 2%

2004 graduates employed in-state: 76%
2004 graduates employed in foreign countries: 0%
Number of states where graduates are employed: 13
Percentage of 2004 graduates working in: New England: 0%, Middle Atlantic: 0%, East North Central: 1%, West North Central: 0%, South Atlantic: 6%, East South Central: 89%, West South Central: 3%, Mountain: N/A, Pacific: 1%, Unknown: 0%

BAR PASSAGE RATES
Based on 2004 graduates taking Summer 2004 or Winter 2005 exams. Most of the school's first-time test takers took the bar in Mississippi.

| 90% |
School's bar passage rate for first-time test takers

| 90% |
Statewide bar passage rate for first-time test takers

University of Missouri–Columbia

■ 203 Hulston Hall, Columbia, MO, 65211-4300
■ http://www.law.missouri.edu
■ Public
■ Year founded: 1872
■ 2005-2006 tuition: In-state: full-time: $13,614, part-time: N/A;
  Out-of-state: full-time: $25,986
■ Enrollment 2005-06 academic year: full-time: 440; part-time: 6
■ U.S. News 2007 law specialty ranking: dispute resolution: 2

3.31-3.74	GPA, 25TH-75TH PERCENTILE
156-160	LSAT, 25TH-75TH PERCENTILE
32%	ACCEPTANCE RATE
60	2007 U.S. NEWS LAW SCHOOL RANKING

ADMISSIONS

Admissions phone number: **(573) 882-6042**
Admissions email address: **umclawadmissions@missouri.edu**
Application website: **http://www.law.missouri.edu/admissions.html**
Application deadline for Fall 2007 admission: **3/01**

Admissions statistics:

Number of applicants for Fall 2005: **977**
Number of acceptances: **314**
Number enrolled: **150**
Acceptance rate: **32%**
GPA, 25th-75th percentile, entering class Fall 2005: **3.31-3.74**
LSAT, 25th-75th percentile, entering class Fall 2005: **156-160**

FINANCIAL AID

Financial aid phone number: **(573) 882-6643**
Financial aid application deadline: **3/01**
Tuition 2005-2006 academic year: In-state: full-time: **$13,614**, part-time: N/A; Out-of-state: full-time: **$25,986**
Room and board: **$7,590**; books: **$1,372**; miscellaneous expenses: **$5,090**
Total of room/board/books/miscellaneous expenses: **$14,052**
University offers graduate student housing for which law students are eligible.

Financial aid profile

Percent of students that received grants for the 2004-2005 academic year: full-time: **53%**
Median grant amount: full-time: **$3,500**
The average law-school debt of those in the Class of 2005 who borrowed: **$57,889**. Proportion who borrowed: **87%**

ACADEMIC PROGRAMS

Calendar: **semester**
Joint degrees awarded: **J.D./M.B.A.; J.D./M.P.A.; J.D./M.S.(Ag Econ); J.D./M.H.A.; J.D./M.A. (Econ);**
J.D./M.A. (HDFS); J.D./M.A. (ELPA); J.D./M.A. (Journalism); J.D./Ph.D. (Journalism); J.D./M.A. (Library & Infomation Science); J.D./M.A. (Consumer & Family Economics); J.D./M.S. (HDFS)
Typical first-year section size: Full-time: **72**
Is there typically a "small section" of the first year class, other than Legal Writing, taught by full-time faculty?: Full-time: **yes**
Number of course titles, beyond the first year curriculum, offered last year: **126**
Percentages of upper division course sections, excluding seminars, with an enrollment of:

Under 25: **70%**		25 to 49: **17%**	
50 to 74: **10%**		75 to 99: **2%**	
100+: **0%**			

Areas of specialization: appellate advocacy, clinical training, dispute resolution, environmental law, healthcare law, intellectual property law, international law, tax law, trial advocacy

Fall 2005 faculty profile

Total teaching faculty: **43**. Full-time: **65%**; **57%** men, **43%** women, **14%** minorities. Part-time: **35%**; **73%** men, **27%** women, **7%** minorities
Student-to-faculty ratio: **13.2**

SPECIAL PROGRAMS (as provided by law school):

Alternative dispute resolution: The nationally recognized Center for the Study of Dispute Resolution is a unique feature of the law school. Our faculty continues to help shape the field of dispute resolution by serving in leadership positions in national and international organizations. Missouri's award-winning program to integrate dispute resolution instruction into the first-year curriculum received widespread attention. Lawyering: Problem Solving and Dispute Resolution exposes students to skills that they will use throughout their careers. The Center also houses a master of laws in dispute resolution degree program, one of the first programs of its kind in the country.

Certificate programs: In addition to a certificate in dispute resolution, MU offers interdisciplinary graduate certificates in journalism, the Digital Globe and the European Union. MU is one of only 10 European Union centers in the United States.

Dual-degree programs: We offer dual degrees in business administration (J.D./M.B.A.), public administration (J.D./M.P.A.), health administration (J.D./M.H.A.), library science (J.D./M.L.S.), and journalism (J.D./M.A. and J.D./Ph.D.).

Study abroad: Through the London Law Consortium, MU students can spend the winter semester in London, participate in a fall semester exchange program at Bucerius University in Hamburg, Germany, or spend the summer in Cape Town, South Africa, studying comparative law.

Clinics and externships: MU provides students many opportunities to gain practical experience, to enhance lawyering skills, and to promote awareness of ethical issues through an active externship program and four clinical programs. MU externs work under the supervision of attorneys or judges in various settings. The Criminal Prosecution Clinic allows students to represent the state at felony preliminary hearings and misdemeanor trials. Students in the Family Violence Clinic represent indigent victims of domestic abuse. The Mediation Clinic allows students to act as mediators in a variety of dispute resolution settings, and finally, our Legislative Clinic allows students to draft legislation, lobby and work on policy initiatives that influence legislation.

STUDENT BODY

Fall 2005 full-time enrollment: 440

Men: 60%	Women: 40%
African-American: 4.8%	American Indian: 1.1%
Asian-American: 2.3%	Mexican-American: 0.0%
Puerto Rican: 0.0%	Other Hisp-Amer: 1.6%
White: 86.4%	International: 0.7%
Unknown: 3.2%	

Fall 2005 part-time enrollment: 6

Men: 67%	Women: 33%
African-American: 16.7%	American Indian: 0.0%
Asian-American: 16.7%	Mexican-American: 0.0%
Puerto Rican: 0.0%	Other Hisp-Amer: 0.0%
White: 50.0%	International: 0.0%
Unknown: 16.7%	

Attrition rates for 2004-2005 full-time students

Percent of students discontinuing law school:

Men: 4%	Women: 4%
First-year students: 9%	Second-year students: 3%
Third-year students: 1%	

LIBRARY RESOURCES

The library holds 191,121 and receives 2,589 current subscriptions.
Total volumes: 363,074

Percentage of the titles in the online catalog: 99%
Total seats available for library users: 469

INFORMATION TECHNOLOGY

Number of wired network connections available to students: 45 total (in the law library, excluding computer labs: 5; in classrooms: 0; in computer labs: 35; elsewhere in the law school: 5)
Law school has a wireless network.
Approximate number of simultaneous users that can be accommodated on wireless network: 750
Students are not required to own a computer.

EMPLOYMENT AND SALARIES

Proportion of 2004 graduates employed at graduation: 59%
Employed 9 months later, as of February 15, 2005: 93%
Salaries in the private sector (law firms, business, industry): $39,000–$78,000 (25th-75th percentile)
Median salary in the private sector: $52,500
Percentage in the private sector who reported salary information: 49%
Median salary in public service (government, judicial clerkships, academic posts, non-profits): $37,000

Percentage of 2004 graduates in:

Law firms: 53%	Bus./industry (legal): 15%
Bus./industry (nonlegal): N/A	Government: 17%
Public interest: 3%	Judicial clerkship: 11%
Academia : 1%	Unknown: 0%

2004 graduates employed in-state: 85%
2004 graduates employed in foreign countries: 0%
Number of states where graduates are employed: 16
Percentage of 2004 graduates working in: New England: 0%, Middle Atlantic: 2%, East North Central: 6%, West North Central: 88%, South Atlantic: 4%, East South Central: 0%, West South Central: 0%, Mountain: 1%, Pacific: 0%, Unknown: 0%

BAR PASSAGE RATES

Based on 2004 graduates taking Summer 2004 or Winter 2005 exams. Most of the school's first-time test takers took the bar in Missouri.

89%
School's bar passage rate for first-time test takers

88%
Statewide bar passage rate for first-time test takers

University of Missouri–Kansas City

- 5100 Rockhill Road, Kansas City, MO, 64110
- http://www.law.umkc.edu
- Public
- Year founded: 1895
- 2005-2006 tuition: In-state: full-time: $12,803, part-time: $9,214; Out-of-state: full-time: $24,504
- Enrollment 2005-06 academic year: full-time: 499; part-time: 24
- U.S. News 2007 law specialty ranking: N/A

3.14-3.66 GPA, 25TH-75TH PERCENTILE

152-156 LSAT, 25TH-75TH PERCENTILE

38% ACCEPTANCE RATE

Tier 3 2007 U.S. NEWS LAW SCHOOL RANKING

ADMISSIONS

Admissions phone number: **(816) 235-1644**
Admissions email address: **law@umkc.edu**
Application website: **http://www1.law.umkc.edu/admissions/**
Application deadline for Fall 2007 admission: **rolling**

Admissions statistics:
Number of applicants for Fall 2005: **1,207**
Number of acceptances: **461**
Number enrolled: **172**
Acceptance rate: **38%**
GPA, 25th-75th percentile, entering class Fall 2005: **3.14-3.66**
LSAT, 25th-75th percentile, entering class Fall 2005: **152-156**

Part-time program:
Number of applicants for Fall 2005: **47**
Number of acceptances: **14**
Number enrolled: **6**
Acceptance rate: **30%**
GPA, 25th-75th percentile, entering class Fall 2005: **2.76-2.95**
LSAT, 25th-75th percentile, entering class Fall 2005: **152-156**

FINANCIAL AID

Financial aid phone number: **(816) 235-1154**
Financial aid application deadline: **N/A**
Tuition 2005-2006 academic year: In-state: full-time: **$12,803**, part-time: **$9,214**; Out-of-state: full-time: **$24,504**
Room and board: **$8,340**; books: **$3,760**; miscellaneous expenses: **$3,640**
Total of room/board/books/miscellaneous expenses: **$15,740**
University offers graduate student housing for which law students are eligible.

Financial aid profile
Percent of students that received grants for the 2004-2005 academic year: full-time: **31%**
Median grant amount: full-time: **$7,454**
The average law-school debt of those in the Class of 2005 who borrowed: **$65,387**. Proportion who borrowed: **88%**

ACADEMIC PROGRAMS

Calendar: **semester**
Joint degrees awarded: **J.D./M.B.A.; J.D./M.P.A.; J.D./LL.M. in Taxation; J.D./LL.M. in Urban Affairs**
Typical first-year section size: Full-time: **60**
Is there typically a "small section" of the first year class, other than Legal Writing, taught by full-time faculty?: Full-time: **no**; Part-time: **no**
Number of course titles, beyond the first year curriculum, offered last year: **94**
Percentages of upper division course sections, excluding seminars, with an enrollment of:

Under 25: **59%**	25 to 49: **22%**
50 to 74: **13%**	75 to 99: **6%**
100+: **0%**	

Areas of specialization: appellate advocacy, clinical training, dispute resolution, environmental law, intellectual property law, international law, tax law, trial advocacy

Fall 2005 faculty profile
Total teaching faculty: **89**. Full-time: **28%**; **72%** men, **28%** women, **12%** minorities. Part-time: **72%**; **77%** men, **23%** women, **5%** minorities
Student-to-faculty ratio: **20.4**

SPECIAL PROGRAMS *(as provided by law school)*:
The School offers students opportunities for summer study, including summer abroad programs in both China and Ireland. Bridging Theory and Practice: Through the Inns of UMKC Program, students receive mentoring and guidance from faculty, attorneys and judges. Students desiring greater experience in the practice of law may complete internships at the School and externships in local governmental agencies.

The School's in-house clinical programs include the Entrepreneurial Law & Practice Clinic. Under faculty supervision, students assist new entrepreneurs by providing start-up companies and their owners legal and business services they cannot otherwise afford. Students receive classroom instruction in client counseling, business planning and the drafting of business documents (articles of incorporation and organization, by-laws, partnership agreements, etc.).

Students may also be involved in other business-related matters ranging from regulatory, consumer, licensing, and taxation requirements; copyrights, trademark, and patent creation; and 501(C)(3) applications for nonprofits. Kansas City Tax Clinic is a project of the UMKC Graduate Tax Law Foundation, and is partially funded by the Internal Revenue Service. In the clinic, students counsel low income clients in federal, state and local tax controversies under the supervision and direction of tax faculty, the clinic director and volunteer attorneys.

Child and Family Services Clinic: Under the supervision and direction of clinic faculty and faculty directors, students assist the Division of Family Services in its role as custodian in providing legal support to children in foster care who are wards of the court and who require legal assistance to help them through the court system.

The Midwestern Innocence Project: Under faculty supervision, students provide pro bono investigative and legal assistance to prisoners in the Midwest with persuasive actual innocence claims, whether provable through scientific evidence or otherwise. In addition to reviewing requests from prisoners to determine which are promising cases, students investigate, research and prepare pleadings and other documents to obtain their release through judicial proceedings or executive clemency. Through MIPSO, our student-run branch of the project, students participate in work-days, working as volunteers on potential innocence cases.

Students desiring to develop a special competence in an area of the law may participate in one of the School's emphasis areas. Current areas of emphasis include Business and Entrepreneurial Law; Family Law; Litigation; and Urban, Land Use and Environmental Law. Each emphasis area includes required coursework, specialized instruction in research and ethical issues as well as a skills requirement.

STUDENT BODY

Fall 2005 full-time enrollment: 499

Men: 56%	Women: 44%
African-American: 3.0%	American Indian: 0.6%
Asian-American: 3.4%	Mexican-American: 0.6%
Puerto Rican: 0.0%	Other Hisp-Amer: 1.4%
White: 82.8%	International: 0.6%
Unknown: 7.6%	

Fall 2005 part-time enrollment: 24

Men: 50%	Women: 50%
African-American: 8.3%	American Indian: 4.2%
Asian-American: 25.0%	Mexican-American: 0.0%
Puerto Rican: 0.0%	Other Hisp-Amer: 0.0%
White: 54.2%	International: 0.0%
Unknown: 8.3%	

Attrition rates for 2004-2005 full-time students

Percent of students discontinuing law school:

Men: 7%	Women: 6%
First-year students: 11%	Second-year students: 7%
Third-year students: N/A	

LIBRARY RESOURCES

The library holds 71,809 and receives 1,812 current subscriptions.
Total volumes: 325,344
Percentage of the titles in the online catalog: 100%
Total seats available for library users: 369

INFORMATION TECHNOLOGY

Number of wired network connections available to students: 18 total (in the law library, excluding computer labs: 0; in classrooms: 0; in computer labs: 0; elsewhere in the law school: 18)
Law school has a wireless network.
Approximate number of simultaneous users that can be accommodated on wireless network: 2,530
Students are not required to own a computer.

EMPLOYMENT AND SALARIES

Proportion of 2004 graduates employed at graduation: N/A
Employed 9 months later, as of February 15, 2005: 88%
Salaries in the private sector (law firms, business, industry): $35,000–$60,000 (25th-75th percentile)
Median salary in the private sector: $40,000
Percentage in the private sector who reported salary information: 61%
Median salary in public service (government, judicial clerkships, academic posts, non-profits): $39,000

Percentage of 2004 graduates in:

Law firms: 55%	Bus./industry (legal): 7%
Bus./industry (nonlegal): 3%	Government: 10%
Public interest: 7%	Judicial clerkship: 12%
Academia : 1%	Unknown: 5%

2004 graduates employed in-state: 77%
2004 graduates employed in foreign countries: 1%
Number of states where graduates are employed: 13
Percentage of 2004 graduates working in: New England: N/A, Middle Atlantic: N/A, East North Central: 1%, West North Central: 91%, South Atlantic: 4%, East South Central: 1%, West South Central: N/A, Mountain: 1%, Pacific: 1%, Unknown: N/A

BAR PASSAGE RATES

Based on 2004 graduates taking Summer 2004 or Winter 2005 exams. Most of the school's first-time test takers took the bar in Missouri.

85%
School's bar passage rate for first-time test takers

88%
Statewide bar passage rate for first-time test takers

University of Montana

- 32 Campus Drive, Missoula, MT, 59812
- http://www.umt.edu/law
- Public
- **2005-2006 tuition:** In-state: full-time: $9,113, part-time: N/A; Out-of-state: full-time: $18,677
- **Enrollment 2005-06 academic year:** full-time: 237
- **U.S. News 2007 law specialty ranking:** N/A

3.17-3.70 GPA, 25TH-75TH PERCENTILE

151-157 LSAT, 25TH-75TH PERCENTILE

38% ACCEPTANCE RATE

Tier 3 2007 U.S. NEWS LAW SCHOOL RANKING

ADMISSIONS

Admissions phone number: **(406) 243-2698**
Admissions email address: **heidi.fanslow@umontana.edu**
Application website:
   http://www.umt.edu/law/applying.htm
Application deadline for Fall 2007 admission: **8/28**

Admissions statistics:
Number of applicants for Fall 2005: **458**
Number of acceptances: **172**
Number enrolled: **85**
Acceptance rate: **38%**
GPA, 25th-75th percentile, entering class Fall 2005:
   3.17-3.70
LSAT, 25th-75th percentile, entering class Fall 2005: **151-157**

FINANCIAL AID

Financial aid phone number: **(406) 243-5524**
Financial aid application deadline: **6/29**
Tuition 2005-2006 academic year: In-state: full-time:
   $9,113, part-time: **N/A**; Out-of-state: full-time: **$18,677**
Room and board: **$9,900**; books: **$1,050**; miscellaneous
   expenses: **$340**
Total of room/board/books/miscellaneous expenses:
   $11,290
University offers graduate student housing for which law
   students are eligible.

Financial aid profile
Percent of students that received grants for the 2004-2005
   academic year: full-time: **42%**
Median grant amount: full-time: **$1,400**
The average law-school debt of those in the Class of 2005
   who borrowed: **$50,325.** Proportion who borrowed: **85%**

ACADEMIC PROGRAMS

Calendar: **semester**
Joint degrees awarded: **J.D./M.B.A.; J.D./MPA;
   J.D./MEVST**
Typical first-year section size: Full-time: **43**

Is there typically a "small section" of the first year class,
   other than Legal Writing, taught by full-time faculty?:
   Full-time: **no**
Number of course titles, beyond the first year curriculum,
   offered last year: **N/A**
Percentages of upper division course sections, excluding
   seminars, with an enrollment of:
   Under 25: **N/A**   25 to 49: **N/A**
   50 to 74: **N/A**   75 to 99: **N/A**
   100+: **N/A**
Areas of specialization: appellate advocacy, clinical training,
   dispute resolution, environmental law, healthcare law,
   intellectual property law, international law, tax law, trial
   advocacy

Fall 2005 faculty profile
Total teaching faculty: **N/A**. Full-time: **N/A; N/A** men, **N/A**
   women, **N/A** minorities. Part-time: **N/A; N/A** men, **N/A**
   women, **N/A** minorities
Student-to-faculty ratio: **18.2**

SPECIAL PROGRAMS (as provided by law school):
The University of Montana is one of a small number of law
schools where all students participate in a clinic before graduating. This requirement reinforces our goal of preparing graduates for the practice of law. All third-year students practice in a
public interest setting, either in an in-house clinic at the law
school or under the supervision of an attorney in the community. Students apply the skills and knowledge from their first
two years of law school to a practice setting where they will be
challenged to identify and resolve ethical and professionalism
issues like those they will face in practice.
   The Mission of the University of Montana School of Law's
required clinical program is to provide for third-year students
faculty-supervised, experience-based learning by representing
clients in clinics serving the public interest. The clinical program engages students in applying, enhancing, and integrating
substantive and skills components of legal education, improves
their ability to identify and resolve ethical and professionalism
issues, and assesses student performance and the law school's
competency-based curriculum. Students can select from the fol-

lowing sixteen clinical offerings: ASUM legal services, the child support enforcement division, the criminal defense clinic, the disability law clinic, the federal defenders of Montana, the Indian law clinic, the judicial clinic, the land use clinic, the mediation clinic, the Missoula city attorney's office, the Missoula county attorney's office, the Montana legal services association, the natural resource law clinic, the office of the USDA general counsel, the Rocky Mountain Elk Foundation, the U.S. Attorney's Office, and the University of Montana Legal Counsel's Office.

The University of Montana believes that a legal education must rest on a solid foundation. Even if a student is dedicated to a career in environmental law, he or she needs to understand the fundamentals of contracts, torts and tax law. After those fundamentals, however, there are ample opportunities for students to focus their studies.

We offer certificate programs in environmental and natural resource law and alternative dispute resolution. The main campus offers a certificate program in natural resources conflict resolution.

Concentrations in environmental and natural resource law, Indian law, trial advocacy, and dispute resolution are offered.

The University of Montana School of Law also offers three joint degree programs: a J.D./M.B.A., a J.D./M.P.A., and a J.D./master's of environmental studies.

STUDENT BODY

Fall 2005 full-time enrollment: 237

Men: 49%	Women: 51%
African-American: 0.4%	American Indian: 5.5%
Asian-American: 1.7%	Mexican-American: 0.0%
Puerto Rican: 0.4%	Other Hisp-Amer: 0.0%
White: 91.6%	International: 0.0%
Unknown: 0.4%	

Attrition rates for 2004-2005 full-time students
Percent of students discontinuing law school:

Men: N/A	Women: N/A
First-year students: N/A	Second-year students: N/A
Third-year students: N/A	

LIBRARY RESOURCES

The library holds 22,531 and receives 1,250 current subscriptions.
Total volumes: 123,661
Percentage of the titles in the online catalog: 97%
Total seats available for library users: 364

INFORMATION TECHNOLOGY

Number of wired network connections available to students: 133 total (in the law library, excluding computer labs: 96; in classrooms: 20; in computer labs: 5; elsewhere in the law school: 12)
Law school has a wireless network.
Approximate number of simultaneous users that can be accommodated on wireless network: 450
Students are not required to own a computer.

EMPLOYMENT AND SALARIES

Proportion of 2004 graduates employed at graduation: N/A
Employed 9 months later, as of February 15, 2005: 89%
Salaries in the private sector (law firms, business, industry): $36,500–$45,000 (25th-75th percentile)
Median salary in the private sector: $40,000
Percentage in the private sector who reported salary information: 72%
Median salary in public service (government, judicial clerkships, academic posts, non-profits): $39,000

Percentage of 2004 graduates in:

Law firms: 48%	Bus./industry (legal): 5%
Bus./industry (nonlegal): 5%	Government: 12%
Public interest: 2%	Judicial clerkship: 28%
Academia : 0%	Unknown: 0%

2004 graduates employed in-state: 75%
2004 graduates employed in foreign countries: 1%
Number of states where graduates are employed: 12
Percentage of 2004 graduates working in: New England: 0%, Middle Atlantic: 1%, East North Central: 0%, West North Central: 2%, South Atlantic: 0%, East South Central: 0%, West South Central: 0%, Mountain: 87%, Pacific: 9%, Unknown: 0%

BAR PASSAGE RATES

Based on 2004 graduates taking Summer 2004 or Winter 2005 exams. Most of the school's first-time test takers took the bar in Montana.

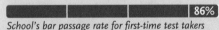

86%

School's bar passage rate for first-time test takers

83%

Statewide bar passage rate for first-time test takers

University of Nebraska–Lincoln

- PO Box 830902, Lincoln, NE, 68583-0902
- http://law.unl.edu
- Public
- Year founded: 1891
- 2005-2006 tuition: In-state: full-time: $8,783, part-time: N/A; Out-of-state: full-time: $20,449
- Enrollment 2005-06 academic year: full-time: 389; part-time: 5
- U.S. News 2007 law specialty ranking: N/A

3.30-3.83 GPA, 25TH-75TH PERCENTILE

153-159 LSAT, 25TH-75TH PERCENTILE

41% ACCEPTANCE RATE

70 2007 U.S. NEWS LAW SCHOOL RANKING

ADMISSIONS

Admissions phone number: **(402) 472-2161**
Admissions email address: **lawadm@unl.edu**
Application website: **http://www.unl.edu/lawcoll/application.html**
Application deadline for Fall 2007 admission: **3/01**

Admissions statistics:

Number of applicants for Fall 2005: **865**
Number of acceptances: **352**
Number enrolled: **136**
Acceptance rate: **41%**
GPA, 25th-75th percentile, entering class Fall 2005: **3.30-3.83**
LSAT, 25th-75th percentile, entering class Fall 2005: **153-159**

FINANCIAL AID

Financial aid phone number: **(402) 472-2161**
Financial aid application deadline: **5/01**
Tuition 2005-2006 academic year: In-state: full-time: **$8,783**, part-time: **N/A**; Out-of-state: full-time: **$20,449**
Room and board: **$6,660**; books: **$1,230**; miscellaneous expenses: **$2,900**
Total of room/board/books/miscellaneous expenses: **$10,790**
University offers graduate student housing for which law students are eligible.

Financial aid profile

Percent of students that received grants for the 2004-2005 academic year: full-time: **47%**
Median grant amount: full-time: **$6,500**
The average law-school debt of those in the Class of 2005 who borrowed: **$40,642**. Proportion who borrowed: **80%**

ACADEMIC PROGRAMS

Calendar: **semester**
Joint degrees awarded: **J.D./M.A. Economics; J.D./M.P.A.; J.D./M.A.Psychology; J.D./M.B.A.; J.D./Ph.D. Education; J.D./Ph.D. Psychology; J.D./M.A. Political Science; J.D./M.C.R.P.; J.D./M.A. International Affairs**

Typical first-year section size: Full-time: **70**
Is there typically a "small section" of the first year class, other than Legal Writing, taught by full-time faculty?: Full-time: **yes**
Number of course titles, beyond the first year curriculum, offered last year: **64**
Percentages of upper division course sections, excluding seminars, with an enrollment of:
Under 25: **45%** 25 to 49: **33%**
50 to 74: **19%** 75 to 99: **3%**
100+: **N/A**
Areas of specialization: appellate advocacy, clinical training, dispute resolution, environmental law, healthcare law, intellectual property law, international law, tax law, trial advocacy

Fall 2005 faculty profile

Total teaching faculty: **63**. Full-time: **41%; 69%** men, **31%** women, **8%** minorities. Part-time: **59%; 70%** men, **30%** women, **0%** minorities
Student-to-faculty ratio: **13.7**

SPECIAL PROGRAMS *(as provided by law school):*

The Law College has a number of very strong interdisciplinary programs, including perhaps the country's foremost program in law and psychology. These programs permit students to obtain a law degree and a graduate degree (usually a master's or a Ph.D.) in less time than would be required to obtain them independently. The college has well-established tracks in litigation and business transactions. In addition, it permits students to develop their own specialized track in virtually any substantive area, in consultation with individual faculty members.

The college offers a wide variety of practice-oriented experiences, including traditional civil and criminal clinics. The college also has active externship and pro bono programs. The college participates in summer programs at Cambridge University in England and the University of Limerick in Ireland.

STUDENT BODY

Fall 2005 full-time enrollment: 389
Men: 54%   Women: 46%
African-American: 3.3%   American Indian: 1.0%
Asian-American: 2.3%   Mexican-American: 2.8%
Puerto Rican: 0.0%   Other Hisp-Amer: 0.0%
White: 89.7%   International: 0.8%
Unknown: 0.0%

Fall 2005 part-time enrollment: 5
Men: 60%   Women: 40%
African-American: 20.0%   American Indian: 0.0%
Asian-American: 40.0%   Mexican-American: 0.0%
Puerto Rican: 0.0%   Other Hisp-Amer: 0.0%
White: 20.0%   International: 20.0%
Unknown: 0.0%

Attrition rates for 2004-2005 full-time students
Percent of students discontinuing law school:
Men: 1%   Women: 5%
First-year students: 8%   Second-year students: N/A
Third-year students: N/A

LIBRARY RESOURCES

The library holds 58,607 and receives 2,571 current
    subscriptions.
Total volumes: 401,745
Percentage of the titles in the online catalog: 68%
Total seats available for library users: 372

INFORMATION TECHNOLOGY

Number of wired network connections available to stu-
    dents: 24 total (in the law library, excluding computer
    labs: 24; in classrooms: 0; in computer labs: 0; else-
    where in the law school: 0)
Law school has a wireless network.
Approximate number of simultaneous users that can be
    accommodated on wireless network: 255
Students are not required to own a computer.

EMPLOYMENT AND SALARIES

Proportion of 2004 graduates employed at graduation: 75%
Employed 9 months later, as of February 15, 2005: 92%
Salaries in the private sector (law firms, business, indus-
    try): $52,000–$123,500 (25th-75th percentile)
Median salary in the private sector: $77,000
Percentage in the private sector who reported salary
    information: 68%
Median salary in public service (government, judicial clerk-
    ships, academic posts, non-profits): $43,000

Percentage of 2004 graduates in:
Law firms: 59%   Bus./industry (legal): 16%
Bus./industry (nonlegal): N/A Government: 16%
Public interest: 3%   Judicial clerkship: 6%
Academia : 2%   Unknown: 0%

2004 graduates employed in-state: 64%
2004 graduates employed in foreign countries: 0%
Number of states where graduates are employed: 20
Percentage of 2004 graduates working in: New England:
    0%, Middle Atlantic: 1%, East North Central: 2%, West
    North Central: 88%, South Atlantic: 2%, East South
    Central: 0%, West South Central: 1%, Mountain: 2%,
    Pacific: 2%, Unknown: 3%

BAR PASSAGE RATES

Based on 2004 graduates taking Summer 2004 or
Winter 2005 exams. Most of the school's first-time test
takers took the bar in Nebraska.

| 90% |
School's bar passage rate for first-time test takers

| 88% |
Statewide bar passage rate for first-time test takers

Univ. of Nevada–Las Vegas (Boyd)

■ 4505 Maryland Parkway, PO Box 451003, Las Vegas, NV, 89154-1003
■ http://www.law.unlv.edu/
■ Public
■ Year founded: 1997
■ 2005-2006 tuition: In-state: full-time: $9,552, part-time: $6,310; Out-of-state: full-time: $18,452
■ Enrollment 2005-06 academic year: full-time: 322; part-time: 157
■ U.S. News 2007 law specialty ranking: clinical training: 27, dispute resolution: 13

3.55-3.67 GPA, 25TH-75TH PERCENTILE

155-160 LSAT, 25TH-75TH PERCENTILE

12% ACCEPTANCE RATE

Tier 3 2007 U.S. NEWS LAW SCHOOL RANKING

ADMISSIONS

Admissions phone number: (702) 895-2440
Admissions email address: request@law.unlv.edu
Application website: http://www.law.unlv.edu/admissions_application.html
Application deadline for Fall 2007 admission: 3/15

Admissions statistics:
Number of applicants for Fall 2005: 2,134
Number of acceptances: 258
Number enrolled: 106
Acceptance rate: 12%
GPA, 25th-75th percentile, entering class Fall 2005: 3.55-3.67
LSAT, 25th-75th percentile, entering class Fall 2005: 155-160

Part-time program:
Number of applicants for Fall 2005: 274
Number of acceptances: 59
Number enrolled: 45
Acceptance rate: 22%
GPA, 25th-75th percentile, entering class Fall 2005: 3.01-3.55
LSAT, 25th-75th percentile, entering class Fall 2005: 152-157

FINANCIAL AID

Financial aid phone number: (702) 895-4112
Financial aid application deadline: 2/01
Tuition 2005-2006 academic year: In-state: full-time: $9,552, part-time: $6,310; Out-of-state: full-time: $18,452
Room and board: $11,680; books: $850; miscellaneous expenses: $230
Total of room/board/books/miscellaneous expenses: $12,760
University does not offer graduate student housing for which law students are eligible.

Financial aid profile
Percent of students that received grants for the 2004-2005 academic year: full-time: 46%; part-time 11%

Median grant amount: full-time: $7,245; part-time: $2,580
The average law-school debt of those in the Class of 2005 who borrowed: $48,810. Proportion who borrowed: 87%

ACADEMIC PROGRAMS

Calendar: semester
Joint degrees awarded: J.D./M.B.A. program; J.D./M.S.W. program
Typical first-year section size: Full-time: 63; Part-time: 40
Is there typically a "small section" of the first year class, other than Legal Writing, taught by full-time faculty?: Full-time: no; Part-time: no
Number of course titles, beyond the first year curriculum, offered last year: 71
Percentages of upper division course sections, excluding seminars, with an enrollment of:

Under 25: 74%	25 to 49: 20%
50 to 74: 4%	75 to 99: 2%
100+: 0%	

Areas of specialization: appellate advocacy, clinical training, dispute resolution, environmental law, healthcare law, intellectual property law, international law, tax law, trial advocacy

Fall 2005 faculty profile
Total teaching faculty: 49. Full-time: 53%; 58% men, 42% women, 27% minorities. Part-time: 47%; 70% men, 30% women, 4% minorities
Student-to-faculty ratio: 15.0

SPECIAL PROGRAMS *(as provided by law school):*

The Thomas and Mack Legal Clinic houses the school's law firm and offers students an integrated academic and practice-based educational experience that teaches students to be reflective practitioners and community-oriented professionals. The clinical program provides service to communities in need of legal assistance and seeks to improve the quality of, and access to, legal systems that affect communities in need in Nevada.

Clinics focus on four areas: child welfare, juvenile justice, capital defense, and immigration. Students in the clinical program may represent clients in the Juvenile Court of Clark

County and other state and federal courts. Clinic students are expected to take the lead in a real case and are responsible for developing the attorney-client relationship and litigation strategy, and for conducting fact investigation, legal research, and trial work. Social work and special education students work with the law students to serve client's needs. Students are supervised by clinical professors devoted full time to clinical teaching. Enrollment is limited to eight students in each clinic.

Externships: Bridging the gap between law practice and law school education is an important goal of the William S. Boyd School of Law. A year-round externship program provides opportunities for approximately 100 students each year with the federal and state judiciary; government and public-service agencies; and Nevada and U.S. legislatures.

Saltman Center for Conflict Resolution: The center, established in 2003, will sponsor lectures, symposia, and other opportunities for exploring both the nature of conflict and methods of dispute resolution. Students may benefit from the insights of nationally and internationally recognized scholars in the field.

Academic Success Program: The program's objective is to provide a comprehensive network of presentations, activities, tutorials, and workshops designed to stimulate learning and amplify the classroom experience. The Academic Success Program supplements the required curriculum and a host of opportunities to enhance learning skills.

The Center for Academic Success and Enrichment: The center, known as CASE, is a component of the Academic Success Program. CASE hosts workshops and presentations to assist students with class preparation, outlining, and exam-taking skills. Tutoring is available in individual subject areas.

STUDENT BODY

Fall 2005 full-time enrollment: 322

Men: 50%	Women: 50%
African-American: 3.1%	American Indian: 0.6%
Asian-American: 12.7%	Mexican-American: 4.7%
Puerto Rican: 0.0%	Other Hisp-Amer: 1.6%
White: 70.5%	International: 0.0%
Unknown: 6.8%	

Fall 2005 part-time enrollment: 157

Men: 54%	Women: 46%
African-American: 5.1%	American Indian: 0.6%
Asian-American: 11.5%	Mexican-American: 7.6%
Puerto Rican: 0.0%	Other Hisp-Amer: 1.3%
White: 65.6%	International: 0.0%
Unknown: 8.3%	

Attrition rates for 2004-2005 full-time students
Percent of students discontinuing law school:

Men: 6%	Women: 5%
First-year students: 12%	Second-year students: 5%
Third-year students: N/A	

LIBRARY RESOURCES
The library holds 186,071 and receives 4,013 current subscriptions.
Total volumes: 284,593
Percentage of the titles in the online catalog: 100%
Total seats available for library users: 327

INFORMATION TECHNOLOGY
Number of wired network connections available to students: 1,004 total (in the law library, excluding computer labs: 475; in classrooms: 310; in computer labs: 50; elsewhere in the law school: 169)
Law school has a wireless network.
Approximate number of simultaneous users that can be accommodated on wireless network: 400
Students are not required to own a computer.

EMPLOYMENT AND SALARIES
Proportion of 2004 graduates employed at graduation: 60%
Employed 9 months later, as of February 15, 2005: 83%
Salaries in the private sector (law firms, business, industry): $50,000–$78,000 (25th-75th percentile)
Median salary in the private sector: $65,000
Percentage in the private sector who reported salary information: 81%
Median salary in public service (government, judicial clerkships, academic posts, non-profits): $48,000

Percentage of 2004 graduates in:

Law firms: 62%	Bus./industry (legal): 2%
Bus./industry (nonlegal): 9%	Government: 6%
Public interest: 1%	Judicial clerkship: 16%
Academia : 2%	Unknown: 1%

2004 graduates employed in-state: 90%
2004 graduates employed in foreign countries: 0%
Number of states where graduates are employed: 6
Percentage of 2004 graduates working in: New England: 0%, Middle Atlantic: 0%, East North Central: 0%, West North Central: 1%, South Atlantic: 3%, East South Central: 0%, West South Central: 1%, Mountain: 94%, Pacific: 1%, Unknown: 0%

BAR PASSAGE RATES
Based on 2004 graduates taking Summer 2004 or Winter 2005 exams. Most of the school's first-time test takers took the bar in Nevada.

65%
School's bar passage rate for first-time test takers

73%
Statewide bar passage rate for first-time test takers

University of New Mexico

- 1117 Stanford Drive NE, Albuquerque, NM, 87131-1431
- http://lawschool.unm.edu
- Public
- Year founded: 1948
- 2005-2006 tuition: In-state: full-time: $8,816, part-time: N/A; Out-of-state: full-time: $21,394
- Enrollment 2005-06 academic year: full-time: 357
- U.S. News 2007 law specialty ranking: clinical training: 7

3.07-3.65 GPA, 25TH-75TH PERCENTILE

150-159 LSAT, 25TH-75TH PERCENTILE

21% ACCEPTANCE RATE

77 2007 U.S. NEWS LAW SCHOOL RANKING

ADMISSIONS

Admissions phone number: **(505) 277-0572**
Admissions email address: **admissions@law.unm.edu**
Application website: **http://lawschool.unm.edu**
Application deadline for Fall 2007 admission: **2/15**

Admissions statistics:

Number of applicants for Fall 2005: **1,161**
Number of acceptances: **242**
Number enrolled: **119**
Acceptance rate: **21%**
GPA, 25th-75th percentile, entering class Fall 2005: **3.07-3.65**
LSAT, 25th-75th percentile, entering class Fall 2005: **150-159**

FINANCIAL AID

Financial aid phone number: **(505) 277-0572**
Financial aid application deadline: **3/01**
Tuition 2005-2006 academic year: In-state: full-time: **$8,816**, part-time: **N/A**; Out-of-state: full-time: **$21,394**
Room and board: **$7,252**; books: **$960**; miscellaneous expenses: **$4,062**
Total of room/board/books/miscellaneous expenses: **$12,274**
University does not offer graduate student housing for which law students are eligible.

Financial aid profile

Percent of students that received grants for the 2004-2005 academic year: full-time: **20%**
Median grant amount: full-time: **$7,568**
The average law-school debt of those in the Class of 2005 who borrowed: **$33,739**. Proportion who borrowed: **97%**

ACADEMIC PROGRAMS

Calendar: **semester**
Joint degrees awarded: **J.D./M.B.A.; J.D./MPA; J.D./MLAS; J.D./Ph.D; J.D./M Engineering**
Typical first-year section size: Full-time: **59**

Is there typically a "small section" of the first year class, other than Legal Writing, taught by full-time faculty?: Full-time: **yes**
Number of course titles, beyond the first year curriculum, offered last year: **81**
Percentages of upper division course sections, excluding seminars, with an enrollment of:

Under 25: **50%**	25 to 49: **29%**
50 to 74: **21%**	75 to 99: **0%**
100+: **0%**	

Areas of specialization: appellate advocacy, clinical training, dispute resolution, environmental law, healthcare law, intellectual property law, international law, tax law, trial advocacy

Fall 2005 faculty profile

Total teaching faculty: **57**. Full-time: **58%**; **55%** men, **45%** women, **30%** minorities. Part-time: **42%**; **71%** men, **29%** women, **21%** minorities
Student-to-faculty ratio: **11.4**

SPECIAL PROGRAMS *(as provided by law school):*

The University of New Mexico School of Law curriculum combines traditional and innovative approaches to the study of law. The curriculum is designed to expose students to the range of interests addressed by the legal system and to engage them in exploration of the historical, theoretical, and practical aspects of law. The curriculum stands out for its clinical, Indian, international, and natural resources law programs.

Economic Development Program: Our newest program combines a curriculum of business and commercial courses, with several aimed at economic development issues, as well as a Community Economic Development Clinic. In the Clinic, the students will work with start-up companies and nonprofits, practicing both transactional and litigation skills in the business context.

Clinical Law Program: The program is nationally recognized as one of the best in the United States. It is one of New Mexico's largest law firms. The law school has offered clinical education as a basic part of its curriculum since 1970, requiring every graduate to complete a semester in clinic.

Indian Law: UNM Law School has led the way in educating lawyers among the American Indian and Alaska Native populations. UNM has one of the most comprehensive Indian law programs in the country. The Indian law program offers the Indian law certificate, Southwest Indian Law Clinic, Tribal Law Journal, Native American Law Students Association, and Native American Economic Development Scholarship.

Guanajuato Summer Law Institute: The law schools of the University of New Mexico, Universidad de Guanajuato, Southwestern University, and Texas Tech University, in cooperation with UNM's Latin American and Iberian Institute, offer four to six weeks of summer law study in Guanajuato, Mexico. The Guanajuato Summer Law Institute features an introduction to Mexican law and international law subjects related to Latin America.

Natural Resources: The law school is widely known for its faculty strength in the areas of natural resources and environmental law. Students who wish to undertake in-depth study of current resources and environmental problems are afforded valuable opportunities through the Natural Resources Journal and the natural resources certificate.

STUDENT BODY

Fall 2005 full-time enrollment: 357

Men: 50%	Women: 50%
African-American: 3.6%	American Indian: 10.6%
Asian-American: 2.2%	Mexican-American: 24.4%
Puerto Rican: 0.0%	Other Hisp-Amer: 0.0%
White: 49.6%	International: 0.0%
Unknown: 9.5%	

Attrition rates for 2004-2005 full-time students

Percent of students discontinuing law school:

Men: 4%	Women: 2%
First-year students: 2%	Second-year students: 5%
Third-year students: 2%	

LIBRARY RESOURCES

The library holds 127,735 and receives 3,239 current subscriptions.
Total volumes: 425,093
Percentage of the titles in the online catalog: 97%
Total seats available for library users: 601

INFORMATION TECHNOLOGY

Number of wired network connections available to students: 323 total (in the law library, excluding computer labs: 143; in classrooms: 156; in computer labs: 12; elsewhere in the law school: 12)

Law school has a wireless network.
Approximate number of simultaneous users that can be accommodated on wireless network: 300
Students are not required to own a computer.

EMPLOYMENT AND SALARIES

Proportion of 2004 graduates employed at graduation: 73%
Employed 9 months later, as of February 15, 2005: 94%
Salaries in the private sector (law firms, business, industry): $40,000–$70,000 (25th-75th percentile)
Median salary in the private sector: $50,000
Percentage in the private sector who reported salary information: 67%
Median salary in public service (government, judicial clerkships, academic posts, non-profits): $37,877

Percentage of 2004 graduates in:

Law firms: 37%	Bus./industry (legal): 6%
Bus./industry (nonlegal): 0%	Government: 24%
Public interest: 20%	Judicial clerkship: 12%
Academia : 0%	Unknown: 1%

2004 graduates employed in-state: 84%
2004 graduates employed in foreign countries: 0%
Number of states where graduates are employed: 11
Percentage of 2004 graduates working in: New England: 0%, Middle Atlantic: 1%, East North Central: 0%, West North Central: 0%, South Atlantic: 4%, East South Central: 0%, West South Central: 4%, Mountain: 89%, Pacific: 3%, Unknown: 0%

BAR PASSAGE RATES

Based on 2004 graduates taking Summer 2004 or Winter 2005 exams. Most of the school's first-time test takers took the bar in New Mexico.

81%
School's bar passage rate for first-time test takers

82%
Statewide bar passage rate for first-time test takers

iv. of North Carolina—Chapel Hill

■ Van Hecke-Wettach Hall, CB No. 3380, Chapel Hill, NC, 27599-3380
■ http://www.law.unc.edu
■ Public
■ Year founded: 1843
■ 2005-2006 tuition: In-state: full-time: $11,981, part-time: N/A;
   Out-of-state: full-time: $24,199
■ Enrollment 2005-06 academic year: full-time: 715
■ U.S. News 2007 law specialty ranking: N/A

3.47-3.84 GPA, 25TH-75TH PERCENTILE

158-164 LSAT, 25TH-75TH PERCENTILE

15% ACCEPTANCE RATE

27 2007 U.S. NEWS LAW SCHOOL RANKING

ADMISSIONS

Admissions phone number: **(919) 962-5109**
Admissions email address: **law_admission@unc.edu**
Application website: **http://www.law.unc.edu/PDFs/lawap-plicationfinal.pdf**
Application deadline for Fall 2007 admission: **2/01**

Admissions statistics:
Number of applicants for Fall 2005: **3,648**
Number of acceptances: **557**
Number enrolled: **231**
Acceptance rate: **15%**
GPA, 25th-75th percentile, entering class Fall 2005:
   3.47-3.84
LSAT, 25th-75th percentile, entering class Fall 2005:
   158-164

FINANCIAL AID

Financial aid phone number: **(919) 962-8396**
Financial aid application deadline: **3/01**
Tuition 2005-2006 academic year: In-state: full-time:
   $11,981, part-time: **N/A**; Out-of-state: full-time: **$24,199**
Room and board: **$11,128**; books: **$1,000**; miscellaneous
   expenses: **$3,904**
Total of room/board/books/miscellaneous expenses:
   $16,032
University offers graduate student housing for which law
   students are eligible.

Financial aid profile
Percent of students that received grants for the 2004-2005
   academic year: full-time: **72%**
Median grant amount: full-time: **$2,250**
The average law-school debt of those in the Class of 2005
   who borrowed: **$52,566**. Proportion who borrowed: **79%**

ACADEMIC PROGRAMS

Calendar: **semester**
Joint degrees awarded: **J.D./M.B.A.; J.D./MPA; J.D./MPP;
   J.D./MPH; J.D./MRP; J.D./MSW**
Typical first-year section size: Full-time: **77**

Is there typically a "small section" of the first year class,
   other than Legal Writing, taught by full-time faculty?:
   Full-time: **yes**
Number of course titles, beyond the first year curriculum,
   offered last year: **106**
Percentages of upper division course sections, excluding
   seminars, with an enrollment of:
   Under 25: **49%**   25 to 49: **27%**
   50 to 74: **12%**   75 to 99: **8%**
   100+: **4%**
Areas of specialization: appellate advocacy, clinical training,
   dispute resolution, environmental law, healthcare law,
   intellectual property law, international law, tax law, trial
   advocacy

Fall 2005 faculty profile
Total teaching faculty: **100**. Full-time: **35%**; **71%** men, **29%**
   women, **20%** minorities. Part-time: **65%**; **66%** men,
   34% women, **17%** minorities
Student-to-faculty ratio: **16.9**

SPECIAL PROGRAMS (as provided by law school):

Carolina Law offers nationally recognized programs in banking
and financial services, civil rights and entrepreneurial law. The
Center for Banking and Finance supports state and national
financial institutions in the evolution of the financial services
industry. The Center studies legal policy issues related to banking
and finance, advances the teaching of banking and finance law
and policy, and sponsors conferences for professionals. The
Center for Civil Rights is committed to the advancement of civil
rights and social justice, especially in the American South. It fosters empirical and analytical research, sponsors student inquiry
and activities, and convenes faculty, visiting scholars, policy advocates, and practicing attorneys to confront legal and social issues
of concern to racial and ethnic minorities, to the poor, and to
other potential beneficiaries of civil rights advances. The Council
for Entrepreneurial Law supports the regional and national entrepreneurial economy. The Council's goals are to facilitate students'
understanding and appreciation of entrepreneurial law and to
support the bar by developing continuing legal education programs in entrepreneurial law. Carolina Law offers four clinics:

civil, criminal, community development, and policy. The clinical programs give students an opportunity to develop competency in practical skills. The law school offers students externship placements in legal positions that have been selected by the faculty for their educational value, the high quality of the host organization's legal work, and the availability of a skilled supervisor. Most placements are in state government offices, nonprofit agencies or judicial chambers. Students interested in international law can participate in foreign study programs at Universite Jean Moulin—Lyon III, France; Katholieke Universiteit Nijmegen, the Netherlands, Universidad Iberoamericana, Mexico; University of Manchester, England; University of Glasgow, Scotland; and the Augsburg University, Germany. The School of Law offers a foreign summer program in Sydney, Australia, in cooperation with The University of Sydney Faculty of Law. The law school participates in a campus-wide initiative leading to the nonprofit leadership certificate. The program was created to enhance the leadership capability of executives and board members of human services, education, arts and other nonprofit organizations throughout North Carolina.

STUDENT BODY

Fall 2005 full-time enrollment: 715

Men: 52%	Women: 48%
African-American: 10.5%	American Indian: 1.7%
Asian-American: 5.2%	Mexican-American: 0.0%
Puerto Rican: 0.0%	Other Hisp-Amer: 4.1%
White: 76.4%	International: 0.0%
Unknown: 2.2%	

Attrition rates for 2004-2005 full-time students
Percent of students discontinuing law school:

Men: 1%	Women: 1%
First-year students: 2%	Second-year students: 0%
Third-year students: 0%	

LIBRARY RESOURCES

The library holds 106,646 and receives 6,725 current subscriptions.
Total volumes: 519,776
Percentage of the titles in the online catalog: 99%
Total seats available for library users: 481

INFORMATION TECHNOLOGY

Number of wired network connections available to students: 564 total (in the law library, excluding computer labs: 175; in classrooms: 165; in computer labs: 0; elsewhere in the law school: 224)

Law school has a wireless network.
Approximate number of simultaneous users that can be accommodated on wireless network: 700
Students are not required to own a computer.

EMPLOYMENT AND SALARIES

Proportion of 2004 graduates employed at graduation: 72%
Employed 9 months later, as of February 15, 2005: 90%
Salaries in the private sector (law firms, business, industry): $70,000–$115,000 (25th-75th percentile)
Median salary in the private sector: $100,000
Percentage in the private sector who reported salary information: 72%
Median salary in public service (government, judicial clerkships, academic posts, non-profits): $44,500

Percentage of 2004 graduates in:

Law firms: 74%	Bus./industry (legal): 4%
Bus./industry (nonlegal): 0%	Government: 9%
Public interest: 3%	Judicial clerkship: 8%
Academia : 2%	Unknown: 0%

2004 graduates employed in-state: 54%
2004 graduates employed in foreign countries: 0%
Number of states where graduates are employed: 24
Percentage of 2004 graduates working in: New England: 4%, Middle Atlantic: 10%, East North Central: 4%, West North Central: 1%, South Atlantic: 75%, East South Central: 2%, West South Central: 1%, Mountain: 4%, Pacific: 1%, Unknown: 1%

BAR PASSAGE RATES

Based on 2004 graduates taking Summer 2004 or Winter 2005 exams. Most of the school's first-time test takers took the bar in North Carolina.

| 85% |

School's bar passage rate for first-time test takers

| 75% |

Statewide bar passage rate for first-time test takers

University of North Dakota

■ PO Box 9003, Grand Forks, ND, 58202
■ http://www.law.und.nodak.edu
■ Public
■ Year founded: 1899
■ 2005-2006 tuition: In-state: full-time: $7,602, part-time: N/A;
  Out-of-state: full-time: $16,220
■ Enrollment 2005-06 academic year: full-time: 224
■ U.S. News 2007 law specialty ranking: N/A

3.25-3.74 GPA, 25ᵀᴴ-75ᵀᴴ PERCENTILE

147-154 LSAT, 25ᵀᴴ-75ᵀᴴ PERCENTILE

45% ACCEPTANCE RATE

Tier 3 2007 U.S. NEWS LAW SCHOOL RANKING

ADMISSIONS

Admissions phone number: **(701) 777-2104**
Admissions email address: **hoffman@law.und.edu**
Application website: **http://www.law.und.nodak.edu/pros-tudents/index.php**
Application deadline for Fall 2007 admission: **6/01**

Admissions statistics:

Number of applicants for Fall 2005: **430**
Number of acceptances: **194**
Number enrolled: **90**
Acceptance rate: **45%**
GPA, 25th-75th percentile, entering class Fall 2005:
  3.25-3.74
LSAT, 25th-75th percentile, entering class Fall 2005:
  147-154

FINANCIAL AID

Financial aid phone number: **(701) 777-6265**
Financial aid application deadline: **4/01**
Tuition 2005-2006 academic year: In-state: full-time:
  $7,602, part-time: **N/A**; Out-of-state: full-time: **$16,220**
Room and board: **$8,200**; books: **$900**; miscellaneous
  expenses: **$4,500**
Total of room/board/books/miscellaneous expenses:
  $13,600
University offers graduate student housing for which law
  students are eligible.

Financial aid profile

Percent of students that received grants for the 2004-2005
  academic year: full-time: **48%**
Median grant amount: full-time: **$1,025**
The average law-school debt of those in the Class of 2005
  who borrowed: **$49,510**. Proportion who borrowed: **94%**

ACADEMIC PROGRAMS

Calendar: **semester**
Joint degrees awarded: **J.D./M.P.A.**
Typical first-year section size: Full-time: **76**

Is there typically a "small section" of the first year class,
  other than Legal Writing, taught by full-time faculty?:
  Full-time: **no**
Number of course titles, beyond the first year curriculum,
  offered last year: **47**
Percentages of upper division course sections, excluding
  seminars, with an enrollment of:
  Under 25: **63%**   25 to 49: **29%**
  50 to 74: **8%**   75 to 99: **N/A**
  100+: **N/A**
Areas of specialization: appellate advocacy, clinical training,
  dispute resolution, environmental law, intellectual property law, international law, tax law, trial advocacy

Fall 2005 faculty profile

Total teaching faculty: **31**. Full-time: **42%**; **46%** men, **54%**
  women, **15%** minorities. Part-time: **58%**; **67%** men, **33%**
  women, **0%** minorities
Student-to-faculty ratio: **19.0**

SPECIAL PROGRAMS *(as provided by law school)*:

Legal Education Clinic: The mission of the University of
North Dakota School of Law's clinical education program is
to further the School of Law's overall pedagogical mission by
educating and preparing highly competent, ethical, and professional future lawyers and instilling in them a commitment to justice within our legal system. The clinical
education program offers students the opportunity to represent clients on actual civil cases within the professional law
firm environment of our in-house clinic; provides clinic students with high-quality education through classes, case-
rounds sessions, and hands-on training, while ensuring that
clinic clients receive high-quality legal representation; and
encourages its faculty, students, and staff to maintain the
highest level of professionalism. In short, the central purpose of our clinical program is to help students make the
transition from doing what students do to doing what
lawyers do, and to make this transition in a thoughtful, pur-
poseful, and reflective manner.
  Externships and internships: Students are offered the opportunity to participate in externships with the U.S. Attorney's

office, the federal District Court, and the Eighth Circuit Court of Appeals. Students are also offered internship opportunities—clerking for District Court judges during the fall and spring and in the Grand Forks, Fargo, and Grafton Counties state's attorney's office during the fall and spring semesters. During the legislative term, students can participate in the legislative internship program, working in Bismarck with various legislative committees and processes.

Oslo exchange program: Since 1982, the School of Law has operated a law student exchange program with the University of Oslo Faculty of Law in Norway. From mid-May until the end of June, UND law students attend lectures taught by members of the Oslo law faculty, government and court officials, and private lawyers in Oslo. Norwegian law students attend UND law school for the spring semester.

Northern Plains Indian Law Center: The center is a clearinghouse for American Indian legal materials and provides a forum for discussing and resolving legal issues confronting Indian tribes, the states, and the federal government. It also supports tribal advocacy training programs. Among the center's programs is the Northern Plains Tribal Judicial Training Institute. The center supports teaching, scholarship, and service that make education in American Indian law a distinctive experience at UND.

STUDENT BODY

Fall 2005 full-time enrollment: 224

Men: 54%	Women: 46%
African-American: 1.8%	American Indian: 2.7%
Asian-American: 3.6%	Mexican-American: 1.3%
Puerto Rican: 0.0%	Other Hisp-Amer: 0.4%
White: 86.6%	International: 3.1%
Unknown: 0.4%	

Attrition rates for 2004-2005 full-time students
Percent of students discontinuing law school:

Men: 6%	Women: 6%
First-year students: 9%	Second-year students: 8%
Third-year students: N/A	

LIBRARY RESOURCES

The library holds 119,245 and receives 2,001 current subscriptions.
Total volumes: 317,000
Percentage of the titles in the online catalog: 100%
Total seats available for library users: 212

INFORMATION TECHNOLOGY

Number of wired network connections available to students: 145 total (in the law library, excluding computer labs: 127; in classrooms: 8; in computer labs: 0; elsewhere in the law school: 10)
Law school has a wireless network.
Approximate number of simultaneous users that can be accommodated on wireless network: 1,500
Students are not required to own a computer.

EMPLOYMENT AND SALARIES

Proportion of 2004 graduates employed at graduation: **N/A**
Employed 9 months later, as of February 15, 2005: **88%**
Salaries in the private sector (law firms, business, industry): **$35,000–$45,000** (25th-75th percentile)
Median salary in the private sector: **$39,500**
Percentage in the private sector who reported salary information: **25%**
Median salary in public service (government, judicial clerkships, academic posts, non-profits): **$40,000**

Percentage of 2004 graduates in:

Law firms: **48%**	Bus./industry (legal): **12%**
Bus./industry (nonlegal): **N/A**	Government: **8%**
Public interest: **8%**	Judicial clerkship: **24%**
Academia : **N/A**	Unknown: **N/A**

2004 graduates employed in-state: **65%**
2004 graduates employed in foreign countries: **N/A**
Number of states where graduates are employed: **10**
Percentage of 2004 graduates working in: New England: **0%**, Middle Atlantic: **0%**, East North Central: **2%**, West North Central: **86%**, South Atlantic: **6%**, East South Central: **0%**, West South Central: **0%**, Mountain: **4%**, Pacific: **2%**, Unknown: **N/A**

BAR PASSAGE RATES

Based on 2004 graduates taking Summer 2004 or Winter 2005 exams. Most of the school's first-time test takers took the bar in North Dakota.

84%	
School's bar passage rate for first-time test takers	

82%	
Statewide bar passage rate for first-time test takers	

University of Notre Dame

- PO Box 780, Notre Dame, IN, 46556-0780
- http://www.lawadmissions.nd.edu
- Private
- Year founded: 1869
- 2005-2006 tuition: full-time: $32,220; part-time: N/A
- Enrollment 2005-06 academic year: full-time: 538; part-time: 1
- U.S. News 2007 law specialty ranking: trial advocacy: 4

3.28-3.78 GPA, 25TH-75TH PERCENTILE

163-167 LSAT, 25TH-75TH PERCENTILE

18% ACCEPTANCE RATE

22 2007 U.S. NEWS LAW SCHOOL RANKING

ADMISSIONS
Admissions phone number: **(574) 631-6626**
Admissions email address: **lawadmit@nd.edu**
Application website:
 http://www.lawadmissions.nd.edu/admissions/meth-ods.html
Application deadline for Fall 2007 admission: **3/01**

Admissions statistics:
Number of applicants for Fall 2005: **3,507**
Number of acceptances: **637**
Number enrolled: **175**
Acceptance rate: **18%**
GPA, 25th-75th percentile, entering class Fall 2005: **3.28-3.78**
LSAT, 25th-75th percentile, entering class Fall 2005: **163-167**

FINANCIAL AID
Financial aid phone number: **(574) 631-6626**
Financial aid application deadline: **2/15**
Tuition 2005-2006 academic year: full-time: **$32,220**; part-time: **N/A**
Room and board: **$6,915**; books: **$1,200**; miscellaneous expenses: **$4,940**
Total of room/board/books/miscellaneous expenses: **$13,055**
University offers graduate student housing for which law students are eligible.

Financial aid profile
Percent of students that received grants for the 2004-2005 academic year: full-time: **65%**
Median grant amount: full-time: **$12,000**
The average law-school debt of those in the Class of 2005 who borrowed: **$79,599**. Proportion who borrowed: **87%**

ACADEMIC PROGRAMS
Calendar: **semester**
Joint degrees awarded: **J.D./M.B.A.; J.D./M.A.; J.D./M.S. ; J.D./Ph.D**
Typical first-year section size: Full-time: **89**

Is there typically a "small section" of the first year class, other than Legal Writing, taught by full-time faculty?:
 Full-time: **no**
Number of course titles, beyond the first year curriculum, offered last year: **109**
Percentages of upper division course sections, excluding seminars, with an enrollment of:
 Under 25: **51%**   25 to 49: **25%**
 50 to 74: **18%**   75 to 99: **6%**
 100+: **1%**
Areas of specialization: appellate advocacy, clinical training, dispute resolution, environmental law, healthcare law, intellectual property law, international law, tax law, trial advocacy

Fall 2005 faculty profile
Total teaching faculty: **92**. Full-time: **37%**; **74%** men, **26%** women, **18%** minorities. Part-time: **63%**; **57%** men, **43%** women, **3%** minorities
Student-to-faculty ratio: **14.3**

SPECIAL PROGRAMS *(as provided by law school):*
Special programs at the University of Notre Dame include trial advocacy, a second year in London, the Center for Civil and Human Rights, and the Legal Aid Clinic.

STUDENT BODY
Fall 2005 full-time enrollment: **538**

Men: **58%**	Women: **42%**
African-American: **5.6%**	American Indian: **1.1%**
Asian-American: **8.2%**	Mexican-American: **1.5%**
Puerto Rican: **1.1%**	Other Hisp-Amer: **5.0%**
White: **68.0%**	International: **1.5%**
Unknown: **8.0%**	

Fall 2005 part-time enrollment: **1**

Men: **0%**	Women: **100%**
African-American: **0.0%**	American Indian: **0.0%**
Asian-American: **0.0%**	Mexican-American: **0.0%**
Puerto Rican: **0.0%**	Other Hisp-Amer: **0.0%**

White: **100.0%**   International: **0.0%**
Unknown: **0.0%**

Attrition rates for 2004-2005 full-time students
Percent of students discontinuing law school:
Men: **1%**   Women: **3%**
First-year students: **3%**   Second-year students: **3%**
Third-year students: **N/A**

LIBRARY RESOURCES
The library holds **201,827** and receives **7,203** current
subscriptions.
Total volumes: **634,905**
Percentage of the titles in the online catalog: **98%**
Total seats available for library users: **416**

INFORMATION TECHNOLOGY
Number of wired network connections available to students: **116** total (in the law library, excluding computer labs: **100**; in classrooms: **6**; in computer labs: **0**; elsewhere in the law school: **10**)
Law school has a wireless network.
Approximate number of simultaneous users that can be accommodated on wireless network: **570**
Students are not required to own a computer.

EMPLOYMENT AND SALARIES
Proportion of 2004 graduates employed at graduation: **87%**
Employed 9 months later, as of February 15, 2005: **98%**
Salaries in the private sector (law firms, business, industry): **$90,000–$125,000** (25th-75th percentile)

Median salary in the private sector: **$100,000**
Percentage in the private sector who reported salary information: **84%**
Median salary in public service (government, judicial clerkships, academic posts, non-profits): **$45,500**

Percentage of 2004 graduates in:
Law firms: **59%**   Bus./industry (legal): **1%**
Bus./industry (nonlegal): **3%**   Government: **11%**
Public interest: **6%**   Judicial clerkship: **20%**
Academia : **0%**   Unknown: **0%**

2004 graduates employed in-state: **9%**
2004 graduates employed in foreign countries: **1%**
Number of states where graduates are employed: **26**
Percentage of 2004 graduates working in: New England: **2%**, Middle Atlantic: **13%**, East North Central: **44%**, West North Central: **3%**, South Atlantic: **15%**, East South Central: **2%**, West South Central: **3%**, Mountain: **6%**, Pacific: **12%**, Unknown: **0%**

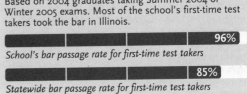

BAR PASSAGE RATES
Based on 2004 graduates taking Summer 2004 or Winter 2005 exams. Most of the school's first-time test takers took the bar in Illinois.

| 96% |
School's bar passage rate for first-time test takers

| 85% |
Statewide bar passage rate for first-time test takers

versity of Oklahoma

■ Andrew M. Coats Hall, 300 Timberdell Road, Norman, OK, 73019-5081
■ http://www.law.ou.edu
■ Public
■ Year founded: 1909
■ 2005-2006 tuition: In-state: full-time: $10,786, part-time: N/A; Out-of-state: full-time: $20,053
■ Enrollment 2005-06 academic year: full-time: 516
■ U.S. News 2007 law specialty ranking: N/A

3.32-3.76 GPA, 25ᵀᴴ-75ᵀᴴ PERCENTILE

154-160 LSAT, 25ᵀᴴ-75ᵀᴴ PERCENTILE

26% ACCEPTANCE RATE

80 2007 U.S. NEWS LAW SCHOOL RANKING

ADMISSIONS

Admissions phone number: **(405) 325-4728**
Admissions email address: **admissions@ou.edu; kmadden@ou.edu**
Application website:
http://www.law.ou.edu/prospective/admissions
Application deadline for Fall 2007 admission: **3/15**

Admissions statistics:

Number of applicants for Fall 2005: **1,278**
Number of acceptances: **336**
Number enrolled: **174**
Acceptance rate: **26%**
GPA, 25th-75th percentile, entering class Fall 2005: **3.32-3.76**
LSAT, 25th-75th percentile, entering class Fall 2005: **154-160**

FINANCIAL AID

Financial aid phone number: **(405) 325-4521**
Financial aid application deadline: **3/01**
Tuition 2005-2006 academic year: In-state: full-time: **$10,786**, part-time: **N/A**; Out-of-state: full-time: **$20,053**
Room and board: **$9,415**; books: **$1,067**; miscellaneous expenses: **$4,703**
Total of room/board/books/miscellaneous expenses: **$15,185**
University offers graduate student housing for which law students are eligible.

Financial aid profile

Percent of students that received grants for the 2004-2005 academic year: full-time: **56%**
Median grant amount: full-time: **$2,500**
The average law-school debt of those in the Class of 2005 who borrowed: **$63,439.** Proportion who borrowed: **64%**

ACADEMIC PROGRAMS

Calendar: **semester**
Joint degrees awarded: **Masters in Business Administration; Masters of Public Health; Dual Degree**

Typical first-year section size: Full-time: **43**
Is there typically a "small section" of the first year class, other than Legal Writing, taught by full-time faculty?: Full-time: **no**
Number of course titles, beyond the first year curriculum, offered last year: **121**
Percentages of upper division course sections, excluding seminars, with an enrollment of:
Under 25: **48%**   25 to 49: **34%**
50 to 74: **11%**   75 to 99: **8%**
100+: **0%**
Areas of specialization: appellate advocacy, clinical training, dispute resolution, environmental law, healthcare law, intellectual property law, international law, tax law, trial advocacy

Fall 2005 faculty profile

Total teaching faculty: **58.** Full-time: **48%**; **79%** men, **21%** women, **14%** minorities. Part-time: **52%**; **73%** men, **27%** women, **0%** minorities
Student-to-faculty ratio: **15.3**

SPECIAL PROGRAMS (as provided by law school):

Clinics: The OU Clinical Legal Education Program allows students to learn skills and values essential to good lawyering and to gain insight into our legal system and the lawyer's role therein by representing real clients in real cases under the direct supervision of one of our Clinic Professors. The OU Clinical Education Program offers students two live-client clinic opportunities, the OU Criminal Defense Clinic and the OU Civil Clinic. Students earn three credit hours per semester while enrolled in either clinic (most students enroll for two consecutive semesters, though with permission of the Director of Clinical Education, students may be authorized to enroll for only one semester). Our students enrolled in the Civil Clinic represent low-income clients in cases, transactions, and administrative proceedings. All of our students in the Civil Clinic will represent at least one client in a litigated family law matter, and every student will serve in at least one litigated matter as court-appointed guardian ad litem for a minor. Additionally, our Civil Clinic students prepare Wills, Living Wills, and powers of attorney for low-income clients, and assist low-income clients in their new home purchases from Habitat for Humanity. The Criminal Defense Clinic interns represent indigent defendants charged with municipal, misdemeanor, and felony offenses. Students plan and perform interviewing, counseling, investigation, negotiation, pretrial motion practice, and trial. Each clinic is complemented by a skills class where students apply substantive knowledge within performance sessions, skills training, and small-group/solo critique.

The OU College of Law offers assorted field placement opportunities in Washington, D.C., supervised by full-time faculty members. The environmental law externship places students with the U.S. Department of Justice Environmental Enforcement Section. The federal Indian law externship gives students the opportunity to work on Indian law litigation and policymaking with the U.S. Department of Justice and the Bureau of Indian Affairs. OU students have also secured externships with the State Department, the Consumer Product Safety Commission, and the Federal Trade Commission, all through individualized programs arranged with College of Law faculty.

International and summer study programs: Students at the College of Law study abroad through student-initiated programs in other host countries and through the summer program at Oxford, England. The summer program, held at Brasenose College, offers students a lovely and lively setting within which to deepen their understanding of American legal institutions and law and the Anglo-American tradition that informs it. Students live and eat on campus with OU and Oxford faculty. Students have also created individual study programs at foreign law schools, for a semester or a year. OU law students have recently attended universities in France, Mexico, the Netherlands, Australia, Germany, and Thailand, among others.

STUDENT BODY
Fall 2005 full-time enrollment: 516

Men: 55%	Women: 45%
African-American: 5.2%	American Indian: 9.7%
Asian-American: 2.7%	Mexican-American: 3.5%
Puerto Rican: 0.0%	Other Hisp-Amer: 0.2%
White: 71.7%	International: 0.2%
Unknown: 6.8%	

Attrition rates for 2004-2005 full-time students
Percent of students discontinuing law school:

Men: 0%	Women: 0%
First-year students: 1%	Second-year students: N/A
Third-year students: 1%	

LIBRARY RESOURCES
The library holds 139,361 and receives 4,914 current subscriptions.

Total volumes: 345,394
Percentage of the titles in the online catalog: 100%
Total seats available for library users: 406

INFORMATION TECHNOLOGY
Number of wired network connections available to students: 106 total (in the law library, excluding computer labs: 92; in classrooms: 14; in computer labs: 0; elsewhere in the law school: 0)
Law school has a wireless network.
Approximate number of simultaneous users that can be accommodated on wireless network: 600
Students are not required to own a computer.

EMPLOYMENT AND SALARIES
Proportion of 2004 graduates employed at graduation: 69%
Employed 9 months later, as of February 15, 2005: 88%
Salaries in the private sector (law firms, business, industry): $37,500–$75,000 (25th-75th percentile)
Median salary in the private sector: $51,000
Percentage in the private sector who reported salary information: 72%
Median salary in public service (government, judicial clerkships, academic posts, non-profits): $40,000

Percentage of 2004 graduates in:

Law firms: 65%	Bus./industry (legal): 2%
Bus./industry (nonlegal): 5%	Government: 21%
Public interest: 4%	Judicial clerkship: 1%
Academia : 1%	Unknown: 0%

2004 graduates employed in-state: 74%
2004 graduates employed in foreign countries: 1%
Number of states where graduates are employed: 13
Percentage of 2004 graduates working in: New England: 0%, Middle Atlantic: 1%, East North Central: 1%, West North Central: 1%, South Atlantic: 4%, East South Central: 1%, West South Central: 86%, Mountain: 3%, Pacific: 1%, Unknown: 1%

BAR PASSAGE RATES
Based on 2004 graduates taking Summer 2004 or Winter 2005 exams. Most of the school's first-time test takers took the bar in Oklahoma.

96%
School's bar passage rate for first-time test takers

83%
Statewide bar passage rate for first-time test takers

University of Oregon

- 1221 University of Oregon, Eugene, OR, 97403-1221
- http://www.law.uoregon.edu
- Public
- Year founded: 1884
- 2005-2006 tuition: In-state: full-time: $17,792, part-time: N/A; Out-of-state: full-time: $22,400
- Enrollment 2005-06 academic year: full-time: 526
- U.S. News 2007 law specialty ranking: dispute resolution: 13, environmental law: 6

3.17-3.66 GPA, 25TH-75TH PERCENTILE

156-160 LSAT, 25TH-75TH PERCENTILE

37% ACCEPTANCE RATE

70 2007 U.S. NEWS LAW SCHOOL RANKING

ADMISSIONS

Admissions phone number: **(541) 346-3846**
Admissions email address: **admissions@law.uoregon.edu**
Application website: **http://www.law.uoregon.edu/admissions**
Application deadline for Fall 2007 admission: **3/01**

Admissions statistics:

Number of applicants for Fall 2005: **1,944**
Number of acceptances: **726**
Number enrolled: **179**
Acceptance rate: **37%**
GPA, 25th-75th percentile, entering class Fall 2005: **3.17-3.66**
LSAT, 25th-75th percentile, entering class Fall 2005: **156-160**

FINANCIAL AID

Financial aid phone number: **(800) 760-6953**
Financial aid application deadline: **3/01**
Tuition 2005-2006 academic year: In-state: full-time: **$17,792**, part-time: **N/A**; Out-of-state: full-time: **$22,400**
Room and board: **$7,758**; books: **$1,700**; miscellaneous expenses: **$2,556**
Total of room/board/books/miscellaneous expenses: **$12,014**
University offers graduate student housing for which law students are eligible.

Financial aid profile

Percent of students that received grants for the 2004-2005 academic year: full-time: **52%**
Median grant amount: full-time: **$3,000**
The average law-school debt of those in the Class of 2005 who borrowed: **$62,151**. Proportion who borrowed: **87%**

ACADEMIC PROGRAMS

Calendar: **semester**
Joint degrees awarded: **Only concurrent degrees**
Typical first-year section size: Full-time: **65**

Is there typically a "small section" of the first year class, other than Legal Writing, taught by full-time faculty?: Full-time: **no**
Number of course titles, beyond the first year curriculum, offered last year: **94**
Percentages of upper division course sections, excluding seminars, with an enrollment of:
Under 25: **34%**   25 to 49: **36%**
50 to 74: **24%**   75 to 99: **5%**
100+: **2%**
Areas of specialization: appellate advocacy, clinical training, dispute resolution, environmental law, healthcare law, intellectual property law, international law, tax law, trial advocacy

Fall 2005 faculty profile

Total teaching faculty: **64**. Full-time: **47%**; **60%** men, **40%** women, **17%** minorities. Part-time: **53%**; **65%** men, **35%** women, **3%** minorities
Student-to-faculty ratio: **19.7**

SPECIAL PROGRAMS (as provided by law school):

The School offers a number of special programs. These include six centers and programs, seven clinical programs, numerous internship and externship opportunities, Orientation, academic support, and a separate master's degree in conflict resolution. Students also may participate in specialized certificate programs and pursue concurrent graduate degrees. Centers & Programs: Six centers and programs enrich the school and link it to the community at large. These include the Appropriate Dispute Resolution Program, the Environmental and Natural Resources Law Center, the Center for Law & Entrepreneurship, the Public Interest / Public Service Program, the Ocean & Coastal Law Center, and The Wayne Morse Center for Law & Politics. Each of these provides students with opportunities to pursue their interests in a professional context. Clinical Programs & Internships: The judicial internship program provides students with an opportunity to work directly with district and appellate court judges. Familiarity with the Oregon political process is gained through the Legislative Issues Workshop. Our seven clinics (Civil Practice, Criminal Defense, Criminal Prosecution,

Domestic Violence, Environmental Law, Mediation, and Small Business) introduce advanced students to the practice of law through supervised experience with actual clients and cases. Orientation & Academic Support Programs: The Orientation Program is a comprehensive transition and academic enrichment program open to all law students in their first year. It includes faculty presentations, skill-building exercises, and social events. Once classes start, all students have the option to participate in biweekly academic support sessions for each first-year course with successful upper level scholars. Certificate Programs: Students who earn certificates of completion gain credibility in the job market for their targeted skills and knowledge. Our certificates recognize students who concentrate in defined practice areas including business law, criminal law practice, public interest/public service law, environmental and natural resources law, estate planning, intellectual property, international law, law and entrepreneurship, ocean and coastal law, and tax law. Concurrent Degree Programs: Combined degree programs enable students to earn a J.D. and a master's degree in a shorter period of time than each degree could be earned separately and to enrich each body of knowledge with the perspective of the other. Current programs include Business and Law (J.D./M.B.A.), Environmental Studies and Law (J.D./M.S.),International Studies and Law (J.D./M.A), and Dispute Resolution and Law(J.D./M.A. or M.S.).

STUDENT BODY

Fall 2005 full-time enrollment: 526

Men: 58%	Women: 42%
African-American: 3.2%	American Indian: 1.5%
Asian-American: 7.8%	Mexican-American: 1.3%
Puerto Rican: 0.4%	Other Hisp-Amer: 3.4%
White: 80.8%	International: 1.5%
Unknown: 0.0%	

Attrition rates for 2004-2005 full-time students
Percent of students discontinuing law school:

Men: 2%	Women: 2%
First-year students: 3%	Second-year students: 2%
Third-year students: 1%	

LIBRARY RESOURCES

The library holds 52,545 and receives 2,814 current subscriptions.
Total volumes: 358,470
Percentage of the titles in the online catalog: 99%
Total seats available for library users: 288

INFORMATION TECHNOLOGY

Number of wired network connections available to students: 1,370 total (in the law library, excluding computer labs: 288; in classrooms: 632; in computer labs: 16; elsewhere in the law school: 434)
Law school has a wireless network.
Approximate number of simultaneous users that can be accommodated on wireless network: 3,200
Students are required to own a computer.

EMPLOYMENT AND SALARIES

Proportion of 2004 graduates employed at graduation: 62%
Employed 9 months later, as of February 15, 2005: 92%
Salaries in the private sector (law firms, business, industry): $45,500–$65,400 (25th-75th percentile)
Median salary in the private sector: $52,500
Percentage in the private sector who reported salary information: 85%
Median salary in public service (government, judicial clerkships, academic posts, non-profits): $40,100

Percentage of 2004 graduates in:

Law firms: 42%	Bus./industry (legal): 5%
Bus./industry (nonlegal): 6%	Government: 17%
Public interest: 7%	Judicial clerkship: 18%
Academia : 5%	Unknown: 0%

2004 graduates employed in-state: 51%
2004 graduates employed in foreign countries: 1%
Number of states where graduates are employed: 19
Percentage of 2004 graduates working in: New England: 0%, Middle Atlantic: 3%, East North Central: 2%, West North Central: 2%, South Atlantic: 7%, East South Central: 0%, West South Central: 2%, Mountain: 13%, Pacific: 71%, Unknown: 0%

BAR PASSAGE RATES

Based on 2004 graduates taking Summer 2004 or Winter 2005 exams. Most of the school's first-time test takers took the bar in Oregon.

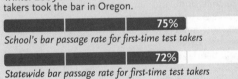

75%
School's bar passage rate for first-time test takers

72%
Statewide bar passage rate for first-time test takers

University of Pennsylvania

- 3400 Chestnut Street, Philadelphia, PA, 19104-6204
- http://www.law.upenn.edu
- Private
- Year founded: 1790
- 2005-2006 tuition: full-time: $37,086; part-time: N/A
- Enrollment 2005-06 academic year: full-time: 777
- U.S. News 2007 law specialty ranking: N/A

3.43-3.85 GPA, 25TH-75TH PERCENTILE

166-171 LSAT, 25TH-75TH PERCENTILE

13% ACCEPTANCE RATE

7 2007 U.S. NEWS LAW SCHOOL RANKING

ADMISSIONS

Admissions phone number: **(215) 898-7400**
Admissions email address: **admissions@law.upenn.edu**
Application website: **http://www.law.upenn.edu/prospective/jd/apply/index.html**
Application deadline for Fall 2007 admission: 2/15

Admissions statistics:

Number of applicants for Fall 2005: **6,396**
Number of acceptances: **801**
Number enrolled: **243**
Acceptance rate: **13%**
GPA, 25th-75th percentile, entering class Fall 2005: **3.43-3.85**
LSAT, 25th-75th percentile, entering class Fall 2005: **166-171**

FINANCIAL AID

Financial aid phone number: **(215) 898-7400**
Financial aid application deadline: **3/01**
Tuition 2005-2006 academic year: full-time: **$37,086**; part-time: **N/A**
Room and board: **$10,884**; books: **$975**; miscellaneous expenses: **$4,555**
Total of room/board/books/miscellaneous expenses: **$16,414**
University offers graduate student housing for which law students are eligible.

Financial aid profile

Percent of students that received grants for the 2004-2005 academic year: full-time: **36%**
Median grant amount: full-time: **$14,180**
The average law-school debt of those in the Class of 2005 who borrowed: **$101,757**. Proportion who borrowed: **84%**

ACADEMIC PROGRAMS

Calendar: **semester**
Joint degrees awarded: **J.D./B.A. or B.S.; J.D./M. Bioethics; J.D./M.B.A.; J.D./M.C.P. - City Planning; J.D./M.A. or M.S. Criminology; J.D./M.A., MsEd; J.D./M.E.S.;** J.D./M.G.A.; J.D./A.M. Islamic Studies; J.D./M.A. Philosophy; J.D./Ph.D. - Communications; J.D./Ph.D. - Economics; J.D./M.P.H.; J.D./M.S.W.; J.D./Ph.D. American Legal History; J.D./B.A./B.S.; J.D./BSE Engineering; J.D./Ph.D. Communications; J.D./Ph.D. Economics; J.D./Ph.D. Philosophy; J.D./D.E.S.S.
Typical first-year section size: Full-time: **85**
Is there typically a "small section" of the first year class, other than Legal Writing, taught by full-time faculty?: Full-time: **no**
Number of course titles, beyond the first year curriculum, offered last year: **92**
Percentages of upper division course sections, excluding seminars, with an enrollment of:

Under 25: **38%**	25 to 49: **23%**
50 to 74: **20%**	75 to 99: **13%**
100+: **6%**	

Areas of specialization: appellate advocacy, clinical training, dispute resolution, environmental law, healthcare law, intellectual property law, international law, tax law, trial advocacy

Fall 2005 faculty profile

Total teaching faculty: **113**. Full-time: **37%**; **81%** men, **19%** women, **10%** minorities. Part-time: **63%**; **72%** men, **28%** women, **13%** minorities
Student-to-faculty ratio: **12.8**

SPECIAL PROGRAMS *(as provided by law school)*:

Penn Law's distinguished history begins with that of our nation. Since that time, Penn Law has been an innovator in legal education, most recently with our unique cross-disciplinary approach to legal education. Our program benefits from being physically adjacent and academically linked to one of the finest arrays of professional schools in the nation such as Wharton, Annenberg School for Communications and the Bioethics program. Many of our faculty hold joint appointments (over 70 percent hold graduate degrees in law-related fields), and students draw on the collective expertise of this Ivy League university.

Our students have the freedom to craft a legal education that suits their interests. Our own curriculum and programs are rich in opportunities to learn about law in relationship to other fields. Students can augment their legal study by taking up to four courses, for law school credit, at any of the university's graduate and professional schools. Some students earn joint degrees in one of our formal joint degree programs or by creating an ad hoc program in their own areas of interest. Many students also participate in our Certificate Program.

Our clinical and public-service programs are also well known for their innovative approaches. Students apply classroom theory to the realities of actual legal problems under faculty supervision in the Gittis Center for Clinical Legal Studies. The program offers choices in every major lawyering area (litigation, transactional lawyering, mediation, and legislation) and in interdisciplinary child advocacy, transnational law, criminal defense, and public-interest lawyering.

Our Public Service Program brings us national renown as the first national law school to create a mandatory pro bono requirement and the first—and only—law school to win the American Bar Association's Pro Bono Public Award. Students work in the community on a variety of issues: environmental justice, family law, governmental practice, health law, immigration, international human rights law, labor law, women's issues, and youth law. Penn's academic program continues to offer the most rigorous foundation in legal study, and builds on this with a cross-disciplinary emphasis that best prepares our graduates for their roles in the legal profession.

STUDENT BODY

Fall 2005 full-time enrollment: 777

Men: 55%	Women: 45%
African-American: 7.9%	American Indian: 0.6%
Asian-American: 14.2%	Mexican-American: 1.0%
Puerto Rican: 1.0%	Other Hisp-Amer: 4.8%
White: 65.6%	International: 3.7%
Unknown: 1.2%	

Attrition rates for 2004-2005 full-time students
Percent of students discontinuing law school:

Men: 2%	Women: 0%
First-year students: 0%	Second-year students: 3%
Third-year students: N/A	

LIBRARY RESOURCES

The library holds 337,237 and receives 7,558 current subscriptions.
Total volumes: 826,096
Percentage of the titles in the online catalog: 98%
Total seats available for library users: 526

INFORMATION TECHNOLOGY

Number of wired network connections available to students: 168 total (in the law library, excluding computer labs: 23; in classrooms: 62; in computer labs: 2; elsewhere in the law school: 81)
Law school has a wireless network.
Approximate number of simultaneous users that can be accommodated on wireless network: 2,160
Students are not required to own a computer.

EMPLOYMENT AND SALARIES

Proportion of 2004 graduates employed at graduation: 99%
Employed 9 months later, as of February 15, 2005: 99%
Salaries in the private sector (law firms, business, industry): $125,000–$125,000 (25th-75th percentile)
Median salary in the private sector: $125,000
Percentage in the private sector who reported salary information: 79%
Median salary in public service (government, judicial clerkships, academic posts, non-profits): $50,250

Percentage of 2004 graduates in:

Law firms: 76%	Bus./industry (legal): 0%
Bus./industry (nonlegal): 2%	Government: 1%
Public interest: 2%	Judicial clerkship: 17%
Academia : 1%	Unknown: 0%

2004 graduates employed in-state: 18%
2004 graduates employed in foreign countries: 3%
Number of states where graduates are employed: 17
Percentage of 2004 graduates working in: New England: 6%, Middle Atlantic: 61%, East North Central: 1%, West North Central: 0%, South Atlantic: 20%, East South Central: 0%, West South Central: 1%, Mountain: 0%, Pacific: 8%, Unknown: 0%

BAR PASSAGE RATES

Based on 2004 graduates taking Summer 2004 or Winter 2005 exams. Most of the school's first-time test takers took the bar in New York.

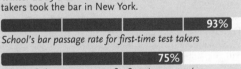

93%
School's bar passage rate for first-time test takers

75%
Statewide bar passage rate for first-time test takers

University of Pittsburgh

- 3900 Forbes Avenue, Pittsburgh, PA, 15260
- http://www.law.pitt.edu
- Public
- **Year founded:** 1895
- **2005-2006 tuition:** In-state: full-time: $19,602, part-time: N/A; Out-of-state: full-time: $28,210
- **Enrollment 2005-06 academic year:** full-time: 691
- **U.S. News 2007 law specialty ranking:** intellecutal property law: 24

3.12-3.63 GPA, 25TH-75TH PERCENTILE

157-161 LSAT, 25TH-75TH PERCENTILE

29% ACCEPTANCE RATE

60 2007 U.S. NEWS LAW SCHOOL RANKING

ADMISSIONS

Admissions phone number: **(412) 648-1415**
Admissions email address: **admissions@law.pitt.edu**
Application website: **N/A**
Application deadline for Fall 2007 admission: **3/01**

Admissions statistics:
Number of applicants for Fall 2005: **2,349**
Number of acceptances: **671**
Number enrolled: **243**
Acceptance rate: **29%**
GPA, 25th-75th percentile, entering class Fall 2005: **3.12-3.63**
LSAT, 25th-75th percentile, entering class Fall 2005: **157-161**

FINANCIAL AID

Financial aid phone number: **(412) 648-1415**
Financial aid application deadline: **3/01**
Tuition 2005-2006 academic year: In-state: full-time: **$19,602**, part-time: **N/A**; Out-of-state: full-time: **$28,210**
Room and board: **$12,490**; books: **$1,500**; miscellaneous expenses: **$580**
Total of room/board/books/miscellaneous expenses: **$14,570**
University does not offer graduate student housing for which law students are eligible.

Financial aid profile
Percent of students that received grants for the 2004-2005 academic year: full-time: **52%**
Median grant amount: full-time: **$10,000**
The average law-school debt of those in the Class of 2005 who borrowed: **$67,294**. Proportion who borrowed: **73%**

ACADEMIC PROGRAMS

Calendar: **semester**
Joint degrees awarded: **J.D./M.B.A.; J.D./MPIA; J.D./M.P.H.; J.D./M.I.D.; J.D./M.A.; J.D./M.S.; J.D./M.P.A.**
Typical first-year section size: Full-time: **84**

Is there typically a "small section" of the first year class, other than Legal Writing, taught by full-time faculty?: Full-time: **yes**
Number of course titles, beyond the first year curriculum, offered last year: **162**
Percentages of upper division course sections, excluding seminars, with an enrollment of:

Under 25: **67%**	25 to 49: **15%**
50 to 74: **7%**	75 to 99: **6%**
100+: **5%**	

Areas of specialization: appellate advocacy, clinical training, dispute resolution, environmental law, healthcare law, intellectual property law, international law, tax law, trial advocacy

Fall 2005 faculty profile
Total teaching faculty: **134.** Full-time: **36%**; 60% men, 40% women, 10% minorities. Part-time: **64%**; 71% men, 29% women, 5% minorities
Student-to-faculty ratio: **14.4**

SPECIAL PROGRAMS *(as provided by law school):*

We have five certificate programs available to J.D. students: health law; environmental law; international and comparative law; the John Gismondi Civil Litigation Program; and intellectual property and technology law. These programs offer students additional opportunities for personal faculty mentoring, give students who are unsure of how to get to their desired career goals a measure of organization and structure, create communities of shared legal interests, and assist graduates in the placement process.

We have live-client, in-house clinics at the law school, in the areas of elder law, health law, environmental law, low-income tax law, family law, and community economic development. We also offer our students two additional live-client clinical practice opportunities, one with Allegheny County Neighborhood Legal Services and one with Washington County Legal Services. In addition, many law students enroll in our practicum/externship program, receiving academic credit for work at approved externship sites by assisting in the provision of legal service to indigents and nonprofit organizations.

Our Center for International Legal Education develops and coordinates numerous programs designed to prepare law students for careers in a global economy and in international law. J.D. students are encouraged to develop individualized programs, including study at foreign law schools.

Our unique Languages for Lawyers Program offers language courses as part of the J.D. curriculum, focused on legal terminology and the use of dialogue from comparative legal experiences. We are widely recognized as a leader in combining the study of language and law. Language courses designed especially for lawyers are regularly offered in Chinese, French, German, Japanese, and Spanish.

It has long been a priority of the School of Law to maintain an effective academic support program. Our Mellon Program and Legal Writing Center assist students in developing the analytical and communication skills needed for success in law school and in the legal profession. The Bar Passage Assistance Program consists of two parts: a BEAT (bar exam accelerated training) program presented by a commercial bar preparation company, the expense of which is defrayed entirely by the school, and our own internal program of assistance.

STUDENT BODY

Fall 2005 full-time enrollment: 691

Men: 55%	Women: 45%
African-American: 6.5%	American Indian: 0.1%
Asian-American: 5.2%	Mexican-American: 0.6%
Puerto Rican: 0.3%	Other Hisp-Amer: 1.3%
White: 60.3%	International: 0.0%
Unknown: 25.6%	

Attrition rates for 2004-2005 full-time students
Percent of students discontinuing law school:

Men: 0%	Women: N/A
First-year students: N/A	Second-year students: 0%
Third-year students: N/A	

LIBRARY RESOURCES

The library holds 249,027 and receives 2,672 current subscriptions.
Total volumes: 440,116
Percentage of the titles in the online catalog: 100%
Total seats available for library users: 436

INFORMATION TECHNOLOGY

Number of wired network connections available to students: 304 total (in the law library, excluding computer labs: 41; in classrooms: 201; in computer labs: 62; elsewhere in the law school: 0)

Law school has a wireless network.
Approximate number of simultaneous users that can be accommodated on wireless network: 425
Students are not required to own a computer.

EMPLOYMENT AND SALARIES

Proportion of 2004 graduates employed at graduation: 76%
Employed 9 months later, as of February 15, 2005: 97%
Salaries in the private sector (law firms, business, industry): $46,000–$100,000 (25th-75th percentile)
Median salary in the private sector: $75,000
Percentage in the private sector who reported salary information: 76%
Median salary in public service (government, judicial clerkships, academic posts, non-profits): $40,000

Percentage of 2004 graduates in:

Law firms: 56%	Bus./industry (legal): 12%
Bus./industry (nonlegal): 8%	Government: 11%
Public interest: 3%	Judicial clerkship: 6%
Academia : 3%	Unknown: 1%

2004 graduates employed in-state: 72%
2004 graduates employed in foreign countries: 2%
Number of states where graduates are employed: 22
Percentage of 2004 graduates working in: New England: 0%, Middle Atlantic: 78%, East North Central: 4%, West North Central: 0%, South Atlantic: 13%, East South Central: 0%, West South Central: 0%, Mountain: 0%, Pacific: 1%, Unknown: 0%

BAR PASSAGE RATES

Based on 2004 graduates taking Summer 2004 or Winter 2005 exams. Most of the school's first-time test takers took the bar in Pennsylvania.

82%
School's bar passage rate for first-time test takers

81%
Statewide bar passage rate for first-time test takers

University of Richmond

- T.C. Williams School of Law, Richmond, VA, 23173
- http://law.richmond.edu
- Private
- Year founded: 1870
- 2005-2006 tuition: full-time: $27,060; part-time: $1,350/credit hour
- Enrollment 2005-06 academic year: full-time: 483; part-time: 2
- U.S. News 2007 law specialty ranking: N/A

3.10-3.54 GPA, 25TH-75TH PERCENTILE

160-163 LSAT, 25TH-75TH PERCENTILE

26% ACCEPTANCE RATE

80 2007 U.S. NEWS LAW SCHOOL RANKING

ADMISSIONS

Admissions phone number: **(804) 289-8189**
Admissions email address: **mrahman@richmond.edu**
Application website:
  http://law.richmond.edu/application/application.htm
Application deadline for Fall 2007 admission: **1/15**

Admissions statistics:
Number of applicants for Fall 2005: **2,203**
Number of acceptances: **581**
Number enrolled: **171**
Acceptance rate: **26%**
GPA, 25th-75th percentile, entering class Fall 2005:
  3.10-3.54
LSAT, 25th-75th percentile, entering class Fall 2005:
  160-163

FINANCIAL AID

Financial aid phone number: **(804) 289-8438**
Financial aid application deadline: **2/25**
Tuition 2005-2006 academic year: full-time: **$27,060**; part-time: **$1,350/credit hour**
Room and board: **$8,415**; books: **$1,200**; miscellaneous expenses: **$3,635**
Total of room/board/books/miscellaneous expenses: **$13,250**
University offers graduate student housing for which law students are eligible.

Financial aid profile
Percent of students that received grants for the 2004-2005 academic year: full-time: **56%**
Median grant amount: full-time: **$5,000**
The average law-school debt of those in the Class of 2005 who borrowed: **$74,780**. Proportion who borrowed: **84%**

ACADEMIC PROGRAMS

Calendar: **semester**
Joint degrees awarded: **J.D./M.B.A.; J.D./MSW; J.D./M. Public Admin.; J.D./M. Health Admin.; J.D./ M. Urban Planning**

Typical first-year section size: Full-time: **85**
Is there typically a "small section" of the first year class, other than Legal Writing, taught by full-time faculty?: Full-time: **yes**
Number of course titles, beyond the first year curriculum, offered last year: **82**
Percentages of upper division course sections, excluding seminars, with an enrollment of:
  Under 25: **68%**   25 to 49: **18%**
  50 to 74: **8%**   75 to 99: **6%**
  100+: **0%**
Areas of specialization: appellate advocacy, clinical training, dispute resolution, environmental law, healthcare law, intellectual property law, international law, tax law, trial advocacy

Fall 2005 faculty profile
Total teaching faculty: **118**. Full-time: **24%**; **64%** men, **36%** women, **14%** minorities. Part-time: **76%**; **69%** men, **31%** women, **3%** minorities
Student-to-faculty ratio: **14.3**

SPECIAL PROGRAMS (as provided by law school):
Special programs include the Juvenile Delinquency Clinic, the Mental Disabilities Clinic, the Clinical Placement Program, the Merhige Environmental Law Center, the John Marshall Scholars Program, and summer study abroad at the University of Cambridge, England.

STUDENT BODY

Fall 2005 full-time enrollment: 483
Men: **58%**	Women: **42%**
African-American: **3.9%**	American Indian: **0.4%**
Asian-American: **4.1%**	Mexican-American: **0.0%**
Puerto Rican: **0.0%**	Other Hisp-Amer: **0.2%**
White: **90.1%**	International: **1.2%**
Unknown: **0.0%**	

Fall 2005 part-time enrollment: 2
Men: **50%**	Women: **50%**
African-American: **0.0%**	American Indian: **0.0%**

Asian-American: 0.0% Mexican-American: 0.0%
Puerto Rican: 0.0% Other Hisp-Amer: 0.0%
White: 100.0% International: 0.0%
Unknown: 0.0%

Attrition rates for 2004-2005 full-time students
Percent of students discontinuing law school:
Men: 3% Women: 2%
First-year students: 7% Second-year students: N/A
Third-year students: N/A

LIBRARY RESOURCES

The library holds 162,374 and receives 4,573 current
 subscriptions.
Total volumes: 382,741
Percentage of the titles in the online catalog: 100%
Total seats available for library users: 643

INFORMATION TECHNOLOGY

Number of wired network connections available to students: 889 total (in the law library, excluding computer
 labs: 480; in classrooms: 380; in computer labs: 5; elsewhere in the law school: 24)
Law school has a wireless network.
Approximate number of simultaneous users that can be
 accommodated on wireless network: 700
Students are required to own a computer.

EMPLOYMENT AND SALARIES

Proportion of 2004 graduates employed at graduation: 57%
Employed 9 months later, as of February 15, 2005: 93%
Salaries in the private sector (law firms, business, indus-
 try): $52,405–$67,114 (25th-75th percentile)

Median salary in the private sector: $60,000
Percentage in the private sector who reported salary
 information: 99%
Median salary in public service (government, judicial clerkships, academic posts, non-profits): $47,658

Percentage of 2004 graduates in:
Law firms: 51% Bus./industry (legal): 14%
Bus./industry (nonlegal): 1% Government: 8%
Public interest: 3% Judicial clerkship: 21%
Academia : 1% Unknown: 1%

2004 graduates employed in-state: 71%
2004 graduates employed in foreign countries: 1%
Number of states where graduates are employed: 19
Percentage of 2004 graduates working in: New England:
 1%, Middle Atlantic: 5%, East North Central: 1%, West
 North Central: 0%, South Atlantic: 88%, East South
 Central: 1%, West South Central: 2%, Mountain: 0%,
 Pacific: 2%, Unknown: 0%

BAR PASSAGE RATES

Based on 2004 graduates taking Summer 2004 or
Winter 2005 exams. Most of the school's first-time test
takers took the bar in Virginia.

75%

School's bar passage rate for first-time test takers

74%

Statewide bar passage rate for first-time test takers

University of San Diego

- 5998 Alcala Park, San Diego, CA, 92110-2492
- http://www.law.sandiego.edu
- Private
- Year founded: 1954
- 2005-2006 tuition: full-time: $33,826; part-time: $24,076
- Enrollment 2005-06 academic year: full-time: 763; part-time: 303
- U.S. News 2007 law specialty ranking: tax law: 9

3.11-3.54 GPA, 25TH-75TH PERCENTILE

160-164 LSAT, 25TH-75TH PERCENTILE

25% ACCEPTANCE RATE

65 2007 U.S. NEWS LAW SCHOOL RANKING

ADMISSIONS

Admissions phone number: **(619) 260-4528**
Admissions email address: **jdinfo@SanDiego.edu**
Application website: **http://www.law.sandiego.edu**
Application deadline for Fall 2007 admission: **2/02**

Admissions statistics:

Number of applicants for Fall 2005: **4,580**
Number of acceptances: **1,139**
Number enrolled: **266**
Acceptance rate: **25%**
GPA, 25th-75th percentile, entering class Fall 2005: **3.11-3.54**
LSAT, 25th-75th percentile, entering class Fall 2005: **160-164**

Part-time program:

Number of applicants for Fall 2005: **538**
Number of acceptances: **235**
Number enrolled: **99**
Acceptance rate: **44%**
GPA, 25th-75th percentile, entering class Fall 2005: **3.08-3.55**
LSAT, 25th-75th percentile, entering class Fall 2005: **156-159**

FINANCIAL AID

Financial aid phone number: **(619) 260-4570**
Financial aid application deadline: **3/01**
Tuition 2005-2006 academic year: full-time: **$33,826**; part-time: **$24,076**
Room and board: **$10,542**; books: **$895**; miscellaneous expenses: **$5,618**
Total of room/board/books/miscellaneous expenses: **$17,055**
University offers graduate student housing for which law students are eligible.

Financial aid profile

Percent of students that received grants for the 2004-2005 academic year: full-time: **38%**; part-time **23%**

Median grant amount: full-time: **$15,000**; part-time: **$9,900**
The average law-school debt of those in the Class of 2005 who borrowed: **$87,905**. Proportion who borrowed: **89%**

ACADEMIC PROGRAMS

Calendar: **semester**
Joint degrees awarded: **N/A**
Typical first-year section size: Full-time: **85**; Part-time: **85**
Is there typically a "small section" of the first year class, other than Legal Writing, taught by full-time faculty?: Full-time: **yes**; Part-time: **yes**
Number of course titles, beyond the first year curriculum, offered last year: **125**
Percentages of upper division course sections, excluding seminars, with an enrollment of:

Under 25: **61%**   25 to 49: **23%**
50 to 74: **7%**   75 to 99: **8%**
100+: **1%**

Areas of specialization: appellate advocacy, clinical training, dispute resolution, environmental law, healthcare law, intellectual property law, international law, tax law, trial advocacy

Fall 2005 faculty profile

Total teaching faculty: **94**. Full-time: **49%**; **74%** men, **26%** women, **13%** minorities. Part-time: **51%**; **81%** men, **19%** women, **8%** minorities
Student-to-faculty ratio: **14.3**

SPECIAL PROGRAMS (as provided by law school):

The University of San Diego School of Law's Clinical Education Program includes the Land Use Clinic; Civil Clinic; Environmental Law Clinic; Child Advocacy Clinic; Immigration Clinic; Criminal Clinic; Small-Claims Clinic; Public Interest Law Clinic; Mental Health Clinic; Entrepreneurship Clinic; Perspectives in Criminal Justice Clinic; Special Education Clinic; and Tax Clinic. The University of San Diego School of Law, in cooperation with foreign universities, sponsors the Institute on International and Comparative Law. This institute conducts summer law study programs in England, France, Ireland, Italy, Mexico, Russia and Spain. The programs introduce American law students to foreign law and legal institutions, and provide intensive study during four- to five-week sessions. All courses are taught in English by institute faculty, and credits can be earned toward degree requirements. Founded in 1980, USD's Center for Public Interest Law (CPIL) serves as an academic center of research, learning and advocacy in administrative law; teaches direct lawyering skills in public interest law; represents the interests of the disadvantaged or underrepresented in state regulatory proceedings; and attempts to make the regulatory functions of state government more efficient and visible by serving as a public monitor of state agencies. The Children's Advocacy Institute (CAI), a project of CPIL, is an academic, research and advocacy center dedicated to promoting the health and well being of California's children. The Institute for Law and Philosophy advances knowledge on legal topics of philosophical significance, particularly those that implicate moral, political, and religious philosophical issues. The institute furthers its missions through roundtables, conferences, public lectures and public debates. The University of San Diego School of Law offers students outstanding internship programs. The Agency Internship Program enables students to earn academic credit for working in a law-related internship position with either a government agency or a nonprofit organization. In the Judicial Internship Program, students earn academic credit for working with judges in the state or federal trial or appellate courts. These placements translate academic legal education into practical adjudicative decision-making, helping students understand how courts work and how attorneys, judges, and litigants succeed and fail in the process.

STUDENT BODY

Fall 2005 full-time enrollment: 763

Men: 55%	Women: 45%
African-American: 3.1%	American Indian: 0.8%
Asian-American: 14.2%	Mexican-American: 4.8%
Puerto Rican: 0.8%	Other Hisp-Amer: 4.5%
White: 71.4%	International: 0.4%
Unknown: 0.0%	

Fall 2005 part-time enrollment: 303

Men: 55%	Women: 45%
African-American: 3.6%	American Indian: 0.3%
Asian-American: 15.2%	Mexican-American: 3.3%
Puerto Rican: 0.3%	Other Hisp-Amer: 3.3%
White: 73.6%	International: 0.3%
Unknown: 0.0%	

Attrition rates for 2004-2005 full-time students
Percent of students discontinuing law school:

Men: 4%	Women: 3%
First-year students: 8%	Second-year students: 2%
Third-year students: 0%	

LIBRARY RESOURCES

The library holds 295,891 and receives 5,034 current subscriptions.
Total volumes: 523,054
Percentage of the titles in the online catalog: 100%
Total seats available for library users: 600

INFORMATION TECHNOLOGY

Number of wired network connections available to students: 222 total (in the law library, excluding computer labs: 202; in classrooms: 0; in computer labs: 0; elsewhere in the law school: 20)
Law school has a wireless network.
Approximate number of simultaneous users that can be accommodated on wireless network: 2,432
Students are not required to own a computer.

EMPLOYMENT AND SALARIES

Proportion of 2004 graduates employed at graduation: 66%
Employed 9 months later, as of February 15, 2005: 89%
Salaries in the private sector (law firms, business, industry): $56,000–$100,000 (25th-75th percentile)
Median salary in the private sector: $68,000
Percentage in the private sector who reported salary information: 76%
Median salary in public service (government, judicial clerkships, academic posts, non-profits): $50,000

Percentage of 2004 graduates in:

Law firms: 63%	Bus./industry (legal): 13%
Bus./industry (nonlegal): 3%	Government: 12%
Public interest: 3%	Judicial clerkship: 3%
Academia : 2%	Unknown: 2%

2004 graduates employed in-state: 86%
2004 graduates employed in foreign countries: 0%
Number of states where graduates are employed: 19
Percentage of 2004 graduates working in: New England: 0%, Middle Atlantic: 1%, East North Central: 2%, West North Central: 0%, South Atlantic: 4%, East South Central: 0%, West South Central: 1%, Mountain: 6%, Pacific: 86%, Unknown: 0%

BAR PASSAGE RATES

Based on 2004 graduates taking Summer 2004 or Winter 2005 exams. Most of the school's first-time test takers took the bar in California.

71%
School's bar passage rate for first-time test takers

61%
Statewide bar passage rate for first-time test takers

University of San Francisco

- 2130 Fulton Street, San Francisco, CA, 94117-1080
- http://www.law.usfca.edu
- Private
- Year founded: 1912
- 2005-2006 tuition: full-time: $30,650; part-time: $1,095/credit hour
- Enrollment 2005-06 academic year: full-time: 599; part-time: 130
- U.S. News 2007 law specialty ranking: N/A

3.13-3.59 GPA, 25TH-75TH PERCENTILE

157-161 LSAT, 25TH-75TH PERCENTILE

32% ACCEPTANCE RATE

93 2007 U.S. NEWS LAW SCHOOL RANKING

ADMISSIONS

Admissions phone number: (415) 422-6586
Admissions email address: lawadmissions@usfca.edu
Application website: http://www.law.usfca.edu
Application deadline for Fall 2007 admission: 2/01

Admissions statistics:
Number of applicants for Fall 2005: 3,674
Number of acceptances: 1,165
Number enrolled: 208
Acceptance rate: 32%
GPA, 25th-75th percentile, entering class Fall 2005:
   3.13-3.59
LSAT, 25th-75th percentile, entering class Fall 2005: 157-161

Part-time program:
Number of applicants for Fall 2005: 480
Number of acceptances: 100
Number enrolled: 51
Acceptance rate: 21%
GPA, 25th-75th percentile, entering class Fall 2005:
   2.94-3.46
LSAT, 25th-75th percentile, entering class Fall 2005:
   154-159

FINANCIAL AID

Financial aid phone number: (415) 422-6210
Financial aid application deadline: 2/01
Tuition 2005-2006 academic year: full-time: $30,650; part-time: $1,095/credit hour
Room and board: $13,500; books: $900; miscellaneous expenses: $4,904
Total of room/board/books/miscellaneous expenses: $19,304
University offers graduate student housing for which law students are eligible.

Financial aid profile
Percent of students that received grants for the 2004-2005 academic year: full-time: 30%; part-time 20%
Median grant amount: full-time: $8,113; part-time: $3,500

The average law-school debt of those in the Class of 2005 who borrowed: $95,327. Proportion who borrowed: 85%

ACADEMIC PROGRAMS

Calendar: **semester**
Joint degrees awarded: **J.D./M.B.A. Concurrent Program**
Typical first-year section size: Full-time: **94**; Part-time: **70**
Is there typically a "small section" of the first year class, other than Legal Writing, taught by full-time faculty?:
   Full-time: **yes**; Part-time: **no**
Number of course titles, beyond the first year curriculum, offered last year: **71**
Percentages of upper division course sections, excluding seminars, with an enrollment of:
   Under 25: **46%**   25 to 49: **32%**
   50 to 74: **9%**   75 to 99: **13%**
   100+: **0%**
Areas of specialization: appellate advocacy, clinical training, dispute resolution, environmental law, intellectual property law, international law, tax law, trial advocacy

Fall 2005 faculty profile
Total teaching faculty: **65**. Full-time: **37%**; **63%** men, **38%** women, **25%** minorities. Part-time: **63%**; **56%** men, **44%** women, **24%** minorities
Student-to-faculty ratio: **16.7**

SPECIAL PROGRAMS *(as provided by law school):*
Clinics: A range of innovative clinical programs are available, including the International Human Rights Clinic (research and present issues before the United Nations in Geneva), the Criminal Justice Clinic (adult misdemeanor criminal defense and juvenile cases),the Child Advocacy Clinic (representing minors in all phases of juvenile dependency proceedings), the Employment Law Mediation Clinic (representing parties in employment discrimination disputes in mediations conducted by the U.S. Equal Employment Opportunity Commission's San Francisco office), the Mediation Clinic (mediating matters before the Small Claims Court), Investor Justice Project (representing clients in National Association of Securities Dealers actions), and the Intellectual Property Internet Justice Project.

Centers and institutes: The Center for Law & Global Justice administers a range of programs, both on campus and abroad. It sponsors legal assistance projects in China and East Timor; administers intern summer programs in the Dominican Republic, the Philippines, India, El Salvador and Switzerland; and provides research opportunities for students at home in investigational projects on human rights violations in Latin America and international business corruption in Africa. The J. Thomas McCarthy Institute for Intellectual Property and Technology Law honors longtime faculty member J. Thomas McCarthy who helped pioneer and define intellectual property law. The Institute promotes ongoing development in IP law.

Summer study: Three summer abroad programs are offered: Trinity College (Dublin), Charles University (Prague, Czech Republic), and Pazmany University (Budapest, Hungary). Also, the Center for Law & Global Justice offers a summer class for USF students in Cambodia.

Internships: The clinical placement and judicial externship programs provide students the opportunity to work in legal agencies or with federal and state judges throughout the San Francisco Bay Area. Students gain practical experience and a real-world perspective about an attorney's professional responsibility.

Other special programs: The summer Intensive Advocacy Program offers pre-trial and trial advocacy skills enrichment. The Inn of Court is a legal mentoring organization. The Law in Motion Service Program is a community service program which reminds students that people without access to the basic needs of life or human rights should be on the minds of lawyers, whose role is to promote justice in society.

STUDENT BODY

Fall 2005 full-time enrollment: 599
Men: 48%	Women: 52%
African-American: 4.0%	American Indian: 0.3%
Asian-American: 19.0%	Mexican-American: 4.0%
Puerto Rican: 0.5%	Other Hisp-Amer: 3.2%
White: 51.4%	International: 0.5%
Unknown: 17.0%	

Fall 2005 part-time enrollment: 130
Men: 51%	Women: 49%
African-American: 5.4%	American Indian: 2.3%
Asian-American: 16.2%	Mexican-American: 4.6%
Puerto Rican: 0.0%	Other Hisp-Amer: 8.5%
White: 51.5%	International: 0.8%
Unknown: 10.8%	

Attrition rates for 2004-2005 full-time students
Percent of students discontinuing law school:
Men: 8%	Women: 7%
First-year students: 18%	Second-year students: 3%
Third-year students: 0%	

LIBRARY RESOURCES
The library holds 184,210 and receives 3,293 current subscriptions.
Total volumes: 354,849
Percentage of the titles in the online catalog: 100%
Total seats available for library users: 428

INFORMATION TECHNOLOGY
Number of wired network connections available to students: 1,285 total (in the law library, excluding computer labs: 700; in classrooms: 490; in computer labs: 60; elsewhere in the law school: 35)
Law school doesn't have a wireless network.
Approximate number of simultaneous users that can be accommodated on wireless network: N/A
Students are not required to own a computer.

EMPLOYMENT AND SALARIES
Proportion of 2004 graduates employed at graduation: N/A
Employed 9 months later, as of February 15, 2005: 95%
Salaries in the private sector (law firms, business, industry): $61,000–$112,800 (25th-75th percentile)
Median salary in the private sector: $75,300
Percentage in the private sector who reported salary information: 35%
Median salary in public service (government, judicial clerkships, academic posts, non-profits): $50,625

Percentage of 2004 graduates in:
Law firms: 49%	Bus./industry (legal): 5%
Bus./industry (nonlegal): 19%	Government: 12%
Public interest: 5%	Judicial clerkship: 4%
Academia : 1%	Unknown: 5%

2004 graduates employed in-state: 79%
2004 graduates employed in foreign countries: 0%
Number of states where graduates are employed: 16
Percentage of 2004 graduates working in: New England: 1%, Middle Atlantic: 2%, East North Central: 0%, West North Central: 1%, South Atlantic: 1%, East South Central: 0%, West South Central: 1%, Mountain: 2%, Pacific: 81%, Unknown: 12%

BAR PASSAGE RATES
Based on 2004 graduates taking Summer 2004 or Winter 2005 exams. Most of the school's first-time test takers took the bar in California.

66%
School's bar passage rate for first-time test takers

61%
Statewide bar passage rate for first-time test takers

University of South Carolina

- 701 S. Main Street, Columbia, SC, 29208
- http://www.law.sc.edu
- Public
- Year founded: 1867
- 2005-2006 tuition: In-state: full-time: $15,264, part-time: $626/credit hour; Out-of-state: full-time: $30,400
- Enrollment 2005-06 academic year: full-time: 739
- U.S. News 2007 law specialty ranking: N/A

3.19-3.68 GPA, 25TH-75TH PERCENTILE

154-160 LSAT, 25TH-75TH PERCENTILE

34% ACCEPTANCE RATE

97 2007 U.S. NEWS LAW SCHOOL RANKING

ADMISSIONS

Admissions phone number: **(803) 777-6605**
Admissions email address: **usclaw@law.law.sc.edu**
Application website: **N/A**
Application deadline for Fall 2007 admission: **4/01**

Admissions statistics:

Number of applicants for Fall 2005: **1,503**
Number of acceptances: **516**
Number enrolled: **225**
Acceptance rate: **34%**
GPA, 25th-75th percentile, entering class Fall 2005: **3.19-3.68**
LSAT, 25th-75th percentile, entering class Fall 2005: **154-160**

FINANCIAL AID

Financial aid phone number: **(803) 777-6605**
Financial aid application deadline: **4/15**
Tuition 2005-2006 academic year: In-state: full-time: **$15,264**, part-time: **$626/credit hour**; Out-of-state: full-time: **$30,400**
Room and board: **$9,840**; books: **$785**; miscellaneous expenses: **$4,721**
Total of room/board/books/miscellaneous expenses: **$15,346**
University offers graduate student housing for which law students are eligible.

Financial aid profile

Percent of students that received grants for the 2004-2005 academic year: full-time: **15%**
Median grant amount: full-time: **$3,000**
The average law-school debt of those in the Class of 2005 who borrowed: **$54,865**. Proportion who borrowed: **78%**

ACADEMIC PROGRAMS

Calendar: **semester**
Joint degrees awarded: **J.D./International MBA; J.D./M.A. Public Administration; J.D./M.A. Criminology &Criminal Justice; J.D./M.A. Human Resources; J.D./M.A.cc; J.D./M.S.W.; J.D./M.S. Health Administration; J.D./M.S. Earth and Env. Resources Mgmt.; J.D./M.B.A.**
Typical first-year section size: Full-time: **75**
Is there typically a "small section" of the first year class, other than Legal Writing, taught by full-time faculty?: Full-time: **no**
Number of course titles, beyond the first year curriculum, offered last year: **105**
Percentages of upper division course sections, excluding seminars, with an enrollment of:

Under 25: **44%**   25 to 49: **22%**
50 to 74: **15%**   75 to 99: **15%**
100+: **4%**

Areas of specialization: appellate advocacy, clinical training, dispute resolution, environmental law, healthcare law, intellectual property law, international law, tax law, trial advocacy

Fall 2005 faculty profile

Total teaching faculty: **92**. Full-time: **42%**; **74%** men, **26%** women, **10%** minorities. Part-time: **58%**; **60%** men, **40%** women, **2%** minorities
Student-to-faculty ratio: **17.8**

SPECIAL PROGRAMS *(as provided by law school)*:

The School of Law recognizes that experiential learning in the area of professional skills is essential to a well-rounded legal education. Under special court rule, third-year law students may represent clients and appear in court when enrolled in a clinical legal education course. The clinical education program offers courses designed to develop critical lawyering skills. The program also offers training in trial advocacy, interviewing, counseling, negotiation, alternative dispute resolution, and legal drafting. Clinics include environmental law, criminal practice, juvenile justice, domestic practice, bankruptcy, and federal litigation. Judicial internships place students with trial and appellate court judges. The Pro Bono Program, one of the longest operating programs of its type, has an outstanding national and local reputation. Under the leaderships of a full-time director and a student board, the program offers students an opportunity to be involved in activities such as income tax assistance,

Habitat for Humanity, and legal research. The School of Law offers a summer study abroad program at Gray's Inn, one of the four Inns of Court, in London, on Transnational Dispute Resolution. In the summer of 2004, 44 law students participated in this program, and in the summer of 2005, 33 law students participated.

STUDENT BODY

Fall 2005 full-time enrollment: 739

Men: 57%	Women: 43%
African-American: 6.4%	American Indian: 0.1%
Asian-American: 1.8%	Mexican-American: 0.0%
Puerto Rican: 0.0%	Other Hisp-Amer: 1.8%
White: 88.2%	International: 1.8%
Unknown: 0.0%	

Attrition rates for 2004-2005 full-time students
Percent of students discontinuing law school:

Men: 1%	Women: 2%
First-year students: 2%	Second-year students: 3%
Third-year students: 0%	

LIBRARY RESOURCES

The library holds 77,494 and receives 3,347 current subscriptions.
Total volumes: 521,597
Percentage of the titles in the online catalog: 100%
Total seats available for library users: 597

INFORMATION TECHNOLOGY

Number of wired network connections available to students: 52 total (in the law library, excluding computer labs: 8; in classrooms: 0; in computer labs: 44; elsewhere in the law school: 0)
Law school has a wireless network.
Approximate number of simultaneous users that can be accommodated on wireless network: 700
Students are not required to own a computer.

EMPLOYMENT AND SALARIES

Proportion of 2004 graduates employed at graduation: 59%
Employed 9 months later, as of February 15, 2005: 95%
Salaries in the private sector (law firms, business, industry): $50,000–$68,000 (25th-75th percentile)
Median salary in the private sector: $61,200
Percentage in the private sector who reported salary information: 58%
Median salary in public service (government, judicial clerkships, academic posts, non-profits): $35,143

Percentage of 2004 graduates in:

Law firms: 54%	Bus./industry (legal): 4%
Bus./industry (nonlegal): 2%	Government: 9%
Public interest: 4%	Judicial clerkship: 27%
Academia : 1%	Unknown: 0%

2004 graduates employed in-state: 86%
2004 graduates employed in foreign countries: 1%
Number of states where graduates are employed: 14
Percentage of 2004 graduates working in: New England: 1%, Middle Atlantic: 1%, East North Central: 1%, West North Central: 0%, South Atlantic: 95%, East South Central: 1%, West South Central: 1%, Mountain: 1%, Pacific: 0%, Unknown: 0%

BAR PASSAGE RATES

Based on 2004 graduates taking Summer 2004 or Winter 2005 exams. Most of the school's first-time test takers took the bar in South Carolina.

87%
School's bar passage rate for first-time test takers

84%
Statewide bar passage rate for first-time test takers

University of South Dakota

- 414 E. Clark Street, Vermillion, SD, 57069-2390
- http://www.usd.edu/law/
- Public
- **Year founded:** 1901
- **2005-2006 tuition:** In-state: full-time: $7,962, part-time: $3,981; Out-of-state: full-time: $15,927
- **Enrollment 2005-06 academic year:** full-time: 247; part-time: 3
- **U.S. News 2007 law specialty ranking:** N/A

2.95-3.74	GPA, 25TH-75TH PERCENTILE
150-156	LSAT, 25TH-75TH PERCENTILE
35%	ACCEPTANCE RATE
Tier 4	2007 U.S. NEWS LAW SCHOOL RANKING

ADMISSIONS
Admissions phone number: **(605) 677-5443**
Admissions email address: **lawreq@usd.edu**
Application website:
  http://www.usd.edu/law/prospective_students/admission.cfm
Application deadline for Fall 2007 admission: **3/01**

Admissions statistics:
Number of applicants for Fall 2005: **516**
Number of acceptances: **180**
Number enrolled: **90**
Acceptance rate: **35%**
GPA, 25th-75th percentile, entering class Fall 2005: **2.95-3.74**
LSAT, 25th-75th percentile, entering class Fall 2005: **150-156**

Part-time program:
Number of applicants for Fall 2005: **3**
Number of acceptances: **1**
Number enrolled: **1**
Acceptance rate: **33%**
GPA, 25th-75th percentile, entering class Fall 2005: **N/A**
LSAT, 25th-75th percentile, entering class Fall 2005: **N/A**

FINANCIAL AID
Financial aid phone number: **(605) 677-5446**
Financial aid application deadline: **3/01**
Tuition 2005-2006 academic year: In-state: full-time: **$7,962**, part-time: **$3,981**; Out-of-state: full-time: **$15,927**
Room and board: **$6,116**; books: **$1,300**; miscellaneous expenses: **$5,502**
Total of room/board/books/miscellaneous expenses: **$12,918**
University offers graduate student housing for which law students are eligible.

Financial aid profile
Percent of students that received grants for the 2004-2005 academic year: full-time: **33%**

Median grant amount: full-time: **$625**
The average law-school debt of those in the Class of 2005 who borrowed: **$58,304**. Proportion who borrowed: **100%**

ACADEMIC PROGRAMS
Calendar: **semester**
Joint degrees awarded: **J.D./M.B.A.; J.D./MA Psy; J.D./MA English; J.D./MPA**
Typical first-year section size: Full-time: **73**
Is there typically a "small section" of the first year class, other than Legal Writing, taught by full-time faculty?: Full-time: **yes**
Number of course titles, beyond the first year curriculum, offered last year: **41**
Percentages of upper division course sections, excluding seminars, with an enrollment of:
  Under 25: **47%**   25 to 49: **32%**
  50 to 74: **13%**   75 to 99: **9%**
  100+: **N/A**
Areas of specialization: appellate advocacy, dispute resolution, environmental law, healthcare law, intellectual property law, international law, tax law, trial advocacy

Fall 2005 faculty profile
Total teaching faculty: **14**. Full-time: **93%**; **77%** men, **23%** women, **8%** minorities. Part-time: **7%**; **100%** men, **N/A** women, **N/A** minorities
Student-to-faculty ratio: **16.1**

SPECIAL PROGRAMS *(as provided by law school):*
Joint degree programs: There are nine programs with other graduate departments, with master's degrees available in professional accountancy, business administration, history, English, psychology, education administration, political science, public administration, and administrative studies. Students may transfer nine hours of approved interdisciplinary coursework for J.D. credit and are able to complete both programs in three years.

Interdisciplinary study: For upper-division students not in a joint degree program, up to six graduate credits in other university divisions may be taken and applied toward the hours required for the J.D. degree. This allows a law student to broaden his or her education by the pursuit of new disciplines.

Curricular tracks: The curriculum provides four special tracks of study. Tracks are informally structured and provide curricular, cocurricular, and extracurricular opportunities for enhancement. Tracks are offered in business law, environmental and natural resources law, Indian law, and trial advocacy.

Flextime program: This program permits certain well-qualified students to take less than the normal load of credits each semester and obtain a J.D. in five years instead of three. The program admits a limited number of students who could not attend law school on a full-time basis. The law school does not offer evening or weekend classes.

Accelerated admission: An applicant may apply for accelerated admission and be admitted to and enroll in law school without final completion of the requirements for the applicant's undergraduate degree. The undergraduate degree must be attained by the applicant before graduation from law school.

Law Honors Scholars Program: High school seniors who are accepted to USD undergraduate Honors Scholars may apply for and receive provisional (automatic) admission to the law school upon successful completion of their undergraduate degree in four years with a 3.5 grade-point average, fulfillment of honors program requirements, and completion of the LSAT for statistical purposes only.

Summer Screening Program: Applicants who are not regularly admitted may be invited to participate in the Summer Screening Program. The program consists of two courses, agency and personal property, offered in five weeks of lectures and finals during the sixth week. Participants are admitted or denied admission on the basis of their performance on final exams, which are graded anonymously.

STUDENT BODY

Fall 2005 full-time enrollment: 247

Men: 57%	Women: 43%
African-American: 0.4%	American Indian: 2.0%
Asian-American: 0.8%	Mexican-American: 0.0%
Puerto Rican: 0.4%	Other Hisp-Amer: 1.6%
White: 94.3%	International: 0.4%
Unknown: 0.0%	

Fall 2005 part-time enrollment: 3

Men: 67%	Women: 33%
African-American: 0.0%	American Indian: 0.0%
Asian-American: 0.0%	Mexican-American: 0.0%
Puerto Rican: 0.0%	Other Hisp-Amer: 0.0%
White: 100.0%	International: 0.0%
Unknown: 0.0%	

Attrition rates for 2004-2005 full-time students

Percent of students discontinuing law school:

Men: 1%	Women: 3%
First-year students: 4%	Second-year students: 2%
Third-year students: N/A	

LIBRARY RESOURCES

The library holds 41,069 and receives 1,874 current subscriptions.

Total volumes: 205,506

Percentage of the titles in the online catalog: 100%

Total seats available for library users: 227

INFORMATION TECHNOLOGY

Number of wired network connections available to students: 227 total (in the law library, excluding computer labs: 188; in classrooms: N/A; in computer labs: N/A; elsewhere in the law school: 39)

Law school has a wireless network.

Approximate number of simultaneous users that can be accommodated on wireless network: 180

Students are not required to own a computer.

EMPLOYMENT AND SALARIES

Proportion of 2004 graduates employed at graduation: 49%

Employed 9 months later, as of February 15, 2005: 75%

Salaries in the private sector (law firms, business, industry): $33,000–$47,000 (25th-75th percentile)

Median salary in the private sector: $38,000

Percentage in the private sector who reported salary information: 48%

Median salary in public service (government, judicial clerkships, academic posts, non-profits): $40,000

Percentage of 2004 graduates in:

Law firms: 46%	Bus./industry (legal): 6%
Bus./industry (nonlegal): N/A	Government: 19%
Public interest: 2%	Judicial clerkship: 27%
Academia : N/A	Unknown: N/A

2004 graduates employed in-state: 63%

2004 graduates employed in foreign countries: 0%

Number of states where graduates are employed: 12

Percentage of 2004 graduates working in: New England: 2%, Middle Atlantic: 0%, East North Central: 4%, West North Central: 83%, South Atlantic: 2%, East South Central: 0%, West South Central: 2%, Mountain: 2%, Pacific: 4%, Unknown: 0%

BAR PASSAGE RATES

Based on 2004 graduates taking Summer 2004 or Winter 2005 exams. Most of the school's first-time test takers took the bar in South Dakota.

69%

School's bar passage rate for first-time test takers

74%

Statewide bar passage rate for first-time test takers

Univ. of Southern California (Gould)

- Los Angeles, CA, 90089-0071
- http://www.usc.edu/law
- Private
- **Year founded:** 1900
- **2005-2006 tuition:** full-time: $37,971; part-time: N/A
- **Enrollment 2005-06 academic year:** full-time: 628
- **U.S. News 2007 law specialty ranking:** tax law: 15

3.51-3.78 GPA, 25TH-75TH PERCENTILE

164-167 LSAT, 25TH-75TH PERCENTILE

20% ACCEPTANCE RATE

17 2007 U.S. NEWS LAW SCHOOL RANKING

ADMISSIONS

Admissions phone number: **(213) 740-2523**
Admissions email address: **admissions@law.usc.edu**
Application website: **http://www.usc.edu/law/admissions**
Application deadline for Fall 2007 admission: 2/01

Admissions statistics:

Number of applicants for Fall 2005: **7,075**
Number of acceptances: **1,438**
Number enrolled: **207**
Acceptance rate: **20%**
GPA, 25th-75th percentile, entering class Fall 2005:
   3.51-3.78
LSAT, 25th-75th percentile, entering class Fall 2005:
   164-167

FINANCIAL AID

Financial aid phone number: **(213) 740-2523**
Financial aid application deadline: 2/15
Tuition 2005-2006 academic year: full-time: **$37,971**; part-time: **N/A**
Room and board: **$11,006**; books: **$1,584**; miscellaneous expenses: **$3,182**
Total of room/board/books/miscellaneous expenses: **$15,772**
University offers graduate student housing for which law students are eligible.

Financial aid profile

Percent of students that received grants for the 2004-2005 academic year: full-time: **58%**
Median grant amount: full-time: **$12,000**
The average law-school debt of those in the Class of 2005 who borrowed: **$90,266**. Proportion who borrowed: **85%**

ACADEMIC PROGRAMS

Calendar: **semester**
Joint degrees awarded: **J.D./MA ECON; J.D./MA IR; J.D./MPA; J.D./MA REL; J.D./MSW; J.D./M.B.A.; J.D./MBT; J.D./MA COMM; J.D./MRED; J.D./MA PHIL; J.D./MA POLS; J.D./MS GER; J.D./MPP; J.D./PhD; J.D./PharmD**
Typical first-year section size: Full-time: **70**
Is there typically a "small section" of the first year class, other than Legal Writing, taught by full-time faculty?: Full-time: **no**
Number of course titles, beyond the first year curriculum, offered last year: **86**
Percentages of upper division course sections, excluding seminars, with an enrollment of:
   Under 25: **53%**   25 to 49: **34%**
   50 to 74: **5%**   75 to 99: **5%**
   100+: **5%**
Areas of specialization: appellate advocacy, clinical training, dispute resolution, environmental law, healthcare law, intellectual property law, international law, tax law, trial advocacy

Fall 2005 faculty profile

Total teaching faculty: **139**. Full-time: **30%**; **64%** men, **36%** women, **12%** minorities. Part-time: **70%**; **73%** men, **27%** women, **15%** minorities
Student-to-faculty ratio: **13.0**

SPECIAL PROGRAMS *(as provided by law school):*

USC Law offers a broad range of programs that allow students to maximize their educational experience and combine academic theory with real-world practice.

   USC Law's unique interdisciplinary focus helps students understand how diverse forces shape the law and how the law shapes other professions and fields. Seven major interdisciplinary research centers offer unique opportunities: the USC-Caltech Center for the Study of Law and Politics; the Initiative and Referendum Institute; the USC Center for Law, History, and Culture; the USC Center for Law, Economics, and Organization; the USC Pacific Center for Health Policy and Ethics; the Center for Law and Philosophy; and the USC Center for Communication Law and Policy.

   Through clinical courses and other programs, students gain hands-on experience representing clients and working in legal agencies. The school's clinics specialize in intellectual property, immigration law, post-conviction matters, children's issues, and employer legal advice. Coordinated by the Office of Public Service, an externship program offers academic credit for work with state and federal judges, and an internship program offers credit for work in legal and public-service organizations. USC Law's Summer Fellows program awards approximately 20 top applicants each year a guaranteed paid position during the summer following the first year of law school. Students spend half the summer at a prestigious law firm and half at a top business or public-interest organization. Taking advantage of USC's location and strong ties to the entertainment industry, the school has established a new entertainment law practicum, which blends study of substantive law with work placements in studios and entertainment businesses.

USC Law also offers opportunities to gain a global perspective of the law. An LL.M. program brings lawyers trained in foreign countries to USC for an intensive one-year program. LL.M. students take courses alongside J.D. students, facilitating extensive interaction among students of diverse cultures. Through a study abroad program, J.D. students may spend a semester at the University of Hong Kong's Faculty of Law. Home to one of the largest and most respected continuing legal education programs in the nation, USC Law offers students opportunities to participate in and work at conferences and institutes attended by top industry leaders.

STUDENT BODY

Fall 2005 full-time enrollment: 628

Men: 52%	Women: 48%
African-American: 9.1%	American Indian: 0.3%
Asian-American: 19.4%	Mexican-American: 6.2%
Puerto Rican: 0.2%	Other Hisp-Amer: 2.4%
White: 52.2%	International: 1.0%
Unknown: 9.2%	

Attrition rates for 2004-2005 full-time students
Percent of students discontinuing law school:

Men: 2%	Women: 2%
First-year students: 5%	Second-year students: 0%
Third-year students: N/A	

LIBRARY RESOURCES

The library holds 170,540 and receives 4,818 current subscriptions.
Total volumes: 413,501
Percentage of the titles in the online catalog: 100%
Total seats available for library users: 281

INFORMATION TECHNOLOGY

Number of wired network connections available to students: 60 total (in the law library, excluding computer labs: 60; in classrooms: 0; in computer labs: 0; elsewhere in the law school: 0)
Law school has a wireless network.
Approximate number of simultaneous users that can be accommodated on wireless network: 650
Students are not required to own a computer.

EMPLOYMENT AND SALARIES

Proportion of 2004 graduates employed at graduation: 88%
Employed 9 months later, as of February 15, 2005: 99%
Salaries in the private sector (law firms, business, industry): $120,000–$125,000 (25th-75th percentile)
Median salary in the private sector: $125,000
Percentage in the private sector who reported salary information: 57%
Median salary in public service (government, judicial clerkships, academic posts, non-profits): $53,000

Percentage of 2004 graduates in:

Law firms: 65%	Bus./industry (legal): 2%
Bus./industry (nonlegal): 10%	Government: 5%
Public interest: 3%	Judicial clerkship: 7%
Academia : 2%	Unknown: 5%

2004 graduates employed in-state: 83%
2004 graduates employed in foreign countries: 1%
Number of states where graduates are employed: 11
Percentage of 2004 graduates working in: New England: 1%, Middle Atlantic: 2%, East North Central: 1%, West North Central: 0%, South Atlantic: 6%, East South Central: 0%, West South Central: 1%, Mountain: 2%, Pacific: 83%, Unknown: 5%

BAR PASSAGE RATES

Based on 2004 graduates taking Summer 2004 or Winter 2005 exams. Most of the school's first-time test takers took the bar in California.

81%
School's bar passage rate for first-time test takers

61%
Statewide bar passage rate for first-time test takers

University of St. Thomas

■ MSL 411, 1000 LaSalle Avenue, Minneapolis, MN, 55403-2015
■ http://www.stthomas.edu/law
■ Private
■ Year founded: 2001
■ 2005-2006 tuition: full-time: $25,404; part-time: N/A
■ Enrollment 2005-06 academic year: full-time: 418
■ U.S. News 2007 law specialty ranking: N/A

3.03-3.60 GPA, 25TH-75TH PERCENTILE

151-158 LSAT, 25TH-75TH PERCENTILE

45% ACCEPTANCE RATE

Unranked 2007 U.S. NEWS LAW SCHOOL RANKING

ADMISSIONS

Admissions phone number: **(651) 962-4895**
Admissions email address: **lawschool@stthomas.edu**
Application website: **http://www.stthomas.edu/law/admissions/applicationinformation.asp**
Application deadline for Fall 2007 admission: **7/01**

Admissions statistics:

Number of applicants for Fall 2005: **1,039**
Number of acceptances: **469**
Number enrolled: **148**
Acceptance rate: **45%**
GPA, 25th-75th percentile, entering class Fall 2005: **3.03-3.60**
LSAT, 25th-75th percentile, entering class Fall 2005: **151-158**

FINANCIAL AID

Financial aid phone number: **(651) 962-4895**
Financial aid application deadline: **6/01**
Tuition 2005-2006 academic year: full-time: **$25,404**; part-time: **N/A**
Room and board: **N/A**; books: **N/A**; miscellaneous expenses: **N/A**
Total of room/board/books/miscellaneous expenses: **$15,662**
University does not offer graduate student housing for which law students are eligible.

Financial aid profile

Percent of students that received grants for the 2004-2005 academic year: full-time: **70%**
Median grant amount: full-time: **$15,000**
The average law-school debt of those in the Class of 2005 who borrowed: **$68,501**. Proportion who borrowed: **85%**

ACADEMIC PROGRAMS

Calendar: **semester**
Joint degrees awarded: **M.A.Catholic Studies; M.A. Educational Leadership; M.B.A.; M.S.W.; M.A. Professional Psychology**
Typical first-year section size: Full-time: **73**

Is there typically a "small section" of the first year class, other than Legal Writing, taught by full-time faculty?: Full-time: **no**
Number of course titles, beyond the first year curriculum, offered last year: **67**
Percentages of upper division course sections, excluding seminars, with an enrollment of:

Under 25: **78%**	25 to 49: **15%**
50 to 74: **7%**	75 to 99: **0%**
100+: **0%**	

Areas of specialization: appellate advocacy, clinical training, dispute resolution, environmental law, healthcare law, intellectual property law, international law, tax law, trial advocacy

Fall 2005 faculty profile

Total teaching faculty: **70**. Full-time: **30%**; **62%** men, **38%** women, **10%** minorities. Part-time: **70%**; **57%** men, **43%** women, **4%** minorities
Student-to-faculty ratio: **15.1**

SPECIAL PROGRAMS (as provided by law school):

The University of St. Thomas School of Law (UST) received full accreditation from the ABA in February 2006. To fulfill its distinctive mission—integrating faith and reason in a search for truth with a focus on morality and social justice—UST has developed a number of special programs. First, UST students participate in its unique, nationally-recognized Mentor Externship Program throughout their years at UST. Paired with a practicing lawyer or judge, students are required to observe lawyers and judges in action. They reflect on these experiences with their mentors and engage in discussions with other students in a classroom setting in which they can integrate readings, observed experiences and personal reflections as they develop a deeper understanding of professionalism and the habit and skill of reflective lawyering. Second, students can participate in the innovative Legal Services Clinic (Clinic) of the Interprofessional Center for Counseling and Legal Services, which offers students exposure to client advocacy and litigation in a supervised interprofessional setting in which law students work side-by-side with graduate students in professional psychology and social work. The Clinic handles a variety of civil cases, representing low-income or nonprofit clients, and is divided into three practice groups: Elder Law, Immigration Law, and Family Law. The Clinic provides students with opportunities to develop competent lawyering practice skills, to apply substantive course work to actual cases and to examine the institutional, ethical and personal problems inherent in the lives of today's practicing lawyers. Finally, UST Law has two research centers—the Terrence J. Murphy Institute for Catholic Thought, Law, and Public Policy and the Center for Ethical Leadership in the Professions. The Murphy Institute is a collaboration between UST Law and the University's Center for Catholic Studies. The Institute "explore[s] the various interactions between law and Catholic thought on topics ranging from workers rights to criminal law to marriage and family. To help provide connections between law and Catholic thought, the Institute will develop curricular resources, facilitate scholarship and scholarly discussions, and engage and serve the church and community through public events and public policy analysis." The Center for Ethical Leadership in the Professions will provide leading-edge interdisciplinary research, curriculum development, and programs focusing holistically on the formation of both students and practicing professionals into accomplished ethical leaders in their communities.

STUDENT BODY

Fall 2005 full-time enrollment: 418

Men: 49%	Women: 51%
African-American: 4.1%	American Indian: 1.0%
Asian-American: 6.2%	Mexican-American: 0.2%
Puerto Rican: 0.2%	Other Hisp-Amer: 2.9%
White: 71.1%	International: 0.0%
Unknown: 14.4%	

Attrition rates for 2004-2005 full-time students
Percent of students discontinuing law school:

Men: 2%	Women: 2%
First-year students: 3%	Second-year students: 2%
Third-year students: 1%	

LIBRARY RESOURCES

The library holds 125,163 and receives 1,474 current subscriptions.
Total volumes: 165,537
Percentage of the titles in the online catalog: 100%
Total seats available for library users: 379

INFORMATION TECHNOLOGY

Number of wired network connections available to students: 595 total (in the law library, excluding computer labs: 335; in classrooms: 165; in computer labs: 0; elsewhere in the law school: 95)
Law school has a wireless network.
Approximate number of simultaneous users that can be accommodated on wireless network: N/A
Students are not required to own a computer.

EMPLOYMENT AND SALARIES

Proportion of 2004 graduates employed at graduation: N/A
Employed 9 months later, as of February 15, 2005: N/A
Salaries in the private sector (law firms, business, industry): N/A–N/A (25th-75th percentile)
Median salary in the private sector: N/A
Percentage in the private sector who reported salary information: N/A
Median salary in public service (government, judicial clerkships, academic posts, non-profits): N/A

Percentage of 2004 graduates in:

Law firms: 42%	Bus./industry (legal): 12%
Bus./industry (nonlegal): N/A	Government: 8%
Public interest: 15%	Judicial clerkship: 18%
Academia : 2%	Unknown: 3%

2004 graduates employed in-state: 80%
2004 graduates employed in foreign countries: 2%
Number of states where graduates are employed: 12
Percentage of 2004 graduates working in: New England: 0%, Middle Atlantic: 0%, East North Central: 3%, West North Central: 84%, South Atlantic: 1%, East South Central: 2%, West South Central: 0%, Mountain: 7%, Pacific: 1%, Unknown: 0%

BAR PASSAGE RATES

Based on 2004 graduates taking Summer 2004 or Winter 2005 exams. Most of the school's first-time test takers took the bar in Minnesota.

N/A
School's bar passage rate for first-time test takers

N/A
Statewide bar passage rate for first-time test takers

University of Tennessee—Knoxville

■ 1505 W. Cumberland Avenue, Knoxville, TN, 37996-1810
■ http://www.law.utk.edu
■ Public
■ Year founded: 1890
■ 2005-2006 tuition: In-state: full-time: $9,412, part-time: N/A;
  Out-of-state: full-time: $24,106
■ Enrollment 2005-06 academic year: full-time: 457
■ U.S. News 2007 law specialty ranking: clinical training: 19

3.36-3.86 GPA, 25TH-75TH PERCENTILE

155-161 LSAT, 25TH-75TH PERCENTILE

20% ACCEPTANCE RATE

60 2007 U.S. NEWS LAW SCHOOL RANKING

ADMISSIONS

Admissions phone number: **(865) 974-4131**
Admissions email address: **lawadmit@libra.law.utk.edu**
Application website: **http://www.law.utk.edu/depart-
ments/admiss/prospecstuhome.htm**
Application deadline for Fall 2007 admission: **3/01**

Admissions statistics:
Number of applicants for Fall 2005: **1,622**
Number of acceptances: **322**
Number enrolled: **158**
Acceptance rate: **20%**
GPA, 25th-75th percentile, entering class Fall 2005:
  3.36-3.86
LSAT, 25th-75th percentile, entering class Fall 2005: **155-161**

FINANCIAL AID

Financial aid phone number: **(865) 974-4131**
Financial aid application deadline: **3/01**
Tuition 2005-2006 academic year: In-state: full-time:
  $9,412, part-time: **N/A**; Out-of-state: full-time: **$24,106**
Room and board: **$7,714**; books: **$1,400**; miscellaneous
  expenses: **$5,074**
Total of room/board/books/miscellaneous expenses:
  $14,188
University offers graduate student housing for which law
  students are eligible.

Financial aid profile
Percent of students that received grants for the 2004-2005
  academic year: full-time: **46%**
Median grant amount: full-time: **$5,000**
The average law-school debt of those in the Class of 2005
  who borrowed: **$45,404**. Proportion who borrowed: **80%**

ACADEMIC PROGRAMS

Calendar: **semester**
Joint degrees awarded: **J.D./M.B.A.; J.D./M.P.A.**
Typical first-year section size: Full-time: **52**

Is there typically a "small section" of the first year class,
  other than Legal Writing, taught by full-time faculty?:
  Full-time: **no**
Number of course titles, beyond the first year curriculum,
  offered last year: **94**
Percentages of upper division course sections, excluding
  seminars, with an enrollment of:
  Under 25: **74%**   25 to 49: **17%**
  50 to 74: **8%**   75 to 99: **1%**
  100+: **0%**
Areas of specialization: appellate advocacy, clinical training,
  dispute resolution, environmental law, healthcare law,
  intellectual property law, international law, tax law, trial
  advocacy

Fall 2005 faculty profile
Total teaching faculty: **96**. Full-time: **30%**; **62%** men, **38%**
  women, **10%** minorities. Part-time: **70%**; **60%** men,
  40% women, **4%** minorities
Student-to-faculty ratio: **12.1**

SPECIAL PROGRAMS *(as provided by law school):*

The University of Tennessee College of Law offers two academic
concentrations that allow students to specialize in particular
areas of the law. The advocacy and dispute resolution track
builds upon the college's long-standing excellence in clinical
training, and the business transactions track provides hands-on
training in the representation of businesses.

   The college also offers a joint J.D./M.B.A. program, in which
students can earn advanced degrees in law and business, as well
as a joint J.D./M.P.A. program for law and public administration degrees.

   The college's Legal Clinic allows third-year students to learn
by doing. Working under faculty supervision, clinic students
represent real clients with real legal problems. In addition, the
Mediation Clinic offers students an alternative method of
resolving disputes between parties.

   In conjunction with other law schools, the UT College of Law
offers a summer study program at the University of Cambridge
in England, which features internationally recognized faculty,
including members of the Tennessee law faculty.

STUDENT BODY

Fall 2005 full-time enrollment: 457

Men: 49%	Women: 51%
African-American: 12.9%	American Indian: 0.4%
Asian-American: 0.9%	Mexican-American: 0.0%
Puerto Rican: 0.0%	Other Hisp-Amer: 0.4%
White: 84.0%	International: 0.0%
Unknown: 1.3%	

Attrition rates for 2004-2005 full-time students

Percent of students discontinuing law school:

Men: 0%	Women: 0%
First-year students: 1%	Second-year students: 1%
Third-year students: N/A	

LIBRARY RESOURCES

The library holds 112,208 and receives 6,650 current subscriptions.

Total volumes: 558,262

Percentage of the titles in the online catalog: 99%

Total seats available for library users: 437

INFORMATION TECHNOLOGY

Number of wired network connections available to students: 164 total (in the law library, excluding computer labs: 105; in classrooms: 0; in computer labs: 59; elsewhere in the law school: 0)

Law school has a wireless network.

Approximate number of simultaneous users that can be accommodated on wireless network: 900

Students are not required to own a computer.

EMPLOYMENT AND SALARIES

Proportion of 2004 graduates employed at graduation: 60%

Employed 9 months later, as of February 15, 2005: 85%

Salaries in the private sector (law firms, business, industry): $50,000–$83,000 (25th-75th percentile)

Median salary in the private sector: $63,000

Percentage in the private sector who reported salary information: 70%

Median salary in public service (government, judicial clerkships, academic posts, non-profits): $42,000

Percentage of 2004 graduates in:

Law firms: 67%	Bus./industry (legal): 0%
Bus./industry (nonlegal): 6%	Government: 15%
Public interest: 3%	Judicial clerkship: 7%
Academia : 2%	Unknown: 0%

2004 graduates employed in-state: 65%

2004 graduates employed in foreign countries: 0%

Number of states where graduates are employed: 20

Percentage of 2004 graduates working in: New England: 0%, Middle Atlantic: 1%, East North Central: 2%, West North Central: 0%, South Atlantic: 24%, East South Central: 68%, West South Central: 2%, Mountain: 3%, Pacific: 0%, Unknown: 0%

BAR PASSAGE RATES

Based on 2004 graduates taking Summer 2004 or Winter 2005 exams. Most of the school's first-time test takers took the bar in Tennessee.

87%

School's bar passage rate for first-time test takers

82%

Statewide bar passage rate for first-time test takers

iversity of Texas–Austin

■ 727 E. Dean Keeton Street, Austin, TX, 78705-3299
■ http://www.utexas.edu/law
■ Public
■ Year founded: 1883
■ 2005-2006 tuition: In-state: full-time: $16,935, part-time: N/A;
  Out-of-state: full-time: $29,291
■ Enrollment 2005-06 academic year: full-time: 1,387
■ U.S. News 2007 law specialty ranking: environmental law: 18, intelle-
  cutal property law: 21, international law: 11, tax law: 15

3.41-3.83 GPA, 25TH-75TH PERCENTILE

161-168 LSAT, 25TH-75TH PERCENTILE

19% ACCEPTANCE RATE

16 2007 U.S. NEWS LAW SCHOOL RANKING

ADMISSIONS

Admissions phone number: **(512) 232-1200**
Admissions email address: **admissions@law.utexas.edu**
Application website:
   http://www.utexas.edu/law/depts/admissions/
Application deadline for Fall 2007 admission: **2/01**

Admissions statistics:
Number of applicants for Fall 2005: **5,442**
Number of acceptances: **1,017**
Number enrolled: **442**
Acceptance rate: **19%**
GPA, 25th-75th percentile, entering class Fall 2005:
   3.41-3.83
LSAT, 25th-75th percentile, entering class Fall 2005:
   161-168

FINANCIAL AID

Financial aid phone number: **(512) 232-1130**
Financial aid application deadline: **3/31**
Tuition 2005-2006 academic year: In-state: full-time:
   $16,935, part-time: **N/A**; Out-of-state: full-time: **$29,291**
Room and board: **$8,000**; books: **$1,000**; miscellaneous
   expenses: **$2,620**
Total of room/board/books/miscellaneous expenses:
   $11,620
University offers graduate student housing for which law
   students are eligible.

Financial aid profile
Percent of students that received grants for the 2004-2005
   academic year: full-time: **86%**
Median grant amount: full-time: **$1,250**
The average law-school debt of those in the Class of 2005
   who borrowed: **$63,240**. Proportion who borrowed: **72%**

ACADEMIC PROGRAMS
Calendar: **semester**
Joint degrees awarded: **J.D./M.B.A.; J.D./MPA; J.D./MA;
   J.D./MSCRP**
Typical first-year section size: Full-time: **106**

Is there typically a "small section" of the first year class,
   other than Legal Writing, taught by full-time faculty?:
   Full-time: **yes**
Number of course titles, beyond the first year curriculum,
   offered last year: **138**
Percentages of upper division course sections, excluding
   seminars, with an enrollment of:
   Under 25: **56%**   25 to 49: **23%**
   50 to 74: **8%**   75 to 99: **4%**
   100+: **9%**
Areas of specialization: appellate advocacy, clinical training,
   dispute resolution, environmental law, healthcare law,
   intellectual property law, international law, tax law, trial
   advocacy

Fall 2005 faculty profile
Total teaching faculty: **112**. Full-time: **54%**; **73%** men, **27%**
   women, **7%** minorities. Part-time: **46%**; **65%** men, **35%**
   women, **12%** minorities
Student-to-faculty ratio: **16.7**

SPECIAL PROGRAMS *(as provided by law school)*:
Clinics: The law school offers clinics in actual innocence, capital
punishment, children's rights, criminal defense, domestic violence, environmental law, housing law, immigration law, juvenile justice, mediation, mental health, prosecution, and
transnational worker rights.
   Internships: Internships are available with federal and state
court judges, nonprofit organizations, government (the
Commission on Environmental Quality, the Texas Legislature,
and others), the International Criminal Tribunal for the Former
Yugoslavia, the International Criminal Tribunal for Rwanda, the
Inter-American Court of Human Rights, Democracy Fellows—
Latin America, and the European Court of Justice in
Luxembourg. Independent international law internships may be
arranged.
   Centers and institutes: Such programs include the Bernard
and Audre Rapoport Center for Human Rights and Justice; the
Center for Law, Business, and Economics; the Center on
Lawyers, Civil Justice, and the Media; the William Wayne Justice
Center for Public Interest Law; the Center for Public Policy and

Dispute Resolution; the Institute for Transnational Law; and the Law and Philosophy Program.

Summer study: The summer school offers more than a dozen courses, internships, seminars, and clinics.

Special study: Eight joint degree programs. Two LLM programs: Latin American and International Law; U.S. Law for Foreign Lawyers. Study abroad: Semester in London program. Exchange programs with: England: University of Nottingham; Scotland: University of Edinburgh; Spain: University of Pais Vasco; France: University of Paris X (Nanterre); Germany: Bucerius Law School; Italy: University of Siena; Australia: Australian National University; University of Melbourne; University of New South Wales; University of Sydney; the Netherlands: University of Leiden; Argentina: Universidad Torcuato di Tella; Universidad de Buenos Aires; Brazil: Universidade Federal do Rio Grande do Sul; Universidade Federal do Para.

STUDENT BODY
Fall 2005 full-time enrollment: 1,387

Men: 57%	Women: 43%
African-American: 5.7%	American Indian: 0.8%
Asian-American: 6.1%	Mexican-American: 14.4%
Puerto Rican: 0.0%	Other Hisp-Amer: 4.8%
White: 57.0%	International: 0.0%
Unknown: 11.2%	

Attrition rates for 2004-2005 full-time students
Percent of students discontinuing law school:

Men: 2%	Women: 2%
First-year students: 3%	Second-year students: 2%
Third-year students: 0%	

LIBRARY RESOURCES
The library holds 379,242 and receives 8,322 current subscriptions.
Total volumes: 1,026,598
Percentage of the titles in the online catalog: 100%
Total seats available for library users: 1,321

INFORMATION TECHNOLOGY
Number of wired network connections available to students: 310 total (in the law library, excluding computer labs: 24; in classrooms: 98; in computer labs: 38; elsewhere in the law school: 150)

Law school has a wireless network.
Approximate number of simultaneous users that can be accommodated on wireless network: 35,000
Students are not required to own a computer.

EMPLOYMENT AND SALARIES
Proportion of 2004 graduates employed at graduation: 95%
Employed 9 months later, as of February 15, 2005: 98%
Salaries in the private sector (law firms, business, industry): $100,000–$120,000 (25th-75th percentile)
Median salary in the private sector: $110,000
Percentage in the private sector who reported salary information: 66%
Median salary in public service (government, judicial clerkships, academic posts, non-profits): $47,000

Percentage of 2004 graduates in:

Law firms: 61%	Bus./industry (legal): 4%
Bus./industry (nonlegal): 3%	Government: 11%
Public interest: 5%	Judicial clerkship: 13%
Academia : 1%	Unknown: 2%

2004 graduates employed in-state: 74%
2004 graduates employed in foreign countries: 0%
Number of states where graduates are employed: 29
Percentage of 2004 graduates working in: New England: 0%, Middle Atlantic: 5%, East North Central: 2%, West North Central: 2%, South Atlantic: 7%, East South Central: 2%, West South Central: 74%, Mountain: 1%, Pacific: 4%, Unknown: 4%

BAR PASSAGE RATES
Based on 2004 graduates taking Summer 2004 or Winter 2005 exams. Most of the school's first-time test takers took the bar in Texas.

92%
School's bar passage rate for first-time test takers

79%
Statewide bar passage rate for first-time test takers

Univ. of the Dist. of Columbia (Clarke)

- 4200 Connecticut Avenue NW, Building 38 & 39, Washington, D.C., 20008
- http://www.law.udc.edu
- Public
- Year founded: 1988
- 2005-2006 tuition: In-state: full-time: $7,000, part-time: N/A; Out-of-state: full-time: $14,000
- Enrollment 2005-06 academic year: full-time: 232
- U.S. News 2007 law specialty ranking: clinical training: 19

2.76-3.23 GPA, 25TH-75TH PERCENTILE

149-155 LSAT, 25TH-75TH PERCENTILE

23% ACCEPTANCE RATE

Tier 4 2007 U.S. NEWS LAW SCHOOL RANKING

ADMISSIONS

Admissions phone number: (202) 274-7341
Admissions email address: vcanty@udc.edu
Application website:
  http://www.law.edu/prospective/apply/html
Application deadline for Fall 2007 admission: 3/15

Admissions statistics:
Number of applicants for Fall 2005: 1,373
Number of acceptances: 316
Number enrolled: 81
Acceptance rate: 23%
GPA, 25th-75th percentile, entering class Fall 2005:
  2.76-3.23
LSAT, 25th-75th percentile, entering class Fall 2005:
  149-155

FINANCIAL AID

Financial aid phone number: (202) 274-7337
Financial aid application deadline: 3/31
Tuition 2005-2006 academic year: In-state: full-time:
  $7,000, part-time: N/A; Out-of-state: full-time: $14,000
Room and board: N/A; books: N/A; miscellaneous
  expenses: N/A
Total of room/board/books/miscellaneous expenses:
  $23,900
University does not offer graduate student housing for
  which law students are eligible.

Financial aid profile
Percent of students that received grants for the 2004-2005
  academic year: full-time: 78%
Median grant amount: full-time: $4,000
The average law-school debt of those in the Class of 2005
  who borrowed: $67,000. Proportion who borrowed:
  100%

ACADEMIC PROGRAMS

Calendar: semester
Joint degrees awarded: N/A
Typical first-year section size: Full-time: 85

Is there typically a "small section" of the first year class,
  other than Legal Writing, taught by full-time faculty?:
  Full-time: yes
Number of course titles, beyond the first year curriculum,
  offered last year: 45
Percentages of upper division course sections, excluding
  seminars, with an enrollment of:
  Under 25: 64%   25 to 49: 21%
  50 to 74: 10%   75 to 99: 5%
  100+: 0%
Areas of specialization: appellate advocacy, clinical training,
  healthcare law, intellectual property law, international
  law, tax law, trial advocacy

Fall 2005 faculty profile
Total teaching faculty: 29. Full-time: 59%; 59% men, 41%
  women, 47% minorities. Part-time: 41%; 67% men, 33%
  women, 67% minorities
Student-to-faculty ratio: 11.5

STUDENT BODY

Fall 2005 full-time enrollment: 232
Men: 38%   Women: 62%
African-American: 30.6%   American Indian: 1.3%
Asian-American: 6.5%   Mexican-American: 1.7%
Puerto Rican: 0.9%   Other Hisp-Amer: 6.5%
White: 46.6%   International: 6.0%
Unknown: 0.0%

Attrition rates for 2004-2005 full-time students
Percent of students discontinuing law school:
Men: 2%   Women: 9%
First-year students: 15%   Second-year students: 3%
Third-year students: N/A

LIBRARY RESOURCES

The library holds 132,760 and receives 1,603 current
  subscriptions.
Total volumes: 243,651
Percentage of the titles in the online catalog: 100%
Total seats available for library users: 251

INFORMATION TECHNOLOGY

Number of wired network connections available to students: **16** total (in the law library, excluding computer labs: **4**; in classrooms: **N/A**; in computer labs: **N/A**; elsewhere in the law school: **12**)

Law school has a wireless network.

Approximate number of simultaneous users that can be accommodated on wireless network: **762**

Students are required to own a computer.

EMPLOYMENT AND SALARIES

Proportion of 2004 graduates employed at graduation: **N/A**

Employed 9 months later, as of February 15, 2005: **78%**

Salaries in the private sector (law firms, business, industry): **N/A–N/A** (25th-75th percentile)

Median salary in the private sector: **N/A**

Percentage in the private sector who reported salary information: **N/A**

Median salary in public service (government, judicial clerkships, academic posts, non-profits): **N/A**

Percentage of 2004 graduates in:

Law firms: **56%**   Bus./industry (legal): **15%**
Bus./industry (nonlegal): **N/A**   Government: **3%**

Public interest: **17%**   Judicial clerkship: **3%**
Academia : **6%**   Unknown: **N/A**

2004 graduates employed in-state: **39%**
2004 graduates employed in foreign countries: **N/A**
Number of states where graduates are employed: **12**
Percentage of 2004 graduates working in: New England: **N/A**, Middle Atlantic: **N/A**, East North Central: **N/A**, West North Central: **N/A**, South Atlantic: **N/A**, East South Central: **N/A**, West South Central: **N/A**, Mountain: **N/A**, Pacific: **N/A**, Unknown: **N/A**

BAR PASSAGE RATES

Based on 2004 graduates taking Summer 2004 or Winter 2005 exams. Most of the school's first-time test takers took the bar in Maryland.

36%
School's bar passage rate for first-time test takers

72%
Statewide bar passage rate for first-time test takers

University of the Pacific (McGeorge)

- 3200 Fifth Avenue, Sacramento, CA, 95817
- http://www.mcgeorge.edu
- Private
- Year founded: 1924
- 2005-2006 tuition: full-time: $31,173; part-time: $20,690
- Enrollment 2005-06 academic year: full-time: 641; part-time: 401
- U.S. News 2007 law specialty ranking: N/A

3.00-3.51 GPA, 25TH-75TH PERCENTILE

156-160 LSAT, 25TH-75TH PERCENTILE

31% ACCEPTANCE RATE

97 2007 U.S. NEWS LAW SCHOOL RANKING

ADMISSIONS

Admissions phone number: **(916) 739-7105**
Admissions email address:
   admissionsmcgeorge@pacific.edu
Application website: **http://www.mcgeorge.edu/admissions/apply/index.htm**
Application deadline for Fall 2007 admission: **rolling**

Admissions statistics:
Number of applicants for Fall 2005: **3,027**
Number of acceptances: **939**
Number enrolled: **243**
Acceptance rate: **31%**
GPA, 25th-75th percentile, entering class Fall 2005:
   3.00-3.51
LSAT, 25th-75th percentile, entering class Fall 2005:
   156-160

Part-time program:
Number of applicants for Fall 2005: **374**
Number of acceptances: **155**
Number enrolled: **97**
Acceptance rate: **41%**
GPA, 25th-75th percentile, entering class Fall 2005:
   2.89-3.42
LSAT, 25th-75th percentile, entering class Fall 2005:
   152-156

FINANCIAL AID

Financial aid phone number: **(916) 739-7158**
Financial aid application deadline: **N/A**
Tuition 2005-2006 academic year: full-time: **$31,173**; part-time: **$20,690**
Room and board: **$11,520**; books: **$800**; miscellaneous expenses: **$6,432**
Total of room/board/books/miscellaneous expenses: **$18,752**
University offers graduate student housing for which law students are eligible.

Financial aid profile
Percent of students that received grants for the 2004-2005 academic year: full-time: **59%**; part-time **42%**
Median grant amount: full-time: **$10,000**; part-time: **$5,000**
The average law-school debt of those in the Class of 2005 who borrowed: **$86,435**. Proportion who borrowed: **96%**

ACADEMIC PROGRAMS

Calendar: **semester**
Joint degrees awarded: **J.D./M.B.A.; J.D./M.S. M.I.S.; J.D./M.P.P.A.; J.D./M.S. Acctg.**
Typical first-year section size: Full-time: **82**; Part-time: **107**
Is there typically a "small section" of the first year class, other than Legal Writing, taught by full-time faculty?: Full-time: **yes**; Part-time: **yes**
Number of course titles, beyond the first year curriculum, offered last year: **129**
Percentages of upper division course sections, excluding seminars, with an enrollment of:

Under 25: **47%**	25 to 49: **25%**
50 to 74: **15%**	75 to 99: **11%**
100+: **2%**	

Areas of specialization: appellate advocacy, clinical training, dispute resolution, environmental law, healthcare law, intellectual property law, international law, tax law, trial advocacy

Fall 2005 faculty profile
Total teaching faculty: **100**. Full-time: **52%**; **62%** men, **38%** women, **13%** minorities. Part-time: **48%**; **67%** men, **33%** women, **13%** minorities
Student-to-faculty ratio: **16.1**

SPECIAL PROGRAMS *(as provided by law school):*
Students at Pacific McGeorge can choose to concentrate in any one of six specialty areas: Advocacy, Criminal Justice, Governmental Law & Policy, Intellectual Property, International Law, or Tax. We also offer extensive clinical, internship, and study abroad programs. Our Advocacy Program is one of the strongest in the nation. That's nothing new—we were the first

winner of the American College of Trial Lawyer's Emil Gumpert Award, the highest national honor for trial advocacy training. We offer a Certificate in Advocacy and Dispute Resolution for students interested in this area. Our Governmental Law & Policy program offers unparalleled advantages to law students seeking careers in government and public policy. By working on actual legislation and helping to develop public policy in California's capital, both in the classroom and in governmental internships, students receive the legal training and practical skills needed to understand and participate in the lawmaking process. Students who complete the program receive a Certificate in Government Law & Policy upon graduation. We are the only law school west of the District of Columbia to offer a graduate law degree in Government Law and Public Policy.

Pacific McGeorge is a leader in international law. We offer 25 courses on international law topics, and allow qualified students to study law abroad for a semester. Students can also attend classes in our summer programs in Austria or China. Finally, our unique LL.M. programs in international law attract graduate students from around the world, giving our campus an international flavor. Our new Pacific McGeorge Center for Global Business and Development promotes scholarship, curricular innovation, and real-world projects to help attorneys and policy makers address the legal issues raised by the global economy. We also offer a Certificate in International Legal Studies for students who wish to focus their studies in this area. Finally, Pacific McGeorge was a pioneer in clinical legal education. We began our on-campus Community Legal Services clinic in 1972, when some in legal education considered it a radical idea. Students in the clinic, supervised by full-time faculty members, represent low-income clients in a variety of matters and receive hands-on training in the practice of law. In total, the clinic serves about 4,000 clients each year. In addition, the clinic building houses the offices for our extensive internship program. Capitalizing on our location in California's capital, we offer over 70 internship opportunities in federal, state, and local agencies and nonprofit organizations.

STUDENT BODY

Fall 2005 full-time enrollment: 641

Men: 56%	Women: 44%
African-American: 1.6%	American Indian: 0.9%
Asian-American: 13.9%	Mexican-American: 2.2%
Puerto Rican: 0.3%	Other Hisp-Amer: 1.1%
White: 77.5%	International: 2.5%
Unknown: 0.0%	

Fall 2005 part-time enrollment: 401

Men: 50%	Women: 50%
African-American: 3.5%	American Indian: 1.2%
Asian-American: 10.0%	Mexican-American: 4.2%
Puerto Rican: 0.2%	Other Hisp-Amer: 4.5%
White: 74.6%	International: 1.7%
Unknown: 0.0%	

Attrition rates for 2004-2005 full-time students
Percent of students discontinuing law school:
Men: 8%   Women: 6%

First-year students: 13%   Second-year students: 8%
Third-year students: 1%

LIBRARY RESOURCES
The library holds 116,357 and receives 4,546 current subscriptions.
Total volumes: 481,402
Percentage of the titles in the online catalog: 100%
Total seats available for library users: 529

INFORMATION TECHNOLOGY
Number of wired network connections available to students: 305 total (in the law library, excluding computer labs: 277; in classrooms: 20; in computer labs: 8; elsewhere in the law school: 0)
Law school has a wireless network.
Approximate number of simultaneous users that can be accommodated on wireless network: 576
Students are not required to own a computer.

EMPLOYMENT AND SALARIES
Proportion of 2004 graduates employed at graduation: N/A
Employed 9 months later, as of February 15, 2005: 96%
Salaries in the private sector (law firms, business, industry): $55,000–$70,000 (25th-75th percentile)
Median salary in the private sector: $62,200
Percentage in the private sector who reported salary information: 51%
Median salary in public service (government, judicial clerkships, academic posts, non-profits): $53,000

Percentage of 2004 graduates in:

Law firms: 52%	Bus./industry (legal): 1%
Bus./industry (nonlegal): 11%	Government: 14%
Public interest: 12%	Judicial clerkship: 6%
Academia : 3%	Unknown: 1%

2004 graduates employed in-state: 89%
2004 graduates employed in foreign countries: 0%
Number of states where graduates are employed: 10
Percentage of 2004 graduates working in: New England: 0%, Middle Atlantic: 0%, East North Central: 0%, West North Central: 0%, South Atlantic: 3%, East South Central: 0%, West South Central: 0%, Mountain: 7%, Pacific: 89%, Unknown: 0%

BAR PASSAGE RATES
Based on 2004 graduates taking Summer 2004 or Winter 2005 exams. Most of the school's first-time test takers took the bar in California.

69%
School's bar passage rate for first-time test takers

61%
Statewide bar passage rate for first-time test takers

University of Toledo

- 2801 W. Bancroft, Toledo, OH, 43606
- http://www.utlaw.edu
- Public
- Year founded: 1906
- 2005-2006 tuition: In-state: full-time: $13,781, part-time: $10,913; Out-of-state: full-time: $24,024
- Enrollment 2005-06 academic year: full-time: 351; part-time: 159
- U.S. News 2007 law specialty ranking: N/A

2.98-3.76 GPA, 25TH-75TH PERCENTILE

155-162 LSAT, 25TH-75TH PERCENTILE

19% ACCEPTANCE RATE

93 2007 U.S. NEWS LAW SCHOOL RANKING

ADMISSIONS
Admissions phone number: **(419) 530-4131**
Admissions email address: **law.admissions@utoledo.edu**
Application website: **http://www.utlaw.edu/admissions**
Application deadline for Fall 2007 admission: **1/07**

Admissions statistics:
Number of applicants for Fall 2005: 1,231
Number of acceptances: 231
Number enrolled: 85
Acceptance rate: 19%
GPA, 25th-75th percentile, entering class Fall 2005: 2.98-3.76
LSAT, 25th-75th percentile, entering class Fall 2005: 155-162

Part-time program:
Number of applicants for Fall 2005: 266
Number of acceptances: 111
Number enrolled: 89
Acceptance rate: 42%
GPA, 25th-75th percentile, entering class Fall 2005: 3.00-3.42
LSAT, 25th-75th percentile, entering class Fall 2005: 152-156

FINANCIAL AID
Financial aid phone number: **(419) 530-7929**
Financial aid application deadline: 1/08
Tuition 2005-2006 academic year: In-state: full-time: $13,781, part-time: $10,913; Out-of-state: full-time: $24,024
Room and board: $7,635; books: $1,750; miscellaneous expenses: $4,179
Total of room/board/books/miscellaneous expenses: $13,564
University does not offer graduate student housing for which law students are eligible.

Financial aid profile
Percent of students that received grants for the 2004-2005 academic year: full-time: 48%; part-time 6%

Median grant amount: full-time: $11,511; part-time: $504
The average law-school debt of those in the Class of 2005 who borrowed: $56,387. Proportion who borrowed: 87%

ACADEMIC PROGRAMS
Calendar: **semester**
Joint degrees awarded: **J.D./M.B.A.; J.D./M.S.E.; J.D./M.P.A.; J.D./MCriminal Justice; J.D./M (Student Designed); J.D./M.P.H. (Public Health)**
Typical first-year section size: Full-time: 57; Part-time: 37
Is there typically a "small section" of the first year class, other than Legal Writing, taught by full-time faculty?: Full-time: **no**; Part-time: **no**
Number of course titles, beyond the first year curriculum, offered last year: **84**
Percentages of upper division course sections, excluding seminars, with an enrollment of:

Under 25: **72%**	25 to 49: **22%**
50 to 74: **5%**	75 to 99: **1%**
100+: **0%**	

Areas of specialization: appellate advocacy, clinical training, dispute resolution, environmental law, healthcare law, intellectual property law, international law, tax law, trial advocacy

Fall 2005 faculty profile
Total teaching faculty: 67. Full-time: 46%; 61% men, 39% women, 6% minorities. Part-time: 54%; 81% men, 19% women, 0% minorities
Student-to-faculty ratio: 13.4

SPECIAL PROGRAMS (as provided by law school):
A pioneer in clinical legal education, the College strives to offer to each student before graduation an actual legal experience with a practicing attorney. The Legal Clinic encourages students to handle cases from initial interview to final disposition. The Criminal Practice Program places student legal interns in prosecutors' offices in Ohio, Michigan, and across the country. Through the Dispute Resolution Clinic, mediation experience is available in a variety of matters, including unruly child complaints and custody and visitation issues in parentage cases in

juvenile court. In the Domestic Violence Clinic students assist with the prosecution of domestic violence cases by performing all of the traditional functions of a prosecutor. The Human Rights Project is a community-based effort to protect the rights of gay, lesbian, bisexual, and transgendered persons through traditional litigation, educational outreach, legislative action, and community activism. Students in the Public Service Externship Clinic are assigned to public service legal entities such as the judiciary, legal services offices, pro bono programs, public defender offices, legislative bodies, government agencies and public interest organizations. The College has five certificate programs that recognize advanced study in Environmental Law, Homeland Security Law, International Law, Intellectual Property Law, and Labor Law. The Certificate Program is one way for employers to identify graduates who can contribute immediately in these areas. The Legal Institute of the Great Lakes (LIGL), a research center that supports research, maintains publications and sponsors conferences on legal, economic and social issues of importance to the Great Lakes Region. LIGL hosts an annual symposium every fall focused on an aspect of Great Lakes water and The National Water Crisis. The Cybersecurities Law Institute focuses on the impact of Internet technology on securities and investment law and sponsors new courses, conferences, research, lectures, and symposia. The Institute positions the College as one of the national leaders in scholarship and teaching on legal issues posed by the growing dominance of the Internet in the area of corporate and securities law. The Cannon Lecture Series has hosted individuals of national prominence. A generous endowment by the Stranahan Foundation sponsors Stranahan National Issues Forum. As part of the Day After Speakers Series, attorneys visit the College the day after they have argued before the U.S. Supreme Court. The lawyers recount their methods of preparation and impressions of their oral arguments. The College's annual Labor Law Speaker Series reflects Northwest Ohio's historical association with the American labor movement.

STUDENT BODY

Fall 2005 full-time enrollment: 351

Men: 60%	Women: 40%
African-American: 3.1%	American Indian: 0.3%
Asian-American: 2.3%	Mexican-American: 0.0%
Puerto Rican: 0.0%	Other Hisp-Amer: 1.7%
White: 63.5%	International: 0.6%
Unknown: 28.5%	

Fall 2005 part-time enrollment: 159

Men: 57%	Women: 43%
African-American: 1.9%	American Indian: 1.3%
Asian-American: 1.9%	Mexican-American: 0.0%
Puerto Rican: 0.0%	Other Hisp-Amer: 0.6%
White: 72.3%	International: 0.0%
Unknown: 22.0%	

Attrition rates for 2004-2005 full-time students
Percent of students discontinuing law school:
Men: 4%   Women: 2%

First-year students: 7%   Second-year students: 1%
Third-year students: 1%

LIBRARY RESOURCES

The library holds 52,821 and receives 3,351 current subscriptions.
Total volumes: 344,863
Percentage of the titles in the online catalog: 100%
Total seats available for library users: 441

INFORMATION TECHNOLOGY

Number of wired network connections available to students: 27 total (in the law library, excluding computer labs: 27; in classrooms: 0; in computer labs: 0; elsewhere in the law school: 0)
Law school has a wireless network.
Approximate number of simultaneous users that can be accommodated on wireless network: 200
Students are not required to own a computer.

EMPLOYMENT AND SALARIES

Proportion of 2004 graduates employed at graduation: 87%
Employed 9 months later, as of February 15, 2005: 92%
Salaries in the private sector (law firms, business, industry): $36,000–$70,000 (25th-75th percentile)
Median salary in the private sector: $55,000
Percentage in the private sector who reported salary information: 30%
Median salary in public service (government, judicial clerkships, academic posts, non-profits): $38,000

Percentage of 2004 graduates in:

Law firms: 43%	Bus./industry (legal): 14%
Bus./industry (nonlegal): 0%	Government: 15%
Public interest: 7%	Judicial clerkship: 11%
Academia : 6%	Unknown: 4%

2004 graduates employed in-state: 68%
2004 graduates employed in foreign countries: 0%
Number of states where graduates are employed: 16
Percentage of 2004 graduates working in: New England: 0%, Middle Atlantic: 2%, East North Central: 83%, West North Central: 2%, South Atlantic: 4%, East South Central: 2%, West South Central: 0%, Mountain: 4%, Pacific: 0%, Unknown: 3%

BAR PASSAGE RATES

Based on 2004 graduates taking Summer 2004 or Winter 2005 exams. Most of the school's first-time test takers took the bar in Ohio.

90%
School's bar passage rate for first-time test takers

81%
Statewide bar passage rate for first-time test takers

University of Tulsa

■ 3120 E. Fourth Place, Tulsa, OK, 74104
■ http://www.law.utulsa.edu
■ Private
■ Year founded: 1923
■ 2005-2006 tuition: full-time: $23,459; part-time: $16,445
■ Enrollment 2005-06 academic year: full-time: 506; part-time: 85
■ U.S. News 2007 law specialty ranking: N/A

2.80-3.50 GPA, 25TH-75TH PERCENTILE

150-154 LSAT, 25TH-75TH PERCENTILE

34% ACCEPTANCE RATE

Tier 4 2007 U.S. NEWS LAW SCHOOL RANKING

ADMISSIONS

Admissions phone number: **(918) 631-2406**
Admissions email address: **lawadmissions@utulsa.edu**
Application website: **http://www.law.utulsa.edu/admissions**
Application deadline for Fall 2007 admission: **rolling**

Admissions statistics:

Number of applicants for Fall 2005: **1,486**
Number of acceptances: **509**
Number enrolled: **188**
Acceptance rate: **34%**
GPA, 25th-75th percentile, entering class Fall 2005:
   2.80-3.50
LSAT, 25th-75th percentile, entering class Fall 2005:
   150-154

Part-time program:

Number of applicants for Fall 2005: **110**
Number of acceptances: **32**
Number enrolled: **20**
Acceptance rate: **29%**
GPA, 25th-75th percentile, entering class Fall 2005:
   3.10-3.60
LSAT, 25th-75th percentile, entering class Fall 2005: **150-153**

FINANCIAL AID

Financial aid phone number: **(918) 631-2526**
Financial aid application deadline: **N/A**
Tuition 2005-2006 academic year: full-time: **$23,459**; part-time: **$16,445**
Room and board: **$7,915**; books: **$3,427**; miscellaneous expenses: **$4,058**
Total of room/board/books/miscellaneous expenses:
   $15,400
University offers graduate student housing for which law students are eligible.

Financial aid profile

Percent of students that received grants for the 2004-2005 academic year: full-time: **34%**; part-time **33%**
Median grant amount: full-time: **$6,500**; part-time: **$5,000**

The average law-school debt of those in the Class of 2005 who borrowed: **$87,032**. Proportion who borrowed: **85%**

ACADEMIC PROGRAMS

Calendar: **semester**
Joint degrees awarded: **J.D./Anthropology; J.D./Accounting; J.D./Biosciences; J.D./English; J.D./History; J.D./M.B.A.; J.D./PSY Clinical&IO; J.D./Taxation; J.D./Geosciences**
Typical first-year section size: Full-time: **76**
Is there typically a "small section" of the first year class, other than Legal Writing, taught by full-time faculty?:
   Full-time: **yes**; Part-time: **yes**
Number of course titles, beyond the first year curriculum, offered last year: **96**
Percentages of upper division course sections, excluding seminars, with an enrollment of:

Under 25: **62%**	25 to 49: **24%**
50 to 74: **10%**	75 to 99: **4%**
100+: **N/A**	

Areas of specialization: appellate advocacy, clinical training, dispute resolution, environmental law, healthcare law, intellectual property law, international law, tax law, trial advocacy

Fall 2005 faculty profile

Total teaching faculty: **62**. Full-time: **50%**; **55%** men, **45%** women, **10%** minorities. Part-time: **50%**; **71%** men, **29%** women, **6%** minorities
Student-to-faculty ratio: **16.3**

SPECIAL PROGRAMS *(as provided by law school)*:

Special programs include the National Energy-Environment Law and Policy Institute, the Native American Law Center, the Comparative and International Law Center, and the Dispute Resolution Program. The law school also offers the following eight certificate programs: Native American law, REEL (resources, energy, and environmental law), alternative dispute resolution, comparative and international law, public policy, health law, lawyering skills, and entrepreneurial law.

The Comparative and International Law Center offers study abroad programs in Buenos Aires, London, Dublin, Geneva, and Leuven, Belgium.

There are three clinics located in the law school's Boesche Legal Clinic. These include the Older Americans' Law Project, the Health Law Project, and the Muscogee (Creek) Nation Indian Law Clinic.

The College of Law offers students the opportunity to work for an attorney through its legal internship program. There is also a supervised judicial internship program, where students can work directly with Oklahoma federal and state judges.

The College of Law offers two advanced degrees, an LL.M. degree in American Indian and indigenous law and an LL.M. degree in American law for foreign graduates.

STUDENT BODY

Fall 2005 full-time enrollment: 506

Men: 67%	Women: 33%
African-American: 2.6%	American Indian: 4.9%
Asian-American: 2.0%	Mexican-American: 3.2%
Puerto Rican: 0.0%	Other Hisp-Amer: 0.0%
White: 71.5%	International: 0.8%
Unknown: 15.0%	

Fall 2005 part-time enrollment: 85

Men: 44%	Women: 56%
African-American: 3.5%	American Indian: 7.1%
Asian-American: 1.2%	Mexican-American: 2.4%
Puerto Rican: 0.0%	Other Hisp-Amer: 0.0%
White: 75.3%	International: 0.0%
Unknown: 10.6%	

Attrition rates for 2004-2005 full-time students
Percent of students discontinuing law school:

Men: 8%	Women: 7%
First-year students: 14%	Second-year students: 8%
Third-year students: N/A	

LIBRARY RESOURCES

The library holds 184,063 and receives 3,293 current subscriptions.

Total volumes: 385,167

Percentage of the titles in the online catalog: 99%

Total seats available for library users: 715

INFORMATION TECHNOLOGY

Number of wired network connections available to students: 405 total (in the law library, excluding computer labs: 269; in classrooms: 136; in computer labs: 0; elsewhere in the law school: 0)

Law school has a wireless network.

Approximate number of simultaneous users that can be accommodated on wireless network: 2,000

Students are not required to own a computer.

EMPLOYMENT AND SALARIES

Proportion of 2004 graduates employed at graduation: 53%

Employed 9 months later, as of February 15, 2005: 87%

Salaries in the private sector (law firms, business, industry): $42,000–$65,000 (25th-75th percentile)

Median salary in the private sector: $50,000

Percentage in the private sector who reported salary information: 34%

Median salary in public service (government, judicial clerkships, academic posts, non-profits): $40,000

Percentage of 2004 graduates in:

Law firms: 58%	Bus./industry (legal): 5%
Bus./industry (nonlegal): 8%	Government: 17%
Public interest: 3%	Judicial clerkship: 4%
Academia : 5%	Unknown: 0%

2004 graduates employed in-state: 63%

2004 graduates employed in foreign countries: 0%

Number of states where graduates are employed: 22

Percentage of 2004 graduates working in: New England: 0%, Middle Atlantic: 3%, East North Central: 1%, West North Central: 8%, South Atlantic: 6%, East South Central: 1%, West South Central: 73%, Mountain: 5%, Pacific: 3%, Unknown: 0%

BAR PASSAGE RATES

Based on 2004 graduates taking Summer 2004 or Winter 2005 exams. Most of the school's first-time test takers took the bar in Oklahoma.

75%
School's bar passage rate for first-time test takers

83%
Statewide bar passage rate for first-time test takers

University of Utah (S.J. Quinney)

- 332 S 1400 E, Room 101, Salt Lake City, UT, 84112
- http://www.law.utah.edu
- Public
- Year founded: 1913
- 2005-2006 tuition: In-state: full-time: $10,782, part-time: N/A; Out-of-state: full-time: $22,987
- Enrollment 2005-06 academic year: full-time: 398
- U.S. News 2007 law specialty ranking: environmental law: 17

3.46-3.81 GPA, 25TH-75TH PERCENTILE

158-162 LSAT, 25TH-75TH PERCENTILE

31% ACCEPTANCE RATE

57 2007 U.S. NEWS LAW SCHOOL RANKING

ADMISSIONS

Admissions phone number: **(801) 581-7479**
Admissions email address: **admissions@law.utah.edu**
Application website: **http://www.law.utah.edu/prospective/admissions.html**
Application deadline for Fall 2007 admission: **2/01**

Admissions statistics:

Number of applicants for Fall 2005: **1,176**
Number of acceptances: **359**
Number enrolled: **127**
Acceptance rate: **31%**
GPA, 25th-75th percentile, entering class Fall 2005: **3.46-3.81**
LSAT, 25th-75th percentile, entering class Fall 2005: **158-162**

FINANCIAL AID

Financial aid phone number: **(801) 581-6211**
Financial aid application deadline: **3/15**
Tuition 2005-2006 academic year: In-state: full-time: **$10,782**, part-time: N/A; Out-of-state: full-time: **$22,987**
Room and board: **$8,334**; books: **$1,592**; miscellaneous expenses: **$4,186**
Total of room/board/books/miscellaneous expenses: **$14,112**
University offers graduate student housing for which law students are eligible.

Financial aid profile

Percent of students that received grants for the 2004-2005 academic year: full-time: **43%**
Median grant amount: full-time: **$1,575**
The average law-school debt of those in the Class of 2005 who borrowed: **$49,981**. Proportion who borrowed: **89%**

ACADEMIC PROGRAMS

Calendar: **semester**
Joint degrees awarded: **J.D./M.B.A.; J.D./MPA**
Typical first-year section size: Full-time: **44**

Is there typically a "small section" of the first year class, other than Legal Writing, taught by full-time faculty?: Full-time: **yes**
Number of course titles, beyond the first year curriculum, offered last year: **96**
Percentages of upper division course sections, excluding seminars, with an enrollment of:

Under 25: **54%**   25 to 49: **30%**
50 to 74: **14%**   75 to 99: **2%**
100+: **0%**

Areas of specialization: appellate advocacy, clinical training, dispute resolution, environmental law, healthcare law, intellectual property law, international law, tax law, trial advocacy

Fall 2005 faculty profile

Total teaching faculty: **47**. Full-time: **62%**; **62%** men, **38%** women, **17%** minorities. Part-time: **38%**; **67%** men, **33%** women, **6%** minorities
Student-to-faculty ratio: **11.5**

SPECIAL PROGRAMS (as provided by law school):

Judicial Clinic: Students intern for judges on state, federal, and tribal courts, as well as in the U.S. Department of the Interior.

Criminal Clinic: Students assist in felony and misdemeanor cases for state and federal prosecutors and public defenders.

Civil Clinic: Students learn skills at public-interest law offices such as Utah Legal Services, the Legal Aid Society of Salt Lake, the Disability Law Center, and the Office of the Guardian Ad Litem.

Environmental Practice Clinic: Students work in government, public-interest, and private law offices on environmental or natural resource cases.

Health Clinic: Students consider the delivery of health care; the health law class collaborates with various public and private offices.

Mediation Clinic: Students serve as mediators, helping parties resolve landlord-tenant, parent visitation, victim-offender, small claims, and other disputes.

Legislative Clinic: Students work with the Office of Legislative Counsel, members of the Utah Legislature, and nonprofit organizations to research and draft proposed legislation and work with the bill's sponsor during the legislative session.

Rocky Mountain Innocence Center: Students help investigate the cases of prisoners in which DNA evidence may be available for testing and assist pro bono attorneys in post-conviction proceedings.

Interdisciplinary and London study: After completing the first year, students may fulfill the requirements for a J.D. degree with some courses in a companion discipline. Students can study in London with the London Law Consortium.

Joint degree programs: J.D./M.B.A., with the David Eccles School of Business, and J.D./M.P.A., with the university's Center for Public Policy and Administration. The University of Utah offers numerous highly regarded master's and doctoral programs. We assist students on a case-by-case basis if they wish to pursue interdisciplinary study.

Summer study: Two five-week summer sessions featuring guest faculty from schools throughout the country are offered.

Wallace Stegner Center for Land, Resources, and the Environment: The center sponsors academic research, conferences, and symposia. We are one of only a few schools in the country that offer a certificate in environmental and natural resources law to J.D. students as well as an LL.M. degree program in environmental and natural resources law.

STUDENT BODY

Fall 2005 full-time enrollment: 398

Men: 62%	Women: 38%
African-American: 0.8%	American Indian: 1.0%
Asian-American: 4.3%	Mexican-American: 1.0%
Puerto Rican: 0.5%	Other Hisp-Amer: 2.8%
White: 77.1%	International: 0.8%
Unknown: 11.8%	

Attrition rates for 2004-2005 full-time students
Percent of students discontinuing law school:

Men: N/A	Women: N/A
First-year students: N/A	Second-year students: N/A
Third-year students: N/A	

LIBRARY RESOURCES

The library holds 131,330 and receives 4,804 current subscriptions.
Total volumes: 334,119
Percentage of the titles in the online catalog: 99%
Total seats available for library users: 356

INFORMATION TECHNOLOGY

Number of wired network connections available to students: 634 total (in the law library, excluding computer labs: 216; in classrooms: 230; in computer labs: 28; elsewhere in the law school: 160)
Law school has a wireless network.
Approximate number of simultaneous users that can be accommodated on wireless network: 400
Students are not required to own a computer.

EMPLOYMENT AND SALARIES

Proportion of 2004 graduates employed at graduation: 69%
Employed 9 months later, as of February 15, 2005: 91%
Salaries in the private sector (law firms, business, industry): $52,000–$90,000 (25th-75th percentile)
Median salary in the private sector: $65,000
Percentage in the private sector who reported salary information: 73%
Median salary in public service (government, judicial clerkships, academic posts, non-profits): $40,000

Percentage of 2004 graduates in:

Law firms: 55%	Bus./industry (legal): 10%
Bus./industry (nonlegal): 9%	Government: 10%
Public interest: 3%	Judicial clerkship: 11%
Academia : 2%	Unknown: 0%

2004 graduates employed in-state: 75%
2004 graduates employed in foreign countries: 0%
Number of states where graduates are employed: 16
Percentage of 2004 graduates working in: New England: 1%, Middle Atlantic: 2%, East North Central: 2%, West North Central: 2%, South Atlantic: 4%, East South Central: 0%, West South Central: 0%, Mountain: 82%, Pacific: 7%, Unknown: 2%

BAR PASSAGE RATES

Based on 2004 graduates taking Summer 2004 or Winter 2005 exams. Most of the school's first-time test takers took the bar in Utah.

89%

School's bar passage rate for first-time test takers

90%

Statewide bar passage rate for first-time test takers

University of Virginia

580 Massie Road, Charlottesville, VA, 22903-1789
http://www.law.virginia.edu
Public
Year founded: 1819
2005-2006 tuition: In-state: full-time: $28,300, part-time: N/A;
Out-of-state: full-time: $33,300
Enrollment 2005-06 academic year: full-time: 1,118
U.S. News 2007 law specialty ranking: international law: 9, tax law: 11

3.53-3.83 GPA, 25TH-75TH PERCENTILE

167-171 LSAT, 25TH-75TH PERCENTILE

20% ACCEPTANCE RATE

8 2007 U.S. NEWS LAW SCHOOL RANKING

ADMISSIONS
Admissions phone number: **(434) 924-7351**
Admissions email address: **lawadmit@virginia.edu**
Application website:
http://www.law.virginia.edu/Main/Application+Forms
Application deadline for Fall 2007 admission: **1/15**

Admissions statistics:
Number of applicants for Fall 2005: **5,495**
Number of acceptances: **1,111**
Number enrolled: **374**
Acceptance rate: **20%**
GPA, 25th-75th percentile, entering class Fall 2005:
3.53-3.83
LSAT, 25th-75th percentile, entering class Fall 2005:
167-171

FINANCIAL AID
Financial aid phone number: **(434) 924-7805**
Financial aid application deadline: **2/15**
Tuition 2005-2006 academic year: In-state: full-time:
$28,300, part-time: N/A; Out-of-state: full-time: **$33,300**
Room and board: **$14,045**; books: **$1,000**; miscellaneous
expenses: **$555**
Total of room/board/books/miscellaneous expenses:
$15,600
University offers graduate student housing for which law
students are eligible.

Financial aid profile
Percent of students that received grants for the 2004-2005
academic year: full-time: **50%**
Median grant amount: full-time: **$10,000**
The average law-school debt of those in the Class of 2005
who borrowed: **$60,000**. Proportion who borrowed: **78%**

ACADEMIC PROGRAMS
Calendar: **semester**
Joint degrees awarded: **J.D./M.A. History; J.D./M.A.
Government; J.D./M.P. Planning; J.D./M.A. Economics;
J.D./M.A. English; J.D./M.A. Philosophy;**

**J.D./M.A.Sociology; J.D./M.A. Bioethics; J.D./M.S.
Accounting; J.D./M.B.A.; J.D./Ph.D. Government;
J.D./Ph.D. History; J.D./M.A. Foreign Affairs**
Typical first-year section size: Full-time: **65**
Is there typically a "small section" of the first year class,
other than Legal Writing, taught by full-time faculty?:
Full-time: **yes**
Number of course titles, beyond the first year curriculum,
offered last year: **242**
Percentages of upper division course sections, excluding
seminars, with an enrollment of:
Under 25: **47%**   25 to 49: **16%**
50 to 74: **18%**   75 to 99: **7%**
100+: **12%**
Areas of specialization: appellate advocacy, clinical training,
dispute resolution, environmental law, healthcare law,
intellectual property law, international law, tax law, trial
advocacy

Fall 2005 faculty profile
Total teaching faculty: **192**. Full-time: **39%**; **73%** men, **27%**
women, **8%** minorities. Part-time: **61%**; **88%** men, **12%**
women, **3%** minorities
Student-to-faculty ratio: **13.0**

SPECIAL PROGRAMS *(as provided by law school):*
Intellectual life is the heart of any great academic institution. At
Virginia, law in its origins, impact, and implications is analyzed
and debated in classes, workshops, lecture programs, student
organizations, and informal faculty-student exchanges. Faculty
members meet with and mentor students, exploring ideas and
fostering understanding and creative scholarship.
Interdisciplinary thinking comes naturally at Virginia, with
nearly half of the law faculty holding advanced degrees in fields
such as psychology, economics, philosophy, history, medicine,
and theological studies. In addition to the vibrant exchanges
that develop freely in a community of accomplished scholars
and superlative students, the law school also promotes debate
and discussion through targeted centers, institutes, and programs of study.

The law school has strength in corporate and commercial law rooted in exceptional faculty and enhanced by close relationships with the Darden Graduate Business School, one of the nation's leading business schools. Its prominence in international law is built on a long tradition, with notable faculty in areas of immigration, human rights, environment, and constitutional law in other countries, as well as private and commercial law in a global community. Its reputation in legal and constitutional history stems from faculty producing influential scholarship. Environmental endeavors draw strength from the Center for Environmental Law and the Virginia Environmental Law Journal.

Students may enroll in several joint degree programs. The J.D./M.B.A. program is a four-year program in conjunction with the Darden school. There are also eight subject areas for M.A. degrees and two for Ph.D. degrees in arts and sciences, an M.S. in accounting, and an M.P. in planning.

The law school provides students an opportunity to develop their lawyering skills through clinical opportunities in the following areas: advocacy for the elderly, appellate litigation, child advocacy, criminal defense, employment law, environmental practice, First Amendment law, housing law, international human-rights law, mental health law, negotiation and public practice, patent and licensing law, and prosecution.

Students also have the opportunity to pursue legal studies through external programs, including study at the Bucerius Law School in Hamburg, Germany, the University of Melbourne, Australia, and the University of Nottingham, England.

STUDENT BODY

Fall 2005 full-time enrollment: 1,118

Men: 59%	Women: 41%
African-American: 7.3%	American Indian: 0.5%
Asian-American: 7.5%	Mexican-American: 0.0%
Puerto Rican: 0.0%	Other Hisp-Amer: 1.6%
White: 63.1%	International: 0.3%
Unknown: 19.7%	

Attrition rates for 2004-2005 full-time students
Percent of students discontinuing law school:

Men: 1%	Women: 1%
First-year students: 1%	Second-year students: 2%
Third-year students: 0%	

LIBRARY RESOURCES

The library holds 275,145 and receives 11,275 current subscriptions.
Total volumes: 882,770
Percentage of the titles in the online catalog: 99%
Total seats available for library users: 785

INFORMATION TECHNOLOGY

Number of wired network connections available to students: 84 total (in the law library, excluding computer labs: 84; in classrooms: 0; in computer labs: 0; elsewhere in the law school: 0)
Law school has a wireless network.
Approximate number of simultaneous users that can be accommodated on wireless network: 1,424
Students are required to own a computer.

EMPLOYMENT AND SALARIES

Proportion of 2004 graduates employed at graduation: 98%
Employed 9 months later, as of February 15, 2005: 99%
Salaries in the private sector (law firms, business, industry): $100,000–$128,000 (25th-75th percentile)
Median salary in the private sector: $118,000
Percentage in the private sector who reported salary information: 100%
Median salary in public service (government, judicial clerkships, academic posts, non-profits): $52,000

Percentage of 2004 graduates in:

Law firms: 75%	Bus./industry (legal): 0%
Bus./industry (nonlegal): 0%	Government: 6%
Public interest: 3%	Judicial clerkship: 15%
Academia : 0%	Unknown: 0%

2004 graduates employed in-state: 12%
2004 graduates employed in foreign countries: 2%
Number of states where graduates are employed: 33
Percentage of 2004 graduates working in: New England: 5%, Middle Atlantic: 21%, East North Central: 5%, West North Central: 2%, South Atlantic: 46%, East South Central: 5%, West South Central: 7%, Mountain: 1%, Pacific: 7%, Unknown: 0%

BAR PASSAGE RATES

Based on 2004 graduates taking Summer 2004 or Winter 2005 exams. Most of the school's first-time test takers took the bar in Virginia.

91%
School's bar passage rate for first-time test takers

74%
Statewide bar passage rate for first-time test takers

University of Washington

■ Campus Box 353020, Seattle, WA, 98195-3020
■ http://www.law.washington.edu
■ Public
■ Year founded: 1899
■ 2005-2006 tuition: In-state: full-time: $14,927, part-time: N/A;
Out-of-state: full-time: $21,857
■ Enrollment 2005-06 academic year: full-time: 561
■ U.S. News 2007 law specialty ranking: environmental law: 19, intelle-
cutal property law: 17, tax law: 13

3.51-3.84 GPA, 25TH-75TH PERCENTILE

159-165 LSAT, 25TH-75TH PERCENTILE

21% ACCEPTANCE RATE

27 2007 U.S. NEWS LAW SCHOOL RANKING

ADMISSIONS
Admissions phone number: **(206) 543-4078**
Admissions email address: **lawadm@u.washington.edu**
Application website: **N/A**
Application deadline for Fall 2007 admission: **1/15**

Admissions statistics:
Number of applicants for Fall 2005: **2,465**
Number of acceptances: **529**
Number enrolled: **180**
Acceptance rate: **21%**
GPA, 25th-75th percentile, entering class Fall 2005:
3.51-3.84
LSAT, 25th-75th percentile, entering class Fall 2005:
159-165

FINANCIAL AID
Financial aid phone number: **(206) 543-4552**
Financial aid application deadline: **2/28**
Tuition 2005-2006 academic year: In-state: full-time:
$14,927, part-time: **N/A**; Out-of-state: full-time: **$21,857**
Room and board: **$10,000**; books: **$1,000**; miscellaneous
expenses: **$3,913**
Total of room/board/books/miscellaneous expenses:
$14,913
University offers graduate student housing for which law
students are eligible.

Financial aid profile
Percent of students that received grants for the 2004-2005
academic year: full-time: **45%**
Median grant amount: full-time: **$7,000**
The average law-school debt of those in the Class of 2005
who borrowed: **$48,450**. Proportion who borrowed: **88%**

ACADEMIC PROGRAMS
Calendar: **quarter**
Joint degrees awarded: **Public Affairs; LL.M. in Taxation;
International Studies; LL.M. in Asian Law; LL.M. in
Sustainable Intl. Development**
Typical first-year section size: Full-time: **62**

Is there typically a "small section" of the first year class,
other than Legal Writing, taught by full-time faculty?:
Full-time: **yes**
Number of course titles, beyond the first year curriculum,
offered last year: **96**
Percentages of upper division course sections, excluding
seminars, with an enrollment of:

Under 25: **52%**	25 to 49: **31%**
50 to 74: **9%**	75 to 99: **8%**
100+: **N/A**	

Areas of specialization: appellate advocacy, clinical training,
dispute resolution, environmental law, healthcare law,
intellectual property law, international law, tax law, trial
advocacy

Fall 2005 faculty profile
Total teaching faculty: **106**. Full-time: **34%**; **64%** men, **36%**
women, **14%** minorities. Part-time: **66%**; **71%** men, **29%**
women, **9%** minorities
Student-to-faculty ratio: **10.9**

SPECIAL PROGRAMS *(as provided by law school):*
The clinical law program offers students an opportunity to serve
people in need of legal assistance in several areas. Students
develop essential professional skills and gain valuable client and
case management experience. Current clinics include the
Innocence Project Northwest Clinic, Unemployment
Compensation Law Clinic, Mediation Clinic, Refugee and
Immigrant Advocacy Clinic, Children and Youth Advocacy
Clinic, Tribal Court Criminal Defense Clinic, Low-Income
Taxpayer Clinic, Berman Environmental Law Clinic, and
Technology Law and Public Policy Clinic.

Centers and Institutes enrich the research, teaching, and
service missions of the Law School and include the Asian Law
Center, the Center for Advanced Study and Research on
Intellectual Property, the Native American Law Center, the Rural
Development Institute, and the Shidler Center for Law,
Commerce and Technology.

All UW law students must perform at least 60 hours of public service legal work as a condition for graduation. Students may
complete public interest externships with government agencies,

nonprofit organizations, state courts, and private law firms working on pro bono matters. Externships typically last three months and may be based with local, national or international organizations such as the Washington State Attorney General, the U.S. Department of Justice, the federal public defender, the Northwest Justice Project, the Northwest Immigrant Rights Project, Columbia Legal Services, the Irish Center for Human Rights, and the European Citizen Action Service.

Beginning in September 2006, the William H. Gates Public Service Law Scholarship Program will provide full scholarships to five new University of Washington law students each year who demonstrate a commitment to careers in public service. A $33.3 million gift from the Bill & Melinda Gates Foundation will fund the full cost of tuition, academic supplies, room and board. The program will also help pay for seminars and internships and for collaborative public interest initiatives with other law schools.

STUDENT BODY
Fall 2005 full-time enrollment: 561

Men: 42%	Women: 58%
African-American: 1.6%	American Indian: 2.5%
Asian-American: 13.0%	Mexican-American: 0.0%
Puerto Rican: 0.0%	Other Hisp-Amer: 2.3%
White: 75.4%	International: 4.3%
Unknown: 0.9%	

Attrition rates for 2004-2005 full-time students
Percent of students discontinuing law school:

Men: 1%	Women: 1%
First-year students: N/A	Second-year students: 3%
Third-year students: N/A	

LIBRARY RESOURCES
The library holds 124,945 and receives 5,550 current subscriptions.
Total volumes: 591,741
Percentage of the titles in the online catalog: 100%
Total seats available for library users: 389

INFORMATION TECHNOLOGY
Number of wired network connections available to students: 0 total (in the law library, excluding computer labs: 0; in classrooms: 0; in computer labs: 0; elsewhere in the law school: 0)

Law school has a wireless network.
Approximate number of simultaneous users that can be accommodated on wireless network: 500
Students are not required to own a computer.

EMPLOYMENT AND SALARIES
Proportion of 2004 graduates employed at graduation: 89%
Employed 9 months later, as of February 15, 2005: 99%
Salaries in the private sector (law firms, business, industry): $57,600–$95,000 (25th-75th percentile)
Median salary in the private sector: $80,000
Percentage in the private sector who reported salary information: 57%
Median salary in public service (government, judicial clerkships, academic posts, non-profits): $40,000

Percentage of 2004 graduates in:

Law firms: 50%	Bus./industry (legal): 7%
Bus./industry (nonlegal): N/A	Government: 18%
Public interest: 4%	Judicial clerkship: 16%
Academia : 4%	Unknown: 1%

2004 graduates employed in-state: 74%
2004 graduates employed in foreign countries: 1%
Number of states where graduates are employed: 15
Percentage of 2004 graduates working in: New England: 1%, Middle Atlantic: 2%, East North Central: 0%, West North Central: 0%, South Atlantic: 6%, East South Central: 0%, West South Central: 1%, Mountain: 10%, Pacific: 80%, Unknown: N/A

BAR PASSAGE RATES
Based on 2004 graduates taking Summer 2004 or Winter 2005 exams. Most of the school's first-time test takers took the bar in Washington.

89%
School's bar passage rate for first-time test takers

79%
Statewide bar passage rate for first-time test takers

University of Wisconsin–Madison

- 975 Bascom Mall, Madison, WI, 53706-1399
- http://www.law.wisc.edu
- Public
- Year founded: 1868
- 2005-2006 tuition: In-state: full-time: $11,658, part-time: $975/credit hour; Out-of-state: full-time: $28,870
- Enrollment 2005-06 academic year: full-time: 801; part-time: 38
- U.S. News 2007 law specialty ranking: N/A

3.30-3.77 GPA, 25TH-75TH PERCENTILE

158-163 LSAT, 25TH-75TH PERCENTILE

24% ACCEPTANCE RATE

32 2007 U.S. NEWS LAW SCHOOL RANKING

ADMISSIONS

Admissions phone number: (608) 262-5914
Admissions email address: **admissions@law.wisc.edu**
Application website:
  http://www.law.wisc.edu/admissions/reqform.htm
Application deadline for Fall 2007 admission: 2/01

Admissions statistics:

Number of applicants for Fall 2005: 3,157
Number of acceptances: 743
Number enrolled: 271
Acceptance rate: 24%
GPA, 25th-75th percentile, entering class Fall 2005:
  3.30-3.77
LSAT, 25th-75th percentile, entering class Fall 2005:
  158-163

FINANCIAL AID

Financial aid phone number: (608) 262-5914
Financial aid application deadline: 3/01
Tuition 2005-2006 academic year: In-state: full-time: $11,658, part-time: $975/credit hour; Out-of-state: full-time: $28,870
Room and board: $7,220; books: $2,040; miscellaneous expenses: $4,330
Total of room/board/books/miscellaneous expenses: $13,590
University offers graduate student housing for which law students are eligible.

Financial aid profile

Percent of students that received grants for the 2004-2005 academic year: full-time: 31%
Median grant amount: full-time: $10,730
The average law-school debt of those in the Class of 2005 who borrowed: $49,751. Proportion who borrowed: 82%

ACADEMIC PROGRAMS

Calendar: **semester**
Joint degrees awarded: **J.D./M.B.A; J.D./ M.A. Education Administration; J.D./M.A.Latin American Studies; J.D./M.S. Environmental Studies; J.D./M.S. Library**
Information Science; J.D./M.A. Philosophy; J.D./M.A. Sociology; J.D./M.A.Urban & Regional Planning; J.D./MA Journalism & Mass Communications; J.D./M.A. Public Affairs; J.D./M.A. Political Science; J.D./M.A. Social Work; J.D./M.S. Medicine
Typical first-year section size: Full-time: **70**
Is there typically a "small section" of the first year class, other than Legal Writing, taught by full-time faculty?: Full-time: **yes**
Number of course titles, beyond the first year curriculum, offered last year: **169**
Percentages of upper division course sections, excluding seminars, with an enrollment of:

Under 25: **63%**	25 to 49: **25%**
50 to 74: **6%**	75 to 99: **4%**
100+: **2%**	

Areas of specialization: appellate advocacy, clinical training, dispute resolution, environmental law, healthcare law, intellectual property law, international law, tax law, trial advocacy

Fall 2005 faculty profile

Total teaching faculty: **116**. Full-time: **46%; 64%** men, **36%** women, **13%** minorities. Part-time: **54%; 52%** men, **48%** women, **8%** minorities
Student-to-faculty ratio: **13.1**

SPECIAL PROGRAMS *(as provided by law school)*:

Dual-degree programs: The University of Wisconsin Law School is known for its interdisciplinary approach and law-in-action philosophy. An extensive curriculum and a rigorous academic program are at the core of the J.D. program. Students can combine the J.D. with another graduate degree. There are eight dual-degree programs; students may develop individualized dual-degrees.

Clinical programs: UW Law is committed to practical experience and offers experiential learning through clinics, judicial internships, government externships, and simulated skills courses. A large program with over 20 faculty and 10+ clinics provides a clinical experience for every interested student. The clinics offer direct-client contact, under direct supervision of clinical faculty in criminal and civil areas. Legal Assistance to Institutionalized Persons provides legal assistance to inmates. Innocence Project investigates and litigates innocence claims. Family Law Project provides assistance on family law issues to prison inmates. Criminal Appeals Project engages students in the appellate process. Restorative Justice Project practices mediation. Consumer Law Clinic represents low/moderate-income consumers in individual and class actions. Neighborhood Law Project provides services to low-income neighborhoods. Legal Defense Program represents indigent persons facing criminal charges or probation revocations. Center for Patient Partnerships advocates on behalf of cancer patients. Communication and Advocacy Program coordinates many opportunities to gain experience and skills in oral and written communication through legal writing, oral presentation, and advocacy. Individualized Instruction Service offers writing instruction tailored to learning styles and particular writing concerns. Moot Court and Mock Trial Teams provide unparalleled experiences in trial and appellate work. Lawyering Skills Program teaches core lawyering skills through simulations in negotiation, oral advocacy and communication, interviewing and counseling, drafting, and problem solving. Students also examine how practicing lawyers address ethical and professional problems, manage their practices, and balance their professional and personal lives.

International law and study abroad: Students can study with one of seven foreign law faculties: in Chile, Germany, Italy, the Netherlands, Peru, South Africa, and the United Kingdom—or participate in foreign study programs of other U.S. law schools. Additional opportunities are available through the East Asian Legal Studies Center.

STUDENT BODY

Fall 2005 full-time enrollment: 801

Men: 54%	Women: 46%
African-American: 7.5%	American Indian: 1.9%
Asian-American: 6.6%	Mexican-American: 4.7%
Puerto Rican: 1.1%	Other Hisp-Amer: 1.9%
White: 71.2%	International: 2.2%
Unknown: 2.9%	

Fall 2005 part-time enrollment: 38

Men: 29%	Women: 71%
African-American: 21.1%	American Indian: 5.3%
Asian-American: 5.3%	Mexican-American: 0.0%
Puerto Rican: 0.0%	Other Hisp-Amer: 7.9%
White: 15.8%	International: 0.0%
Unknown: 44.7%	

Attrition rates for 2004-2005 full-time students

Percent of students discontinuing law school:

Men: 2%	Women: 1%
First-year students: N/A	Second-year students: 4%
Third-year students: N/A	

LIBRARY RESOURCES

The library holds 287,215 and receives 6,173 current subscriptions.
Total volumes: 553,997
Percentage of the titles in the online catalog: 99%
Total seats available for library users: 615

INFORMATION TECHNOLOGY

Number of wired network connections available to students: 309 total (in the law library, excluding computer labs: 278; in classrooms: 0; in computer labs: 0; elsewhere in the law school: 31)
Law school has a wireless network.
Approximate number of simultaneous users that can be accommodated on wireless network: 1,000
Students are required to own a computer.

EMPLOYMENT AND SALARIES

Proportion of 2004 graduates employed at graduation: 73%
Employed 9 months later, as of February 15, 2005: 97%
Salaries in the private sector (law firms, business, industry): $50,000–$95,000 (25th-75th percentile)
Median salary in the private sector: $70,000
Percentage in the private sector who reported salary information: 52%
Median salary in public service (government, judicial clerkships, academic posts, non-profits): $40,000

Percentage of 2004 graduates in:

Law firms: 55%	Bus./industry (legal): 3%
Bus./industry (nonlegal): 13%	Government: 11%
Public interest: 7%	Judicial clerkship: 7%
Academia : 4%	Unknown: 0%

2004 graduates employed in-state: 58%
2004 graduates employed in foreign countries: 2%
Number of states where graduates are employed: 22
Percentage of 2004 graduates working in: New England: 0%, Middle Atlantic: 6%, East North Central: 70%, West North Central: 7%, South Atlantic: 6%, East South Central: 1%, West South Central: 0%, Mountain: 1%, Pacific: 6%, Unknown: 1%

BAR PASSAGE RATES

Based on 2004 graduates taking Summer 2004 or Winter 2005 exams. Most of the school's first-time test takers took the bar in Wisconsin.

100%
School's bar passage rate for first-time test takers

84%
Statewide bar passage rate for first-time test takers

University of Wyoming

- Department 3035, 1000 E. University Avenue, Laramie, WY, 82071
- http://www.uwyo.edu/law
- Public
- Year founded: 1920
- 2005-2006 tuition: In-state: full-time: $6,519, part-time: N/A; Out-of-state: full-time: $13,799
- Enrollment 2005-06 academic year: full-time: 227
- U.S. News 2007 law specialty ranking: N/A

3.06-3.65 GPA, 25TH-75TH PERCENTILE

149-156 LSAT, 25TH-75TH PERCENTILE

26% ACCEPTANCE RATE

Tier 4 2007 U.S. NEWS LAW SCHOOL RANKING

ADMISSIONS

Admissions phone number: **(307) 766-6416**
Admissions email address: **lawadmis@uwyo.edu**
Application website: **N/A**
Application deadline for Fall 2007 admission: **3/01**

Admissions statistics:

Number of applicants for Fall 2005: **728**
Number of acceptances: **188**
Number enrolled: **80**
Acceptance rate: **26%**
GPA, 25th-75th percentile, entering class Fall 2005: **3.06-3.65**
LSAT, 25th-75th percentile, entering class Fall 2005: **149-156**

FINANCIAL AID

Financial aid phone number: **(307) 766-2116**
Financial aid application deadline: **3/01**
Tuition 2005-2006 academic year: In-state: full-time: **$6,519**, part-time: N/A; Out-of-state: full-time: **$13,799**
Room and board: **$7,703**; books: **$1,200**; miscellaneous expenses: **$2,759**
Total of room/board/books/miscellaneous expenses: **$11,662**
University offers graduate student housing for which law students are eligible.

Financial aid profile

Percent of students that received grants for the 2004-2005 academic year: full-time: **77%**
Median grant amount: full-time: **$1,000**
The average law-school debt of those in the Class of 2005 who borrowed: **$38,542**. Proportion who borrowed: **81%**

ACADEMIC PROGRAMS

Calendar: **semester**
Joint degrees awarded: **J.D./M.P.A.; J.D./M.B.A.**
Typical first-year section size: Full-time: **78**

Is there typically a "small section" of the first year class, other than Legal Writing, taught by full-time faculty?: Full-time: **no**
Number of course titles, beyond the first year curriculum, offered last year: **56**
Percentages of upper division course sections, excluding seminars, with an enrollment of:

Under 25: **67%**   25 to 49: **14%**
50 to 74: **18%**   75 to 99: **2%**
100+: **0%**

Areas of specialization: appellate advocacy, clinical training, dispute resolution, environmental law, healthcare law, intellectual property law, international law, tax law, trial advocacy

Fall 2005 faculty profile

Total teaching faculty: **16**. Full-time: **69%**; **73%** men, **27%** women, **18%** minorities. Part-time: **31%**; **20%** men, **80%** women, **0%** minorities
Student-to-faculty ratio: **17.2**

SPECIAL PROGRAMS *(as provided by law school)*:

The University of Wyoming College of Law has five clinical programs: Legal Services Clinic (dealing with civil problems of low-income clients), Prosecution Assistance Clinic (assisting the state with appeals and assisting state prosecutors at the trial level), Defender Aid Clinic (assisting the state public defender with post conviction relief and appeals), Domestic Violence Clinic (providing civil legal assistance to victims of domestic violence, sexual assault, and stalking); and the ASUW clinic (providing civil legal assistance to enrolled students of the University of Wyoming). The college also has an externship program that places students in experiential learning with, for example, state and federal judges, government agencies, and environmental groups to gain hands-on legal experience for academic credit.

STUDENT BODY

Fall 2005 full-time enrollment: 227
Men: **56%**   Women: **44%**
African-American: **0.9%**   American Indian: **1.8%**

Asian-American: **1.3%** Mexican-American: **1.3%**
Puerto Rican: **0.4%** Other Hisp-Amer: **1.8%**
White: **80.6%** International: **1.8%**
Unknown: **10.1%**

Attrition rates for 2004-2005 full-time students
Percent of students discontinuing law school:
Men: **2%** Women: **2%**
First-year students: **1%** Second-year students: **4%**
Third-year students: **N/A**

LIBRARY RESOURCES
The library holds **25,561** and receives **1,852** current subscriptions.
Total volumes: **285,827**
Percentage of the titles in the online catalog: **99%**
Total seats available for library users: **250**

INFORMATION TECHNOLOGY
Number of wired network connections available to students: **189** total (in the law library, excluding computer labs: **12**; in classrooms: **164**; in computer labs: **10**; elsewhere in the law school: **3**)
Law school has a wireless network.
Approximate number of simultaneous users that can be accommodated on wireless network: **180**
Students are not required to own a computer.

EMPLOYMENT AND SALARIES
Proportion of 2004 graduates employed at graduation: **N/A**
Employed 9 months later, as of February 15, 2005: **83%**
Salaries in the private sector (law firms, business, industry): **$33,000–$88,000** (25th-75th percentile)

Median salary in the private sector: **$45,714**
Percentage in the private sector who reported salary information: **64%**
Median salary in public service (government, judicial clerkships, academic posts, non-profits): **$43,452**

Percentage of 2004 graduates in:
Law firms: **47%** Bus./industry (legal): **5%**
Bus./industry (nonlegal): **0%** Government: **22%**
Public interest: **5%** Judicial clerkship: **22%**
Academia : **0%** Unknown: **0%**

2004 graduates employed in-state: **63%**
2004 graduates employed in foreign countries: **0%**
Number of states where graduates are employed: **9**
Percentage of 2004 graduates working in: New England: **0%**, Middle Atlantic: **0%**, East North Central: **0%**, West North Central: **0%**, South Atlantic: **2%**, East South Central: **0%**, West South Central: **0%**, Mountain: **88%**, Pacific: **10%**, Unknown: **0%**

BAR PASSAGE RATES
Based on 2004 graduates taking Summer 2004 or Winter 2005 exams. Most of the school's first-time test takers took the bar in Wyoming.

70%

School's bar passage rate for first-time test takers

68%

Statewide bar passage rate for first-time test takers

Valparaiso University

- 656 S. Greenwich Street, Wesemann Hall, Valparaiso, IN, 46383
- http://www.valpo.edu/law
- Private
- Year founded: 1879
- 2005-2006 tuition: full-time: $27,063; part-time: $1,057/credit hour
- Enrollment 2005-06 academic year: full-time: 479; part-time: 47
- U.S. News 2007 law specialty ranking: N/A

2.97-3.58 GPA, 25TH-75TH PERCENTILE

150-155 LSAT, 25TH-75TH PERCENTILE

21% ACCEPTANCE RATE

Tier 4 2007 U.S. NEWS LAW SCHOOL RANKING

ADMISSIONS

Admissions phone number: **(219) 548-7703**
Admissions email address: **valpolaw@valpo.edu**
Application website: **https://www.valpo.edu/law/admissions/apply**
Application deadline for Fall 2007 admission: **4/01**

Admissions statistics:
Number of applicants for Fall 2005: **2,918**
Number of acceptances: **627**
Number enrolled: **172**
Acceptance rate: **21%**
GPA, 25th-75th percentile, entering class Fall 2005: **2.97-3.58**
LSAT, 25th-75th percentile, entering class Fall 2005: **150-155**

Part-time program:
Number of applicants for Fall 2005: **175**
Number of acceptances: **55**
Number enrolled: **27**
Acceptance rate: **31%**
GPA, 25th-75th percentile, entering class Fall 2005: **2.78-3.29**
LSAT, 25th-75th percentile, entering class Fall 2005: **144-148**

FINANCIAL AID

Financial aid phone number: **(219) 465-7818**
Financial aid application deadline: **3/01**
Tuition 2005-2006 academic year: full-time: **$27,063**; part-time: **$1,057/credit hour**
Room and board: **$6,600**; books: **$1,000**; miscellaneous expenses: **$2,610**
Total of room/board/books/miscellaneous expenses: **$10,210**
University does not offer graduate student housing for which law students are eligible.

Financial aid profile
Percent of students that received grants for the 2004-2005 academic year: full-time: **32%**

Median grant amount: full-time: **$12,335**
The average law-school debt of those in the Class of 2005 who borrowed: **$53,454**. Proportion who borrowed: **94%**

ACADEMIC PROGRAMS
Calendar: **semester**
Joint degrees awarded: **J.D./MA-Psych; J.D./MA-CMHC; J.D./M.B.A.; J.D./MALS; J.D./MSICP; J.D./MSSports**
Typical first-year section size: Full-time: **93**
Is there typically a "small section" of the first year class, other than Legal Writing, taught by full-time faculty?: Full-time: **no**; Part-time: **no**
Number of course titles, beyond the first year curriculum, offered last year: **99**
Percentages of upper division course sections, excluding seminars, with an enrollment of:
Under 25: **58%**   25 to 49: **25%**
50 to 74: **7%**   75 to 99: **7%**
100+: **2%**
Areas of specialization: appellate advocacy, clinical training, dispute resolution, environmental law, healthcare law, intellectual property law, international law, tax law, trial advocacy

Fall 2005 faculty profile
Total teaching faculty: **71**. Full-time: **38%**; **59%** men, **41%** women, **4%** minorities. Part-time: **62%**; **73%** men, **27%** women, **0%** minorities
Student-to-faculty ratio: **15.5**

SPECIAL PROGRAMS (as provided by law school):
The Valparaiso University School of Law is renowned for the following four traits.

Law as a Calling: We are a community dedicated to imparting not just skills and knowledge, but values, the sense of self, and the commitment to service.

Enduring Core Competencies: There are certain constants in the legal world: the ability to engage in critical, analytical, and creative thinking, and the ability to communicate clearly and cleanly. These core competencies comprise the cornerstone of your Valpo Law education.

Exceptional Legal Research and Writing: We have three years of both legal writing and legal research. This is a professional activity in which every Valpo Law alumnus/a excels.

Truly Personal Manner of Teaching and Learning: Every pedagogical component, including the intentionally smaller student body, is designed to help you, as an individual, succeed in your professional endeavors.

Notable program offerings include:

Externships: We offer over 60 different extern employers (work for academic credit) from a wide range of both public and private agencies and entities.

Summer Study Abroad: Our interest in international and comparative law is enhanced with a Summer Study Abroad Program in Cambridge, England. A program in South America is under development.

Honors Program: The Honors Program is designed to offer a special academic challenge to highly talented students.

Summer Public Interest Scholarships: Each year we award Summer Public Interest Scholarships to students who work in a public interest capacity.

Loan Repayment Assistance Program: Encourages law students to accept public service jobs upon graduation by offering financial assistance to graduates who chose public service employment.

Academic Success Program: Designed to assist students with the transition from college or the work force to law school and to assure their academic success.

Law Clinic: A multi-practice area, in-house, live-client legal assistance program that provides a chance to actually practice law while a law student.

Degree Options: full-time J.D., part-time J.D., two-year J.D., LL.M., dual degrees.

Dual Degree: Complement your J.D. with a master's degree in: psychology, clinical mental health counseling, liberal studies, business administration, sports administration, or international commerce and policy.

STUDENT BODY

Fall 2005 full-time enrollment: 479

Men: 53%	Women: 47%
African-American: 4.2%	American Indian: 0.4%
Asian-American: 1.9%	Mexican-American: 1.5%
Puerto Rican: 0.0%	Other Hisp-Amer: 2.5%
White: 88.1%	International: 1.3%
Unknown: 0.2%	

Fall 2005 part-time enrollment: 47

Men: 62%	Women: 38%
African-American: 17.0%	American Indian: 0.0%
Asian-American: 2.1%	Mexican-American: 4.3%
Puerto Rican: 0.0%	Other Hisp-Amer: 2.1%
White: 74.5%	International: 0.0%
Unknown: 0.0%	

Attrition rates for 2004-2005 full-time students
Percent of students discontinuing law school:
Men: 9%   Women: 6%

First-year students: 16%   Second-year students: 4%
Third-year students: 2%

LIBRARY RESOURCES
The library holds 132,248 and receives 2,348 current subscriptions.
Total volumes: 319,604
Percentage of the titles in the online catalog: 100%
Total seats available for library users: 351

INFORMATION TECHNOLOGY
Number of wired network connections available to students: 58 total (in the law library, excluding computer labs: 45; in classrooms: 3; in computer labs: 0; elsewhere in the law school: 10)
Law school has a wireless network.
Approximate number of simultaneous users that can be accommodated on wireless network: 2,500
Students are not required to own a computer.

EMPLOYMENT AND SALARIES
Proportion of 2004 graduates employed at graduation: 33%
Employed 9 months later, as of February 15, 2005: 81%
Salaries in the private sector (law firms, business, industry): $40,500–$56,300 (25th-75th percentile)
Median salary in the private sector: $47,500
Percentage in the private sector who reported salary information: 47%
Median salary in public service (government, judicial clerkships, academic posts, non-profits): $41,000

Percentage of 2004 graduates in:
Law firms: 63%	Bus./industry (legal): 2%
Bus./industry (nonlegal): 14%	Government: 12%
Public interest: 2%	Judicial clerkship: 4%
Academia : 1%	Unknown: 3%

2004 graduates employed in-state: 47%
2004 graduates employed in foreign countries: 1%
Number of states where graduates are employed: 19
Percentage of 2004 graduates working in: New England: 1%, Middle Atlantic: 1%, East North Central: 85%, West North Central: 2%, South Atlantic: 5%, East South Central: 1%, West South Central: 1%, Mountain: 3%, Pacific: 2%, Unknown: 0%

BAR PASSAGE RATES
Based on 2004 graduates taking Summer 2004 or Winter 2005 exams. Most of the school's first-time test takers took the bar in Indiana.

83%
School's bar passage rate for first-time test takers

84%
Statewide bar passage rate for first-time test takers

Vanderbilt University

- 131 21st Avenue S, Nashville, TN, 37203-1181
- http://www.vanderbilt.edu/law/
- Private
- Year founded: 1874
- 2005-2006 tuition: full-time: $34,036; part-time: N/A
- Enrollment 2005-06 academic year: full-time: 626; part-time: 1
- U.S. News 2007 law specialty ranking: clinical training: 30, international law: 13

3.52-3.85 GPA, 25TH-75TH PERCENTILE

163-167 LSAT, 25TH-75TH PERCENTILE

23% ACCEPTANCE RATE

17 2007 U.S. NEWS LAW SCHOOL RANKING

ADMISSIONS

Admissions phone number: **(615) 322-6452**
Admissions email address: **admissions@law.vanderbilt.edu**
Application website:
  http://law.vanderbilt.edu/admiss/forms.html
Application deadline for Fall 2007 admission: **3/15**

Admissions statistics:

Number of applicants for Fall 2005: **3,437**
Number of acceptances: **791**
Number enrolled: **200**
Acceptance rate: **23%**
GPA, 25th-75th percentile, entering class Fall 2005:
  3.52-3.85
LSAT, 25th-75th percentile, entering class Fall 2005:
  163-167

FINANCIAL AID

Financial aid phone number: **(615) 322-6452**
Financial aid application deadline: **2/15**
Tuition 2005-2006 academic year: full-time: **$34,036**; part-time: **N/A**
Room and board: **$11,268**; books: **$1,484**; miscellaneous expenses: **$6,064**
Total of room/board/books/miscellaneous expenses: **$18,816**
University offers graduate student housing for which law students are eligible.

Financial aid profile

Percent of students that received grants for the 2004-2005 academic year: full-time: **63%**
Median grant amount: full-time: **$14,000**
The average law-school debt of those in the Class of 2005 who borrowed: **$92,809**. Proportion who borrowed: **84%**

ACADEMIC PROGRAMS

Calendar: **semester**
Joint degrees awarded: **J.D./M.B.A; J.D./MTS; J.D./MDiv; J.D./MA; J.D./Ph.D; J.D./MD; J.D./MPP**
Typical first-year section size: Full-time: **100**

Is there typically a "small section" of the first year class, other than Legal Writing, taught by full-time faculty?:
  Full-time: **yes**
Number of course titles, beyond the first year curriculum, offered last year: **132**
Percentages of upper division course sections, excluding seminars, with an enrollment of:
  Under 25: **57%**   25 to 49: **16%**
  50 to 74: **18%**   75 to 99: **6%**
  100+: **2%**
Areas of specialization: appellate advocacy, clinical training, dispute resolution, environmental law, healthcare law, intellectual property law, international law, tax law, trial advocacy

Fall 2005 faculty profile

Total teaching faculty: **102**. Full-time: **37%**; **68%** men, **32%** women, **16%** minorities. Part-time: **63%**; **75%** men, **25%** women, **6%** minorities
Student-to-faculty ratio: **16.4**

SPECIAL PROGRAMS (as provided by law school):

Vanderbilt offers a broad array of opportunities to allow students to craft the legal education that most fits their goals. In addition to courses in the traditional areas of study, the school strives to enhance a student's preparation for the practice of law through a variety of nontraditional options. Vanderbilt was the first major law school to launch a law and business program. The program consists of specially designed courses that are co-taught by law school and business school professors and that are taken by both J.D. and M.B.A. students. The program allows students to familiarize themselves with common business decisions and future business leaders so that they can be more effective when representing their clients.

Curricular specializations are also being developed in Litigation and Dispute Resolution, International Law, and Entertainment and Technology Law.

Vanderbilt also offers a summer program in Venice. Taught by faculty members of the law school and the University of Venice, the program provides in-depth training in various aspects of world legal systems. For those interested in combining a law degree with a degree in another field, Vanderbilt has standing joint degree programs with the medical school, divinity school, graduate school, the public policy program, and the Owen Graduate School of Management. Students may also craft an individualized joint degree program.

Vanderbilt offers a number of vehicles through which students can hone their legal skills. The school has six in-house, live-client clinical courses: Criminal Practice Clinic, Civil Practice Clinic, Juvenile Practice Clinic, Domestic Violence Clinic, Business Law Clinic, and Community and Economic Development Clinic. In each of these courses, small groups of students (no more than eight per class) represent clients under the close supervision of clinical faculty members. Vanderbilt offers externship opportunities to students during both the summer and the academic year.

STUDENT BODY

Fall 2005 full-time enrollment: 626

Men: 54%	Women: 46%
African-American: 9.9%	American Indian: 0.5%
Asian-American: 6.1%	Mexican-American: 0.0%
Puerto Rican: 0.0%	Other Hisp-Amer: 3.7%
White: 70.4%	International: 3.5%
Unknown: 5.9%	

Fall 2005 part-time enrollment: 1

Men: 0%	Women: 100%
African-American: 0.0%	American Indian: 0.0%
Asian-American: 0.0%	Mexican-American: 0.0%
Puerto Rican: 0.0%	Other Hisp-Amer: 0.0%
White: 100.0%	International: 0.0%
Unknown: 0.0%	

Attrition rates for 2004-2005 full-time students

Percent of students discontinuing law school:

Men: 3%	Women: 1%
First-year students: 2%	Second-year students: 5%
Third-year students: N/A	

LIBRARY RESOURCES

The library holds 152,324 and receives 6,959 current subscriptions.
Total volumes: 588,413
Percentage of the titles in the online catalog: 100%
Total seats available for library users: 309

INFORMATION TECHNOLOGY

Number of wired network connections available to students: 405 total (in the law library, excluding computer labs: 185; in classrooms: 150; in computer labs: 0; elsewhere in the law school: 70)
Law school has a wireless network.
Approximate number of simultaneous users that can be accommodated on wireless network: 1,000
Students are not required to own a computer.

EMPLOYMENT AND SALARIES

Proportion of 2004 graduates employed at graduation: 92%
Employed 9 months later, as of February 15, 2005: 97%
Salaries in the private sector (law firms, business, industry): $83,000–$115,000 (25th-75th percentile)
Median salary in the private sector: $100,000
Percentage in the private sector who reported salary information: 78%
Median salary in public service (government, judicial clerkships, academic posts, non-profits): $47,500

Percentage of 2004 graduates in:

Law firms: 73%	Bus./industry (legal): 1%
Bus./industry (nonlegal): 4%	Government: 7%
Public interest: 3%	Judicial clerkship: 11%
Academia : 1%	Unknown: 1%

2004 graduates employed in-state: 22%
2004 graduates employed in foreign countries: 0%
Number of states where graduates are employed: 29
Percentage of 2004 graduates working in: New England: 2%, Middle Atlantic: 8%, East North Central: 7%, West North Central: 4%, South Atlantic: 34%, East South Central: 29%, West South Central: 8%, Mountain: 2%, Pacific: 5%, Unknown: 1%

BAR PASSAGE RATES

Based on 2004 graduates taking Summer 2004 or Winter 2005 exams. Most of the school's first-time test takers took the bar in Tennessee.

91%
School's bar passage rate for first-time test takers

82%
Statewide bar passage rate for first-time test takers

Vermont Law School

- Chelsea Street, South Royalton, VT, 05068-0096
- http://www.vermontlaw.edu
- Private
- **Year founded:** 1972
- **2005-2006 tuition:** full-time: $28,114; part-time: N/A
- **Enrollment 2005-06 academic year:** full-time: 562; part-time: 2
- **U.S. News 2007 law specialty ranking:** environmental law: 2

2.89-3.47 GPA, 25TH-75TH PERCENTILE

151-158 LSAT, 25TH-75TH PERCENTILE

51% ACCEPTANCE RATE

Tier 3 2007 U.S. NEWS LAW SCHOOL RANKING

ADMISSIONS

Admissions phone number: **(888) 277-5985**
Admissions email address: **admiss@vermontlaw.edu**
Application website: **N/A**
Application deadline for Fall 2007 admission: **3/01**

Admissions statistics:
Number of applicants for Fall 2005: **1,116**
Number of acceptances: **565**
Number enrolled: **196**
Acceptance rate: **51%**
GPA, 25th-75th percentile, entering class Fall 2005: **2.89-3.47**
LSAT, 25th-75th percentile, entering class Fall 2005: **151-158**

FINANCIAL AID

Financial aid phone number: **(888) 277-5985**
Financial aid application deadline: **3/01**
Tuition 2005-2006 academic year: full-time: **$28,114**; part-time: **N/A**
Room and board: **$9,530**; books: **$950**; miscellaneous expenses: **$7,052**
Total of room/board/books/miscellaneous expenses: **$17,532**
University does not offer graduate student housing for which law students are eligible.

Financial aid profile
Percent of students that received grants for the 2004-2005 academic year: full-time: **59%**
Median grant amount: full-time: **$5,000**
The average law-school debt of those in the Class of 2005 who borrowed: **$99,810**. Proportion who borrowed: **89%**

ACADEMIC PROGRAMS

Calendar: **semester**
Joint degrees awarded: **J.D./M.S.E.L.**
Typical first-year section size: Full-time: **68**
Is there typically a "small section" of the first year class, other than Legal Writing, taught by full-time faculty?: Full-time: **yes**

Number of course titles, beyond the first year curriculum, offered last year: **120**
Percentages of upper division course sections, excluding seminars, with an enrollment of:

Under 25: **66%**   25 to 49: **19%**
50 to 74: **11%**   75 to 99: **3%**
100+: **0%**

Areas of specialization: appellate advocacy, clinical training, dispute resolution, environmental law, intellectual property law, international law, tax law, trial advocacy

Fall 2005 faculty profile
Total teaching faculty: **70**. Full-time: **54%**; **53%** men, **47%** women, **8%** minorities. Part-time: **46%**; **63%** men, **38%** women, N/A minorities
Student-to-faculty ratio: **13.3**

SPECIAL PROGRAMS *(as provided by law school):*
Clinics offered are Semester in Practice and Legislation Clinic. Also there are the Environmental Semester in Washington, D.C.; Environmental and Natural Resources Law Clinic., South Royalton Legal Clinic and General Practice Program. There are Judicial Externships, Mediation Clinic, MSEL and LL.M. Environmental internships and J.D. Internships.

STUDENT BODY

Fall 2005 full-time enrollment: 562
Men: **49%**	Women: **51%**
African-American: **6.6%**	American Indian: **1.2%**
Asian-American: **2.5%**	Mexican-American: **0.2%**
Puerto Rican: **0.0%**	Other Hisp-Amer: **5.3%**
White: **76.0%**	International: **0.7%**
Unknown: **7.5%**	

Fall 2005 part-time enrollment: 2
Men: **50%**	Women: **50%**
African-American: **0.0%**	American Indian: **0.0%**
Asian-American: **0.0%**	Mexican-American: **0.0%**
Puerto Rican: **0.0%**	Other Hisp-Amer: **50.0%**
White: **50.0%**	International: **0.0%**
Unknown: **0.0%**	

Attrition rates for 2004-2005 full-time students

Percent of students discontinuing law school:

Men: 3%   Women: 5%

First-year students: 12%   Second-year students: N/A

Third-year students: N/A

LIBRARY RESOURCES

The library holds 45,813 and receives 1,856 current subscriptions.

Total volumes: 239,606

Percentage of the titles in the online catalog: 100%

Total seats available for library users: 382

INFORMATION TECHNOLOGY

Number of wired network connections available to students: 110 total (in the law library, excluding computer labs: 54; in classrooms: 45; in computer labs: 1; elsewhere in the law school: 10)

Law school has a wireless network.

Approximate number of simultaneous users that can be accommodated on wireless network: 400

Students are not required to own a computer.

EMPLOYMENT AND SALARIES

Proportion of 2004 graduates employed at graduation: N/A

Employed 9 months later, as of February 15, 2005: 94%

Salaries in the private sector (law firms, business, industry): $35,000–$50,000 (25th-75th percentile)

Median salary in the private sector: $40,000

Percentage in the private sector who reported salary information: 58%

Median salary in public service (government, judicial clerkships, academic posts, non-profits): $35,958

Percentage of 2004 graduates in:

Law firms: 40%	Bus./industry (legal): 18%
Bus./industry (nonlegal): 0%	Government: 12%
Public interest: 13%	Judicial clerkship: 14%
Academia : 3%	Unknown: 0%

2004 graduates employed in-state: 25%

2004 graduates employed in foreign countries: 0%

Number of states where graduates are employed: 32

Percentage of 2004 graduates working in: New England: 42%, Middle Atlantic: 7%, East North Central: 7%, West North Central: 0%, South Atlantic: 20%, East South Central: 5%, West South Central: 5%, Mountain: 5%, Pacific: 9%, Unknown: 1%

BAR PASSAGE RATES

Based on 2004 graduates taking Summer 2004 or Winter 2005 exams. Most of the school's first-time test takers took the bar in Vermont.

74%

School's bar passage rate for first-time test takers

85%

Statewide bar passage rate for first-time test takers

Villanova University

- 299 N. Spring Mill Road, Villanova, PA, 19085
- http://www.law.villanova.edu/
- Private
- Year founded: 1953
- 2005-2006 tuition: full-time: $27,830; part-time: N/A
- Enrollment 2005-06 academic year: full-time: 748
- U.S. News 2007 law specialty ranking: tax law: 19

3.30-3.66 GPA, 25TH-75TH PERCENTILE

161-163 LSAT, 25TH-75TH PERCENTILE

32% ACCEPTANCE RATE

60 2007 U.S. NEWS LAW SCHOOL RANKING

ADMISSIONS

Admissions phone number: **(610) 519-7010**
Admissions email address: **admissions@law.villanova.edu**
Application website: **N/A**
Application deadline for Fall 2007 admission: **rolling**

Admissions statistics:

Number of applicants for Fall 2005: **2,994**
Number of acceptances: **945**
Number enrolled: **245**
Acceptance rate: **32%**
GPA, 25th-75th percentile, entering class Fall 2005:
3.30-3.66
LSAT, 25th-75th percentile, entering class Fall 2005:
161-163

FINANCIAL AID

Financial aid phone number: **(610) 519-7015**
Financial aid application deadline: **N/A**
Tuition 2005-2006 academic year: full-time: **$27,830**; part-time: **N/A**
Room and board: **$12,600**; books: **$1,200**; miscellaneous expenses: **$2,975**
Total of room/board/books/miscellaneous expenses: **$16,775**
University does not offer graduate student housing for which law students are eligible.

Financial aid profile

Percent of students that received grants for the 2004-2005 academic year: full-time: **18%**
Median grant amount: full-time: **$5,000**
The average law-school debt of those in the Class of 2005 who borrowed: **$92,263**. Proportion who borrowed: **85%**

ACADEMIC PROGRAMS

Calendar: **semester**
Joint degrees awarded: **J.D./Ph.D.; J.D./M.B.A.; J.D./LL.M.**
Typical first-year section size: Full-time: **109**

Is there typically a "small section" of the first year class, other than Legal Writing, taught by full-time faculty?:
Full-time: **yes**
Number of course titles, beyond the first year curriculum, offered last year: **109**
Percentages of upper division course sections, excluding seminars, with an enrollment of:
Under 25: **59%**   25 to 49: **15%**
50 to 74: **13%**   75 to 99: **9%**
100+: **3%**
Areas of specialization: appellate advocacy, clinical training, dispute resolution, environmental law, healthcare law, intellectual property law, international law, tax law, trial advocacy

Fall 2005 faculty profile

Total teaching faculty: **87**. Full-time: **43%**; **68%** men, **32%** women, **11%** minorities. Part-time: **57%**; **68%** men, **32%** women, **6%** minorities
Student-to-faculty ratio: **17.7**

SPECIAL PROGRAMS (as provided by law school):

Clinics, practicums, externships: Villanova Law School's clinical programs (asylum, civil justice, farm workers, tax and advanced) offer students the chance to apply classroom learning to representing real clients in real cases, with the safety net of close supervision by a full-time faculty member who is an expert in the field. Students assume primary responsibility for the cases. Practicums also offer supervised real world experience. The Death Penalty Practicum offers the opportunity to represent death-row inmates in appeals, working with the elite Federal Defenders Capital Habeas Unit, and our Mediation Practicum allows students to work as front line mediators in the courts and other nonprofits. In addition, students may elect from more than 20 externships, or may design their own. All are closely supervised by a full-time faculty member.

Public-interest programs: Lawyering Together, a pioneer program, pairs students with alumni to handle a pro bono case. Public-interest scholarships are available to three students per entering class, and a variety of pro bono and volunteer opportunities are coordinated through the Director of Pro Bono and Public Interest Programs.

Joint degrees: The law school offers a J.D./Ph.D. in law and psychology, J.D. LL.M in taxation and a J.D./M.B.A.

LL.M. Program: The law school offers an LL.M. in taxation. The presence of this highly regarded graduate program draws top-notch professors, and allows the law school to offer a large number of sophisticated tax courses to J.D. students.

Sentencing workshop: The workshop brings 12 VLS students, two VLS professors, eight judges, a prosecutor, a defense lawyer, and one correctional/treatment professional together for three intensive weekend sessions to discuss the crucial issues of sentencing and punishment, viewing them through the lens of real cases.

Specialty course guides: While the law school does not offer certifications in specialty areas of practice, the faculty has developed course guides in a number of practice areas.

Study abroad: VLS has a summer abroad program at the University of Montreal. Students may also participate in summer study abroad through accredited programs.

STUDENT BODY

Fall 2005 full-time enrollment: 748

Men: 52%	Women: 48%
African-American: 4.5%	American Indian: 0.4%
Asian-American: 7.1%	Mexican-American: 0.0%
Puerto Rican: 0.0%	Other Hisp-Amer: 4.8%
White: 80.3%	International: 0.9%
Unknown: 1.9%	

Attrition rates for 2004-2005 full-time students
Percent of students discontinuing law school:

Men: 1%	Women: 1%
First-year students: 3%	Second-year students: N/A
Third-year students: N/A	

LIBRARY RESOURCES

The library holds 144,579 and receives 3,554 current subscriptions.
Total volumes: 516,273
Percentage of the titles in the online catalog: 56%
Total seats available for library users: 368

INFORMATION TECHNOLOGY

Number of wired network connections available to students: 327 total (in the law library, excluding computer labs: 94; in classrooms: 81; in computer labs: 98; elsewhere in the law school: 54)

Law school has a wireless network.
Approximate number of simultaneous users that can be accommodated on wireless network: 640
Students are not required to own a computer.

EMPLOYMENT AND SALARIES

Proportion of 2004 graduates employed at graduation: 67%
Employed 9 months later, as of February 15, 2005: 98%
Salaries in the private sector (law firms, business, industry): $60,000–$107,000 (25th-75th percentile)
Median salary in the private sector: $80,000
Percentage in the private sector who reported salary information: 77%
Median salary in public service (government, judicial clerkships, academic posts, non-profits): $42,000

Percentage of 2004 graduates in:

Law firms: 62%	Bus./industry (legal): 4%
Bus./industry (nonlegal): 4%	Government: 8%
Public interest: 1%	Judicial clerkship: 21%
Academia : 0%	Unknown: 1%

2004 graduates employed in-state: 60%
2004 graduates employed in foreign countries: 1%
Number of states where graduates are employed: 16
Percentage of 2004 graduates working in: New England: 3%, Middle Atlantic: 78%, East North Central: 1%, West North Central: 0%, South Atlantic: 16%, East South Central: 0%, West South Central: 0%, Mountain: 1%, Pacific: 1%, Unknown: 0%

BAR PASSAGE RATES

Based on 2004 graduates taking Summer 2004 or Winter 2005 exams. Most of the school's first-time test takers took the bar in Pennsylvania.

79%
School's bar passage rate for first-time test takers

81%
Statewide bar passage rate for first-time test takers

Wake Forest University

- Reynolda Station, PO Box 7206, Winston-Salem, NC, 27109
- http://www.law.wfu.edu
- Private
- Year founded: 1894
- 2005-2006 tuition: full-time: $27,900; part-time: N/A
- Enrollment 2005-06 academic year: full-time: 468; part-time: 20
- U.S. News 2007 law specialty ranking: N/A

3.17-3.62 GPA, 25TH-75TH PERCENTILE

162-166 LSAT, 25TH-75TH PERCENTILE

24% ACCEPTANCE RATE

39 2007 U.S. NEWS LAW SCHOOL RANKING

ADMISSIONS

Admissions phone number: **(336) 758-5437**
Admissions email address: **admissions@law.wfu.edu**
Application website: **https://www4.lsac.org/school/wake-forest.htm**
Application deadline for Fall 2007 admission: **3/01**

Admissions statistics:
Number of applicants for Fall 2005: **2,424**
Number of acceptances: **571**
Number enrolled: **154**
Acceptance rate: **24%**
GPA, 25th-75th percentile, entering class Fall 2005: **3.17-3.62**
LSAT, 25th-75th percentile, entering class Fall 2005: **162-166**

FINANCIAL AID

Financial aid phone number: **(336) 758-5437**
Financial aid application deadline: **4/01**
Tuition 2005-2006 academic year: full-time: **$27,900**; part-time: **N/A**
Room and board: **$8,550**; books: **$800**; miscellaneous expenses: **$6,440**
Total of room/board/books/miscellaneous expenses: **$15,790**
University does not offer graduate student housing for which law students are eligible.

Financial aid profile
Percent of students that received grants for the 2004-2005 academic year: full-time: **35%**
Median grant amount: full-time: **$19,800**
The average law-school debt of those in the Class of 2005 who borrowed: **$75,418**. Proportion who borrowed: **95%**

ACADEMIC PROGRAMS

Calendar: **semester**
Joint degrees awarded: **J.D./M.B.A.**
Typical first-year section size: Full-time: **40**

Is there typically a "small section" of the first year class, other than Legal Writing, taught by full-time faculty?: Full-time: **yes**
Number of course titles, beyond the first year curriculum, offered last year: **87**
Percentages of upper division course sections, excluding seminars, with an enrollment of:
Under 25: **49%**   25 to 49: **37%**
50 to 74: **14%**   75 to 99: **N/A**
100+: **N/A**
Areas of specialization: appellate advocacy, clinical training, dispute resolution, environmental law, healthcare law, intellectual property law, international law, tax law, trial advocacy

Fall 2005 faculty profile
Total teaching faculty: **55**. Full-time: **71%**; **62%** men, **38%** women, **8%** minorities. Part-time: **29%**; **81%** men, **19%** women, **0%** minorities
Student-to-faculty ratio: **10.2**

SPECIAL PROGRAMS *(as provided by law school):*

Clinical opportunities: Wake Forest offers two clinical programs, the Litigation Clinic and the Elder Law Clinic. The Litigation Clinic is a semester-long experience with a combined focus on both civil and criminal law. Students learn from their supervising attorneys in various civil law settings and spend six weeks in offices handling criminal law. The Elder Law Clinic, a collaboration between WFU's School of Law and School of Medicine, exposes students to both the legal issues and medical aspects of this practice area. The clinic is located in the WFU Medical Center and has been noted as one of the nation's premier intern programs in the field of elder law. Students represent low- to moderate-income clients in matters including wills, guardianship, and fraud. They also take two classes taught by the medical school faculty in the Memory Disorders Program.

Summer abroad opportunities: Wake Forest offers four-week international academic programs in London, Venice, and Vienna. In London, students live and study at the Worrell House, a stately, four-story Victorian mansion. In Italy, students live and study at Wake Forest's house in Venice, Casa Artom on the Grand Canal. In Austria, students study comparative law at the University of Vienna. Each program exposes students to distinguished foreign lawyers, jurists, and academics.

Litigation education: Wake Forest's litigation education program has been hailed as one of the best in the country. It received the Emil Gumpert Award from the American College of Trial Lawyers for the nation's best trial advocacy program. Students begin by taking a course in pretrial practice and procedure that walks them through preliminary steps in the litigation process, from interviewing the client through filing a motion. Then, they take trial practice, where they work with a team of six students, simulating trial skills such as direct examination and closing argument. In the end, they combine these skills to conduct a mock jury trial. In addition to these courses, students develop counseling and negotiation skills through simulated exercises in a dispute resolution course. The litigation curriculum is capstoned with the Litigation Clinic or the Elder Law Clinic, where the skills learned are put into practice while assisting real clients with real legal problems.

STUDENT BODY

Fall 2005 full-time enrollment: 468

Men: 55%	Women: 45%
African-American: 6.6%	American Indian: 0.0%
Asian-American: 2.6%	Mexican-American: 0.0%
Puerto Rican: 0.0%	Other Hisp-Amer: 4.7%
White: 84.8%	International: 0.9%
Unknown: 0.4%	

Fall 2005 part-time enrollment: 20

Men: 50%	Women: 50%
African-American: 0.0%	American Indian: 0.0%
Asian-American: 10.0%	Mexican-American: 0.0%
Puerto Rican: 0.0%	Other Hisp-Amer: 5.0%
White: 80.0%	International: 5.0%
Unknown: 0.0%	

Attrition rates for 2004-2005 full-time students
Percent of students discontinuing law school:

Men: 0%	Women: 1%
First-year students: N/A	Second-year students: 2%
Third-year students: N/A	

LIBRARY RESOURCES

The library holds 240,417 and receives 5,442 current subscriptions.
Total volumes: 432,306
Percentage of the titles in the online catalog: 100%
Total seats available for library users: 593

INFORMATION TECHNOLOGY

Number of wired network connections available to students: 110 total (in the law library, excluding computer labs: 64; in classrooms: 0; in computer labs: 30; elsewhere in the law school: 16)
Law school has a wireless network.
Approximate number of simultaneous users that can be accommodated on wireless network: 1,600
Students are required to own a computer.

EMPLOYMENT AND SALARIES

Proportion of 2004 graduates employed at graduation: 77%
Employed 9 months later, as of February 15, 2005: 92%
Salaries in the private sector (law firms, business, industry): $50,000–$100,000 (25th-75th percentile)
Median salary in the private sector: $70,000
Percentage in the private sector who reported salary information: 69%
Median salary in public service (government, judicial clerkships, academic posts, non-profits): $40,000

Percentage of 2004 graduates in:

Law firms: 63%	Bus./industry (legal): 1%
Bus./industry (nonlegal): 4%	Government: 16%
Public interest: 2%	Judicial clerkship: 12%
Academia : 1%	Unknown: 1%

2004 graduates employed in-state: 53%
2004 graduates employed in foreign countries: 1%
Number of states where graduates are employed: 25
Percentage of 2004 graduates working in: New England: 2%, Middle Atlantic: 8%, East North Central: 2%, West North Central: 1%, South Atlantic: 74%, East South Central: 4%, West South Central: 2%, Mountain: 3%, Pacific: 4%, Unknown: 0%

BAR PASSAGE RATES

Based on 2004 graduates taking Summer 2004 or Winter 2005 exams. Most of the school's first-time test takers took the bar in North Carolina.

88%
School's bar passage rate for first-time test takers

75%
Statewide bar passage rate for first-time test takers

Washburn University

■ 1700 College, Topeka, KS, 66621
■ http://washburnlaw.edu
■ Public
■ **Year founded:** 1903
■ **2005-2006 tuition:** In-state: $420/credit hour; Out-of-state: $691/credit hour
■ **Enrollment 2005-06 academic year:** full-time: 451
■ **U.S. News 2007 law specialty ranking:** N/A

3.04-3.66 GPA, 25TH-75TH PERCENTILE

151-155 LSAT, 25TH-75TH PERCENTILE

36% ACCEPTANCE RATE

Tier 3 2007 U.S. NEWS LAW SCHOOL RANKING

ADMISSIONS

Admissions phone number: **(785) 231-1185**
Admissions email address: **admissions@washburnlaw.edu**
Application website: **http://washburnlaw.edu/applyonline/**
Application deadline for Fall 2007 admission: **4/01**

Admissions statistics:

Number of applicants for Fall 2005: **1,105**
Number of acceptances: **397**
Number enrolled: **152**
Acceptance rate: **36%**
GPA, 25th-75th percentile, entering class Fall 2005: **3.04-3.66**
LSAT, 25th-75th percentile, entering class Fall 2005: **151-155**

FINANCIAL AID

Financial aid phone number: **(785) 231-1151**
Financial aid application deadline: **N/A**
Tuition 2005-2006 academic year: In-state: **$420/credit hour**; Out-of-state: **$691/credit hour**
Room and board: **$7,390**; books: **$1,617**; miscellaneous expenses: **$4,798**
Total of room/board/books/miscellaneous expenses: **$13,805**
University offers graduate student housing for which law students are eligible.

Financial aid profile

Percent of students that received grants for the 2004-2005 academic year: full-time: **42%**
Median grant amount: full-time: **$5,000**
The average law-school debt of those in the Class of 2005 who borrowed: **$56,200**. Proportion who borrowed: **86%**

ACADEMIC PROGRAMS

Calendar: **semester**
Joint degrees awarded: **N/A**
Typical first-year section size: Full-time: **75**
Is there typically a "small section" of the first year class, other than Legal Writing, taught by full-time faculty?: Full-time: **yes**

Number of course titles, beyond the first year curriculum, offered last year: **83**
Percentages of upper division course sections, excluding seminars, with an enrollment of:
Under 25: **51%**   25 to 49: **22%**
50 to 74: **15%**   75 to 99: **13%**
100+: **0%**
Areas of specialization: appellate advocacy, clinical training, dispute resolution, environmental law, healthcare law, intellectual property law, international law, tax law, trial advocacy

Fall 2005 faculty profile

Total teaching faculty: **59**. Full-time: **44%**; **69%** men, **31%** women, **23%** minorities. Part-time: **56%**; **79%** men, **21%** women, **0%** minorities
Student-to-faculty ratio: **14.4**

SPECIAL PROGRAMS (as provided by law school):

In 1970 Washburn became one of the first law schools in the nation to offer a program of clinical legal education. The law clinic offers students an opportunity to represent clients in real cases involving criminal defense, family law, and a variety of civil matters. Clinical programs in Native American Law and Transactional Law have been recently added to the curriculum.

Three centers of excellence provide students with opportunities to focus their legal education. The Business and Transactional Law Center offers students an innovative education in all aspects of transactional law, including coursework in crucial skills. Students prepare themselves for successful careers in diverse fields including corporate and securities law, banking, agribusiness, entrepreneurial law, oil and gas law, real estate development, or a general business practice. The Children and Family Law Center supports education, interdisciplinary research, advocacy, and training services focused on children and families involved in the legal system. Washburn houses the American Bar Association's Family Law Quarterly. Students working in the center have the opportunity to take a range of courses related to children and families and to participate in the Washburn Law Clinic representing clients. The Center for Excellence in Advocacy trains law students in skillful use of advocacy techniques. The center also supports research in trial behavior, trial process, and effective advocacy. Students hone their advocacy skills in Washburn's live-client law clinic. The Robinson Courtroom/Bianchino Technology Center contains state-of-the-art equipment that provides students the opportunity for training and experience in the use of the latest technology as a tool in persuasive advocacy. The center coordinates student participation in trial advocacy and moot court competitions that offer students a chance to excel as trial and appellate advocates, matching their skills against competitors from across the United States.

Washburn also offers certificates of specialization in advocacy, corporate law, estate planning, family law, natural resources law, tax law and transactional law. The certificate programs allow students to fully develop their legal interests in these fields. Students who earn certificates graduate with a highly developed working knowledge of the practice area.

Washburn offers a summer program at the University of Utrecht in the Netherlands. For six weeks, participating U.S. and European students take courses co-taught by Washburn and Utrecht faculty.

The Sam A. Crow American Inn of Court, with 75 active members, offers students an opportunity to learn side-by-side with the most experienced judges and lawyers in the community.

STUDENT BODY

Fall 2005 full-time enrollment: 451

Men: 57%	Women: 43%
African-American: 4.2%	American Indian: 1.1%
Asian-American: 4.0%	Mexican-American: 1.8%
Puerto Rican: 0.2%	Other Hisp-Amer: 2.4%
White: 85.4%	International: 0.9%
Unknown: 0.0%	

Attrition rates for 2004-2005 full-time students
Percent of students discontinuing law school:

Men: 2%	Women: 4%
First-year students: 6%	Second-year students: 1%
Third-year students: 1%	

LIBRARY RESOURCES

The library holds 243,240 and receives 4,064 current subscriptions.
Total volumes: 379,814
Percentage of the titles in the online catalog: 100%
Total seats available for library users: 360

INFORMATION TECHNOLOGY

Number of wired network connections available to students: 88 total (in the law library, excluding computer labs: 23; in classrooms: 0; in computer labs: 45; elsewhere in the law school: 20)
Law school has a wireless network.
Approximate number of simultaneous users that can be accommodated on wireless network: 3,060
Students are not required to own a computer.

EMPLOYMENT AND SALARIES

Proportion of 2004 graduates employed at graduation: N/A
Employed 9 months later, as of February 15, 2005: 92%
Salaries in the private sector (law firms, business, industry): $40,000–$58,000 (25th-75th percentile)
Median salary in the private sector: $50,000
Percentage in the private sector who reported salary information: 27%
Median salary in public service (government, judicial clerkships, academic posts, non-profits): $40,000

Percentage of 2004 graduates in:

Law firms: 48%	Bus./industry (legal): 6%
Bus./industry (nonlegal): 14%	Government: 19%
Public interest: 6%	Judicial clerkship: 6%
Academia : N/A	Unknown: N/A

2004 graduates employed in-state: 65%
2004 graduates employed in foreign countries: 1%
Number of states where graduates are employed: 24
Percentage of 2004 graduates working in: New England: N/A, Middle Atlantic: 2%, East North Central: 1%, West North Central: 75%, South Atlantic: 4%, East South Central: 2%, West South Central: 1%, Mountain: 10%, Pacific: 5%, Unknown: 0%

BAR PASSAGE RATES

Based on 2004 graduates taking Summer 2004 or Winter 2005 exams. Most of the school's first-time test takers took the bar in Kansas.

71%
School's bar passage rate for first-time test takers

81%
Statewide bar passage rate for first-time test takers

Washington and Lee University

- Sydney Lewis Hall, Lexington, VA, 24450-0303
- http://law.wlu.edu
- Private
- Year founded: 1849
- 2005-2006 tuition: full-time: $27,981; part-time: N/A
- Enrollment 2005-06 academic year: full-time: 387
- U.S. News 2007 law specialty ranking: N/A

3.25-3.79 GPA, 25ᵀᴴ-75ᵀᴴ PERCENTILE

163-167 LSAT, 25ᵀᴴ-75ᵀᴴ PERCENTILE

21% ACCEPTANCE RATE

22 2007 U.S. NEWS LAW SCHOOL RANKING

ADMISSIONS

Admissions phone number: **(540) 458-8504**
Admissions email address: **lawadm@wlu.edu**
Application website: **http://law.wlu.edu/admissions/application/index.asp**
Application deadline for Fall 2007 admission: **rolling**

Admissions statistics:
Number of applicants for Fall 2005: **4,007**
Number of acceptances: **847**
Number enrolled: **136**
Acceptance rate: **21%**
GPA, 25th-75th percentile, entering class Fall 2005: **3.25-3.79**
LSAT, 25th-75th percentile, entering class Fall 2005: **163-167**

FINANCIAL AID

Financial aid phone number: **(540) 458-8729**
Financial aid application deadline: **N/A**
Tuition 2005-2006 academic year: full-time: **$27,981**; part-time: **N/A**
Room and board: **$8,065**; books: **$1,300**; miscellaneous expenses: **$5,674**
Total of room/board/books/miscellaneous expenses: **$15,039**
University offers graduate student housing for which law students are eligible.

Financial aid profile
Percent of students that received grants for the 2004-2005 academic year: full-time: **76%**
Median grant amount: full-time: **$11,000**
The average law-school debt of those in the Class of 2005 who borrowed: **$60,495**. Proportion who borrowed: **86%**

ACADEMIC PROGRAMS

Calendar: **semester**
Joint degrees awarded: **N/A**
Typical first-year section size: Full-time: **57**
Is there typically a "small section" of the first year class, other than Legal Writing, taught by full-time faculty?: Full-time: **yes**

Number of course titles, beyond the first year curriculum, offered last year: **72**
Percentages of upper division course sections, excluding seminars, with an enrollment of:
Under 25: **54%**   25 to 49: **27%**
50 to 74: **13%**   75 to 99: **6%**
100+: **0%**
Areas of specialization: appellate advocacy, clinical training, dispute resolution, environmental law, healthcare law, intellectual property law, international law, tax law, trial advocacy

Fall 2005 faculty profile
Total teaching faculty: **N/A**. Full-time: **N/A**; **N/A** men, **N/A** women, **N/A** minorities. Part-time: **N/A**; **N/A** men, **N/A** women, **N/A** minorities
Student-to-faculty ratio: **10.5**

SPECIAL PROGRAMS *(as provided by law school):*

Washington and Lee law students have many clinical opportunities. The Legal Clinic has three components: the Community Legal Practice Center, the Black Lung Benefits Program, and placements outside the law school with lawyers in public-service positions. Each component offers a different clinical experience. Students in the Virginia Capital Case Clearinghouse research and write on issues involving capital punishment in Virginia and provide assistance to attorneys involved in capital cases. The Shepherd Poverty Alliance sponsors eight-week summer service-learning student internships.

The law school has exchange programs with the Bucerius Law School in Hamburg, Germany; Trinity College, Dublin; and the University of Western Ontario.

The Center for Law and History conducts workshops and sponsors a lecture during the academic year.

STUDENT BODY

Fall 2005 full-time enrollment: **387**
Men: **58%**   Women: **42%**
African-American: **5.2%**   American Indian: **1.3%**
Asian-American: **7.0%**   Mexican-American: **0.3%**
Puerto Rican: **0.0%**   Other Hisp-Amer: **0.8%**

White: 82.9% International: 2.6%
Unknown: 0.0%

Attrition rates for 2004-2005 full-time students
Percent of students discontinuing law school:
Men: 4% Women: 3%
First-year students: N/A Second-year students: 10%
Third-year students: 1%

LIBRARY RESOURCES
The library holds 160,453 and receives 4,086 current
  subscriptions.
Total volumes: 427,978
Percentage of the titles in the online catalog: 98%
Total seats available for library users: 540

INFORMATION TECHNOLOGY
Number of wired network connections available to students: 325 total (in the law library, excluding computer
  labs: 0; in classrooms: 315; in computer labs: 5; elsewhere in the law school: 5)
Law school has a wireless network.
Approximate number of simultaneous users that can be
  accommodated on wireless network: 2,000
Students are not required to own a computer.

EMPLOYMENT AND SALARIES
Proportion of 2004 graduates employed at graduation:
  77%
Employed 9 months later, as of February 15, 2005: 91%
Salaries in the private sector (law firms, business, indus-
  try): $60,000–$110,000 (25th-75th percentile)
Median salary in the private sector: $83,500

Percentage in the private sector who reported salary
  information: 70%
Median salary in public service (government, judicial clerkships, academic posts, non-profits): $48,974

Percentage of 2004 graduates in:
Law firms: 58% Bus./industry (legal): 7%
Bus./industry (nonlegal): N/A Government: 5%
Public interest: 3% Judicial clerkship: 25%
Academia : 2% Unknown: 0%

2004 graduates employed in-state: 33%
2004 graduates employed in foreign countries: 1%
Number of states where graduates are employed: 21
Percentage of 2004 graduates working in: New England:
  1%, Middle Atlantic: 9%, East North Central: 6%, West
  North Central: 2%, South Atlantic: 65%, East South
  Central: 4%, West South Central: 3%, Mountain: 1%,
  Pacific: 7%, Unknown: 2%

BAR PASSAGE RATES
Based on 2004 graduates taking Summer 2004 or
Winter 2005 exams. Most of the school's first-time test
takers took the bar in Virginia.

| 86% |

School's bar passage rate for first-time test takers

| 74% |

Statewide bar passage rate for first-time test takers

Washington University in St. Louis

- 1 Brookings Drive, Box 1120, St. Louis, MO, 63130
- http://www.law.wustl.edu/
- Private
- Year founded: 1867
- 2005-2006 tuition: full-time: $34,981; part-time: N/A
- Enrollment 2005-06 academic year: full-time: 743; part-time: 2
- U.S. News 2007 law specialty ranking: clinical training: 4, intellecutal property law: 27, international law: 18, tax law: 25, trial advocacy: 7

3.20-3.70	GPA, 25TH-75TH PERCENTILE
161-167	LSAT, 25TH-75TH PERCENTILE
25%	ACCEPTANCE RATE
19	2007 U.S. NEWS LAW SCHOOL RANKING

ADMISSIONS

Admissions phone number: **(314) 935-4525**
Admissions email address: **admiss@wulaw.wustl.edu**
Application website:
https://www.law.wustl.edu/Admissions/wuforms
Application deadline for Fall 2007 admission: **3/01**

Admissions statistics:

Number of applicants for Fall 2005: **3,767**
Number of acceptances: **954**
Number enrolled: **222**
Acceptance rate: **25%**
GPA, 25th-75th percentile, entering class Fall 2005:
3.20-3.70
LSAT, 25th-75th percentile, entering class Fall 2005:
161-167

FINANCIAL AID

Financial aid phone number: **(314) 935-4605**
Financial aid application deadline: **3/01**
Tuition 2005-2006 academic year: full-time: **$34,981**; part-time: **N/A**
Room and board: **$11,000**; books: **$2,000**; miscellaneous expenses: **$6,300**
Total of room/board/books/miscellaneous expenses: **$19,300**
University offers graduate student housing for which law students are eligible.

Financial aid profile

Percent of students that received grants for the 2004-2005 academic year: full-time: **66%**
Median grant amount: full-time: **$10,000**
The average law-school debt of those in the Class of 2005 who borrowed: **$86,371**. Proportion who borrowed: **78%**

ACADEMIC PROGRAMS

Calendar: **semester**
Joint degrees awarded: **Business Administration; East Asian Studies; Social Work; European Studies; Biology; Health Administration; Engineering & Policy; Political Science; Islamic Studies; International Affairs; History; Environmental Engineering**
Typical first-year section size: Full-time: **85**
Is there typically a "small section" of the first year class, other than Legal Writing, taught by full-time faculty?: Full-time: **yes**
Number of course titles, beyond the first year curriculum, offered last year: **123**
Percentages of upper division course sections, excluding seminars, with an enrollment of:

Under 25: **59%**	25 to 49: **20%**
50 to 74: **12%**	75 to 99: **3%**
100+: **6%**	

Areas of specialization: appellate advocacy, clinical training, dispute resolution, environmental law, healthcare law, intellectual property law, international law, tax law, trial advocacy

Fall 2005 faculty profile

Total teaching faculty: **174**. Full-time: **29%**; **49%** men, **51%** women, **10%** minorities. Part-time: **71%**; **76%** men, **24%** women, **10%** minorities
Student-to-faculty ratio: **13.2**

SPECIAL PROGRAMS *(as provided by law school):*

Washington University in St. Louis offers three specialized centers. The Center for Interdisciplinary Studies sponsors annual programs and research that focus on cutting-edge legal issues requiring expertise from various disciplines. The Whitney R. Harris Institute for Global Legal Studies functions as a center for instruction and research in international and comparative law. Among its programs are conferences, student fellowships, an international law journal, and an international moot court team. The Center for Research on Innovation and Entrepreneurship supports conferences and research to benefit the St. Louis economic community, as well as other academic, governmental, and private sector entities nationally. The School of Law offers nine clinical courses, some based in the law school, others based in the community, and one based in Washington, D.C. They are: Appellate Clinic (appellate cases in the U.S. Court of Appeals for the Eighth Circuit); Civil Justice

Clinic (domestic violence, guardian ad litem, predatory lending, clemency, and homelessness issues); Civil Rights and Community Justice Clinic (civil rights law, public policy, client advocacy, and dispute resolution); Congressional and Administrative Law Clinic (the oldest, full-time legal internship program on Capitol Hill); Criminal Justice Clinic (lawyering experience with a public defender's office); Government Lawyering Clinic (experience with a U.S. attorney's office); Intellectual Property & Business Formation Legal Clinic (early-stage legal assistance for innovators, entrepreneurs, research centers, and community and business development organizations); Interdisciplinary Environmental Clinic (pro bono legal and technical consulting services on environmental and health issues); and Judicial Clerkship Clinic (hands-on exposure to civil and criminal litigation from the judicial perspective). The courses are predominantly taught by tenure-track faculty and most have a student/faculty ratio of 8:1. The summer school program includes traditional courses, as well as externships with judges or government agencies. In 2005, the School of Law began offering the Summer Institute for Global Justice, in the Netherlands. The summer institute focuses on courses related to comparative law, as well as to the international institutions located in the Hague (such as the International Court of Justice) and the European institutions located in Brussels.

STUDENT BODY

Fall 2005 full-time enrollment: 743

Men: 59%	Women: 41%
African-American: 6.3%	American Indian: 0.5%
Asian-American: 9.0%	Mexican-American: 0.4%
Puerto Rican: 0.0%	Other Hisp-Amer: 0.8%
White: 58.4%	International: 4.2%
Unknown: 20.3%	

Fall 2005 part-time enrollment: 2

Men: 50%	Women: 50%
African-American: 50.0%	American Indian: 0.0%
Asian-American: 0.0%	Mexican-American: 0.0%
Puerto Rican: 0.0%	Other Hisp-Amer: 0.0%
White: 50.0%	International: 0.0%
Unknown: 0.0%	

Attrition rates for 2004-2005 full-time students
Percent of students discontinuing law school:

Men: 3%	Women: 1%
First-year students: 6%	Second-year students: 1%
Third-year students: N/A	

LIBRARY RESOURCES

The library holds 148,270 and receives 6,109 current subscriptions.

Total volumes: 675,776
Percentage of the titles in the online catalog: 99%
Total seats available for library users: 485

INFORMATION TECHNOLOGY

Number of wired network connections available to students: 760 total (in the law library, excluding computer labs: 430; in classrooms: 200; in computer labs: 45; elsewhere in the law school: 85)
Law school has a wireless network.
Approximate number of simultaneous users that can be accommodated on wireless network: 600
Students are not required to own a computer.

EMPLOYMENT AND SALARIES

Proportion of 2004 graduates employed at graduation: 88%
Employed 9 months later, as of February 15, 2005: 99%
Salaries in the private sector (law firms, business, industry): $82,000–$125,000 (25th-75th percentile)
Median salary in the private sector: $90,000
Percentage in the private sector who reported salary information: 42%
Median salary in public service (government, judicial clerkships, academic posts, non-profits): $49,105

Percentage of 2004 graduates in:

Law firms: 63%	Bus./industry (legal): 6%
Bus./industry (nonlegal): N/A	Government: 16%
Public interest: 5%	Judicial clerkship: 9%
Academia : 0%	Unknown: 1%

2004 graduates employed in-state: 34%
2004 graduates employed in foreign countries: 2%
Number of states where graduates are employed: 33
Percentage of 2004 graduates working in: New England: 1%, Middle Atlantic: 11%, East North Central: 21%, West North Central: 38%, South Atlantic: 11%, East South Central: 3%, West South Central: 3%, Mountain: 1%, Pacific: 5%, Unknown: 4%

BAR PASSAGE RATES

Based on 2004 graduates taking Summer 2004 or Winter 2005 exams. Most of the school's first-time test takers took the bar in Missouri.

96%
School's bar passage rate for first-time test takers

88%
Statewide bar passage rate for first-time test takers

Wayne State University

■ 471 W. Palmer Street, Detroit, MI, 48202
■ http://www.law.wayne.edu
■ Public
■ **Year founded:** 1927
■ **2005-2006 tuition:** In-state: full-time: $17,507, part-time: $9,779; Out-of-state: full-time: $32,570
■ **Enrollment 2005-06 academic year:** full-time: 549; part-time: 162
■ **U.S. News 2007 law specialty ranking:** N/A

3.33-3.72 GPA, 25TH-75TH PERCENTILE

153-159 LSAT, 25TH-75TH PERCENTILE

40% ACCEPTANCE RATE

Tier 3 2007 U.S. NEWS LAW SCHOOL RANKING

ADMISSIONS

Admissions phone number: **(313) 577-3937**
Admissions email address: **lawinquire@wayne.edu**
Application website: **http://www.law.wayne.edu**
Application deadline for Fall 2007 admission: **3/15**

Admissions statistics:

Number of applicants for Fall 2005: **1,206**
Number of acceptances: **477**
Number enrolled: **207**
Acceptance rate: **40%**
GPA, 25th-75th percentile, entering class Fall 2005: **3.33-3.72**
LSAT, 25th-75th percentile, entering class Fall 2005: **153-159**

Part-time program:

Number of applicants for Fall 2005: **156**
Number of acceptances: **42**
Number enrolled: **31**
Acceptance rate: **27%**
GPA, 25th-75th percentile, entering class Fall 2005: **3.28-3.69**
LSAT, 25th-75th percentile, entering class Fall 2005: **151-159**

FINANCIAL AID

Financial aid phone number: **(313) 577-5142**
Financial aid application deadline: **6/06**
Tuition 2005-2006 academic year: In-state: full-time: **$17,507**, part-time: **$9,779**; Out-of-state: full-time: **$32,570**
Room and board: **$11,978**; books: **$1,000**; miscellaneous expenses: **$7,950**
Total of room/board/books/miscellaneous expenses: **$20,928**
University offers graduate student housing for which law students are eligible.

Financial aid profile

Percent of students that received grants for the 2004-2005 academic year: full-time: **80%**; part-time **7%**
Median grant amount: full-time: **$2,000**; part-time: **$2,000**

The average law-school debt of those in the Class of 2005 who borrowed: **$46,344**. Proportion who borrowed: **82%**

ACADEMIC PROGRAMS

Calendar: **semester**
Joint degrees awarded: **J.D./MA History; J.D./MA Poli. Sci.; J.D./M.B.A.; J.D./MA Disp. Res.**
Typical first-year section size: Full-time: **89**; Part-time: **30**
Is there typically a "small section" of the first year class, other than Legal Writing, taught by full-time faculty?: Full-time: **no**; Part-time: **no**
Number of course titles, beyond the first year curriculum, offered last year: **72**
Percentages of upper division course sections, excluding seminars, with an enrollment of:
Under 25: **40%**   25 to 49: **33%**
50 to 74: **16%**   75 to 99: **4%**
100+: **7%**
Areas of specialization: appellate advocacy, clinical training, dispute resolution, environmental law, healthcare law, intellectual property law, international law, tax law, trial advocacy

Fall 2005 faculty profile

Total teaching faculty: **79**. Full-time: **53%**; **62%** men, **38%** women, **10%** minorities. Part-time: **47%**; **84%** men, **16%** women, **3%** minorities
Student-to-faculty ratio: **19.6**

SPECIAL PROGRAMS *(as provided by law school)*:

Wayne State University Law School offers five live-client clinics, where students get a chance, under supervision, to have first chair responsibility in a choice of settings while serving the needs of Detroit's urban community.

Civil Rights Litigation Clinic: Students assist in representation of an indigent prisoner who has filed a civil rights action in U.S. District Court.

Criminal Appellate Practice Clinic: Each student meets with a real client incarcerated in a Michigan prison and prepares a criminal appellate brief on the client's behalf.

Disability Law Clinic: Students assist low-income individuals with disabilities in a range of legal issues.

Free Legal Aid Clinic: Students provide legal assistance in state court on family law matters, such as custody, support, visitation, and divorce.

Nonprofit Corporations and Urban Development Law Clinic: Students serve the legal needs of nonprofit organizations that develop affordable housing, job training, or other services.

Internships: The law school offers students a broad range of opportunities for practical legal training through its internship program. The work of student interns is supervised directly by practicing attorneys and results in academic credit.

Intellectual Property Law Institute: Law school students may take courses at other Detroit-area law schools through the institute, a cooperative effort of the law faculties of Wayne State University, the University of Detroit Mercy, and the University of Windsor in Ontario. The institute offers a rich curriculum in patent, copyright, trademark, computer and related technology, communications and media law, and entertainment law.

Center for Legal Studies: The center is a forum for communication, collaboration, and research on legal issues between the law school and other departments at Wayne State.

International programs: The law school offers many courses in the area of international law. In addition to the courses at Wayne State, students can take courses at the University of Windsor Faculty of Law just across the border in Canada. The law school also sponsors two international student exchange programs and a fellowship for summer study at The Hague, the Netherlands, and houses a leading publication project in the field of international and comparative criminal law.

STUDENT BODY

Fall 2005 full-time enrollment: 549

Men: 51%	Women: 49%
African-American: 8.2%	American Indian: 1.3%
Asian-American: 5.5%	Mexican-American: 1.1%
Puerto Rican: 0.2%	Other Hisp-Amer: 2.9%
White: 80.9%	International: 0.0%
Unknown: 0.0%	

Fall 2005 part-time enrollment: 162

Men: 47%	Women: 53%
African-American: 16.7%	American Indian: 0.6%
Asian-American: 8.0%	Mexican-American: 1.2%
Puerto Rican: 0.0%	Other Hisp-Amer: 1.2%
White: 72.2%	International: 0.0%
Unknown: 0.0%	

Attrition rates for 2004-2005 full-time students
Percent of students discontinuing law school:

Men: 3%	Women: 3%
First-year students: 9%	Second-year students: 2%
Third-year students: 1%	

LIBRARY RESOURCES

The library holds 254,251 and receives 4,863 current subscriptions.
Total volumes: 620,018
Percentage of the titles in the online catalog: 100%
Total seats available for library users: 461

INFORMATION TECHNOLOGY

Number of wired network connections available to students: 151 total (in the law library, excluding computer labs: 68; in classrooms: 50; in computer labs: 3; elsewhere in the law school: 30)
Law school has a wireless network.
Approximate number of simultaneous users that can be accommodated on wireless network: 360
Students are not required to own a computer.

EMPLOYMENT AND SALARIES

Proportion of 2004 graduates employed at graduation: N/A
Employed 9 months later, as of February 15, 2005: 84%
Salaries in the private sector (law firms, business, industry): $50,000–$90,000 (25th-75th percentile)
Median salary in the private sector: $63,700
Percentage in the private sector who reported salary information: 85%
Median salary in public service (government, judicial clerkships, academic posts, non-profits): $50,000

Percentage of 2004 graduates in:

Law firms: 67%	Bus./industry (legal): 18%
Bus./industry (nonlegal): N/A	Government: 8%
Public interest: 1%	Judicial clerkship: 3%
Academia : 1%	Unknown: 2%

2004 graduates employed in-state: 93%
2004 graduates employed in foreign countries: 0%
Number of states where graduates are employed: 9
Percentage of 2004 graduates working in: New England: 1%, Middle Atlantic: 1%, East North Central: 94%, West North Central: 0%, South Atlantic: 2%, East South Central: 0%, West South Central: 0%, Mountain: 0%, Pacific: 2%, Unknown: 1%

BAR PASSAGE RATES

Based on 2004 graduates taking Summer 2004 or Winter 2005 exams. Most of the school's first-time test takers took the bar in Michigan.

84%
School's bar passage rate for first-time test takers

74%
Statewide bar passage rate for first-time test takers

West Virginia University

- PO Box 6130, Morgantown, WV, 26506-6130
- http://www.wvu.edu/~law
- Public
- Year founded: 1878
- 2005-2006 tuition: In-state: full-time: $8,690, part-time: N/A; Out-of-state: full-time: $20,406
- Enrollment 2005-06 academic year: full-time: 463; part-time: 4
- U.S. News 2007 law specialty ranking: N/A

3.19-3.79 GPA, 25TH-75TH PERCENTILE

148-155 LSAT, 25TH-75TH PERCENTILE

39% ACCEPTANCE RATE

Tier 4 2007 U.S. NEWS LAW SCHOOL RANKING

ADMISSIONS

Admissions phone number: **(304) 293-5304**
Admissions email address:
wvulaw.admissions@mail.wvu.edu
Application website: **N/A**
Application deadline for Fall 2007 admission: **2/01**

Admissions statistics:
Number of applicants for Fall 2005: **830**
Number of acceptances: **324**
Number enrolled: **151**
Acceptance rate: **39%**
GPA, 25th-75th percentile, entering class Fall 2005: **3.19-3.79**
LSAT, 25th-75th percentile, entering class Fall 2005: **148-155**

Part-time program:
Number of applicants for Fall 2005: **1**
Number of acceptances: **1**
Number enrolled: **1**
Acceptance rate: **100%**
GPA, 25th-75th percentile, entering class Fall 2005: **N/A**
LSAT, 25th-75th percentile, entering class Fall 2005: **N/A**

FINANCIAL AID

Financial aid phone number: **(304) 293-5302**
Financial aid application deadline: **4/01**
Tuition 2005-2006 academic year: In-state: full-time: **$8,690**, part-time: **N/A**; Out-of-state: full-time: **$20,406**
Room and board: **$8,226**; books: **$1,075**; miscellaneous expenses: **$2,637**
Total of room/board/books/miscellaneous expenses: **$11,938**
University offers graduate student housing for which law students are eligible.

Financial aid profile
Percent of students that received grants for the 2004-2005 academic year: full-time: **33%**
Median grant amount: full-time: **$1,800**

The average law-school debt of those in the Class of 2005 who borrowed: **$46,953**. Proportion who borrowed: **88%**

ACADEMIC PROGRAMS

Calendar: **semester**
Joint degrees awarded: **J.D./M.B.A.; J.D./MPA**
Typical first-year section size: Full-time: **75**
Is there typically a "small section" of the first year class, other than Legal Writing, taught by full-time faculty?: Full-time: **no**; Part-time: **no**
Number of course titles, beyond the first year curriculum, offered last year: **73**
Percentages of upper division course sections, excluding seminars, with an enrollment of:
Under 25: **40%**   25 to 49: **32%**
50 to 74: **19%**   75 to 99: **6%**
100+: **3%**
Areas of specialization: appellate advocacy, clinical training, dispute resolution, environmental law, healthcare law, intellectual property law, international law, tax law, trial advocacy

Fall 2005 faculty profile
Total teaching faculty: **40**. Full-time: **48%**; **63%** men, **37%** women, **16%** minorities. Part-time: **53%**; **76%** men, **24%** women, **N/A** minorities
Student-to-faculty ratio: **23.2**

SPECIAL PROGRAMS *(as provided by law school):*
The West Virginia University College of Law offers a live-client clinical program handling civil cases, as well as the Federal Judicial Externship Program.

STUDENT BODY
Fall 2005 full-time enrollment: 463
Men: **51%**   Women: **49%**
African-American: **5.0%**   American Indian: **0.6%**
Asian-American: **1.1%**   Mexican-American: **0.2%**
Puerto Rican: **0.0%**   Other Hisp-Amer: **1.1%**
White: **91.4%**   International: **0.4%**
Unknown: **0.2%**

Fall 2005 part-time enrollment: 4

Men: 50%	Women: 50%
African-American: 0.0%	American Indian: 0.0%
Asian-American: 0.0%	Mexican-American: 0.0%
Puerto Rican: 0.0%	Other Hisp-Amer: 0.0%
White: 75.0%	International: 25.0%
Unknown: 0.0%	

Attrition rates for 2004-2005 full-time students
Percent of students discontinuing law school:

Men: 2%	Women: 2%
First-year students: 5%	Second-year students: N/A
Third-year students: N/A	

LIBRARY RESOURCES

The library holds 58,351 and receives 3,222 current sub-scriptions.
Total volumes: 347,393
Percentage of the titles in the online catalog: 100%
Total seats available for library users: 274

INFORMATION TECHNOLOGY

Number of wired network connections available to students: 86 total (in the law library, excluding computer labs: 86; in classrooms: 0; in computer labs: 0; elsewhere in the law school: 0)
Law school has a wireless network.
Approximate number of simultaneous users that can be accommodated on wireless network: 200
Students are not required to own a computer.

EMPLOYMENT AND SALARIES

Proportion of 2004 graduates employed at graduation: N/A
Employed 9 months later, as of February 15, 2005: 79%
Salaries in the private sector (law firms, business, industry): $45,000–$57,500 (25th-75th percentile)

Median salary in the private sector: $49,250
Percentage in the private sector who reported salary information: 22%
Median salary in public service (government, judicial clerkships, academic posts, non-profits): $37,515

Percentage of 2004 graduates in:

Law firms: 65%	Bus./industry (legal): N/A
Bus./industry (nonlegal): 5%	Government: 8%
Public interest: 1%	Judicial clerkship: 18%
Academia : 0%	Unknown: 3%

2004 graduates employed in-state: 80%
2004 graduates employed in foreign countries: 0%
Number of states where graduates are employed: 11
Percentage of 2004 graduates working in: New England: N/A, Middle Atlantic: 6%, East North Central: N/A, West North Central: N/A, South Atlantic: 90%, East South Central: 1%, West South Central: N/A, Mountain: 2%, Pacific: 1%, Unknown: 0%

BAR PASSAGE RATES

Based on 2004 graduates taking Summer 2004 or Winter 2005 exams. Most of the school's first-time test takers took the bar in West Virginia.

80%
School's bar passage rate for first-time test takers

78%
Statewide bar passage rate for first-time test takers

Western New England College

- 1215 Wilbraham Road, Springfield, MA, 01119-2684
- http://www.law.wnec.edu
- Private
- Year founded: 1919
- 2005-2006 tuition: full-time: $27,814; part-time: $20,860
- Enrollment 2005-06 academic year: full-time: 416; part-time: 160
- U.S. News 2007 law specialty ranking: N/A

2.70-3.32 GPA, 25TH-75TH PERCENTILE

151-156 LSAT, 25TH-75TH PERCENTILE

43% ACCEPTANCE RATE

Tier 4 2007 U.S. NEWS LAW SCHOOL RANKING

ADMISSIONS
Admissions phone number: **(413) 782-1406**
Admissions email address: **admissions@law.wnec.edu**
Application website:
http://wneclaw.wnec.edu/inquiries.html
Application deadline for Fall 2007 admission: **3/15**

Admissions statistics:
Number of applicants for Fall 2005: **1,600**
Number of acceptances: **688**
Number enrolled: **139**
Acceptance rate: **43%**
GPA, 25th-75th percentile, entering class Fall 2005:
2.70-3.32
LSAT, 25th-75th percentile, entering class Fall 2005: **151-156**

Part-time program:
Number of applicants for Fall 2005: **249**
Number of acceptances: **109**
Number enrolled: **53**
Acceptance rate: **44%**
GPA, 25th-75th percentile, entering class Fall 2005:
2.78-3.36
LSAT, 25th-75th percentile, entering class Fall 2005:
149-151

FINANCIAL AID
Financial aid phone number: **(413) 796-2080**
Financial aid application deadline: **N/A**
Tuition 2005-2006 academic year: full-time: **$27,814**; part-time: **$20,860**
Room and board: **$10,065**; books: **$1,200**; miscellaneous expenses: **$3,935**
Total of room/board/books/miscellaneous expenses:
$15,200
University offers graduate student housing for which law students are eligible.

Financial aid profile
Percent of students that received grants for the 2004-2005 academic year: full-time: **58%**; part-time **36%**

Median grant amount: full-time: **$13,000**; part-time: **$4,000**
The average law-school debt of those in the Class of 2005 who borrowed: **$78,190**. Proportion who borrowed: **81%**

ACADEMIC PROGRAMS
Calendar: **semester**
Joint degrees awarded: **J.D./M.S.W. (with Springfield College); JD/MRP (with U of Massachusetts-Amherst); J.D./M.B.A.**
Typical first-year section size: Full-time: **70**; Part-time: **50**
Is there typically a "small section" of the first year class, other than Legal Writing, taught by full-time faculty?:
Full-time: **no**; Part-time: **no**
Number of course titles, beyond the first year curriculum, offered last year: **92**
Percentages of upper division course sections, excluding seminars, with an enrollment of:
Under 25: **48%**   25 to 49: **40%**
50 to 74: **8%**   75 to 99: **3%**
100+: **0%**
Areas of specialization: appellate advocacy, clinical training, dispute resolution, environmental law, healthcare law, intellectual property law, international law, tax law, trial advocacy

Fall 2005 faculty profile
Total teaching faculty: **64**. Full-time: **48%**; 52% men, 48% women, 6% minorities. Part-time: **52%**; 70% men, 30% women, 3% minorities
Student-to-faculty ratio: **16.5**

SPECIAL PROGRAMS (as provided by law school):
The law school offers five clinics. Students in the Criminal Law Clinic practice as student assistant district attorneys prosecuting criminal matters. In the Consumer Protection Clinic students work through the city of Springfield's law department assisting aggrieved consumers to pursue their claims. Students enrolled in the Legal Services Clinic work with the Western Massachusetts Legal Services Office to serve indigent persons needing legal assistance with family, unemployment, housing,

and other poverty-law issues. The Small Business Clinic allows students to engage in transactional practice, providing a wide range of legal services to small businesses throughout the Greater Springfield area. Students in the Real Property Practice Practicum are placed with attorneys who practice in the real-property area, both commercial and residential.

The law school also has a vigorous externship program in which students have the opportunity to intern with state and federal judges at the trial and appellate levels, or in a governmental law practice, such as the public defender, a federal agency such as the Internal Revenue Service, or a state agency such as the Department of Social Services. If a student's interest is in private practice, internships are available in the offices of corporate counsel or in a nongovernmental public-interest agency, such as the HIV/AIDS Consortium.

The Legislative and Governmental Affairs Institute links students to internships from among the legislatures of three states as well as in city and local governments. The institute is very active in sponsoring presentations and bringing governmental bodies, such as legislative committees, on campus to conduct their business. Similarly, the Law and Business Center for Advancing Entrepreneurship provides a range of programming focusing on the intersection of business and law.

The law school offers well-developed simulation courses, both in litigation courses and transactional courses. The law school also sponsors many moot court teams in appellate and trial competitions, along with a negotiation team. Students may pursue advanced independent study with faculty members. They are also encouraged to study abroad in American Bar Association-sanctioned programs.

STUDENT BODY

Fall 2005 full-time enrollment: 416

Men: 55%	Women: 45%
African-American: 1.7%	American Indian: 0.2%
Asian-American: 4.6%	Mexican-American: 1.0%
Puerto Rican: 0.5%	Other Hisp-Amer: 2.6%
White: 64.4%	International: 5.0%
Unknown: 20.0%	

Fall 2005 part-time enrollment: 160

Men: 53%	Women: 47%
African-American: 3.8%	American Indian: 0.0%
Asian-American: 0.0%	Mexican-American: 0.0%
Puerto Rican: 1.3%	Other Hisp-Amer: 1.3%
White: 63.8%	International: 2.5%
Unknown: 27.5%	

Attrition rates for 2004-2005 full-time students

Percent of students discontinuing law school:

Men: 4%	Women: 3%
First-year students: 9%	Second-year students: 1%
Third-year students: N/A	

LIBRARY RESOURCES

The library holds 145,403 and receives 5,170 current subscriptions.
Total volumes: 384,167
Percentage of the titles in the online catalog: 100%
Total seats available for library users: 320

INFORMATION TECHNOLOGY

Number of wired network connections available to students: 43 total (in the law library, excluding computer labs: 14; in classrooms: 6; in computer labs: 23; elsewhere in the law school: 0)
Law school has a wireless network.
Approximate number of simultaneous users that can be accommodated on wireless network: 1,152
Students are not required to own a computer.

EMPLOYMENT AND SALARIES

Proportion of 2004 graduates employed at graduation: 55%
Employed 9 months later, as of February 15, 2005: 80%
Salaries in the private sector (law firms, business, industry): $35,000–$75,000 (25th-75th percentile)
Median salary in the private sector: $48,000
Percentage in the private sector who reported salary information: 57%
Median salary in public service (government, judicial clerkships, academic posts, non-profits): $43,000

Percentage of 2004 graduates in:

Law firms: 39%	Bus./industry (legal): 5%
Bus./industry (nonlegal): 24%	Government: 17%
Public interest: 3%	Judicial clerkship: 11%
Academia : 1%	Unknown: 0%

2004 graduates employed in-state: 45%
2004 graduates employed in foreign countries: 0%
Number of states where graduates are employed: 13
Percentage of 2004 graduates working in: New England: 77%, Middle Atlantic: 11%, East North Central: 1%, West North Central: 0%, South Atlantic: 5%, East South Central: 2%, West South Central: 1%, Mountain: 1%, Pacific: 0%, Unknown: 2%

BAR PASSAGE RATES

Based on 2004 graduates taking Summer 2004 or Winter 2005 exams. Most of the school's first-time test takers took the bar in Connecticut.

68%
School's bar passage rate for first-time test takers

82%
Statewide bar passage rate for first-time test takers

Whittier Law School

■ 3333 Harbor Boulevard, Costa Mesa, CA, 92626-1501
■ http://www.law.whittier.edu
■ Private
■ Year founded: 1975
■ 2005-2006 tuition: full-time: $29,230; part-time: $17,554
■ Enrollment 2005-06 academic year: full-time: 499; part-time: 372
■ U.S. News 2007 law specialty ranking: N/A

2.86-3.32 GPA, 25TH-75TH PERCENTILE

152-155 LSAT, 25TH-75TH PERCENTILE

30% ACCEPTANCE RATE

Tier 4 2007 U.S. NEWS LAW SCHOOL RANKING

ADMISSIONS

Admissions phone number: **(800) 808-8188**
Admissions email address: **info@law.whittier.edu**
Application website:
  http://www4.Isac.org/LSACD_on_the_web/login/open.a spx
Application deadline for Fall 2007 admission: **3/15**

Admissions statistics:

Number of applicants for Fall 2005: **2,526**
Number of acceptances: **747**
Number enrolled: **162**
Acceptance rate: **30%**
GPA, 25th-75th percentile, entering class Fall 2005:
  2.86-3.32
LSAT, 25th-75th percentile, entering class Fall 2005: **152-155**

Part-time program:

Number of applicants for Fall 2005: **618**
Number of acceptances: **235**
Number enrolled: **111**
Acceptance rate: **38%**
GPA, 25th-75th percentile, entering class Fall 2005:
  2.69-3.28
LSAT, 25th-75th percentile, entering class Fall 2005: **150-153**

FINANCIAL AID

Financial aid phone number: **(714) 444-4141**
Financial aid application deadline: **5/01**
Tuition 2005-2006 academic year: full-time: **$29,230**; part-time: **$17,554**
Room and board: **$10,084**; books: **$1,008**; miscellaneous expenses: **$5,398**
Total of room/board/books/miscellaneous expenses:
  $16,490
University does not offer graduate student housing for which law students are eligible.

Financial aid profile

Percent of students that received grants for the 2004-2005 academic year: full-time: **54%**; part-time **31%**

Median grant amount: full-time: **$6,938**; part-time: **$4,950**
The average law-school debt of those in the Class of 2005 who borrowed: **$87,651.** Proportion who borrowed: **96%**

ACADEMIC PROGRAMS

Calendar: **semester**
Joint degrees awarded: **N/A**
Typical first-year section size: Full-time: **64**; Part-time: **75**
Is there typically a "small section" of the first year class, other than Legal Writing, taught by full-time faculty?:
  Full-time: **no**; Part-time: **no**
Number of course titles, beyond the first year curriculum, offered last year: **85**
Percentages of upper division course sections, excluding seminars, with an enrollment of:
  Under 25: **67%**   25 to 49: **17%**
  50 to 74: **12%**   75 to 99: **4%**
  100+: **0%**
Areas of specialization: appellate advocacy, clinical training, dispute resolution, environmental law, healthcare law, intellectual property law, international law, tax law, trial advocacy

Fall 2005 faculty profile

Total teaching faculty: **69.** Full-time: **41%**; **61%** men, **39%** women, **14%** minorities. Part-time: **59%**; **54%** men, **46%** women, **17%** minorities
Student-to-faculty ratio: **16.6**

SPECIAL PROGRAMS (as provided by law school):

Whittier Law School is committed to providing a variety of clinical legal education opportunities for all of its students. At present, law students can choose from numerous live-client clinics, including the Children's Advocacy Clinic (legal guardianship matters), Family Violence Clinic (combining the law with mental health, counseling, and other social services), Special Education Clinic (providing parents information about rights and services), and Healthcare Access Clinic (providing services for indigent families). In addition, the law school's Legal Policy Clinic focuses on legal policy analysis and advocacy. These clinics provide students with a hands-on working experience.

The law school offers externships in a variety of practice settings, including public-interest law firms, the courts, and public agencies. The law school's Public Interest Law Program offers more than two dozen courses, many clinics, and externships.

Our centers in intellectual property, international and comparative law, and children's rights provide an array of offerings in fellowships and externships. The Center for Intellectual Property also has a certificate program, a distinguished speaker series, the National IP Law Moot Court Competition, a summer institute, and a seminar series. The Center for International and Comparative Law offers an exchange and summer abroad program, LL.M. degree in U.S. legal studies, certificate program, and the annual International Law Symposium. The Center for Children's Rights has the clinics, National Juvenile Law Moot Court Competition, annual symposia, and the Whittier Journal of Child and Family Advocacy.

During the summer session, a limited number of upper-division courses are offered that typically meet in the evening. Full-time students can accelerate their program by taking summer courses, and they can become part-time students in their last semester in order to work or study for the bar examination.

Exchange programs are offered in France and Spain, as well as an LL.M. degree for foreign lawyers. Whittier Law School presently has five American Bar Association-accredited summer abroad programs at: the Universidad de Cantabria in Santander, Spain; Bar-Ilan University in Ramat Gan, Israel, near Tel Aviv; Nanjing University, China; University of Toulouse, France; and Amsterdam Law School in Holland.

STUDENT BODY

Fall 2005 full-time enrollment: 499

Men: 48%	Women: 52%
African-American: 3.2%	American Indian: 0.0%
Asian-American: 20.8%	Mexican-American: 4.8%
Puerto Rican: 0.0%	Other Hisp-Amer: 6.0%
White: 44.5%	International: 0.6%
Unknown: 20.0%	

Fall 2005 part-time enrollment: 372

Men: 49%	Women: 51%
African-American: 6.5%	American Indian: 0.5%
Asian-American: 17.5%	Mexican-American: 5.9%
Puerto Rican: 0.0%	Other Hisp-Amer: 6.7%
White: 47.8%	International: 0.3%
Unknown: 14.8%	

Attrition rates for 2004-2005 full-time students

Percent of students discontinuing law school:

Men: 16%	Women: 15%
First-year students: 31%	Second-year students: 7%
Third-year students: 4%	

LIBRARY RESOURCES

The library holds 179,037 and receives 3,791 current subscriptions.

Total volumes: 421,678
Percentage of the titles in the online catalog: 40%
Total seats available for library users: 386

INFORMATION TECHNOLOGY

Number of wired network connections available to students: 203 total (in the law library, excluding computer labs: 110; in classrooms: 0; in computer labs: 48; elsewhere in the law school: 45)
Law school doesn't have a wireless network.
Approximate number of simultaneous users that can be accommodated on wireless network: N/A
Students are not required to own a computer.

EMPLOYMENT AND SALARIES

Proportion of 2004 graduates employed at graduation: 54%
Employed 9 months later, as of February 15, 2005: 91%
Salaries in the private sector (law firms, business, industry): $58,000–$75,000 (25th-75th percentile)
Median salary in the private sector: $65,000
Percentage in the private sector who reported salary information: 53%
Median salary in public service (government, judicial clerkships, academic posts, non-profits): $56,600

Percentage of 2004 graduates in:

Law firms: 53%	Bus./industry (legal): 9%
Bus./industry (nonlegal): 18%	Government: 10%
Public interest: 5%	Judicial clerkship: 0%
Academia : 5%	Unknown: 0%

2004 graduates employed in-state: 89%
2004 graduates employed in foreign countries: 2%
Number of states where graduates are employed: 9
Percentage of 2004 graduates working in: New England: 0%, Middle Atlantic: 1%, East North Central: 1%, West North Central: 0%, South Atlantic: 0%, East South Central: 0%, West South Central: 2%, Mountain: 4%, Pacific: 91%, Unknown: 0%

BAR PASSAGE RATES

Based on 2004 graduates taking Summer 2004 or Winter 2005 exams. Most of the school's first-time test takers took the bar in California.

40%
School's bar passage rate for first-time test takers

61%
Statewide bar passage rate for first-time test takers

Widener University

- PO Box 7474, Wilmington, DE, 19803-0474
- http://www.law.widener.edu
- Private
- **Year founded:** 1971
- **2005-2006 tuition:** full-time: $28,300; part-time: $21,200
- **Enrollment 2005-06 academic year:** full-time: 997; part-time: 574
- **U.S. News 2007 law specialty ranking:** healthcare law: 8

2.81-3.46	GPA, 25TH-75TH PERCENTILE
150-154	LSAT, 25TH-75TH PERCENTILE
36%	ACCEPTANCE RATE
Tier 4	2007 U.S. NEWS LAW SCHOOL RANKING

ADMISSIONS

Admissions phone number: **(302) 477-2162**
Admissions email address:
  law.admissions@law.widener.edu
Application website: **http://www.law.widener.edu**
Application deadline for Fall 2007 admission: **5/15**

Admissions statistics:

Number of applicants for Fall 2005: **2,932**
Number of acceptances: **1,067**
Number enrolled: **375**
Acceptance rate: **36%**
GPA, 25th-75th percentile, entering class Fall 2005:
  2.81-3.46
LSAT, 25th-75th percentile, entering class Fall 2005:
  150-154

Part-time program:

Number of applicants for Fall 2005: **717**
Number of acceptances: **303**
Number enrolled: **175**
Acceptance rate: **42%**
GPA, 25th-75th percentile, entering class Fall 2005:
  2.75-3.39
LSAT, 25th-75th percentile, entering class Fall 2005:
  149-153

FINANCIAL AID

Financial aid phone number: **(302) 477-2272**
Financial aid application deadline: **4/01**
Tuition 2005-2006 academic year: full-time: **$28,300**; part-time: **$21,200**
Room and board: **$8,300**; books: **$1,000**; miscellaneous expenses: **$3,940**
Total of room/board/books/miscellaneous expenses:
  $13,240
University offers graduate student housing for which law students are eligible.

Financial aid profile

Percent of students that received grants for the 2004-2005 academic year: full-time: **30%**; part-time **15%**
Median grant amount: full-time: **$3,000**; part-time: **$3,250**
The average law-school debt of those in the Class of 2005 who borrowed: **$70,429**. Proportion who borrowed: **90%**

ACADEMIC PROGRAMS

Calendar: **semester**
Joint degrees awarded: **J.D./PsyD; J.D./M.B.A.; J.D./MSLS; J.D./MMP**
Typical first-year section size: Full-time: **75**; Part-time: **55**
Is there typically a "small section" of the first year class, other than Legal Writing, taught by full-time faculty?:
  Full-time: **yes**; Part-time: **yes**
Number of course titles, beyond the first year curriculum, offered last year: **203**
Percentages of upper division course sections, excluding seminars, with an enrollment of:

Under 25: **57%**	25 to 49: **28%**
50 to 74: **12%**	75 to 99: **2%**
100+: **1%**	

Areas of specialization: appellate advocacy, clinical training, dispute resolution, environmental law, healthcare law, intellectual property law, international law, tax law, trial advocacy

Fall 2005 faculty profile

Total teaching faculty: **135**. Full-time: **54%**; **53%** men, **47%** women, **5%** minorities. Part-time: **46%**; **73%** men, **27%** women, **2%** minorities
Student-to-faculty ratio: **17.5**

SPECIAL PROGRAMS (as provided by law school):

Widener is a leader in developing a coordinated lawyering skills program, which includes clinical practice, externship placements, and comprehensive simulations.

  Clinics are designed to permit students to represent clients under the supervision of the clinic director before Pennsylvania and Delaware courts and administrative boards. Widener operates environmental law and criminal defense clinics; Delaware,

Harrisburg, and Pennsylvania civil clinics; the Family Violence/Outreach Clinic; and the Veterans Assistance Clinic. An extensive judicial externship program places students with state and federal courts at both the trial and appellate levels in Delaware, Pennsylvania, New Jersey, Maryland, Virginia, and the District of Columbia.

Widener houses four institutes where students can specialize and, in addition to their J.D. degree, graduate with certificates in health law, corporate law, trial advocacy, and law and government.

The Law and Government Institute in Harrisburg, Pennsylvania, provides hands-on experience with the operation and structure of government agencies. Students are offered a variety of opportunities with state courts, the government, and affiliated agencies in Pennsylvania's state capital.

The nationally ranked Health Law Institute in Delaware provides research, policy analysis, and specialty education under the directorship of one of the leading health law authorities in the country.

Delaware's Corporate Law Institute offers students the opportunity to learn under the tutelage of the leading corporate law decision makers in Delaware's Chancery and Supreme courts in the nation's corporate capital.

The Trial Advocacy Institutes in Delaware and Harrisburg offer students the Intensive Trial Advocacy Program—a one-week boot camp offered each semester where trial skills are honed by over 150 judges and trial attorneys from throughout the United States. This program has been awarded the Emil Gumpert Trial Advocacy Award.

Widener offers several joint degree programs: the J.D./M.B.A. and J.D./Psy.D. in conjunction with Widener University; a J.D./M.M.P. with the University of Delaware; and a J.D./M.S.L.S. in Harrisburg with Clarion University.

Widener has four international summer law institutes, which draw students from all over the United States to programs each summer in Sydney, Geneva, Venice, and Nairobi, Kenya.

STUDENT BODY

Fall 2005 full-time enrollment: 997

Men: 56%	Women: 44%
African-American: 3.1%	American Indian: 0.2%
Asian-American: 6.1%	Mexican-American: 0.0%
Puerto Rican: 0.0%	Other Hisp-Amer: 1.9%
White: 76.1%	International: 0.7%
Unknown: 11.8%	

Fall 2005 part-time enrollment: 574

Men: 52%	Women: 48%
African-American: 7.1%	American Indian: 0.5%
Asian-American: 4.7%	Mexican-American: 0.0%
Puerto Rican: 0.0%	Other Hisp-Amer: 1.7%
White: 71.3%	International: 0.7%
Unknown: 13.9%	

Attrition rates for 2004-2005 full-time students
Percent of students discontinuing law school:
Men: 9%　　　　　Women: 11%

First-year students: 21%　　　Second-year students: 6%
Third-year students: 1%

LIBRARY RESOURCES

The library holds 98,796 and receives 7,354 current subscriptions.
Total volumes: 603,963
Percentage of the titles in the online catalog: 100%
Total seats available for library users: 771

INFORMATION TECHNOLOGY

Number of wired network connections available to students: 85 total (in the law library, excluding computer labs: 60; in classrooms: 25; in computer labs: 0; elsewhere in the law school: 0)
Law school has a wireless network.
Approximate number of simultaneous users that can be accommodated on wireless network: 525
Students are not required to own a computer.

EMPLOYMENT AND SALARIES

Proportion of 2004 graduates employed at graduation: 54%
Employed 9 months later, as of February 15, 2005: 87%
Salaries in the private sector (law firms, business, industry): $45,000–$80,000 (25th-75th percentile)
Median salary in the private sector: $55,000
Percentage in the private sector who reported salary information: 33%
Median salary in public service (government, judicial clerkships, academic posts, non-profits): $40,000

Percentage of 2004 graduates in:

Law firms: 39%	Bus./industry (legal): 3%
Bus./industry (nonlegal): 19%	Government: 14%
Public interest: 2%	Judicial clerkship: 19%
Academia : 1%	Unknown: 3%

2004 graduates employed in-state: 18%
2004 graduates employed in foreign countries: 0%
Number of states where graduates are employed: 13
Percentage of 2004 graduates working in: New England: 1%, Middle Atlantic: 65%, East North Central: 0%, West North Central: 0%, South Atlantic: 24%, East South Central: 0%, West South Central: 1%, Mountain: 0%, Pacific: 1%, Unknown: 8%

BAR PASSAGE RATES

Based on 2004 graduates taking Summer 2004 or Winter 2005 exams. Most of the school's first-time test takers took the bar in Pennsylvania.

72%
School's bar passage rate for first-time test takers

81%
Statewide bar passage rate for first-time test takers

Willamette University (Collins)

■ 245 Winter Street SE, Salem, OR, 97301
■ http://www.willamette.edu/wucl
■ Private
■ Year founded: 1883
■ 2005-2006 tuition: full-time: $25,280; part-time: N/A
■ Enrollment 2005-06 academic year: full-time: 438; part-time: 5
■ U.S. News 2007 law specialty ranking: dispute resolution: 8

3.12-3.62 GPA, 25TH-75TH PERCENTILE

153-157 LSAT, 25TH-75TH PERCENTILE

35% ACCEPTANCE RATE

Tier 3 2007 U.S. NEWS LAW SCHOOL RANKING

ADMISSIONS

Admissions phone number: (503) 370-6282
Admissions email address: law-admission@willamette.edu
Application website:
http://apply.embark.com/grad/willamette/default.asp
Application deadline for Fall 2007 admission: 4/01

Admissions statistics:

Number of applicants for Fall 2005: 1,554
Number of acceptances: 546
Number enrolled: 145
Acceptance rate: 35%
GPA, 25th-75th percentile, entering class Fall 2005:
3.12-3.62
LSAT, 25th-75th percentile, entering class Fall 2005: 153-157

FINANCIAL AID

Financial aid phone number: (503) 370-6273
Financial aid application deadline: 2/01
Tuition 2005-2006 academic year: full-time: $25,280; part-time: N/A
Room and board: $12,930; books: $0; miscellaneous expenses: $0
Total of room/board/books/miscellaneous expenses: $12,930
University offers graduate student housing for which law students are eligible.

Financial aid profile

Percent of students that received grants for the 2004-2005 academic year: full-time: 43%; part-time 100%
Median grant amount: full-time: $9,300; part-time: $7,500
The average law-school debt of those in the Class of 2005 who borrowed: $57,414. Proportion who borrowed: 81%

ACADEMIC PROGRAMS

Calendar: semester
Joint degrees awarded: J.D./M.B.A.
Typical first-year section size: Full-time: 70

Is there typically a "small section" of the first year class, other than Legal Writing, taught by full-time faculty?:
Full-time: yes; Part-time: no
Number of course titles, beyond the first year curriculum, offered last year: 96
Percentages of upper division course sections, excluding seminars, with an enrollment of:
Under 25: 56%   25 to 49: 26%
50 to 74: 11%   75 to 99: 6%
100+: 1%
Areas of specialization: appellate advocacy, clinical training, dispute resolution, environmental law, healthcare law, intellectual property law, international law, tax law, trial advocacy

Fall 2005 faculty profile

Total teaching faculty: 67. Full-time: 72%; 77% men, 23% women, 10% minorities. Part-time: 28%; 74% men, 26% women, 5% minorities
Student-to-faculty ratio: 15.6

SPECIAL PROGRAMS (as provided by law school):

Willamette University College of Law offers several specialty programs for its students. Four certificate programs offer students the opportunity to specialize in business law, international and comparative law, dispute resolution, and law and government. Students who specialize in these programs have the opportunity to study in depth in their chosen areas of specialty.

Students may enroll in a joint degree program that offers an M.B.A. through the Atkinson Graduate School of Management in addition to the J.D. from the College of Law. The law school has recently created an LL.M. program in transnational law that combines the strengths of the school's comprehensive curriculum in domestic law with its well-established foreign programs and transnational course offerings taught by internationally recognized scholars and teachers.

The College of Law offers several programs in foreign study that give its students opportunities to study law in different countries. Off-campus study programs in China, Ecuador, and Germany offer invaluable experience abroad.

STUDENT BODY

Fall 2005 full-time enrollment: 438

Men: 56%	Women: 44%
African-American: 0.9%	American Indian: 1.8%
Asian-American: 3.7%	Mexican-American: 1.4%
Puerto Rican: 0.0%	Other Hisp-Amer: 1.4%
White: 78.1%	International: 0.2%
Unknown: 12.6%	

Fall 2005 part-time enrollment: 5

Men: 60%	Women: 40%
African-American: 0.0%	American Indian: 0.0%
Asian-American: 20.0%	Mexican-American: 0.0%
Puerto Rican: 0.0%	Other Hisp-Amer: 0.0%
White: 60.0%	International: 0.0%
Unknown: 20.0%	

Attrition rates for 2004-2005 full-time students

Percent of students discontinuing law school:

Men: 4%	Women: 4%
First-year students: 8%	Second-year students: 3%
Third-year students: N/A	

LIBRARY RESOURCES

The library holds 39,858 and receives 3,110 current subscriptions.
Total volumes: 288,204
Percentage of the titles in the online catalog: 100%
Total seats available for library users: 492

INFORMATION TECHNOLOGY

Number of wired network connections available to students: 122 total (in the law library, excluding computer labs: 86; in classrooms: 0; in computer labs: 0; elsewhere in the law school: 36)
Law school has a wireless network.
Approximate number of simultaneous users that can be accommodated on wireless network: 700
Students are not required to own a computer.

EMPLOYMENT AND SALARIES

Proportion of 2004 graduates employed at graduation: N/A
Employed 9 months later, as of February 15, 2005: 85%
Salaries in the private sector (law firms, business, industry): $40,800–$72,500 (25th-75th percentile)
Median salary in the private sector: $50,000
Percentage in the private sector who reported salary information: 72%
Median salary in public service (government, judicial clerkships, academic posts, non-profits): $42,500

Percentage of 2004 graduates in:

Law firms: 57%	Bus./industry (legal): 14%
Bus./industry (nonlegal): 0%	Government: 18%
Public interest: 2%	Judicial clerkship: 6%
Academia : 1%	Unknown: 2%

2004 graduates employed in-state: 57%
2004 graduates employed in foreign countries: 0%
Number of states where graduates are employed: 23
Percentage of 2004 graduates working in: New England: 0%, Middle Atlantic: 0%, East North Central: 1%, West North Central: 0%, South Atlantic: 6%, East South Central: 1%, West South Central: 3%, Mountain: 14%, Pacific: 75%, Unknown: 0%

BAR PASSAGE RATES

Based on 2004 graduates taking Summer 2004 or Winter 2005 exams. Most of the school's first-time test takers took the bar in Oregon.

83%

School's bar passage rate for first-time test takers

72%

Statewide bar passage rate for first-time test takers

William Mitchell College of Law

■ 875 Summit Avenue, St. Paul, MN, 55105-3076
■ http://www.wmitchell.edu
■ Private
■ **Year founded:** 1900
■ **2005-2006 tuition:** full-time: $25,950; part-time: $18,780
■ **Enrollment 2005-06 academic year:** full-time: 732; part-time: 382
■ **U.S. News 2007 law specialty ranking:** clinical training: 24, intellectual property law: 28

3.24-3.66 GPA, 25TH-75TH PERCENTILE

151-158 LSAT, 25TH-75TH PERCENTILE

48% ACCEPTANCE RATE

Tier 4 2007 U.S. NEWS LAW SCHOOL RANKING

ADMISSIONS

Admissions phone number: **(651) 290-6476**
Admissions email address: **admissions@wmitchell.edu**
Application website: **http://www.wmitchell.edu/admissions/apply/online.html**
Application deadline for Fall 2007 admission: **5/01**

Admissions statistics:

Number of applicants for Fall 2005: **1,591**
Number of acceptances: **763**
Number enrolled: **271**
Acceptance rate: **48%**
GPA, 25th-75th percentile, entering class Fall 2005:
3.24-3.66
LSAT, 25th-75th percentile, entering class Fall 2005: **151-158**

FINANCIAL AID

Financial aid phone number: **(651) 290-6403**
Financial aid application deadline: **3/15**
Tuition 2005-2006 academic year: full-time: **$25,950**; part-time: **$18,780**
Room and board: **$12,400**; books: **$1,100**; miscellaneous expenses: **$800**
Total of room/board/books/miscellaneous expenses: **$14,300**
University does not offer graduate student housing for which law students are eligible.

Financial aid profile

Percent of students that received grants for the 2004-2005 academic year: full-time: **34%**; part-time **34%**
Median grant amount: full-time: **$6,125**; part-time: **$4,433**
The average law-school debt of those in the Class of 2005 who borrowed: **$69,642**. Proportion who borrowed: **90%**

ACADEMIC PROGRAMS

Calendar: **semester**
Joint degrees awarded: **J.D./MS Womens Studies; J.D./MA Public Administration; J.D./MS Community Health**
Typical first-year section size: Full-time: **78**; Part-time: **70**

Is there typically a "small section" of the first year class, other than Legal Writing, taught by full-time faculty?:
Full-time: **no**; Part-time: **no**
Number of course titles, beyond the first year curriculum, offered last year: **125**
Percentages of upper division course sections, excluding seminars, with an enrollment of:

Under 25: **42%**   25 to 49: **39%**
50 to 74: **16%**   75 to 99: **3%**
100+: **0%**

Areas of specialization: appellate advocacy, clinical training, dispute resolution, environmental law, healthcare law, intellectual property law, international law, tax law, trial advocacy

Fall 2005 faculty profile

Total teaching faculty: **220**. Full-time: **15%**; **65%** men, **35%** women, **15%** minorities. Part-time: **85%**; **55%** men, **45%** women, **17%** minorities
Student-to-faculty ratio: **23.6**

SPECIAL PROGRAMS (as provided by law school):

With more than 100 courses, clinics, and externships, the William Mitchell academic program strikes a balance between the intellectual and practical components of a legal education. All first-year students participate in a rigorous and highly praised skills course called Writing & Representation: Advice & Persuasion (WRAP), mastering research, reasoning, and writing skills, client interviewing and counseling, contract negotiation and drafting, dispute mediation, and pretrial litigation. In the second or third year, students take Writing & Representation: Advocacy, an introduction to researching legislative process and administrative materials, conducting discovery, examining witnesses, introducing exhibits, making opening and closing statements, and presenting appellate arguments in writing and orally.

The clinical program is designed to offer hands-on experience in practicing law as well as convey the importance of public service. This nationally recognized program was one of the first to be established at a U.S. law school. The legal practicum program provides students the opportunity to work as a two-person law firm handling a series of simulated cases, under the supervision of a faculty member and practicing lawyers and judges from the community.

The externship program puts students to work as clerks, advocates, or researchers with judges, administrative agencies, and government or advocacy organizations. The comprehensive curriculum includes the following areas of focus: alternative dispute resolution, business law, commercial law, criminal law, employment law, estate planning, family law, government, intellectual property law, international and comparative law, personal injury and torts, real-estate law, taxation, and trial advocacy.

The college belongs to the Consortium for Innovative Legal Education (CILE) in a partnership with California Western School of Law in San Diego, New England School of Law in Boston, and South Texas College of Law in Houston. CILE is the only consortium program of its kind in the United States, offering students an opportunity to participate in programs and classes at any of the other three CILE law schools. There are summer foreign programs in Galway, Ireland; London; and the island nation of Malta, and semester abroad programs in Aarhus, Denmark, and Leiden, the Netherlands.

William Mitchell also offers dual-degree programs in partnership with Minnesota State University-Mankato, in community healh, public administration, and women's studies.

STUDENT BODY

Fall 2005 full-time enrollment: 732

Men: 48%	Women: 52%
African-American: 2.2%	American Indian: 0.4%
Asian-American: 4.1%	Mexican-American: 0.8%
Puerto Rican: 0.3%	Other Hisp-Amer: 1.1%
White: 77.2%	International: 0.4%
Unknown: 13.5%	

Fall 2005 part-time enrollment: 382

Men: 48%	Women: 52%
African-American: 6.5%	American Indian: 0.5%
Asian-American: 6.3%	Mexican-American: 0.8%
Puerto Rican: 0.3%	Other Hisp-Amer: 1.8%
White: 73.6%	International: 0.8%
Unknown: 9.4%	

Attrition rates for 2004-2005 full-time students

Percent of students discontinuing law school:

Men: 3%	Women: 2%
First-year students: 6%	Second-year students: 1%
Third-year students: 2%	

LIBRARY RESOURCES

The library holds 193,971 and receives 3,988 current subscriptions.

Total volumes: 334,632
Percentage of the titles in the online catalog: 100%
Total seats available for library users: 671

INFORMATION TECHNOLOGY

Number of wired network connections available to students: 240 total (in the law library, excluding computer labs: 20; in classrooms: 140; in computer labs: 60; elsewhere in the law school: 20)

Law school has a wireless network.

Approximate number of simultaneous users that can be accommodated on wireless network: 1,048

Students are required to own a computer.

EMPLOYMENT AND SALARIES

Proportion of 2004 graduates employed at graduation: 54%

Employed 9 months later, as of February 15, 2005: 84%

Salaries in the private sector (law firms, business, industry): $45,000–$80,000 (25th-75th percentile)

Median salary in the private sector: $63,883

Percentage in the private sector who reported salary information: 56%

Median salary in public service (government, judicial clerkships, academic posts, non-profits): $40,000

Percentage of 2004 graduates in:

Law firms: 42%	Bus./industry (legal): 5%
Bus./industry (nonlegal): 22%	Government: 13%
Public interest: 7%	Judicial clerkship: 8%
Academia : 1%	Unknown: 2%

2004 graduates employed in-state: 90%
2004 graduates employed in foreign countries: 0%
Number of states where graduates are employed: 16
Percentage of 2004 graduates working in: New England: 0%, Middle Atlantic: 0%, East North Central: 4%, West North Central: 91%, South Atlantic: 2%, East South Central: 0%, West South Central: 0%, Mountain: 1%, Pacific: 0%, Unknown: 0%

BAR PASSAGE RATES

Based on 2004 graduates taking Summer 2004 or Winter 2005 exams. Most of the school's first-time test takers took the bar in Minnesota.

89%

School's bar passage rate for first-time test takers

91%

Statewide bar passage rate for first-time test takers

Yale University

- PO Box 208215, New Haven, CT, 06520-8215
- http://www.law.yale.edu
- Private
- Year founded: 1824
- 2005-2006 tuition: full-time: $38,800; part-time: $9,700
- Enrollment 2005-06 academic year: full-time: 585; part-time: 1
- U.S. News 2007 law specialty ranking: clinical training: 8, international law: 5, tax law: 11

3.79-3.95 GPA, 25TH-75TH PERCENTILE

168-175 LSAT, 25TH-75TH PERCENTILE

6% ACCEPTANCE RATE

1 2007 U.S. NEWS LAW SCHOOL RANKING

ADMISSIONS

Admissions phone number: **(203) 432-4995**
Admissions email address: **admissions.law@yale.edu**
Application website: **http://www.law.yale.edu/admissions**
Application deadline for Fall 2007 admission: **2/01**

Admissions statistics:

Number of applicants for Fall 2005: **3,778**
Number of acceptances: **235**
Number enrolled: **199**
Acceptance rate: **6%**
GPA, 25th-75th percentile, entering class Fall 2005: **3.79-3.95**
LSAT, 25th-75th percentile, entering class Fall 2005: **168-175**

FINANCIAL AID

Financial aid phone number: **(203) 432-1688**
Financial aid application deadline: **3/15**
Tuition 2005-2006 academic year: full-time: **$38,800**; part-time: **$9,700**
Room and board: **$14,200**; books: **$950**; miscellaneous expenses: **$0**
Total of room/board/books/miscellaneous expenses: **$15,150**
University offers graduate student housing for which law students are eligible.

Financial aid profile

Percent of students that received grants for the 2004-2005 academic year: full-time: **44%**
Median grant amount: full-time: **$15,990**
The average law-school debt of those in the Class of 2005 who borrowed: **$89,908**. Proportion who borrowed: **91%**

ACADEMIC PROGRAMS

Calendar: **semester**
Joint degrees awarded: **Ph.D. - Philosophy; Ph.D. - History; Ph.D - American Studies; Ph.D. - Political Science; M.P.P.M.; M.E.S. Forestry; M.A. - Arts & Sciences; M.D. ; M.A. Statistics; Ph.D. - Sociology; M.A. International Relations; M.A.R. Ethics; Ph.D. - Economics; M.F.S.**
Forestry; M.B.A.; M.A. East Asian Studies; M.P.H.; M.E.M. Forestry; M.P.P.; M.A. - Economics
Typical first-year section size: Full-time: **65**
Is there typically a "small section" of the first year class, other than Legal Writing, taught by full-time faculty?: Full-time: **yes**
Number of course titles, beyond the first year curriculum, offered last year: **143**
Percentages of upper division course sections, excluding seminars, with an enrollment of:

Under 25: **30%**	25 to 49: **45%**
50 to 74: **12%**	75 to 99: **9%**
100+: **4%**	

Areas of specialization: appellate advocacy, clinical training, dispute resolution, environmental law, healthcare law, intellectual property law, international law, tax law, trial advocacy

Fall 2005 faculty profile

Total teaching faculty: **108**. Full-time: **61%**; **79%** men, **21%** women, **14%** minorities. Part-time: **39%**; **67%** men, **33%** women, **19%** minorities
Student-to-faculty ratio: **7.8**

SPECIAL PROGRAMS (as provided by law school):

Please see our bulletin and/or website for this information.

STUDENT BODY

Fall 2005 full-time enrollment: 585

Men: **56%**	Women: **44%**
African-American: **8.9%**	American Indian: **0.0%**
Asian-American: **13.2%**	Mexican-American: **2.6%**
Puerto Rican: **0.9%**	Other Hisp-Amer: **6.2%**
White: **60.9%**	International: **4.1%**
Unknown: **3.4%**	

Fall 2005 part-time enrollment: 1

Men: **0%**	Women: **100%**
African-American: **0.0%**	American Indian: **0.0%**
Asian-American: **0.0%**	Mexican-American: **0.0%**
Puerto Rican: **0.0%**	Other Hisp-Amer: **0.0%**

White: 100.0%   International: 0.0%
Unknown: 0.0%

Attrition rates for 2004-2005 full-time students
Percent of students discontinuing law school:
Men: 1%   Women: N/A
First-year students: 1%   Second-year students: 1%
Third-year students: N/A

LIBRARY RESOURCES
The library holds 328,668 and receives 11,103 current
   subscriptions.
Total volumes: 1,129,973
Percentage of the titles in the online catalog: 100%
Total seats available for library users: 414

INFORMATION TECHNOLOGY
Number of wired network connections available to students: 1,009 total (in the law library, excluding computer
   labs: 414; in classrooms: 581; in computer labs: 4; elsewhere in the law school: 10)
Law school has a wireless network.
Approximate number of simultaneous users that can be
   accommodated on wireless network: 600
Students are not required to own a computer.

EMPLOYMENT AND SALARIES
Proportion of 2004 graduates employed at graduation:
   97%
Employed 9 months later, as of February 15, 2005: 99%
Salaries in the private sector (law firms, business, indus-
   try): $125,000–$125,000 (25th-75th percentile)
Median salary in the private sector: $125,000

Percentage in the private sector who reported salary
   information: 96%
Median salary in public service (government, judicial clerkships, academic posts, non-profits): $51,635

Percentage of 2004 graduates in:
Law firms: 45%   Bus./industry (legal): 0%
Bus./industry (nonlegal): 2%   Government: 3%
Public interest: 5%   Judicial clerkship: 43%
Academia : 2%   Unknown: 0%

2004 graduates employed in-state: 7%
2004 graduates employed in foreign countries: 2%
Number of states where graduates are employed: 28
Percentage of 2004 graduates working in: New England:
   13%, Middle Atlantic: 36%, East North Central: 5%, West
   North Central: 1%, South Atlantic: 19%, East South
   Central: 1%, West South Central: 3%, Mountain: 4%,
   Pacific: 15%, Unknown: 1%

BAR PASSAGE RATES
Based on 2004 graduates taking Summer 2004 or
Winter 2005 exams. Most of the school's first-time test
takers took the bar in New York.

94%

School's bar passage rate for first-time test takers

75%

Statewide bar passage rate for first-time test takers

Non-responding Schools

APPALACHIAN SCHOOL OF LAW
- P.O. Box 2825, Grundy, VA 24614-2825
- http://www.asl.edu
- Private
- Admissions phone number: (800) 895-7411
- Admissions email address: aslinfo@asl.edu
- 2005 U.S.News Law School Ranking: Unranked

CATHOLIC UNIVERSITY
- 2250 Avendia Las Americas, Suite 584, Ponce, Puerto Rico, 00717-0777
- http://www.pucpr.edu
- Private
- Admissions phone number: (787) 841-2000
- Admissions email address: admissions@pucpr.edu
- 2005 U.S.News Law School Ranking: Unranked

INTER-AMERICAN UNIVERSITY
- P.O. Box 70351, San Juan, Puerto Rico 00936-8351
- http://www.metro.inter.edu
- Private
- Admissions phone number: (787) 765-1270
- Admissions email address: edmendez@inter.edu
- 2005 U.S.News Law School Ranking: Unranked

JOHN MARSHALL LAW SCHOOL–ATLANTA
- 1422 W. Peachtree Street NW, Atlanta, GA 30309
- http://www.johnmarshall.edu
- Private
- Admissions phone number: (404) 872-3593
- 2005 U.S.News Law School Ranking: Unranked

SOUTHERN UNIVERSITY
- PO Box 9294, Baton Rouge, LA, 70813
- http://www.sulc.edu/index.html
- Public
- Admissions phone number: (225) 771-5340
- Admissions email address: Admissions@sulc.sus.edu
- GPA, 25th-75th Percentile: 2.66-3.25
- LSAT, 25th-75th Percentile: 1434149
- Acceptance Rate: 22%
- 2005 U.S.News Law School Ranking: Tier 4

UNIVERSITY OF PUERTO RICO
- PO Box 23303 Estacion Universidad, Rio Piedras, Puerto Rico, 00931-3302
- http://www.upr.edu
- Public
- Admissions phone number: (787) 764-0000
- Admissions email address: admissions@upr.edu
- 2005 U.S.News Law School Ranking: Unranked

WESTERN STATE UNIVERSITY
- 1111 N. State College Boulevard, Fullerton, CA, 92831
- http://www.wsulaw.edu
- Private
- Admissions phone number: (714) 459-1101
- Admissions email address: adm@wsulaw.edu
- 2005 U.S.News Law School Ranking: Unranked

Alphabetical Index of Schools

Index of Schools by State

Alabama

Samford University (Cumberland), 276

University of Alabama–Tuscaloosa, 328

Arizona

Arizona State University, 126

University of Arizona (Rogers), 330

Arkansas

University of Arkansas–Fayetteville, 332

University of Arkansas–Little Rock (Bowen), 334

California

California Western School of Law, 142

Chapman University, 154

Golden Gate University, 198

Loyola Law School, 222

Pepperdine University (McConnell), 264

Santa Clara University, 278

Southwestern University School of Law, 290

Stanford University, 300

Thomas Jefferson School of Law, 316

University of California (Hastings), 338

University of California–Berkeley, 340

University of California–Davis, 342

University of California–Los Angeles, 344

University of San Diego, 422

University of San Francisco, 424

University of Southern California (Gould), 430

University of the Pacific (McGeorge), 440

Western State University, 488

Whittier Law School, 478

University of Colorado–Boulder, 350

University of Denver (Sturm), 356

Connecticut

Quinnipiac University, 266

University of Connecticut, 352

Yale University, 486

Delaware

Widener University, 480

District of Columbia

American University (Washington), 124

Catholic University of America (Columbus), 152

George Washington University, 192

Georgetown University, 194

Howard University, 208

University of the District of Columbia (Clarke), 438

Florida

Barry University, 130

Florida A&M University, 178

Florida Coastal School of Law, 180

Florida International University, 182

Florida State University, 184

Nova Southeastern University (Broad), 252

St. Thomas University, 298

Stetson University, 302

University of Florida (Levin), 360

University of Miami, 386

Georgia

Emory University, 176

Georgia State University, 196

John Marshall Law School–Atlanta, 488

Mercer University, 230

University of Georgia, 362

Hawaii

University of Hawaii (Richardson), 364

Idaho

University of Idaho, 368

Illinois

DePaul University, 168

Illinois Institute of Technology (Chicago-Kent),
  210

John Marshall Law School, 216

Loyola University Chicago, 224

Northern Illinois University, 246

Northwestern University, 250

Southern Illinois University–Carbondale, 286

University of Chicago, 346

University of Illinois–Urbana-Champaign, 370

Indiana

Indiana University–Bloomington, 212

Indiana University–Indianapolis, 214

University of Notre Dame, 410

Valparaiso University, 456

Iowa

Drake University, 170

University of Iowa, 372

Kansas

University of Kansas, 374

Washburn University, 466

Kentucky

Northern Kentucky University (Chase), 248

University of Kentucky, 376

University of Louisville (Brandeis), 378

Louisiana

Louisiana State University–Baton Rouge, 220

Loyola University New Orleans, 226

Southern University, 488

Tulane University, 322

Maine

University of Maine, 380

Maryland

University of Baltimore, 336

University of Maryland, 382

Massachusetts

Boston College, 134

Boston University, 136

Harvard University, 204

New England School of Law, 236

Northeastern University, 244

Suffolk University, 304

Western New England College, 476

Michigan

Ave Maria School of Law, 128

Michigan State University, 232

Thomas M. Cooley Law School, 318

University of Detroit Mercy, 358

University of Michigan–Ann Arbor, 388

Wayne State University, 472

Minnesota

Hamline University, 202

University of Minnesota–Twin Cities, 390

University of St. Thomas, 432

William Mitchell College of Law, 484

Mississippi

Mississippi College, 234
University of Mississippi, 392

Missouri

St. Louis University, 294
University of Missouri–Columbia, 394
University of Missouri–Kansas City, 396
Washington University in St. Louis, 470

Montana

University of Montana, 398

Nebraska

Creighton University, 164
University of Nebraska–Lincoln, 400

Nevada

University of Nevada–Las Vegas (Boyd), 402

New Hampshire

Franklin Pierce Law Center, 188

New Jersey

Rutgers State University–Camden, 272
Rutgers State University–Newark, 274
Seton Hall University, 282

New Mexico

University of New Mexico, 404

New York

Albany Law School-Union University, 122
Brooklyn Law School, 140
Cardozo-Yeshiva University, 148
Columbia University, 160
Cornell University, 162
CUNY–Queens College, 166

Fordham University, 186
Hofstra University, 206
New York Law School, 238
New York University, 240
Pace University, 260
St. John's University, 292
Syracuse University, 306
Touro College (Fuchsberg), 320
University at Buffalo–SUNY, 324

North Carolina

Campbell University (Wiggins), 144
Duke University, 172
North Carolina Central University, 242
University of North Carolina–Chapel Hill, 406
Wake Forest University, 464

North Dakota

University of North Dakota, 408

Ohio

Capital University, 146
Case Western Reserve University, 150
Cleveland State University (Cleveland-Marshall), 156
Ohio Northern University (Pettit), 254
Ohio State University (Moritz), 256
University of Akron, 326
University of Cincinnati, 348
University of Dayton, 354
University of Toledo, 442

Oklahoma

Oklahoma City University, 258
University of Oklahoma, 412
University of Tulsa, 444

Oregon

Lewis and Clark College (Northwestern), 218

University of Oregon, 414

Willamette University (Collins), 482

Pennsylvania

Duquesne University, 174

Pennsylvania State University (Dickinson), 262

Temple University (Beasley), 308

University of Pennsylvania, 416

University of Pittsburgh, 418

Villanova University, 462

Puerto Rico

Catholic University, 488

Inter-American University, 488

University of Puerto Rico, 488

Rhode Island

Roger Williams University (Papitto), 270

South Carolina

University of South Carolina, 426

South Dakota

University of South Dakota, 428

University of Memphis (Humphreys), 384

Tennessee

University of Tennessee–Knoxville, 434

Vanderbilt University, 458

Texas

Baylor University, 132

South Texas College of Law, 284

Southern Methodist University, 288

St. Mary's University, 296

Texas Southern University (Marshall), 310

Texas Tech University, 312

Texas Wesleyan University, 314

University of Houston, 366

University of Texas–Austin, 436

Utah

Brigham Young University (Clark), 138

University of Utah (S.J. Quinney), 446

Vermont

Vermont Law School, 460

Virginia

Appalachian School of Law, 488

College of William and Mary (Marshall-Wythe), 158

George Mason University, 190

Regent University, 268

University of Richmond, 420

University of Virginia, 448

Washington and Lee University, 468

Washington

Gonzaga University, 200

Seattle University, 280

University of Washington, 450

West Virginia

West Virginia University, 474

Wisconsin

Marquette University, 228

University of Wisconsin–Madison, 452

Wyoming

University of Wyoming, 454

About the Authors & Editors

Founded in 1933, Washington, D.C.-based *U.S.News & World Report* delivers a unique brand of weekly magazine journalism to its 12.2 million readers. In 1983, *U.S. News* began its exclusive annual rankings of American colleges and universities. The *U.S. News* education franchise is second to none, with its annual college and graduate school rankings among the most eagerly anticipated magazine issues in the country.

Anne McGrath, the book's lead writer, is a deputy editor at *U.S.News & World Report*. She has written about higher education and previously was managing editor of "America's Best Colleges" and "America's Best Graduate Schools," the two *U.S. News* annual publications featuring rankings of the country's colleges and universities.

Robert Morse is the director of data research at *U.S.News & World Report*. He is in charge of the research, data collection, methodologies, and survey design for the annual "America's Best Colleges" rankings and the "America's Best Graduate Schools" rankings.

Brian Kelly is the executive editor of *U.S.News & World Report*. As the magazine's No. 2 editor, he oversees the weekly magazine, the website, and a series of newsstand books. He is a former editor at the *Washington Post* and the author of three books.

Other writers who contributed chapters or passages to the book are Carolyn Kleiner Butler, Kristin Davis, Anna Mulrine, Dan Gilgoff, Betsy Streisand, Jill Rachlin Marbaix, and Samantha Stainburn. The work involved in producing the directory and *U.S. News* Insider's Index was handled by deputy director of data research Sam Flanigan.

Notes

Schools: ASU, Baylor, Franklin Pierce Law Center, George Mason, Lewis + Clark Coll., Penn State, Santa Clara, South Texas, SMU, Syracuse, Arkansas, University of Denver, UGA, Houston, Kansas, Kentucky, UNC, Oklahoma, UT

Notes

Notes

- ✻ Finish what you start
- Do your talking on the field
- Maintain a good attitude
- Most importantly! Never give up